# Waka Paddle to Gas Pedal

## The First Century of Auckland Transport

Keith Mexsom

Copyright © Keith Mexsom

First Published October 2016

Second (Revised) Edition June 2019

Third (Revised) Edition January 2020

ISBN: 978-0-6485129-2-9

# Contents

| | | |
|---|---|---|
| Acknowledgements: | | i |
| Introduction: | | 1 |
| Chapter One: | The Inland Waterways – Paper Canals | 3 |
| Chapter Two: | Across the Waitemata – The Ferries | 9 |
| Chapter Three: | Auckland Canals and the Inland Waterways Commission | 21 |
| Chapter Four: | The Harbour Bridge | 26 |
| Chapter Five: | Trails Through the Fern | 101 |
| Chapter Six: | Trails of Steel – The Railway | 107 |
| Chapter Seven: | The Omnibuses – The Ancillaries Vie for Supremacy | 246 |
| Chapter Eight: | On Your Bike | 259 |
| Chapter Nine: | The Dominance of the Centre Line – The Age of Trams | 262 |
| Chapter Ten: | The Motor Car Cometh | 441 |
| Afterword: | | 480 |
| References: | | 482 |
| Index: | | 532 |

**Acknowledgements**

First and foremost, my thanks to The Bruce Jesson Foundation which, way back in 2008, thought my ambition to write of the commercial influences on Auckland transport planning worthy of the Bruce Jesson Critical Writing Award for that year. Originally, the award was meant to support my preliminary research of the topic's previous sixty years. However, it soon became obvious that Auckland's transport planning, or lack thereof, began much earlier – as far back as the arrival of Auckland's first men of business.

Consequently, Waka Paddle to Gas Pedal – The First Century of Auckland Transport – sets the stage for the decisions and non-decisions that have compounded Auckland's transport difficulties since the Second World War. That subsequent story is to be related in a second volume – Gas Pedal to Back-Pedal – to follow in due course.

My thanks, also, to New Zealand Media and Entertainment, publishers of The New Zealand Herald, and to Fairfax Media, copyright holders of the bygone Auckland Star, for their permission to republish the material written by their unsung journalists of pencil, pen and typewriter – Pitman shorthand practitioners who diligently observed and reported when the art of 'cut and paste' required real scissors and glue; when the term 'story' meant so much more than it does today.

Relevant excerpts from the work of many other learned authors and commentators are also included herewith with what I trust will be viewed by all as fair representation and attribution.

Finally, my great appreciation for the 'Papers Past' newspaper archives provided online by the National Library of New Zealand without which I could never have discovered and traced the sequence of events integral to this narrative; and to the Special Collections Librarians of the Auckland City Library who, for several weeks, kindly allowed me access to the papers of the late Sir Dove-Myer Robinson and other documents.

Cover Design: Graham Kennedy

# Waka Paddle to Gas Pedal

## The First Century of Auckland Transport–1840 to 1940

*"To those who study it, transport is an unjustly neglected branch of history. It is a key social driver – it has such a decisive effect on the entire pattern of our lives, our society and our culture – and yet it is frequently overlooked when the story of lives, our society and cultures is told."* [1] (McCrystal 2007).

### Introduction

In its editorial of 4 September 1914, The New Zealand Herald and Daily Southern Cross commented on the plans recently proposed by the then railways general manager, Mr Ernest Haviland Hiley, for the modernisation and extension of Auckland's railway system. Mr Hiley's report, considered by the Government of the day to be, in Prime Minister William Massey's words, "…the most important Railways Statement ever submitted to Parliament", comprehensively included plans for public transport infrastructure still needed in Auckland a century later.

The Herald editorial anticipated that future need when its writer reminded readers of past realities insofar as actual progress was concerned: "In this proposal is improvement indeed. We cannot be amazed at its extent, however, for the experience of the City, the Province and the North Island in the past is that our railway facilities are never by any chance equal to the public demand. Every belated improvement which has been made has failed to keep ahead of urgent requirements and the result is a perpetual congestion and chronic dissatisfaction." [1]

Not only is this comment a unique example of how little has changed during the preceding century, but also a reminder that, throughout history, the progress of nations and their cities has been driven by visionaries, such as Ernest Hiley, and their ambitions. But only those ambitions realised are remembered. The misses, even the near misses, are soon archived and forgotten.

During the development of their various transport systems, there has been no lack of ambition expressed by Aucklanders as they struggled with the challenges of travelling and trading across their isthmus and beyond.

Unfortunately for the present-day commuter and trader, and for reasons as diverse as the thousands of vehicles that now choke Auckland's roads, precious few ambitions were realised. This is a narrative of those that succeeded, but mostly of those that failed, and why.

Perhaps this account will provide some explanation to those thousands of motorists who now crawl, seemingly forever, along Auckland's roads; those with plenty of time to ask not only, 'Why have I been here so long?' but also, 'How did I get here?'

*Chapter One*

# The Inland Waterways – Paper Canals

One could speculate how, in 1840, a precedent was well and truly set for at least the next 180 years. It was then that New Zealand's earliest (acting) surveyor-general, Felton Mathew, stood on the summit of Mount Wellington and at once saw what is now Panmure on the Tamaki River as the best site for the colony's new capital.

He envisaged a canal to facilitate the transportation of goods to and from the deeper water of the south side of the Waitemata Harbour (now Parnell), to the new colony at Panmure. The proposed canal would link the Orakei and Panmure Basins by way of the Purewa and Omaru Creeks.

No doubt, Felton Mathew's preference for a canal was very much based on the predominant mode of travel and the way goods were transported at the time. During the first years of serious Pakeha colonisation of the Auckland region, food staples and trade goods were carried around the isthmus by ship and inland by waka along the district's many inlets, rivers and creeks. From about 1854, the Maoris expanded their canoe fleet to include small, western-style sailing vessels often referred to as 'the horses and carts of the first decades of settlement'. [1]

Felton Mathew's vision also extended to a railway connection between Karetu (just south of Panmure) and Onehunga. Not only would the railway connect the Tamaki River with the Waitemata and Manukau Harbours, but also further facilitate the movement of settlers, goods and produce to and from the fertile lands of the Waikato and the Hauraki Plains to the south. [2]

Although this might seem an astonishing plan to have been conceived in the 1840s, it should be remembered that the transportation of goods by means of canal and steam railway was then quite common in Felton Mathew's homeland of Britain. But this was not Britain and Felton Mathew's vision was soon archived, just as many future studies and plans for the development of an effective Auckland transport system would be. Time and budget constraints, set to become a precedent for so many fundamentally-important, transport decisions, no doubt influenced Governor William Hobson's eventual decision to found the new settlement at its present site on the Waitemata Harbour.

Nevertheless, the concept of canals, particularly one linking the Waitemata with the Manukau, remained another of those transport options that, according to an editorial published in the Te Aroha News in 1884, "…is a topic which crops out continually, the writers in its favour being usually those who have land interests on one or other of the alternative lines for the proposed canal, or else have failed to make themselves acquainted with what has been done in the past in this matter.

"...the project of a canal connecting the Waitemata and Manukau is a chimerical scheme in the present position of the city: what may happen when a dense population covers the entire isthmus of Auckland is, of course, another matter altogether...In the nearer but still distant future the wants of man will cause them to be joined together again, but that may not be in our day. The almighty dollar governs every undertaking of the sort in these days, and the voice of the financial augurs is against the project at present." [3]

By 1908, the 'financial augurs' of the 1880s depression had been forgotten and the prospect of a canal was again proposed with the passage of the Auckland and Manukau Canal Act in October of that year. The Act empowered "...the Auckland Harbour Board to acquire Land for the Construction of a Canal connecting the Waitemata with the Manukau Harbour." [4]

The canal proposed by the Act was to connect the two harbours utilising parts of the Whau River and smaller streams between what is now known as Avondale and the northern coast of the Manukau Harbour in the vicinity of Lynfield and Hillsborough. An alternative proposal called for the canal to run from the Tamaki River to the eastern and shallower end of the Manukau.

Of course, in keeping with a ruinous spirit of land speculation exercised by many of Auckland's prominent businessmen from the first days of the colony's founding, and as previously speculated by the Te Aroha News, much of the land through which the canals were expected to pass had long since been purchased by business interests. Five years before the Auckland and Manukau Canal Act, the Auckland Star published details of just such a speculative venture:

"A company has been registered called the Waitemata and Manukau Canal Promotion Co. Ltd. of which the provisional directors are Messrs J. M. Mennie, M. A. Clark, R. Cameron, C. V. Houghton, H. Atkinson, W. R. Wilson, W. H. Smith, Thos. Finlayson, D. R. Caldwell, L. D. Nathan, J. J. Craig, W. Bailey, C. Ranson, Geo. Winstone, J. Leyland, and F. Jagger. Mr Arthur J. Furness has been appointed secretary, and Mr Harrison to do the necessary survey over a certain section of the route." [5]

However, speculation is just that, and so not always successful:

"The (Auckland Harbour Board) sub-committee appointed to consider the question of the construction of the Waitemata-Manukau Canal stated that letters from the Waitemata-Manukau Canal Promotion Co., in relation to canal, via Whau, offering land and plans for sale, together with Messrs. Vaile and Sons' valuation, dated September 7, 1909, were submitted, and it was resolved: That the offer made by the Waitemata-Manukau Canal Promotion Co. be declined." [6]

Just how much the inflated cost of land needed for the proposal may have delayed a start on the Waitemata- Manukau Canal in 1909 is not known. The engineering challenges were certainly not as great as the even more ambitious proposal to link the Manukau Harbour with the Waikato River, via Waiuku. This was another waterways project very much under consideration at the time:

"Considerable enthusiasm has lately been displayed in the Dominion in projects for the improvement of our facilities for internal water carriage. Our attention was again drawn to this matter this week by the inspection by various Chambers of Commerce and representatives of local bodies of the suggested route for connection between the Waikato River and Manukau Harbour. Carriage by water is cheaper than can be effected by the most economically run railway…

"The gathering of business men who this week inspected the route by which the water of the Waikato could be partially diverted by a navigable canal into the Manukau Harbour will, we trust, mark an important epoch in the history of the districts more immediately concerned.

"The Waikato is a very fine river, navigable to suitable boats for about 130 miles through a rich pastoral agricultural and coal-bearing district. Its commercial utility is depreciated by a bad bar entrance, and a reasonable scheme by which sufficient of its waters could be taken to make a negotiable channel through to Waiuku, on the Manukau, would be of the greatest importance to a very large proportion of the provincial population.

"We gather from what transpired at the lay inspection earlier in the week that no very detailed investigation has been made, but that sufficient has been ascertained to show that there are no insuperable difficulties in putting through a canal at quite moderate cost. The actual cutting that would be necessary to provide a channel 8 feet deep and 25 feet wide has been estimated to cost £100,681. The length of the cutting to be made is about six miles, and the amount of material to be removed is computed at less than two million cubic yards." [7]

But despite the optimism of earlier years, neither canal had been started by 1914. Nevertheless, the apparent commercial advantages to be gained from one or both systems was such that it was at least time to inquire and discuss the ideas again: "A Royal Commission has been appointed by the Government to report upon the various proposals for the construction of canals and other measures for the more profitable utilisation of the inland waterways in the Auckland Province." [8]

Surprisingly, the Royal Commission brief was to include modes of transport over, as well as along, Auckland's waterways, as reported by The New Zealand Herald on 21 April 1914:

"The necessity for a bridge over the Waitemata Harbour, to facilitate communication between the northern and southern sides was urged by a deputation which waited on the Prime Minister (the Right Hon. W. F. Massey) yesterday afternoon.

"The members of the deputation were Captain A. Whitney, and Messrs. W. Wallace (Mayor of Birkenhead), George Fraser (Mayor of Northcote), and H. Hunt, F. M. King, and A. Bartlett (members of the Birkenhead Borough Council). Captain Whitney said that a suggestion had been made some years ago that a bridge should be constructed over the harbour. (Captain Whitney is thought to be alluding to an 1860 harbour bridge proposal described by the prospectus of the North Shore Bridge Company, as detailed in Chapter Four.) The value of such a bridge would be immense. The interest on the expenditure on the bridge could be paid by a toll on the cattle alone which would be taken over it.

"The Prime Minister: Are the local bodies prepared to find any part of the money? Captain Whitney: I cannot say. That is out of my province. Mr Wallace said the question of a bridge over the harbour might be included in the order of reference of the Inland Waterways Commission that had been set up to consider, the matter of the better utilisation of the waterways of the Auckland Province.

"There was no denying the benefits that would arise from the construction of the bridge. The time would come when a bridge would be absolutely necessary. It would shorten the route to Helensville by about eleven miles. The speaker was opposed to any tolls being levied, and was of opinion that the landowners would be prepared to assist towards the cost of construction, because their land would be improved in value by the bridge.

"After other members of the deputation had spoken in support of the proposal, the Prime Minister said the matter was far too important a one to be disposed of immediately, simply by an affirmative or a negative answer. He was aware of its importance to the whole of the Auckland provincial district. If the scope of the Waterways Commission could be enlarged so as to include a report on the proposed bridge, then he had no objection to its being done. He did not know whether or not it could be included, but he would ask that it should be done." [9]

However, by August 1914, consideration of the harbour bridge vision by the Waterways Commission was overtaken by the outbreak of the First World War. It wasn't until 1919 that government and civic leaders dared to contemplate, once more, the future of Auckland in terms of infrastructure. As might be expected, the Auckland Harbour Board still viewed inland waterways as a viable and important means of transportation: "The prospects of the carrying out of the Waitemata-Manukau canal scheme was discussed at yesterday's meeting of the Auckland Harbour Board apropos of a motion to appoint the Manukau Harbour committee for the year.

"Mr J. S. Bond expressed the hope that the new committee would consider the question of the construction of the Waiuku canal, in particular, which was a matter of great importance, not only to the Manukau district, but also to the whole of Auckland. Mr J. B. Teasdale said the proposed canal would be of great benefit to the Waikato, as well as to the city and neighbouring districts. He was sure it could be undertaken within a short time.

"Mr H. K. Mackenzie said that any man would be lacking in foresight who would say that the Waitemata-Manukau canals would not be constructed within the next 20 years. They might even be carried out within 10 years. Any man of ordinary intelligence must know that this city was the coming port of New Zealand. It was the duty of the board to see that Auckland was pushed ahead, and these canal schemes were going to be an important factor in ensuring the progress of the port." [10]

But regardless of how important the canals were considered to be by the Harbour Board and other idealists, an attempt to re-establish the Inland Waterways Commission in July 1919 did not succeed: "Mr H. D. Heather, chairman of the Auckland Harbour Board, has asked the Prime Minister whether there is any likelihood of the Inland Waterways Commission being revived at an early date. Mr Massey replied that this Commission was suspended during the war, and only one member now remains, Mr J. E. Watson having died and Mr Parry having left the Dominion.

"Cabinet had not yet decided upon their successors. Mr Heather in reply asked on behalf of the Auckland Harbour Board that in the interests of Auckland city and harbour the Commission be revived, so that information already obtained could be used. The Premier handed this request to the Hon. W. H. Herries (Minister of Marine) who has replied that the resuscitation of the Commission will be considered, though at present Mr W. Ferguson is the only remaining member." [11]

While the Parliamentarians promised only more inquiry, locals nevertheless continued to present plans and proposals based on aspirations decades old and rarely realised:

"Plans of a proposed reinforced concrete bridge across the Tamaki River, at Otahuhu were submitted to the Auckland Harbour Board this afternoon by the Marine Department for comment. It is proposed to build a bridge of sixteen spans of 25ft each, with a 7ft clearance under the centre span at high tides.

"…the acting-engineer to the Board (Mr D. Holderness) and harbourmaster (Capt. H. H. Sergeant), called attention to the future possibility of connecting this arm of the Tamaki River by canal with Pukaki Creek, in the Manukau. The report continued: There is a quite possible route for the canal up this arm of the river, and, pending further investigation by the Inland Waterways Commission, we are of opinion that provision should be made for a greater opening between piers, and more headroom under the centre span at high water." [12]

Unfortunately, local aspirations were not always in agreement – a state of affairs often exploited by those in power at Wellington as illustrated throughout this narrative. The possible construction of a canal between the Manukau Harbour and the Waikato River was no exception. In September 1920, a meeting was convened by the Waikato River Board which represented the interests of those settlements and towns adjacent to the river. The Board's prime objective was to improve the navigation and drainage of the Waikato River and its tributaries and that of the meeting to decide "…upon means of impressing upon the Government the necessity of immediately appointing a Royal Commission to investigate and outline a comprehensive scheme." [13]

The River Board's representatives at the meeting had good reason to point out that the Waikato had some "…500 miles of navigable waters which…were capable of being greatly improved. With regard to drainage, hundreds of thousands of acres of swamp land which were useless at present could be made a valuable asset to New Zealand. It had recently been definitely promised that Cabinet would appoint a Royal Commission to report fully upon the most efficient method of improving the navigation of the river and draining the flooded lands, but nothing had resulted.

"The inland settlers not in close touch with the railway were carrying on under great difficulties and heavy expense. The development of industries had been definitely delayed and the loss to the country, as well as to the individuals concerned was incalculable. Mr H. E. R. L. Wily (Frankton) questioned whether it would be advisable to ask for a commission to deal solely with the Waikato River. He did not think they had the slightest chance of getting a separate commission as the Inland Waterways Commission was already in existence.

"Their best plan would be to urge the Government to instruct the commission to report on the Waikato River before dealing with the question of canals. Canals would not be possible for a number of years. He had the assurance of the Minister that the commission appointed in 1914 was to be revived. He moved: That the Government be urged to direct the Inland Waterways Commission to report first on the Waikato River." [13]

*Chapter Two*

# Across the Waitemata – The Ferries

"When the land beyond the river, as it (the North Shore) was called in early and less pretentious days, was purchased, in 1841, the Government allowed the use of the land on grazing leases, but about 1844 the land behind Stokes Point (now Northcote) was surveyed and put up for auction; a little later land round the lake was similarly dealt with, and in 1851, the township at the Flagstaff (Devonport) was cut up into suburban farms. The selling of the land brought more people to reside on the North Shore, and the question of having something like reasonable access to the city became acute.

"The settlers immediately on the waterfront generally had a boat of their own, but those further away were denied this opportunity. Despite the fact that these were the 'good old days,' the farmers had recourse to a practice that is yet much used—they petitioned the Government to do something for them. Governor Grey exercised the power in the commonweal, and after some negotiations he, in the latter part of 1853, instructed, the then harbourmaster, Captain Isaac Burgess, to report on the most desirable points on the Shore to which a ferry service could run.

"The captain handed in his report on December 31, 1853...The report stated that three terminal points on the Shore were needed for ferry purposes—one at Stokes Point, one at Barry's Point (near the orphanage at Takapuna) and the last at the Flagstaff...The Flagstaff service would meet the needs of the population as far away as Wade and Whangaparaoa, for there was a good beach track from those areas.

"On January 4, 1854, Colonel Wynyard, who had assumed the acting-Governorship, called tenders for 'A daily ferry to North Shore, Sundays excepted'. Four-oared whaleboats were specified as requisite and the fare was limited to 6d each way, and a further charge of 6d was to be levied for each 50lb of produce or merchandise above 100lb carried by any passenger on any trip.

"Only one tender was received, that of Mr John Reid, of Stokes Point, who undertook to carry out the three ferries for the sum of £37 10/ per quarter year. His boat was not quite satisfactory, but he was allowed to carry out the contract conditionally on finding another boat so soon as traffic warranted it.

"The first service arranged was: Leave Stokes Point on Mondays, Wednesdays, Thursdays and Saturdays, at 9 a.m., returning from the town at 3 p.m. From the Flagstaff the service was on Fridays only. The ferry boat was an open sailing boat, with a crew of two men. In January of 1854, a meeting of Lake and Flagstaff settlers was held at the residence of Mr Hammond at the Flagstaff, presided over by Mr Alex Alison sen., father of two men who later established the Devonport Ferry Co., Ltd.

"The meeting urged that three separate services were essential, and matter was to be brought before the Provincial Government. The representations must have been successful for very shortly afterwards the Barry's Point service was let to Messrs. D. O'Connor and W. Nicholson…In the year 1858 the number of passengers carried was 6046."[1]

"Barry's Point was always the gateway to Takapuna, as it proved a convenient landing place for passengers, cattle and goods. It was here that the first wharf was built with a shop and a hotel soon afterwards…Once begun, the ferry service improved steadily over the years."[2]

One of those improvements to first ply the Waitemata and the Hauraki Gulf included the paddle wheel steamer, Emu. Skippered by its owner, Capt. F. C. Kreeft, the Emu arrived at Auckland on 8 March 1860, carrying six boxes of apples and one passenger, as reported by the Daily Southern Cross: "The paddle-wheel steamer Emu (36 tons), Capt. F. C. Kreeft, from Nelson, arrived in harbour on Wednesday, the 8th...Her coals by this time running short, economy became necessary; notwithstanding this, however, she rounded the North Head about 6 p.m., and steamed up the harbour bravely, taking her berth at once alongside the Queen-street Wharf.

"It will thus be seen that the little vessel has in 8½ days at sea accomplished a voyage of over 770 miles, surmounting the usual dangers and difficulties of the East Coast of New Zealand, in a manner which at once exhibits her sea-going capabilities, and speaks well for the way in which she has been handled. She is a very neat compact little craft, and is provided with what we were really surprised to see in so small a vessel — a comfortable Saloon, capable of accommodating at least 30 persons, without the slightest inconvenience to each other. By the Melbourne Government Steam Inspectors, she is authorised to carry 80 passengers, and in this and every other respect appears well adapted for the rising traffic in the harbour and in the neighbouring ports."[3]

The Emu wasted no time getting to work with its first excursion on the 10th of March 1860:

"With an alacrity we were scarcely prepared for, we observe, by an advertisement which appears in this day's issue, that the steamer Emu will be ready tomorrow afternoon to afford an opportunity to all who may choose to avail themselves of a pleasant little trip and a breath of fresh air, at a nominal charge. For parties having business to transact, two trips are to be made in the morning to Stokes Bay (Northcote Point) and the Pilot Station (Devonport). With a continuance of the present fine weather, such trips can be and, we doubt not, will be fully enjoyed." [4]

For some months, the Emu continued with excursions across and around the Waitemata and as far afield as the Mahurangi Peninsula. Unfortunately, the service was not to last, as reported by the Colonist on 13 November 1860: "The Southern Cross announce that the Emu steamer has received very serious damage by striking on a rock in Kai Morirua Bay, Motutapu, on Saturday evening, at about 6 o'clock, p.m. We also learn that she has suffered much further injury from the strong gale which blew on the following day. The event is much to be regretted on account of the loss of a great public convenience, but still more on account of Captain Kreeft, the owner; who, with a large family dependent on him, finds himself suddenly deprived of all he possessed. Commodore Loring, with his usual good nature, sent off two boats from the Iris to bring away the passengers." [5]

A later news report advised that all was not lost for Captain Kreeft. A few days after the loss of the Emu, he accepted command of the merchantman, Rosetta, and sailed from the Bay of Islands to Montevideo and Liverpool with a cargo of very valuable china. No mention was made of his large family. [6]

Although the Emu had proved to be a fine vessel for the Waitemata, the services it provided during its short tenure were rather haphazard – catering as much for the excursionist and outlying settler as for the commuter wishing to just cross the harbour. It wasn't until 1865 that the North Shore boat builders, the Holmes Brothers, aspired to satisfy the growing demand for a regular and reliable means of harbour crossing:

"Messrs. Holmes Bros.' fine new No. 1 Ferry steamer Enterprise, was launched from their yard, North Shore, at 12 p m. yesterday. The steamer which has not yet received her machinery, is to be of 22-horse power, and is expected to obtain a high rate of speed. She will ply between Queen-street wharf and the Flagstaff (Devonport), only, and will run every hour. The advantage of regular communication cannot fail to be felt by the residents on both sides of the Waitemata, and we trust the enterprise of Messrs. Holmes may be duly appreciated and rewarded by the public.

"The owners of the Enterprise intend running her regularly between the Queen-street Wharf and Flagstaff Pier, every day from 7.30 a.m. until 8 p.m., and seem determined to give every satisfaction to the public. The Enterprise…is fitted with two saloons, of spacious accommodation, one capable of providing for 30 and the other for 20 passengers; the boat herself is capable of carrying 200 people." [7]

Of course, a regular ferry service meant more than a reliable timetable. It provided easier access to more land and profits to those who had gone before, as reported by The New Zealand Herald on 15 January 1867: "Tenders for a steam ferry service between the Queen-street wharf and Stokes' Point, on the North Shore, three times a day for one year, have been received from Messrs. Holmes Bros, by the Superintendent, and have been accepted.

"We congratulate the North Shore and North country settlers on this undertaking, which will bring them into sure and regular communication with Auckland. The direct road from Mahurangi, Matakana, and even Wangarei (sic) is by the Wade to Stokes' Point, via Lucas's Creek; and now that regular and frequent steam communication is fairly started between Stokes' Point and Auckland, we may expect not only to see an advanced value put upon property on the North Shore itself, but the settlement and cultivation of the lands back from it, north, go rapidly ahead." [8]

This may also have been the first instance that an Auckland transport service was recognised by the Government to be of such value as to warrant a subsidy: "The cost of the subsidy, £200, will be over and over again saved to the province by the increased value which it will put upon the Government township of Woodside, at Stokes' Point, for sale on Thursday next. This township, instead of being as far off Auckland as if it was a dozen miles inland, and even less accessible, will now really become like the land about the flagstaff suburban property.

"A person residing there will now be certain, if he come into town in the morning of being able to return at regular hours, midday or evening, and again of being able to go over to Auckland again next day, let the weather be what it may. And once started and carried on for one year, the ferry is not likely to be given up at a future time. The purchasers of Philip Callan's township, sold nearly a twelvemonth ago, and which joins the Government township of Woodside (Northcote), may consider their venture on that occasion fortunate one, as the establishment of a steam ferry will more than have doubled the value of the property they then purchased." [8]

As the North Shore became more accessible, so did the need for larger and more adaptable ferries such as the Devonport: "The handsome little composite steamer which has just been completed by Mr Beddoes, at his new yards, at the North Shore, to the order of F. J. Somerfield, Esq. was launched on Tuesday, the 1st instant (November 1870).

"...the new vessel is 80 feet overall, with a beam of 11 feet and that instead of the usual timbers of pohutukawa she has frames of angle iron throughout. This is, we believe, the first composite vessel built in our harbour and the main object is, of course, to secure a light draught of water without materially reducing the carrying capacity or strength of build. These objects appear to have been gained to the utmost extreme in the Devonport, for the new craft, although the largest ferry-boat in our harbour, only draws 12 inches aft and about 10 inches forward. The engine and boiler and a day's supply of water and fuel will scarcely put her down in the water to the extent of two feet. We may add that the new craft is universally admired for the beautiful proportions and exceeding symmetry of her lines.

"Now that the necessary iron-work for vessels of this class can be wrought in Auckland as cheaply as in Sydney, we hope to see many vessels of this kind floating on the waters of this province. Our bar harbours will then no longer be inaccessible or dangerous to our steam fleet, and sandspits and mudbanks be infinitely less of a bugbear for the future. The success obtained by Mr Beddoes in this boat puts an end to the question of extending the North Shore wharves, as the new boat will be able to go alongside at low springs without any difficulty...The Devonport, we are informed, will commence plying as a regular ferry-boat between Auckland and the North Shore on the 1st December next." [9]

That date proved to be slightly optimistic and the Devonport didn't start until the 14th but its arrival was nonetheless welcomed by breeze inhalers and prospective residents, if not the existing competition: "It will be of interest to all residents on the North Shore, and all citizens who at times desire to inhale the invigorating breezes of that delightful locality to learn that Mr Somerfield's new steamer, the Devonport has to-day commenced running. It is to be hoped that the opposition boats proprietors will only manifest an amicable rivalry, and if they both consent to run a late night boat, alternately, the number of residents who would avail themselves of the North Shore as a place of residence would so increase as to give more than occupation to the rival companies." [10]

But the harbour infrastructure did not always keep pace with the growth of the ferry industry and this led to unavoidable delays, as reported by the Auckland Star on 10 September 1872:

(At an Auckland Harbour Board meeting) "A letter from Messrs. Holmes Bros was read, stating that as the wharf was at present at the North Shore it would be impossible for them to keep time with their boats, as at low tide they could not go alongside. They asked to have the wharf extended 60 feet. The letter was referred to the Wharf Committee to report at next meeting." [11]

In the meantime, competition intensified with the founding of the Auckland and North Shore Steam Ferry Company Limited on 30 August 1872. It didn't then have a boat, but tenders were soon called "…for the building of a suitable ferry steamer fully furnished and provided with all the necessary appliances…" [12]

As the Auckland Star reported on 7 September 1872:

"Only two tenders were received, and that of Mr H. Niccol was accepted for £2,375, being the lower of the two. The chief peculiarities of the plan consist of a house on deck, the sides filled in principally with glass…Around this there is an open deck space of five feet wide extending round the vessel. There is also a ladies' cabin, nine feet by seven, fitted with wash-stands and all conveniences. Forward there is a smoking saloon, also on deck; the sides in like manner filled in with glass, all the windows sliding.

"A hurricane deck above gives a promenade of sixty-five feet by sixteen, and in the forward part of the vessel's deck, space is reserved for carriages, &c; so arranged that vehicles can be driven aboard and ashore without the necessity of turning. The specifications include every fixture complete, the saloons cushioned, carpeted, &c; even mirrors and spittoons being supplied. Under penalty, in default, the whole is to be completed and the boat delivered over to the directors with steam up within three months of the signing of the contract, so that by the seventh or eighth of December we may hope to see on our waters the most handsome and commodious and elegant ferry steamer in the colonies." [13]

The steam ferry, 'Takapuna' was duly launched from Mr Niccol & Son's shipyard on 2 December 1872: "Then, with a well-directed blow, the champagne bottle was shivered into a thousand: the vessel shook through all her length and shot into the water like an arrow. One, apparently, no friend to the cause, was overheard to say I hope she will go in lop-sided. But there was nothing lop-sided about her, but straight forward nose on and far away out into the stream she shot as if she had been under steam. The burst of applause that announced the launch may be accepted as the death knell of the system of irregular hours, and indifference to the public, and dirty boats under which people have so long grumbled in vain." [14]

Unfortunately, acceptance of the lower tender had not been the best choice. Beneath its elegance, the Takapuna was not all it seemed. This was subsequently described at a general meeting of Auckland and North Shore Steam Ferry Company shareholders held on 13 January 1873: "The Chairman said the next business was to determine the steps to be taken in connection with the completion of the p. s. (paddle steamer) Takapuna.

"Mr Leck said the contract had not been carried out by Mr Niccol. The boat was to have gone nine knots, and it did not. The shareholders could, if they chose, put new machinery in the boat at Mr Niccol's expense; or, if they liked, they could leave the boat on Mr Niccol's hands and demand their money back. Several documents and reports were read, namely, the contract between the shareholders and Mr Niccol, and the specifications. These stated that the engines were to give the boat a speed of not less than nine knots an hour.

"Several engineers' reports were read. They stated generally that the boiler had seen considerable service; that several of the pieces of machinery, pipes, cocks, &c, required to be replaced by new ones. Indeed, the first report, by Mr G. W. Heslop, was an almost general condemnation of the machinery. The second report, by Mr Masefield, stated that at least £200 would be required to place the engines in good working order. His opinion was that the whole of the machinery should be disconnected." [15]

After "...important additions, alterations, and improvements have been made in the machinery and boiler, as well as in every part of the ship...at an expense of about two hundred pounds..." the Takapuna began her regular service across the harbour on 25 January 1873. She was then declared by the Auckland Star to be: "...in a state of thorough efficiency...Irrespective of the elegant accommodation in spacious cabin, lady's cabin, smoking saloon, hurricane deck, &c, which has never been equalled by any ferry steamer in the Southern colonies, we have every confidence that the public will support a steamer which has been started solely for the public good." [16]

However, while the launch of the Takapuna upon Auckland's sparkling waters was seen as a great benefit to the travelling public, competition from the new ferry soon proved too much for the owners of the Enterprise and the Devonport. Within six months, the Holmes Bros and their associates sold their interests to the Auckland and North Shore Steam Ferry Company which funded its acquisition by means of a share issue:

"We would direct attention to the advertisement in another column respecting the disposal of shares in the Auckland and North Shore Steam Ferry Company. The opposition having now come to an end by the satisfactory purchase of the two steamers Devonport and Enterprise, the ferry service cannot fail to become exceedingly remunerative, and as the shares in the company are almost exclusively held by North Shore people and those having large vested interests in the North Shore, the prospects of any future opposition to the company would be particularly hopeless. There are already about two thousand paid up shares held, and the purchase of the Devonport and Enterprise necessitates the sale of two thousand more, the cost of these two boats being two thousand pounds cash and five hundred shares." [17]

While the acquisition of the Holmes Bros' ferries by the Auckland and North Shore Steam Ferry Company may have been to the detriment of future fare control, some preference, by way of a shareholding, was prudently given to the ferry company's North Shore customer base: "Although, the amount of the new shares to be taken will be required to be paid up at once, a proportion of shares, in small parcels, from five to twenty, will be reserved for residents and small property holders in the North Shore and Lake districts, and the terms of payment will be so arranged as to extend over twelve months. These will be exceptional cases, and for the purpose of making the basis of the company as wide as possible, and to identify it with the interests of all those who will be its most constant and reliable supporters." [17]

Without real competition and a growing customer base, it's no wonder that the Directors of the Auckland and North Shore Steam Ferry Company expressed great optimism for the future during its annual meeting, held on 2 February 1874: "The directors, in presenting to the shareholders the balance sheet of the company for the past year, desire to remind the shareholders that the operations of the company for the first six months were conducted under great disadvantage and loss – its position then being competitive, and the rates not remunerative.

"In the interests of the company your directors deemed it advisable to purchase the steamers, plant, and good will of the Messrs. Holmes, which transaction was completed in the month of July for the sum of £2,500. Your directors have to report that since that time the company have progressed favorably, and they trust that at the expiration of the current year, with the increased number of boats, and rising importance of the Devonport and Woodside districts, a better result may be expected." [18]

However, only some seven years later, the Auckland and North Shore Steam Ferry Company was itself subject to a takeover by the Devonport Steam Ferry Company formed in August 1881 by brothers, Ewen and Alexander Alison: "The (Auckland and) North Shore Steam Ferry Company has disposed of its interest in the North Shore and Stokes' Point Ferry Service to the newly-formed Devonport Ferry Company. The steamers Tainui, Devonport, Takapuna, and the ferry boat now building by Mr Holmes at the North Shore (to be the p. s. Victoria), also the plant connected with the service, and the North Shore Company's good-will, have been purchased for £9000." [19]

That good-will was obviously something the new ferry company wished to retain: "The new Devonport Ferry Company have lost no time in assuring the residents that though they have bought up their opponents, and now hold the entire trade, they do not mean to depart from their original intention of cheapening the cost of transit. By advertisement in another column, they announce that the return fare to and from Devonport will only be 6d on and after Monday next." [20]

And, according to the Auckland Star of 10 October 1881, it seemed to work: "The reduction in the fare between the city and Devonport by the new ferry company is well-received by the public, judging by the crowds who took passages on the ferry steamers yesterday. The weather was by no means good, but in several trips there was scarcely standing room on the decks. If the new Company go on as they have begun, we predict a successful career for them." [21]

Indeed, the new venture proved to be very much a success but "Success did not come easily, however; The Alisons had to fight off a substantial challenge from George Quick's Eagle and Osprey in 1887-88 and cope with the depressed trading conditions of the late 1880s and early 1890s." [22]

George Quick and others had incorporated a second company by the name of Auckland and North Shore Steam Ferry Company in 1885 but the company's two Glasgow paddle steamers, Eagle and Osprey, were found to need considerable modifications before they could be used on the Waitemata. Then there was also the established competition to deal with: "The new ferry service which was started several months ago in opposition to the Devonport Ferry Company, under the title of the Auckland and North Shore Ferry Company, have not had a run of luck by any means. The delay of twelve months caused by extensive alterations which were found necessary after the new steamers arrived from Glasgow was a severe drawback to commence with, and since then things have generally been against them. The consequence is that the Company have now intimated that the ferry service is suspended until further notice…

"The Secretary stated that the steamers Eagle and Osprey had met with accidents last week, which caused them to be laid up for a short time, and that now it was found that the service was not paying, and the time table had been temporarily suspended pending a private meeting of shareholders to be held on Tuesday next. He said that the fact of the matter was that the steamers had not been paying owing to the low fares charged by the old

Ferry Company, and that the inclination of shareholders appeared to be that it was better to lay the boats up rather than run them at a loss. If the fare to Devonport and back were raised, however, it is considered probable that the Eagle and Osprey would again take up the running.

"It will be remembered that when the Auckland and North Shore Ferry Company took up the running in opposition to the Devonport Company the return fare was sixpence. The new company soon cut to 3d return and the Devonport retaliated by cutting to 2d for the return voyage. The new Company continued to run at 3d and their opponents at 2d until the former suspended their service. It is now for the shareholders to decide whether the Devonport Ferry service shall be continued or whether some new field shall be chosen for their steamers. We understand that the Devonport Ferry Company will maintain the return fares at 2d, at all events till the end of the month, the holiday traffic being considerably greater than when higher rates were levied." [23]

With £9000 owed to the bank and about £1100 to other creditors, the decision was soon made and the Auckland and North Shore Ferry Company was wound up on 24 January 1888. During the subsequent liquidation process, the steamers and plant were offered for sale by auction, but failed to meet the reserve and were eventually purchased by the Devonport Ferry Company for £6,000. [24]

Subsequently, "...by the turn of the century, the Devonport Steam Ferry Company had control of all the major harbour crossings. In 1904 the Albatross was launched; this was the first of the two-decked double-ended wooden screw-ferries which were to become the Auckland standard. The first of the vehicular ferries which were to carry all of the harbour traffic until the opening of the harbour bridge were also introduced." [25]

By December 1925, The New Zealand Herald was celebrating:

"The distinguished record of the Devonport Steam Ferry Company Limited...For more than 44 years have their ferries plied between Auckland City and the North Shore. The ferry service covers the North Shore generally, including Devonport, Stanley Bay, Takapuna, Milford, Birkenhead, Chelsea and Northcote, through tickets also being issued for Brown's Bay, Castor Bay, and Murray's Bay, while special excursion steamers make frequent trips on the lovely Waitemata Harbour, and to Pine Island and Rangitoto.

"With the construction of the new concrete roads the traffic on the vehicular ferries is greatly on the increase...The company has recently added to their already large fleet the Toroa, and a further contract has now been placed with Mr George Niccol for a new vehicular steamer of the same dimensions as the Mollyhawk, which will be put into service before the 1926 summer season." [26]

However, not all of the ferry company's passengers were celebrating in 1929, as illustrated by this letter published by the Auckland Star on 17 July that year: "The citizens of Devonport are surely mostly a patient body. A comparison of time-tables on the Devonport service will demonstrate and prove that practically the same time-table is in force as provided years ago when the traffic was much smaller and travelling facilities in general much slower. Steamers capable of doing a smart and creditable trip, leisurely do about six or seven knots an hour and vexatious and tiresome calls are made at Stanley Bay. Last week one trip took half an hour, and another 25 minutes, before passengers stepped ashore at the city end. By the present service, the Ferry Company are furthering the harbour bridge project. Arthur O'Halloran." [27]

But by 1940, with little sign that a bridge might be built anytime soon, the financial position of the Devonport Steam Ferry Company remained strong: "The profit of the Devonport Steam Ferry Company, Ltd., Auckland, for the year ended April 30 (1940) was £21,077, an increase of £4620. The directors propose a final dividend of 2½ per cent., making 5 per cent., unchanged, for the year." [28]

However, while ferry-boat accommodation expanded to accommodate the population growth of the North Shore and the needs of excursionists and motorists, those who had settled along much of the long, Waitemata shoreline remained without a service – and, in fact, had done so since at least 1881, as one writer complained in a letter published by the Auckland Star on 13 June of that year: "Why should Devonport and North Shore monopolise the whole of the ferry-boat accommodation? Ponsonby, which is our most important suburb, appears to have been ignored altogether..."[29]

And even some forty years later, still long before adequate roads and bridges had reached them, settlers along the upper Waitemata ardently encouraged any aspirations that could result in a ferry service that might replicate that once provided by the trading canoes and scows of the 1800s – something like the proposal reported by the Auckland Star on 25 September 1920: "A movement of considerable importance to the Auckland district, and fraught with the greatest possibilities in converting the peaceful slopes of the upper reaches of the Waitemata Harbour into hives of industry, has been initiated by Mr J. H. Witheford, who has been in communication with the Minister of Marine in connection with the development of Auckland's inland waterways, particularly dealing with that section of the Waitemata River from Birkdale to Riverhead, where, he points out, there is ample scope and facilities to provide townships, and establish factories as well as homesteads.

"If developed on right lines, Mr Witheford says, these areas would absorb thousands of the city population, providing them with healthier surroundings and relieving the undesirable congestion in the city. The main feature of his scheme is a fast ferry service — cheap passenger and freight — with the junction at Birkdale, where a central wharf should be provided, with a bridge across the harbour from Hobsonville, and other bridges and roads on both sides of the river, to serve as feeders to the main centre of deep water ferry berthage at Birkdale.

"Mr Witheford addressed a large meeting of the Birkdale Fruitgrowers and Ratepayers Association last night, presided over by Mr E. C. Walton, when correspondence in connection with the project was read, and the progress of the negotiations explained. "The Hon. Sir William H. Herries, in his Capacity as Minister of Marine, wrote that the suggested development of the upper reaches of the Waitemata River by means of a fast ferry service would be included in the order of reference of the Inland Waterways Commission, and an opportunity would be afforded Mr Witheford and others interested in the Waitemata River development to give evidence before the commission. Letters were received from Hobsonville settlers in support of the movement." [30]

*Chapter Three*

# Auckland Canals and the Inland Waterways Commission

The appointment of members to the Auckland Canals and Inland Waterways Commission, originally proposed in 1914, was finally announced on 17 December 1920: "The appointment of the commission to inquire into and report as to a system of canals and inland waterways and other transport improvements in the Auckland district is announced in the Gazette tonight. The commission consists of Messrs. W. Ferguson, J. Begg, and A. Hunter. The report is to reach the Government not later than March 31 next.

The matters referred to the commission include the following – "What should be the route or routes of one or more canals and the working expenses of these canals, including maintenance, interest, and sinking fund? The form of control or management of any such works. Whether any concession should be granted by the General Government or local governing authorities? Whether a bridge should be constructed across the Waitemata Harbour to connect the city of Auckland with the northern districts." [1]

As usual, the reporting date for such an inquiry was quite optimistic and the Commission did not actually start its work until 11 April 1921. It then heard its first submissions at Mercer for the improvement of the Waikato River and its tributaries from the Waikato River Navigation and Vigilance Committee, the Hamilton Chamber of Commerce, and others. [2]

Additional hearings at Auckland included:

"Evidence concerning the cutting of the proposed canal across the isthmus between Waitemata and Manukau Harbours…There are alternative suggestions, one being that the canal should be constructed via the Tamaki River, and the other favouring its construction via Whau Creek. A large number of witnesses are to be examined and old plans dealing with the proposed work to be inspected." [3]

The 27-page report of Auckland Canals and Inland Waterways Commission was eventually completed on 25 August 1921 and tabled in Parliament on 13 December that year. In its introduction, the report outlined the matters investigated:

"The Commission restricted itself to inquiries as to proposed canals

(a) between the Waitemata Harbour and the Kaipara Harbour at Helensville;

(b) between the Waitemata and the Manukau Harbours by alternative routes known as the Whau and Tamaki routes;

(c) between the Manukau Harbour and the River Waikato;

(d) between the Waikato River and the Thames Gulf, through the Mangawara Creek and the Piako River.

"The Commission also inquired into the navigation and possible canalization or improvement of the Waikato River and its tributary creeks, and as to the effect of the works carried out by the Waikato River Board; also into the question of the connection of the northern and southern sides of the Waitemata Harbour by means of a bridge. Evidence was tendered by 126 witnesses, but it was upon the whole incomplete and unsatisfactory, and it was clear that the interest in, and the enthusiasm for, the question of inland waterways on a large scale in the Auckland District that existed some years ago had greatly decreased.

"Beyond general statements as to the advantages to be gained, by waterway communication, there were few or no statistics furnished (except in respect to part of the trade or suggested trade on the Waikato River) with the intent of proving that such schemes might be commercially successful. Promises to prepare and furnish statistics to the Commission were made, but have not been adequately fulfilled, and the motive underlying a great deal of the evidence given was undoubtedly (a) a desire to have public moneys spent in the various districts, irrespective of whether the schemes proposed were likely to be commercially successful or not, and (b) a feeling that if water communication existed the dealings of the Railway Department with the public might be placed on a different and more satisfactory footing through the passing-away of a monopoly of transit." [4]

The Commission's report included a great deal of technical information pertaining to the suitability or otherwise of various canal routes and analysis of the engineering, construction and cost that would be required. Its main findings included:

"Waitemata–Kaipara (Helensville) Canal

We have considered the volume of trade that would be likely to be carried by a canal of either class, and, although the data that we were able to obtain as a guide in that respect was somewhat meagre, we easily concluded that there would not be at the present time any justification for a canal, and have therefore not worked out any scheme in detail. [5]

"Waitemata–Manukau Canal (Whau and Tamaki routes)

We are of opinion that the popular view that there would be a considerable saving in time and money through the construction of a ship-canal by the Whau route for vessels trading from Auckland to Australia is fallacious. The saving in distance to Sydney of from 70 to 75 miles would be fully offset by the risk involved in navigating the Manukau bar by deep-draught vessels and by the canal dues that would have to be paid. The saving in time, owing to the slow navigation through the canal and locks and in the shallow waters of the harbour, would be negligible. [6]

"With regard to the Tamaki route there appears to be more justification, and we have looked into the matter in more detail…As the control of the Waitemata and Manukau Harbours is vested in the Auckland Harbour Board, it appears clear that the construction and management of the canal should be in the hands of that body. We therefore recommend that powers be given to the Auckland Harbour Board to carry out the work and to levy tolls on vessels and goods passing through the canal. [7]

"Waiuku–Waikato Canal

Although the Tamaki barge-canal is of importance as giving Onehunga and the harbour of the Manukau water communication with the wharves at Auckland, its value would be very much increased if barge traffic could be established with the Waikato. If this could be done, coal and agricultural produce could be loaded on barges upon the river or its tributaries, and delivered without transhipment at the wharves in the Waitemata.

"The proposal to construct a canal from the Waiuku River, a branch of the Manukau Harbour, past the Town of Waiuku and through a comparatively low saddle to connect with the Awarua Creek, which falls into the northern channel of the delta of the Waikato River, is a project that has been under consideration for many years. [8]

"As the efficiency and success of such canal schemes must be largely locked up with the navigation of the Waikato River, we deem it to be desirable that as soon as the Waiuku connection is started the Auckland Harbour Board should have representation upon any body having control of works affecting that river. As the utility of the Waiuku canal depends wholly upon the possibility of so improving the Waikato River as to make it navigable at all seasons for any vessels using the Waiuku canal or railway, we recommend that no steps be taken in furtherance of such a scheme until it is definitely certain that improvements in the Waikato River can be permanently effected.

"Mangawara–Piako Canal

For many years the idea has been entertained that a canal could be constructed between the upper portion of the Piako River and the Mangawara Creek, which discharges into the Waikato River at Taupiri. If such a canal were constructed of a suitable size, direct communication by means of small coastal steamers could be obtained via the Thames Gulf between Auckland and the Waikato. [9]

"This scheme having been brought under our notice, we are reluctantly compelled to advise that the scheme of constructing a canal from the Waikato River by the Mangawara Valley to the Piako River is, at the present time, not economically desirable. [10]

"Bridge Across Waitemata Harbour

Considerable evidence was placed before the Commission upon the desirability of the construction of a bridge across the Waitemata Harbour to connect the City of Auckland with the northern districts. It was, however, largely of a general character, showing the inconveniences under which residents in the northern suburbs suffer, largely due to alleged deficiencies in the harbour ferry services and more especially in the ferries dealing with vehicular traffic.

"Three sites have been suggested for a bridge crossing the Waitemata Harbour.

Site A, known as the Point Chevalier-Kauri Point site...The length of a bridge upon this site would be some 10,600 ft., or about 2 miles. Site B, between Point Erin and Northcote Point, is about 5,000 ft. in length; whilst Site C, between the north-west corner of the Freeman's Bay reclamation and Northcote Point, is approximately 1 mile in length. [11]

"For a roadway-bridge, with provision for carrying tramways, upon site B, the estimate shows that the cost would be approximately £950,000. Present-day prices for labour and material have been adopted in estimating...If provision be made for a single line of railway in addition to the roadway and tramways on the bridge, the cost on site B would be raised to not less than £1,500,000.

"In view of the probability of a main arterial road being constructed from some point near Northcote to the far north, and also in view of the advent of increased electric current for tramway-extension purposes, we are inclined to the opinion that a bridge erected on site B, constructed to carry a single line of railway with a roadway above the line of rails, having a width of 40 ft. and with provision for a double track of tram-cars, would probably be the scheme best suited to all the conditions. Such a bridge, exclusive of road approaches and of the tramways and railway, might be erected at a cost which for the purpose of this inquiry should not be taken at less than £1,500,000.

"However desirable it is from many aspects to construct a bridge over the Waitemata, the expediency must be judged by the question as to how the annual charges can be met. Whilst some evidence was tendered from residents on the northern side of the harbour of their willingness to be rated in proportion to the benefits they would derive, no material evidence was received from the citizens of Auckland in support of the proposal, and it is therefore reasonably assumed that they do not look for any substantial benefits to be derived by them from the construction of a bridge, and consequently would not be willing to be rated for it. [12]

"We have insufficient data before us on which to form anything more than rough estimates, but it appears to us to be fairly obvious that a maximum rate of 1d. in each pound of the capital value would be considered excessive in proportion to the benefits to be derived. It is impossible for us to say to what extent it would repay the Railway Department to contribute a large sum towards the cost of the bridge, how far it would suit Auckland City to contribute for the purpose of obtaining tramway communication to the northern suburbs, and whether the population of the districts affected, taken as a whole, would consent to being rated to anything like the extent that would be necessary.

"As the prospect of the construction of such bridge appears to be remote, we have not proceeded with the inquiry, particularly as the final decision must rest with the ratepayers, and could only be determined by submitting the question to a poll based upon some definite scheme complete in all its details, and including the whole development and lay-out of the suburban districts on the northern side of the Waitemata. [13]

(In conclusion) "We are of opinion that with the present population the expenditure that would be necessary (to construct the bridge) is not justified." [14]

*Chapter Four*

# The Harbour Bridge

Those living on the North Shore, and particularly the farmers, had for many years sought a cheaper and more efficient way than the ferries to travel and deliver their produce and stock to the more populated City.

"As far back as April, 1860, a proposal was put forward by the late Mr T. T. Masefield to construct a telescopic and pontoon bridge to connect the northern and southern shores of the Waitemata. A counter scheme was also put forward that further west, about the Watchman (Island), the city and north shore could be connected by a viaduct, a chain bridge and a drawbridge. A critic suggested that if neither of the two schemes materialised it might be possible to get a large steam-propelled floating bridge." [1]

While none of these early schemes to span the Waitemata 'materialised', it wasn't because of a lack of vision or planning. Some seventy years later, on 30 June 1931, as government and city administrators continued to procrastinate, the Auckland Star published details of another of the nineteenth century proposals:

"It is often said that there is nothing new under the sun, and the proposal to build a bridge across the Waitemata is almost as old as Auckland itself. For 70 years the prospectus of a concern which was to have been known as the North Shore Bridge Company, together with plans and estimates for a bridge, has lain at the bottom of a chest which originally belonged to a pioneer who farmed at the Three Lamps, Ponsonby. The papers were recently unearthed by Mr M. C. Tomlinson, of Dominion Road, a grandson of the late Mr Fred A. Bell, who as long ago as 1860 was the engineer and architect to the company.

"The information that the proposal to bridge the harbour in much the same place as is now planned is over half a century old, will come as a surprise to many people who are interested, directly and otherwise, in the present project. The prospectus of the old company, which, allowed for a capital of £16,000 in £2 shares, is hand written on light blue legal document paper. In order to develop the resources and capabilities of the northern part of the province of Auckland and bring the north shore in closer proximity to the city, it has been determined on forming a joint stock company for the purpose of erecting a telescope bridge and pontoons, with joints to barges and approaches, extending from shore to shore, navigation being preserved unimpeded to the breadth of 60 feet by a telescope bridge, commences the prospectus.

"The Provincial Council last year, the document reads on, placed £600 to be paid as an annual subsidy to any person who would establish a communication between Stokes Point on the North Shore and the wharf at Auckland by means of a steam boat, which was to make daily trips, but this has proved impossible without a subsidy of £1200. A bridge, as opposed to a steamer, has no expenses except a percentage for depreciation and repairs and the management of the concern, whilst its revenue goes on amassing night and day.

"A bridge will open up the whole country and convert its wildernesses into cultivated fields, gardens and towns, whilst the value of the portions at present under cultivation or built upon will be greatly enhanced, the social state of the present inhabitants will be greatly improved and their conveniences and means of wealth and economy brought to a par with the neighbouring city. After referring to the beneficial effect a bridge would have on the Devonport and Takapuna districts and to the advantage it would be to cattle and horse breeders, the prospectus says: The benefits to the city of Auckland will be very great, as the supply of provisions to the markets will be greatly increased und the internal commerce of the back country will be brought to Auckland direct through first hands.

"In order to support this bridge, it is proposed to apply to the Governor and General Government for a charter of incorporation and an Act from the Provincial Council, authorising the company to construct the necessary buildings and appliances, and to levy certain tolls on passengers, cattle, horses, sheep and all sorts of live and dead stock and produce, etc. The prospectus is signed by Mr Bell at Dedwood Terrace, Ponsonby, and is dated January 3, 1860. It was estimated by the North Shore Bridge Company that the cost of spanning the harbour would amount to £15,562 16/ (note the 16/). The main item shown in the estimates is a sum of £9165, being the estimated cost of 14 solid built timber stages, 40ft by 30ft, clamped, trussed and pinned, with iron rods and nuts and screws, covering the whole length of 5625 ft.

"The estimated cost of 137 boats to form pontoons, each 40ft long, covering 5480 ft, is shown at £3014, and that of 274 mooring chains, averaging 20 fathoms, is entered at £1534 8/. Other items shown in the list of estimates are:—Approaches at each shore, £140; five piers of 12 piles totara, totalling in length 3000 ft, £375; frame work and machinery for erecting telescope bridge, £150; 274 mooring blocks of scoria from Rangitoto, £82 4/; cost of boring blocks, £82 4/; 800 loads of scoria, £160; iron work for shoeing piles and sundries, £200; two small toll houses and gates, £100; two 'tell-tale' check gates, £10; cost of tarring whole bridge, £150; labour, £400.

"The estimated annual revenue of the bridge is shown at £3798 12/6. Assuming that 40,560 persons would use the bridge during the course of a year (the Provincial Government returns showed that the sailing ferry traffic averaged 1690 per quarter) the pedestrian fees were estimated at £2028. Other items were: Drays and carts, £273 15/; working horses not in carts, £13 17/6; saddle horses and riders at 1/6 a time, £547 10/; cattle, £104; sheep and goats, £65; pigs, £26; fees for opening bridge to allow boats to pass, at 2d a time, £36 10/; wharfage charges, £104; Government subsidy, £600.

"The annual charges are shown as: Repairs and depreciation, £1167 3/; salary of managing director, £150; wages for toll collectors £200; rent and incidental expenses, £1617; 3/. These figures show an excess of revenue over annual charges of £2181 9/6. Of this figure it was proposed that £1600 should be paid to shareholders, and that the balance should be placed to a reserve fund.

"In his explanation of the viaduct and pontoons, Mr Bell says that the distance from the south shore to the north shore, according to Captain Drury's chart, was 5625 ft. Apparently the design of the bridge was not definitely decided upon, as Mr Bell details both a system of movable barges, and also what he terms a 'telescope' bridge. For some reason which is not given, the original harbour bridge scheme of 1860 never became an actual fact, but the discovery of the old documents at least proves that the present scheme is not the new brain wave that many people think it is." [2]

Certainly not a new idea and, despite the negative conclusion expressed by the Auckland Canals and Inland Waterways Commissioners in 1921, the ambition for a bridge to span the Waitemata remained strong. It was therefore not surprising that, despite the Commission's findings, "...Mr A Harris (Waitemata) devoted some attention to that portion of the report dealing with the Waitemata bridge. This work, he maintained, was eventually bound to be necessary. In view of the spreading of capital cost over about five years, and the facilities the work would give for relieving unemployment, the present was not such an inopportune time for such an undertaking as it might be thought." [3]

An Auckland Star comment of 17 December 1921 also expressed some optimism that, because of its necessity, the construction of a harbour bridge would soon eventuate:

"It is considered that the matter should be thoroughly investigated with a view to the construction of the bridge in the near future, owing to the importance of the shorter route to the North Auckland districts. Many North Shore residents are optimistic that the financial side of the question can be readily adjusted, and, in any case, is insignificant alongside the advantages that would be secured by the construction of the bridge and appurtenances." [4]

But despite the optimism expressed by many, their ambition was unfortunately tempered by those whose ultimate interests would not benefit from the financing of a bridge instead of their own projects. For instance, in its submission to the Auckland Canals and Inland Waterways Commission, the Auckland Harbour Board expressed concern that a bridge across the harbour might interfere with its future operations: "The harbourmaster, Captain H. H. Sergeant, reported (to the Commission)…It must be realised…that the future possibilities of the Port of Auckland are enormous and that it may be necessary to make use of the valuable foreshore between Freeman s Bay and Point Chevalier reef on the southern shore and between Kauri Point and Chelsea on the northern shore for additional harbour works at some future date. It is therefore of vital importance that the harbour as far west as Kauri Point should not be obstructed in any way." [5]

Nor did the proposed bridge receive much support from the Auckland City Council and even less from the local bodies to the south. The City Council had recently taken over the tramway service and needed to make that pay in the face of increasing motor bus competition, as well as extend its tramway lines to the suburbs. There was also a great deal of southern-shore preference for the extension of the railway by means of a tunnel to the northern line at Morningside. The railway was seen by those living on the city-side of the Waitemata as a more realistic and cost-effective means of traversing the isthmus than the bridge.

The residents of North Auckland naturally disagreed, as per the letter to the editor of The New Zealand Herald, published on 26 January 1929:

"Sir, —Some time ago I noticed a very sensible suggestion made by one of your correspondents about the proposed harbour bridge. He said that it would be much better if the money to be spent on the (Morningside) tunnel were spent upon the bridge instead. To us, living in the North, this is just as it should be. The tunnel will shorten the time by train, certainly, but it will not open up a square yard of new country nor add sixpence to the products of the North. On the other hand, the bridge across the harbour will make available thousands of acres that at present are not payable; it will popularise the many magnificent beaches from Cheltenham to Waiwera; bring a great increase in the population of the four Northern suburbs of the city and increase the trade and enhance the importance of the city itself.

"Further, I believe that the cost of each project is about the same, but the tunnel will save something less than a mile, whereas the bridge will save nearly 20 miles. I do not wish to put any obstacle in the way of those who desire the tunnel, but first things must come first. The bridge will not kill the tunnel project. The increased prosperity brought about by the bridge will ultimately make the tunnel a feasible proposition, but that time is not yet. North Auckland." [6]

Meanwhile, by late 1924, neither the tunnel nor the bridge had been started and the issues were still being debated: "The adoption by the Government of the proposal of the chief engineer of railways to construct a tunnel under the city to Morningside is apparently viewed with envious eyes by those who have long advocated the construction of a bridge across the Waitemata. Their attitude was given expression to at a meeting of the Takapuna Borough Council last evening.

"Mr M. E. Thompson said that, in view of the Government's decision, the time was opportune for a declaration of the council's view on the matter and an affirmation that the natural outlet to the North was via the North Shore boroughs. Instead of spending a large sum of money in making a tunnel under the city, surveys should be taken for the construction of a bridge across the harbour. If a tunnel is built in the city we will never get the bridge, he declared. Mr T. B. Arthur said that, while supporting the idea of a bridge over the harbour, the fact could not be overlooked that nine-tenths of the people who would use the tunnel would never use the bridge." [7]

Almost two years later, Auckland's village pump mentality continued to weaken any regional, united front that could have made a difference to the Government. A prime example of contrasting perspectives was reported by The New Zealand Herald on 11 March 1926: "The unanimous support of the Birkenhead Borough Council was given by resolution last evening to the proposal to bridge the Waitemata Harbour.

"The Mayor, Mr E. G. Skeates, said people were all in favour of a bridge across the Waitemata, which would be an excellent thing, not only for Birkenhead, but also for all the boroughs on the northern side of the harbour. There was no feeling that the bridge must come to Birkenhead or Northcote. There was to be no quarrel as to where the bridge was to be located. They wanted the bridge, wherever it went, as the connection of the northern and southern shores was most essential for the progress of the marine boroughs and the districts right up to the far north. Parochialism was to be discouraged in all deliberations if success was to be achieved.

Get the bridge—wherever it crosses, was the attitude of the committee, he stated." [8]

In the meantime, there was still no railway tunnel and certainly no prospect of a start on the bridge. Little did the proponents of either project know that it would be more than thirty years before only one of their aspirations would be realised. Neither did the councillors of the Birkenhead Borough Council then realise how prophetic the comments of one of their number at the Council meeting would be: "Mr A. Hadfield pointed out that only a few years ago, when Grafton Bridge was erected there was a large public feeling that it was too elaborate, and much before its time. Already it was found that the bridge was altogether inadequate." [8]

Meanwhile, on the other side of the harbour...at Newmarket...parochialism was alive and well..."There is a possibility that we would be levied to help pay for construction, and if we are too keen with our support at present we may be levied accordingly, said Mr F. G. O'Meara, when the opinion of the Newmarket Borough Council on the proposal to connect the city and northern suburbs by bridge was sought last evening in a letter from the Waitemata Bridge Committee.

"Mr G. Smerdon said a body similar to the Power Board would probably be formed if it was decided to proceed with the project. In his opinion the population of Auckland and of the northern suburbs in particular was too sparse at present to warrant the construction of the bridge.

"Mr N. Kelleway said he thought the proposal was certainly progressive, although if they were asked to give financial assistance he did not think he would be keen to give his support. The borough was so close to the city that they were almost sure to be called upon. It was considered that no good could come of entering upon a protracted discussion at the present stage." [9]

While Councillor Kelleway thought the proposal 'progressive', a bridge over the Waitemata was nothing more than common sense and a necessity to both the businessman and recreationist alike, as expressed in a letter to The New Zealand Herald published on 16 March 1926: "Sir, —As a resident of Birkenhead I have been much interested in reading the reports and letters relative to the proposed bridge over the Waitemata...which from a business point of view together with that of its general utility, is most desirable.

"When I refer to the business point of view I have in mind the charges now made for transit across the harbour. I know of two among many cases, one of which during 12 months paid the sum of £800 in freight charges on his lorry, while another (myself), with a 30cwt two-ton lorry, paid £220. When we consider that these heavy charges are paid and that people are hampered by boat-time running and other inconveniences and limitations, the necessity for a bridge becomes apparent. Then again from the general utility point of view, there may be urged the case of the thousands who travel by motor-car and otherwise who would avail themselves of a bridge in their pursuit of business or recreation.

"I have spoken to many on the subject and have found a general expression of willingness to pay a toll commensurate with the benefits conferred and this supplemented by a toll on foot traffic would no doubt be equal to the amount charged for interest on cost of construction. Then, too, what an impetus would be given to the growth and advancement of our marine boroughs! Tis a consummation devoutly to be wished. L. C. Castleton. Birkenhead, March 12, 1926." [10]

But the 'consummation' needed to realise this ambition could only come from those with the power, funds and, most importantly, the vision. No doubt motivated as much by self-interest as a vision, one group of North Shore politicians and businessmen had, by March 1926, formed the 'Waitemata Bridge' Committee (later known as the 'Auckland Harbour Bridge Committee').

In order to gauge what support there was for their cause, the Committee asked a good number of Auckland's local bodies and 'prominent public men' three questions:

"Do you favour the construction of a bridge across the Waitemata?

"Do you agree that the time is opportune?

"Will you support the efforts of this or any other committee or organisation to further the project?" [11]

Later, the secretary of the Waitemata Bridge Committee "...Mr Arthur W. Marks, reported that 195 circulars had been sent out to prominent public men and local bodies. To those 102 replies had come to hand, and he had made an analysis of these and the accompanying remarks. At least 35 were wholly favourable to the project. [12]

But some, such as members of the Mt Albert Borough Council, simply found the questions beyond them: "It's a big question, gentlemen, and unless you have data to work on it is difficult to answer these questions, said Mr L. E. Rhodes, Mayor of Mt. Albert last evening when a letter was read at the council from the secretary of the Waitemata Bridge Committee.

"It's impossible for us to say at this stage whether we are in favour of constructing a bridge, he continued, and we can't do so till further information is before us. Devonport, Northcote and such places are vitally affected in this matter, but we are not." [13]

Others, such as the Auckland City Council, decided that the concept of a bridge was certainly worth some further consideration:

"The Auckland City Council is not disposed to brush aside lightly the suggestions now being made for a revival of the proposal to construct a bridge across the Waitemata Harbour…In moving that the matter be referred to the finance and legal committee for a report, Mr T. Bloodworth said that to his mind the bridge was of more importance than the waterfront roadway to Orakei, which was already served by good roads.

"Mr S. A. Crookes said he thought that a conference of all the local bodies on both sides of the harbour interested should be called. It would take some years to work up the scheme, but there was no doubt it would assist the development of the district to the north of the harbour. Such a bridge would carry water pipes, telephone and electric power lines and districts saving money by this means might well be asked to make an additional contribution toward the cost of the bridge. The matter was referred to the Finance and Legal Committee." [14]

As might be expected from the Council's 'Finance Committee' its subsequent reply was somewhat less than encouraging: "That while the bridge would probably be an advantage, the council cannot express an opinion until more definite information as to cost and location are available. Mr Bloodworth thought they might well omit the word 'probable' as the advantage of a bridge was surely undoubted.

However, "Mr Entrican was not in favour of wasting time over the idea, which would run into an immense amount of money and was too chimerical at the present time. Some people got together formed a perfectly irresponsible body, and the council was asked to give its support. They should treat the thing as absurd.

"Miss Melville mildly explained that the (finance) committee's reply really conveyed Mr Entrican's meaning, but in more polite phraseology. The reply will be duly forwarded to the Waitemata Bridge Committee." [15]

Obviously, there was far more enthusiasm at the home of the 'irresponsible' Waitemata Bridge Committee, across the harbour: "Enthusiastic support for the proposed bridge across the harbour is manifest at Birkenhead, and a series of resolutions by the Birkenhead Borough Council last evening were characterised by absolute unanimity. These declared in favour of the construction of a bridge across the Waitemata; that the time was opportune; and pledging support for the efforts of the Waitemata Bridge Committee, or any committee or organisation to further the project.

"The Mayor (Mr E. G. Skeates), who is chairman of the Bridge Committee, said there was no desire for any hole-and-corner affair. The committee desired the broadest outlook taken, and was quite willing to allow the local bodies to carry on with the arrangement of future details. Parochialism in respect to the particular location of the bridge was undesirable, and would be discouraged. They wanted the bridge across the harbour—wherever it went. He had inquired from Mr A. Harris, M.P., whether the Government would undertake the construction of the bridge as a national affair, as part of the railway system. Mr Harris had stated there was not the slightest hope of that." [16]

Mr Harris was certainly not wrong about the Government's lack of enthusiasm for a bridge, as reported by The New Zealand Herald on 1 April 1926: "The Hon. J. G. Coates, Prime Minister, replied specifically to the questions put, as follows: Do you favour the construction of a bridge across the Waitemata? —Yes, some day. Do you agree that the time is opportune?—No. Will you support the efforts of this or any committee or organisation to further the project?—Not at present." [17]

Just in case the financing of the bridge could be the Government's problem, "The Waitemata Bridge Committee, by 14 votes to six, adopted a resolution to promote legislation empowering the raising of £1,000,000 by lottery, £750,000 of this amount to be allocated for the erection of a bridge to connect the City of Auckland and the northern districts." [18]

Unfortunately, legislation for funding the bridge by means of a lottery was rejected:

"The Government has declined to entertain the proposal of the Waitemata Bridge Committee for legislative authority for the inauguration of a million pounds lottery for the purpose of constructing a bridge across the harbour…

"Mr E. G. Skeates, Mayor of Birkenhead, who is chairman of the committee, in referring to the subject last evening, said the Government was inconsistent regarding these matters. Permits had been given for quite a number of smaller art unions…The present session of Parliament had also passed a Gaming Bill, which gave greater opportunities than ever to racing clubs. Yet, Cabinet saw fit to turn down a bill giving a community an opportunity to raise funds in an open, above-board method, for a great community work, of unlimited advantage to the whole population of the Auckland Province, and of great use to the people of New Zealand generally…" [19]

But, while Wellington and the city-side of the Waitemata remained aloof, support for a bridge across the harbour or at least one further west, connecting Hobsonville with Greenhithe, remained strong. In a letter published by The New Zealand Herald on 10 May 1926, the aptly-named 'Progress' commented: "Whangarei is becoming such an important centre that a saving of 20 miles between it and Auckland is an important consideration; secondly, an immense development has taken place on the East Coast in the way of seaside subdivisions and a line running parallel to the coast and feeding the different beaches by motor-bus services would not only pay well, but also be of great value to the general public who need fresh air and sea breezes, but cannot afford motor-cars.

"If this is the case now, it is certain that in a few years the necessity for a line will be many times greater; so will be the cost of acquiring the land. Let the north-eastern settlers and the supporters of both bridge schemes unite to ask that the Railway Department make a thorough inspection of all routes, decide on one and acquire the necessary land. This mode of action has the advantage of uniting a greater effort and giving it a better chance of success. If it succeeds the Railway Department's decision will no doubt influence the growth of rural settlement and prevent the many anomalies arising from railways being built long after the growth of towns and villages. 'Union and foresight' is an inestimable motto. I recommend one to the governed and the other to the Government. PROGRESS." [20]

Naturally, such comment only served to fuel the resolve of the Waitemata Bridge Committee: "Following the decision of the Government not to permit a lottery to be promoted to raise £1,000,000 for the construction of a bridge across Auckland Harbour, the Waitemata Bridge Committee last evening decided to endeavour to have the bridge erected by other means. It was decided to circulate a petition in favour of the proposed bridge, for presentation to Parliament.

"Mr S. Jones mentioned that a group of financiers in England were desirous, under certain conditions, of becoming interested in financing the erection of the bridge. A sub-committee was empowered to confer with the Auckland representative of this group for the purpose of obtaining further information. Donations of five guineas each were received from the Takapuna Borough Council and the Auckland Automobile Association toward the preliminary expenses of the committee." [21]

On 25 September 1926, the Auckland Star published 'an engineer's conception of the bridge' superimposed on 'a photograph taken from Birkenhead', the combination of which must have convinced even the most sceptical of its readers that the construction of such a span was indeed very possible:

"A project to span the harbour with a bridge, thereby giving more direct access to the North, has had a fair measure of support for a number of years. Here is an engineer's conception of the bridge combined with a photograph taken from Birkenhead. The termini of the bridge are a point on the reclamation and the Northcote Heads. The approach to the bridge from Queen Street would be along a level road with an upgrade from the bridge portal 1 in 40 to the navigation span, which would give a clearance for ships of 85 feet above the water, the grade then falling at 1 in 100 to Northcote Point.

"The design shown provides for a width of 50 feet between parapets, including a carriageway width of 40 feet. The bridge would be founded on caissons sunk to the papa bed of the harbour, piers and abutments being built in concrete. Piers flanking the navigation span would be approximately 220 feet high from the foundation level to the portal heads. The superstructure would consist of steel trusses with a reinforced concrete deck. Designed to carry the heaviest traffic, the bridge is estimated by the Waitemata Bridge Committee's engineers, Messrs Jones and Adams, to cost £650,000." [22]

The national need for the bridge was obvious to the Waitemata Bridge Committee, and its means of financing a formality, as illustrated by a report of an October 1926 meeting of the Committee:

"Reporting last evening to the meeting of the Waitemata Bridge Committee, the secretary (Mr Arthur W. Marks) stated that a deputation had discussed the matter with Mr Robert Burns, of Auckland. The latter offered the opinion that the scheme could be carried out under the British Trade Facilities Act, under which the British Government would advance the money to build the bridge on the basis of a toll, provided the consent of the Government was obtained and power given to a board, constituted by statutory authority, to levy a rate to cover the interest, and a sinking fund of 1½ to 2 per cent; in case the toll should not be sufficient to repay the amount necessary to be expended.

"The material used in the construction of the bridge would need to be obtained in the British Empire. Mr Burns thought it would be a short-dated loan, say, about 20 years, and considered there would be no difficulty in obtaining the money, but understood that Mr Baldwin, the British Prime Minister, thought of bringing the Act to an end in March of next year.

"It was resolved to send a cablegram to the Prime Minister, the Hon. J. G. Coates, to the effect that the committee is desirous of his co-operation towards raising one million sterling for the construction of a traffic bridge to connect the north and southern shores of the Waitemata. Fuller details are to be forwarded by letter. The circulation of a petition, praying Parliament to take all steps necessary for the construction of a bridge across the Waitemata as a work of national importance, was authorised. A deputation is to urge the claims of the bridge during the next visit of the Minister of Public Works to Auckland." [23]

All that remained was to convince the Government. One way of doing that was to compare Sydney's original reluctance to construct a harbour bridge (started 1924 and completed 1932) with that of Auckland, as reported by The New Zealand Herald on 23 November 1926: "After, going fully into the details of the construction of the harbour bridge in Sydney in the interests of the Waitemata Bridge Committee, of which he is chairman, Mr E. G. Skeates, Mayor of Birkenhead, returned by the Aorangi from Sydney last evening.

"He stated the Auckland project was a feasible one. I will have a report to make to the bridge committee and in it I will point out the very great opposition that met the scheme of having a bridge over Sydney Harbour, Mr Skeates said. All this has been reversed now. The general feeling is that Sydney should have had a harbour bridge 25 years ago; in fact, they are now wondering how they managed to get along without it. I feel there is not the slightest doubt that there should be a traffic bridge across the Waitemata linking up the north and south sides of the harbour. Some, I know, think the time is not ripe, but I think the sooner it is constructed the sooner the North Shore boroughs will go ahead. In short, the bridge will attract people to reside on that side of the harbour." [24]

However, for some, the enthusiastic and somewhat visionary lobbying by members of the Waitemata Bridge Committee was somewhat misplaced – a criticism voiced by the Waitemata County Council's engineer, Mr G. A. Jackson, who commented in a January 1927 report to the Council: "…that a petition to Parliament for the construction of a harbour bridge was being circulated by the secretary of the bridge committee, and the chairman (of the Waitemata County Council) had been asked for his assistance to secure signatures.

"The petition gave no indication of the proposed site or probable cost of a bridge, or what proportion of the cost was likely to be provided by the petitioners. The document was far too vague to call for the consideration of Parliament. There is no doubt that the harbour will be bridged someday, said Mr Jackson, but a bridge can only result from the combined efforts of the local bodies interested. Parliament is not likely to act at the instance of an irresponsible self-constructed association, and therefore the Waitemata Bridge Committee would be better advised to limit its operations to organising the local bodies interested, than to waste the time of Parliament by presenting a petition such as is being circulated." [25]

While those local bodies south of the harbour provided little vocal support for the bridge, they were not altogether resistant to the possibilities, as reflected by their 'generous' donations to the coffers of the Waitemata Bridge Committee. For instance, during the August 1927 meeting of the Mount Eden Borough Council, it was decided to donate the princely sum of £2 2 shillings to the Committee (and £3 3s to the Labour Day sports committee). [26] While not much, it was far more than that donated by the Onehunga Borough Council which had earlier declined a request from the Waitemata Bridge Committee. [27]

The Mount Albert Borough Council also declined to contribute to the funds of the Bridge Committee with wardsman, Mr R. J Allingham, commenting, "I do not hold with the ratepayers' money being thrown about in that manner...The best bridge would be to reduce the rates of our own ratepayers.

"A little later, the question of expenditure again came up, this time in connection with a request from the Labour Day Committee for a contribution to its funds. Mr Langley: I move that no action be taken. It is not the sum of two guineas I object to, but the principle. If a ratepayer comes along and wants a bit of work done to his footpath, we have no money, yet we can lavish money on things like this. I'll vote against them every meeting at which they come up. It was finally decided to donate two guineas to the Labour Day Committee." [28]

While both political disunity and a lack of foresight prevailed, letters writers to newspaper editors continued to complain about the time and inconvenience of their daily commute. Some ninety years later, the mode of travel may have changed but the doleful complaint by 'Silverton', published by The New Zealand Herald on 2 May 1927, remains somewhat familiar:

"The loss of time occasioned to the many thousands travelling to their daily businesses in Auckland is in itself an enormous and preventable waste. The time taken at present by the ferry system may be averaged both ways at 40 minutes daily for the whole shore, instead of, say, 6 minutes for both ways by buses across a bridge. Add to this the great waste of time and expense necessitated by the ferrying of vehicles and goods, adding materially to the cost of living on the north side of the harbour.

"A fast-growing population of at present some 28,000 should not be penalised in this manner – we are apt to forget that the North Shore boroughs constitute the fifth largest city in the Dominion. For picturesqueness no part of Auckland south can compare with parts of this district; the roads generally are excellent, and there is no doubt that within a very few years the census returns will pass the 50,000 mark. Given the bridge people do not realise that practically the whole of the district for, say, three miles inland, would be as near to, say, the chief post office as is Mount Albert or the Dominion Road. Putting aside the huge increment in land values that would most assuredly accrue, I would like to emphasise that the annual liability incurred by building the bridge would be as nothing to the time and opportunities wasted, and increased cost of living occasioned by the present manner of transport.

"Another subject of interest to intending home builders is the fact that south of the harbour, four miles from the C.P.O., land is costing at least, £300 to £400 a quarter-acre, while at the same distance from the C.P.O. on the Shore it can be purchased at £120 to £200 per acre. Silverton." [29]

Of course, even in 1927, there had to be those who advocated that funds should be expended on nothing but roads first – but seemingly with good reason in this case:

"Sir,—I notice a tremendous lot of correspondence in your columns advocating the immediate construction of a half million harbour bridge, almost to the exclusion of everything else. Someday there will be a harbour bridge, but everything should be taken in its proper place of urgency; and there are more pressing needs than a bridge. The crying necessity of to-day is for proper roading of the main traffic route with the North, which is via Devonport and Silverdale. Until this is properly done and the perpetual menace of being bogged removed by the Highway Board and other authorities who are deliberately keeping the popular route with the North in mud, any clamour for diverting large sums of money in non-urgent directions in these days of painful money scarcity can hardly arouse enthusiasm among motor-owners and farmers who are being taxed for roads. North Shore." [30]

While Prime Minister Coates appeared happy to look at the transport situation north of the Waitemata, there was precious little debate and certainly no commitment, as reported by The New Zealand Herald on 20 January 1928:

"The Waitemata Harbour bridge and the Auckland-Whangarei Main Highway were discussed at some length by settlers whom the Prime Minister met yesterday on his trip through the northern districts. Mr Coates declined to take part in local differences about the choice of routes for the highway, and stated definitely that the Government could not commit itself in any way concerning the bridge scheme.

"Several settlers whom the Prime Minister met at Albany seemed especially interested in the harbour bridge scheme, and asked what the Government could do to help it forward. Mr Coates said there was a schedule of important public works yet to be carried out, and until these had been completed he could not commit the Government in any way to the bridge scheme. The cost was not known, because no boring had been done, and no reliable estimate could be made without that. Personally, he doubted whether the bridge would be built for £1,000,000, as had been suggested. He wondered how capital charges on such a sum would be met.

One of those present suggested tolls, but Mr Coates remarked that the public was not likely to endorse such a proposal. Another settler suggested that a lottery should be organised to provide funds. Mr Coates: That is right out of the question. I am not a puritan, but I can say at once that that would not be allowed under any consideration." [31]

Fortunately, there were still many with the resolve and ambition to continue their crusade for a harbour bridge, including some with the apparent expertise to know what they were talking about: "Sir, —It is a pity that a douche of cold water should have been administered to a scheme of national importance by a Minister of the Crown, and he the Prime Minister. Surely to say the least of it here is throwing cold water on progress. Without a bridge across the harbour progress north of Auckland is undoubtedly held back. There are thousands on the north of the Waitemata harbour crying out for this bridge and the Prime Minister tells them it is out of the question.

"Again, the Prime Minister states that no reliable estimate could be made because no boring had been done and that he personally could not believe it could be built for one million pounds. We have not asked the Prime Minister to estimate the cost, and further, since he states that no reliable estimate can be given. I respectfully ask, why does he volunteer his own opinion. Capable and reliable engineers have quoted figures ranging as low as £650,000, and the latter figure is my own, based upon an allowance for an average depth of 100 ft. below low-water to rock for the whole length of the bridge. However, I don't fear the Prime Minister's cold douche, as every endeavour will be made to bring about the fulfilment of the harbour bridge scheme. Civil Engineer. R. F. Moore." [32]

Part of that endeavour was an attempt by the governed to formalise its unified front, as reported by The New Zealand Herald on 3 February 1928:

"The Auckland Harbour (Waitemata) Bridge Committee met last evening, Mr J. B. Tonar presiding. It was decided to form an incorporated society under the name of the Auckland Harbour Bridge Association, and rules were adopted. The annual subscription was fixed at five shillings. The secretary, Mr A. W. Marks, stated so far 13,200 signatures had been attached to the petition to Parliament in favour of the bridge. It was agreed that further petitions should be issued for signature at public meetings which it is intended to hold in connection with a publicity campaign. It was decided to obtain at least 20,000 signatures to the petition before presenting it to Parliament." [33]

Following its incorporation on 2 February 1928, the Auckland Harbour Bridge Association wasted no time conveying its legitimacy and vision by way of a letter to the editor of The New Zealand Herald:

"Sir, —As chairman of the Auckland Harbour Bridge Association, I have been much interested in the letters that have appeared in the Herald on this subject. One correspondent, 'Shoreite,' has been giving the scheme a pretty good thrashing, and in so doing has not been as fair or as sensible as he might have been. His last contribution on the subject of dreams seems to call for an answer from one who knows the position regarding the Bayswater people, or dreamers, as 'Shoreite' calls them.

"The Waitemata Bridge Committee, now the Auckland Harbour Bridge Association, was formed in Birkenhead about two years ago, when all local bodies, ratepayers' associations, etc., on the North Shore were asked to appoint delegates to the committee. This they did, with the result that the association's committee now consists of three of the Mayors of North Shore boroughs, several members of North Shore borough councils, the chairman and some members of the Waitemata County Council, well-known civil engineers resident on the North Shore, and members of several ratepayers' and other associations.

"This committee, with its local engineers, together with such prominent engineers as Messrs. Jones and Adams and Mr R. F. Moore, have gone very carefully into the proposal and have come to the conclusion that a bridge is not only very necessary, but that it is reasonable and possible. We are quite aware that we could spend £5,000,000 or double that figure on a bridge, and we could construct a bridge that would be better than the ferry service for vehicles for £100,000, but the desire of the association is to propose and see constructed, a bridge that will serve its purpose well, without any unnecessary expenditure. If that is done, it will not be a burden, but a blessing, to all the boroughs and counties north of the Waitemata.

"Mr Blampied is one of our most energetic and sensible members and his statements…are all perfectly correct and true…It is a fact that hundreds of travellers coming from the north would use the bridge as a short cut to the city in preference to going round Henderson way. Mr Blampied did not say that neither Birkenhead or Devonport people would use the bridge. He said the ordinary ferry passengers from those places would still use the ferry; that does not take away the advantage of the bridge to the large number of motor vehicles carrying passengers, to say nothing of great quantities of building material and general merchandise that would be carried over it.

"If 'Shoreite' would take a feather out of the cap of Mr Blampied and dream a little, he might be able to see into the future clearly enough to be with us in this great and important movement. E. G. Skeates." [34]

But even great and important movements require funds to realise their dreams: "The Bridge Association was now making an effort to raise funds to carry out boring operations to ascertain the nature of the harbour bed for the foundations of the bridge. An approximate estimate of the cost of the bridge would then be- more definitely given. Preliminary estimates ranged up to £700,000.

"He (Mr E. Powell, C.E., a member of the executive of the Bridge Association) pointed out that all important bridges had received financial assistance from the public fund, and considered the suggested undertaking was of such national importance as to have a strong claim for a substantial contribution from the Government. He named several bridges which had been supported from the public purse to the extent of one-third to one-half of the total cost." [35]

By 14 July 1928, the petition target of 20,000 signatures had not quite been reached but, no doubt to maintain some sense of urgency, the petition was nevertheless presented to Parliament: "The agitation for the construction of the Waitemata Harbour bridge was advanced a stage to-day, when Mr A. Harris (Waitemata) presented to the House a petition asking that the necessary steps be taken by Parliament for the erection of the bridge. The member for Waitemata, in presenting the petition, dumped on the top of his desk several bundles of printed petitions, all fully signed—17,000 all told.

"The petition sets out that the Waitemata Bridge Committee is representative of all interests advantageously affected. It says the committee has unquestionable evidence of the advantages to be gained by the direct connection of the northern and southern shores of the Waitemata by means of a bridge. Having consulted many influential persons and organisations, the committee is convinced that the measure has strong support in the Auckland province. Parliament is asked to take the necessary steps towards the construction of the bridge as a work of national importance." [36]

To those who viewed the proposed bridge as more than just a span across the Waitemata Harbour, but as a vital link connecting the country's overall roading network, and therefore of 'national importance', the funding solution was quite clear:

"One of the functions of the Highways Board is to subsidise the construction of bridges on main roads. The bridge suggested for the spanning of the Waitemata would certainly link the highways radiating from Auckland with the North Shore, and as such, the structure might be within the jurisdiction of the board. The position seems to be indistinguishable from that of a bridge across a river, with the exception that perhaps difficulties might arise because the immediate access to the bridge would be by roads entirely controlled by the (Auckland) City Council.

"The attitude of the Highways Board on the matter has not been sought, but since the bridge scheme is supported by motorists, it is certain that owners of cars would approve of the use of main highway funds for subsidy. Tallies taken on vehicular ferries at the end of February show that an average of 750 vehicles crossed the harbour daily." [37]

That support by motorists could only increase when the ferries failed to cope, as reported by The New Zealand Herald on 24 November 1928: "For the last two Sundays there has been considerable delay at the Devonport wharf owing to the number of motorists wishing to return to the city after having spent the day or the week-end at the East Coast Beaches. Last Sunday 22 cars were shut out from the 7 p.m. boat, and by the time the next steamer arrived at 7.40 p.m. there was a long line of cars parked in Victoria Street. It was not until 8 p.m. that the congestion was relieved.

"With the improvement of the main highway to Birkenhead many motorists prefer that route, but as the last boat leaves about 5 p.m. it is necessary for them to follow the metal route to Albany and then divert back to Takapuna to reach Devonport. In the long waiting lines of cars last week many remarks were heard in favour of the harbour bridge, and there was much conjecture as to whether the outcome of the present political situation would help forward the harbour bridge agitation." [38]

Nevertheless, when the attitude of the Highways Board was sought, some months later, the news was not good: "Little hope of financial assistance for the proposed harbour bridge was given members of the Harbour Bridge Association who waited on the Main Highways Board yesterday morning to enlist the board's sympathy with the scheme. The acting-chairman of the Main Highways Board, Mr A. E. Jull, said he was sorry that the spirit of enthusiasm for the bridge had not crossed the harbour and no one from the Auckland side had appeared in support of the proposal.

"If the bridge were to be self-supporting why had the association approached the board? If the structure were subsidised by the proceeds of the petrol tax it would not be possible to put a toll on motorists. I want you to quite understand that the board is engaged in construction work in North Auckland which rather threatens the nerves of members. You have a road running to the North and a service which you may not consider desirable, but which is nevertheless available at a small cost. Would you spend all your money on a gate and leave none for the paths radiating from that gate?

"We are told everywhere when any project is brought forward for which assistance is asked that the work is a national one. We would have been disappointed had we not been told that the bridge is entirely of a national character. The board will go into the matter, now that we have the view of the North Shore representatives before us but to be successful it is necessary to get the people in the city more interested than they are at present. It would be idle for me to pretend that the board can take into consideration the construction of this bridge within the next few years in view of our commitments in both the North and South Islands. I suggest that you secure the cooperation of the 200,000 people on the city side of the harbour and show the board that the bridge is necessary when the time arrives. I can tell you that for the next few years the board cannot take into consideration the expenditure of such a sum—it cannot be done in 1929.

"Mr Aldridge (Mayor of Devonport): Well, make it 1950. Mr Jull: Make it 1939 if you like. (Laughter.) We have our commitments for a considerable time ahead." [39]

The Highways Board's less-than-positive response was just one of a series of similar attitudes faced by the Harbour Bridge Association during its attempts to garner support for the bridge at this time. The Auckland Harbour Board was one of the most powerful fence-sitters; not just because of what it saw as a threat to its command of the harbour, but also because of what money it could lose by way of land taken for the bridge approaches.

The Auckland Star reported some of what was discussed during a Harbour Board meeting held on 28 August 1928: "While not expressing its attitude towards the proposal to erect a bridge across the Waitemata Harbour in definite terms, the Auckland Harbour Board came to conclusions at its meeting yesterday that indicate that it considers the time inopportune to proceed with the project. Findings made in accordance with reports furnished by executive officers of the board, which will be directed to the Harbour Bridge Association, read as follows:—

> "(1) That the erection of a bridge across the Waitemata Harbour is not a harbour work to which the board as such should be asked to contribute;
>
> "(2) that the board, while not opposed to a bridge across the Waitemata when circumstances warrant such a structure as an economic necessity, must protect the present and future port requirements as its paramount obligation;

"(3) that, from the board's standpoint, the type, height and site of any bridge across the Waitemata should not be settled without the board's approval or after the decision of a tribunal on which the board has substantial representation, and after careful investigation and reports by experts;

"(4) that the site suggested will require the careful consideration of the board, it having been advised by its engineer and harbourmaster that the site suggested is not satisfactory as interfering with the present and future port requirements; and

"(5) that at the present time the board does not consider there is any necessity to set up a special committee of the board as requested.

"Examination of the estimates of revenue from the vehicular traffic across the harbour submitted by the association showed that it had greatly over-estimated the amount received by the Devonport Steam Ferry Company. This miscalculation upset all the estimates of revenue from tolls. The statements that the people were already paying for the cost of the bridge through the vehicular traffic ferry, and that the bridge toll would be 25 per cent of the present charge also cannot be sustained. If the board thought a bridge across the harbour was seriously contemplated within the next few years, it was unthinkable that it would have approved the expenditure of £65,000 on the new ferry wharf at Devonport, and £40,000 on two vehicular stages on this side of the harbour. In any case, the scheme laid before the board by the association was so nebulous that the most careful consideration should be given it before a decision was reached.

"The traffic manager (Mr W. R. Golden), said passenger ferry services were run with sufficient frequency to meet all reasonable requirements, and the vehicular services were running to the capacity of their landing stage at Auckland. When the new traffic landing at Mechanics' Bay was completed, traffic should be well catered for." [40]

In a typical case of obfuscation, the Auckland City Council also remained firmly on the fence in October 1928: "The Auckland City Council, replying to the association's communication for support, expressed the opinion that the construction of a bridge is not at present warranted, but that its future construction could be considered as a likely possibility, and provision might be made both on the northern and southern shores for the approaches thereto in any town planning schemes which may be entered into by the local authorities concerned." [41]

And again in January 1929: "The sympathy of the Auckland City Council in the project to span the Waitemata Harbour with a bridge was sought by a deputation from the Harbour Bridge Association which waited on the Mayor, Mr G. Baildon...Mr Baildon emphasised that he could not commit the council, but he gave it as his opinion that the project was one that should be investigated by a committee of experts, and when their report was available the council would have something definite to go upon. All they know now was that there was a desire for the bridge, and although he readily admitted its desirability it was for experts to say whether its construction was justified and to recommend a suitable type." [42]

The former response prompted this query from 'G.E.L.' published by The New Zealand Herald on 9 October 1928: "It would be very interesting to know why the City Council is so timid in its opinion and so vague in its expression. The construction of the bridge is not a necessity, nor a probability, not even a possibility, but only, 'could be considered' as a 'possibility'. It is cheering, however, to note that the council is of opinion that the 'possibility' is a 'likely' one. Is it too much to ask the City Council why it considers the bridge unwarranted, seeing that it will be a splendid thing for the city and need not cost the council anything? G.E.L." [43]

But while Auckland's local government showed little enthusiasm for the Waitemata Bridge, by October 1928, the Auckland Harbour Bridge Association had at last persuaded national government to grant a nominal sum to enable preliminary investigations to be undertaken.

"Satisfaction with the action of the Government in making a grant of £500 for preliminary investigations was expressed at a meeting of the Auckland Harbour Bridge Association last evening...Mr A. Harris, M.P. (Waitemata) said the deputation to Wellington...put the case for the bridge well, and created a deep impression. The bridge had been brought within the bounds of practicable achievement in the next five years. He was firmly convinced the Prime Minister would support the bridge rather than oppose it, realising the strong public demand behind the movement. The project enjoys more prominence to-day than at any previous stage, and I look forward to the opening ceremony, Mr Harris said." [44]

Unfortunately for the aspirations of Alex Harris and the Auckland Harbour Bridge Association, an opening ceremony in five years was not to be. Nor was the £500 grant immediately forthcoming. Indeed, it wasn't until 4 June 1929 that the grant was again offered by the new Prime Minister, Sir Joseph Ward, during his visit to Auckland, as reported by the Auckland Star: "Evidence of the large body of public opinion in favour of the proposal to span the Waitemata Harbour with a traffic bridge, was manifested at the Prime Minister's meeting in the Town Hall last evening, when prolonged applause interrupted Sir Joseph's first reference to the subject.

"I appreciate that the bridge proposal meets with the general acceptation of the majority of those present, said Sir Joseph, after the storm of applause had subsided. Personally, I am in favour of it. (Renewed applause) I am in favour of a preliminary examination being made, and for that purpose I propose to set aside £500 for the preliminary expenses of that examination. The sum of £500 will give it a start, and allow a competent authority to investigate the possibilities of a harbour bridge, the probable amount of expenditure involved and the likelihood of its meeting the requirements of the people." [45]

It was all a big disappointment for Waitemata's Member of Parliament: "I am profoundly disappointed said Mr A. Harris, M.P. for Waitemata, to-day. I expected some definite lead from the Prime Minister, particularly as the matter has been before Cabinet over and over again ever since the Government took office. The £500 referred to was promised in October last by the late Prime Minister, the Hon. J. G. Coates, following the favourable recommendation made to the Government by the Public Petitions Committee which considered a petition bearing 25,000 signatures, presented to Parliament by myself, in support of the harbour bridge.

"Sir Joseph has merely given effect to a commitment of his predecessor. The one gratifying feature of last night's announcement was the spontaneous outburst of continued applause when the Prime Minister intimated his intention of speaking on the harbour bridge question. That should at least convince him that there is a very definite and pronounced public opinion behind the movement—certainly not confined only to North Shore." [46]

Of course there remained those who continued to oppose any progress toward the construction of a bridge across the Waitemata. Some naturally sought to protect their vested interests and none had more to lose than the ferry operators, as reported by the Auckland Star on 13 June 1929: "Shareholders will doubtless anticipate some remarks being made with reference to the suggested bridge across the Waitemata Harbour said the Hon. E. W. Alison, chairman of directors of the Devonport Steam Ferry Company, at the annual meeting this afternoon. I do not propose to enlarge upon either the proposal or the published propaganda however misleading many of the published statements in connection therewith may be...

"My reason for withholding criticism of the bridge proposition is that the Government is intending to set up a commission to inquire into and report upon the whole proposal. It was freely circulated recently that the present Government was prepared to undertake the erection of a bridge across the Waitemata as a national work and that no financial responsibility would be imposed upon property owners. The probability of the Government doing so, is, however, in my opinion, very remote, and it is unthinkable that property owners will agree to the borrowing of the enormous sum which would be required to construct a bridge across the Waitemata Harbour and the approaches thereto, and saddle themselves with the excessive taxation which would undoubtedly have to be imposed to meet the huge annual deficit in receipts over expenditure which would be entailed.

"The erection of a bridge across the Waitemata, as proposed by the Bridge Association, is as premature and unnecessary as when the Auckland Canals and Inland Waterways Commission reported in 1921…" [47]

In his letter to the Editor of the Auckland Star, John Guiniven responded with a call for progress: "It is obvious that the chairman of directors of the Devonport Steam Ferry Company could not reasonably be expected to advocate any progressive scheme, such as the harbour bridge project, which might lessen the company's profits and end the existing monopoly of cross-harbour transport.

"No advantage is gained by our opponents in quoting the decision of the 1921 commission, which was unfavourable to the construction of the bridge. Circumstances are now totally different. We have a progressive Government in power with Sir Joseph Ward as leader, whose slogan is 'Progress,' and the rapid development of the country. Obsolete methods of transport must go; vehicular ferry boats are as old-fashioned as Noah's Ark. I feel positive that the present Government realises that the bridge is a national concern and will bear the cost of construction... John Guiniven." [48]

Perhaps in anticipation that a bridge could actually be built…one day…the discussion by mid-1929 had broadened from the debate as to its placement and financing to include its construction and design, as reported by The New Zealand Herald on 3 July of that year:

"A plea for the closer co-operation of engineer and architect in the designing of bridges, illustrated with examples of some of the finest structures in the world, was made by Mr W. H. Gummer in the course of a lecture on bridge architecture delivered at the Auckland University College last evening…Mr Gummer then dealt with the proposed bridge across the Waitemata Harbour, stating that such a bridge to be satisfactory must be not only of sound construction, but also aesthetically perfect to fit in with its surroundings. It must add to, not detract from, the beauty of the harbour." [49]

When presenting his lecture, little did Mr Gummer know how prescient (and ignored) his advice would be during the eventual planning and construction of the bridge some 29 years later…"Mr Gummer did not give any figures as to the width desirable in the proposed bridge, but uttered a warning against planning on too small lines. It was frequently the experience in structures of this nature that they were made so small that they were found inadequate as soon as they were completed. If finance compelled the building of a bridge with the width strictly limited to immediate needs, some provision should be made for the economical widening at any time in the future." [50]

But before the dream of an 'aesthetically perfect' bridge across the Waitemata could be realised, there loomed the nightmares of the depression and the political parochialism of Parliament to spoil everything. The latter torment was illustrated by a Parliamentary debate that took place on 27 July 1929: "Advocating that the Government should go on with the proposal to construct a bridge across the Waitemata Harbour, as a national undertaking, Mr A. Harris (Waitemata) stated in the House of Representatives this afternoon that the work would absorb great numbers of unemployed men. Indeed, added Mr Harris, our unemployment problem in Auckland could be ended with a stroke of the pen.

"Mr Coates had stated in the House last October that the Government would grant £500 towards a survey of the harbour bed and later Mr Coates promised to convene a conference of interested bodies. However, when Mr Coates went out of office he could do nothing more for the bridge and Sir Joseph Ward was then approached. Sir Joseph had given an assurance that the tribunal would be set up. I can't understand why nothing is done, complained Mr Harris. I seem to be up against a stone wall. I get very nice replies, but you don't get very far on nice replies.

"A Southern Member: Where is the Waitemata? The Hon. T. M. Wilford: Will the hon. gentleman vote to fill the South Island railway gap if I vote for his bridge? Mr Harris: I won't give any undertaking just now. There is no comparison between the two undertakings. Our bridge will pay handsomely, but I don't know about the other. People are becoming irritated at the unnecessary delay. Mr Harris added that the tribunal should be set up as soon as possible. The Government had to take care of the people of Auckland." [51]

Finally, what appeared to be a decision made on a real start to the bridge project was reported on 20 August 1929: "An assurance that the £1000 promised by the Government for preliminary work on the harbour bridge scheme would be spent entirely on investigations of the harbour bed was given yesterday afternoon by the Minister of Public Works, the Hon. E. A. Ransom, to the president of the Harbour Bridge Association, Mr R. H. Greville. The Minister stated the Government would in addition pay the costs of the commission which will shortly be set up." [52]

And, a few days later, it seemed that all was ready for the borings and the feasibility study to begin: "Arrangements may be made to begin preliminary borings for the proposed Auckland Harbour bridge sometime next week. Mr R. H. Greville, president of the Auckland Harbour Bridge Association, who returned from Wellington on Saturday, stated that the Prime Minister, Sir Joseph Ward, had promised him that Cabinet would consider this week the personnel of the proposed Royal Commission which is to inquire into the feasibility of the bridge project. Matters connected with the expenditure of the £1000 promised for borings on the harbour bed would also be considered." [53]

Surely…it could not be so straightforward…and, of course…it was not. For a start, the all-powerful, Auckland Harbour Board had a hand to play: "The statement on the harbour bridge made to the Harbour Board yesterday by the chairman was clear and convincing, and the Board very properly supported his views. The Board is the harbour trustee for the people of the city and the province. Commercially the harbour is the 'all-in-all' of Auckland, and it is the Board's primary duty to protect the port against any encroachment that would interfere with its present or future operations.

"If the Harbour Board can give good reasons for objecting to a site for a bridge, that should be sufficient to condemn it. Mr Wynyard (Board Chairman) was quite right in asking that the Board be consulted by the Government before the personnel of the Commission is fixed. He is also justified in suggesting that the definition of an acceptable site area should precede boring, for the money spent on such tests would be wasted if the Commission did not approve of the position." [54]

A later report published by the Auckland Star on 4 September 1929 revealed the political influence that could be wielded by the Harbour Board: "The Auckland Harbour Board is content in the knowledge that the personnel of the commission to investigate the desirability of building the Waitemata Harbour bridge will not be finalised before consultation with it. At yesterday's meeting of the board approval was given the recommendation of the board in committee disapproving of the commission suggested by the Harbour Bridge Association as not possessing the necessary qualifications for determining such a vital harbour question. The recommendation expressed the opinion that the commission should include an independent engineer, such as the engineer of the Public Works Department; a nautical expert, such as the harbourmaster of Sydney, and a harbour engineer of standing.

"Mr E. Aldridge reported that he had conveyed the board's opinion to the Prime Minister (Sir Joseph Ward) when in Wellington recently. Sir Joseph had intimated that the personnel of the board had not yet been selected and every consideration would be given the board's recommendations. Mr Wynyard said he had had several communications from members of Parliament and Ministers of the Crown in regard to the commission. The assurance given in the House that the board would be consulted before the personnel of the commission was fixed appeared satisfactory." [55]

But while members of the Harbour Board were receiving communications from Wellington, by 5 September, the Auckland Harbour Bridge Association were still awaiting for instructions to start work. That is, until told by the Prime Minister that he'd had second thoughts (but not that he might have been influenced in any way).

"No word has been received in Auckland regarding the preliminary borings in connection with the Auckland Harbour Bridge scheme for which it was thought arrangements would have been made by the beginning of the present week. On his return from Wellington over a week ago, Mr R. H. Greville, president of the Auckland Harbour Bridge Association, stated that as a result of an interview with the Prime Minister, Sir Joseph Ward, he expected that authority to begin the work would be received in Auckland before the end of last week.

"Yesterday Mr Greville stated that he had been in telegraphic communication with the Prime Minister, and as far as he could gather it was not intended to commence the preliminary work until the proposed Royal Commission had inquired into the feasibility of the bridge project. It seemed unlikely to him that any boring work would be carried out until the commission had been set up and had defined an area within which the bridge might be built." [56]

And the Auckland Harbour Board was not the only organisation calling for professionals to be involved in the consultation process. The Auckland Town-planning Association was advocating that far more planning on a regional scale was needed – as reported by The New Zealand Herald on 18 September 1929: "The necessity for carrying out regional planning before the harbour bridge site is chosen is urged in a letter to be forwarded to the Director of Town Planning by the Auckland Town-planning Association. It is pointed out that although the construction of the bridge is not opposed the site should not be selected unless due regard is given to a comprehensive planning on both shores of the Waitemata Harbour.

"The bridge site was a major regional activity and could not be considered without an extensive survey of the whole region, with particular reference to the main traffic routes, both local and provincial. It was more important to make the bridge and consequential works fit the regional plan than to embark on costly street reconstruction schemes to make the plan fit the bridge Regional planning on both sides of the harbour should be expedited in its relation to the proposed bridge site. The association's comments were in no sense antagonistic to the bridge scheme, although it was believed if the proposal were studied on the lines suggested more support would be accorded it." [57]

But neither the regional nor national significance of such a piece of infrastructure came close to being realised by those holding the purse strings and who were subject to parochial influences, as reported by the Auckland Star on 28 September 1929: "Who will pay for the Waitemata Harbour Bridge? Reference to the vital question of finance was made by the Prime Minister (Sir Joseph Ward) in the course of his speech early this morning. He had been answering the pleas of Auckland members for important Auckland works, and he said that four 'items' totalled £4,720,000.

"On top of that, said Sir Joseph, Mr A. Harris (Waitemata) had asked that the Waitemata Harbour Bridge be built at the expense of New Zealand. That had never previously been suggested. Up till now the Government had only been asked for survey facilities, and he had undertaken to do that. As a matter of fact, Cabinet had just appointed two members of the Commission, and it was waiting for the Auckland Harbour Board to approve the third before making the name public. It was surprising to hear Mr Harris suggest that the bridge be built at the cost of the New Zealand taxpayer. The Government had always understood Auckland would build it." [58]

"Referring to the Auckland members' representations early this morning, Sir Joseph Ward said that Aucklanders must be reasonable in their demands. The sum of £1,000,000 was being expended at present on the railway station and yards, and the Westfield deviation would cost £700,000. The Morningside tunnel was estimated to cost £1,000,000, and the Paeroa-Pokeno railway would cost £1,020,000. Those four items totalled *£4,720,000." [59] (*That the actual total is £3,720,000 seems to have been accepted as a political embellishment.)

The Harbour Bridge Commissioners were finally named by the Government on 10 October 1929: "There were only three members: Mr F.

W. Furkert, engineer-in-chief of the Public Works Department, Mr James Marchbanks, general manager and chief engineer of the Wellington Harbour Board. Captain Coll McDonald, retired shipmaster, of MacAndrew Bay, Dunedin. Captain McDonald will represent the Auckland Harbour Board.

"The Minister said the order of reference had not been decided upon, but it was in course of preparation by the Public Works Department, and it would be announced in a few days' time, when the question of borings and all other essential matters would be finalised." [60]

Naturally, the formation of the Harbour Bridge Commission was widely criticised and, from a town-planning and regional point of view, with some justification, as it turned out: "The personnel of the commission appointed by the Government to hear evidence concerning the proposed bridge across the Waitemata Harbour was criticised at a meeting of the Auckland Town Planning Association executive last evening. Deference was made to the fact that none of the members was an acknowledged expert in town planning...It is rather extraordinary that no town-planning expert is to be associated with the commission, Mr E. V. Blake said. I think that we should certainly protest.

"An able engineer has been appointed at the head of the commission, but that does not say that he will have time to study the town-planning principles involved. While the bridge commission might select the bridge site purely from the aspect of its location, I do not think that it will go out of its way to study it in relation to the amenities of Auckland.

"Mr C. K. Grierson said he was afraid that by the appointment of the commission the Government was only throwing out a sop to the agitation that had been going on. The finding of the commission would be wasted. The £1500 to be spent on the commission could be better spent in other ways. I am afraid that it is perfectly useless making any suggestion to the Harbour Bridge Association, Mr Grierson said. Its members will be absolutely satisfied at their next meeting. They have the commission appointed, and they think that the millennium is in sight. Any suggestions made now will be howled down. I do not think that we as a town-planning association should take much notice of this commission, but as ratepayers I think that we should deplore the fact that another £1500 are being thrown into the waste-paper basket.

"The chairman said that nothing could be done until the question had been considered by the regional committee. It was still uncertain whether the commission was going to investigate and report upon the best site for the bridge or whether it would merely confine itself to the desirability of a bridge at all at the present time. Mr T. Bloodworth: It looks as though the bridge is being considered solely from the viewpoint of navigation. On the motion of Mr Blake, seconded by Mr Bloodworth, it was resolved to approach the Government with a view to having an expert in town-planning included on the commission in order to bring the whole question within the viewpoint of regional town planning.

"The Chairman: You do not suggest that this is one of the Government's means to find work for the unemployed within five weeks? I cannot see that anything of a practical nature will arise from the commission. It will certainly spend the £1500, but beyond that it may be years before anything is done. I think that we will use the ferry for a while yet." [61]

Fervent protest as to the commissioners appointed was also voiced by two Auckland Members of Parliament during a debate reported by the Auckland Star on 18 October 1929: "Emphatic protests against the appointment of Mr F. W. Furkert, engineer in chief to the Public Works Department, as member of the Auckland Harbour bridge Commission, were voiced in the House of Representatives to-day by Mr J. S. Fletcher (Grey Lynn) and Mr H. G. R. Mason (Auckland Suburbs).

"Mr Fletcher said he was making no complaint concerning the personal ability of Mr Furkert, but the trouble was that that officer was overburdened with work, and could not possibly give full attention to his many duties. In addition to being engineer in chief, he was also under-secretary of the Public Works Department, chief marine engineer, chairman of the Main Highways Board, chairman of the Engineers' Registration Board and a member of the Office Accommodation Board and the Local Bodies Loans Board.

"One would think that ships were going to use this bridge, instead of motor traffic, said Mr Mason, because the other gentlemen appointed to the commission are connected with shipping interests. To my mind the question of town planning should be considered. A town planner should be the first consideration, but apparently there is to be no representation in that respect." [62]

The following day, on 19 October 1929: "The order of reference for the commission appointed by the Government to consider the advisability or otherwise of building a bridge across the Waitemata Harbour was made public by the Minister of Public Works, the Hon. A. E. Ransom.

"The commission is asked to determine the following questions, and its report is to be presented within six months:

(1) The present Waitemata Harbour transit facilities.
(2) The present and future harbour transit requirements.

(3) The means by which such requirements may best be provided, and in particular the following matters: (1) The necessity or otherwise for the building of a bridge across the Waitemata Harbour.

"In considering the question the commission shall take into consideration the adequacy, efficiency and suitability of the existing harbour transit facilities, in view of the population, capital value of the north shore boroughs, and adjacent Waitemata County areas; the travelling population; the number of motor vehicles likely to require transport facilities across the harbour; the distance from the present ferry routes to the harbour bridge sites suggested by the Auckland Harbour Bridge Association, incorporated, or any other practicable site; the probable passenger fares and times taken from various termini by any proposed route to the city compared with the present ferry and vehicular charges and times; the liabilities of any proposed rating area if rated to cover the whole or portion of the cost of the bridge and its approaches, or alternatively the probable tolls chargeable on those using the bridge.

"If the former question is answered in the negative, then the commission shall consider the period of time within which the probable growth of population and use of motor vehicles, together with other methods of transport, shall so increase the necessity for increased transit facilities across the harbour as to render the bridge necessary." [63]

The Harbour Bridge Commissioners began their inquiries on 14 November 1929 with an inspection of the Waitemata Harbour and a motor tour of the North Shore as far north as Warkworth and Matakana and as far west as the Kaipara. During the Commission's hearings, some sixty-two witnesses were examined including representatives of the Auckland Harbour Bridge Association, the Auckland Harbour Board, the Auckland City Council, local borough councils, the Auckland Transport Board, the Waitemata Electric Power Board, the Automobile Association, the Auckland Town-planning Association, the Devonport Steam Ferry Company, various bridge designers and engineers, and others presenting evidence for and against the construction of a bridge at its various proposed locations.

When the Commission's report was completed on 22 April 1930, it first summed up the harbour transit facilities then provided by the 'well-organized' Devonport Steam Ferry Company: "The fleet comprises nine passenger ferry-boats and four vehicular ferries. There are landing-places at five points on the North Shore and three on the city or southern side of the harbour, to and from which these vessels ply. Of these landing-places two on the city side and three on the North Shore are available for embarkation and disembarkation of vehicles. The evidence showed that the passenger ferry service in the daytime is very efficient, entirely adequate, and extremely cheap. The passenger-carrying facilities after midnight, however, are meagre, though a small vessel is always kept available for emergencies.

"For a considerable number of years it will be possible to adequately provide for the requirements of harbour transit at Auckland by a progressive increase, both in size and numbers, in the ferry fleet, plus further landing-stages at each end. A time will arrive, however, as it has arrived within recent years in Sydney, and in New York in respect to the ferry services between Staten Island and New Jersey and between Manhattan and New Jersey, when no increase in the number of ferryboats will adequately cope with the demand, and then provision for unrestricted traffic between the northern and southern shores of the harbour by bridge or tunnel will become imperative. The time when such provision will become necessary at present appears to be well in the future, especially when one considers the size to which such cities as Sydney, New York, &c., grew before the large expenditure involved in the construction of bridges was entertained.

"After careful consideration of the whole question, your Commissioners are of the opinion that the day has not yet arrived when a bridge is necessary. With the only practicable site for a bridge, the distance to be travelled by road and bridge between Queen Street and the centre of Devonport—which is by far the most populous of the North Shore suburbs – would be so great that a bus service could not be carried on except at a figure very much in advance of the present ferry charges; further, the time occupied on the journey would be longer. With regard to private motor-cars, though these would have the advantage of being able to go and come across the harbour at any time if a bridge were constructed, the running-costs on a mileage basis would exceed the charge for which cars are now carried on the ferries.

"A great deal of evidence was submitted to the Commission in support of the probability of vast development taking place in that portion of the Waitemata County immediately adjacent to the North Shore boroughs, as a result of the construction of a harbour bridge. We examined this area of country and found that it was in a very backward state. This is explainable by two causes, quite unconnected with the present lack of bridge connection with the City of Auckland. Firstly, the land in parts is extremely poor in quality, and, secondly, the roads are in a very backward condition, there not being even one continuous first-class metalled road in this area.

"The greater part of the advantage derived from the construction of a bridge would be reaped by the owners of motor-vehicles resident in Auckland desiring to visit points on the North Shore for recreation purposes, which factor was greatly stressed in the evidence, and to a lesser degree by motor carrying firms engaged in the delivery of goods from merchants' warehouses in the city to customers on the North Shore. The bridge would provide no advantage to the ordinary passengers, as apart from the motorist driving his own vehicle. It would also enable a considerable number of comparatively well-to-do people resident on the North Shore to own and drive their own motor-vehicles; these people are at present deterred from investing in cars by the fact that they would in practice be restricted to a very small mileage of road unless they incurred the inconvenience, risk, and delay of ferry transport.

"The representatives of practically every shade of opinion who gave evidence, while expressing the general view that the bridge would be a great convenience, repudiated, any willingness to contribute towards its cost. It appeared to be the generally accepted view that the bridge should be financed with tolls levied on motor-vehicles; but the official representative of the organized Automobile Association repudiated any willingness on the part of his members to pay tolls for crossing the bridge, submitting that the motor-vehicle was already sufficiently taxed, and that the bridge should be regarded as portion of the roading system of the Dominion, and should be constructed and maintained by the State out of the Public Works Fund. Under cross-examination, however, this witness stated that he would prefer a toll bridge to the continuation of the existing system, which is in effect a toll.

"The official representatives of almost every local authority who were examined stated that their Councils were opposed to any proposal to levy rates for financing the bridge, and expressed the opinion that the necessary funds should be obtained by tolls, both for the upkeep of the bridge and as security for the raising of the requisite capital for first construction. After careful consideration of all the evidence, and after investigations made in the districts, your Commissioners are of the opinion that the time for the erection of a bridge across the Waitemata Harbour will not arrive in less than twenty years, though it might be advisable in, say, ten years' time to have the position reviewed again." [64]

All good news for the Devonport Steam Ferry Company which celebrated its fiftieth anniversary on 16 June 1931: "...when the Hon. E. W. Alison, M.L.C., was warmly complimented by the shareholders who attended the annual meeting, on completing half a century as chairman of the company. Congratulatory reference was made to the company's remarkable record of achievement, in that not one serious accident had been met with during the 50 years it had been in operation, not a single strike of any character had occurred, and not a single year had elapsed during which the directors did not recommend the payment of a dividend of not less than 7½ per cent.

"In moving the adoption of the report and balance-sheet, details of which had already been published, Mr Alison said the accounts must be considered fairly satisfactory in view of economic conditions. After making an allowance for depreciation on steamers and plant, the net profit for the year was £11,230 5s. To that sum had to be added the amount of £544 13s 11d brought forward from last year, making a total of £11,774 18s 11d. It may interest shareholders to be informed that when the company was promoted in 1881, the capital was £10,000 in 10,000 £1 shares. In 1895 the capital was increased to £50,000 in £1 shares, of which £25,000 were then issued. Later on, in 1913, the capital was increased to £150,000, and again in 1927 it was further increased to £250,000, of which £150,000 was issued, and which is the amount of issued capital at date.

"The population of Devonport in 1881 numbered 1316, and the revenue of the then local public body, the Devonport Road Board, at March 31, was £462 6s. Contrast these figures with the statistical returns for Devonport at March 31, 1931, namely, population, 10,400; revenue, £84,430. Shareholders will expect some reference to be made to the proposal to build a bridge across the Waitemata, continued Mr Alison…Personally, I am certain the proposal is premature and such a large expenditure unwarranted. However, if outside capital can be secured to complete the building of a suitable bridge with necessary approaches, and the public interests are fully protected in the bill before Parliament, all well, but if the required finance is secured, those who find the money can be looked upon as philanthropists, not business men." [65]

The 'bill before Parliament' referred to by Mr Alison was the Auckland Harbour Bridge Empowering Act 1931 which essentially privatised the proposed, national resource. While the bridge Commissioners had decided that a bridge over the Waitemata was twenty years ahead of its time, "…Members of the Harbour Bridge Association were undeterred, and in November 1930, the Auckland Harbour Bridge Company was registered with a capital of £5000 in £1 shares. After negotiations with representatives of Dorman, Long and Company, contractors for the Sydney Harbour Bridge, a bill authorising the company to obtain a charter to carry out the work was introduced into Parliament. Various delays occurred, and the measure was considerably amended before it became law the following October." [66]

The Auckland Harbour Bridge Empowering Act 1931 empowered: "...the Auckland Harbour Bridge Company, Limited to erect a Bridge across the Auckland Harbour and impose and collect Tolls for the Use of the Same...WHEREAS a company limited by shares has been incorporated...under the name of The Auckland Harbour Bridge Company, Limited, having for its objects the erection, maintenance, and control of a bridge across the Auckland Harbour from a point in Fanshawe Street, in the City of Auckland, to a point in the Borough of Northcote..." [67]

The legislation stipulated that of the minimum number of seven and maximum of twelve Directors making up the Board of the Auckland Harbour Bridge Company, one each should be appointed by the Auckland City Council, the Auckland Harbour Board, and the Northcote Borough Council. The remainder were to be elected by the company's shareholders.

But while there was public representation, that did not mean there could be any public liability. Clause 99 of the Act clearly stated: "Notwithstanding anything contained in this Act to the contrary, neither the Crown nor any authority or corporation, municipal or otherwise, other than the company, shall be called upon or become in any way whatever liable to pay for the cost or any part of the cost of or in connection with the bridge." [68]

"In its original form the bill gave the company two years and three months from the commencement of the Act in which to begin the erection of the bridge, failing which the charter and the Act were to lapse. However, by a later amendment it was provided that the company must begin the work of erection within two years after it had received the 'approved plans' of the structure from the Governor-General-in-Council, otherwise the charter and the act would lapse." [69]

Not long after the passage of the original bill, preliminary discussions to have the bridge privately constructed were under way, as reported by the Auckland Star on 14 December 1931: "A conference was held in Wellington to-day between members of the Auckland Harbour Bridge Association and Mr L. Ennis, engineer to Messrs. Dorman, Long and Co., of London, the contractors for the Sydney Harbour bridge.

"The discussions on the Auckland Harbour bridge were in the very early stages, Mr Ennis said, but he was optimistic that the bridging of the Waitemata would shortly be an accomplished fact. Apart from unforeseen difficulties, he believed the bridge could be built in 4½ years. They say the bridge is 20 years ahead of its time, he remarked. I do not agree with that statement. I say the bridge is wanted. The situation is ideal, and the north shore would progress more rapidly if the harbour were spanned." [70]

Accordingly, the Auckland Harbour Bridge Company and Messrs. Dorman, Long and Co wasted no time preparing design plans for the proposed bridge, as reported by The New Zealand Herald on 11 February 1932: "Advice that a design and general plans for the Auckland Harbour Bridge have been completed for Dorman, Long and Company by Mr Ralph Freeman, designing and consulting engineer of London, has been received by Mr C. H. M. Wills, chairman of directors of the Harbour Bridge Company.

"The information to Mr Wills was verbal and confirmation by mail is expected shortly. Mr Wills said yesterday that the plans were probably now in the hands of English financiers, to whom it was most important that an engineer of Mr Freeman's standing should be in charge of the design. Mr Freeman was the designer of the Sydney harbour bridge. It was expected that a copy of the plans would reach Auckland in two months, Mr Wills said. They would be considered by experts in New Zealand and the Marine Department would have to give final approval. Mr Wills said the company was negotiating with other bridge-building firms and competition for the work was by no means closed. He understood that other firms were also preparing plans." [71]

Unfortunately, 1932 was not the most opportune time for potential investors to consider underwriting what was viewed as a speculative project at that time. At least that was the view of the deputy-chairman of Dorman, Long and Co: "The Auckland harbour bridge project was referred to this morning by the Hon. Roland D. Kitson, a director of the Bank of England and deputy-chairman of Dorman, Long and Co., Ltd., builders of the Sydney Bridge. Mr Kitson went to Australia to attend the bridge festivities in Sydney, and is a through passenger by the Niagara. Mr Kitson said he was here quite informally, and directors of the Auckland Harbour Bridge Co. would discuss the project with him in an unofficial way.

"He referred to statistics that had been compiled as to the wheeled traffic that used the vehicular ferries, and commented that the figures were not very encouraging. There had been an estimate prepared of the traffic that was likely to use the bridge, but it was always difficult to substantiate figures of that character when the question of providing the finance was concerned. Those who are asked to provide the money, he said, must be convinced beyond doubt that the traffic is there before the necessary finance can be secured…The Royal Commission of 1930 which reported on the project, said Mr Kitson, distinctly states that from a financial point of view the bridge is not warranted for twenty years, but that it may be worthwhile reconsidering the proposal in ten years. In the circumstances it may be we are discussing the bridge a little too early...in any case the arranging of finance at the present time was a difficult matter in view of world conditions...The investing public in England, said Mr Kitson in conclusion, are like the investing public everywhere else; they are looking for a good security, and they must be firmly convinced before they put their money into a venture that it is sound." [72]

Not unexpectedly, then, the investing public of England could not be convinced that a bridge across the Waitemata was a sound investment. Nevertheless, the Auckland Harbour Bridge Company remained undeterred, as reported by the Auckland Star on 6 September 1932: "Negotiations between the Auckland Harbour Bridge Company, Ltd. and Messrs. Dorman Long and Company, and other English construction companies for the raising of the money for the erection of the proposed bridge across the Auckland harbour at an estimated cost of £1,250,000, have not proved successful. An announcement to this effect is contained in a circular which was sent to shareholders in the bridge company last evening." [73]

"In view of the position that has now arisen the directors of the bridge company recommend that the Government be asked to authorise the Unemployment Board to find the interest on a loan of £500,000 for four years or until the bridge is opened, so that other arrangements may be made for the letting of a contract for the construction of the bridge, using largely unemployed labour. These proposals are to be considered at a meeting of shareholders next Tuesday.

"After setting out the result of the negotiations with English construction companies, the directors express the view that a further effort should be made to raise some of the money required for the bridge project, from public and private sources within the Dominion. The estimated time required for erecting the bridge was four years and the average number of men required would be 500." [74]

At the subsequent board meeting, support for the Directors' efforts remained strong and optimistic, as reported by the Auckland Star on 13 September 1932: "At a meeting of the Harbour Bridge Association held last evening, Sir Walter Stringer presiding, the shareholders approved the suggestion of the directors that an endeavour be made to obtain the assistance of the Unemployment Board to raise money to start, the building of the bridge. Mr M. H. Wynyard, representing the Harbour Board, and Mr T. Bloodworth, representing the City Council, accorded the proposal strong support. The shareholders gave the directors very wide powers to further the project.

"It was suggested by some shareholders that the directors should call a meeting and invite representatives of the local bodies, the power boards, the Harbour Board, trades union representatives, and a representative of the Unemployment Board so that the directors' proposals could be fully discussed and the support of the various bodies obtained. The directors promised to consider the suggestion and do something on the lines suggested." [75]

But not all shared the optimism of the Harbour Bridge Company, as per this letter to the Auckland Star published 15 September 1932: "It is very interesting to read the deliberations and intentions of the Harbour Bridge enthusiasts. I quite realise their anxiety when their bridge account exchequer is diminished to the infinitesimal sum of £62, as disclosed by the balance-sheet. The Parliament of this country entered into specific and complete details as to what procedure the bridge authorities should take; the bridge commission also stated most emphatically that the bridge was not required for at least 10 or 20 years.

"The bridge enthusiasts painted a most glorified picture as to how the necessary capital might be raised, and so many shares were disposed of. But that astute firm of financiers, Dorman, Long and Company, hardly focused the position in the same optimistic light. Could one expect a firm of financiers to expend a couple of millions (only a part of the cost of the proposed bridge) and wait until the first motorist crossed the bridge before any financial return would be forthcoming? The Sydney Bridge was to have cost five millions, but it finally cost 100 per cent more. The latest scheme is to ask the Unemployment Board to advance a few thousands 'just to keep the unemployed busy.' If the board advanced £100,000 it would end in waste, for the balance to be expended might not be raised for 20 years. Does the bridge management seriously think that the board will acquiesce in such a foolish expenditure? Devonport." [76]

The shareholders of the Auckland Harbour Bridge Company were also showing some impatience with the company's directors following their failure to raise the necessary funds. This came to a head during the company's first annual meeting which took place on 16 September 1932: "After a lively discussion for over three hours, the first annual meeting of the Auckland Harbour Bridge Company, Limited, held in the Chamber of Commerce Hall last evening, broke up in confusion when the chairman of directors, Sir Walter Stringer, vacated the chair and said he would leave the shareholders 'to their own devices'.

"Sir Walter made an appeal for order and then left the meeting in company with three other directors…It was stated subsequently that very little business was transacted, the time being occupied chiefly with discussing motions and amendments and challenges to both. There were frequent interjections. A motion was passed asking the directors to resign and most of those present, including Sir Walter Stringer, expressed their willingness to do so." [77]

Following the public display of disunity at the Auckland Harbour Bridge Company meeting, those civic leaders still interested in keeping the bridge project alive, decided that a meeting of their own was needed to consider how they might best do that, as reported by the Auckland Star on 29 September 1932: "The Mayor, Mr G. W. Hutchison, said this morning that an invitation had been received by the City Council to be represented at a meeting of local bodies to be held next week to consider the harbour bridge project. It is evident from reports of meetings of the Bridge Company that no progress has been made, said Mr Hutchison, and it must be apparent to shareholders that the discord which seems to exist in the company is not likely to enhance the chance of bringing the proposal to a successful conclusion.

"The attitude which the council adopted when the bridge legislation was before Parliament was to the effect that as long as the interests of the council were protected and it was not involved financially, it would be pleased to see the bridge erected. Personally, I have been a supporter of the bridge all along. I think the proposal of Mr J. Guiniven, Mayor of Takapuna, to have the charter vested in some responsible local authority pending a favourable opportunity to finance the undertaking is on the right lines, but I would have preferred the offer to come from the company itself, as soon as shareholders had made up their minds that the company could not carry out its objective, and that there was no alternative but liquidation.

"If the meeting that has been called results in a conference between representatives of the company and the local bodies, it will be all to the good. From the point of view of providing employment, the scheme is worthy of fresh examination to ascertain what proportion of the cost the Government and local bodies might be justified in contributing. It is very evident that without some such contribution no contracting firm or financial institution would favourably consider building the bridge...The company has certainly done its best to forward the project, but the question of finance has prevented the negotiations ending satisfactorily.

"There is a sum of approximately £300,000 needed to meet the interest charges while the bridge is building, and it is practically impossible to get any company to finance the undertaking unless the interest account is assured. In the circumstances the local bodies interested should, in my opinion, step into the breach, and the Government should be asked for a subsidy covering the interest charges or a sum approaching the amount needed under that head." [78]

Many believed that councils beyond the greater Auckland area should also be involved, as their businesses and residents were sure to benefit from the bridge and its enhancement of the main highway system – as suggested by a letter published by The New Zealand Herald on 3 October 1932: "Sir, — As a shareholder in the Harbour Bridge Company, I am heartily in accord with the proposals initiated by the Mayor of Takapuna. The company was created as a necessary legal entity to whom the charter could be granted on behalf of the city and province of Auckland. Indeed, it has been rightly deemed a Dominion proposition. The company, therefore, being custodians and not, as the directors assume, proprietors of the charter, competent control as indicated by Mr Guiniven is overdue. I suggest, however, in view of the increasing volume of traffic on both main highway systems northwards that both Rodney and Whangarei Councils are also vitally concerned and should be represented at next Wednesday's meeting. DICTYS." [79]

Unfortunately, the concept that a bridge to connect the country's main highway system should be a 'Dominion proposition', and therefore driven by all Auckland region local bodies, was not valued. Any support for the bridge that might encourage a financial liability was to be avoided, regardless of regional benefits that could eventuate: "Opposition to the suggestion that interested local authorities should take over the charter of the Auckland Harbour Bridge Company was expressed at a meeting of the Mount Eden Borough Council last evening. The council received a notification that Mr J. Guiniven, Mayor of Takapuna, had convened a meeting for to-day to discuss the advisability of approaching the Government to bring down legislation vesting the charter in the local bodies, with a view to bringing about the early construction of the bridge. The council decided to be represented at the meeting, the delegates being instructed that Mount Eden would not accept financial liability, and did not view with favour a charter involving local authorities." [80]

Nevertheless, some consensus was reached during the subsequent meeting called by the mayor of Takapuna, as reported by the Auckland Star on 6 October 1932: "The general opinion at the present time is that the bridge will never be built by the Harbour Bridge Company, and the most feasible way to bring it about is for the local bodies to form a board of control, said Mr J. Guiniven, Mayor of Takapuna, who presided at a meeting yesterday of about 30 representatives of local bodies which he convened. The meeting was called to consider the advisability of approaching the Government to vest the charter, which was granted to the company, in the local authorities.

"Mr Guiniven said that though he did not desire to disclose anything of a confidential nature, he was of the opinion that if fresh money was not available within a month the Harbour Bridge Company would go into liquidation. He thought the bridge scheme should be regarded as a metropolitan, if not a national, matter. It was part of the national highway from one end of the island to the other, and just as important as any bridge on the Main Trunk railway. It should not be looked upon in a parochial light. After the donnybrook at the company meeting the other night I don't think they are going to get far with the scheme, he added.

"Mr Guiniven then said that the Harbour Bridge Empowering Act provided that in the event of the company failing to complete the bridge, or going into liquidation, the charter conferring authority to build the structure should be transferred to whatever authority the City Council or the Northcote Borough Council should determine. He was firmly of the opinion that the company was 'fizzling out' and it was either a question of letting the charter go or getting it transferred to a board of control.

"Mr T. Bloodworth, the City Council representative, pointed out that he could not vote on any new proposal. The attitude of the City Council was that it would give moral but not financial support. Personally, he held the opinion that had been expressed, that the bridge could not be built without some guaranteed security. It seemed unthinkable that any company would guarantee to find the money to build the bridge without any security. In the last analysis it meant a public body rate, and, as had been pointed out, there was only a remote chance of it being collected, but, nevertheless, it was there to be collected if the occasion arose.

"Mr Guiniven: I don't think there is any chance of a special rate being collected His idea was that the meeting should appoint representatives to approach the company, for he was sure many of the shareholders were anxious to get rid of their responsibilities. After further discussion, a committee comprised of the Mayors of the North Shore boroughs and Messrs. Bishop and J. C. Rennie, of the Waitemata County Council, was appointed to confer with the directors of the company in a friendly spirit to see what could be done to further the project." [81]

In the meantime, as the world's depression continued to bite, any start on expensive projects such as the harbour bridge seemed as remote as ever. Paradoxically, as unemployment rose, there was so much for those out of work to do. The frustration was expressed by Waitemata's Member of Parliament, Alex Harris, during a House of Representative debate on 14 October 1932: "I am not going to sit down quietly and submit to 173 homes in my constituency being broken, said Mr A. Harris (Coalition, Waitemata) during the Imprest Supply debate in the House of Representatives this morning. The gloves have got to come off.

"Mr Harris said he wanted a declaration of policy from the Government on the question of sending married men to camps in the country. The Takapuna Borough Council had advised him that 173 married men had to be put off to-morrow and go to camps. He wanted an assurance from the Government that these 173 homes were not going to be broken up. It was not a question of not being able to find reproductive work. The Takapuna Borough Council had officially intimated that reproductive work was waiting for all married men who were registered as unemployed, and the council was prepared to employ these men as long as work lasted. With 78,000 unemployed in the Dominion, Mr Harris maintained there was no need to drive married men into the country.

"He suggested that with a little investigation and a little business acumen displayed, reproductive works in towns could be found. As an example, he cited the approaches to the proposed Auckland Harbour Bridge which would keep from 600 to 1000 men employed for three or four years." [82]

Additional comment about the apparent wasting of money and effort expended on negligible infrastructure was reported by The New Zealand Herald on 10 December 1932: "The revelations recently made regarding the wastefulness of a great deal of the relief work at present in progress in the city and suburbs have called public attention to a state of affairs that urgently demands remedy. The facts disclosed are only a fraction of the details that could be gathered, yet they show that £16,200, which was raised by unemployment taxation, has been spent on four relief schemes which private contractors could have completed for £3750.

"When work, even relief work, costs the taxpayer four times what it could be done for under efficient management and supervision, a general overhaul of all relief undertakings appears to be called for. Two important factors contribute to the high cost of relief schemes — lack of incentive to work on the part of the men so engaged and lack of up-to-date equipment to cheapen and speed up the work. In both these respects the relief schemes at present in operation in the Auckland district are deplorably deficient. Authorities who have examined the problem carefully frankly admit that the class of work at present allotted to the unemployed is uninspiring. The construction of elaborate playgrounds for children who would just as soon appreciate a simple grass paddock for their games is not the kind of work, concerning which, men can display any enthusiasm.

"An Auckland business man suggested that the construction of the long-discussed Auckland-Manukau Canal was the type of work that the unemployed forces of the community should be put to. The canal is bound to come in time, he said. It would provide useful work for practically all the men now engaged on useless relief schemes, and it would supply that incentive which is so sadly lacking in the ornamental rock gardens, stone walls, playing fields, cycle tracks and vegetable gardens that at present result in such an enormous amount of wasted energy and squandered money. The canal would be revenue-producing as soon as it was built and would provide Auckland with an asset for all time. He added that a work of almost equivalent value would be the construction of the approaches of the harbour bridge, which is bound to come in future and which would, in the long run, be revenue producing." [83]

And just when a consolidation of resources and enlightened leadership was required, the shareholder-appointed directors of the Auckland Harbour Bridge Company thought the opposite. At a meeting of directors on 31 October 1932, it was decided that the company's three local body directors, representing the City Council, the Northcote Borough Council, and the Harbour Board, were to be excluded from deliberations and decisions made by the company's board – other than those decisions vital "…to complete negotiations for raising finance or to sign a contract for building the bridge." [84]

After having been deprived of their normal rights as directors, the three quickly resigned, leaving the Harbour Bridge Company to its own private devices. This, and the lack of any progress toward achieving its goal, didn't exactly inspire confidence in the company but the apparently wasted time did inspire alternatives to a harbour bridge, as expressed by Edward C. Walton in his letter to the editor of the Auckland Star, published on 24 December 1932: "Now that it must have become evident, even to its most optimistic supporters, that the chances of the harbour bridge project being fulfilled are not nearly so rosy as they had been led to believe, and, in fact, that the possibility of early construction has receded into the dim distance, perhaps it would not be amiss to suggest an alternative scheme which, to my mind, has many attractive features not possessed by the bridge proposal.

"Nature has already in the form of a reef of solid rock provided the foundation of a roadway for 7500 ft from Point Chevalier towards Kauri Point. Of the remaining 2300 ft there is but 850 ft of deep water, varying from five to 13 fathoms, to fill in to complete the roadway from shore to shore. By the construction of a dam carrying a roadway at this point, not only would the crossing of the harbour be secured, but by the provision of a lock and the impounding of the water at a constant high tide level, great areas of shallow water would be rendered navigable at all times, and also, looking to the future, the dredging of the main channel for deep draught shipping obviated.

"Much would thus be added to the value of Auckland's great water heritage, instead of risking the obstruction to expansion which might be occasioned by a bridge. In addition to improving the shipping facilities of the port by adding to the navigable water, a valuable asset would be given to the city in the acquisition of what would shortly become a great freshwater lake at its front door. From a tourist attraction and pleasure resort point of view great possibilities would thereby be opened up.

"A bridge means imported steel and skilled labour, as well as costly maintenance. The alternative proposal would utilise local material, maintenance would be lower, and no more useful work could be contemplated to give employment to many men in the city and neighbourhood close to their homes practically immediately, thus obviating the consideration of country camps. Edward. C. Walton." [85]

Unfortunately, such imagination and enterprise needed to drive a realistic and affordable means of crossing the Waitemata remained submerged by political debate. Increasingly spurred by a growing public demand for a bridge, the local bodies most affected were pressed to state their positions on the matter. Two of the councils representing the residents most likely to benefit from a bridge, Birkenhead and Takapuna, believed that local bodies such as theirs should now be in charge of negotiating contracts to build it – particularly as the Auckland City Council, the Auckland Harbour Board and the Northcote Borough Council were no longer represented on the board of the Harbour Bridge Company.

As reported by the Auckland Star on 26 January 1933: "The history of the Harbour Bridge project is always that something is going to happen in the future. This company is only wasting time, said Mr J. Macdonald, when speaking about a letter from the Local Bodies' Harbour Bridge Committee at the meeting of the Birkenhead Borough Council last night. We cannot stand for this any longer, in view of the state of the country's affairs, and of what the construction of the bridge would mean in the alleviation of unemployment, continued Mr Macdonald. He moved: That it be a recommendation to the Local Bodies' Committee that if something definite was not done in three months, the Government should be asked to transfer the charter to the local bodies." [86]

About four weeks later, the Birkenhead and Takapuna Councils were calling for the end of private enterprise attempts to build the bridge with a winding up of the Harbour Bridge Company: "The Birkenhead Borough

Council last night decided to follow the example of Takapuna and send a letter to the Prime Minister suggesting that the time is opportune for the Government to investigate the affairs of the Auckland Harbour Bridge Co., Ltd. The best thing would be to wind the company up, said Mr P. Dennen.

"The company, as such, was governed by the Companies Act. He thought the shareholders would not object to making an end of the company. Mrs J. Prickett said the company had recently issued a call on shares. Some of the shareholders had refused to pay any more, and those who had paid obviously supported the present directorate." [87]

But the Auckland Harbour Bridge Company was far from capitulating to the councillors, as reported by The New Zealand Herald on 6 March 1933: "A further circular from the directors of the Auckland Harbour Bridge Company has been received by shareholders. It is signed by Mr C. Harris, as chairman, by order of the board. The circular is as follows: The nearer your company approaches success, the fiercer is the antagonism of our opponents. This fierceness, recently intensified, proves that our opponents realise our closeness to success. They know that negotiations are so far advanced that the final stages are in sight.

"Fortunately, the hard-headed financiers and contractors with whom we are negotiating will probably never know about the attacks made to crush your company, and if they do, being used to such tactics, they will completely ignore them. No matter what opponents (unaware of the facts) may say, you are assured that the objects for which your company exists are being carried out with an outstanding chance of success, but it would be a tactical mistake at present to disclose details." [88]

By 19 June 1933, more of those details were known and they indicated that the bridge was to become a reality after all, thanks to Waitemata M.P., Alex Harris, as reported by the Auckland Star: "A highly important development in connection with the proposal to construct a bridge across the Waitemata Harbour is announced. This, it is authoritatively predicted, will make the prospects of an early start with the undertaking assured. Following a meeting of directors this morning, the following official statement was issued: The Auckland Harbour Bridge Company, Ltd. has received advice from England to the effect that £1,500,000 is ready and available to build the bridge, provided that certain financial details are settled locally. During the past few days negotiations have been made whereby these details have been satisfactorily adjusted as far as New Zealand is concerned.

"All that now remains is for these details to be finalised in London. A cablegram has been sent to-day by the company with that object in view. These negotiations have been pushed to a conclusion by Mr A. Harris,

M.P. for Waitemata, whose ability and perseverance have produced this highly satisfactory result." [89]

Indeed, the practical involvement of Mr Harris had far exceeded that of any politician so far, and more was to come: "As the outcome of further developments in connection with the Auckland Harbour Bridge proposal, Mr A. Harris, M.P. for Waitemata, will leave Auckland for Australia by the Wanganella to-morrow afternoon to make inquiries in the Commonwealth regarding supplies of material...This action is rendered necessary owing to the fact that inquiries from England indicate the probability of certain supplies, needed for the bridge, being required from the Commonwealth." [90]

Later developments would render the return of Alex Harris from Australia on 13 September 1933 a precursor of Neville Chamberlain's return from Munich in 1938. In the meantime, as with the 'peace in our time' delusion, hope sprung eternal that the Waitemata Harbour would very soon be spanned by a sturdy bridge.

"The directors of the Auckland Harbour Bridge Company Limited are now in a position to say that the negotiations for financing the construction of the harbour bridge have reached a very satisfactory stage and one which should enable finality to be reached in the comparatively near future. At this stage the directors cannot make a more detailed statement, but they give the assurance that as soon as it is possible to do so, the public will be taken into their entire confidence. Prior to his departure for Wellington last evening, Mr Harris said that prospects of ultimate success were never brighter than at present." [91]

But not everyone trusted the opinion of Mr Harris, including former Auckland mayor (1911-1915), parliamentarian and Minister (1914-1925), and high commissioner to London (1926-1929 & 1933-1936), Christopher James Parr, who expressed his feelings in a letter published by The New Zealand Herald on 4 November 1933:

"Sir, — I observe Mr Harris M.P. complains that he was not notified of the recent deputation led by me to Ministers about the Bridge Company. But why should we notify him when we know that we can expect no help whatever from Mr Harris, who has identified himself lately as the company's active agent and apologist?

"It is evident Mr Harris prefers the company's interests to those of many of his constituents, who have lost all patience with this procrastinating corporation. Mr Harris tells us to be patient as the company is doing good work. Mr Harris, I hope, will forgive me when I say that I consider this statement is not lacking in assurance in view of the fact that though the company got its charter over two years ago not even a single plan has as yet been prepared and lodged with the Minister, as required by the Statute. Further, is it not four months ago since Mr Harris in the public press begged myself and other doubters to be silent lest we should upset delicate negotiations which were almost on the point of being completed for the construction of the bridge? I then accepted Mr Harris' representation. I was thus misled into a quiescent attitude, but I decline to be humbugged again. Lastly, Mr Harris' statement that I am the only legislator dissatisfied with the Bridge Company is quite incorrect. C. J. Parr. Crown Hill, Takapuna." [92]

Mr Parr was not the only person to question the role of Mr Harris. The Mayor of Takapuna, John Guiniven, also had his doubts about the MP's involvement:

"When Mr Alex Harris, M.P. for Waitemata, assured the public some months ago that work would soon commence in connection with the construction of the Harbour Bridge members of the Local Bodies Bridge Committee regarded his statements as a joke, realising that although no private firm would undertake to construct the bridge unless interest payments in connection with the cost of the bridge during the course of erection were guaranteed, the Government had never at any time agreed to share any portion of the responsibility.

"The committee further realised that ratepayers would not be in favour of being rated in connection with the necessary interest payments, that construction firms would not be satisfied with the prospect of getting their money back in the form of tolls alone, and after careful consideration decided to press for a commission. Until a commission of inquiry is held, nothing substantial will ever come of the project. The only feasible method of obtaining progress is by joint action by the local bodies and the Unemployment Board, and this is only possible when Mr Harris and the company stand aside." [93]

Far from standing aside, the Auckland Harbour Bridge Company was pressing on, buoyed by the good news from London announced on 8 December 1933: "Reputable underwriters here have definitely undertaken to provide finance for the construction of the Auckland Harbour Bridge. This was part of a cablegram from the High Commissioner in London to the Prime Minister, read by Mr A. Harris, M.P., at the annual meeting of the Auckland Harbour Bridge Company this morning. Confidence in the directors and a conviction that the prospects of the bridge were never brighter than they were at present were expressed." [94]

With finance from London apparently almost guaranteed, there seemed to be little that could go wrong and confidence was maintained by assurances from Mr Harris, published by The New Zealand Herald on 3

February 1934: "Every condition imposed by London financiers in connection with the harbour bridge scheme has been complied with by the Auckland Harbour Bridge Company, Limited, according to a statement made by Mr A. Harris, M.P., yesterday, on his return from Wellington.

"All information required, and statements asked for from the Auckland City Council, the Auckland Harbour Board and the Northcote Borough Council, have now been supplied, said Mr Harris. A cablegram of a satisfactory nature, the contents of which he could not at present reveal, had been sent by the Government to the High Commissioner in London, to be forwarded to the financial interests concerned. Nothing further remains to be done at this end, said Mr Harris. The next move is from London." [95]

A month later and the chance of London finance now seemed to be a formality according to a New Zealand Herald report of 5 March 1934:

"The Auckland Harbour Bridge Company has been advised of the receipt at the week-end by an Auckland legal firm of a cablegram referring to the progress of negotiations for raising the necessary finance in London for the harbour bridge. The message states that 'all contracts and trust deeds relative to the Auckland harbour bridge will be ready for signature during the ensuing week'. The information is unofficial, and so far the Auckland Harbour Bridge Company has not been similarly advised. It should be pointed out that any signature will be provisional, as all documents in connection with the contract will have to be sent to New Zealand for execution by the Auckland Harbour Bridge Company." [96]

But just when a united front was needed to convince overseas financiers that an Auckland harbour bridge would prove a most lucrative investment, those locals who stood to benefit the most, once more confined their ambition to the parish pump.

"The report of the delegates to the recent conference concerning the amalgamation of the four North Shore boroughs of Devonport, Takapuna, Birkenhead and Northcote was presented to the Takapuna Borough Council at last night's meeting. Several members regretted that Devonport would not co-operate. Mr T. M. Rollo said further consideration should be deferred, as the boroughs could not hope to get far without the support of Devonport. He hoped that it might yet be possible to get Devonport to agree to the scheme. Without Devonport the whole thing will fall flat, said Mr Rollo. Devonport is like Newmarket, said the Mayor. It means to remain self-contained. Look at the Auckland City Council, which has been trying for years to get Newmarket to amalgamate, but it refuses." [97]

Nevertheless, hopes remained high that any local friction would be overlooked and the finance needed to construct the harbour bridge would soon be forthcoming from London. Those hopes continued to spring eternal with every bit of news eagerly passed to the press by the Auckland Harbour Bridge Company:

"Following a wireless telephone conversation with London on Thursday, the Auckland Harbour Bridge Company has been notified by the solicitors for the English financiers who are concerned with the bridge project that, they are hopeful that the negotiations will be completed early this month. The conversation, which came through particularly clearly, confirmed recent important cables and indicated that successful completion of the negotiations was not likely to be long delayed. It is possible that it may be necessary for a representative of the company to leave for London at an early date." [98]

But, by May 1934, the London arrangement had come to nothing with the British Treasury abrogating the deal, as reported by the Auckland Star on 10 May 1934: "A statement concerning the negotiations in progress to further the interests of the harbour bridge was made this morning by Mr John Guiniven, Mayor of Takapuna.

"Judging by statements made recently by Mr Harris, M.P., and Mr W. Parkinson (Chairman of the Harbour Bridge Company), the chances of the harbour bridge being constructed by the company are more remote than ever, he said. The whole scheme obviously is fizzling out, as the above-mentioned gentlemen have already admitted that the Government has refused to give any guarantee in connection with interest payments necessary during the period of construction, and also the project has been turned down by the British Treasury." [99]

A further report also seemed to cite the lack of official Government support for the otherwise private enterprise:

"The (Auckland Harbour Bridge) company...was advised by the solicitors to the financiers in London that finality would be reached by the third week in April, but when that date arrived a cablegram was received to the effect that the British Treasury would not sanction the loan pending a more favourable attitude on the part of the authorities." [100]

While a lack of moral and financial Government support for Auckland infrastructure projects surprised few, some questioned the need for any outside help at all: "If we cannot finance our own national undertakings when we have materials and labour available, surely it is time we questioned the utility of our methods of finance. If it is true that whatever we can do, we can pay for; if it is true that paying is doing; if it is true that most of our money is only figures in books to be written when service has been rendered or sure to be rendered, then why do we need to send to London for permission to get busy and do the work we can do? Can we not do our own bookkeeping without incurring debts to others? Are we not yet convinced that New Zealand money must be created in New Zealand for all our national and private undertakings, and that foreign borrowing is quite unnecessary to provide money tickets? Peter Mellor." [101]

But any such locally-financed projects very definitely required wholehearted community support – the kind of support so rare in the Auckland region that successive national Governments could easily ignore any entreaties between elections. By June 1934, the harbour bridge proponents knew that local attitudes had to change if a bridge was to be built soon:

"Are the ratepayers of the North Shore prepared to guarantee the payment of interest on the cost of the proposed harbour bridge? According to Mr J. Guiniven, Mayor, of Takapuna, and a member of the Local Bodies' Harbour Bridge Committee, there is no possibility of the bridge being built until such a guarantee is provided." [102]

By August 1934, at least two Mayors were talking to each other about a reconsideration of the best way forward, as reported by the Auckland Star:

"The proposed harbour bridge figured again among the items of business at last night's meeting of the City Council. The Mayor (Mr G. W. Hutchison) reported that Mr Mills (Mayor of Birkenhead) had waited upon him on July 16 and stated that there did not appear to be any prospect of the Harbour Bridge Company succeeding in making the necessary arrangements for the construction of the bridge, and he suggested that the time had arrived when the local bodies should reconsider their attitude towards the proposal. Mr Mills expressed the opinion that if the local bodies took the matter up, and obtained the support of the Unemployment Board, the bridge could be constructed. That would mean fresh legislation vesting the charter in the trustees for the local bodies, and possibly a commission to allocate such part of the costs as the local bodies were prepared to bear as their contribution.

"It was decided that the Mayor be asked to convene a conference of Mayors of local bodies to consider the harbour bridge proposals and to ascertain what prospects there are of the Harbour Bridge Company putting the proposal into operation at an early date." [103]

However, in the meantime, the Government maintained its aloofness, failing to take a leadership role that could involve it as any sort of guarantor: "A letter (addressed to Mr A. Harris. M.P.) from the Minister of Finance, Mr Coates, regarding financial negotiations for the construction of the Auckland Harbour bridge, was read at a meeting of the Northcote Borough Council last night.

"The letter from the Minister referred to an earlier communication to Mr Harris, in which Mr Coates stated: With reference to your representations asking for a cable to be sent to the underwriters with whom the Auckland Harbour Bridge Company, Limited, is negotiating. I may point out that in such matters as this an accepted principle in Government finance prevents my complying with your wishes. Consequently, I regret that it is not possible to associate the Government with any expression of opinion that may be obtained regarding the financial prospects or traffic of the Auckland Harbour bridge. However, a cable will be sent to the High Commissioner informing him why the Government cannot, by implication or otherwise, express an opinion on the matter." [104]

Failing any commitment from the Government, could Auckland's local bodies, for the first time, unite in a common cause? By October 1934, as the need for discussion became more immediate, there was every incentive to do so: "The possibility of local bodies in the Auckland Metropolitan area meeting to discuss proposals for the construction of the Auckland Harbour bridge was mentioned at the meeting of the Auckland City Council last evening.

"The matter was introduced by Mr J. W. Yarnall, who, in the course of a lengthy question concerning remedies for unemployment, suggested that the council should call a conference of all local bodies in and round Auckland to consider ways and means of taking over the charter granted to the Auckland Harbour Bridge Company, Limited, with a view to having the charter vested in the local bodies as representing the people of Auckland for the purpose of having the question of erecting the bridge examined as a suitable work to provide employment and a much desired public utility." [105]

Since it was granted the charter in 1931, the Auckland Harbour Bridge Company had more or less shunned any support offered by Auckland's local bodies, believing the company could arrange the funding well enough on its own. Unfortunately, probably based on past experiences, London financiers needed more than the Auckland Harbour Bridge Company could deliver by way of assurances that the bridge was a sound investment.

By November 1934, the support of the locals had become important after all, as reported by The New Zealand Herald on 7 November 1934:

"The directors of the Auckland Harbour Bridge Company met the Mayors of Northcote and Birkenhead, Mr R. Martin and Mr G. Mills, in conference on Monday. The object was to ascertain the progress made with the project, and whether the local bodies could reasonably help in any direction in furthering proposals for financing the construction of the bridge.

"A report received from the company's London correspondent stated: 'We feel quite certain that the money can be obtained here if you can provide for the financiers in London some official report to offset the only official report at present existing—that of the Royal Commission of 1929. All that was required of the Government and the Auckland City Council was to lend officialdom to the compilation of data required to show that the bridge, if constructed, would prove a sound investment." [105]

The compilation of data to show investors how viable a bridge would be obviously included some idea of the traffic that would use it. Here was a way the local bodies such as Northcote and Birkenhead could contribute:

"That the vehicular traffic between Auckland and the North Shore has substantially increased since the Royal Commission reported in 1929 on the prospects of the proposed harbour bridge was shown by the tally submitted by the Mayor of Northcote, Mr R. Martin, to the borough council last night. Mr Martin stated that the traffic tallies of vehicles carried on the ferries between North Shore and the city had been taken last Friday, Saturday and Sunday. The details were: —Friday: To and from Devonport, 818; to and from Northcote and Birkenhead, 183; total, 1001. Saturday: Devonport, 932; Northcote and Birkenhead, 164; total, 1096. Sunday: Devonport, 844; Northcote and Birkenhead, 96; total, 940. The total for the three days was 3037, or a daily average of 1012.

"The Mayor said a tally of bus traffic from the North Shore ferries also had been taken last Friday. This showed that 294 buses departed from the Devonport wharf, 112 from Bayswater wharf, 59 from Birkenhead wharf, and 44 from Northcote wharf; a total of 509 bus trips for the day. Mr N. S. Davidson, the representative of the council on the bridge company, said the figures now available were 40 per cent above those obtained at the census of traffic taken in February preceding the sitting of the Royal Commission." [107]

'Not true' said the Devonport Steam Ferry Company which quickly supplied its own figures to show that the net increase of vehicles crossing the harbour as from the date of the Harbour Bridge Commission (1930 to October 1934) to be 17.39 per cent. [108]

Nevertheless, as 1934 came to an end, the Auckland Harbour Bridge Company retained its optimistic attitude that a deal to finance the construction of a harbour bridge was soon to be finalised. At least that was the message delivered at the company's third annual meeting held on 3 December 1934: "Every confidence in the successful completion of the negotiations for the financing of the harbour bridge is expressed by the chairman of directors, Mr C. Hams, in the annual report of the Auckland Harbour Bridge Company, Limited, to be presented at the third annual meeting of shareholders to-day.

"After reviewing negotiations, the report states that a firm of financiers in London with which the directors had dealt had so far achieved success that now little remained to be done to bring the project into finality. Co-operation not only on the part of the boroughs continguous (sic) to the harbour, but also of those further north and south of the harbour, had assisted. Also, the result of the recent trans-harbour tally, showing 40 per cent increase in three years, was helping considerably." [109]

By the end of January 1935, that optimism had spread to at least one local body: "A statement that all necessary preliminaries had been completed locally in the negotiations for the financing of the proposed Auckland harbour bridge was made by the Mayor of Birkenhead, Mr G. Mills, at a meeting of the Birkenhead Borough Council last night.

"Mr Mills said certain information had already come to hand, but it could not be divulged at present. Documents had to be sent from England for perusal and it was hardly to be expected that £1,250,000 or £1,500,000 could be raised at a moment's notice. Mr Mills added that he was hopeful that the bridge would be a reality in the near future." [110]

But, despite the Birkenhead Borough Council's enthusiasm and that of the Auckland Harbour Bridge Company, impatience with the lack of progress again precipitated disunity among the councils, as reported by The New Zealand Herald on 15 February 1935: "The forfeiture of the Auckland Harbour Bridge Company's charter and the repeal of its empowering Act were recommended by the Auckland City Council after a discussion in committee at the close of ordinary business last night. The Mayor, Mr G. W. Hutchison, stated after the meeting that the council had discussed at some length certain proposals that had been submitted to it in connection with the proposed Auckland Harbour Bridge.

"The council, the Mayor said, had unanimously decided that it must be a condition precedent to the giving of any fresh consideration to the council's attitude toward the bridge proposal that the charter held by the Auckland Harbour Bridge Company Limited, should be surrendered to the Government and that the Auckland Harbour Bridge Empowering Act, 1931, be repealed." [111]

With that decision, any possibility of a united city bridging the Waitemata was once more submerged at the parish pump. The immediate reaction from north shore politicians was published by the Auckland Star:

"The following combined statement was made this morning by the Mayor of Northcote, Mr R. Martin, the Mayor of Takapuna, Mr J. Guiniven, the Mayor of Birkenhead, Mr G. Mills, and the Takapuna riding member on the Waitemata County Council, Mr J. C. Rennie:

"We cannot but be surprised and hurt by what we must regard as the extraordinary action of the Auckland City Council. In common with nearly all the local authorities around Auckland, the city joined in sending strong cables to London supporting the bridge project. Then it was felt advisable that the local bodies should take a more prominent part in the scheme than was originally proposed. A scheme was prepared by the mayors and county representative named above, and submitted to the Auckland Harbour Bridge Company for its approval.

"Since the only object of the latter is to have the bridge built they cordially agreed to the proposals, which were those placed before the City Council. It should be emphasised that these did not emanate from the Bridge Company, but from those holding responsible offices on the North Shore. Under the scheme submitted to the city there would have been a minimum of borrowing from outside sources, large scale and useful employment at standard rates would have been found, and the local bodies would from the inception of building have had practical control, since they were to have nine seats out of twelve on the company's directorate.

"The scheme was submitted to the Auckland City Council in all good faith, and those responsible feel extremely hurt by the cavalier treatment accorded it by the City Council last night. The proposals submitted would have secured a serviceable, toll-free bridge in a minimum period. We feel that the City Council must accept a grave responsibility for its refusal to consider the scheme submitted by us—not by the Bridge Company. We feel most strongly that the only practicable method to secure the harbour bridge is to co-operate with the company, and, instead of cancelling the charter, work along lines which will ensure public and representative control of finance, construction and operation from the very outset." [112]

The North Shore politicians were not the only ones to express their displeasure at the City Council's departure from what was thought to have been the beginnings of a unified approach to the bridge project. If the Harbour Bridge Company was to be believed, indications from London were that a prompt start on the bridge could be made if only the locals could agree:

"Objection to certain references in the latest statement by the Mayor of Auckland, Mr G. W. Hutchison, on the Auckland Harbour Bridge proposal was taken yesterday by Mr T. A. Felton, of Felton and Orr, public accountants, Auckland agents for Mr F. W. Strack, who is at present carrying on negotiations in London for financing the undertaking.

"From these references the public might infer that the negotiations in London had failed, said Mr Felton. On the contrary, they were still in progress, and Mr Strack had recently informed him by cablegram that the full amount required to build the bridge was available at 4½ per cent, provided that four Auckland local bodies, including the City Council, guaranteed the payment of interest and sinking fund. On these terms a loan could be arranged immediately.

"Mr Felton added that negotiations for a loan without guarantee had been carried on successfully up to a point at which it had been deemed advisable to seek means of obtaining a lower rate of interest than that offered by the underwriters. It was now felt that if legislative and other arrangements could be made for a guarantee it should be possible to free the bridge from tolls much earlier —say, within 20 years —than if the company built it unaided. Even on the most conservative official estimates of traffic, the risk that the guarantor local bodies would be called upon was very remote, and the saving in interest would be substantial." [113]

Because of New Zealand's strong ties with the 'Home Country', another proposal of February 1935 was not taken up: "The interest of Krupps, the great German steel and armament firm, in the financing and building of the proposed Auckland Harbour Bridge was revealed yesterday when an offer from that concern was conveyed to the Auckland Harbour Bridge Company, Limited, by the Mayor of Birkenhead, Mr G. Mills." [114]

In the meantime, there was a domestic alternative to be tried by the North Shore local bodies, as reported by the Auckland Star on 6 March 1935: "A subsidy of £400,000 from the Unemployment Board and Main Highways Board to ensure the construction of the Auckland Harbour Bridge was applied for by a deputation of North Shore Mayors and members of the Waitemata County Council which waited on the Minister of Employment, Sir Alexander Young, to-day.

"It was estimated by the contractors that £663,000 would be expended in labour costs in the construction of the bridge approaches and causeways, and that at least 1000 men would be employed for three years on the work. As the men would be drawn from the ranks of the unemployed at standard rates of pay the Unemployment Board's funds would be relieved to the extent of £93,600 per annum or a total sum in three years of £280,000 (sic). To supplement this saving must be added the amount contributed by wages taxation on £663,000, which amounted to £27,625, resulting in a direct saving to the board's funds of £27,625, plus £280,800, equalling £308,425.

According to Mr Julius Hogben, a director of the (Auckland Harbour Bridge) company, capital was ready for the construction of the bridge and the contracts were ready for signature. The company required to be able to assure the London financiers that £400,000 was available in New Zealand by way of guarantee. They understood the Unemployment Board had promised a subsidy of £100,000." [115]

Not so, replied the Minister, who seemed very keen not to describe any Unemployment Board payment made to Auckland as any kind of 'subsidy'. "The Minister: Let us clear that up at once. That is not the position. There has been a good deal of misrepresentation about this, and a sum of £100,000 has been 'handed out' in Auckland. There was no promise of a subsidy of £100,000 from the board. What the board did was to agree tentatively to grant a subsidy on the wages paid to men in New Zealand engaged on the fabrication of steel up to £100,000. It is as well that that point be cleared up now." [116]

Despite what seemed to be a realistic financial solution proposed by the North Shore delegation – one that could not only provide a national asset but also relieve the unemployment situation, nothing came of the visit. The Minister's denial that any sort of subsidy would be forthcoming from the Unemployment Board seemed to be just another example of the Government's lack of motivation.

By August 1935, with no progress being made, the Auckland Harbour Bridge Company was accused by Auckland City's deputy mayor of demonstrating the same attitude: "Dissatisfaction with the Auckland Harbour Bridge Company was expressed at the meeting of the City Council last night by the deputy-mayor, Mr Martin, who had asked for a report setting out the council's position in connection with the project. "Mr Martin thought it was not in the interests of Auckland that the company should retain its monopoly, while apparently doing nothing. The matter could not be allowed to remain as it was, and the Government should be called on to withdraw the charter given to the company." [117]

But just when it was thought the Harbour Bridge Company could be on the ropes, there was always talk of another agreement having been reached with finance assured, as reported by the Auckland Star on 10 October 1935:

"A special meeting of directors of the Harbour Bridge (Company) yesterday afternoon confirmed an agreement made in Sydney by the secretary, Captain C. G. Ashdowne, with an Australian group for the financing of the project, a condition being that financial arrangements must be completed within twelve months. Captain Ashdowne said to-day, however, that he expected that the group, whose names he would not disclose, would be ready to start before the expiry of the time fixed.

"In terms of the agreement, Captain Ashdowne said, steps would be taken to increase the capital of the company from £5000 to £300,000. They had been greatly assisted in their negotiations with the New Zealand

Government by Mr Harris, the member for Waitemata. It was entirely through his energetic efforts that the Unemployment Board's subsidy for the work had been increased to 35/. The amount which would be payable under that subsidy was estimated at not less than £150,000." [118]

Of course, it was also nearly election time again. With the possibility of a first win by Michael Joseph Savage's Labour Party, there was bound to be more optimism for the construction of a harbour bridge, particularly from Government politicians who had remained silent beforehand: "Questions regarding the possibility of the Auckland Harbour bridge being started in the near future were addressed to the Minister of Finance, Mr Coates, during his election meeting at Brown's Bay to-day.

"Personally, I am all in favour of the idea, said Mr Coates. I am given to understand that the money is now available for the work, and in that case the bridge should be started shortly. There is clear-cut evidence that the capital will be subscribed, said Mr Coates. The Bridge Company got to the point where all the initial capital was arranged and then one of the interested parties died. However, associated groups took up the matter, and I understand that capital is now available. If the money is not forthcoming on this occasion the Harbour Bridge Act can be amended." [119]

Indeed, with the 1935 general election to be held on 27 November, the early part of that month was chock-full of optimism for an early start on the bridge: "It has been my dream for 24 years, and I believe that it is about to be realised, said Mr A. Harris, Independent National Government candidate for Waitemata, at Bayswater last night when he was asked, 'What about the harbour bridge?'

"Mr Harris said it was quite possible that the work would be started soon after Easter. He also stated that he understood that the City Council was going to spend £250,000 on the approaches. A large sum had been paid for the right to underwrite the whole amount required for the construction of the bridge and during the next few weeks 'two eminent men from Australia' would arrive to confer. Finance had been made possible by the Government agreeing to grant a subsidy on wages through the Unemployment Board up to £150,000. Without that negotiations could not have been finalised." [120]

However, the Mayor of Takapuna, Mr J. Guiniven, was sceptical:

"A statement that the public was being misled regarding the early commencement of the building of the Auckland Harbour Bridge was made by the Mayor of Takapuna, Mr J. Guiniven, at a meeting of the Takapuna Borough Council last night. There is nothing in the rumour that the bridge will be commenced by Easter of next year, said Mr Guiniven. I have made careful investigations regarding the matter and have found no foundation for the opinion." [121]

Nevertheless, an Easter start remained a certainty, according to Mr Harris during his address to electors at the North Shore suburb of Belmont on 15 November 1935: "In replying to a question concerning the Auckland Harbour Bridge, Mr Harris said that the London principals with whom the Auckland Harbour Bridge Company had been negotiating for finance had already paid £1000 to the company for preliminary investigation work. I cannot see any possibility of a hitch occurring now, said Mr Harris, and there seems every chance of the project being really under way by Easter of next year." [122]

However, after 24 years of representing Waitemata in Parliament, Alexander Harris failed to be re-elected at the 1935 election and was succeeded by Labour's William John (Jack) Lyon.

As the prospect of an early start to the construction of a harbour bridge seemed to disappear with Mr Harris, electors pondered the future:

"Sir, – Now that the elections are over and that allusions to the harbour bridge can no longer have any political significance, the public has a right to demand the truth about the bridge. Mr Lyon, the Waitemata parliamentary representative, has stated publicly that the Labour Government is prepared to treat the bridge as a national undertaking. This being so we are entitled to know: who or what stands in the way? The local bodies should insist on getting an answer with corroborative proof and should afterward make the information public. M. Irwin. Greenhithe." [123]

In the meantime, the Auckland Harbour Bridge Company remained as optimistic as ever, as demonstrated by the report of its fourth annual general meeting held in December 1935: "The directors are desirous of informing you that, contrary to rumours and reports, the progress of matters relating to the proposed Auckland Harbour bridge is such that the completion of the proposal is perceptibly nearer than is generally believed, stated the report presented at the fourth annual meeting of the Auckland Harbour Bridge Company.

"At the present time, financiers and also constructors are busily engaged on the proposition, and, although it is not possible for the directors to state the probable time, yet it is likely that an early commencement may be made, continued the report. The chairman, Mr Charles Hams, reviewed the activities of the past year, which had been mainly directed toward arranging finance for building the bridge. Dealing with the negotiations at present proceeding with the syndicate in Sydney, he explained that these had been delayed somewhat owing to the shipping strike and the change of Government in New Zealand. Now that the policy of the new Government had been explained, it was expected that matters would move more quickly." [124]

Needless to say, by March 1936, nothing had eventuated, prompting the Auckland branch of the Automobile Association to comment: "We have heard these stories before, remarked the president, Mr A. Grayson, at last night's meeting of the council of the Automobile Association (Auckland), when a letter was received from the Auckland Harbour Bridge Company Limited, advising that the negotiations for the raising of money for the bridge were well advanced. The association had previously requested the company to report progress.

"Personally, I have lost all faith in this company, Mr Grayson said. This matter is of pressing interest to all motorists, but the bridge is as far off as ever. The public is always being led to believe that things are about to be started, and that the financial arrangements are nearly completed. On the motion of the president, it was decided to request the Minister of Public Works, Hon. R. Semple, whom Mr Grayson described as 'a really vigorous Minister' to do all he could to facilitate the construction of a bridge, preferably as a national undertaking." [125]

A national undertaking it most certainly had to be because, by April 1936, any hope of just an Auckland initiative had once more dissolved into parochialism, as reported by the Auckland Star: "A decision not to support either the Auckland Harbour bridge or harbour tunnel proposals was made by the Auckland City Council last evening. A letter was received from the Waitemata County Council stating that the Takapuna Borough Council had requested support of the Auckland Harbour bridge as a national undertaking. The Waitemata County Council was prepared to support any representations which the City Council might make, and asked what the City Council's views were.

"The finance committee reported that it had given careful consideration to both the bridge and tunnel proposals. The issue was generally controversial, and if construction of the bridge were undertaken under conditions which would safeguard the city from any antecedent or post-constructional liability the council should have no comment to make. The committee pointed out that in the city there were undeveloped areas which would provide for an additional 34,000 buildings, with an equal number of potential ratepayers. In view of that fact alone the city could not lend support to either connecting project. The eastern area of the city was developed to an extent of only 6 per cent, and the city ratepayers had still to carry the burden of interest and sinking fund charges on £254,000 of the amount expended.

"The committee considered that the city should first look to the settlement of the vacant spaces before supporting a plan which would take the population northward. There was much at stake. The effect on the business community, who contributed heavily to the city treasury, and also on those responsible for the provision of essential services, could not be ignored. The committee referred to a report by the city valuer who pointed out that only a third of the area in the city usable for building had been utilised to date, and that there was an undeveloped portion of 9000 acres." [126]

At least one 'Greater Aucklander', wise beyond his time, viewed the City Council's lack of vision as 'pathetic'. His Letter to the Editor was published by The New Zealand Herald on 4 April 1936:

"Sir, — The Auckland City Council is entitled to denounce the Harbour Bridge project, but the reason given for its disapproval is pathetic. It says any benefit should be denied to the North Auckland Peninsula because there are vacant sections for sale in the city. But the position will be exactly the same 100 years hence, and the City Council's attitude does not speak well for the ideal of a Greater Auckland. Surely a broader and less parochial view might be taken by our leading local body. Greater Auckland." [127]

Undeterred by the insular attitude taken by the Auckland City Council, its northern neighbours continued to promote the need for a steel and concrete connection, preferably provided by the Government:

"A campaign to urge the Government to construct the proposed Auckland Harbour Bridge was opened last night in the Foresters' Hall, Birkenhead. The deputy-Mayor of Birkenhead, Mr A Hadfield, presided. Mr J. Littlejohn, Birkenhead riding member of the Waitemata County Council, said the promoters of the campaign came forward in no spirit of antagonism to any other body desirous of having the bridge built, but in order to consolidate expression of opinion that the bridge was urgent.

"It was intended to hold a series of meetings on the North Shore and in surrounding districts, and to forward resolutions to the Government urging the necessity for proceeding with the bridge immediately. It was desired that the Government should announce its intention of building the bridge before bringing down the housing scheme, in order that people would build on the northern side of the harbour. Large numbers would live on the northern side if they knew the bridge was to be built. They were convinced that the only body capable of building the bridge was the Government…A resolution urging the Government to build the bridge was carried unanimously." [128]

"The view that the proposed Auckland harbour bridge should be built by the Government as a national undertaking, and should be free of tolls, was expressed by several speakers at a public meeting held at Milford. Mr J. Littlejohn, member for the Birkenhead riding of the Waitemata County Council, said that the present method of transport across the harbour was obsolete, and entirely inadequate for present-day needs. A great volume of employment would be created by the building of the bridge, and the development works that would naturally follow on the north side of the bridge. As the Government proposed to build 20,000 to 30,000 houses, its views on the bridge should be announced, for if there was a prospect of the bridge being built in the near future, hundreds of people would build on the North Shore. Otherwise they would be forced to build on the southern outskirts of the city.

"There is no doubt that the people of the north urgently want a bridge across the harbour, stated Mr C. H. M. Willis (sic – should have read Wills). But to achieve success it is essential for them to express their desires definitely to the Government. It will only be by constant agitation and pressure of public opinion that the Government will be persuaded that the bridge is needed urgently. Mr Willis added that following upon the holding of numerous meetings throughout the north within the next few weeks, it was proposed that a large representative deputation should wait upon the Prime Minister and other Cabinet Ministers during the coming Parliamentary recess.

"Mr W. B. Darlow, a member of the Auckland Harbour Board and the Waitemata Electric Power Board, said everybody was tired of waiting for the bridge company to do anything. According to the company, it was always just on the point of finalising matters, but nothing ever eventuated. In his opinion the company was more of a hindrance than a help. The meeting carried a resolution urging upon the Government the necessity for building the harbour bridge as a national undertaking free of tolls." [129]

Unfortunately, by June 1936, the 'constant agitation and pressure of public opinion' called for by the North Shore local bodies had not quite persuaded the Government that the bridge was urgently needed. Not surprisingly, it was the Government's opinion that more dialogue, by which to gauge Auckland's apparently-important unity on the matter, was required first:

"The necessity for local bodies interested in the Auckland harbour bridge project to reach some common understanding as a preliminary to a full examination of the scheme was stressed in-an interview yesterday by the Prime Minister, Mr Savage.

"There appeared to be widely divergent views on what was chiefly an Auckland matter, the Prime Minister said, and until a measure of unanimity prevailed among the local bodies concerned no great progress could be made. Mr Savage said he had discussed the bridge project some weeks ago with representatives of the Australian syndicate with which the Auckland Harbour Bridge Company had been carrying on negotiations. He had asked for a report from the Public Works Department on the whole scheme, and since then there had been preliminary discussions on the matter in the Cabinet.

"However, there had been no decision as to any definite line of Government action. Supporters of the bridge scheme appear to be convinced that the bridge would be a decided asset to Auckland and the district to the north, Mr Savage added. However, it has to be remembered that the bridge is only one of a number of major works which the Government has been asked to investigate. If the Auckland local bodies could manage to sink their differences and reach some common basis of understanding, the way would be open for the Government to give further consideration to the matter." [130]

At least the ardent supporters for the bridge now knew where the project stood with the new Labour Government. With the Prime Minister's pronouncement that more investigation and discussion was required, bridge supporters were absolutely back to square one; they were virtually back to the negative findings of the Waterways Commission of 1921 and of the Harbour Bridge Commission of 1930.

Little had really changed since the bridge was first mooted, including any 'measure of unanimity' among Auckland's local bodies – always a factor readily made the most of by insincere Governments and opposing entities with their own interests to protect. That's why it was so important for the North Shore, at least, to project a united front to the Government, as reported by the Auckland Star on 10 July 1936: "That the construction of the Auckland harbour bridge should be undertaken by the Government as a national project, leaving local bodies free from financial responsibility, was the decision reached last night by a conference of northern local bodies held at Takapuna.

"Mr Guiniven stressed the need for unanimity in placing the matter before the Government, and said that in his opinion the only way to approach the Government was to press for a national undertaking. He could not see any hope of North Shore local bodies sharing in the cost of the undertaking, not even for maintenance. The Government should be approached on the single issue of asking for a toll-free bridge as a national undertaking." [131]

But if the North Shore local bodies were to project a sense of national unity during their petitioning of the Government for a bridge, that unity had to include the support of the Auckland City Council. Until 1936, Auckland's history of self-interest had not provided much of a foundation on which to support any kind of regional consensus and, by August 1936, that was not about to change:

"The first local body objection to contributing toward the initial cost of the projected Waitakere Ridge road, as proposed by the Mayor of Auckland, Mr Ernest Davis, was raised at a meeting of the Birkenhead Borough Council last evening on the grounds that the Auckland City Council had turned down the harbour bridge proposals put forward by Birkenhead some months ago.

"As soon as a circular tetter from the City Council recommending the road proposal to local bodies was received, the Mayor, Mr G. Mills, stated that he felt very strongly over the matter and did not consider that the City Council should expect any help from Birkenhead until it had helped Birkenhead...The Auckland City Council has played a selfish part in refusing to support proposals for the bridge. Mr Mills added that he had just returned from a visit to the North and had found great enthusiasm for the bridge there. During his trip he met the mayors of Whangarei and Dargaville, both of whom had realised the potential value of the harbour bridge." [132]

Unfortunately, 'great enthusiasm' did not always mean full support, as reported by The New Zealand Herald on 15 August 1936:

"A decision not to support the building of an Auckland Harbour Bridge as a national undertaking was made by the Whangarei County Council today. The matter was raised when support was sought for a petition to the Government on the subject...The motion was defeated by five votes to four." [133]

The neutral position held by the Auckland Harbour Board was hardly helpful either: "The determination of the Auckland Harbour Board to maintain a neutral attitude toward the harbour bridge project was emphasised at yesterday's meeting of the board by the chairman, Mr C. G. Macindoe.

"Above all things it must be the duty of this board, as the port authority, to make it assured that the construction of a bridge does not interfere with the operation of port activities, said Mr Macindoe. However, the board had always maintained an attitude of neutrality toward the desirability of promoting the bridge project, and that attitude had not changed." [134]

Nevertheless, by November 1936, such neutrality seemed inconsequential compared to the positive interest being shown by an Australian entrepreneur, as reported by the Auckland Star:

"The Government is at present considering an offer to build the proposed Auckland harbour bridge from Fanshawe Street to Northcote Point at a total estimated cost of £1,800,000. The offer was made last week by Mr M. R. Hornibrook, managing director of the M. R. Hornibrook Proprietary, Ltd., Brisbane, and should the Government agree to certain conditions, it is stated that work could be begun in three months from the time approval was granted, giving work to some 730 men for four years.

"The cost of the bridge is estimated by Mr Hornibrook at £1,400,000 but with viaducts and other incidentals the total cost could reach £1,800,000. It is understood that the Government attitude to the proposal and to any proposal for building the bridge is that no money should be brought in from Australia or from overseas at all; but the bridge will be built if the local bodies require it to be built and if the Auckland City Council, as the sole dissenting authority, agrees that the bridge should be constructed as a Government measure. In a statement submitted to the Government, Mr Hornibrook said that if the Government would guarantee interest on a loan of £1,500,000 the work could be put in hand immediately. All the capital required and the plant were available." [135]

To an outsider from a city with three toll bridges, justification for an Auckland bridge in economic and practical terms seemed a foregone conclusion:

"The need for a bridge to connect the north side of the harbour with the south was no doubt past due, said Mr Hornibrook, making a comparison between Brisbane, where there were three toll bridges, and Auckland. Speaking of Auckland, Mr Hornibrook said that up to the present a ferry service had answered its purpose, but the time had come when something more was required to meet the growing demands of the city and the North Shore. A bridge was the logical thing. Either Brisbane was making a mistake in building another toll bridge, or else Auckland was backward in not having a bridge.

"A bridge in Auckland would not increase the rates in the city or in the North Shore boroughs, and it would not be a charge on the taxpayer. The user would pay for it. It would, on the contrary, be a big cash saving to the motorist in comparison with the present ferry charges, as well as a great saving of time to the residents of both sides. Mr Hornibrook added that the vehicular traffic using the Auckland ferries had doubled in the past eight years, although the Bridge Commission of 1929 had estimated an increase of 25 per cent in 10 years. For vehicles going north, 20 miles would be saved by using the bridge. The Public Works Department had taken a count and stated that 1000 vehicles each 24 hours passed Silverdale by the main road. Apparently these motorists were prepared to travel the extra 20 miles rather than use the ferry." [136]

Nevertheless, as Mr Hornibrook prepared to leave a bridgeless Auckland for home, the Government continued to dodge any national responsibility by blaming Auckland's local bodies for failing to agree that a bridge was needed. Until then, in the opinion of the Minister of Public Works, any schemes advocated by the likes of Mr Hornibrook would be ignored while still having 'an open mind on the matter':

"The statement that the whole question of Government consideration of the Auckland harbour bridge proposal hinged on the desire of the local bodies, and that before the Government would take any action there would have to be unanimity, was made by the Minister of Public Works, the Hon. R. Semple, to-day.

"The first essential is for the Auckland people generally affected by the proposal to make up their minds, said the Minister, and then only, will it be time for the Government, in my opinion, to think seriously about the question. Until that unanimity is shown and a general demand is made for the bridge service the Government would not be wise to rush into the matter. Personally, as Minister of Public Works, I am not going to be influenced by company promoters or the representatives of contracting firms. I have an open mind on the matter." [137]

All very well but, surprisingly, those sitting upon their lofty fences failed to recognise the cost and inconvenience of those forced to use the 'hopelessly antiquated, inadequate and highly expensive method of reaching the northern shores':

"Sir, —As a humble motorist who is thoroughly conversant with the needs of thousands of other humble motorists, I am delighted to see that the Auckland Automobile Association is supporting the harbour bridge proposal. Any other policy would be ludicrous.

"So far, so good, but in the Herald's report of the Auckland Automobile Association's meeting, I am astounded to see an anomaly incomprehensible to progress. The committee re-affirmed its previous opinion that the bridge is highly desirable, but that it should be regarded as a national, not a local undertaking! Does the committee imply that until a bridge is provided free from cost or toll to motorists, the present hopelessly antiquated, inadequate and highly expensive method of reaching the northern shores must obtain? Does it imply that a decision adopted nine years ago is not to be reconsidered to-day, when the demands for the bridge have increased far beyond the most optimistic calculations and prophecies of the Royal Commission and of the city engineer, to say nothing of the huge further increase which must necessarily take place before the bridge is completed? Surely this is beyond belief. Motorist." [138]

As 1936 closed, with no progress having been made toward the construction of a harbour bridge, Auckland's ferry service continued to struggle with increasing demand and inadequate infrastructure:

"Sir, —It will surprise many that the Devonport Steam Ferry Company has decided to supply another ferry boat for cars. Ferries of any type are out of date, and obviously the proposed new boat is intended to further retard the commencement of the harbour bridge. Even with an additional boat there is certain to be congestion and delay during certain holidays, and on Saturdays and Sundays because during those times at present four ferry boats are employed, but owing to insufficient and inadequate landing stages these boats often have to wait in mid-stream because of the time occupied in loading and unloading the cars. Motorists and others should wake up and do their best to improve the transport facilities between the city and the North Shore. PROGRESS." [139]

Little did the City's motorists appreciate that, even by March 1937, their frustration was not a major concern for those who could make a difference:

"Telling a deputation from North Shore boroughs that they represented only half the argument on the question of the Auckland harbour bridge the Prime Minister, the Right Hon. M. J. Savage, expressed himself in plain terms on the whole proposal this morning. He demanded that they should first prove to the Government that the people of Auckland wanted the bridge. Good heavens, is it too much to ask the people of Auckland to say this is an essential work, and we want it? he said. I can't see any violent enthusiasm at all.

"The only people who have come to me up to now are the bridge company. The less we say about that the better. I am not concerned with the company, but with the bridge. We won't run out of a job for quite a long time. We have already had a Public Works report on the matter. I am going to get a Treasury report, and analyse some of the figures that have been spilled about for years. I have reason to believe that that report will be a very different thing from what we have seen on circulars for some years. The Treasury Department has asked me, before there is any decision, to get their point of view. I am going to get that done as soon as I get to Wellington. I am suggesting to you that you get the people of the locality to say that they want the bridge. That isn't too much to ask for. You haven't convinced the City Council yet.

"It was pointed out by members of the deputation that the North Shore districts regarded the building of the bridge as a vital necessity. The attitude of the Auckland City Council was a selfish one in that it felt that there were still large areas of land on the city side of the harbour that should be settled before a bridge was built, encouraging city residents to go over to the other side. All local bodies in the Far North were anxious to see the bridge undertaken, as they were sure that the lack of a bridge was retarding their development.

"Speaking on behalf of the Devonport Borough Council, Mr S. Green said that while they were grateful for the service that they were getting from the Ferry Company at present, the present ferry facilities were not equal to the needs. From Christmas Eve to January 3 a total of 20,350 vehicles had entered Devonport by the vehicular ferry. This was equivalent to 2000 cars a day of eight hours. At rush times it took 57 minutes for a car to board the ferry, covering a distance of three-eighths of a mile, and the car was then from 12 to 15 minutes on the crossing. In rush times six vehicular ferries left each hour, carrying a total of 169 cars an hour. Mr Green urged that a Departmental inquiry should be made in regard to the matter.

"I don't know that I can say anything other than what I have said a dozen times already, said Mr Savage, in reply. We want the people in this locality to say they want the bridge. You say that it is essential that this bridge should be built as a national undertaking. We want proof of that. What is the answer of a member for Dunedin going to be to that? He sees it from the national aspect, too. Mr Savage then spoke straightly to the deputation, telling them that he wanted an adequate, representative opinion on the matter. He did not ask them to take a referendum, but they could get the opinion of responsible bodies, representing large sections of the people, who were directly concerned. When we get that we'll do the job, said Mr Savage. I can't say anything more than that."

"Isn't this deputation representative enough? asked Mr Guiniven. It represents one side of the argument, only, said Mr Savage. I am not here to debate the question. All I want is a greater unanimity of opinion — including the City Council." [140]

Sadly, the Auckland City Council was in no mood to take any responsibility for the sanctioning of any bridge proposal – apparently for financial reasons only, and most definitely not because of the Mayor's alleged conflict of interest – reported the Auckland Star on 25 June 1937:

"The city is not in a position to undertake any financial responsibility for the erection of the bridge, concluded a statement adopted last night as an expression of the attitude of the Auckland City Council towards the erection of a bridge across Auckland Harbour.

"The statement, prepared by the finance committee, mentioned that for some reason not fully explained there had been a tendency in the direction of placing upon the council the responsibility of a decision as to the necessity or otherwise at present of a bridge. It seemed probable that a bridge would some day become an established fact, but the committee considered that primarily it was not the responsibility of the council to take a lead on the question, although it agreed that to some extent the citizens of Auckland were interested.

"The Mayor, Sir Ernest Davis, said he wished to make his position clear. First I must nail the canard that I am opposed to the bridge because I am a director of the Devonport Steam Ferry Company, Limited, he said. That was so much stuff and nonsense and would be ignored by him but for the fact that it was kept in persistent circulation. He was not opposed to the proposal because of his association with the ferry company. He had tendered his resignation as a director of the company, but his co-directors declined to accept it on the ground that such a step was unnecessary. They had authorised him to inform the Government that the company would place no obstacle in the way of the construction of the bridge, although it felt, as he did, that the proposition from the viewpoint of the Government, the local authorities concerned and the travelling public was neither economic nor necessary. The question could be determined finally only by expert investigation and analysis. I suppose it is largely due to the existence of rumour-mongering and character blackening that many a man whose qualifications would be an asset to public life prefers the obscurity of successful business, he added." [141]

Obviously more mindful of its possible loss of revenue from toll-paying ferry passengers, the Auckland Harbour Board also remained firmly astride its fence, with purse strings firmly knotted:

"A policy of caution in approaching the question of improved vehicular ferry terminals was recommended to the Auckland Harbour Board yesterday by the superintendent and engineer. His view was that until the Government had made a definite pronouncement on the subject of a harbour bridge, or alternatively, a tunnel, the board could not reasonably be expected to commit itself to substantial expenditure on increased ferry facilities. It is true that if a bridge were built the vehicular service would undoubtedly cease at once for lack of demand.

"Whether all the passenger services would disappear as promptly is a more open question, but it cannot be argued to finality at present. If the bridge were in immediate prospect, the board would be justified in hesitating about spending money on what would at best be a short-lived asset. But is it in prospect? Its most ardent advocates are not able to offer very convincing evidence that it is, and the Government, very sensibly, shows no sign of committing itself to the project without considerable thought." [142]

All very well but, as the City Council and the Harbour Board fiddled, its citizens from both sides of the harbour had to make do with what they had, as the following 'Letters to the Editor' testify:

"In endorsing the sentiment expressed by W. S. Gilbert, in the refrain of his song, 'that the punishment should fit the crime', I would suggest that our city Mayor and councillors should be compelled for twelve months to travel daily on the 5.10 boat to Devonport or the 5.20 to Bayswater, laden with the usual amount of baggage carried by many city workers. Methinks by the end of that period they would realise that no private interest should be allowed on any consideration to stand in the way of the building of the harbour bridge. Doubtless boats to other North Shore suburbs are equally crowded, so how much longer must the people allow their comfort and security to be set at naught. In case of a collision on a foggy evening one shudders to contemplate what the results might be.

"Can we imagine that the old-fashioned gangways provided are the latest invented and the mad rush and scramble which ensues when the passengers embark and disembark may some time cause a bad accident whilst the second wild rush for buses is a blot on our so-called civilisation. Passenger." [143]

"Sir, — How much longer is the harbour bridge to be delayed? That it is a necessity there can be no question. On a recent crossing there was a strong westerly wind blowing, and six cars were packed on the weather side of the boat. Four of them, my own included, were drenched with spray. As a result of the salt water drenching, I had to take the car straight into a garage and have it washed. On another occasion I had to have the mudguard repaired and touched up, which all means loss of time. If the Government does not wish to proceed with the bridge let a private company get on with the job. The objection raised to the toll system is all rubbish. The present means of transport across the harbour is in the hands of a private company and printed on the ticket for one to read is the enlightening information that fourpence is paid as toll to the Auckland Harbour Board.

"The Sydney bridge is a big success under the toll system, and users of a harbour bridge here would be quite willing to pay for the privilege of using it. Also, it would be the users who would pay, and not the non-users. Speaking of the toll system, the excellent roads of Taranaki were made possible in this way, and to-day they are free to everyone. One extra boat will make no difference in the summer. How much longer is this necessary traffic link with the other side of the harbour to be side-stepped and allowed to be dropped? The present system is inadequate, inconvenient and inefficient. P. H. Dawson." [144]

"Sir, – The fiasco of considerably more than 200 cars (vide Herald report) being held up at Devonport on Labour Day for lack of harbour transport has at last stirred our A.A. into action. For many years long queues of waiting cars have by no means been uncommon. What will be the position by the time a bridge is built 'gives one furiously to think'. Inconvenience to motorists, however, is the mildest factor in the absurdity of depending upon steam punts for transharbour traffic. The loss to trade and the retardation of development of the North are the vital factors bearing upon the matter. Surely no other city in the world would suffer the protracted delay in building a bridge. Some 12 months ago the Prime Minister promised action should unanimity among the local bodies he forthcoming. The City Council was the sole local body lacking the vision to see the potentialities of a bridge. But even the council, in June last, expressed its opinion, 'that undoubtedly the Auckland Harbour bridge would be an asset to the whole of metropolitan Auckland'…Hauraki." [145]

"Sir, —Anent the letter in your issue of November 1, pointing out the necessity for the immediate construction of a bridge across the Waitemata Harbour may I allude to the fact that in August, 1928, 30,000 Auckland citizens signed a petition praying for the erection of the bridge, and that the petition was presented to Parliament by Mr A. Harris, M.P.? Surely the number of signatories would be trebled today. In May, 1929, specially-selected delegates, urging the erection of the bridge, waited upon the Minister of Internal Affairs at Wellington, representing the Auckland City Council, the Borough Councils of Devonport, Birkenhead, Northcote, Takapuna and Waitemata, the Auckland Hospital Board and the Harbour Bridge Association. How much longer will the citizens of Auckland permit themselves to be subjugated to a policy of apathetic procrastination in a matter of such outstanding importance to the whole of the province? Petrol." [146]

What's the problem? asked Prime Minister Savage, who had obviously spent his 1937 Labour weekend far from the shores of the Waitemata:

"The facilities provided are adequate to deal with the normal flow of traffic across the harbour, and it seems to me that motorists must expect a certain amount of delay on such exceptional occasions, stated the Prime Minister, Mr Savage, in a letter received by the Automobile Association (Auckland). The letter was a reply to a protest forwarded to the Prime

Minister, and signed by a large number of drivers who suffered delays on Labour Day in being transported across the harbour.

"Mr Savage said he had had inquiries made following receipt of the letter regarding the inadequacy of the trans-harbour vehicular transport facilities. It appears that the delay and inconvenience caused on the occasion referred to, Labour Day, were due to exceptional conditions, a fall of rain in the early evening causing a general speeding-up of motorists city-bound from the north, Mr Savage said, in his letter. Also, a certain amount of congestion was inevitable in view of cars which crossed the harbour on Saturday, Sunday and Monday all wishing to return at the close of the holiday. The Prime Minister added that he was informed that the ferry company expected to have an additional ferry boat available in time for Christmas, and this would do much to relieve the position during peak periods.

"An official of the Automobile Association said yesterday that suggestions recently made that the Government might intend seriously to interest itself in a harbour bridge appeared to be discounted by the Prime Minister's remarks. No doubt advocates of the bridge would be disappointed at this further set-back. He added that some definite opinion regarding the relief which the new ferry could afford would be gained during the present holiday period." [147]

To the supporters of the harbour bridge, another set-back came as no surprise and it was the opinion of some, such as the Mayor of Takapuna, John Guiniven, that the delays were politically motivated:

"Sir, — Your correspondent Enid Ellis wonders why nobody has protested against Mr Savage's remarks in connection with cross-harbour transport facilities. Your correspondent seems to forget that vested interests contribute to the party's political fighting fund and that the present Government is opposed to any modern system of communication which might interfere with the existing obsolete railway system.

"As a matter of fact, Mr Savage is to be congratulated for assuring us that the Government will not build the bridge, especially as some other members of Parliament are running with the hare and hounds. As Labour secured a large majority at last election, personally I have no quarrel with Sir Savage and his colleagues, just because they are not in favour of the Government building the bridge, but I do blame them from spragging the wheels of private enterprise.

"Mr Hornibrook had sufficient capital to build the bridge, but the Government refused to allow him to do so. The bridge has not been built because the necessary enthusiasm and organisation was lacking on the northern side of the harbour, and because city people took no interest in the development of the north. If the members of the Automobile Association, together with those living north of the harbour, gave Mr Savage to understand that they would not support his Government at next election unless the bridge was built as a national undertaking the work would soon be commenced.

"The danger lies in the Government taking over the obsolete ferries, and thus putting the chance of getting a bridge off for 30 or 40 years. Of course, the Labour Party will use the bridge as a slogan before next election: a large number of electors will be fooled as usual, but if re-elected the Government will not build the bridge. Some time ago I endeavoured to arouse interested parties in the city with a view of getting the bridge built, but Labour was allowed to butt in and the whole scheme fell through. With a Labour majority in the House and in the City Council there is not the remotest chance of the bridge being built, nationally or privately. However, it seems that a lot of North Shore people like being fooled by shrewd opportunists. Takapuna, John Guiniven." [148]

The newly-formed Waitemata Harbour Bridge Association Incorporated advanced its argument for a bridge using facts and figures to illustrate the obvious need, as per the Association's letter to the Editor of The New Zealand Herald, published on 16 June 1938:

"Sir, —In your issue of June 14 the following statement, included in the report of the chairman of directors of the Devonport Steam Ferry Company, Limited, is worthy of comment: —'If the vehicular traffic continued to increase, which was almost too much to expect, it would be necessary to have additional landing facilities.'

"Why this diffidence? Let us examine the increase in traffic during last 18 years. According to schedule No. 7 handed in in evidence to the Royal Commission in 1930 by the Devonport Ferry Company, the total number of vehicles carried per annum by the vehicular ferries had increased from 106,580 in 1920 to 284,690 in 1929 – a total increase of 267 per cent, or an average annual increase of nearly 30 per cent. The amount of tolls paid in respect of vehicular traffic by the Ferry Company to the Auckland Harbour Board in 1929 was £4099 19s 5d, and it is estimated from the returns of such tolls paid to March 31, 1938, that this figure will increase to £7656, or an increase of 86 per cent for the year ending September 30, 1938. This represents 534,000 vehicles per annum at present being carried.

"The traffic actually declined somewhat during the depression, but during the last five years has increased over 100 per cent. The total increase over the 18-year period is over 500 per cent. Can we therefore anticipate as traffic increases a string of vehicular wharves on each side of the harbour, and is this a logical solution of the difficulty? There is only one method of solving the problem, that is the immediate erection of the harbour bridge. R. H. Greville, LL.M. Secretary, Waitemata Harbour Bridge Association (Incorporated.)" [149]

By December 1938, little had changed, including the Government's indifference to the increasingly urgent need for a bridge:

"In response to representations in regard to the congestion of vehicular traffic across the Auckland Harbour, the Prime Minister, Mr Savage, advised the Automobile Association (Auckland) in a message received at a meeting of the council last night, that in his opinion fresh inquiries should be made concerning the proposal to build a harbour bridge before any action was taken. Mr Savage stated that recently the Cabinet had this question under review, but decided to withhold action in the meantime.

"Reports and complaints from motorists who had been shut off vehicular ferries during November were received by the council. Disappointment was expressed at the inadequacy of the present service to meet the requirements of travellers, especially at holiday or rush periods. It was decided to make further endeavours to secure an improvement in the Birkenhead and Northcote services, in order to relieve the congestion at the Devonport landing." [150]

While 1939 was to include events of devastating importance to the world with far-reaching consequences, those events were not to include the bridging of the Waitemata. This was despite the hopelessly-inadequate, trans-harbour service provided by the ferries, as described by Auckland's Automobile Association and reported by the Auckland Star on 27 January of that year:

"The harbour bridge controversy was revived last evening, when the Automobile Association (Auckland) submitted figures which, it was claimed, showed the inadequacy of the vehicular ferry service between the city and North Shore. It was suggested that the Auckland city had now reached such a stage in its development, and the density of the traffic was so great, that the present system of trans-harbour transport could not adequately serve the public. The association is of the opinion that the matter is so serious as to demand active steps, firstly to provide adequate service immediately, and secondly, to bring about a permanent solution by the provision of a traffic bridge across the harbour…" [151]

Prime Minister Savage had long since advocated a conference comprising all interested parties to discuss the need for a bridge. However, such a conference was never a priority for the Government and became even less so as each day of 1939 passed:

"A letter from the Prime Minister, Mr Savage, advising that, in view of more urgent matters, it was not possible to state definitely when the suggested conference concerning the Waitemata Harbour bridge project would be held, was received at last night's meeting of the Takapuna Borough Council. It was decided to communicate with the Prime Minister, reminding him of his former promises, pointing out that the question of urgency was a matter of opinion, and stating that the council considered the reply most unsatisfactory.

"The Mayor, Mr J. Guiniven, said he considered the Prime Minister was the greatest stumbling block to the construction of the bridge. The scheme was of greater importance to North Auckland than to either Northcote or Takapuna. The Prime Minister had no interest in the development of the North Shore boroughs, and still less in the North. Thousands of acres of land in the North could not be opened because of the lack of the bridge." [152]

Then, by the end of July 1939, it was decided (seemingly by both the Devonport Steam Ferry Company and the Harbour Board) that Northcote would no longer be a ferry destination. The reaction of the Northcote Borough Council was reported by the New Zealand Herald on 27 July 1939:

"Following a discussion at a meeting of the Northcote Borough Council on Tuesday night a letter was sent to the Devonport Steam Ferry Company yesterday making a 'strong and urgent protest' against the decision to delete Northcote from the vehicular ferry service from next Sunday.

"When the Mayor of Northcote, Mr R. Martin, heard of the proposals on Tuesday he got into touch with members of the company's staff, who claimed that the service was to be eliminated on the recommendation of the Harbour Board…The chairman of the board, Mr W. B. Darlow, denied that this was the case and said the board would continue to maintain the wharf. It was difficult to understand the action of the company in deciding without reference to the council to discontinue a service which had been in existence for many years and which, although not entirely satisfactory, was vital to the district." [153]

Northcote's Mayor was not the only one to feel aggrieved about the termination of ferry services to the borough:

"The discontinuance by the Devonport Steam Ferry Company of the vehicular service to Northcote was discussed in the King's Theatre last night at one of the largest meetings ever held in the borough. The crowd of approximately 1000 overflowed the large hall and extended to the post office on the opposite side of the street. Loud-speakers kept those outside informed of the proceedings. The Mayor, Mr R. Martin, who presided, said he had invited the Ferry Company to be represented, but a reply had been received that no useful purpose would be served by attending a protest meeting." [154]

Indeed, after nearly twenty years of argument and protest by those for and against the bridge, no useful purpose had been served at all. As reported by The New Zealand Herald on 25 August 1939, the frustration of many was summed up by Takapuna's long-serving Mayor, John Guiniven:

"We must prove to the Government's satisfaction that the findings of the commission which investigated the question of the Waitemata Harbour Bridge in 1929 were wrong, said the Mayor of Takapuna, Mr J. Guiniven, at a public meeting held in the Takapuna Borough Chambers last night to press for the institution of a Government inquiry.

"We at Takapuna have passed countless resolutions for a harbour bridge and sent them to the Government with no tangible result. Therefore, we must get the inquiry going. The Waitemata Harbour Bridge Association is in a position to upset the theories promulgated by the commission, the members of which were not sympathetic with the project. In the past, the city's attitude had not been in favour of the bridge, continued Mr Guiniven, because they considered that there were about 30,000 sections on their side of the harbour which should be settled first. However, he considered that with unanimity on the North Shore a good case could he built up which would force the Government's hand. If the Government had not the money it should say so, and the association could arrange some other scheme.

"Mr Guiniven expressed sympathy with the ferry company. It was doing its best with an obsolete means of transport, and could not be expected to spend money trying to better it while the bridge question was still unsettled. He mentioned the vast areas of arable land in the north which would be opened up by the bridge. Mr R. H. Greville, secretary of the Waitemata Harbour Bridge Association, said that only one good thing came from the findings of the 1929 commission, and that was the site and style for the bridge. All the rest of its findings, regarding methods of finance, cost, etc., had since been proved hopelessly pessimistic.

"Whereas the commission had considered it would take 33 years for trans-harbour traffic to double itself, an increase of almost 20 per cent took place yearly. The condition of traffic on the harbour in another five years was difficult to contemplate. The meeting unanimously passed a resolution stating that the erection of a harbour bridge was considered an urgent necessity, and requesting the Government to set up the promised inquiry forthwith." [155]

Unfortunately, the days of 1939 had been marching toward Armageddon and a month later there came another war…a major blow to the ambitions of all bridge supporters. Their appeals to Government were suddenly rendered pointless, as conveyed by The New Zealand Herald report of 19 September 1939:

"At a meeting of the Northcote Women's Progressive League…The secretary of the Waitemata Harbour Bridge Association, Mr R. H. Greville, who was to have addressed the gathering, intimated that, in view of the outbreak of war, the association would refrain from appealing to the public for the time being." [156]

Indeed, it would not be until 1959, another twenty years, before traffic would at last cross the Auckland Harbour by way of a bridge – but first there was another war to be fought…

*Chapter Five*

# Trails Through the Fern

By the time Felton Mathew's vision of a canal to the Tamaki and a connecting railway to Onehunga had reached the archives, the first settlers extended their beachhead south, trampling trails across the scoria and through the hillside fern. But even the most sure-footed horses and rudimentary carts needed roads a little wider and firmer than those trodden ferns and the single-file, Maori tracks that bisected the Auckland isthmus at the time. Highways and byways that did not become morasses of mud in winter and ruts of dust in summer were needed if the Auckland settlement was to grow in a sustainable manner.

William Hobson died in 1842 and when Robert Fitzroy became New Zealand's second Governor in December the following year, he soon found there was little treasury money available for the provision of public services such as roads. However, there was a surfeit of labour in the form of new immigrants who were without private employment and the means to acquire land.

Captain David Rough (1815-1899), appointed Auckland's Harbour Master in 1841 and Immigration Officer in 1842, was placed in charge of the formation of some of the colony's first roads, as Auckland's superintendent of works. Under Captain Rough's supervision, those immigrants were organised to set about the formation of Queen Street, Shortland Street and Princes Street and to cut new roads to Newmarket (Khyber Pass) and to the Tamaki and Onehunga districts. [1]

By 1850, there was still little money for infrastructure and a lot of work still to be done. This was graphically described in an article published by the Daily Southern Cross on 26 February of that year:

"The Surveyor, who first projected Auckland, must certainly have had the Multum-in-Parvo (a great deal in a small place) principle strongly impressed, and assiduously inculcated. Broad, open, well ventilated streets, intersecting each other at right angles, must, to his contracted vision have appeared an extravagance of conception on no account to be indulged.

"Sewers to carry off pool or puddle, it is clear, entered not into the scheme of his political economy. He may have read, very probably, that manure, both solid and liquid, is a source of considerable wealth to a city corporation possessed of soil-carts, scavengers, and the other ministers of purification; but, knowing that Auckland was as guiltless of such corporate intelligence as New Zealand's Nominee Councils are of political independence, our projector may have deemed it but fair to dam our thoroughfares, and so to leave at every man's door that fair proportion of filth to which he may be reasonably and lawfully entitled.

"Drains indeed! Drains are expensive affairs to deal with and should one, by miracle, be attempted, to render practicable the slough to the receipt of custom, it must be undertaken in such utter defiance of the simplest rules of art, that it is sure to break down in disgust under the pelting of a more than ordinarily energetic summer shower. West Queen-street yet continues a frightful canal for the confluence of animal and vegetable putrescency. Queen-street and Shortland street rejoice in numerous untended ruts which winter will convert to deep and dangerous pitfalls. As for the others, most are mere sludgy tracks, wind and water worn, or else they are so many sloughs of despond into which nothing but necessity would induce the unwary to intrude.

"In fact, the thoroughfares, be they leading or lonely ones, are in such a condition that the passenger will never be able to thread them without difficulty and disgust, whilst, as if in solemn mockery of the prevailing nastiness, we have stringent foot-path ordinances, but not a street with a foot-path to protect. We have again and again directed attention to the wasteful expenditure lavished in the formation of Upper Queen-street, and we again call upon the Authorities to exhibit some little foresight in yet saving a portion of the money and material sunk in that injudicious quagmire. If there be not some channels prepared by which the wash of the high grounds may be carried into the Queen-street tunnel, we shall find the main approach to our city an all but impassable gutter. In seeking thus again to blazon our grievances, we can scarcely entertain the silly expectation that the authorities will attempt the slightest remedy. Whatever way our cash is squandered, there is none to be spared in promotion of the traffic or the health of the town through whose commerce our revenue is chiefly derived." [2]

With the granting of a 'Representative Constitution to the Colony of New Zealand' by the British Parliament in 1852, the country's two provinces, unimaginatively named New Ulster and New Munster, were replaced by the six provinces of Auckland, New Plymouth (later renamed Taranaki), Wellington, Nelson, Canterbury, and Otago. The number of provinces was later increased to nine with the inclusion of Hawkes Bay in 1858, Marlborough in 1859, and Westland (as a fully autonomous province) in 1873.

Until the provinces were replaced by a county system in 1876, each was governed by a Superintendent and a Provincial Council responsible to its citizens under The Provincial Councils Powers Act 1856. This and other empowering legislation, such as the Highways Act of 1867 and the Highway Boards Empowering Acts of 1871 and 1872, allowed each province to govern its local, day-to-day affairs in much the same way as District and City Councils do today.

The Highway Boards Empowering Acts provided for the establishment of Highway Boards within each municipality and the sphere of influence of these Boards more or less came to define the local body boundaries in which they were located.

"Between 1855 and 1892, substantial sums of money were allocated by the Provincial Government for the survey, formation and upkeep of roads. However, these funds were not sufficient for every need and so under the Local Improvement Act 1858, agreements were made with property occupiers permitting them to collectively meet part of the cost to improve roads and footpaths. Among those who took advantage of this were the residents and shopkeepers of Queen Street who contributed to construct a footpath on the eastern side." [3]

The Highway Boards Empowering Acts and the later Main Highways Act of 1922 certainly demonstrated the importance placed on the construction and maintenance of roads as a necessary part of the nation's growth and prosperity. But the early establishment of Highway and Roads Boards was not just to supervise the layout and construction of highways and roads. These Boards could do more than that.

As originally constituted, they were empowered "...to impose rates on such lands and the occupiers and owners thereof...to make by-laws for certain purposes and by such by-laws to provide for the imposition of a penalty for the breach thereof and to enable such Boards or other bodies to take land compulsorily for certain purposes without first obtaining a special Act or Ordinance." [4]

The first of these Boards to be formed in the province of Auckland included the (West) Tamaki Road Board, established in 1862; and the Remuera Road Board, and the One Tree Hill, Parnell, and Panmure Highway Boards formed in 1863. These were followed by the establishment of Highway Boards representing Otahuhu in 1865, Mt Albert in1866, Mt Eden and Mt Roskill in 1867, and Grey Lynn, Whau (later Avondale), Newmarket, Onehunga, Ponsonby, and Karangahape in 1868.

Naturally, as the city's population and geographical size increased, much of the legislation governing this growth needed to be regularly amended. As a result, the Auckland Provincial Council passed such Acts as the Auckland Provincial Highways Act 1862, later refined by amending legislation of 1867 and 1874. And there were a few instances when Provincial legislation had to be amended by the country's Parliament. Such an instance occurred in 1875, when a special rate had to be added to the general road rate "...for the purpose of raising funds to be applied to the lighting of the several streets and roads of the district with gas or other illuminating material." [5]

The Auckland Highway Districts Validation Act of 1877 is of particular interest in that it was needed to hurriedly correct certain notifications made by Sir George Grey who served as Auckland Provincial Superintendent from March 1875 to October 1876. These notifications, made pursuant to the powers contained in the 1874 Highways Act, related to the division of certain portions of the Auckland Province into various Highway districts. [6]

Unfortunately, the wording of these notices omitted to inform that they were issued "By advice and consent of the Executive Council..." [7] This omission, according to the judgement given on 25 July 1877 by Supreme Court Judge Gillies in the appeal case, Aitken v Bremner, rendered the Highways Act notifications of Superintendent Grey invalid.

Judge Gillies' decision, described the following day by the Waikato Times as "fatal", reversed an earlier finding of the lower court - this time in favour of wealthy, Auckland real estate agent, William Aitken, against Alexander Bremner, then employed by the Waitoa Highway District Board as secretary and rate collector.

"The decision is important," the paper noted, "as it is believed the large majority of highway districts in the Province (Auckland) have been similarly constituted, and are liable to defeat in the recovery of rates." [8]

According to a Waikato Times report, the case brought by William Aitken centred around "... rates for Judge Fenton's land in the Waitoa Highway District." [9]

How William Aitken came to be involved in Judge Fenton's rate dispute, except perhaps as his agent, is not known but the amending legislation, the Auckland Highway Districts Validation Act 1877, which became law by October of that year, specifically included a clause providing "...that nothing in this Act contained shall affect an action recently tried on appeal by the Supreme Court in Auckland between William Aitken, appellant, and Alexander Bremner, respondent." [10]

Presumably, that meant that the learned Judge Fenton and a good many other Auckland Provincial landowners, did not have to pay their rates, for that year at least. No wonder the amending legislation was processed as a matter of urgency. Indeed, according to the Southland Times, the new Bill was introduced by way of an interruption to Parliament's normal business when "...Mr Rees obtained leave to introduce a bill to validate certain actions of highway boards, and in respect to which a decision adverse to the boards was recently given by Judge Gillies; without such a measure they would, he said, be unable to exist." [11]

While, after its establishment in 1870, the Government's Public Works Department supervised and controlled most of the nation's road construction, a large proportion of the work within the boundaries governed by the Highway Boards was paid for by their respective local authorities. This funding was of course acquired from the rates imposed on 'local lands and the occupiers and owners thereof'. But by the time the Auckland City Council was created in April 1871, Auckland's street network was potentially a bottomless pit of expenditure and more roads were desperately needed. It is no wonder that by October 1877, it was realised that, despite their revenue generating capacity, the Highway Boards and the provinces in general were struggling to maintain a national, road-building programme.

According to a Bay of Plenty Times report of October 6, 1877:

"...Mr De Latour (for the Government) brought forward the motion – That in the opinion of this House, it being now established that the counties are unable to make provision for the construction and maintenance of the main arterial roads of the colony, it is imperative that immediate and permanent provision should be made by the Government for the gradual construction and maintenance of the same. As Mr De Latour truly said, unless some such motion be carried, traffic in the inland districts must inevitably be suspended during several months in the year, and the commerce of the country, from want of roads, severely handicapped." [12]

Such early differences between national and regional aspirations, severe enough to impact the legislative and practical implementation of transport systems, should come as no surprise to the 21st-century Aucklander. And nor should certain other similarities between contemporary attitudes and conditions and those of the 1800s. At a time when successful settlement not only relied on reliable transport routes but also a steady inflow of colonists to use and subsidise them, a conflict soon arose as to how the expenditure on public works was to be allocated. In many cases, an individual's preferences very much depended on whether he or she lived in town or suburbia. It was a conflict that was to last, to some extent, until well after the invention of Auckland as a 'super city' of the 21st century.

In 1858, Auckland's Daily Southern Cross knew where it stood on the matter:

"Our readers are aware that in making choice among the many public works required, we have always laid great stress upon giving the preference to such as were most likely to be of a re productive character. And whilst admitting the necessity of providing the towns with such sanatory (sic) improvements as are essential to the health or convenience to the inhabitants, we have expressed our conviction that, as a general rule, money expended in opening up the country would benefit both country and town infinitely more than the same sum spent on works of doubtful utility in the city.

"This being a question of mere profit or loss to every individual in the community can be fairly examined without the aid of those partisan feelings which mystify every scheme for the good of the province. Our country readers will of course agree with us in opinion. Our city readers will probably do the same, if they can be induced to look at the question in its simplest point of view, and ask themselves, does the city really gain or lose, by the large sums of money voted for its use?" [13]

This debate about how limited funds were to be spent – whether on the consolidation and improvement of current city amenities or on the city's expansion to outlying districts – obviously determined the progress of the Auckland province as a whole. As Felton Mathew had earlier foreseen, expansion south, toward the fertile Waikato District, was the obvious choice.

*Chapter Six*

# Trails of Steel – The Railway

"Early in 1862, the Provincial Council Superintendent brought to the consideration of members a project for a railway connecting Auckland with Drury. Members debated the merits or demerits of construction of such a railway, how far this railway should go, and the cost and who should bear this…The end result was that it was agreed that necessary surveys should be completed for a proposed line of railway from Auckland to Drury.

"The first survey for the Auckland to Drury Railway was undertaken in 1862 by Samuel Harding and James Stewart (both Civil Engineers). It took most of the year for the survey to be completed along with the preparation of plans and estimates for the route selected. The initial route proposed was from an Auckland terminus outside Fort Britomart, winding around the bay, crossing the road at Mechanics Bay, and then striking high ground near the Parnell brickworks, with a tunnel under the Epsom Road and on to Newmarket, then from there almost paralleling the Great South Road to Ellerslie where a line branched off to Onehunga.

"The main railway continued on towards Papakura, avoiding the head and branches of the Tamaki River, and passing within about a quarter of a mile of Manurewa Mountain, then onwards via Papakura to the proposed terminus on the Great South Road at Drury. Stewart and Harding presented the plans and report to Provincial Council in early 1863. Then began the long months of debate, planning, preparation and raising of finance by the Provincial Council to construct this railway. The outbreak of the Waikato war in July 1863 temporarily delayed matters. However, in September 1863 the Auckland Provincial Superintendent applied to General Assembly for leave to bring the Auckland and Drury Railways Bill before the assembly." [1]

The Auckland and Drury Railway Act was passed on 14 December 1863 and the Auckland Provincial Council met on 18 December to consider, among other things, the appropriation of £100,000 for the purpose of building the Auckland and Drury Railway, with a branch line to Onehunga. During the ensuing debate, it was obvious that not all the Provincial Council's esteemed members agreed as to whether or not their limited funds should be used to finance a project that was not overtly beneficial to the city.

As reported by the Daily Southern Cross on 19 December 1863, the diverse opinions of Council members not only reflected a certain lack of collective purpose, often repeated as the City grew, but also a degree of suspicion as to which of the Council members might also benefit from the construction of the railway. It was also one of the first times that such a body was to debate the merits of road use compared to those of rail. In this instance, after debating the Railway Appropriation Bill, rail prevailed, but that was not a result that was to be repeated too many times at future meetings of Auckland's civic leaders.

"Mr Wynn moved the second reading of a bill to appropriate the sum of £100,000 for the purpose of constructing a railway between Auckland and Drury. The principle of the bill he said was in accordance with the resolution passed in the previous part of this session.

"Mr J O'Neill protested against the diversion of this money from its original purpose, while other works of greater importance were neglected, and especially as they had heard there would be very little surplus revenue this year. He believed in railways, but thought they could be better carried out by private companies. He also thought that so large a work should be undertaken by an in-coming rather than by an out-going Government.

"Mr Harrop said he believed in private enterprise alone, and was sure that the Government would find the undertaking more difficult than they had calculated upon.

"Mr Lynch was also entirely opposed to this vote at the present time. He considered it unjust thus to take advantage of a loan, to be raised for great public purposes, by the consent of members who were opposed to a railway. He would rather see immigration and land purchase carried on first. The interest and sinking fund of this loan would greatly decrease the revenue of this province for a long time; and he thought that, seeing that all the attention of the General and Provincial Government was being entirely directed to the South at this time, they might rest satisfied without this railway.

"He was convinced that there was no revenue to spare for interest and sinking fund; it was all required for public works. He would consent to giving a guarantee to a private company. He had no faith in the proposed commissioners; believing that they would disagree with the Government in a few months, and the work fall through. He trusted to see the bill modified in committee, so as only to go to Onehunga at present. He would not object to that, but thought the settlement of the South not sufficiently developed to enable them to determine in what direction the main line should run.

"Mr Ross also opposed the bill. There was no security for the outlay, as in case of the Tamaki bridge; nor would the speculation be a paying one. Mr Foley considered that the people in the Southern district should guarantee the interest and sinking fund for the railway. If not, he should oppose the people of Tamaki giving it for the bridge. Mr George opposed this Government project as an expensive affair which would decrease our revenue, already very small.

"Captain Rattray had come to the conclusion that it would be very well to have a railway, provided that the means were legitimately obtained, but the present scheme appeared to him rather one-sided, when it was known that not three miles of the North Road was in a good state. It was not the £100,000 he stuck at, but that would not be a third enough. There was no information as to the cost of the land through which it passed. He was decidedly of opinion that only the Onehunga line should be proceeded with at present. He objected to the scheme proposed, as not only premature, but unfair to the Northern Division. He complained of the public works for which the loan was raised had not been proceeded with at once. He could not but think with Mr Lynch that there was self-interest in this matter, and must vote against the bill.

"Mr King challenged the last speaker to show that any vote proposed for the Northern Division had ever been opposed. The Northern part of the country, he remarked had such a sea-board, that they were not in the same need of a railway as the South, and in the South a railway must be made if Auckland was again to become an exporting colony. When the loan was raised it was not known what a change would take place in the condition of the interior, and he thought it would now be very unwise to let so much money lie idle, knowing, as they did, that a portion of the £90,000 raised for land purchase seven years ago was still unexpended.

"As to the South taxing themselves, they were doing so by paying tolls on the South Road. The railway could not stop at Drury, but must be the first joint of a grand trunk railway through the country. He contended that the cost of the railway was not assumed, but calculated and known with certainty; and that the expenditure would benefit the whole colony, and not the South alone. As to the revenue not being sufficient to pay the interest, there was nothing that would so tend to increase the revenue as opening the way for settlers to get to their land. The immediate construction of a permanent work would also be much cheaper than continuing to make shift with metalled roads.

"He trusted that the House would pass this bill, believing that the General Government would assist them to make a railway right through the country. The loan proposed to be expended on roads he thought would be far better spent in making a Waikato Railway. £8,000 a year was all the province could lose by the present scheme, and they would save that by diminished expenditure on the Great South Road.

"Mr Rowe had hoped that this question would not have required another discussion. He was sorry that the member for City West and others should come to the Council with such narrow-minded arguments — the course of which was simply south against north. The promoters believed that they were benefitting the whole province, and did not believe that one shilling would be taken from the expenditure on the north. He was sure, indeed, that amongst the promoters of this railway the north might count its best friends. Further the warmest promoters of this had no private interest in it whatever. He asked if it would not have been far better to have laid down the railway years ago instead of squandering so much on the Great South Road.

"Mr Gallaugher insisted that it was not those who supported, but those who opposed the railway that were actuated by selfish motives, as it would bring down produce cheaper than it now came from the North.

"Mr Cadman thought the speech of the member for City East (Dr Pollen), in a previous debate had completely settled this question. No road paid directly, and it was only a question between the cost of common roads and of railroads. He was prepared to show that it would cost £75,000 to make the Great South Road, and £20,000 a year to keep it in repair; an expense which the province would get cheaply out of by making the railroad. It had been a matter of regret to him that a railroad or tram road had not been made long ago. It was wonderful to find people in the 19th century opposing a railway, especially when the very youngest province of this colony was now actually constructing one. He was sure, moreover, that the work would not only after a little while pay the interest and sinking fund, but also leave the Government a large profit.

"He also believed that the construction of a railroad would tend to the permanent pacification of the country. The proposed Waikato settlers must raise a great amount of produce, and altogether he thought the Council would be very unwise to reject this bill. He should support it with a deal of pleasure.

"Mr Buckland remarked that when this question was introduced there was a majority against it, which had steadily changed till there was a majority for it, a circumstance with which he was much pleased. He also maintained that they had no right to go to private companies and demand of them to invest their means for the public weal. He held that this investment would be first rate, but that was nothing to do with it. The Waikato was, indeed, a fine country; but it was shut up, and we must either continue to import our grain or make a road to open the country up; and not only assist the settlers, but by inducing the Maoris to cultivate, assist in civilizing and keeping them peaceful. To those members who wished the railway to stop at Onehunga he said, let the second reading pass and fight out the question where it should go to afterwards.

"The question was then put that the bill be read a second time, and the Council divided as follows: — Ayes, 14 – Noes, 5. The bill was then read a second time and the Council went into committee upon it." [2]

Once the vote of £100,000 was in place, the Auckland and Drury Railway bill was enacted. Clause IV of the Bill was specific as to the route it was to take:

"It shall be lawful for the Superintendent to make and maintain a Railway commencing on the Sea Beach at or near the Easterly end of Customhouse-street in the City of Auckland and passing from in through or into the several townships places or other territorial divisions following that is to say Auckland Waitemata Parnell Epsom Newmarket Remuera Manurewa Otahuhu Opaheke Papakura and Drury and terminating in an allotment in the occupation of George Graham at or near the North Eastern corner of the town of Drury as laid down in the official plan thereof with a Branch Railway from the same terminating in the Public Reserve near Geddes' Basin at or near to the Town of Onehunga all in the said Province as the same is more particularly delineated and described in the said plan and section or within the limits of deviation set forth on the said plan..." [3]

However, because of the uncertainties of railway construction through such varied terrain, Clause XI of the Act also allowed that, "The Superintendent in constructing the Railway may deviate from the line of works laid down in the plan..." [4]

And, as might be expected, there were many commentators who strongly believed that 'the line of works laid down in the plan' should be changed. While many of these opinions were naturally self-serving, some were of a more practical nature – such as that expressed in a letter to the editor by 'A Dweller on the Coast' published by The New Zealand Herald on 1 April 1864:

"In perusing your just remarks upon the course proposed for the line of the Drury Railway, in to-day's paper I was struck with an idea suggested by your observations. It was with reference to one of the probable disadvantages likely to accrue from running the line along by the margin of, or straight across one of the exposed Bays on the coast in the immediate neighbourhood of Auckland.

"As it is now, there have been gales in Auckland Harbour when it would have been impossible for a man to stand upon the Queen-street Wharf without being blown bodily over into the water. The Bays are far more exposed to the force of the wind; the North Head not affording even the same break there that it does to the Queen-street Wharf higher up the harbour. What then will be the effect of one of these strong gales upon the extent of surface exposed to it by a Railway train while passing along the proposed raised embankment from Fort Britomart across Official and Mechanic's Bays. It strikes me that that part of the line would be impassable, or that some time there would occur an accident of a terrible character. A gale that will bowl a house bodily down in Parnell would not make much of a Railway Train on the sea shore." [5]

Nevertheless, the enthusiasm for the Auckland and Drury Railway, by whatever route, was maintained and, indeed, a start was eagerly anticipated by the Daily Southern Cross:

"Our readers will be glad to learn that tenders have been called for the construction of the Auckland and Drury Railway, with a branch line to Onehunga, and an announcement to that effect from Mr Cheeseman, the Chairman of the Railway Board, will be seen in another column. The length of the line between Auckland and Drury is twenty-two miles. Plans and specifications will be ready at the office of the Board on and after the 1st June, and tenders will be received until noon of August 1, 1864.

"Tenders are also invited (for the same work) for the supply of about 30,000 sleepers, of either puriri, kauri, or blue gum. These tenders are to be sent in not later than the 1st June. There is nothing like making a beginning, and when we see the first ground broken, we shall begin to realise in perspective the luxury of railway travelling." [6]

However, the anticipation of a successfully completed line between Auckland and Drury was not shared by all. In a long editorial published on 15 July 1864, The New Zealand Herald expressed its serious reservations about both the financial and practical means of the Railway Commissioners to complete the task:

"Seeing the vast importance of our first efforts in Railway making, there needs no apology for constantly referring to the subject in our columns. A false step now may plunge us into expense and grievous losses, which will long lie a heavy incubus upon us and paralyse further efforts in this direction. The difference between wisdom and foolishness acted now may cost us thousands of pounds, as well as greatly retard the extension of railways among us, and so in effect greatly retard the successful colonization of this island.

"And having the experience both of the mother country and of Australia to guide and warn us, nothing but sheer ignorance and stupidity can prevent us from avoiding the bogs which have, in their ease, swallowed up such enormous amounts of money. The Commissioners to whom is entrusted the construction of the Auckland and Drury Railway may either do us an incalculable amount of harm or good, and we much fear that the course they are pursuing is likely to tend to the injury of the Province." [7]

At the same time, the Herald called for a more visionary approach to the whole scheme:

"The Auckland and Drury Railway Commissioners must rise to a higher level than that on which they started when first they were appointed. They must extend their horizon and view a large breadth of country beyond Drury, as imperatively requiring their consideration. The latter place must not shut in and bound their view. The name of the proposed railway does not now meet the necessities of the changed circumstances, and it will still less do so twelve months hence.

"Land that was the other day entirely in possession of the natives will shortly be planted with young and thriving settlements, and it needs no prophetic eye to see from the tops of the hills of the Waikato Ranges numberless homesteads that will dot the adjoining valleys; villages and towns springing rapidly into existence; the rich portions of that large and fertile district covered with golden grain and feeding herds of cattle, and flocks of sheep.

"The busy hum of industry will take the place of the silence and solitude of the desert; and the population that will doubtless be quickly located in that region, if proper wisdom and prudence only be shown, will imperatively require every facility for carrying the produce of their fields, their orchards, and their dairies to a ready market, and for obtaining necessary supplies in exchange for them. Now this can best be effected by a railway carried direct into the Waikato. The present name, the Auckland and Drury Railway, is a, misnomer under present circumstances. It must be changed to the Auckland and Waikato Railway, though, for the present, only to be made between Newmarket and Waikato. No one who is able to think at all upon the subject will come to any other conclusion.

"The scheme, then, as at present decided upon had far better be allowed to remain in abeyance, so far as the Auckland end of it is concerned, till the whole question can be gone into by both the General and the Provincial Governments. That the present scheme cannot be carried out for the sum appropriated for that purpose is a fact which cannot for a moment be doubted. To attempt to make the line from Auckland to Drury for the amount voted and in the manner contemplated by the committee will be utterly foolishness. It will be swallowed up long before Drury is reached, and will leave Onehunga just as it is at the present moment. The portion of the line from Auckland to Newmarket will take a very large portion of the money. The absurd scheme of the sea wall and the nature of the country will cause this short first length to be very costly, much more so than many people would imagine.

"If we put £40,000 for the line from Auckland to Newmarket, not quite two miles, we shall not be very far wrong. And we leave our readers to calculate, if they can, how far the remainder of the amount voted, taking into consideration the unnecessary costly schemes of the committee, will carry the line on to Drury and a branch to Onehunga. Those who are sanguine enough to dream that the balance of money remaining after the line has been made to Newmarket will carry it onward to Drury in the expensive manner intended are day dreamers, pure et simple, but they will one day awake to the stern reality that will be presented to them of a demand upon the Provincial Council of another £100,000 to prevent the first £100,000 from having been uselessly expended.

"The fact is that the funds at the disposal of the Commissioners are totally inadequate for carrying out their idea of the requirements for a line of railway from Auckland to Drury…we ought to do the best we possibly can with the means at our disposal, and secure the greatest amount of good which will unquestionably be obtained by commencing at Newmarket, and so avoiding, for the present, by far the most expensive portion of the line, and pushing it on to Waikato."[3]

Of course, the twenty-first century reader, with all the hindsight that confers, will be familiar with the concerns of underfunding expressed by The New Zealand Herald. At least, in this case, some action was being taken by decision makers, underfunded or not. Despite the apprehension expressed, by the Herald and others, tenders for the construction of the railway were called and some twelve firms, three from Auckland and the remainder from Otago, Melbourne and Sydney, had tendered for the opportunity to construct the Auckland and Drury Railway.

By early October, those tenders had been considered by the Railway Commissioners and details of their acceptance were published by a comparatively more enthusiastic Herald on 11 October 1864:

"We are able to inform our readers that the progress of this undertaking is now so far towards consummation that it may be expected to be an accomplished fact in a short time, inasmuch as the line has been competed for by thirteen tenderers for works, and seven for fencing, and that the Commissioners have decided upon accepting the lowest of the tenders for works, namely, that of Mr G. Blandford, whose estimate for the works amounts to £86,000, in round numbers; the others being respectively £106,000, £129,000, £140,000, £145,000, and £146,000.

"These several estimates include the fencing with the works on the railway proper: for the fencing, separate, there were tenders varying from £9,000 to £14,000; but between the lowest tender for works and the next there exists a difference of £20,000; the fencing will, therefore, go with the lowest tenderer, that of .Mr G Blandford, who was formerly engineer to the City Board. This estimate, certainly, is low, and the Province may congratulate itself on the small cost of so important a work. Besides which the Commissioners have wisely reserved the power of substituting or altering the nature of the works, and will thus have it in their power to lessen the expense of the line by some £18,000.

"The line will not differ in its route, materially, from that laid down on the original Parliamentary plan, but the gradient and curves have been much improved and the whole work, from Auckland to Drury, including the branch to Onehunga, is now estimated to cost a less sum than £150,000; this amount includes the works, fencing, permanent way, and rolling stock of sufficient capacity to meet the requirements for a lengthened period, and the purchase of land with stations erected thereon.

"The station, for the time being, will be of a character suited to the means, rather than of a grand scale. It may be anticipated that the work will be commenced in a few weeks, and at several points along the line, at once, in order to allow the embankments sufficient time to consolidate, and be in a fit state to receive the permanent rails, which, with locomotives and other things, have already been ordered from England. We may add that the sleepers are now being prepared, and there is every prospect of the line being opened for traffic by the time named in the specification, namely, eighteen months." [9]

Unfortunately, all this enthusiasm for the tender process and its result was not to last, although hope sprung eternal at The New Zealand Herald on 17 October 1864:

"The works of the above railway have for the past week been the subject of much solicitude amongst our local contractors. It was known that the lowest tender was that of Mr Blandford of this city, and it was anticipated that by the works being performed by Auckland contractors the greater amount of money would thus be retained in the Province. We hear, however, that after every reasonable latitude as to time for furnishing the required deposit had been given by the Commissioners, the gentleman furnishing the lowest tender has been unable to satisfy the Board as to his ability to carry out the undertaking, and his tender is consequently null and void.

"The next lowest tender is that of Messrs Higgins and Bloomfield, of Victoria, well-known contractors, and whose name is a guarantee that if they undertake the works, they will not fail to complete them satisfactorily. The Commissioners will do well to close with those gentlemen as early as possible, and we believe such is their intention so as to take advantage of the season of fine weather which is now setting in." [10]

However, there was a bit more to it than just the inability of Mr Blandford to justify his tender. It seems that in order to have an even cheaper job done, the Auckland and Drury Railway Commissioners had shifted the goalposts a little. At least, that is how the comment published in the Daily Southern Cross on 22 December 1864 read:

"We understand that the last accepted tender for the Auckland and Drury Railway has, like the previous one, fallen through. It will be remembered that on Mr Blandford failing to provide the required sureties for the performance of this work the Commissioners accepted the tender of Messrs Higgins and Bloomfield and those gentlemen were communicated with to that effect.

"At the time this communication reached Melbourne Mr Higgins was absent, we believe in another colony but a telegram was received from his partner stating that he would be in Auckland shortly, but not intimating the acceptance of the tender. After considerable delay, however, a letter was received from Mr Higgins by the 'Auckland' in which, after raising some ground of complaint, whether imaginary or otherwise we are not prepared to say, he declined to carry out the contract unless the original amount of it was adhered to.

"It will here be necessary to explain that the work was tendered for at scheduled prices at so much per cubic yard for earth-work, cuttings, &c; and that in the specifications the Commissioners reserved to themselves the power of altering or amending any of the works. This, we are informed, is a usual reservation, and it was one that was absolutely necessary in this case, as the plans or the details of them had not been completed by the engineers. Subsequently to the tenders being received, the Commissioners determined to reduce the cost of the work by substituting embankments for expensive viaducts, and making other alterations, to lessen the expenditure. At the scheduled prices this reduced the sum total of the two lowest tenders, Mr Blandford's, and Messrs Higgins and Bloomfield's, by about from £15,000 to £20,000 each, so that the tender of the last named contractors would be – we cannot quote the figures at this moment precisely – instead of about £100,000, only £80,000.

"This is Messrs Higgins and Bloomfield's cause of complaint, and as we have said they decline to proceed with the work unless they receive the original amount of their tender. This of course the Commissioners decline to accede to, and after great loss of time and labour the matter rests pretty much where it was when the tenders were first called for, with the exception that the plans are now perfect…we regret that so much time should be lost in the prosecution of such an important work from this cause. However, we must remember the old proverb that it is of no use crying over spilt milk we are glad to hear that the Commissioners have taken immediate action towards having the work commenced forthwith. They propose, we understand, to let the work in small sections to local contractors, whose means may only enable them to undertake a small portion of it.

"There has always been a considerable difference of opinion as to the propriety or otherwise of letting the work to outsider persons not resident in the colony and the principal reason given for the adverse view on that point is, that with local contractors the money would be kept in the province. We fully admit that if the work could be done as well and as cheaply by local contractors it should be given to them." [11]

In its editorial of 31 December, summing up the events of 1864, The New Zealand Herald optimistically commented on the Auckland and Drury Railway:

"We had also to congratulate our readers early in the year on the passing of the Auckland and Drury Railway Bill, and we should have been glad if we could now after the lapse of twelve months, offer our congratulations to the public on account of its being proceeded with at a rapid rate. From one circumstance however or another it is not yet commenced, the Commissioners apparently proceeding on the motto 'tis quick enough if well enough'. We trust, however, that the turning of the first sod will not be long delayed, and that 1865 will see the rapid progress and completion for traffic of our first railway, and that it will be carried on to the Waikato." [12]

Indeed, there was hardly any delay and that first sod was officially turned on 16 February 1865, as described on the following day by the Daily Southern Cross:

"It is certainly a cause for congratulation that this province has made such an important stride in the march of improvement as that indicated by the turning of the first sod of the Auckland and Drury Railway. This important event took place yesterday, at Newmarket, in a field belonging to Mr Dilworth; and the ceremony of turning the sod was performed by his Honor the Superintendent (Robert Graham). On account of the short notice that was given, it was not intended, we believe, that there should be any very special demonstration, and, consequently, the public did not assemble in any large numbers, 200 persons being about the maximum of those who were present." [13]

Prior to turning that first, historic sod on a day described by the Daily Southern Cross as "very fine" and in a landscape "...very attractive, Mount Eden, and the many pretty villas which ornament its side and base, forming a pleasing and conspicuous part of it", Mr Graham observed, in part:

"The Auckland and Drury Railway would for the present be between Auckland and Onehunga, but it must enter the Waikato and connect it with Auckland. Until they went there they had failed in their object. (Cheers) With proper steamers there they should open up a magnificent country, which would be available and be the backbone of Auckland.

"If the work had been undertaken four years ago they would have saved the expense to the Imperial Government of four times the cost of constructing; so that every day's delay was a loss to the community, to the county, and to the Imperial Government, because it must be acknowledged that railways were the great civilizers of the age.

"With those few remarks, he would commence and show them that he was not a great navvy, but that he would do his best. His Honor the Superintendent then took the spade from Mr Cheeseman, the chairman of the Railway Board, and turned the sod in a workmanlike manner and having filled the barrow, wheeled it outside the circle of spectators, and then tipped it amid the acclamations of the assemblage." [14]

Four months later, the newspaper's enthusiasm for the Auckland and Drury Railway had not diminished, but its editorial of 13 June 1865 hinted at more than a little difficulty ahead, caused by both the weather and officialdom:

"Four months have scarcely elapsed since the first soil of the Auckland and Drury Railway was turned by his Honor the Superintendent…The immense importance to the province of Auckland of the undertaking initiated on that occasion cannot be over-estimated by the commercial community, finding, as they must, their exertions cramped and impeded from the want of direct and rapid communication with the interior of the country.

"In the earlier stages of our colonization, when the wave of civilisation had extended but a short distance inland, the requirements of the settlers in the vicinity of Auckland were easily met by the formation of roads and bridging of creeks to enable them to visit the city occasionally; but the recent rapid rise of settlements far removed from the city, and the confiscation of the Waikato district, necessitated an alteration in the modes of communication; and although many vexatious delays have taken place in carrying out the railway project, the works we are pleased to say are now being pushed forward with considerable spirit.

"It requires no weighty reasoning to prove the great value to agriculturists of the iron road, to enable them to bring their produce to market and profitably compete with Australian and South American growers for cereal crops; and we may therefore expect that, access being given by its means to the broad lands of the Waikato, that fertile tract of country will not remain much longer unproductive and unremunerative, but will be quickly turned to profitable account. As we have said, the works are being pushed forward vigorously, but the recent wet and wintry weather has impeded them. Another great hindrance to the progress of the works nearer Auckland and the construction of bridges has been the obstructiveness of the City Board of Commissioners.

"The Railway Board of Commissioners and the City Board are at variance as to the desirability of having a level crossing at the Strand, Mechanics' Bay, or, in place thereof, a bridge erected at a certain height, and beneath which foot passengers and vehicles can pass. It is not our intention here to speak in advocacy of one plan or the other, but simply to express a hope that some decision may quickly be arrived at, in order that no further delays in this portion of the work may ensue. As speedily as possible after the turning of the first sod by his Honor the Superintendent, the requisite legal notices were given by the Board of Commissioners to the occupiers and owners of premises and ground over which the line was to be carried…". [15]

But from the turning of that sod in Dilworth's field in 1865, the construction of Auckland's first government-funded railway was beset with difficulties.

"It was found that not enough care had been taken in preparation, especially when it came to buying the land over which the line was to run. This purchase of land had already cost twice what had been expected, and had involved some rather hard negotiations with private land owners. Other items that proved very expensive were the Mechanics Bay viaduct and the Parnell Tunnel." [16]

Amazingly, in a nation where, from the very beginning, land speculation had been a primary industry, the budget allocated to the Auckland and Drury Railway project did not fully include the cost of acquiring the land through which the line was to pass. Even the purchase of Dilworth's field had not been settled before that first sod was turned.

"Well-to-do settlers were aware from what had happened in Sydney and Adelaide that a royal road to wealth for men with capital was to buy cheap land early in the life of a settlement and to see property rise dramatically in value over time as the community grew up around it. But in pioneer Auckland, the attempt to reap a harvest of capital gains by speculating in land became so naked and so well developed a characteristic that it gave rise to the southern jibe that Auckland settlers seemed more interested in trading in land than in actually farming it.

"Government officials in Auckland itself, in fact, first made that charge. In June 1844, the Colonial Secretary, Dr Andrew Sinclair, complained in the Legislative Council that many of Auckland's first settlers were men who would rather speculate in land or merchandise than produce anything from the soil." [17]

"By the 1860s this feisty little colonial town had precipitated out a ruling business elite. Some of the names of those involved are still prominent in the affairs of the city well over a century later. The group they constituted was known to all as 'the limited circle'. They comprised largely those whose business affairs encompassed a series of interlocking interests in banking, mining, agricultural processing and, in particular and ultimately, land speculation." [18]

"They called themselves gentlemen of fortune. Settlers to the south referred to them as landsharks and speculators, men with an eye for the main chance. So there was from the very beginning a particularity, something distinctive…And clinging to this 'otherness' was the whiff of disrepute." [19]

While there is no doubt that were it not for the entrepreneurial skills and investment of 'the limited circle' Aucklanders would still be trading from tents on the beach, the modus operandi of such founding fathers as John Logan Campbell, Josiah Clifton Firth, Thomas Russell, Frederick Whitaker, Thomas Morrin, James Dilworth and others was not entirely without suspicion of scandal and political intrigue.

James Dilworth arrived at Auckland in 1841 from Ireland and New South Wales. "Equipped with capital (presumably from his family) he had already turned to land buying. Late in 1842 he had bought six acres of Parnell land on which he put a house, and in 1845 bought nearly 100 acres at Takapuna. In 1844 he had acquired more than 150 acres between Mt St John and Mt Hobson.

"Setting himself up as a farmer he continued to add to this estate, which became in time the most valuable of all the farms in this vicinity. He also acquired properties in the township and throughout the Auckland province. He was the astutest of land buyers. In the 1860s Dilworth prospered. With the continued growth of Auckland's population his suburban farm, three miles from town, shot up remarkably in value. He also had two strokes of luck: the outbreak of the New Zealand wars led to valuable commissariat contracts, and the government decision to run the tracks of the trunk railway through his estate put generous compensation money into his pocket." [20]

Generous, perhaps, but still not the amount James Dilworth had originally claimed for the incursion of the railway destined to run for some 86 chains through his property at Newmarket. He claimed £13,400 as damages from the Railway Commissioners who had offered him £4,500. Both the Daily Southern Cross and The New Zealand Herald considered the dispute to be of fundamental importance and provided extensive coverage of the hearing which began at the Auckland Supreme Court on 8 January 1866, after arbitration had failed to resolve the matter.

"Yesterday, counsel were heard before Mr Beckham, at the Supreme Court room, as to the compensation to be awarded to Mr Dilworth by the Commissioners of the Auckland and Drury Railway, for the line passing through his land at Newmarket. Mr Brookfield and Mr Wynn appeared on behalf of Mr Dilworth and Mr Gillies for the Railway Commissioners.

"Before the arbitrators ten witnesses had been examined as to the value of the land taken, and of that number seven agreed that compensation should be given for severance the other three apparently estimated only the intrinsic value of the particular position of the land taken. Those seven gave an average amount of damages of £13,200. The Railway Commissioners objected, on the ground that this was prospective damage but he (Mr Brookfield for Mr Dilworth) should endeavour to prove that it was not.

"He (Mr Brookfield) contended that it was proved that the land was damaged to the extent of £9,000 or £10,000 as consequential damage, beyond the intrinsic damage, which was pretty well settled by the witnesses at about £5,000. Where the injury could be ascertained, consequential damage might be given, and that was what was now sought. Mr Dilworth was entitled to claim damage for the severance, and also for being prevented from carrying out those plans which otherwise he would have completed.

"Mr Gillies, for the Commissioners, said he admitted that Mr Dilworth was entitled to claim compensation for damages arising necessarily and obviously from the operations of the railway, and also to damages for severance, according to, the provisions of the Lands Clauses Consolidation Act. But the question was not as to damages arising from severance, or from the operations of the Railway Company, but as to prospective or contingent damages.

"Prospective damage might be allowed when it was obviously ascertainable at present, but when it was contingent— that was, when it might, or might not occur, according to circumstances – it was contrary to law to allow it. The taking of land by a railway company was somewhat of the nature of a trespass, but without the element of illegality, and the owner of the land was entitled to the damage which he can show he has sustained, or will necessarily sustain.

"When they looked at Mr Dilworth's claim, or rather at the evidence offered in support of it, they would see that from beginning to end it was based upon a supposititious value. The evidence was not that the land was worth so much, and so much more for damage for severance, but it was what the land might possibly be worth if cut up into building allotments at some future time. That was all a myth. Who could say that that land might not be absolutely worthless for building sites? Mr Gillies said the amount of damage would be the best price Mr Dilworth could get for the land at the time when notice was given, whether cut up or not, but not what he might get if he held it over for a number of years. This was agreed to as the principle upon which compensation would be awarded, and certain queries are to be agreed to by counsel to put to witnesses." [21]

The hearing, which lasted for several days during January and February 1866, heard evidence from a number of engineers, surveyors, contractors and land agents who suggested various values for James Dilworth's land, based on their experience and judgement. These values varied greatly, depending on whether certain lots were considered as grazing or arable land, or as residential allotments, with or without road or rail frontages and access to water sources. Of course, the debate centred around the damage that the proposed railway line would do to those present and projected values, and based on which of those values compensation should be calculated.

In his final summing up on 10 February 1866, Mr Brookfield for James Dilworth projected the latter's motives for adequate compensation as completely acceptable despite the Railway Commissioners' argument that "...the railway, being for public benefit, all private considerations and convenience were to be given up to it."

As reported by the Daily Southern Cross, Mr Brookfield continued:
"Now this, as an axiom, may be very good, and were the private convenience only of Mr Dilworth interfered with (as, for instance, by smoke from the engine occasionally coming into his house) then, perhaps, he would not be entitled to consideration; but when a permanent injury is

done to him, which might be prevented by inquiry, were it not sanctioned by legislative enactment, then the case is widely different, and full compensation ought to be granted; and this, no doubt, was the feeling of the framers of the Land Clauses Consolidation Act, when they enacted that compensation should be granted for all injuries done or to be caused by the line.

"Now, my friend (Mr Gillies for the Railway Commissioners) urged upon you that the only question for you to consider was whether one paddock was cut off from the water, and whether any extra expense would be incurred in cultivating the lands in consequence of the severance. But we contend that this is not the only question. It has been proved to you that the water is cut off by the railway from by far the largest portion of the farm, and that the cattle can only have access by bridges, of which Mr Stewart thinks two will be sufficient; and I need not hardly tell you that it is injurious to cattle not to have an opportunity of roaming about, and that it will entail much loss and inconvenience to Mr Dilworth to employ men to drive his cattle to water two or three times a day.

"My friend also asserts that if Mr Dilworth had sold his frontage to Remuera road, before the railway was started, the purchaser could not obtain damage in consequence of a railway crossing that road; granted. But will my friend venture to say that the value of those frontages is now as great as before the line was projected? I think not.

"My friend, and one or two of his witnesses, say that damage by severance is to be calculated on the land taken; that appears to me to be absurd, because what possible damage can be done to the .land taken? Surely the damage is to that which is left, and therefore the percentage to be allowed for severance must be calculated upon the value of that which is left, taking into consideration the purposes for which it is available.

"My learned friend admitted at the outset that Mr Dilworth was entitled to a liberal and fair consideration of his claim for compensation for the lands taken, for forced sale, and for severance. The questions therefore for the Umpire to decide are: 1st. The quantity of land taken and its value. 2nd. Compensation for forced sale. 3rd. Compensation for severance by reason of the railway passing through, and thus dividing one portion of Mr Dilworth's property from the other.

"I would call the Umpire's particular attention, first, to the nature of Mr Dilworth's land and its configuration secondly, to its nearness to Auckland, and its position as to frontages to Roads, i.e., it has a frontage of its entire length to the Great South Road, the same to the Remuera Road, and also a frontage to a cross road running through from the Great South Road to the Remuera Road. The estate itself is but a narrow one, and is encircled by one entire fence of quickthorn, thus forming one of the most beautiful and compact properties near Auckland, although narrow in its length— this very narrowness rendering the injury sustained by severance, of much greater importance and extent.

"It is stated that here in this province public works of this character are in their infancy, and that it is of the utmost importance that the true principle for ascertaining the value of lands taken compulsorily, should be fully investigated, and laid down; and it is much to be regretted that the Commissioners were not a little more particular in the selection of their witnesses, for the purpose of truly ascertaining and fixing this great principle. Before concluding, I wish again to call the attention of the Umpire to an abstract of the figure, as before stated, the average of the value and compensation, as given by Mr Dilworth's witness, £16,673 19s. 6d.

"On the other side it is difficult to come to an accurate calculation; three only of the witnesses make an actual calculation, viz., Mr R. Ridings, of an average of £8,299 19 9. Add to this the average on the other side, viz.: £16,673 19s. 6d. we have a grand total of £24,973 19s. 3d. the whole mean average of these 13 persons being £12,416 19s. 7d." [22]

Several days later, the Umpire and Resident Magistrate, Mr Thomas Beckham, awarded James Dilworth the sum of £6,343 3s. [23]

However, the matter did not quite end there, as reported by the Daily Southern Cross on 26 April 1866:

"At the Supreme Court yesterday, Thomas Beckham, Esq. and D B Thornton, Esq. JP, held a sitting to receive evidence relative to the kind and number of accommodation works (bridges) to be executed by the Superintendent, on behalf of the Railway Company, on Mr Dilworth's land, at Remuera.

"By the Lands Clauses Consolidation Act it is provided that, when differences arise with regard to accommodation works in regard to any public undertaking, the company is empowered to summon the persons who may consider themselves aggrieved, before two justices of the peace, for the full investigation of the claim.

"On behalf of the Railway Company there were examined Mr Baber, Mr Weaver, Mr Stewart, Mr Shepherd, Mr Baddeley, and Mr Austin; the general tendency of their evidence being that from three to five crossings would be sufficient on Mr Dilworth's property.

"On behalf of Mr Dilworth, there were examined Mr Dilworth, Mr Reader Wood, and Mr Joseph Cochrane, who gave evidence to the effect that proper accommodation could not be given to Mr Dilworth with less than ten bridges. After the witnesses had been examined, Mr Beckham said that the evidence had been in entirely different directions. Mr Thornton and himself would proceed to the ground and inspect the place themselves. Their decision would then be given in a few days." [24]

The decision of Messrs Beckham and Thornton was delivered relatively quickly, as reported by the Daily Southern Cross on 3 May 1866:

"Now the said Justices, having heard evidence on behalf of both parties, and after due consideration thereof, do direct that the said James Dilworth shall be accommodated with three crossings, by bridges sufficient for the traffic of carts, and two level crossings, which accommodation works shall be completed within a term of six calendar months from this date. Given under our hands and seals this 2nd day of May, 1866 - Thomas Beckham R.M. (and) D. B. Thornton J.P." [25]

However, by this time, the Railway Commissioners were struggling to complete work on the line itself and had offered James Dilworth funds in lieu of the construction of the bridges and level crossings on his land – an offer not entirely agreed upon again, as highlighted during a meeting of the Auckland Provincial Council held on 30 November 1866:

"Mr May moved, That this Council regrets to hear from the Waste Lands Commissioner that his Honor the Superintendent has paid Mr Dilworth the sum of one thousand pounds on account of £2050 awarded for accommodation works on the railway through Mr Dilworth's land, and hopes for the future to see all such works executed by the Provincial Government.

"He said that Mr Dilworth had required accommodation. If money were given, the person should not be allowed to pocket the money, and do without the accommodation; whenever money was paid in this way they should take care that it was expended in the way required. There were a great many going about unable to find work. Money so paid should have been expended in giving employment.

"Mr Cheeseman explained at considerable length the arrangements made with Mr Dilworth. Two Justices had been appointed to decide upon the matter. Twelve crossings were demanded. The Judges awarded three crossings by bridges and two level crossings. The Justices were Mr Beckham and Mr D B Thornton. Mr Dilworth demanded that the bridges should be in a certain position, which brought on a new dispute, in which it was found that Mr Dilworth had the advantage in a legal sense. The estimate for building these accommodations was £1807. Mr Dilworth then said he would undertake to carry out the work. He put in claims for maintenance of the works and £200 was agreed to be given, making in all £2007.

"Mr Dilworth objected to accept the sum. Eventually £242 was offered. The final arrangement had been deferred till his Honor came from Wellington and the £1000 was paid to him on account. Here the matter rested at present. Mr Cheeseman, in reply to Captain Cooper, said that the money was not part of Mr Dilworth's compensation, and Mr Dilworth might keep the money without constructing the work if he thought fit. Mr May suggested that the House should go into Committee, the question being one involving the expenditure of money. The House went into Committee; Mr Ball in the chair.

"Mr Cheeseman said that Mr Dilworth's letter was to the effect that he wanted the payment to justify him in proceeding with the bridges. At the same time he (Mr Cheeseman) thought the line would be better without the bridges—they would certainly become obstructions. Mr Wynn said that the question how money spent in such a work should be utilized and not, as it were, sunk in a well.

"The Waste Lands Commissioner said, had those accommodation works being made by the Government, the Government would have been chargeable with their maintenance. It was therefore a question whether a compromise should not have been made and a less sum paid than was awarded, if a less sum would have been received. Mr Dignan said that the hon. gentleman (Mr May) he would be as exacting to obtain his rights perhaps as Mr Dilworth appeared to be. Mr May said he had not been grasping any period of his life. He pitied those who were wrapt up in money. The motion was negatived." [26]

By this time, November 1866, the money had just about run out and the whole project was grinding to a halt, a result that had been forecast by the Railway Commissioners' second report to the Provincial Council in January that year. In that report, the Railway Board Chairman, Thomas Cheeseman, defended the numerous delays and additional costs that had been sustained since work had started. Those additional costs naturally included the compensation claimed by those "as exacting to obtain his rights perhaps as Mr Dilworth appeared to be".

In part, the January report included an "...accompanying schedule of expenditure (in which) it is shown that the purchase of land and claims for compensation amount to more than £32,000, exceeding the original estimate by fully £18,000." [27]

The report then detailed the engineering difficulties experienced, together with an indication that the local contractors, chosen when the larger firms had withdrawn their tenders, had ultimately proved incapable of completing the work:

"The line to Onehunga was divided into four sections, and contracted for at prices effecting a saving on previous tenders to the amount of £9,000. As it relates to the progress of the works generally, the Commissioners regret that upon No. 1 section considerable delays have been occasioned, not only by the entire absence of suitable plant in the province, but a most unusually wet winter, and frequent misunderstandings between the contractor and his workmen. A better state of things, however, is anticipated, and the works are expected to be prosecuted, with vigour. Contract No. 2 would have been finished within the specified time, but for the large beds of scoria rock met with in Mr Dilworth's field. Sections 3 and 4 are rapidly approaching completion, and will shortly be ready to receive the permanent way. A fuller and more particular description of the entire line is given in the subjoined report by the Engineers of the Board." [28]

Not only did the accompanying Engineers' Report, completed by the Railway's engineers, James Stewart and Samuel Harding, comment on the adverse weather experienced and their contractors' lack of resources, but also indicated a degree of poor forward planning:

"Delays, however, have occurred, which render it unlikely that the contractors will finish within time. The contractors were not alive to the necessity of preparing for the work on a large scale, and hence allowed a great deal of fine weather to pass away with little work done. The weather during winter and spring was very severe. In section No. 1 the land was not procured so soon as it ought to have been. Additional works have also been thrown on the contractors, such as an addition to the length of the tunnel, and the construction of a viaduct in Mechanics' Bay.

"These extra, works have been wisely ordered by the Board. The tunnel, by being lengthened, will tend materially to ensure the safety of Mr Kempthorne's house, which otherwise would have been in danger of a landslip. The viaduct has been decided on, in order to economise the valuable land fronting the Strand, which, if traversed by an embankment, would have been of little use, especially as the action of the City Board led to the heightening of the proposed level of the railway. The raising of the bridges over the Strand and tan-work road alone will cost nearly £400.

"Another source of increased expense on this section lies in the necessity which exists for lining with brickwork the sides of the tunnel. It was at one time considered that, by abutting the crown arch well into the sides, the latter would stand, as the rock was hard enough. On the rock being examined by a long drive, however, it was found so jointy and treacherous that it would have been worse than folly to have risked the original design of construction. This extra work adds about £4,300 to the cost of the tunnel, and is a very fortunate one for the contractor, as his rate for it is very high. He is, notwithstanding, exceedingly backward in pushing it on and although new arrangements are made to do so, yet time has been lost." [29]

Indeed, just about all was lost for the Auckland and Drury Railway and The New Zealand Herald of 20 January 1866 certainly showed no sympathy for the Railway Commissioners in its summation of their report:

"Everything *would* have happened right, *but* that everything happened wrong. No. 1 section *would* have progressed satisfactorily *but* for certain very satisfactory reasons given, and No. 2 *would* have been finished within the specified time, *but* for the large beds of scoria rock met with in Mr Dilworth's field. We are not told what the scoria rock was doing when it was met with, nor whether it should be looked upon as a poacher or trespasser, or a friend taking an early morning constitutional or not.

"The Commissioners, so far as we can judge from their report, find that they have made a mess of the work, but do not like to make a clean breast of it, and say so in plain English. Their language is that of one conscious of guilt, but who wishes to keep up a respectable appearance to the last, avoiding strong assertions of innocence equally with distinct avowals of guilt. They also try to make capital out of events which, when followed to the end, only make more glaring their mistakes, to use a mild word, of the Commissioners." [30]

Concluding its damning editorial, of which this is just a portion, The Herald provided what must have been one of the first cost-benefit analysis of rail and road transport alternatives. Little did the editorial writer realise that, in doing so, he had started an argument that would continue in Auckland, ad infinitum, well into the 21st century:

"But we wish just to point out what might have been done with the £117,000 that it will take, according to the Commissioners' own estimates, to make the railway from Auckland to Onehunga, within a few yards, as far as it goes, of an excellent macadamised road.

"The cutting of a bush road twelve feet wide would cost about seven shillings a chain. Wages of three pounds a week per man could be made at that rate. Let us say ten shillings a chain, and include in this any necessary bush bridges. This £117,000 then would have cleared 2925 miles of bush road in the Province! But supposing it had been met by say one-third, to take a low estimate, from settlers, then we should have had a sum of £156,000, which would have cut 3900 Miles Of Bush Road And Bridged it!

"What a difference would these miles of road have made in developing the resources of this Province? How many Waikato and Northern settlers would that money have given partial employment to, and capital to enable them to fight the battle and conquer and subdue the patch of land they had? How much additional agricultural produce would it have caused to be raised and sold in the Province and so have prevented thousands upon thousands of pounds being sent out of the Province, and thus done something to prevent the present tightness of the money market?

"Spent in the way we have indicated it would even now be reproductive. Will any man tell us that making this railway to Onehunga will benefit the Province of Auckland to one thousandth part of the extent which the making of 3900 miles of bush roads would do? How many blocks of land would then be approachable, how many people might in such a case go and settle on their land?" [31]

By the time the Chairman of the Railways Commissioners, Thomas Cheeseman, reported to the Provincial Council on 31 October 1866, the money and the incentive to spend more had run out:

"In compliance with your Honor's verbal instructions of the 20th instant, the several contractors have been written to, and desired to complete their various engagements on or before the 30th of November, 1866. The instructions given by your Honor, previous to your departure for Wellington, regarding the reduction of this establishment, have been complied with and the office of clerk has been abolished, the Inspector of Works and the Assistant Engineer discharged; and, at the beginning of the month, the engineering department was placed under the care of the Engineer-in-Chief.

"On the 30th of the last month, the total expenditure amounted to £98,191 11s. 6d…To meet this expenditure, there was appropriated by the last Council the sum of £117,000 from which there is an unexpended balance of £19,809 11s. 6d. The only outstanding claims for land and compensation not yet dealt with relate to properties near Mount Smart belonging to Messrs Dilworth, Rooney, Goulding, and Walker, and they are all capable of easy adjustment.

"But I cannot dismiss this part of my report without directing your Honor's attention to the fact that the purchase of land will absorb the sum of about £36,000, an amount exceeding, fully by one-half, the most liberal estimate of its real value. And until landowners, who derive more pecuniary benefit from railways than any other persons, are prepared to surrender the land required, at its fair market price, it is futile to expect any further extension of the railway system." [32]

The issue of fair compensation for land taken for the railway was to fester with Thomas Cheeseman for many years. His preoccupation with the subject was still evident in his 1872 correspondence with the Daily

Southern Cross a portion of which rebuts the newspaper's assertion that he (Cheeseman) "...had a bad cause to defend". A part of his rebuttal, published by the Daily Southern Cross on 3 September 1872, included:

"To the Editor: Sir, — My letter, which appeared in the Cross of last Friday, was no 'defence of Provincial mismanagement' but a statement of facts relative to the Auckland and Drury Railway, and a comparison of that work with some branches of General Government administration. I made no 'damaging admission' by stating that £36,000 were paid for land and compensation; nor did I attempt to defend so large an amount. You distinctly deny that there is anything in the Land Clauses or Railway Clauses Consolidation Acts to compel the Commissioners to purchase land above its real value, and desire me to point out the machinery in them that would lead to such a result.

"I have no objection to enlighten you on this matter and request you, therefore, to turn to the Auckland and Drury Railway Act, General Assembly, 1863. At clause 6, you will find that 'all persons being owners of, or having any lease, estate, or interest in land which may be taken or damaged by the construction of the said railway, shall be entitled to receive compensation, the amount whereof shall be ascertained in the manner set forth in the Land Clauses Consolidation Act of the General Assembly, 1863, which said Act for that and other purposes shall be incorporated with this Act'.

"In all cases of disputed compensation, the Lands Clauses and also the Railway Clauses Consolidation Acts, give the claimants the option of going either to arbitration or a jury and arbitration was resorted to by the claimants against the Railway Commissioners in every disputed case. And on that account I stated that the Commissioners were placed at the mercy of grasping landowners. Had we been able to go to a jury, fully £10,000 would have been saved. You affirm that, 'if the Provincial Government were at the mercy of landowners at all, it was due to their own short sightedness in not having made arrangement for the land before the work was commenced'. I must say that you display a marvellous talent in refusing to discern anything favourable either to the Provincial Government or Railway Commissioners.

"In the proceedings of the Provincial Council for April, 1863, you will find the report of a Railway Committee, in which it is stated that 60 circulars were sent to landowners along the line of railway, requesting to know the terms on which they would dispose of their interest in the lands required. Twenty-two answers were received, and in no instance was any objection raised to the undertaking. Some owners of large blocks offered to give their land; and the general reply was that they were willing to receive a fair compensation. But how different the result, when those same gentlemen were served with the legal notices by the Superintendent. The sums they demanded for the land between Auckland and. Onehunga amounted to £56,744!

"Your next assertion is that 'enormous sums paid for compensation were winked at'. The undermentioned claims were the most enormous and it would be interesting to know from you which of them was winked at. The proprietors of a certain Auckland newspaper demanded, for 2 acres and 20 perches, £1,000. A gentleman farmer, for 11½ acres, £13,426. An independent gentleman, for 1¼ acres, £5,057. Another, for 1½ acres, £3,000. A third, for 1 acre and 3 roods, £3,118. For a four year's leasehold in Mechanics' Bay £4,000 were asked; and for the freehold of the same, 410 links by 137, the sum of £3,000. Now these seven claims, amounting to £32,175 were reduced, by the action of the Railway Commissioners, to £11,101. What credence, then, is to be placed in your remarks, when you say that these enormous payments were winked at?" [33]

But the enormous profits expected to be made from land sales, winked at or not, were hardly surprising in the domain of laissez-faire capitalists whose land speculation continued to dominate private investment in the country's infrastructure. These entrepreneurs soon realised that their prosperity depended on transport services to open up the country and its towns to settlers keen to buy their land and they saw little reason why they should differentiate between those settlers and the Railway. As early as 1841, Ernest Dieffenbach, during his exploration of New Zealand on behalf of the New Zealand Company, observed:

"The government town of Auckland, considering the short time it has existed, has made considerable progress. Its population, which amounts to more than 2000, has been drawn together from all parts of the island. A bank has been formed, fine barracks have been built of scoriae; and were it not for a general spirit of over-speculation in land, without any attempt to explore the home resources of the island, there would be every ground for hoping that the place would gradually and steadily rise into importance." [34]

Of course, much of this land had already been unfairly acquired from its original inhabitants – unfairly, in the sense that the Maori had not, at first, realised their land's true trade value – not until their traditional role as custodians was so suddenly threatened by the greedy Pakeha hordes.

As journalist, Bruce Jesson, described it in 'Behind the Mirror Glass':

"The British colonists represented an invading culture that systematically eradicated any Maori authority in New Zealand. In particular, it was necessary to the colonial project that the Maori relationship with the land be broken. Freedom to buy and sell land was basic to the development of colonial capitalism. Accordingly, the Maori were deprived of their lands and consigned to the margins of the developing colonial economy." [35]

"One of the key characteristics of colonial New Zealand was that it was a land of quite limited opportunity. As a colony, it was a creation of industry, technology and capital, but it didn't possess these things itself and depended on industrial imports from England. Our external economy was controlled by British and Australian finance capital." [36]

However, by 1870, there wasn't quite so much of that finance capital forthcoming and New Zealand was experiencing the first of its many cyclical depressions. Wool prices had dropped, gold production had tapered off and there was open warfare with the Maoris. As a result, the country was no longer such a favoured destination for immigrants and investment although that soon changed with the appointment of Julius Vogel as the country's Colonial Treasurer in 1869. He sought to boost the country's prospects by means of both financial and immigrant investment with the passage of his Immigration and Public Works Loan Act 1870. It was Vogel's vision to unite the nation by way of infilling the very hostile frontier between its various settlements and he saw the rapid construction of extensive rail, road and waterworks as the best means of accomplishing that.

The 1870 Act authorised the appointment of Agents in Great Britain and elsewhere to facilitate the raising of a "Loan secured on the Consolidated Revenue of New Zealand funds for the Roads Railways Waterworks and Immigration purposes which the Governor is authorized to construct and undertake by 'The Immigration and Public Works Act 1870 and for repaying certain moneys already advanced out of the Consolidated Fund for the construction of certain roads in the North Island of New Zealand and for the construction of Telegraphs…" [37]

The initial Schedule of the Act prescribed the apportionment of £2 million for railway construction, £1 million for immigration (including assisted passages), £400,000 for road construction and £300,000 for waterworks (used mainly for the mining of gold). From today's perspective, the sum initially allocated in the 1870s to rail, compared to that for road construction, would seem to have been disproportionate. However the 1870's allocation of funds for rail construction and operation was of course intended to facilitate the transportation of the populace and goods over long and extremely rugged distances between the country's main centres and not for the local transport needs within the settlements.

But while the construction of the national railway network was intended to provide a safe and efficient mass transportation system, a good return on the investment was also expected.

"As the advance of the railways enhanced the value of the land through which they passed, so the progressive sale of the reserved lands would enable the Government to pay off the principal and interest on the loans." [38]

It was this expectation of economic viability and profit from mineral and timber resources and, of course, settlement land that drove much of New Zealand's mad dash into the construction of its railway networks. At least that was the plan. During his visit to Britain in early 1871, Julius Vogel subsequently negotiated, "…a loan of £1,200,000 for New Zealand, mainly for immigration and public works. After a very short notice the whole amount asked for was subscribed, at a price which, allowing for all deductions, represented about £95 15s. This loan is of the 'unguaranteed debentures', the £1,000,000 previously guaranteed by the Imperial Government remaining to be used in fact, as a reserved fund.

"The main object, however, of Mr Vogel's visit to this country (Britain) has been the carrying out of the policy of the present Government connected with public works and immigration, a policy with which his name will probably henceforward be honourably associated. Negotiations for the construction of railroad were opened by Mr Vogel with Messrs John Brogden and Sons, the extensive contractors, and with other gentlemen…we are informed that, within an hour or two of his departure from London, a most important contract with Messrs Brogden and Sons was signed for the construction of railways in the colony, either upon a system of direct guarantee, or by guarantees in connection with a system of land grants and with emigration, the Government being at liberty to elect between the two systems.

"The details of these contracts are as yet necessarily private, but the engineering staff proceeds to the colony by the present mail, and the Messrs Brogden in proof of their bona fides, have deposited with the Government bankers in London securities to the value of £25,000." [39]

By September 1871, Julius Vogel had returned to New Zealand and reported to Parliament, laying before it what The New Zealand Herald of 9 September 1871 described as 'both voluminous and important':

"Perhaps the most important business detailed in the papers, next to the negotiation of the loan, is the arrangements partly entered into on behalf of the colony with the eminent railway contractors, Messrs Brogden & Sons, of London. These have reference to the construction of such works as shall be finally decided on by the Government. The agreements between Mr

Vogel and the contractors, allow of substitution, and alteration in various important particulars. In fact, there, are, as in the instance of the Mail Service Contract, separate sets of agreements, leaving it optional with the New Zealand Government to make choice as to which shall be eventually acted on, either as respects the whole of the works to be contracted for, or any part of them.

"One arrangement proposes part-payment in land, in which event a certain proportion of immigrants, to be approved by the Government agent in England, shall be introduced from time to time by the contractors, to be settled on such land. But the principal feature in both sets of arrangements is the guarantee of 5¼ to 5½ per cent interest on the amount expended on railway works by the contractors. When the net profits exceed 8 per cent, the balance is to be divided, in one instance in equal proportions, and in the other one-fourth to the Government, and three-fourths to the contractors."

"These are among the general outlines embraced in the provisional arrangements entered into with the contractors, by Mr Vogel. Of course everything will depend upon the view the Assembly may take of the matter, as to the extent to which these arrangements shall be eventually acted on. Looking at the arrangements under which similar works have been recently undertaken in India and elsewhere, it would appear that the conditions obtained by Mr Vogel, as detailed in the papers before us, are, on the whole, very favourable to the colony. We think it doubtful whether better terms can be effected than those set forth under the first of these agreements. If even we are to have such works carried out in the colony, there cannot be a more favourable time to enter upon them than the present." [40]

However, as usual, not everyone agreed, particularly with the employment of contractors from outside the colony. In his letter to the Editor of Otago Daily Times, published 17 October 1871, 'Fair Play' wrote:

"I have heard it stated by one or two out and out defenders of Mr Vogel that the present outcry against the proposed Brogden Railway Contracts has been got up and is fomented by the Southern League. I wish, so far as I am concerned, to say that I doubt this very much and to say, further, that if it were, the public would be very much obliged to the League for drawing public attention to so very unwise, unjust, and unsound a system as is embodied in the scheme of Mr Vogel with regard to the railway contracts.

"I will say, further, that I will find twenty men in this Colony, within a month, if desired, who would most thankfully and readily offer to make as many miles of railway as might be necessary, the prices being fixed by arbitration; would be only too glad to do so, without the additional five per cent which Mr Brogden is to get; and would, moreover, as colonists, acquainted with the nature and requirements of Colonial railways, know their business much better than a firm of English iron founders, however respectable they may be, can be expected to know about railway machinery." [41]

But there was also some concern, expressed by 'Fair Play', that any repudiation of the preliminary contracts with Messrs Brogden & Sons could affect the entire financing arrangement and the confidence of investors:

"A fear has been expressed that if the Colonial Government were to repudiate these contracts, and pay Mr Brogden an amount in lieu of damages, the Colonial security in England would suffer, and that capitalists would have no confidence in us or our undertakings. I should think the result would be exactly the reverse, and that every prudent investor would consider it to have been much more judicious to get quit of an unwise and hastily contrived contract, than to have the Colony bound hand and foot, and at the mercy of men whose only object, and I do not blame them for it, is to make money at the expense of the Colony and to go home again to spend it.

"I believe if Mr Vogel were to ask for a vote of so much to pay Mr Brogden for a relinquishment of his contract and of all his claims under it, it would be immediately and thankfully voted, and that throughout the length and breadth of the Colony a feeling of thankfulness would arise for deliverance, even-at this expense, from a scheme which I have never heard one individual attempt to defend." [42]

Although much pessimism and uncertainty as to the probable success of Vogel's ambitious plans for immigration and railway construction continued through to the end of the parliamentary session of 1871, The New Zealand Herald editorial of 1 November of that year continued to view the railway contracts, at least, to be "...far from unfavourable to the colony...The work of legislation has steadily proceeded at Wellington during the past month, and probably another fortnight will see the dispersion of members to their homes, and the somewhat unusual circumstance in New Zealand, of a Ministry outliving its second session of Parliament. Opposition there has been, but to the extent only of moderating, not of overthrowing, the ministerial policy. As might have been looked for, the chief opposition has been levelled against the railway scheme of the Government, and especially against the Brogden contracts.

"There exists, however, not only within the Assembly, but without it, a considerable amount of doubt whether it is advisable that the colony shall enter on so large an expenditure in railroad construction as that proposed in the more comprehensive of the two contracts, and we should not, therefore, be surprised to learn that the Legislature had, with the consent of the Ministry, agreed to a reconsideration and reconstruction of that part of the colonial scheme." [43]

The two contracts referred to by the Herald were those previously agreed between Julius Vogel and Brogden and Sons. They were very flexible as to costs to be paid to the contractor; designed to be refined in greater detail as each railway line was tendered for. This was explained by the nation's newspapers on 20 December 1871 following an official statement issued by the Government the previous day. A part of the Otago Daily Times report included:

"We understand that the question of the construction of the railways authorised by the Assembly has constantly occupied the attention of the Government since the close of the session, and that after considerable negotiations with Mr James Brogden, preliminary arrangements have been made with that gentleman on behalf of his firm and a determination has also been generally arrived at respecting all the authorised railways.

"The arrangement come to with Mr Brogden is to this effect: With as little delay as possible the Government will place in his hands data sufficient to enable the firm to tender for the construction of various railways. If the Government are able to make arrangements with Messrs Brogden for railways to the extent of £700,000, then Contract No. 2, as entered into by Mr Vogel with the firm in England, is to be cancelled otherwise it will remain in force. Several months must elapse before the necessary data as to all the railways can be given to Mr Brogden but as the data for each line are given, he is, on behalf of his firm, within one month to send in a tender for its construction, and if the Government should not consider such tender to be reasonable, they will be at liberty to call for public tenders for the particular work.

"During the interval before final arrangements can be completed, the Government may give to Messrs Brogden and Sons the construction of such portions of railways as may be resolved upon, and the works are to be executed under direction of the Engineer-in-Chief; the firm receiving payment at the rate of 10 per cent over and above the actual outlay, and all expenditure being under the control and by the direction of the Government. This provision will enable work to be commenced without delay upon such lines in different parts of the country as the engineers may have ready for commencement. On the other hand, if the railways be not included in the contract, the Government have power at any time to end the ten per cent arrangement and call for public tenders." [44]

By 1871, John Brogden and Sons was a firm of important railway contractors and pioneers of the early industrial development of iron and coal in the British Midlands and South Wales. Following the death of its principal, John Brogden, in December 1869, the firm remained a family business, run by his eldest three sons, Alexander, Henry and James. It was James Brogden who travelled to New Zealand to negotiate the finer points of the country's railway construction, leaving Liverpool on the 19th of August 1871 and returning to England early in 1873.

"The diary he kept during his visit shows that he was engaged in protracted and difficult negotiations. The Brogdens first proposed a very comprehensive building programme involving an expenditure of some £4,500,000 which the New Zealand government rejected, and the modified proposals they subsequently made were also turned down. However, in 1872 the Company was given six contracts for sections of railway totalling 159 miles of construction at a cost of £808,000. In order to carry out these contracts, the firm sent out a fleet of fifteen ships carrying more than 2,000 navvies with wives, children and equipment.

"Despite the scale of these preparations and the reputation the firm enjoyed in this country, evidence in New Zealand reveals that the Brogdens were not more successful than the local contractors. The New Zealand venture by John Brogden & Sons undoubtedly turned out to be a great disappointment. The first proposals the Brogdens made indicate that they originally saw the project as an opportunity of taking over the colony's whole railway construction programme: it ended, however, in their obtaining only half a dozen relatively small contracts.

"The venture was also not a success financially. Some Brogden correspondence relating to 1879 contains references to the firm's outstanding claims against the New Zealand Government and to a proposal to send James out again to press for payment. Evidence from New Zealand, however, reveals that its government rejected the claim by the Brogdens that large sums due to them under the terms of their contracts had been unfairly withheld.

"The failure of their attempt to take over the coal and iron undertakings in Mid-Glamorgan and the resulting loss of their own very valuable properties, the financially very disappointing results of their New Zealand venture, their very costly litigation with the Metropolitan Railway Company and the money problems connected with their father's will ultimately resulted in John Brogden & Sons becoming insolvent.

"Subsequently, on the 31st of July 1880, the partnership between Alexander Brogden, Henry Brogden and James Brogden, trading as John Brogden & Sons and carrying on business as contractors and coal and iron masters at No. 52 Queen Victoria Street in the City of London, was dissolved as from the 26th of July 1880 by an order of the Chancery Division of Her Majesty's High Court of Justice. The result of the failure of the family firm was described in a letter written by the son of one of the partners as a plunge from well-being into poverty." [45]

In the meantime, Julius Vogel's initiatives meant that work on the Auckland and Drury Railway, with its branch line to Onehunga, could be resumed. Indeed, in early January 1872, this was one of the first lines to be considered by James Brogden who, with "...his engineer Mr Henderson, and the Colonial Engineer, Mr Carruthers, and staff proceeded to Auckland by the Luna for the purpose of pushing on the working survey and placing everything in train for the commencement of the line." [46]

The previous Auckland and Drury Railway Engineers, James Stewart and Samuel Harding, were back on the job and such was the finance available this time, the line had been re-surveyed to include Mercer as the terminus. But while more funding might be in place, there were obviously some labour issues to be sorted out, particularly before the arrival of what were to become known as 'Brogden's Navvies'.

The Auckland Star of 22 January 1872 reported that the first signs of trouble arose the previous weekend:

"On Saturday afternoon Mr Hope, the ganger of the men employed on the Waikato Railway, informed the employees that they would be required to work until five o'clock on that day. This they declined to accede to; and, on the clock striking four, knocked off work. This morning the following notice was issued to the workmen, whereupon the men refused to proceed:—

"Notice.—All men accepting employment, engage to work, nine hours for every week day, with the exception of every second Saturday, when the work will terminate at 4 p.m. Payment for wages will be made every four weeks, but money may be paid on account two weeks before the general pay day. The pay sheet will be made up to Thursday night, being two days preceding the monthly pay day. At a meeting of the workmen, held subsequently, it was unanimously resolved that 'the workmen are willing to work overtime, but refuse to work nine hours a day, it being contrary to the established usages of the colony'. The works are consequently at a standstill." [47]

In its editorial published in the same edition, the Auckland Star presented its opinion of the strike and suggested that it was well timed to set the stage for the railway works to be undertaken by outside contractors:

"We should be sorry to speak a word tending to bring labour and capital into collision, or to advocate the principle of strikes which have wrought so much mischief in the manufacturing districts of England. But there are times when the claims of humanity cannot be repressed, even though they should become allied with an objectionable system.

"At the present hour the workmen on the recently recommenced Waikato (Auckland and Drury) Railway are on strike, and the cause in the present case is such that public sympathy must be on the side of the men. They simply ask that the working day should consist of eight hours instead of nine, and the claim is so reasonable that, so long as the men confine themselves to moral and legitimate means, they may calculate on public sympathy and support, and on eventual success.

"There can be no doubt that eight hours of hard manual labour are as much as the human system is capable of enduring, without injury. And it is as well that now, in the inception of our great colonial public works, the question of the hours of labour should be at once solved. Nigger driving does not find favour in any of the colonies, and the eight-hour system is becoming almost everywhere established. It is in the highest degree important that at once the system should be accepted on our railway works.

"Sooner or later it must come to this, and the sooner the better, if we desire to avoid those heart-burnings and strife that otherwise will become chronic on our public works. But there is an additional reason why the hours of labour should be at once fixed. Mr Brogdens' contracts are not fully arranged, and it is important to the satisfactory arrangement of terms, that the matter should be distinctly understood.

"At present, as we understand, the contractors are proceeding on the provisional arrangement, by which they receive a percentage on the money actually expended in the construction of the works. It is therefore at present of no consequence to the contractors, whether the hours are eight hours or nine. In fact so important is it to the contractors that the hours should be at once and definitely fixed, that we should not be surprised if their agents are not averse to the present strike, and have done something more than merely winking at it. But this we only say in a whisper, and would not for the world have it spoken about.

"However this may be, we cordially wish success to the eight hours movement among the men. If it is to be at the cost of the country, it does not much signify for there is not a constituency in New Zealand that would be in favour of nigger driving, or would instruct its representative to throw an obstacle in the way of the eight hours movement. And as the country will not object to pay for its railways, by a fair day's wage for a fair day's work, we trust that Mr Brogden will make all his calculations and all his terms of contract with the Government, on the basis of a day of eight hours. This, we can assure him, is what it will come to; and we should regret that his firm, being strangers to the colony, should be misled by the supposition that nine hours can be compelled." [48]

But apart from the number of hours to be fairly worked, there was also the issue of how wages were to be paid by contractors to their workers. By the end of 1871 and before New Zealand's great works were to commence, it was the view of many that the 'truck system' of payment to workers should be discontinued. The 'truck system' enabled an employer to pay wages otherwise than in the current coin of the realm – for instance, by way of an advance of provisions from their own shops. These advances are then paid for at a premium on paydays, the periods between which can be quite long so as to encourage more debt.

The New Zealand Herald of 7 December 1871 denounced the practice of trucking as one affecting not just the prosperity of the workers but that of the entire colony:

"From all parts of the colony a cry is heard against the proposed truck system which is at present part and parcel of the Brogden contracts. We have explained before, when speaking on this question, of what this system consists, and have pointed out some of the evils which must on the face of the matter arise from it. An important portion of the Public Works and Immigration theory of the Government, as understood by the people, has always been the employment of fresh immigrants upon public works, immediately upon their arrival, in order that they may be enabled to save a sufficiency of funds whilst kept in regular employment, to permit them to become permanent settlers on land granted to them.

"We shall not be wrong in saying that this is, in the opinion of most people, one of the most important parts of the Government scheme. But observe how the truck system must strike at the root of any hopes that might otherwise have been indulged of any such good results. The whole aim and object of this objectionable system is to create improvident habits, to induce the workmen to adopt a continuous system of credit, to promote habits of intemperance and recklessness, and to ruin, in body and mind, those to whom we are looking as the future colonizers and redeemers of our desert wastes.

"In point of fact, should this system be carried out, no money will be put in circulation. The workmen will never have any funds at their disposal, and the whole of the loan, not only in the shape of contract payments, but every shilling of workmen's wages, will find its way into the pockets of the Messrs Brogden and be forwarded to England. Thus, instead of an industrious, thrifty class of horny-handed, steady, country settlers, we shall be training up, at the expense of the country, a mob of dissolute and improvident men, too many of whom, when the contracts are finished, and they are thrown out of employment, will, partly through vicious habits, and partly through necessity, join the criminal classes, whilst the land, which should have been covered with prosperous farms and villages, will remain a wilderness, and commerce unrefreshed by any wide circulation of money, must languish day by day.

"All these evils we can clearly see in store for us, following at the heels of the truck system. It is possible that the Government may not have sufficiently considered the question. Attention, however, will have been aroused by the notice which is at present being taken of the matter by the entire Colonial Press, and we trust that the utmost consideration will be given to the subject before the truck clause of the contracts is permitted to become law." [49]

Once some of these workforce ground rules had been established, a good restart was finally made on the Auckland and (now to) Mercer Railway in early 1872. "Parnell Hill was pierced by a tunnel on July 31st, 1872, and the Auckland-Onehunga portion of the line was opened on December 24th, 1873." [50]

**The First Train from Auckland**

"Hale and hearty, though eighty-three years of age, Mr Wm. Baker, of Claudelands, Hamilton, vividly recalls Auckland's first two-carriage train which blazed the railway trail in the run to Onehunga on the day before Christmas, 1873. Being the official issuer of tickets on that pioneer trip, which was regarded as a development extraordinary at the time, Mr Baker has a happy recollection of the event.

"The train started from Fort Britomart, which was the high embankment just about the foot of where Anzac Avenue now is. I remember we used to have to climb up there what we called 'Jacob's Ladder,' and the Presbyterian Church (St. Andrew's) was on the crest before it was shifted to its present location. When the time came for the train to start on December 24, Mr Hardington, who ran coaches between Onehunga and Auckland, suspended his service, as he thought it would be no use competing against the regular train.

"The contractors for the railway line ran the first train, and continued to do so for some little time until the railway was taken over by the Government. We left Fort Britomart on the first trip at 8 a.m. and carried a big crowd, as the races were on at Ellerslie. We continued past the racecourse, and also brought back people from the Onehunga terminus. Several trips each way were done that day without a hitch, the speed being 15 miles per hour." [51]

Until Auckland and Wellington were directly connected by the main trunk line in 1908, one option for those wishing to journey to and from the Capital was to take the train to Onehunga and then board the steamer to New Plymouth from where they could then complete their journey to the Capital by rail. When the Onehunga line eventually closed in 1973, it was at a time when motor vehicle use had well and truly put paid to passenger train patronage. Ironically, the line was re-opened some 37 years later, on 19 September 2010. The reason: 'to reduce the need for motor vehicle use'.

That ideal was articulated by Auckland Regional Council chairman, Mike Lee, who rather optimistically pronounced at the 2010 opening that, "…people would look back on September 2010 as the day the phrase 'Aucklanders never get out of their cars' lost its meaning." [52]

In the meantime, long before the car was invented, the momentum of the 1870s continued, and patronage of the railway line to Onehunga was such that it was drawing crowds of excursionists much to the chagrin of the more traditional transport providers:

"The railway continues to be a great attraction on Sunday, numbers availing themselves of it and the fine weather to visit Onehunga. The North Shore appears to be deserted on Sundays now, and the ferry-boats must suffer accordingly." [53]

However, The New Zealand Herald of 19 January 1874 obviously felt that the etiquette shown aboard this new mode of transport left something to be desired:

"We would suggest that smoking should be strictly prohibited, and also that gentlemen should be taught to exercise some little gallantry towards lady passengers, and not retain their seats whilst ladies stand in the centre of the carriage during the whole distance of the run to Onehunga. If the guard would, as an example, turn out one or two of the many youthful snobs who persistently keep their seats whilst ladies stand, and, at the same time, puff away at a bad cigar like a steam engine, they would receive the thanks of lady passengers, and be only doing their duty." [54]

"On 26 March 1874, a passenger excursion train reached Otahuhu. Six days later the first produce from the area was shipped to Auckland by train – a load of 12 tons of potatoes. On 20 May 1875 passenger services began between Auckland and Mercer. At that time the stops along the route included Penrose, Otahuhu, Papatoetoe, Manurewa, Papakura, Hunua, Drury, Pukekohe, Buckland, Tuakau and Pokeno." [55]

While the new railway south may have caused some initial downturn for the ferries carrying excursionists across the Waitemata, it would be another railway and then roads that would ultimately prove to be the death knell of water transportation to the north.

## Rail to the Kaipara

The broad, sparkling waters of the Waitemata Harbour had been a highway of commerce since long before the colonists arrived. From the Mahurangi Peninsula to the Rangitoto Channel, the Thames Estuary and the upper reaches to Riverhead, the users of this waterway had no need to borrow for construction and, apart from buoyage and sometimes dredging, this highway needed little maintenance.

Indeed, this waterway was considered to be so important to the settlement and exporting potential of the resource-rich Kaipara region that a canal, a tramway and then a railway line for the trans-shipment of passengers and goods between Riverhead, via Kumeu, to Helensville was first proposed during the 1860s.

However, it was not until January 1871 that the Kaipara Railway Act was passed by the Auckland Provincial Council and arrangements were made to survey and acquire the land for the line. The Act sanctioned the spending of no more than £27,000 or £2,200 per mile, including rolling stock and stations, for the project.

Clause 4 of the Act stipulated that:

"Such Railway shall not be commenced or contracted for until the land over which the same shall pass together with the land necessary for stations and other necessaries for the line shall have been acquired by the Superintendent free from any compensation therefor and the surveys route and termini of line approved of by the Provincial Engineer." [56]

During a visit to the district during the following month, a Member for the Northern Division and Secretary of the Auckland Provincial Council, John Sheehan, "...obtained the verbal sanction of every native, over whose land the railway passed, to give the land as a gift. Yesterday afternoon (23 February 1871) he left again for the same district, with the necessary legal documents, to obtain a formal cession of the land for railway purposes.

"The few Europeans over whose land the line must pass, seeing such an example set by the natives, may be looked upon as far-sighted as to what will advance the district, and it is hoped an equal liberality will be shown by them. The land required is trifling, compared with the increased value the railway will give their properties." [57]

Unlike the conditions that existed at the start of the Auckland and Drury Railway, there would seem to have been nothing to impede an early start at the Kaipara. However, for reasons that could only be surmised by The New Zealand Herald in its editorial of 28 April 1871, there was, indeed, an inexplicable and frustrating delay:

"We cannot help regarding it as a serious public loss that so much valuable time has been frittered away before commencing operations in the matter of the Kaipara railway. The most favourable season of the year is being allowed to pass unimproved, while nothing practical is accomplished or any decision arrived at respecting this important provincial undertaking.

"In accordance with the provision contained in the fourth clause of the Kaipara Railway Act, the Provincial Engineer-in-Chief was instructed by his Honor the Superintendent to proceed to the ground, and determine the route the railway should take, and fix the termini of the line. Mr O'Neill, we understand, has carried out his instructions in this respect, and sent in his report to the Government more than a month ago. What has become of this report? What was its purport? Why has it not been given to the public, that the information it contains might be allowed to speak for itself?

"It is clear, from the wording of the Act, that the main, if not sole responsibility of deciding as to the proper sites for the termini of the line devolves absolutely on the Provincial Engineer for the time being.

"We are aware that another survey has since been ordered, the cost of which, we suppose, must be borne ultimately by the taxpayers of the province? On what ground this can be justified, or by whose authority this additional expense is incurred, we are at a loss to conceive. If it is true, as we have heard it stated, that the sending in of his report by the Engineer-in-Chief, was immediately followed by an intimation from the Superintendent that his services were no longer required—then we can understand that there are, possibly, influences at work in fixing the termini of the railway of a character which the public had not previously calculated on. How far these influences are legitimate or otherwise time only will determine.

"It will be understood that there are three sites named for the terminus at Riverhead, all of which, it may be stated for the sake of illustration, lead respectively to a neutral point on the line, at Kumeu Creek, some two and a-half miles inland. The site at Lamb's landing would require a detour from the point named of two and three-quarter miles in a northerly direction, taking the railway a mile and a-half further up the river than the direct route would do. The site at the Bluff requires a detour of three and a-half miles from the main line at Kumeu Creek, leading south in the direction of Auckland, crossing Brigham's Creek, entailing the erection of an expensive bridge there, lengthening the line by a mile or thereabout, and otherwise involving considerable additional outlay.

"The site at Harkin's Point is in direct continuation of the main line, slightly diverging toward Auckland. After leaving Kumeu Creek till the landing place is reached, a distance of two miles and a-half, as contrasted with three miles and a-half to the Bluff, and two miles and three-quarters to Lamb's landing. In the event of the line being extended to Auckland at a future day, a mile of the route from Kumeu to Harkin's Point would be available for that purpose; whereas, if the terminus were taken to Lamb's, two miles and three-quarters of the railway would have to be sacrificed altogether.

"But in whatever way these questions may be reconciled by professional men, something, we trust, will now at length be determined on by the Government. The public, naturally, is impatient of so much circumlocution, from which only one result is certain to follow, the throwing back the work into the rainy season, and additional cost to the country in the shape of duplicate professional charges, the expediency of which may well be doubted, and the authority for which will probably be called in question." [58]

Thanks to what appeared to be a lack of official communication, what was referred to as 'the battle of the termini', certainly attracted its share of conspiracy theories. Many Letters to the Editor expressed dismay that what seemed to be political favour, endemic to national railway construction, had eventually steamed its way to the Auckland Province. In a letter published by The New Zealand Herald on 2 May 1871, 'Practical' wrote, in part:

"The late Provincial Engineer, Mr C. O'Neill, reported in favour of Harkin's Point, and against Mr Harding's (surveyor) proposal to have the terminus in Lamb's paddock, for which he (Mr O'Neill) was summarily dismissed, and Mr (Henry) Wrigg was appointed Provincial Engineer for a fortnight, to report upon the terminus, in hopes possibly that he will be more pliant than Mr O'Neill.

"If not, I suppose he will also be sent to the right-about, and some other person tried, until a more supple individual is found to hold the appointment of Provincial Engineer for a few days, and sign the necessary documents required by law. If Lamb's paddock were the best site for the terminus, would all this be necessary? If not, why should any person have the power to entail all this extra cost, and cause all this unnecessary delay?" [59]

Although another correspondent in his letter to the Editor of The New Zealand Herald, 'Toka Toka', disagreed with 'Practical's' suggestion that "...there would appear to have been a foregone conclusion that certain persons should specially benefit by the expenditure of the public money in the construction of the railway", he did question the suppression of the engineers' reports and comment, "To my dull comprehension, the whole affair looks very like a job; and it is a job for which there is no possible justification."

"...the Act was passed before the end of January. It is now the 2nd of May, and nothing has been done. One Provincial Engineer has been dismissed for differing with the Executive as to the most desirable terminus, and another has been appointed to revise his work, in the hope that he may be more plastic, and report that a longer and more costly line starting at Riverhead (a private township) is more desirable than a shorter, cheaper, and more direct line, uniting Kaipara with Auckland." [60]

One of the 'certain persons', suggested by Toka Toka', who 'should specially benefit by the expenditure of the public money in the construction of the railway', was of course the owner of Lamb's paddock, John Lamb. Lamb was a prominent businessman who operated the Waitemata Flour Mill and Biscuit Factory at Riverhead for 30 years and had his own freight vessel, the SS Scotchman. [61]

But, according to John Lamb's letter of rebuttal to The New Zealand Herald, dated 2 May 1871, even he was apparently unable to access any of the Engineers' reports, despite having personally called on the Superintendent. [62]

Then came the shock announcement that the whole project had been put in the too-hard basket, as reported by The New Zealand Herald of 3 May 1871:

"The Kaipara Railway Bill has been disallowed by His Excellency the Governor, and this, we suppose, will end the battle of the termini, which has raged hot and furious for some time past. From what we learn, the *causa belli*, as in the case of the celebrated dispute, where the two nations went to war upon the question whether an egg should be broken at the round or pointed end, was a matter of inconsiderable moment — a question of nine minutes difference in the route.

"The disallowance of this Act cuts through the Gordian knot of the difficulty, the 4th clause, which bound the Government to abide in the matter of termini by the report of the Engineer-in-Chief. Now the Superintendent and Executive are left free to act upon their own discretion, and since they have now the report of Mr Wrigg before them, as well as that of Mr O'Neill, the late Engineer-in-Chief, they will, we trust, be able in a few days to come to a decision satisfactory to the public at large, and that they may disarm all jealousy, we sincerely recommend them, by publishing in *extenso*, the reports of both Engineers, to give the public an opportunity of understanding the reasons which lead to the decision arrived at.

"There is one matter now only to be considered, and that having been satisfactorily disposed of, the sooner the work is commenced the better, and that is: will the £27,000 available suffice? If it will not, then by all means let us save the province from such an engineering blunder and abortion as its first essay at railway-making entailed upon it. We shall anxiously wait to see if Mr Wrigg's report in any way bears upon the probable entire cost of the work." [63]

The following day, The New Zealand Herald editorial graphically described the failure of the Railway project as, "...the long-talked-of undertaking, like an untimely birth, falls still-born into the hands of the disappointed operators. And, in truth, the miscarriage of so important a public work, though but for a time, will prove a disappointment to many in more respects than one. Not that it was felt that the work was certain to be carried out under the happiest auspices. Late events had tended to qualify public expectation on that head, but, notwithstanding, the general conviction was so far in favour of improved speedy communication with our numerous valuable northern settlements, that the prospect of the Kaipara Railway becoming an accomplished fact was eagerly looked forward to as some indication of progress in the right direction.

"We now see it was not to be so! Indeed, who ever heard of a railway in the Province of Auckland? Who ever imagined that the timber was grown, or the iron forged, that should be employed in the construction of the first locomotive train to press the soil of a province where progress is frowned on by authority, and where energy and enterprise are fugitives from the face of the powers that be. Then where is the impediment? What has gone wrong? ...Is it possible that this is only the sport of men in power? That a little stubbornness, a little wilfulness, on the part of one man, has brought about consequences of a magnitude affecting the prospects of thousands and involving a question of progress or stagnation to half the Province?

"Yet this is what we hear. We understand the General Government— true to its bargain with the Province— is most anxious to facilitate the work in every way...and that it never contemplated finding itself in the position of being compelled to veto the Act. It appears the matter for correction was of the simplest kind—a negative rather than a positive defect. No provision had been made for crossings and other minor matters of the sort, usually attended to in the most ordinary Railway legislation, and the Colonial Government required an assurance that these omissions would be made good at the proper time. This, we understand, the Superintendent declines to accede to, whether or not on the advice of his Executive we cannot say. But we are certain the public will desire to know where the responsibility lies, and the sooner this is made to appear the better.

"There should be no overstrained secrecy in these matters. The public has a right to be informed of what is being done. No sooner was the survey of the line of railway held, and duly reported, under the hands of the engineering staff of the Government, but we hear of that survey being set aside, the party making it quietly displaced from office, and another staff engaged expressly for the purpose of performing a particular work. Can anyone doubt the meaning of all this? To what purpose, we ask, was this second survey ordered? Who is to decide between two rival engineers' reports —each equally reliable and authoritative, the work of successive Engineers-in- Chief, battle-doored in and out of office, apparently with no other reason than can be discerned in the part they have been expected to play in a very questionable episode of provincial history?

"This is what it comes to: another year must be lost. The cause of settlement in our northern districts is to be temporarily sacrificed out of deference to the tricks of experts and the intrigue of office…It is a blow to our provincial status. It is a loss to our prestige, and a bar to settlement, for some time, in a direction where it is exceedingly desirable to encourage enterprise and increase population." [64]

Eventually, the first report of Provincial Engineer, Charles O'Neill, and then that of his successor, Henry Wrigg, were released by the Provincial Engineer's Office in May 1871 and subsequently published in the press for the public to scrutinise. Charles O'Neill undertook his survey of the various line options for the Kaipara Railway during February and March 1871 and the date of his report was dated 30 March that year. Henry Wrigg's survey was undertaken barely a month later and he resigned as Provincial Engineer after submitting his report on 1 May 1871.

While both engineers more or less agreed as to where the Helensville terminus should be, they differed greatly as to whether the line should start at Harkin's Point or Mr Lamb's Paddock. Many valid reasons were given by Charles O'Neill for the start to be made from Harkin's Point, including its shorter and more direct route to Helensville, its suitability to form part of a future line from Auckland and its easy proximity to the deeper water of the channel (the Rangitopuni River) leading to the Waitemata. [65]

That was in contrast to Henry Wrigg's recommendations which seemed to place greater emphasis on "…the purposes of a local trade daily growing into more importance" – in other words, the business that John Lamb operated not far from Henry Wrigg's terminus choice of Lamb's Paddock. [66]

Whether or not this second report was another case of political bias was again summed up by 'Practical' in a rather sarcastic Letter to the Editor of The New Zealand Herald, published on 23 May 1871:

"The public should be much obliged to you for publishing the reports of the two late Provincial Engineers on the above railway, and I trust they will read them both, and weigh the reasons adduced in the report of the second Provincial Engineer, who was evidently appointed for the express purpose of reporting in favour of the terminus being at Lamb's paddock; if not, what other reason could there be for appointing him Provincial Engineer for a fortnight, immediately after the dismissal of Mr C O'Neill? —as the only duty he performed in the capacity of Provincial Engineer was the production of the report alluded to. Doubtless, had he not been found sufficiently plastic, we should have had a third, or perhaps a fourth, Provincial Engineer appointed, until a suitable report was obtained from someone of them; and Mr Wrigg may be deserving of our thanks for having saved the country the expense that would have been incurred in these appointments, by at once doing what was required of him." [67]

In the meantime, the stalemate continued, much to the frustration of the likes of Samuel Edgar who wrote to the Editor of The New Zealand Herald in August 1871, parts of which included:

"You have frequently called attention to the difficulties of the Northern settlers, and the danger there is of many of them being driven out of the country. I do not think you have at all exaggerated the matter. It seems to me, however, not quite fair to lay all the blame on the present Government. The fact is, that for the last nine years, to my knowledge, neglect of the North has disheartened the most patient and industrious settlers, and thinned their ranks beyond all computation.

"If it goes on much longer, many districts will be deserted. The evil is, I think, that the country is governed from Auckland, by men who, however good their intentions, are quite ignorant of the wants of the country, and therefore incapable of legislating so as to meet those wants. I see no hope for the province, till we are governed by men who really understand the country districts. Nor is that ever likely to come to pass, till local are substituted for Provincial Institutions, with one economical central Government.

"There are very many men in the North who have laboured hard and successfully to found for themselves and their children comfortable homesteads. But nine years of weary disappointment, without the least prospect of any improvement, may well leave them heartless. The vanishing of the Kaipara Railway illusion will probably complete the despair that will for ever alienate and banish many from New Zealand.

Since writing the above, I have read Mr Munro's letter—the truth of the whole of which is confirmed by my nine years' experience of Auckland. Mr Vogel's scheme I from the first regarded, and still regard, as one of the gigantic swindles which many of us may live bitterly to repent, unless we are able and well enough to leave the colony in time. It is not bringing immigrants here that we want, but enabling those who are here to live and prosper permanently." [68]

However, only a couple of days later, the Kaipara railway illusion was on its way to becoming reality, as The New Zealand Herald announced:

"We understand that at a meeting of the Provincial Executive held yesterday, it was agreed to proceed with the construction of the Kaipara railway, and accept the lowest tender received—Mr Matthew Edgar's subject to the satisfactory completion of certain necessary preliminary arrangements. The amount of Mr Edgar's tender is £42,620 from Lamb's Point, and £42,321 from Harkin's Point." [69]

While the start of the line may not then have been determined, plans for perhaps the most important aspect of the project, the sod-turning ceremony, were nevertheless underway:

"This long talked of and important work is to be begun on Thursday, the 31st instant, when the ceremony of turning the first sod will be performed at the Riverhead end of the line. The steamer Lady Bowen, which has been chartered for the occasion, will leave the Queen-street wharf on that day at 9 o'clock a.m. conveying the Deputy Superintendent, the Executive, and those members of the Provincial Council who may desire to be present on the occasion, returning to town about 3 p.m. the same day.

"A large number of European settlers and natives are expected to be present on the occasion. The event will be one of no small importance, and we have no doubt that there will be a large assemblage of people who are interested in matters so deeply connected with the future development of the province." [70]

Indeed, there was a large assemblage of dignitaries, settlers, and Maori to witness the official start of the construction of the Kaipara Railway on 31 August 1871:

"The first step toward this most important work was inaugurated yesterday at Harkin's Point, Riverhead. The Deputy Superintendent turned the first sod and wheeled the first barrow-load of earth for the railway between Kaipara and Riverhead." [71]

The editorial of the Daily Southern Cross, published the following day, summed up the 'turning the first sod' event as one of hope that, now the ceremonies were over, an Auckland railway project would be completed this time, and without the greed so evident during the Auckland and Drury debacle:

"Yesterday will be marked as a red-letter day in the annals of Auckland province, but especially in the records that treat of the progress and development of the country lying north of this city. The long-projected railway that is to connect the head waters of the Waitemata, on the east coast, with the vast inland sea of Kaipara, on the west, has at length been begun.

"The formal ceremony of 'turning the first sod' is over, and the remainder of the work is now fairly committed, for completion, to the hands of Mr Edgar, the contractor, and his brawny navvies. This much is, so far, well, but it is not the first time we have been called upon to chronicle the 'turning of the first sod' for a railway in this province, but we have never yet had the pleasure of attending the opening of a line for traffic, although an expenditure of nearly £130,000 was the result of turning that sod. As a community, therefore, we might incline to deprecate any jubilant expressions on this, the second time that the sod-turning ceremony has been performed, and plead for our stoicism the severe and expensive lessons of the past.

"We do not choose to pursue this course, however, but join heartily in the general rejoicing at the successful inauguration of a work which, if faithfully carried out, will more rapidly tend to the development of our great internal resources than almost any other work requiring a similar expenditure of public money. But, apart from these reflections, we have more hope of this line being made within a reasonable time than ever we entertained of the Auckland and Drury Railway. The ruinous spirit of land speculation which is so characteristically condemned by Dieffenbach's 'Travels in New Zealand' which he observed springing up from the very time that Auckland was selected by Captain Hobson for the site of the capital of the colony, were very observable in 1864.

"We could name many instances where people purchased allotments and blocks of land on or near the supposed line of the Auckland and Drury Railway, after it was spoken about and before anything definitely was done, a few months afterwards demanding the most exorbitant price for the same land when wanted by the Railway Commissioners. That was the 'public spirit' and that was the conduct which prevented the Auckland and Drury Railway from ever becoming an accomplished fact.

"Had the Assembly passed a short Act enabling the Provincial Government or the Railway Commissioners to take the land they required at a reasonable price, the position of Auckland would have been different to-day; for, by unscrupulous greed, the goose was killed which would have laid the golden eggs in the future. The Kaipara railway has been differently managed, for the land over which it is to pass has been made a free gift, both by its European and Maori owners. This is a step in the right direction, and one from which the donors will, we have no doubt, yet reap a rich reward; and a concession which has been made to the Provincial Government solely through the tact and management of Mr Sheehan, the Provincial Treasurer." [72]

After what must have been a few more barrow-loads of rock and earth, the Kaipara Railway opened on 29 October 1875. This was to be some six years before the rail connection between Helensville and Auckland was made. The first trips from Riverhead (Harkin's Point) to Helensville took about one hour and forty minutes, depending on the load.

"Occasionally the engine got off the line, but the pace was so slow that no damage was done to the train, and the engine driver always carried a jack to get the engine on again. If the line was a little out of plumb where the engine had run off, the guard and engine driver would go to the nearest gully and get some small pungas to prop up the rails level again." [73]

Despite the difficulties, the purpose of the new line was considered by the Auckland Star to be as much a conveyance for excursionists as for any commercial purpose:

"Captain Casey announces special trips to connect with the line, thus bringing a picnic at Helensville and return the same day within the possibilities of these go-ahead days. To those who make up their minds for the journey we would say a word of caution against allowing their imaginations to revel in anticipations of delightful scenery—alternating shades of woodland, fertile plains, babbling brooks, and crystal streams. The line runs through a very uninteresting country, commencing with unproductive gum flats, and ending in three or four miles of swamp.

"There is some very fair land in the vicinity of the Kumeu and when the swamps are drained there could be no more fertile soil, but at present the tourist is disposed to ask what will support the line? The great benefit that is expected to flow from the opening of this railway pertains not to the land through which it passes but to the many districts North, abutting on the great Kaipara harbour." [74]

By early 1876, the railway from Riverhead to Helensville had certainly generated an interest in excursions to that part of the country, as announced by the Auckland Star of 28 January that year:

"A splendid opportunity for crossing the Kaipara railway and seeing the Helensville district will be afforded by the excursion provided by Captain Casey. The Gemini leaves Auckland at ten o'clock, meeting the train at Riverhead at noon. The excursionists will have two or three hours at

Helensville, and be back in time to connect with the Gemini at Riverhead at five o' clock, arriving in town before dark." [75]

From the early 1860s, Captain Casey "…was the owner at various times of a large number of trading craft. To his private enterprise is due in a large measure the regular steam communication enjoyed by many flourishing country settlements, and this is notably the case with the Mahurangi and Hot Springs and also the Riverhead and Kaipara trade. A great deal of the progress of these settlements may be attributed to the advantages the settlers derived from the regular trips of Captain Casey's steamers, which succeeded the old cargo boats and cutters that had previously monopolised the trade." [76]

When Captain Casey died on 6 July 1881, his death was described by the Auckland Star as "Another old colonist has passed over to the 'great majority'…at the advanced age of 61." [77]

This was just 12 days before the opening of the Auckland to Helensville line on 18 July 1881 but, by then, he had sold all but two of his vessels to the Kaipara Steamship Company Limited which soon struggled with the new competition. Indeed, as reported by The New Zealand Herald of 3 October 1882, the bottom line and future prospects of the Kaipara Steamship Company Limited was directly affected barely a year after the opening of the railway to Helensville.

"The Chairman (of the Kaipara Steamship Company Limited), in moving the adoption of the report and balance-sheet, said the object in changing the time of the yearly meeting was to enable the directors to try to induce the capitalists of Auckland to take up shares at the present valuation of the company, as ascertained by actual valuation, and thus relieve the company of the debt at the bank, and put the company as they had not yet been—on a sound footing. He need not say anything as to the value of the shares. The company was doing well, and they would have been paying dividends if they had been out of debt. Unfortunately, through the completion of the railway line to Helensville, some of the boats had been thrown out of use. The company would have been prosperous under other circumstances than the present. He did not think he need say more." [78]

But while the railway to Helensville from Auckland would in time eclipse the Waitemata ship trade altogether, a waterway transportation system between the two centres was still being mooted as late as 1911.

In what The New Zealand Herald sub-headlined as "A Stupendous Proposal", the paper reported on 7 September 1911:

"The project of constructing a canal to connect the Kaipara and Waitemata waterways has been raised by the member for Kaipara (Mr J.

Stallworthy) in the House of Representatives. Discussing the scheme this afternoon the Minister for Marine said that the canal would require to extend from below Helensville, on the Kaipara River, to some distance on the Auckland side of Riverhead, and would require to follow generally the course of the Kaipara and the Kumeu Rivers, and of the abandoned railway between the main line and Riverhead.

"The distance from Helensville to Riverhead, along the line of a canal, would be about 15½ miles, but dredging would require to be carried out for several miles, as the head of the Waitemata Harbour in the vicinity of Riverhead is very shallow, as is also the Kaipara River for some distance below Helensville. The top of the ridge between the Kumeu River and Riverhead is about 130 ft above high water spring tides, and the height of the Kumeu River, near the Kumeu railway station, is about 70ft above high water. It will therefore be seen that, without taking into consideration the construction of the necessary locks to deal with the difference in tide levels, the undertaking would be a stupendous one, the cost of which could not be estimated without a survey in detail." [79]

As with the various canals suggested as a means of connecting the Waitemata and Manukau Harbours, the Kaipara member's proposal occasionally resurfaced but was eventually forgotten as a credible alternative to rail and road, both of which continued to be constructed throughout the country during the 1870s.

Indeed, "For the colony as a whole, the 1870s was a decade of great capital formation, investment, and business expansion. A boom was unleashed when the Vogel scheme of borrowing and development was immoderately and rapidly put into operation." [80]

And, of course, this "Borrowing, public and private, and the immigration of the 1870s obviously had much to do with the way the population of the (Auckland) province grew during the decade from about 60,000 to 95,000…" [81]

And that was all to the good, according to Julius Vogel (by then Sir Julius Vogel) who, while in England in 1878, wrote:

"No doubt it was a bold policy: it was a policy virtually forced on the Colony by the abandonment of the Mother Country of the duties it had contracted by the Treaty of Waitangi. That the remedy of the colonists was in opening up the land and increasing the population, was recognised by the Government of this country (England), for after great reluctance they passed through Parliament a Bill authorising an imperial guarantee to be given to a million sterling of Colonial debentures. All doubts as to the soundness of the policy are at rest. Already it has been found necessary to make the railways fifty per cent more substantial than was at first contemplated. The value of private property in the country has much more than doubled. The value of the public estate has equally advanced." [82]

Whether forced on the colony or not, there was still plenty of evidence to suggest, "The history of public works from 1870 to 1890 (and indeed well into the twentieth century) is in many ways the history of public, private and political pressure for private, political, and parochial ends." [83]

As already illustrated, that fulfilling of private, political, and parochial ambition, particularly if that ambition included the accumulation of private wealth, was certainly a priority in the name of progress and in keeping with the laissez-fare attitudes of the time. Indeed, those attitudes and the excesses they generated were easily accepted as a means of progress by a populace otherwise too busy with their own struggles. Nevertheless, in order to implement some of the lessons learned during the acquisition of land for the Auckland and Drury Railway and to cement in a few ground rules by way of legislation for all this "…great capital formation, investment, and business expansion" of the 1870s, Parliament eventually enacted 'An Act for Consolidating the Laws relating to Public Works' in the form of the Public Works Act of 1876.

The Act was divided into several parts which included provisions for the taking of lands for public works, the rates of compensation that could be paid and the definition of and management of roads, railways, drainage and water supply for the goldfields. Some parts of this Act certainly seek to cover every eventuality, using language that today might not be viewed as quite so politically correct, such as that used in Clause 34:

*"A claim for compensation may be made by any person seized, possessed of, or entitled to such lands or to any estate or interest therein, whether such person has or has not the power to sell and convey the same, or by any executor or administrator; and any such claim on behalf of cestuique trusts, wards, lunatics or idiots, may be made by their trustees, guardians, or committees respectively."* [84]

And Clause 100 was particularly prescient with its warning that:

*"If any person is drunk when in charge of any animal or vehicle upon a road, he shall be liable to a penalty of not more than five pounds, or at the discretion of the Justices to be imprisoned, with or without hard labour, for not more than fourteen days."* [85]

"By 1879, New Zealand had 1,136 miles of operational railways. Unfortunately, (and despite the Public Works Act) things were not quite what they seemed. A good deal of the construction completed and that which was to continue over the next decade despite much shaking of heads and the uttering of dark prophecies about where it would all end, had been undertaken with an insouciance that in retrospect can only be described as breath-taking. "Groups of local entrepreneurs, blinded to reality by the prospects of quick profits, projected and commenced railway lines that never had a chance of delivering a profitable return at all, let alone sufficient income to meet loan costs." [86]

"According to the (Public Works) department's critics, inefficient and confused administration was the reason for the working railways' failure to pay the interest on the loans raised for their construction. As well as providing an insufficient return on the money invested in them, the railways were also offering allegedly inadequate services." [87]

"In the seventies public works in an area assured prosperity through employment opportunities, rising land values, and increased settlement. Public pressure for works, particularly railway lines, was widespread." [88]

"Of course politicians pressured for railway lines not only for private ends but also for political ones – and parochial interests served usually meant political ends gained. The Minister of Public Works, James MacAndrew, was described as 'the very impersonation of local selfishness'. In the 1878 public works proposals his province of Otago was allocated eight branch lines, including 160 miles of the Otago Central railway. This despite the unfavourable report on the latter line. The Otago Central and the Midland line were classic examples. Three unfavourable reports were compiled by department staff on the latter line. But it went ahead because of the private interests of some politicians including Vogel and Stout." (Robert Stout, MP Dunedin East) [89]

"Groups of local entrepreneurs, blinded to reality by the prospects of quick profits, projected and commenced railway lines that never had a chance of delivering a profitable return at all, let alone sufficient income to meet loan costs. The parliamentary record is littered with reports of enquiries into these expensive white elephants." [90]

The cronyism, the perceived waste of public money and concerns about the economic performance of the rail network became so bad that such an inquiry, by way of a Royal Commission, was decided upon as the best means by which the matter could be resolved. In an editorial published on 23 December 1879, the West Coast Times repeated the concerns previously reported by the Lyttelton Times:

"The Lyttelton Times, in a recent article, pointed out the reckless manner in which the Public Works Policy is administered. Neither the Ministry or anyone else seems to know or care whether money is thrown away or not. Mr Oliver (Richard Oliver – Minister of Public Works) confessed that Ministers had no time to devote to a close inquiry into the manner in which the ever recurring loans are spent.

"Hence the proposal for a Royal Commission to examine into the prospects of the railways under construction is proposed. It is indeed high time that the system adopted by successive Ministries, since the Vogel scheme of public works was first introduced, should be altered. The Lyttelton Times truly observes that some of the railways of New Zealand represent the result of a gigantic system of log rolling. One member voted for a railway to another member's paddock, because he of the paddock had agreed to the construction of a railway which would make his stable site valuable. Another insisted on a railway because his constituents wanted it, and Governments pressed forward railways because votes were given accordingly.

"It is very remarkable to find a Public Works Minister making a protest against such a state of things, because it is a state of things by which Ministers live. A Minister who has the courage of such an opinion is decidedly greater than the average politician. It remains to be seen whether the courage of Mr Oliver and his colleagues is of the right kind. We are very much afraid that Mr Oliver and his colleagues will turn out to be log rollers of the highest capabilities. The present Ministry have shown themselves adept in the art of bringing over political opponents.

"The Lyttelton Times does not think the House of Representatives to blame because the representatives are only what the people make them. Our contemporary goes on to say: In the majority of the elections, who is it that carries the day? The man who makes the biggest promises. The man who pledges himself to railways, harbour works, roads, bridges, and many other works, of which he knows little, and cares less.

"The Royal Commission, if it does its work properly, will discover that many districts have been scandalously neglected, that people who have for years contributed largely to the revenue, have received no adequate return, and that certain parts of the Colony have been left in comparative isolation, while railway communication far in excess of what was wanted has been given in others quarters." [91]

The Royal Commission, comprising five prominent persons from around the country, was convened in 1879 and reported to both Houses of Parliament on 26 July 1880. The Commissioners' main findings included:
- stations were over-staffed;
- train services were too frequent;
- wages were too high;
- political interference in response to pressure from sectional and regional interests was affecting capital expenditure and operational decisions; and

- excessive railway construction had occurred in advance of demand. [92]

One of the Royal Commission's principal recommendations was reported by The New Zealand Herald of 27 July 1880:

"Our recommendation in reference to train mileage, in short, amounts to this: That the running of trains should everywhere be reduced to the number that actually pay, and the results would be found not only in the reduction of what is strictly speaking current expenditure, but probably still more in diminution of wear and tear of permanent way and rolling stock of lines thus relieved. It is only right that we should say that action has recently been taken in some of the directions we have indicated, and with good effect, but much more remains to be done." [93]

"By 1880, New Zealand Railways (NZR) was operating more than 1,900 kilometres of track and carrying almost 3 million passengers and 830,000 tons of freight a year." [94]

Despite the Royal Commission's findings and much navel gazing, the nation's railway infrastructure was not deemed to be sufficient, and the fast pace of railway construction continued well into the twentieth century. But, despite all the adverse history and negative publicity, not all of these lines were white elephants. Some, like those constructed to access resource-rich regions, such as west and north-west Auckland were, in fact, essential to their continued development.

Indeed, "Nothing was more influential in bringing suburban blocks on to the market than the provision of these transport facilities. It was the completion of the railway link between Newmarket and Henderson that enabled the boosters of Mt Albert land, 'healthily and cheerfully situate' within the sound of the Kaipara train as it passed and repassed regularly throughout the day, to claim that purchasers would have 'TOWN COMFORTS – COUNTRY LUXURIES'." [95]

The first part of this link, from Newmarket to Glen Eden, opened on 29 March 1880, as described by The New Zealand Herald:

"The first section of the railway to the North was opened yesterday under somewhat favourable auspices, the occasion being the race meeting at Henderson's Mill. The train started from the Auckland station at half-past 10 o'clock, with a good row of carriages and a large crowd of passengers. On leaving the Newmarket station there were nine carriages attached to the engine, and as these were filled, and extra passengers were taken up at the intermediate stations, the load became a trying one. After passing the Whau this fact became manifest sensibly, for it was found necessary to detach a portion of the carriages, and go on with the remainder. Fortunately, the distance was short, so that those left in waiting were, after all, in good time to witness the races. The return journey was accomplished without interruption." [96]

This first ten miles of what was to become known as the Northern Railway had six stations along its length from Newmarket: Mt Eden, Kingsland, Mt Albert, Avondale, New Lynn and Waikomiti (Glen Eden).

The line comprised "...five road bridges, and about forty crossings. The longest cutting is near Khyber Pass. It is about a quarter of a mile in length and twenty-five feet at its greatest depth. The heaviest cutting was through rock, at or near Mount Albert. It is six chains in length, and twenty-three feet deep. Beyond this there is a stone breastwork filling of the same height – twenty-three feet." [97]

The line through to Kumeu and then Helensville (connecting with the existing Riverhead/Helensville line at Kumeu) was officially opened on 18 July 1881, an event that, according to the Auckland Star of that date, "...caused a good deal of interest and excitement. The country all along the line looks well. Persons are beginning to settle. Shops, stores and hotels are seen here and there. All along the Kumeu swamp gum diggers are located earning in various places over 40s a week.

"The Kumeu station is small but good. The shed is equal to most on any line. There is no road within 3/4 mile of the Kumeu Junction. This speaks badly for the district. The Railway Inspector scarcely knew where to erect the crossing gates, there being no roads. There seems to be great delight among the people at seeing the first through train, which will give an impetus to the districts. All along the line boundary and at Helensville in particular, business is brisk among the shipping. The grass crop on the farms all around looks magnificent and promising. Large logs are abundant in the river. Men are getting them into shipshape. It is thought that in a few months this railway will pay well, provided the freight is reasonable." [98]

While the coming of the railway was none too soon for most of the north-western settlements, many still lacked an efficient means by which they could transport their produce and goods to and from their farms to the railway and thence to the city. Citing their lack of roads, some had threatened to ignore the property tax increases imposed in the late 1870s. In a 'Letter to the Editor', published by the Auckland Star on 6 February 1880, a 'Northern Settler' commented:

"You have no conception of our primitive condition here. Before a railway can benefit us, we must be able to transport our produce by dray to the railway, and not on the pack-saddle. Here we have no dray road within ten miles of the nearest station on that line. I am surrounded on all sides but seaward by settlers who are in a similar position...You have no idea of the discontent and heart burnings here from Manukau to the Kaipara Heads.

"I venture to say there are not five settlers who would clear out if they could, and yet these men, one and all say they have no fault with soil or climate. In fact they all speak highly of the soil. Auckland from this district, could be partly supplied with butter, poultry, bacon, cheese and garden produce, if there were roads or access to the railway when opened." [99]

So, despite lines such as the Northern and the Southern opening vast areas of hinterland to settlement and ultimate prosperity to the country, the railway remained a one-dimensional transport system without adequate road access as well. And it wasn't just the connection needs of the 'Northern Settler' to be met. Access to a district's settlers and natural resources was expected to return a profit to the railways and its investors.

Unfortunately, in the words of the Evening Star when commenting on the planned line to the Kaipara, much of the railway building in New Zealand "…tended more to enrich a comparatively small class of rather too well-to-do settlers, has caused an increase in speculation in land rather than an increase of settlement.

"In Great Britain and older countries, of course, the purely commercial idea prevails, and thus railways, for the most part, came into competition with well-made roads and canals in affording speedier and cheaper transit between centres of population. But in a new country, almost uninhabited, with millions of acres of land awaiting occupation and cultivation, and the successful settlement of which constitutes the development of the Colony, railways have a different function to perform. Undoubtedly, when a railway scheme is proposed and entered upon, the whole cost of which is intended to be defrayed out of the consolidated revenue, it is absolutely imperative that those lines should be constructed first which will most speedily utilise the public estate, so as to spread population, stimulate and increase production. For the most part these principles have not been complied with in New Zealand." [100]

Of course, to be profitable, the services provided by the railway had not only to be accessible by means of stations that were conveniently deployed for its customers, but not so close together as to limit the efficiency and speed of steam-engine journeys. It was part of the raw principle referred to by the Evening Star – the principle that also called for a good balance between a district's railway and a road network as essential to providing a successful transportation solution for both rural and urban environments. It is a concept that was to be recommended as a solution to Auckland's transport problems by countless, future studies, but rarely actioned.

During the late 1800s, the apparent lack of concern for their needs encouraged passionate citizens along the northern and southern railway corridors to form 'leagues' to promote or, in the vernacular of the time, 'boost' the chances of their districts or townships to acquire improvements to their rail and road services. Often led by local body office holders and men of prominence in the communities they represented, such leagues are a concept as old as colonisation and one that continues today in many forms, ranging from tourism promotion to parliamentary lobbying.

By 1900, at a time when rowdy meetings in drafty community halls were common, leagues had become very vocal in their representations to officials with the power to satisfy their demands. In the case of the railways, those officials included the Minister of Railways and District Engineers.

While the timetable along a single-track line over such a distance as that between Newmarket and the farthest suburb of Waitakere was always going to be less than satisfactory, the settlers of early, twentieth-century West Auckland were of the opinion that the service could nevertheless be improved and so set up a lobby group called the North Auckland Railway League. However, because of the relatively small population of West Auckland at the turn of the twentieth century, the North Auckland Railway League sought the help of the much larger and experienced, North Island Main Trunk Railway League.

As reported by The New Zealand Herald of 13 July 1901, an application by the North Auckland Railway League for amalgamation with the North Island Main Trunk Railway League was considered by members of both groups at the City Council Chambers on 12 July 1901:

"In opening the proceedings the Chairman (the Hon. E Mitchelson) said that...Not many people realised the benefits which would accrue to this district from the North Auckland line. According to the last census the European population north of the Waitemata was over 38,000, and the native population over 9000, so that combined there were upwards of 47,000.

"When that number was contrasted against the sparsely populated Otago district they would be amazed, and more so if they compared the figures of expenditure on the two lines. Since the first sod of the North Auckland railway was cut, some 32 years ago, it had not progressed at the rate of more than two miles per year. For every 100 persons the Southern railways benefited, railways in the North would benefit 1000. The people of Auckland had shown some apathy in not recognising that the future prosperity of Auckland was bound up in the North Auckland railway. He favoured the amalgamation of the two leagues, and thought they would gain in strength by union." [101]

After much debate, it was agreed by members of both leagues "That a new body be now formed, to be called the Auckland Main Trunk Railway League..." and that..."The importance of the North Auckland line required to be forced upon the public as the importance of the Main Trunk line had been. If anything, the former line was of more importance to Auckland than the latter, the speedy continuation of which, the probabilities were, would be pushed forward with expedition." [102]

By August 1911, a newly-formed Northern Suburban Railway League, obviously focused more on the improvement of suburban railway services, was pressing for better railway facilities between Auckland and Swanson.

Following its representations to the Railways Department, a reply from the Railways General Manager, Mr T Ronayne, to the League and the League's reaction was reported by The New Zealand Herald on 11 November 1911:

"About two months ago the Northern Suburban Railway League communicated with the Railway Department, urging the need for improvements in the suburban railway service on the north line. Special stress was laid on the need for extra and faster trains, for shelters at the principal crossings on the line traversed by the motor train, and for workmen's trains between Auckland and Swanson.

"The president of the league (Mr M. J. Coyle) has now received a reply from the General Manager of Railways (Mr T. Ronayne) stating that it is not practicable to maintain the ordinary time-table on the Auckland-Henderson service at holiday times, when the bulk of the people are on pleasure bent, and railway arrangements have necessarily to a large extent to be made to fit in with the various local attractions along the route served by the railway.

"Regarding the request for additional trains on Sundays between Auckland and Henderson, Mr Ronayne says he regrets that the request cannot be complied with. He adds that the general experience of the Department has been that strong objection is invariably manifested in respect of any proposal for increasing the number of Sunday trains, first by the public, and then by members of the railway staff.

"Mr Coyle said last evening that the reply of the General Manager is regarded by the members of the league as being far from satisfactory. It does not refer at all to the major points of the league's requests. The members of the league felt that they had just cause for complaint, and that their requests were all reasonable and well grounded. People would not go into the further suburbs unless they could get to and from their work with facility, and at convenient hours. It was not expected that the improved train service would pay at first in the direct sense; but by encouraging the population it would increase the revenue in other directions. Kingsland illustrated the way in which transport induced the growth of the population. Before the trams ran there the place was fairly settled but in the subsequent years the population had increased at least fourfold. The league felt that it was unfortunate that the Minister was unable to go into questions of this sort personally.

"In view of the unsatisfactory nature of the Departmental reply, a meeting of the executive of the league is to be held on Monday night, to decide upon a plan of action. The league does not intend to let the matter rest where it is, and will agitate until some improvement is effected. Mr Coyle proposes that all the candidates for election in the Auckland district should be asked to support the league in its endeavour to have the service improved. He suggested last night that in a case of this sort the whole of Auckland should interest itself, and fight the question of suburban services. If necessary, a league, not trespassing upon the province of the present Railway League, which is concerned with railway expansion, should be formed to deal with traffic matters." [103]

At a subsequent meeting of the Northern Suburban Railway League, held on 20 December 1911 to discuss the increased train service to Avondale as proposed by Mr Ronayne, the executive of the League "…deemed the proposed increases totally inadequate to the requirements of the growing districts represented by them, and considered that the trains should have been extended to Swanson. It was stated that members of the league had requested indignation meetings to be called at New Lynn, Waikumete, Henderson, and Swanson, and after discussion the executive resolved to conform to their wishes as soon as the holidays were over." [104]

One of these 'indignation' meetings was held at Henderson on 28 February 1912:

"This consistent refusal of the Minister for Railways to cater for the oft-stated needs of the residents of the suburbs of Auckland has passed into a by-word. Definite protest has now been made by the many suburban people who have to suffer by the way in which the suburban section of the Kaipara line is mismanaged. In response to repeated requests from a considerable number of people residing in Waikumete, Henderson, and Swanson, the executive of the Northern Suburban Railway League journeyed to Henderson on Wednesday night to take part in an indignation meeting to protest against the inaction of the Minister as regards the provision of more frequent and faster trains to and from Auckland. The meeting was held in the Henderson Public Hall, and people came from several miles around to voice the opinions generally held throughout the rapidly-growing districts named.

"Mr A. Cochrane (chairman of the Waitemata County Council) presided, and amongst those who supported him were Mr R Knox (Swanson), Messrs M. J. Coyle, T. B. Clay, and E. Freeman (Mayor and Councillors of Mount Albert), Messrs Grandison and Parker (New Lynn Town Board), Mr Campbell (Avondale Road Board), and a large number of representative Henderson residents.

"The chairman briefly referred to the amount of progress the league had made since its inception. He voiced the very general complaint of the fruit growers of these districts as to the disadvantages they had to put up with through the totally insufficient facilities provided by the Department for the transit of fruit. Mr Coyle went on to remark that the two additional trains recently put on by the Department, and for which Avondale had been made the terminus, were by no means what the league were agitating for. The league had been consistently advocating Swanson as a reasonable terminus for the suburban area in view of the rapid settlement of the district all along the line.

"The Government, moreover, was the owner of a considerable block of land close to Swanson station which is very suitable for subdivision into small areas adaptable for workmen's homes, if only trains were run to suit the needs of the workers. The railway line passes through 1400 acres of idle Government land, and yet the Department failed to see the expediency of putting on trains which would allow of this big block being brought into close settlement.

"As showing that the requests made by the league, where granted, had been proved to be reasonable ones, and profit-earning to the Department, Mr Coyle instanced the inauguration of what is known as the motor (express) service some years ago. This for a long time the Department refused to start, on the grounds that it would never pay to run. When it was started it was only in the nature of an experiment for three months, the assumption being that it would prove such a failure in that time that agitation would cease. On the contrary, the experiment had proved an unqualified success, and not only had the service remained permanent, but the Department had been forced to put on several additional coaches for each trip; and there was no talk now of discontinuing the motor service (Cheers).

"Mr Clay read extracts from an official document which he had secured when on a visit to Australia. This revealed the enterprise displayed by the railway management there in granting every inducement to city toilers to live in the clear air of the suburbs. The contrast between' the methods of

Australian managements and those of the New Zealand Railway Department did not by any means show up the latter as a shining light for other countries to follow...

"Mr Knox (Swanson) moved the following resolution: That this representative meeting of the inhabitants of Henderson, Waikumete, and Swanson, urges the absolute necessity of improving the present service by an early train from Swanson to Auckland, and that the present 5.15 p.m. train to Henderson be extended to Swanson. Mr Knox stated that he himself knew fifty or sixty persons in Auckland who owned land in Swanson and would: come out there to live were reasonable train services available.

"Mr Campbell (Avondale) then, moved: That in view of the ever-increasing traffic between Auckland, New Lynn, Waikumete, Henderson, and Swanson, the Railway Department is totally neglecting and ignoring the requirements of these districts, for increased and more frequent means of communication with Auckland; that the time has now arrived when the workmen's trains should be extended to Swanson; that the two extra trains added lately are totally inadequate as they only run to Avondale. It is plainly evident, that the residents in these suburbs are keenly alive to the disadvantages they labour under as compared with other suburbs served by -the train service. Quite a formidable number of new members joined the league at the close of the meeting." [105]

This complaint that the railway system did not always cater to the needs of the suburbs and the convenience and expectations of the travelling public, particularly the workers, was one that seems to have persisted from the 1880s. In 1882, The New Zealand Herald pointed out the folly of the Railways Department providing only half the service required on the Southern line:

"The experiment of running an evening train to Otahuhu is fully justifying the wisdom of the railway authorities in adopting the step. The residents of the township, however, state that half the value of the train as a means of promoting settlement there, is lost through there being no early morning train as is the case at Onehunga.

"Provision is made for getting people out at night at a convenient hour, but the only opportunity in the morning is the down from Mercer, which reaches town about quarter to 10 o'clock—an hour which is too for late workmen, or even for shopkeepers and others. The evening Otahuhu train returns back to town at 7 o'clock, and it is followed three-quarters of an hour subsequently by the Waikato down train which gives the Otahuhu people thus two opportunities of coming to town in the evening. It has been suggested that the convenience of the residents would be fully met in that respect by the Waikato train and that if the present evening Otahuhu train remained on the 'lie-by' overnight and started like the Onehunga train for town at 7 a.m. an immense stimulus would be given to settlement in the district. [106]

But an inflexible timetable was not the only inconvenience that early railway commuters experienced. The economic and carrying capacity of the railway network very much depended on the disposition of stations along the route. Many stations were too close together for the economical running of a steam train of that era. Others, such as Auckland's main railway station, would continue to be poorly positioned for the convenience of passengers.

As The New Zealand Herald of 7 January 1878 pointed out, even a relatively short extension of the Waikato Railway to lower Queen Street would ease the congestion then experienced at the main station at Fort Britomart (at the foot of what is now Anzac Street):

"It would appear that the matter of extending the Waikato Railway to the Queen Street Wharf, and forming a passenger and parcel station there, so as to lessen the great inconveniencies which arise from the present out-of-the-way position of the terminus, has not made such progress as the public generally supposed.

"Sir George Grey has transmitted to Mr Macfarlane the following copy of a telegram which he had received in reply to his own from the Hon. Colonel Whitmore, Colonial Secretary: 'Re the Auckland Railway terminus, it appears that the Government did not agree to any plans, so far as the Department is aware.

"Your telegram apparently refers to a proposal which would cost £30,000; for which a substitute of a back shunt has been proposed, to cost £9,000. The question has been considered by each successive Ministry but has never been settled by any because it appears that the expenditure would not do the least good to the railway, but would seriously lessen the revenue of the Harbour Board. The alterations of the £9000 proposal would only give a platform and a small station shed. Perhaps it would be advisable to defer the discussion till the Cabinet meets — G. S. Whitmore.

"The land reclaimed by carrying the line to the spot proposed would in the end more than recoup the cost of the work. But it is said that there has been some obstacle thrown in the way of this improvement by the Harbour Board, and people are disposed to conclude that the ulterior motive for any such obstruction is a selfish one. This portion of the mud flat was, we are informed, made a reserve for railway purposes, but if it was not used for such purposes within a certain time the property will fall in to the hands of the Harbour Trustees. We cannot believe that this is the cause of the objection. Even a shunt line with a passenger and parcel station would be a great boon. The goods station could remain at the present terminus." [107]

By 1885, the need for a new Auckland railway station had prevailed and the line was subsequently extended to its present site at Britomart. Britomart had been Point Britomart until the cliff was levelled to fill in Commercial Bay, across which the railway from the south was extended to terminate to the east of the City's main thoroughfare, lower Queen Street.

A New Zealand Herald article described some of the construction of the new station before its eventual opening on 30 November 1885:

"The new railway station building contract is progressing apace. The contractor, Mr Ahern, has the plastering of the rooms in the top storey well in hand, and as soon as it is finished, the joiners will be able to get on. A large quantity of asphalt materials has been laid down, and a start will be made on asphalting the floors of the arrival and departure sheds as soon as the weather gets settled. The sections of asphalt will be 700 and 850 feet in length respectively.

"Over £3000 was sunk alone in the foundations of the station, the piling being 36 feet with nine feet of concrete on top. There is a splendid view from the tower of the city and harbour, the Auckland railway station being the only railway station in the colony which is two storeys in height. Some idea of the difficulties the contractor labours under in getting orders for material executed, may be gathered from one instance. The spouting for the building was ordered from Home about a year ago, and it only arrived at Dunedin last week. Temporary spouting had to be fixed on the building in order to permit of the men getting on with the work, all of which will have again to be removed." [108]

While the new station became known as the Queen Street station, its two-storey brick façade actually fronted Galway Street. As services increased, two island platforms were constructed so that the station eventually had six platforms. [109]

However, before reaching the Queen Street station terminus, the railway crossed Breakwater Road which was then a main connecting road between Customs and Quay Streets. Not only was Breakwater Road a busy arterial route between the commercial heart of the city and its port, but its intersection with the railway soon became an early battleground in the growing conflict between road users and the railway.

On the 2nd of November 1908, Mr J W Kenah and his son, Mr W Kenah, of Papatoetoe were apparently not the first to crash their motor car into a train at the Breakwater Road crossing and nor were they to be the last. According to the New Zealand Herald, the two travelling at "the ordinary pace" failed to see the signalman or the train as it left the station and because of the noise made by their motor car after "Mr Kenah senior, who was driving, threw the machine on to the lower gear" they did not hear it either. Although the son was thrown from the vehicle as it impacted the first truck behind the engine and he actually hit the truck as well, he "escaped with a severe shaking and a few bruises". [110]

Disagreements as to whether the trains or the motorist had the right of way at level crossings continued for many years. During a suit for damages against the Railway Department by a motorist heard at the Supreme Court in August 1913, the Department's district railway engineer, Mr D T McIntosh, made it clear that:

"Though it may not be generally known a person who walks or drives over a level railway crossing when an approaching train is within half a mile, is, under the railway by-laws, a trespasser, and is liable for prosecution." [111]

But despite these early conflicts, the consolidation of the Auckland Railway Station next to the City's main thoroughfare and the port provided a more convenient public access to the railway network. Indeed, that worthy concept of public and commercial convenience continued for more than thirty years, until the Government decided that the Queen Street frontage of the railway station would also be an ideal site for the City's new Post Office.

By the early 1900s, the width of the railway station was already constricted by the commercial buildings fronting the adjacent Quay and Customs Streets and even before the new Post Office opened in November 1912, the station's length was considerably reduced as well. As W K O'Hara described "The Development of Auckland's Railway Station", published in a 1927 edition of The New Zealand Railways Magazine, "Old colonists tell of occasions when the vans of trains were pushed through the old iron fence right out into Queen Street. Frequent additions have been made, from time to time, to serve the needs of the fast increasing business, but it was early realised that the present station was entirely unsuited to meet the requirements of a great city." [112]

By July 1909, work on the new post office and, as a consequence, the necessary remodelling of the railway station, was well underway. The New Zealand Herald of 9 July that year described the scene as one of "strange confusion" and added, "The railway traffic at Auckland involves the despatch and arrival of nearly a hundred trains daily, and in this traffic, of course, there must be no interruption. In the midst of disorder, order prevails, and trains continue to come and go with their accustomed order and regularity.

"The cause of the altered appearance and the general transformation of the yard is twofold. First there is the commencement of work by the contractors for the new post office, which takes the 'front seat' of the railway premises; and, secondly, there is the alteration of the platform system, rendered necessary by the completion of the duplication works between the station and the (Parnell) tunnel.

"The taking of the site for the post office and the provision of the roadway at what will be the back of the new building has curtailed the length of the railway metals at the Queen-street end by some 200 ft. This has, of course, entailed the Railway Department taking a back seat, and the moving back of its network of lines, sidings, and points to that extent. Several sets of points have had to be taken up, and relaid, and the signal box, which formerly stood just inside the entrance, has had to find a new abiding place nearer the present station buildings.

"Pending the decision as to a new railway station, all these arrangements and extensions are, of course, of only a temporary nature, and the edges of the new portion of the platforms on this account are of wood. The works, which are being carried out by Mr D. T. McIntosh, district railway engineer, will probably take another two months to complete. What will probably be the most inconvenient feature of the new arrangement — which, although only temporary, will have to suffice for some considerable time will be the fact that when the longer trains are drawn up along the platforms they will frequently extend across the level crossing at Breakwater Road, and thus for the time block the numerous vehicles that have occasion to use that crossing.

"The selection of the railway site for the post office has, the railway authorities point out, rendered this encroachment unavoidable, and it seems that the public will have to make the best of the inconvenience that must ensue when the larger trains are at the platforms. Some time ago plans were prepared, which provided for the closing of Breakwater Road as a public thoroughfare, and the substitution of an overhead traffic bridge.

"This would, of course, have obviated the difficulty; but the scheme, owing to the large expenditure that it would entail, has been left in abeyance. The cost of such a work, including the construction of the bridge and the purchase of land required for the approaches, will probably run into £35,000 or £40,000, and whilst the Government is expending hundreds of thousands on such works as the Midland railway — commencing at and leading to nowhere it cannot, of course, spare the money required for such an urgently-needed work in the busiest part of the largest city of the Dominion. Therefore, Aucklanders must again wait." [113]

Two years later and Aucklanders were still waiting for improved and not 'temporary' conditions. In its editorial of 3 August 1911, The New Zealand Herald and Daily Southern Cross expressed the frustration of many of Auckland's railway travellers of the time. In language that would hardly be used in the same newspaper today, the Herald's opinion was particularly scathing of the then Minister of Railways, John Andrew Millar, and his Department's treatment of the commuter:

"The usual Spring movement to obtain better suburban train facilities is already visible, steps being taken on both the Main Line and the Henderson Line to present the case of the regular traveller, who works in the city and resides in the suburbs, to the dull ears of railway authority. In this connection we would point out that very little consideration can be expected from the Department in this respect until a new Auckland Railway Station is erected for the simple but sufficient reason that the station has practically reached its limit of accommodation.

"Mr Millar regards all money spent by his Department in Auckland as entirely wasted, but it is quite impossible to carry on the railway business, however inadequately, without making constant additions to the whole railway equipment. Not only have more carriages to be built, more engines to be obtained, more men to be employed, in order to meet the ever-increasing demands of Auckland Province, but no administrative invention can do without platform accommodation and station buildings of some sort, if business insists on expanding. No assertions that railway stations are 'luxuries,' and that there is no money to 'fool away' upon them, can alter the arbitrary conditions which are greater than Ministers. It is probable that more money is dribbled away upon casual makeshifts and impermanent additions to the Auckland Railway Station than would suffice to erect an establishment adequate for current uses and immediate prospects.

"Mr Millar prefers to dribble money, grudgingly and ineffectively, where Auckland is concerned, but he is driven to admit that some increased accommodation may be required shortly. The present buildings and platform only meet requirements, and cannot well be increased to do more...However, a new station costs money, and though Auckland Province and Auckland City are graciously permitted to supply more than their share of railway earnings they must not hope for further recognition.

"With a tunnel which cannot carry any much heavier passenger traffic in the 'rush' hours; with a station so limited in its platform accommodation that every additional train disturbs the official mind; and with a Minister determined to do anything rather than allow Auckland to have the 'luxury' of an adequate station and the necessity of a duplicated line on the most important railway section in the Dominion, what prospect is there of any marked improvement in the suburban train service?" [114]

By early 1912, the beleaguered John Andrew Millar had been replaced as Minister of Railways by his Liberal Party colleague, Arthur Myers. However, it was not long before Myers was also replaced following the election win of William Massey's Reform Party in July of that year. The new Minister, William Herbert Herries, was to remain the Minister of Railways for some seven years.

In one of his first responses to a question about the Auckland Railway Station in the House of Representatives in August 1912, the new Minister acknowledged that a new Auckland railway station, "...when provided, should afford all modern conveniences necessary for dealing with the present and prospective railway traffic in the northern city for many years to come."

However, the Hon. William Herries continued, "I am not prepared at the present time to submit plans and specifications for the new railway station at Auckland. A very large amount of preliminary work is necessary before anything can be done in respect to the construction of the new station, and considering the expenditure that will be involved it is essential that any proposals made should be very carefully considered. The work, however, is entirely dependent on funds being available, and I regret that at the present moment I am unable to give any indication as to when the work will be commenced." [115]

While funds remained unavailable, "In 1912 a definite move was made to remedy conditions. The late Mr D. T. McIntosh (Daniel Thomas McIntosh), then District Engineer, went fully into the question of providing for future development. By this time the proposed Auckland-Westfield deviation and the Northern Tunnel outlet to the Kaipara line had been mooted. The provision of suitable connections to serve these various routes required careful consideration. After much scheming the problem was solved. The skeleton outline, on which our new station has been designed, was definitely developed.

"From the higher positions above Beach Road, a fine bird's eye view of the whole yard is obtained, and it is said that Mr McIntosh conceived his great scheme when, one evening, he viewed the panorama from the roof promenade of Cargen Hotel. Auckland owes much to this fine engineer. Our new station will stand as a fitting tribute to his wisdom and foresight." [116]

"He (McIntosh) was appointed engineer in charge of the Auckland District in 1905. Under his supervision the duplication of the railway line between Auckland and Penrose, the construction of the new Parnell tunnel, the grade easements between Otahuhu and Mercer, and the extension and rearrangement of practically every important station yard in the Auckland district have been carried out." [117]

Unfortunately, Mr McIntosh did not get to see the opening of the new railway station he had envisaged. He retired on 12 August 1920 after some 46 years of service with the Public Works and Railways Departments and died on or about 17 November 1926 – just four years before the completion of the station which, as described by the Auckland Star, "…was evolved by Mr McIntosh personally and remains as one of the many monuments to his skill as a railway engineer." [118]

In the meantime, by July 1914, the Hon. William Herries was still answering questions as to when a new Auckland railway station might eventuate. Just as he did two years previously, the Minister continued to express, very much in political terms, his willingness to plan for the future in this reply in the House on 9 July 1914:

"The desirability of providing increased facilities at Auckland is engaging attention, and in view of the expansion of the traffic that is taking place it is necessary to look well ahead, so that any provision that is made will be ample for meeting all requirements of the existing and prospective traffic for many years. As a large expenditure will be involved, the matter must be dealt with in a comprehensive way." [119]

The term, 'engaging attention', used by Minister Herries, was to prove to be a gross understatement as congestion at the Auckland Railway Station continued through to the 1920s. In fact, business at the station had doubled during the eight years to 1914, and was expected to double again by 1922. But it wasn't just a case of building a new railway station. The increased business of railway transport was growing at such an abnormal rate that facilities were in desperate need of renewal and expansion and it was the latter, the need for more space for passengers and freight that caused the most concern.

During a debate in the House of Representatives on 24 October 1914, former Prime Minister, Sir Joseph Ward, commented. "…the possibility of having an up-to-date railway station in Auckland on the present site had been spoiled by the erection of the new post office. The post office was a good one, but it was in the wrong place…It is one of the finest sites in Auckland." [120]

This debate resulted from the introduction of a comprehensive review of the country's railway system to the House on 3 September 1914. The review had been undertaken by Englishman, Mr E H Hiley, who had been appointed General Manager of the New Zealand Railways Department following the retirement of Mr Ronayne on 1 November 1913.

Mr Hiley had only arrived in Auckland from Britain on 24 September 1913 after a three-week stopover in Canada to study that country's railway network. While his travels around New Zealand were hampered somewhat by a smallpox epidemic and a waterside workers' strike, he nevertheless wasted no time in summing up the organisation and its shortcomings. In his report to the Railways Minister in August 1914, the new General Manager advised that a more sensible management approach to the running of the country's railway network was necessary and urgent:

"The arrangements under which new railways are authorized and built in the Dominion are, I would respectfully suggest, capable of considerable improvement. At the present time a new line is undertaken without any consultation with the Railway Department, and in consequence the only official estimate available before the country is committed to additional expenditure is the Public Works Engineer's estimate of the cost of construction.

"The Department which will ultimately take over and work the new railway is not consulted as to the route, grades, and alignment, nor are the plans submitted to it before the new line is commenced. No estimate is obtained from the Railway Department as to the cost of building the additional rolling-stock required. No estimate is made of the annual cost in the shape of working-expenses, and no figures are prepared by the Railway Department as to the probable revenue from the proposed line, therefore no reliable calculation can be made as to whether the net revenue will represent a profit or a loss.

"The practice in New Zealand is to hand new railways over to the Working Railways Department entirely bare of rolling-stock, the expense for providing which has to come out of the annual grant of 'Additions to open lines' which has often been inadequate for the purpose. This has contributed in no small degree to the shortage of rolling-stock now prevailing. I believe I am correct in stating that there are over twenty new railways in course of construction at the present time, and I submit that this is not an economical method of procedure. It must be obvious that if the work of construction was concentrated upon, say, five of these railways, the cost of supervision would be lower and the speed at which the railways would be finished and become traffic-bearing and revenue-earning would be at least four times as rapid. Over twenty uncompleted and unremunerative railways are a serious handicap to a comparatively small undertaking. The Working Railways Department is vitally interested in economical construction, because the expenditure ultimately becomes a portion of the capital upon which interest has to be earned." [121]

What became known as the 'Hiley Report' soon caught the imagination of the media and those who felt that railway time in New Zealand had stood still for too long. Indeed, from beginning to end, Mr Hiley's report to the Government was all-encompassing and very much to the point:

"The conclusion arrived at after reviewing the railway situation in New Zealand is that the system has outgrown its present organization. Established, no doubt, on sound lines in the first instance, it is evident that the rapid growth of the system and expansion of business has rendered the machinery for traffic control unequal to the demands put upon it by existing circumstances. The staff requires to be strengthened and the staff arrangements remodelled in some cases. This is particularly necessary in the Traffic branches.

"The Department is short of engine-power and rolling-stock for dealing promptly with the business now offering. The terminal accommodation is inadequate at several important centres, and a forward policy is necessary in regard to duplication of congested suburban lines, regrading of main lines, bridge-strengthening, and additional signalling equipment if the traffic of the Dominion is to be fostered and handled economically, safely, and expeditiously." [122]

The body of Mr Hiley's report then went on to detail the railway system's managerial and material shortcomings up and down the country. Customer relations came in for some particular attention when he advocated what must have been a first for a Government-run service – the appointment of a 'Commercial Agent' to undertake what, today, would be called public relations and marketing duties.

"There is frequently a tendency to overlook the fact that the New Zealand Railway Department, although a State concern, is nevertheless a business undertaking established for the purpose of selling transport. In no other concern in which capital exceeding £32,000,000 has been invested would the organization be considered complete without the inclusion of a responsible official whose sole duty would be the development of new revenue-producing business. It is, however, a fact that there is no such official attached to the New Zealand railways.

"The Commercial Agent will be free from the routine of preparation of time-tables, traffic advertisements, or rates revision, but he should nevertheless be required to keep a watchful eye on these matters as well as on the cleanliness of passenger stock, smoothness of railway-track, running of trains, efficiency of the dining-car service, civility of staff, and convenience of facilities for dealing with traffic at passenger and goods stations, &c, because these and kindred matters tend towards the attraction or repulsion of business. Complaints from the public will concern the

Commercial Agent, because the public are his particular care, therefore it is clear that the position of Commercial Agent will not be a sinecure in a country where grumbling is not yet a lost art." [123]

Additional matters relating to the carrying of passengers and of concern to Mr Hiley included:

"The passenger accommodation is insufficient to meet the requirements of the traffic. There are a number of cars under construction in the railway workshops, and an effort will be made to increase the output. I am not convinced that it is necessary at the present juncture to go outside the Dominion for cars, and I am anxious to avoid this if possible.

"It would be uneconomical to provide cars sufficient to meet the heaviest demand made by rushes of traffic during the holiday season; nevertheless I am strongly of opinion that the practice of withdrawing a large number of wagons from traffic for utilization as passenger-vehicles is objectionable from both the departmental and the public point of view, and should be gradually restricted. The question of substituting electric lighting for gas on the main through trains is having consideration. Electric light has obvious advantages, but its installation on a large scale in New Zealand passenger-trains would involve too serious an expenditure to be contemplated at the present time." [124]

Mr Hiley's concern for passenger comfort and safety also extended to the interaction between rail and road users at level crossings. Slower-paced carters and their horses could better hear and see and react to oncoming trains, unlike the motor car driver more intent on the superiority of his mechanical propulsion. By 1914, the latter were very much in the ascendancy.

"The advent of the motor-car and other forms of motor traction has materially increased the danger at level crossings owing to the high rate of speed road vehicles now attain. Distant warning notices are therefore desirable in the interests of the users of the road, and the road authorities should undertake some responsibility in connection with the maintenance of such notices. I (propose) communicating further with them on the matter, which is of general public interest." [125]

The need for urgency was particularly noticeable when his report referred to the needs of the North Island and especially the Auckland region:

"The duplication from Penrose to Papakura is required both as a relief to the main line and to develop the Auckland suburban business. The capacity of the single line between these stations has reached its limit, yet there is every prospect of the suburbs spreading rapidly. The Department is not in a position to cope with additional traffic, and therefore the duplication should be taken in hand without delay. The work, which will cost £80,000, will take three years to complete. The new Parnell Tunnel, which is already in hand, will simplify the problem of handling the Auckland suburban traffic, and every effort is being made to push forward with the tunnelling-work." [126]

The 'new' Parnell Tunnel, started in April 1914 and completed in March 1915, provided a double set of railway lines between the Auckland station to as far as Penrose. Running parallel to the original tunnel under the Parnell rise, the gradient of the lines running through the new tunnel was far less than the old, where heavily-loaded trains had often come to a stop. [127]

Ernest Hiley's Report continued to describe the Auckland region's more pressing railway system needs and the expenditure that would be required to satisfy them:

"The most serious question that has to be faced by the Department at the present moment, because of the expenditure involved, is the rebuilding of the stations and increasing the terminal accommodation in the principal towns in the Dominion—viz., Auckland, Wellington, and Christchurch. It is most unfortunate that the work at all the centres should have to be undertaken simultaneously, but the necessity for further accommodation is so urgent in each case that it is quite out of the question postponing the raising of the necessary loan any longer than is avoidable.

"Statistics have been compiled to arrive at the extent of the present accommodation, the amount of traffic now being handled, and the growth of business, and it is evident from these records that if the rate of increase of recent years be maintained at Auckland and Wellington the railway traffic offering in eight years' time will be double what it is now, whilst the rate of progress beyond that period may be expected to be at least at the same ratio. In both the towns mentioned and at Christchurch the accommodation for both passenger and goods traffic is even now below requirements at busy seasons, and therefore it is evident that no time should be lost in undertaking the new works, having regard to the fact that they cannot be completed in much less than five years from commencement of operations." [128]

When reporting the Auckland situation, Mr Hiley suggested that a number of problems could be solved with a repositioning of the Auckland station (along the lines suggested by the District Engineer, D T McIntosh) and his reasons certainly seemed to make sense – but only if his recommendations could be carried out in their entirety:

"The accommodation at the existing station is already overtaxed, the business only being carried out at much inconvenience to the public and at excessive cost to the Department. Sufficient accommodation for the future cannot be provided on the present site, owing to its cramped position, being bounded on either side by Customs and Quay Streets, by the post-office at the west end, and by Breakwater Road at the east end. The platforms are too short, and to lengthen them would entail the closing of Breakwater Road, an undesirable proceeding.

"In order to obtain sufficient space for a passenger-station capable of dealing with the Auckland traffic of the future and yet maintain a connection with the existing line to Kaipara and Penrose via Newmarket, a site on Beach Road opposite Eden Street has been selected, the suburban station, with connections to Newmarket, being elevated about 15ft. above and to the south of the main-line station.

"The intention in designing the new station is that the traffic north via the Kaipara line and the suburban traffic to Onehunga and south via Remuera will be dealt with at the High Level station (Upper Queen Street), south main-line traffic being handled at the Low Level station (Beach Road) and travelling on the proposed new line via Hobson and Orakei Bays and joining the present Main Trunk Railway at Westfield.

"The large area of land which the Department has been in process of acquiring by reclamation in Mechanic's Bay since 1911 as a site for the new station and yard all lies east of the Parnell junction with the present Main Trunk Railway, and in view of the situation it would be impossible to utilize this land to proper advantage and to lay out a workable station and yard without an alternative to the present outlet for south-bound traffic. The route via Hobson Bay is an admirable solution of the problem; by this means full advantage is made of the reclaimed ground, and the railway can be laid down with a maximum grade of 1 in 132 to Westfield, as against 1 in 43 via Newmarket, the difference in grade giving an increased engine-load of 150 per cent.

"The new railway will open out an entirely new suburban area for Auckland, bringing Orakei, Panmure, and the desirable country in this neighbourhood within a few minutes by train of the business centre of the city. A glance at the map accompanying this report ……. will show that when the new railway to Westfield is completed and the present main line duplicated it will be possible to run an inner suburban circle service from the Auckland High Level Station via Orakei, Panmure, Westfield, Remuera, back to Auckland. The cost of the new station and marshalling-yard will be £450,000, and the cost of the new railway via Hobson Bay £375,000. Both will take about five years to complete.

"Ultimately a credit of £220,000 can be placed against this expenditure, being the value of the land between the post-office and Breakwater Road, at present occupied by the passenger-station. At some future period when the traffic north of Auckland increases sufficiently to justify the expense it will be desirable to extend the Main Trunk line straight through Auckland Station, carrying the line westward over Queen Street and through the suburb of Ponsonby, and joining the present railway to Kaipara at either New Lynn or Kumeu.

"A railway on this route would enable traffic from the north to be brought into Auckland over easier grades and by a shorter route than the present line via New Lynn and Newmarket, and will open out a suburban area not now served by a station. The site selected for the new station renders this extension possible.

"The development of the suburban business on the Kaipara Branch, together with the increasing traffic from the district north of Auckland, renders necessary the duplication of the railway from Newmarket to New Lynn, together with a direct junction at Newmarket for trains running between Auckland and the stations on the Kaipara Branch. The severe gradients on this branch (1 in 40) tend to slow down the running, and emphasize the difficulty of working heavy traffic on a single track. The opportunity will be taken whilst duplicating the line to dispense with a number of level crossings and somewhat improve the grades. The work will cost £200,000, and will take five years to complete.

"The improvements to the working railways referred to in this report entail a total estimated expenditure of £3,250,000, spread over a period of five years…The amount asked for appears large, but nothing has been included without the most careful consideration and investigation, and I am convinced it is absolutely necessary if the transport business of the Dominion is to be conducted in a satisfactory manner." [129]

Early comments about Mr Hiley's report were varied. An editorial published in The New Zealand Herald and Daily Southern Cross of 4 September 1914 expressed particular enthusiasm for Mr Hiley's proposals despite the advent of war and associated financial difficulties:

"Even amid war and rumours of war, the public business of the Dominion claims attention, although it is necessarily affected by the financial and industrial disturbances incidental to international hostilities. Under ordinary circumstances the report by the general manager upon the railways of the Dominion and his recommendation of improvements designed to place them upon a sound basis would attract extraordinary interest.

"Mr Hiley's report is deserving of special consideration for its purpose is to improve transit and transport facilities and thus to foster the progress of the community and the development of our resources. The Mayor of

Auckland and the chairman of the Auckland Harbour Board were fully consulted by responsible railway officers in the drafting of the proposed scheme of local improvement, with the result that this district has every reason to be satisfied with the plans yesterday submitted to Parliament.

"It is unfortunate that financial considerations may now interfere with the prompt commencement of urgent public work, but on this point much is to be said...we take it for granted that both Government and Opposition will be sympathetic with schemes which promise to remove multitudinous difficulties and widespread dissatisfaction. Among Mr Hiley's wise suggestions is one for the appointment of a commercial agent who would keep the Railways Department in touch with the needs of the community. This should prove wholly satisfactory for it would help to place the public service upon a businesslike footing.

"The proposed outlet by Hobson Bay and the proposed duplication to New Lynn have an important bearing upon the suburban problem, always acute in growing Auckland in spite of the great facilities offered by the tramway system. Mr Hiley has evidently a very keen sense of the value of the suburban passenger business and points out that the Hobson Bay line would enable a railway 'circle' to be established with Westfield as its outer radius and would bring the Orakei and Panmure lands into the city's residential area." [130]

But despite his enthusiasm, the writer of the Herald editorial felt compelled to remind readers of past realities insofar as actual progress was concerned:

"In this proposal is improvement indeed. We cannot be amazed at its extent, however, for the experience of the City, the Province and the North Island in the past is that our railway facilities are never by any chance equal to the public demand. Every belated improvement which has been made has failed to keep ahead of urgent requirements and the result is a perpetual congestion and chronic dissatisfaction." [131]

Little did the Herald writer know that his opinion of the insubstantial progress of railway facilities up to 1914 would be just as relevant more than a century later. In fact, his description of 'perpetual congestion and chronic dissatisfaction' could apply to the whole of Auckland's twenty-first century, transport network. In the meantime, despite the Prime Minister William Massey's description of the Hiley Report as "...the most important Railways Statement ever submitted to Parliament", the procrastination of those holding the purse strings continued.

Following the September 1914 tabling of the report, other parliamentarians such as the Liberal, Arthur Myers, (who donated the land now known as Myers Park off Upper Queen Street) agreed that the Hiley

Report was of some significance and expressed the view that "...he was heartily in accord with the recommendation made by Mr Hiley, who had justified his appointment by the comprehensive grasp that he had of the various matters dealt with in his report."

However, "At the same time he could not but say that the bringing in of a Bill at the present juncture providing for such a large expenditure could only be done for political purposes...The proper thing to have done at present was to have made provision for only such urgent works as duplications, grade easements, level crossing improvements, better workshops, and bridge strengthening." [132]

While the economic uncertainties concerning New Zealand's contribution to the Great War no doubt posed an enormous burden, this was otherwise to be just another of the many instances where the advice of an expert with much overseas experience, obtained at substantial cost, was ignored by the New Zealand legislators for no better reason than the expense that the proposals would incur.

But the Free Lance, one of New Zealand's most popular weekly pictorial newspapers, first published in Wellington in 1900, suggested that Parliament's reaction to the Hiley report had more to do with political positioning than economic constraints:

"Mr E H Hiley's long-expected report on our railway system has at length been presented to Parliament. It is a very comprehensive document and at all points very interesting. Mr Hiley's recommendations are open to discussion, but it is made plain that he is a railwayman of high capacity and independence. Thus, he makes no bones about criticising some of the evil effects of political control. 'At the present time,' he says, 'a new line is undertaken without any consultation with the Railway Department.' Put bluntly like that, the thing seems incredible, and it only serves to show how far the stupidity of political control will go.

"In common-sense and fairness, the skilled heads of the Railway Department should be consulted before any statement of railway policy is made. No manager can be expected to control a system to the best effect, if his plans and actions – the whole laboriously systemised working of his department – are liable at any moment to be hampered or upset by Ministerial interference due wholly and solely to political influence and schemes. The proposal to import twenty costly American locomotives needs explanation. If engines as good for the purpose can be got within the Empire, we should not go to America for them." [133]

The Opposition was also somewhat critical of Mr Hiley's plans to import railway engines from America and this concern was echoed by many with a view to preserving the country's ties to the Empire –

particularly at a time of world conflict when patriotism to the mother country was essential:

"Objection was raised particularly to the recommendation that sufficient locomotives should be imported to supply the immediate needs of the railway system. The proposals for expenditure upon railway stations and yards were also criticised.

"A reply to some of these objections was made by the Prime Minister. He explained that it was unlikely that the Government would be able to carry out any of the proposals during the present financial year, but the report would provide a programme for years to come. No part of the proposed loan would be raised this year." [134]

But, for some concerned Aucklanders, the availability of finance was the least worrisome aspect of Mr Hiley's proposals. More importantly, for the forerunners of the present Green movement, was the route that a planned outlet to the east of the City from a new station at Beach Road would take. There was also the effect that any construction of marshalling yards and sheds would have on the pristine, Waitemata waterfront.

By March 1915, the Auckland Star was keen to advise its readers of the consequences of the planned eastern railway outlet which had, by then, been approved by Parliament but "The people of Auckland, who are chiefly concerned, seem to know little or nothing about the matter; at all events, they have never been consulted." [135]

The rail outlet to the east was described by the Auckland Star of 12 March 1915 as a:

"...railway running along the Waitemata eastward from King's Wharf, cutting through Campbell's Point and across Judge's Bay to Point Resolution and thence across Hobson Bay, giving an outlet to our traffic on that side of the city. The effect of this scheme will be to block off the whole of the waterfront on this side from the city, to destroy Campbell's Point, admittedly the most attractive feature of the picturesque Waitemata landscape; and to fill in Judge's Bay, thus depriving the city of one of its best yacht harbours and most beautiful beaches, and at the same time defeating the chief object for which Gillies Park was purchased. It seems to us that such wholesale destruction of scenic beauty would need very urgent reasons to justify it; but so far we have been unable to discover them.

"As to the plea that Campbell's Point and the coastline generally ought to be sacrificed to the Harbour Board's plan of running a broad picturesque esplanade along the harbour point, that is entirely misleading. But the strangest feature of the whole business is, it seems to us, that Mr Hiley's railway can be carried out of the city by a different route quite easily and economically without injuring the harbour foreshore anywhere.

"The plans we publish today show that the line could be carried through from St George's Bay to Hobson Bay by means of a tunnel only 30 chains long, and we have reason to believe that neither the engineering difficulties nor the expense of this construction would be formidable. In this way Campbell's Point and Judge's Bay would be left intact; one of the most beautiful portions of our lovely harbour foreshore would survive to give delight to future generations; and Gillies Park would remain what it was meant to be, an approach to the most perfect and best-protected of all our harbour beaches." [136]

The Star's sketch maps did indeed illustrate what it deemed to be a "perfectly feasible" alternative to "...the wanton and needless spoliation of our city and its surroundings which Mr Hiley now contemplates." [137]

With a succession of headlines and sub-headings, "Hand Of The Spoiler Already At Work", "Destruction of Campbell's Point", "Point Resolution To Go Next", "Judge's Bay To Disappear" and "A Prominent Engineer's Prediction", the Auckland Star did its best to alert the Auckland public to the fact that:

"Hundreds of tons of earth have come down at Campbell's Point, leaving an ugly gaping wound. It is the first result of the hand of the spoiler. Earth. Millions of tons of it, is wanted for a waterfront railway, and the harbour's beauty spots are being demolished, ostensibly to make way for the iron rails, but in reality to provide spoil for the embankments and reclamations which will efface bays and beauty spots." [138]

In its editorial of 15 March 1915, the Auckland Star tried to rally public interest against "...breaking down the foreshore and tumbling it into the harbour...We hope that the citizens of Auckland will take vigorous steps to urge their opinions on this subject upon the attention of the Government, and to make it plain that they will leave no expedient untried to protect our city's splendid heritage of natural beauty from the hand of the spoiler." [139]

And the Star's tunnel solution was sanctioned by many, including "...Mr H H Metcalfe, one of Auckland's best known civil engineers" who was quoted by the paper to declare: "It is not too late for the people to stop this wilful destruction of the waterfront. The damage done to Campbell's Point, though bad enough, is not irreparable. The city authorities have been completely gulled. The Mayor was told that Judge's Bay would not be spoiled – that it would still be possible to use it as a boat haven, and for ordinary beach purposes." [140]

Another who approved of the tunnel alternative was the Mayor of Newmarket, Mr D Teed, who was described by the Auckland Star as

"...one of those most emphatic in the opinion that the public should refuse to allow the spoliation of these beauty spots to proceed."

Said Mr Teed, "The Railway Department is simply taking the nearest and easiest route, quite irrespective of what Auckland citizens may desire in regard to the preservation of the natural beauties of the harbour. It suits them to go round the waterfront, and so they calmly proceed to saw off as much of Campbell's Point as stands in the way, and no doubt the same will be done with Point Resolution, unless the public wakes up and cries 'hands off'. I think that the various local bodies should at once communicate with the Mayor of Auckland, on his return from Wellington, and ask that a conference be held. We should ask the Government to devise some other route, and refuse absolutely to allow the present scheme to proceed. I will certainly favour some such action." [141]

However, as it turned out, the citizens of Auckland had more to contend with than just the Government and it was all too late for protesting anyway. The Auckland City Council, the Railways Department (Government) and the powerful Auckland Harbour Board had already done a deal. And the reason for the Auckland Council's change of mind was, in the end, all about straight line stuff, as the Auckland Mayor explained in an interview published by the Auckland Star on 15 March 1915:

"This morning a 'Star' representative asked the Mayor (Mr C J Parr) to explain why the City Council, which a year ago violently opposed the waterfront railway proposition, had now approved of Mr Hiley's scheme.

"The history of the waterfront railway is quite clear," said the Mayor. "A year ago a proposal was made to the Council from Harbour Board quarters which meant cutting down the whole of Campbell's Point. No mention whatever was made of the railway, nor was any offer made of the valuable concessions in the way of a waterfront road, which I was afterwards able to obtain. Consequently, the City Council, at my suggestion, turned down the proposal of the Harbour Board.

"Six months later Mr Hiley, General Manager of the New Zealand Railways, came to me with a very different and much more important proposition. He indicated that the Government was prepared to spend £2,000,000 in providing an up-to-date railway station and equipping extensive goods yards and accommodation on the reclamation, and for a railway running round the waterfront through Orakei, and out at Westfield.

"It will be admitted that the City Council was bound to give such a great scheme, meaning so much for Auckland, its careful consideration. I went very fully into the question of whether there was another way out. Every possible route was inquired into, including that now proposed by Mr

Metcalfe. In fact, I insisted that the question of a tunnel should be very carefully considered. And it was. The result was that it was believed to be quite impracticable. One of the fatal objections was that the tunnel scheme would make it impossible to provide accommodation for handling the passenger traffic, to say nothing of the goods traffic.

"I say, advisedly, that Mr Metcalfe's scheme is quite useless. It would tap only about half the reclaimed area that the Government considers necessary for goods and passenger traffic. It would mean moreover, if Mr Metcalfe's scheme were adopted, that no adequate goods station or yards could be provided in Auckland, and the eastern end of the reclaimed land would be quite useless. The only means of providing adequate accommodation for the growing Auckland business is the plan adopted, which utilises the whole of the reclaimed area, and provides for the inevitable development of the city and province. So much for the tunnel alternative, which I have shown to be quite impossible. The City Council considered the interests of the 120,000 people of the city of Auckland, and the other 120,000 people of the province, whose material prosperity depends so largely on adequate railway facilities.

"Most people are quite unacquainted with the phenomenal growth of the Auckland traffic. In six years it has doubled itself, and in less than two years, unless some remedy of a comprehensive nature can be found, it will be almost impossible to carry on the work. When I found that a railway scheme was inevitable I stood for concessions, and I got them. The department has agreed to widen Beach Road and Breakwater Road, to build an esplanade right along the waterfront, to provide a passenger bridge from Parnell Park, to the new road, thus bringing that end of Parnell within ten minutes of the city. I am satisfied, after months of negotiations and investigation, that the only way of adequately providing for Auckland's needs is contained in Mr Hiley's scheme." [142]

A week later, The New Zealand Herald of 22 March 1915 also confirmed its support for the waterfront railway outlet by publishing an interview with Mr Hiley himself. Under what it headlined as 'Opponents Criticised' and 'An Effective Reply', the Herald sought to provide:

"An effective reply to those who are seeking to create an eleventh hour agitation against the carrying out of the waterfront railway scheme…"

According to the Herald article, Mr Hiley regretted the effect of the eleventh hour agitation "…for the reason that any suggestion of lack of unanimity on the part of Auckland citizens in accepting the waterfront scheme might conceivably discourage the Government from allocating money for its initiation at a time when the funds available for urgent public works were strictly limited. Delay of this kind would be truly lamentable, said Mr Hiley, because Auckland was urgently in need of increased railway accommodation for immediate use.

"The insuperable objections to the adoption of the outlet advocated by Mr Metcalfe are, I think, obvious even to the man in the street, if the situation of this outlet is considered in relation to the land available in Auckland for railway purposes. It will be clearly seen from a reference to the diagram published with my report of August 1 last, as presented to Parliament...that the reclaimed land available in Mechanics' Bay is a long narrow strip, bounded on the west by Breakwater Road and on the east by Campbell's Point. Every inch of this land will be required...for passenger stations, car sidings, car washing facilities, goods shed, marshalling sidings, etc., within at least 15 years, at the present rate of progress of Auckland's business. After 15 years it will be necessary to find auxiliary accommodation for the purposes named outside Auckland.

"In the scheme advocated by the Department, the outlet for the line is at the extreme eastern end, and the whole area is readily accessible for railway purposes...On the other hand Mr Metcalfe's proposed outlet strikes the area on the south side near the centre, and at an awkward angle, and, in consequence, from 35 per cent to 50 per cent of the space would be lost for railway purposes owing to inaccessibility. I can see considerable objection and danger in submitting and leaving the fate of a highly-technical and elaborate scheme such as is being discussed for Auckland to the verdict of 10 gentlemen (Civil Engineer Metcalfe, Arthur Myers and other concerned Aucklanders objecting to the destruction of Campbell's Point) elected by acclamation at a meeting of self-interested or otherwise biased persons, said Mr Hiley, in conclusion." [143]

And that is just how The New Zealand Herald saw it with its editorial and just about the final word on the subject of 22 March 1915:

"The interview with Mr Hiley, General Manager of Railways, published in another column, should convince all reasonable citizens that nothing is to be gained by opposition to the waterfront railway scheme. Mr Hiley shows clearly that the space available for railway yards can only be fully, utilised if the outlet is at the eastern end. The tunnel scheme provides an outlet on the south which Mr Hiley, from expert knowledge, states would render 35 per cent to 50 per cent of the available space useless for railway purposes. This is a crushing condemnation of the alternative proposal which even the strongest opponent of a waterfront line will find it difficult to answer.

"The importance of pushing on the work to relieve railway congestion is also urged by Mr Hiley, who deplores the possibility of a lamentable delay which may result from the present agitation...the city engineer has given unhesitating support to the scheme, and it is well known that the whole proposal is also endorsed by the harbour engineer. The Chamber of Commerce has wisely condemned the present agitation as adverse, to the interests of Auckland.

"On the whole the opponents of the foreshore railway, if they are open to conviction, must by this time be conscious of the weakness of their case. One of the statements on which they have built their claim for an inquiry is that there has been a lack of publicity in connection with the negotiations. This is entirely erroneous. Mr Hiley's report was laid before Parliament in August last, and was fully debated in the House in September.

"In the beginning of this year the results of negotiations between the City Council and the Railway Department were published and on January 22 the whole scheme in its relation to city properties was publicly discussed by the City Council and unanimously approved. The fullest publicity has been given to every phase of the proposal. To state- that there has been any mystery or anything hidden from the public can only argue a lack of acquaintance with the facts." [144]

But while there seemed little doubt as to the best route for the eastern outlet from the proposed site for the new Auckland Railway Station and sidings, more than a year later, there were still some misgivings about the remoteness of it all. The Hiley report recommended the Beach Road position as the best place from which more direct routes with easier gradients could connect to stations to the south and, eventually, the north of the City. However, many believed that the distance between the new station and the city centre and its bus, tram and ferry services, would prove to be extremely detrimental to the City's suburban railway network.

In November 1916, Auckland City Councillor, Ernest Davis, put a notice of motion to the Council proposing:

"That a special committee of the council be set up to consider the proposal of the Railway Department to remove the Auckland railway station from the foot of Queen Street to the foot of Eden Street (Beach Road), and that such committee be empowered, if they so think fit, to call a conference of local bodies to co-operate with it in protesting against any such alterations as retrogressive and detrimental to the best interests of the city." [145]

According to The New Zealand Herald of 17 November 1916:

"In a note attached to his notice of motion, Mr Davis points out the advantage of the present central position of the station, and stated that if the new station were erected where proposed all the North Shore and other suburban railway passengers on arriving at the foot of Queen Street would be put to the expense and inconvenience of a second trip by tram or taxi to the station. The business houses and shops in Queen Street would suffer severely through the proposed change, as passengers catching trains will cease to buy goods freely on their way home if they were forced to travel laden with packages from the foot of Queen Street to the proposed site.

"The losses thus incurred would depreciate the taxable value of Queen Street, from which a large proportion of the city rates were drawn. These objections were so serious that if in the opinion of the Railway Department there was not sufficient accommodation for the metropolitan traffic where the station now stands, it would pay the people of the city and province to buy the whole surrounding block and enlarge the station, financing the cost of the resumption by striking a rate over the whole district. In any case, he considered a change of such importance should not be left to the discretion of any Government Department. The opinion of the local bodies, and more especially of the City Council, should be taken before the matter was finally settled." [146]

Unfortunately for Auckland's future suburban commuters, the motion to reconsider the repositioning of the city's railway station was not carried by the Council after it debated the issue on 30 November 1916.

"Those City Councillors present during the debate included the Mayor, Mr J. H. Gunson, Miss E. Melville, Messrs. A J Entrican, M Casey, H D Heather, W. Burton, G Baildon, E Davis, G Knight, G W Murray, F W Brinsden, S Moore-Jones, P J Nerheny, J Dempsey, R T Michaels, J A Warnock, E J Carr, P McElwain, H N Bagnall, A Hall-Skelton, and P M Mackay.

Those who spoke against the motion included:

"Mr H N Bagnall said that the proper time for raising this question would have been before the site facing Queen Street was taken for the purposes of the post office. For six years the Railway Department had been spending enormous sums in the preparations for putting the station at Eden Street. Now the council was asked to go behind the work of railway engineers who had studied every phase of the question, and had fixed upon one site as the most suitable. The council would stultify itself, and become the laughing-stock of the whole of New Zealand if it now attempted to interfere with the decision of the Government experts. The only business places likely to be affected by the removal of the railway station nearer Parnell was that of the hotelkeepers. The extra tram fare to the site chosen by the Government would be only a penny. That too, would be paid by the travelling public, and not saddled upon the whole community for all time.

"Mr H. D. Heather suggested that the time had gone by when the proposal could be considered. The purchase of the properties surrounding the present railway station would be an enormous undertaking at present values. It was exhaustively examined two years ago, and considered inadvisable. Mr A J Entrican moved as an amendment that the matter be referred to the Finance and Legal Committee. That committee had had the handling of the complicated arrangements already made between the City Council, the Harbour Board, and the Railway Department, and was familiar with the details of the position.

"The Mayor, Mr J H Gunson, considered it inadvisable to carry either motion or amendment. The matter of the station site had long ceased to be a 'proposal'. It was now an actual signed and sealed contract between the citizens of Auckland — as represented by the City Council and the Harbour Board — and the Railway Department. Under that contract the city had received what was considered in 1914 to be a quid pro quo for the change in the station site.

"There was then an exhaustive inquiry, as the result of which the removal of the passenger station to Eden Street was generally approved. The compensations conceded by the Department included 30ft of Beach Road, and also land for the widening of Breakwater Road to 100ft, and various other considerations, including the payment of £4000 to the Harbour Board, and certain alterations in the Department's scheme of works which are to the advantage of Auckland. "The Eden Street site was adopted after most mature consideration. By carrying the motion the council would stultify itself and repudiate a contract in respect of which it had already taken payment.

"Mr Davis said he was sure the majority of the people of Auckland were unaware of the facts just stated by the Mayor. He was prepared to withdraw his motion, but he must say he considered that a retrograde step had been taken in the adoption of the Eden Street site. Leave was given for the withdrawal of the motion." [147]

Of course, the matter didn't end there and couldn't be expected to until some of the railway proposals, suggested by Mr Hiley in 1914, were actually put in place. However, because of the economic uncertainties and resource shortages experienced during the First World War, very few of his recommendations were implemented despite an urgent need for many of them. And some cosmetic progress was made during the War years. For instance, the reshaping of Point Resolution and the reclamation of Mechanics Bay, the future site of the Auckland station and marshalling yards, continued.

Auckland's railway commuters also kept up the pressure for improvements to the existing railway network, making their needs known through public meetings organised by their various railway leagues. One of the most significant of these meetings was held at St Thomas' Hall, New Lynn on 3 July 1918 when a New Lynn branch of the Suburban Railway League was formed to promote an alternative to Mr Hiley's 1914 recommendations – referred to as the 'Town Hall deviation scheme', variations of which later became known as the 'Morningside deviation'.

At that meeting, Mr C F Gardner (a member of the Avondale Road Board and later the first Mayor of New Lynn) explained this new initiative which proposed the extension of the southern line to directly connect with the North Auckland line at Morningside by means of a tunnel from near the Auckland Town Hall at Upper Queen Street. [148]

This differed from Mr Hiley's plan to connect the two lines, "at some future period", by means of an extension of the main trunk line "…when the traffic work of Auckland increases sufficiently to justify the expense…straight through Auckland station (Beach Road) carrying the line westward over Queen Street and through the suburb of Ponsonby and joining the present railway to Kaipara at either New Lynn or Kumeu." [149]

The 1914 plan to connect the city centre with the northern districts by means of a railway line was by no means a unique idea. Indeed, such a scheme was proposed not long after a detachment of Royal Engineers was despatched to Auckland in 1860 "…upon a surveying expedition to this colony…not only to make an entire survey of the interior of New Zealand, but also to assist in the formation of necessary trunk roads, the erection of bridges, &c." [150]

In an article published on 4 September 1926, the Auckland Star recalled the earlier survey of a railway route undertaken by the Royal Engineers:

"In the early days when the Royal Engineers were stationed in Auckland they actually made a rough survey for a railway line north. The idea was to have the central station near where the Town Hall stands, tunnel under the hill to the old cemetery gully, run one line north and put a second tunnel south to Newmarket. Along the Arch Hill gully the land for the railway line of the future was stated to have been reserved.

"It is a case of history almost repeating itself and it actually does so far as part of the tunnelling scheme is concerned, but more particularly in regard to placing a central underground station in the vicinity of the Town Hall. For some considerable time the Northern Suburban Railway League has been advocating the construction of the line in question, and on many occasions that body has approached the Government and has pointed out the many advantages to be gained by the Railway Department. The league has left no stone unturned, and has petitioned Parliament with a view to having a start made without delay, so that the completion of the proposed scheme would synchronise with the completion of the new Auckland railway yards and station as well as the Westfield deviation." [151]

Indeed, subsequent meetings promoting the Town Hall deviation scheme continued to be held throughout the district and the promotion attracted so much public support that the Railways Department agreed to undertake a survey of the proposed route. While that would have been an exciting first step for the Suburban Railway League, little did they know that many variations of their scheme would be explored and reported on for nearly a century – and still the connection would not be realised.

On 6 June 1919, sometime after that first Government undertaking to survey the Morningside route, The New Zealand Herald reported on what was to be an account of the beginning of all that procrastination to follow:

"A survey of the proposed new railway route between Morningside and the city was promised some time ago by the Railway Department at the request of the originators of the scheme. Mr C. F. Gardner, a member of the Avondale Road Board, reported at the last meeting of that body that he had waited upon the Minister for Railways, the Hon. W H Herries, during the latter's present visit to Auckland, and urged that the survey be undertaken. The Minister explained that the scarcity of suitable labour had hitherto prevented the work being commenced. He assured Mr Gardner, however, that it would be put in hand almost immediately." [152]

In a letter to the Editor of the Auckland Star, published 20 June 1919, C F Gardner, then the President of the North Suburban Railway League, New Lynn, apparently had every faith in the Minister of Railways to eventually honour his commitment:

"...please permit me space to say that the work of organising the Suburban Railway League is going steadily on, and its views and desires are, from time to time, as opportunity offers, being placed before local organisations with a view to securing additional support. This is all that for the time can be done, as on his last visit to Auckland the Hon. Minister for Railways undertook that the long-promised survey, Town Hall to Morningside, would be made immediately. It is interesting to note that even during the war period and with a greatly curtailed service, the suburban traffic on the north line has greatly increased, and this increase will for the future doubtlessly be greatly accelerated." [153]

However, by June 1921, the Hon. W H Herries had been replaced as Minister of Railways by the premier, William Massey and there had still been no decision, let alone any progress, made on the Town Hall to Morningside deviation. With William Massey overseas, the Northern Suburban Railway League found itself talking to the Minister for Education and Public Health about its concerns.

The League's approach was twofold:

"A deputation from the Northern Suburban Railway League, headed by Mr [H] A Robertson, was received yesterday by the Hon. C J Parr, Minister for Education and Public Health. The deputation asked for an opportunity to place before the General Manager of Railways, Mr R W McVilly, proposals for the modification of the Hiley scheme for shortening the northern route. The Hiley scheme is to shorten the route by a new line from Kumeu, along the foreshore of the Waitemata and through Ponsonby and Freeman's Bay.

"The Minister said he would refer the matter to Mr McVilly, who, no doubt, would be pleased to hear anything of practical value that they might lay before him." (Mr Hiley retired as Railways General Manager in favour of his loyal deputy, R W McVilly, on 15 February 1919.)

"The deputation also discussed the Town Hall to Morningside tunnel project. Mr Parr said it was of course quite out of practical politics at the present time to expect any government to find a large sum of money — estimated by the departmental officers as at least £500,000 — for this work. The deputation replied that it was recognised that Parliament could not be expected to provide a vote for this work in the present financial condition of the country, but it was felt they would be able to suggest to Mr McVilly certain improvements to the present service. Mr Parr promised to do everything he could to assist them in this matter." [154]

After some seven years of increasing inefficiency and inaction suffered by Auckland's railway commuters since the Hiley report, the understanding shown by the Northern Suburban Railway League at this meeting would seem to have been somewhat lame. However, the country had slipped into another of its recessions by this time. The supporters of Massey's Reform Party "...became more insistent that taxes should be lowered, government spending cut, public servants dismissed and wage demands rejected." [155]

Under the circumstances, it would seem that the League could do little more than remind the Government of its members' needs as often as it could. In the meantime, the overall transport needs of Auckland were not lost on the city's engineer, Mr W E Bush, who spoke of 'The future development of Auckland City and Suburbs' at a Rotary Club luncheon on 18 July 1921. His speech was published by the Auckland Star and parts then relevant to Auckland's transport situation included:

"To estimate the growth of the future...it is necessary to survey the past. In 1906, when I arrived here to take up the duties of city engineer, the population of Auckland City was 38,000, and its area 1,762 acres; today the population of the city is 81,718 and its area 8,311 acres, while the population of the metropolitan area south of the harbour has increased from 74,000 to 137,672, and of the metropolitan area from 82,000 to 157,750.

"Looking forward it will be realised that if the same rate of increase, is maintained, the population of the metropolitan area will, in 15 years' time, be not less than 250,000, and in 60 years' time 750,000. In other words the Auckland of 60 years hence must be visualised as that of the Sydney of to-day, with this difference that Auckland to-day is in some respects more advanced municipally than Sydney to-day, and in all respects is far ahead of the Sydney of 60 years ago. The first point that claims attention is the harbour and the facilities it offers…the provision for ferries will inevitably require large expansion, and the exact location of this must be considered in relation to tramway and road facilities…The second point for consideration is the passenger and freight railway facilities, and it presents the most difficult and pressing problem of any.

"In the scheme outlined in Mr Hiley's report of 1914, a solution is offered for the traffic problem south of Auckland and for dealing with the area east of Queen's wharf, by the location of the passenger and freight stations between Beach Road and the King's Drive, as the eastern extension of Quay Street is now called. But the almost certain necessity of utilising some portions of Hobson Bay as a marshalling yard and possibly for the discharge of goods, suggests the desirability of an easy grade road on the south side of the proposed railway tracks between the eastern breakwater and Hobson Bay, involving the sacrifice at some future date of the Parnell baths and a portion of Point Resolution, so that access by road can be obtained on either side of the railway.

"The problem of railway provision to the North has not yet been solved and is extremely complicated and is bound up with the linking up of the railway with the wharves, west of Queen's wharf, and the idea of railway tracks right along the waterfront similar to those now in Quay Street East is not an agreeable one, and yet it is hard to see how it is to be avoided if such linking up of railway and wharves is to be effected. There are possible alternative routes to the north, and it is clear, however, that a better solution must be found than that now existing.

"Coupled with the question of main railway facilities is the very important one of suburban traffic, which must be catered for on far more generous lines than those existing to-day, for no large city can depend upon tramways and motor vehicles for the transport of its industrial and commercial population between their work and their homes. This brings us, naturally, to the third point, that of the tramway facilities and this is not merely one of extension, a comparatively simple matter, but most vitally one of city terminals and loading and discharging points.

"We are all familiar with the 5 o'clock scramble for cars, and although much may be done by better regulation of the traffic and of the public using the cars, the provision of better terminal facilities in the city must be provided. The exact location of these facilities depends, to some extent, on the future position of city ferry terminals, for it is obvious that a large population will be housed on the northern suburbs and those eastern and western suburbs close to the waterfront, but who will be either occupied during the day in the city or travel there for the purpose of doing business and shopping or engaging in study, recreation or pleasure. It is here that the example of Sydney and San Francisco should prove helpful in suggesting means of overcoming the very real difficulties that exist now and will be much increased with the growth of the city.

"The speaker touched also upon the value of the motor bus as a transit auxiliary to the other services, instancing the success of these vehicles in London, Paris and New York. Its flexibility of movement was referred to as one of its most attractive features, but importance was laid on the necessity of such vehicles being under one control, and allowed to run only on routes where first-class roads could be provided. Another matter which would require careful consideration, said Mr Bush, was accommodation for the parking of motor cars, and stands for taxis and light parcel vans and motors, while the possibilities of air transport raised the question of the location of aerodromes and landing stations for aircraft." [156]

The Rotary Club audience no doubt appreciated Mr Bush's vision of what was to be and what would be required to create a modern transport system to meet the future needs of Auckland; and no doubt some of that audience were decision makers or at least members of the City's 'limited circle' who could influence decision makers if they chose to.

Unfortunately, they did not, or were not successful if they tried. So, by August 1922, it was left to the likes of the Northern Suburban Railway League to continue pressing for a survey of a rail connection, any connection, from the city to the Northern line.

At a meeting held at Kumeu on 8 August 1922, the vice-president of the League, Mr H A Robertson, illustrated the growing numbers travelling on the line by comparing the number of season tickets sold at Avondale in 1912 (14,554) with those issued during 1921 (39,635).

Those season tickets sold further along the line, at Henderson in 1912 (7851), were also compared with those issued in 1921 (10,577). Mr Robertson estimated that, in a year, a daily passenger travelling between the Northern line to and from the city, spent an unnecessary 300 hours travelling 900 miles by detouring through Newmarket during each journey. It was the League's view that unnecessary travelling time was also expended because the line west from Newmarket also "...contained very many difficult grades." [157]

At the time, the Northern Suburban Railway League was advocating a Morningside scheme that included:

"...an Auckland central station at Marmion Street, in the Wakefield Gully. A double line would connect direct with Morningside. From the Auckland main station the line would come along Stanley Street, somewhere underneath St Paul's Church, to the central station. The line would then go under Karangahape Road, coming out at the head of the Newton Gully, where a station would be erected. This would give Karangahape Road and Symonds Street an impetus which they would never otherwise secure. The line would then go along the Newton Gully to Morningside. There was no way of getting out at Auckland except by bridges or tunnels. The grade to Morningside would be 1 in 100 instead of 1 in 43, as it was at one place on the present line. Two miles would be saved if the duplicate line were constructed.

"From Morningside it was proposed a line should go, with a grade of no more than 1 in 100, and with a very slight curve, across the Whau River to Kumeu. This would be 14½ miles from Kumeu to the Auckland central station, instead of 25 miles as at present. Kumeu would then be a junction for the main northern line. Between the present and the proposed line all the land, which included Government blocks, would be thickly populated in a very short time. They were not asking the Government to commit itself, concluded Mr Robertson. What they wanted was the fulfilment of the 1918 promise that a survey of the proposed route be made to verify the estimated grade." [158]

"Mr J Lambden (Chairman) said the district was positively languishing because of the poor railway service. While Kumeu was over the maximum distance from Auckland (20 miles), it was contended that the mileage should count from the Mount Eden station, which was the real city station as far as passengers from the North were concerned. The meeting decided to approach the Minister for Railways on the matter. It was also resolved that efforts be made to secure a Sunday train from Helensville to Auckland. If this train ran, Kumeu settlers could make contracts and supply whole milk to the City of Auckland." [159]

Meanwhile, back at the station…in 1922, the Auckland City terminus is still that, squeezed in behind the new Post Office and, apart from some cosmetic changes and add-ons, it is the same as that described in the Hiley report of 1914:

"The accommodation at the existing station is already overtaxed, the business only being carried out at much inconvenience to the public and at excessive cost to the Department. Sufficient accommodation for the future cannot be provided on the present site, owing to its cramped position, being bounded on either side by Customs and Quay Streets, by the post-office at the west end, and by Breakwater Road at the east end. The platforms are too short, and to lengthen them would entail the closing of Breakwater Road, an undesirable proceeding." [160]

By way of its editorial of 22 December 1922, The New Zealand Herald bluntly expressed its frustration at the state of the Auckland station:

"The state of affairs at the Auckland railway station during these days of early holiday traffic has become a positive scandal. All that has been said by way of criticism of the present management of our Dominion's railway system is more than justified by the happenings at this important station at the present moment. It is difficult to describe the conditions now obtaining at the Auckland station; it is quite impossible to exaggerate the vexatious discomfort to which intending travellers are subjected. It is no matter for surprise that some are deterred from embarking on a railway journey from that point of departure.

"It might reasonably be expected that the simple matter of buying a ticket or booking a reserved seat would be easily accomplished by anyone sufficiently able-bodied to go on a journey in a New Zealand train. Instead, these things involve a severe physical strain and are consequently provocative of considerable vexation. The main facts are dealt with elsewhere in this issue. Knowledge of them must fill Aucklanders with a sense of abject indignity, although the disgrace is not theirs. The arrangements for ticket-selling are so terribly inadequate that sometimes more than sixty people are kept in a queue for a long period before they can be attended to, and the conditions under which reserved seats may be booked are hopelessly primitive.

"The public of this city is strangely long-suffering if its patience, already sorely tried by railway inconveniences, does not break down utterly under the strain of this holiday muddle. That public has rights in the matter. The railways, owned by the people of the country, are supposed to be run for their use, not their annoyance.

"It is not Auckland alone that is enduring this horror. The muddle at its central city station is more or less typical of an inefficiency throughout the Dominion. The fault lies with the Minister for Railways and the General Manager (Mr R W McVilly). There was — it has been previously acknowledged — a measure of improvement under Mr McVilly's management during days when the country's financial stress checked the volume of traffic. Useful economies, at least, were effected in running costs. But this does not exonerate him from responsibility for the present fiasco. He has lamentably failed to take advantage of improving conditions. It was his business to anticipate a recovery in the general volume of traffic, and especially to anticipate this holiday demand, and that business has been palpably neglected.

"Nor can the Minister escape responsibility. If Mr McVilly complains of political interference with his plans, both he and the Minister are at fault—he for not resisting the politicians, and the Minister for not supporting his executive officer. If the Minister complains of managerial incompetence, then both he and the General Manager are at fault — he for not insisting on the vigorous prosecution of managerial duty and the General Manager for neglect or incapacity, or both. The Minister and Mr McVilly may be left to settle between them the nice point as to the exact division of their responsibility.

"What the public is concerned about is the urgent desirability of having the present arrangement ended or mended. Auckland has specific grievances. Its railway terminal facilities, to say nothing now of suburban requirements, are shockingly bad. The present station accommodation is woefully insufficient and effete. It would be a disgrace to a city a third of the size of Auckland. A new station is an immediate necessity. A booking office should long ago have been opened in some central position in the business part of the city. Had the Board of Management appointed by the Government done its duty, such a booking centre would have been opened up within forty-eight hours of its recent official visit. The Board did nothing — in complete harmony with the tradition steadily becoming associated with New Zealand railway management.

"The only way to cope with the situation that has arisen is to dispense with political control and appoint an independent manager for a definite term of years. In the light of our own bitter experience and the approval of this method elsewhere, it is the only safe refuge from a condition of things of which the Auckland station chaos is the nearest appalling example." [161]

Christmas holiday travellers obviously added to the overcrowding and emphasised the inefficiency of Auckland's suburban services:

"The disorganisation of suburban railway traffic as a result of the holiday congestion at the Auckland railway station on Friday and Saturday (22 and 23 December 1922) was the subject of bitter complaint from exasperated travellers on both days. On Friday evening, as might have been expected, there were enormous crowds to be conveyed home, and when the 9.45 p.m. Papakura train arrived at Newmarket, 20 minutes late, those waiting were compelled to crowd on to an already hopelessly overcrowded train.

"So great was the crush on some of the platforms, that the safety gates actually could not be closed, men standing on the steps and clinging to the upright stanchion for support. On one platform no less than 20 passengers were jammed into one heated, uncomfortable pack, and the feelings of the Newmarket passengers were in no way soothed by the fact that a few moments previously, they had seen the Henderson train pass through with two empty carriages, and vacant seats in all parts of the train. On Saturday morning, suburban travellers were held up for an hour by the late departure of the south-bound expresses, and so great was the congestion at Auckland station at times that in order to make headway, scores of people left the platform and walked along the railway tracks." [162]

As some measure of progress, one cannot help but compare that New Zealand Herald report of December 1922 with another, published by the same newspaper on 10 September 2011, when New Zealand hosted the Rugby World Cup:

"Nelson man Robert Paul said he had been in a train carriage at Britomart for 40 minutes waiting for it to leave for Eden Park. He had arrived in good time to get to the All Blacks v Tonga game and was upset he would not make it in time. He said some frustrated passengers got out of the train and began walking up the tracks towards Eden Park. Thousands of commuters had their night disrupted by trains, buses and ferries that were unable to cope with the number of people wanting to join in the festivities...Last night, huge crowds also built up at Britomart station in the central city as people waited for hours to catch a train home." [163]

Apart from a larger population, little would seem to have changed during the intervening 89 years except that, by 2011, Auckland had twice relocated its main railway station. By 1923, that first relocation from lower Queen Street to the Beach Road site recommended in the Hiley report was becoming ever more necessary. That's not to say that, thanks to some clever organisation, the Queen Street station wasn't able to handle record numbers of passengers at peak times when it had to. But Easter 1923 was obviously a challenge, as described by The New Zealand Herald:

"The traffic at Auckland railway station last evening was exceptionally heavy, over 1100 passengers leaving by the two Main Trunk expresses, while the inward and outward suburban trains were also very large ones. The first express, which got away promptly to time, consisted of eight cars and one sleeper, and carried 350 passengers.

"As soon as the train left, the gates were opened for the second express, and for the next half-hour the scene on the platform was one of great activity. It was soon evident that the train would be a very heavy one, and eight carriages, which were standing in readiness, were coupled up, making a total of 18 cars and two sleepers. The word soon flashed down the platform, 'Plenty of room in front' and the crowd surged toward the empty carriages, with the result that when the train left, about a quarter of an hour late, it carried 750 comfortably-seated passengers.

"The traffic this Easter, both incoming and outgoing, has been unusually heavy, and the returns will probably constitute a record. Special preparation was made by the railway staff to cope with very heavy traffic, and the officials state that the arrangements have worked so smoothly that no complaints have been received at headquarters. The arrangements for dealing with the suburban traffic have worked admirably, and no overcrowding, such as occurred at Christmas-time, has marred the holiday coming-and-going of suburban residents." [164]

Nevertheless, the Northern Suburban Railway League continued to lobby for improvements and, as reported by The New Zealand Herald on 26 May 1923, put certain proposals to Prime Minister William Massey during his visit to Auckland. Those proposals included:

"To have the suburban railway radius extended to Kumeu. This did not mean that they were asking for more trains, but that workers out to that point should get the benefit of suburban fares. They also asked that workers' tickets should be available to those who arrived in the city shortly before 9 a.m. as the present restriction to 8 a.m. worked harshly against many office girls who had not now the benefit of the cheaper rate. The extension of the 12-trip concession tickets to 14 days instead of six, to enable wives to take full advantage of the concession, was also desired.

"The complaint was made that on race days ordinary trains were often side-tracked to enable race trains to proceed, thus delaying workers who had already spent a long time away from their homes. It was suggested that an hourly - service of small trains from Mount Eden to Henderson could profitably be instituted. It was further asked that the department submit suggestions for any serious alterations in the time-table to the league. Mr Massey: And make you responsible? I like the idea.

"Mr Robertson (of the League) further asked that children under 16 years should be allowed to travel at half fares, the age limit at present being 12. He said this would result in a larger number of families settling in the suburbs and would benefit the service. Mr Massey said the whole service was now under consideration, and certain changes were pending in the railway department which would make a considerable difference in favour of the district. He added that Auckland was growing so rapidly that it was difficult to keep up with the requirements of the city and suburbs, but the work had to be tackled, and he thought it could be carried out. He welcomed the formation and attitude of the league and said he thought it would prove useful." [165]

Again, The New Zealand Herald supported the requests of the Northern Suburban Railway League and reported, "The justice of their complaints was frankly admitted by Mr Massey, with a promise of changes of benefit to the district." [166]

The Herald editorial, entitled 'Behind The Times', then weighed in with its opinion of what needed to be done:

"Those changes must be drastic and far-reaching to effect any substantial improvement, for the department has for so long been out of step with the progress of the country that it will not easily bring its services up to the modern standard of efficiency and present-day needs. Its deficiencies are largely due to wrong outlook.

"As an excuse for its failure to provide for the suburban development of Auckland, it has given Mr Massey the explanation that Auckland has grown rapidly. That is not a defence but a condemnation of its policy and its methods. Private enterprise finds in the growth of Auckland a source of continual encouragement to wider efforts and greater expansion. It fosters that growth by providing this year for next year's larger population, and has its reward in public satisfaction and comfortable profits.

"In railway management, no class of business is more easily developed than suburban passenger traffic, more reliable when once established, more easily carried since its volume is free from fluctuations, nor more profitable. Yet the Railway Department is aggrieved at the growth of Auckland's suburbs, and so neglects the opportunity to increase its profits that tramways run in competition within a stone's throw of its lines.

"Public necessity demands the awakening of the department from this condition of apathy, even hostility. The department must realise that the Auckland railway station is both a disgrace to the system and a handicap on its operations. It must reorganise the suburban services to meet immediate needs and to encourage further expansion in the suburbs. It must revise the provincial time-table in the light of the conditions created in the rapid growth of population. Such reforms as these should actually be the foundation of railway policy. If Mr Massey's statement means that they are seriously intended, its importance cannot be exaggerated." [167]

Seriously intended or not, by June 1923, there was a new Minister for Railways, Joseph Gordon Coates, who, according to The New Zealand Herald, was then "…engaged in the onerous task of inspecting lines and facilities throughout the Dominion, so that a programme of urgently-needed improvements may be devised. The undertaking is exacting not because he will have any difficulty in finding work for his hands to do, but because the list of improvements calling imperatively to be effected is so great." [168]

But what the Herald didn't mention was that by the time Joseph Coates was first made Minister of Public Works in March 1920, the economic boom which had greatly inflated public expectations at the end of the war were collapsing fast as export prices dropped.

"The challenge for Coates was to produce results at a time when money was in short supply. This he did by diverting money from a myriad of branch railway lines, concentrating instead on completing the three main trunk lines: the Midland, East Coast and North Auckland lines." [169]

That meant that just as with the 1914 review, at the end of another study in 1923, there was again little money to meet the needs of Auckland. This is despite the Hiley report having 'categorically condemned the Auckland railway station, platforms and yards' some nine years previously. The (Hiley) report stated that the accommodation was overtaxed. Business was being carried out at much inconvenience to the public, and at excessive cost to the department. When, therefore, improvements are being listed in order of urgency, it is obvious that the Auckland station and the question of the railway outlet from the city must take a foremost place.

Not only did the Hiley report condemn the Auckland station and its appointments, it declared the impossibility of real amelioration with the present site retained. The position cramped and constricted, Quay Street and Customs Street bounding the sides, the post office sealing one end and Breakwater Road cutting across the other, was classified as hopeless for the expansion required by existent and potential traffic.

"Many Aucklanders may be disposed to question the wisdom of taking the railway terminus further away from Queen Street than the present site. But what is the alternative? If new station buildings would suffice to meet existing and future needs, there would be an arguable case for retaining the old position. But they will not. More platforms, sheds, yards and sidings are needed. The present site could be utilised to better advantage than at present, but the position is too cramped for the principal station of a great city like Auckland. The city is growing in every other way. In railway facilities alone it stands still. The present station was condemned in 1914, and nothing happening since has given any cause to reverse the sentence.

"Now, when a Minister fresh to the department and full of energy (Joseph Coates) is preparing a programme of improvements, it is essential that full weight should be given to Auckland's claim to be rescued from the present hopeless condition of the city's railway outlet." [170]

Ever optimistic, the Northern Suburban Railway League, still represented by its honorary secretary, Mr H A Robertson, continued its lobbying for both public and financial support to help fund its two-tunnel proposal joining the projected new station at Beach Road with Morningside. By September 1923, the League was promoting the future benefits for those who had businesses trading along the proposed city rail route.

As reported by The New Zealand Herald, Auckland businessmen met with the League on 25 September 1923 when the following was highlighted by Mr Robertson:

"From the point of view of Queen Street and Karangahape Road business men, the proposal should have considerable appeal, as the proposed central station at Marmion Street would certainly be the alighting platform for the majority of the North Auckland and suburban shoppers, who, if they continued the journey into the new Auckland station at Mechanics' Bay, would have a considerable walk into the foot of Queen Street.

"The construction of the proposed outlet, said Mr Robertson, would not involve the purchase of expensive land. The whole scheme was estimated by the Railway Department to cost £600,000. The speaker suggested that the business men of Queen Street and Karangahape Road should find the sum of £5000 per annum for a period of five years to assist the department in carrying out what was sure to be an invaluable factor in the expansion of business in Queen Street and Karangahape Road. Figures were quoted showing the large amount of passenger traffic on the northern suburban line; Mr Robertson pointing out that the completion of the links with Whangarei and Dargaville would mean a considerable increase in this traffic. If any improvement was expected in the matter of routes, now was the time to act.

"After some discussion, Mr Fowlds, representing the Queen Street interests of those present, and Mr M J Bennett, on behalf of Karangahape Road interests, were appointed to accompany a deputation which is to wait upon the Minister for Railways, the Hon. J. G. Coates, this morning in connection with the matter. The delegates were instructed to watch the proceedings and report to a later meeting." [171]

But while The New Zealand Herald had favoured the immediate implementation of the improvements recommended in the 1914 Hiley Report, the newspaper's editorial of 27 September 1923 now advocated some patience while the new Minister familiarised himself with the needs of the Auckland network and the country as a whole. The Herald's editorial suggested:

"Conditions have changed materially since it (the Hiley Report) was drafted. As one indication, it is not possible that the schedule of costs contained in it would apply to-day. Prices for many things have risen, yet on the other hand the progressive utilisation of labour-saving machinery promises a reduction in labour costs for which the Hiley scheme could not allow. Since then also the prospects of electrifying suburban lines have improved. Mr Hiley did not take this definitely into account. In fact the Railway Department has not yet given it detailed consideration. The suggestion of a new outlet to the North, with fairly extensive tunnelling naturally hinges upon the possibility of an electrified service.

"It is not impossible, as the deputation submitted, to conceive of the scheme with ordinary coal-burning locomotives but, even so, it is easily realised that with electric traction the prospect of tunnel travelling would be more readily faced by the public. Such details must be taken carefully into account in estimating the worth of the proposed route. What requires to be clearly understood is that there should be no point-blank demand for immediate acceptance of the scheme and an instant beginning with the work. Its advocates have certainly reinforced their urgings by the suggestion that there would be public financial support. Even that, however, should not be taken as justifying an attempt to stampede the Minister into a decision. The position is simply that Mr Coates is endeavouring to find what needs doing to bring the railway system into line with the requirements of traffic.

"He is evidently impressed with the woeful inadequacy of Auckland's facilities. He has to consider the whole Dominion, and bring into correct perspective all the many works which await the doing. It is reasonable to consider also whether a larger scheme for Auckland would not be feasible, practical, and ultimately economical. In the circumstances the new northern outlet is a proposition which he and his officers must weigh carefully. They can gather the evidence and decide how the difficulties of route can be best overcome and view the whole project in relation to the possibilities of the early electrification of the suburban services. The important thing is that the sum of Auckland's needs should be placed in the right focus when means for relieving the present railway congestion are under review." [172]

On the same day, an Auckland Star article also reported Mr Coates' comments and observed that the bigger picture had to be considered:

"The proposal that a railway line be driven under Karangahape Road to shorten the suburban railway journey to the west opens up the whole question of the railway outlets of Auckland. The Minister admitted at yesterday's interview that the service has reached its limit in that it is impossible to run any more trains at the rush hours, and he points out that in the next few years large additions to open lines will centre more traffic in Auckland. The problem is complicated one. The first work on the Department's schedule, we take it, is the erection of the new station in Mechanics' Bay and the construction of the line via Tamaki, designed to avoid the heavy grade to Remuera. This, however, will give no relief to the northern line.

"A point that does not seem to have been given its due importance is that if the present line is maintained as the sole western outlet it will have to be duplicated. Mr Hiley's plan of 1914 has 'proposed duplication' marked on the section between Newmarket and New Lynn. This will be a costly work, and in considering such a proposal as the tunnel under Karangahape Road we must bear in mind that if this was adopted, some of this cost of duplication would be saved. This proposal of a short cut well merits the expert investigation that the Minister has promised it shall have. It should, however, be treated not merely as an isolated idea, but as part of the whole problem of the exits and entrances of a city whose contours, while varied and beautiful, are a permanent nuisance to the railway man." [173]

As the latest review conducted by the Minister for Railways and his staff extended to the end of 1923 and into 1924, the press continued to report the congestion experienced at Auckland station and the inadequacy of its facilities for the numbers using them:

"The lack of proper platform facilities at the Auckland railway station was again evident last evening when the Main Trunk express, due to leave at 7.40 p.m., was 12 minutes late in departing. Since the despatch of a second evening express, it has been found necessary on practically every occasion to add extra cars to the train after the departure of the first express.

"The reason is that the length of the platform does not permit of more than ten cars being accommodated at one time. During shunting operations, which caused the delay, fully 100 passengers were obliged to wait at the end of the platform. When the carriages were eventually linked up there was the usual scramble for seats, some passengers having to walk along the rails to board the train, which comprised 16 cars. The 7.10 p.m. express consisted of 12 cars and a postal van. Over 900 people travelled South on the two trains." [174]

But while it may not have seemed like it to those passengers who had to 'scramble for seats' after a 'walk along the rails to board the train', the numbers using the trains were down during the 1923/1924 holiday season.

Between 9 December 1923 and 5 January 1924, "...the total number of travellers, in both the ordinary and holiday services, to leave Auckland by rail was 42,213, and the revenue derived was £30,876. The comparative figures for the corresponding period a year ago were: Passengers, 43,500; revenue £28,915." [175]

In what may have been one of the first indications of how other modes of transport may be impacting the fortunes of the suburban railway service, The New Zealand Herald surmised in January 1924:

"That fewer people travelled during the recent period is probably attributable to the fact that 12 months ago the tram service to Ellerslie was not in operation." [176]

However, the drop in patronage between the two holiday seasons could not be attributed entirely to just the competitiveness of suburban services, as demonstrated by the reduced patronage and income derived from longer journeys and excursions:

"In addition to the foregoing returns, figures are available in respect of travellers from Auckland by excursion and special trains, including trains to Whangarei and to Ellerslie races. The number carried this season between December 9 and January 5 was 10,583, yielding a revenue of £2814. Comparative figures for the corresponding period a year ago are Passengers: 16,037; and revenue, £3216." [177]

By 1924, the country's railway service was not just competing with trams but, as roads became more numerous and driveable, there was also the new kid on the block, the motor car, to contend with. There were more than 30,000 cars in New Zealand by 1920 and Gordon Coates, who was also the Minister of Public Works and therefore in charge of road building, soon recognised that this new form of transport could only be worked with and not opposed.

During a January 1924 inspection tour of Northland with the railways general manager, R W McVilly; chief railways engineer, F J Jones; and the inspecting engineer of the Public Works Department, C J McKenzie, Coates made it clear that if the railways were to remain profitable, no longer could lines be laid or operated without taking this new 'transport factor' into account:

"The policy of the Government is to construct roads that will be feeders to the railways, and to ports. It is endeavouring to get the people to the railways on good roads instead of letting them flounder their way through mud," said the Minister for Railways and Public works, the Hon. J G Coates, in addressing a meeting of settlers at Kaeo this evening. I recognise that railways are of cardinal importance, but I also recognise the great importance of the new transport factor represented by petrol-driven vehicles on roads. We are anxious now, and the time has arrived, to fix the point at which the North Auckland railway or other railways should stop. That point should be where it can most usefully serve all the roads that concentrate upon it, and we want also to see that people have the roads to reach the railways."[178]

In the case of Waipu, that policy of rail giving way to road was demonstrated the following month when a decision was made by Gordon Coates, as the Minister of Public Works, to replace the previously-started railway access with "...the early completion of a good metalled road (which) would meet all the wants of this isolated area for a long time to come."[179]

Some ten years after Mr Hiley completed his tour of the country's railway network and furnished his report to Parliament, the Hon. J G Coates had nearly finished his six-month tour of inspection:

"When the Minister for Railways, the Hon. J. G. Coates, completes a coming three-weeks' tour, including Dunedin, Invercargill and Central Otago, he will have inspected the whole of the New Zealand railways – a work which he commenced in September last. He will then, as previously stated, frame a programme of railway improvement, on which attention will be concentrated until they are completed, as was done in the case of the Public Works railways construction. The Minister will leave Wellington next Thursday."[180]

During February 1924, there was a good deal of optimism expressed by the press that this latest inspection would generate a quick and positive response to the long-suffering transport needs of Auckland:

"The survey being made by the Minister and his staff of existing railway facilities and the need for improvement is nearing its end. Soon the whole sum of work to be done will have to be considered in order that the most urgent may be selected for immediate attention. Having regard to the logic of facts, it is impossible to believe otherwise than that a new railway station and yards at Auckland will prove the most urgently necessary work in sight. This conclusion must be reached not simply because Auckland wants a new station, though the city has wanted one long enough and waited for one far too long.

"It is not a question of Auckland's wishes, or of the desire for a station more in keeping with the size and deserts of the city. It is entirely a case of providing for the working railways facilities to handle the traffic offering at the most populous and most rapidly expanding centre to which trains are run. It is no secret, it is a commonplace, that at the busy periods of the day, the staff cannot bring another train into or out of the Auckland station.

"Those at present run (sic) tax the existing facilities to the last limit. Is the case so desperate anywhere else? Are the prospects of increased traffic equalled at any other point on the whole railway system? Is there any railway station in New Zealand where the traffic returns more profit to the railway revenue? A negative answers all these questions.

"If, or rather when, it is announced that this essential undertaking must begin forthwith, it is quite conceivable that Minister and department will be assailed by the advocates of other works. It will be an occasion, if ever there was one, for Auckland to show a united front, and give the Minister all possible support. Members of Parliament and public alike will need to be on guard to see that politics are not permitted to obscure a question which should be settled in the light of plain common sense.

"Unless the railway facilities are brought into line with the city's growth, that growth must stop, or at best lose pace. Such a possibility is far too serious to be suffered. The needs of the present are easily visible, those of the future inevitable. One serious aspect of the situation is that they cannot be adequately met in a week or a year. The construction of a station and of yards which will meet present needs and leave adequate room for future expansion is an undertaking of considerable magnitude.

"This is only one more reason for grappling promptly with the problems. Provision of effective connection with the northern line, the station, and the existing main line has difficulties calling for the greatest skill and nicety in their overcoming. Meantime work on the actual station and yards could proceed. There is another part of the scheme which could commence forthwith, the new eastern outlet via Hobson Bay, and on to Westfield. It is generally understood that everything is in readiness for this to begin. It might well be pushed forward vigorously while the subsidiary problems were being solved. The actual order in which the work is done matters little. The dominating need is to ease the pressure, long grown intolerable, at the Auckland station." [181]

But, surprisingly, the Minister's lengthy and, no doubt, expensive enquiry was not the only one undertaken in 1924. Two British rail experts, Sir Sam Fay and Sir Vincent Raven, were commissioned by the New Zealand Government to inquire into the country's railway system once they had completed a similar survey in New South Wales.

"The order of reference of the Commission is the same as that given in New South Wales. The Commissioners will inquire into the management, equipment, and general working, including the finance, administration, control, and economy of the railway service, and more particularly:

"(1) The organisation and running of the passenger and goods traffic, the services rendered, the scale of fares and freights operating, and the financial returns.

"(2) Matters appertaining to the organisation and conduct of the mechanical section of the system, in relation to the respective types of locomotives and rolling stock adopted, cost, economy of life and use, equipment, renewal, and maintenance charges.

"(3) Matters relating to the construction, renewal, and maintenance of the permanent way, including station equipment, and the systems of signalling and interlocking adopted.

"The experts have power to call before them all persons necessary for the production of books, papers, and-other documents, and to inspect such offices and premises as they may judge necessary to the inquiry. Arrangements will be made for the Commission of Inquiry to make a, comprehensive tour of the railway system, in order to ascertain at first hand the circumstances and traffic conditions of the various lines—and to get the atmosphere as it were. This is regarded as essential if the inquiries are to be conducted on an adequate basis. An investigation will be made into the arrangements of the different departments and the methods adopted." [182]

As the arrival of the Commissioners in New Zealand was expected to coincide with the completion of the Minister's report in October 1924, some doubts were expressed as to the need for a second, costly enquiry which would more or less duplicate the Minister's endeavours.

(As previously mentioned, on a smaller scale, and for no apparently logical reason, a similar dual survey of the line between Riverhead and Kaipara was also undertaken in 1871.)

The Evening Post's editorial of 2 June 1924 summed up the thoughts of many and yet also justified the need for the Commission's independent evaluation of what was otherwise very much a political animal:

"When it was suggested that a Royal Commission should be appointed to report upon the railways we raised the objection that such an appointment would imply lack of confidence in the Minister of Railways, the General Manager, and the staff. It must be admitted that the circumstances of the appointment since announced lessen this implication.

"The Government has really only taken advantage of the presence of experts in Australia to obtain an opinion of the working of our railways compared with other systems. At the same time, it appears to us that it would have been better to await the results of the complete investigation made by the Minister of Railways before obtaining the opinion of a Commission upon the whole organisation.

"The English experts, with all their experience, will be new to the conditions obtaining in New Zealand, and they will have to spend some weeks in endeavouring to become seized of these conditions. They will follow in Mr Coates's footsteps, hearing the requests that he has heard, and receiving information that has already been given to him. If our railways were to be run henceforth as a business organisation, with no political, economic, or social objects which did not fit into a business policy, there might, even so, be some advantage in obtaining outside advice. But can the English experts be expected to appreciate, after a few weeks of inquiry, all the aims which enter into the railways policy? Will they understand how the railways are expected to aid settlement, to foster agriculture, to assist education, and even to promote the growth of social life?

"All these are worthy objects for a State, and as the State in New Zealand owns the railways, it uses them as a means for attainment of economic and social aims. Can English experts be expected even to understand the objection to a reduction of staffs in a politically controlled railway system? Possibly the experts will be able to plot out for us a straightforward business policy, with no concessions to this or that, no unprofitable lines kept open for the convenience of settlers—in- fact, none of the anomalies now present.

"But most of these anomalies are perfectly well known now. Many of them have been cited in reports by the General Manager, and they are still maintained. The Royal Commission from abroad will certainly be unable to enforce the adoption of a business policy, though its members, being prophets of another country, may be heeded where the advice of the local experts has been disregarded. To the public also the Commission may render service by giving an impartial judgment upon freights and fares, salaries and wages. These possibilities excuse in a measure the appointment of the Commission; but it must always be remembered that the Commission's powers are strictly limited. It can advise but it cannot compel the politicians to accept the advice. In the end the reorganisation of the railways is the work of those who have the ruling authority—the Minister and Parliament. And the responsibility is theirs also." [183]

Of course, it was also the responsibility of Parliament to account for and justify the cost of these enquiries. When word reached New Zealand that the Commission's New South Wales costs were estimated to be in the region of £14,000, the expected cost to New Zealand was naturally put by way of a Parliamentary question to the Minister of Railways in July 1924:

"Apparently the questioner does not know this Government very well, replied the Hon. J. G. Coates, who gave a prompt assurance that before arrangements were made with Sir Samuel Fay, Sir Vincent Raven, and the three others associated with them to hold an inquiry into the New Zealand railways, it ascertained the cost. Speaking from memory, it would not exceed £6000." [184]

But, for once, the dire need for improvements to Auckland's railway facilities could no longer wait for the completion of either the Minister's enquiry or that of the British Commissioners. A 'preliminary' start was initiated by the Government and proclaimed by The New Zealand Herald on 18 July 1924:

"A start has been made with the preliminary work in connection with the construction of a new railway station and goods yard at Auckland and of the deviation via Hobson and Orakei Bays to Westfield. The work was recommended by Mr E H Hiley in 1914, and was estimated by him to cost £965,000 including £140,000 for a new engine depot and approach lines. No estimate has been given of the cost at present rates of wages and prices generally, but it will probably be no less; than one and a half millions if the scheme is carried through in its entirety.

"Mr Hiley estimated that the work would take five years to complete, therefore in calculating the annual expenditure on railways in the province during the next few years it will not be outside the mark to allow £300,000 a year for the next five years for the Auckland station, and new outlet. This work is precisely in the same category as all other Government undertakings in the province, it is an absolute necessity and its neglect would reflect upon the whole Dominion.

"In 1914, when the Auckland railway traffic was much less than it is to-day, the station and yard facilities were overtaxed and the steep gradient to Newmarket had begun to cause traffic congestion. The war compelled the postponement of the work and now, almost exactly 10 years after the recommendation was made and when traffic congestion is not only causing extreme inconvenience but also financial loss for the department and for merchants and manufacturers, a start is being made.

"Although no announcement has been made as to the actual plans of the new station and yard it is understood that there are to be eight platforms, which will thus provide 16 sets of rails. The buildings will be of brick or concrete, and they will be double-storeyed, and will have sufficient accommodation for the administrative staff now occupying part of the Post Office building. The site will be in the vicinity of Beach Road. While traffic considerations are the only questions of consequence in connection with the construction of the deviation to Westfield, the line will yet serve another great purpose as far as the city is concerned. It will run through pleasant country possessing every requirement of suburban residential areas.

"Owing to the absence of ready means of communication with the West Tamaki districts that are not within reach of the harbour, these rolling lands of extraordinary fertility have remained farms while suburbs have sprung up much further from the city. The reason is that railway communication existed. When the Westfield line is opened there is not the slightest doubt that suburban settlements will quickly appear along it. The line will pull the city to the east and in view of the extent of open land that is available every opportunity will be afforded for building suburbs according to town-planning principles.

"For some years the Government has been acquiring areas of native land at Orakei as the site of a model suburb and this will be served by the railway. The fact that an early start will be made with the construction of the line affords much gratification. It will mean the solution of the Auckland traffic problem as well as being a great civic asset." [185]

At last, the Minister of Railways, the Hon. J G Coates, tabled his railways improvement statement to the House of Representatives, as reported by the Auckland Star on 3 October 1924:

"The long-promised statement of the Minister of Railways, setting forth the programme of works which the Department intends to carry into effect, was presented to the House of Representatives last night. The scheme, an extension of that evolved by Mr Hiley, formerly General Manager of Railways, which was interrupted by the war, and it involves a total expenditure of £8,000,000, spread over a period of eight years.

"With the greater development of the North the bulk of the expenditure will be incurred in the North Island, the total being £5,809.000 against £717,000 for the South. Items which involve both islands account for the remaining million and a half. The programme for Auckland includes works long familiar to the public, such as the low-level deviation to Westfield, the duplication to Papakura and the new yard at the Auckland station, while the Minister has definitely committed himself to the proposed tunnel under the city to Morningside, in order to shorten the Northern journey, and duplication of the line as far as New Lynn." [186]

The Auckland Star was certainly in favour of the Minister's plans for improvements to the Auckland railway network:

"In a programme of railway improvements which is the most important thing of its kind since the Hiley report of 1914, and probably the largest single set of proposals since the days of Vogel, the Minister of Railways puts forward plans that will mean an expenditure of eight millions in eight years. He has been all over the Dominion seeing how the land lies; he has taken some months to think over the whole problem; and he disclaims any political bias.

"This assurance should be accepted, though one cannot hope that the proposals will be received everywhere dispassionately. As all our readers should know, these railway improvements are long overdue. Auckland City is to get not only the terminus and the deviation to Westfield outlined by Mr Hiley, but, sometime in the future, a new route to the outer suburbs on the Northern line, and this route, we presume, will also carry the traffic to the North. The idea of tunnelling under the city is a bold one, but it would give a much quicker run, and save a great deal in working expenses. The Northern line has about reached its limit of capacity, and travelling by the roundabout route is long and tedious. Duplication would cost about half the estimate for the proposed short-cut line, and there would be no comparison between the efficiency of the two services." [187]

Such was the importance of these latest, promised improvements to Auckland's railway facilities that newspapers such as the Auckland Star gave the Minister's report widespread publicity. In a separate article, published on 3 October 1924, the Star outlined the precise route to be followed by the new line to Morningside:

"In submitting proposals in regard to the Newmarket-New Lynn duplication, the General Manager and Chief Engineer of Railways included details of an alternative route from Auckland's new station to Morningside, crossing Beach Road by an over-bridge, and tunnelling under the city by a tunnel 116 chains long.

"The route is from the new station site, across Beach Road, and then by a tunnel in a straight line to a point beneath the Normal School. The tunnel then takes a slight curve to Wakefield Street, where the proposed underground station will be situated, with a double-line platform. Thence the route is by the tunnel to the vicinity of the bottom of Newton Road. An open line continues along the gully to Morningside, where there will be another short tunnel. From the schedule of expenditure, it appears that the construction of the new line is to be commenced in the third year, and completed in five years.

"The allocations are as follow:—Third year, £50,000; fourth, £100,000; fifth, £175,000; sixth, £250,000; seventh, £41,000. Total £616,000. The work of duplicating between Newmarket and New Lynn was estimated to cost £300,000, as against the duplicated tunnel route costing:—Auckland City to Morningside £449,000, Morningside-New Lynn duplication £167,000, total £610,000. This route will reduce the distance from Auckland to Morningside by approximately one mile and a half and the travelling time by about 15 minutes. The bulk of the suburban traffic to and from that direction will be much better provided for by the alternative route than by the existing train and tram facilities. One underground station would be required in the vicinity of the Town Hall.

"In view of the decided advantages to be obtained and the comparative costs of the two works the Government has decided to adopt the major scheme. So far as electrification is concerned this section will be included in those to be reported on by Messrs Merz and McLellan, the English consulting engineers.

"The chief engineer at Auckland, in discussing the cost of construction, said: If such a line were constructed it would be necessary to electrify it, and presumably if such were done, the whole of the lines in the Auckland suburban area would be electrified at the same time. The matter can therefore be considered from a broad standpoint only. Apart from the question of electrification, the saving in working expenses should almost pay interest on the cost of construction.

"Thus 50 trains a day saving 1½ miles each would equal £12,000 per annum. The difference in cost is £316,000; at 4 per cent this would equal £12,640. The question of the electrification of the Auckland suburban area is worth investigation. From near Morningside on the city route it will in the future be possible to junction with a low level line to Kumeu if such becomes advisable." [188]

The English consulting engineers, referred to by the Auckland Star, Merz McLellan, were described at the time to be "…among the leading consulting engineers of the world on railway electrification. By mid-November 1924, the firm's chief electrical engineer, Mr E P Grove, had completed a survey of North Island requirements and was heading to the South Island. His brief was to "…state the cost of electrifying the four suburban railway systems of the Dominion, and generally to indicate the running conditions and costs under electrification." [189]

This meant that during 1924, no fewer than three surveys of the country's railway network were undertaken – first by the Minister, then the Railway Commissioners, Fay and Raven, and, finally, by Mr Grove of Merz McLellan.

Could there have been a more studied transportation system anywhere in the world? Possibly, but to what end? Following the report of Railways Minister Coates, in October 1926, the findings of the Commissioners, Fay and Raven, "…were eagerly anticipated in railway circles, more especially as it has been mooted that important changes in administration have been deferred pending the disclosure of the commission's recommendation." [190]

Those possible, 'important changes in administration' were indeed widely mooted, as described by the NZ Truth in its article entitled, What Will Fay And Raven Say?, published on 8 November 1924:

"Cut The Apron Strings – Railways Are Old Enough To Raise Their Own Loans – They Should Be Independent, Pay Their Own Way, Build Reserves, And Be Honest. Are the New Zealand railways, old enough to set up housekeeping on their own account? Or are they still such irresponsible infants that they must live in the old man's counting house, and pay into and draw on the Consolidated Fund of a paternal Government?

"If the railways had their own banking account, and were responsible for their own loans (old and new), they would gain in authority and self-respect, and the true strength and weakness of their position would be made more perceptible to their owners (the people); but — the politicians would lose in power! That the British Railway experts (Sir Sam Fay and Sir Vincent Raven) who are now inspecting the New Zealand railways will report in favour of taking railway finance out of the Treasury's control, and of making non-political and independent railway commissioners responsible for such finance (including loans, loan-renewals, and new loans), is hardly to be doubted, because the same experts recently made that recommendation in the parallel case of New South Wales.

"But what chance is there of establishing an independent railway-control, with independent finance, when Masseyism and Liberalism are honeycombed with laissez-faire, and when Hollandite Labor's enthusiasm is no for efficiency, but for some form of Syndicalistic control of the public railways by persons who ought to be public servants, but who aspire to be the public's masters? A State railway service in New Zealand or Australia is a tree of irregular growth, which has thrown out branches and roots more or less haphazard, in a weird political reticulation. An old bush tree, thick with parasitic vines and perching plants, green in parts and dead in parts — such composite growth fairly typifies the New Zealand railways.

"Such a composite undertaking ought to be made to keep its own accounts and do its own borrowing. So long as the railways tree continues to lean on the tree of the State, the rotten spots will be masked. In other words, the railway service should be thrown on its own responsibility. The Fay-Raven duo recommended so much in New South Wales; and can surely not recommend any less in New Zealand. But to entrust the railways management with authority and responsibility — for the two go together — means not only robbing the politicians of power, but means allowing the railways management to refuse to compromise its own efforts at self-support by carrying the baby for non-paying 'developmental' transport schemes." [191]

Indeed, in their 70-page report released on 12 December 1924, the British Railway Commissioners, Sir Sam Fay and Sir Vincent Raven, criticised the funding of the country's railway network, and much more:

"Important recommendations are made by Sir Sam Fay and Sir Vincent Raven, English experts, who recently investigated the working of the New Zealand Government Railways. (Their 35 recommendations included) That railway finance be taken out of the control of the Treasury, and the Railway Department be given full control of its own funds...That reserve funds be established to provide for obsolescence and wasting assets of permanent way and rolling stock." [192]

"Some interesting points in regard to railway finance are dealt with by the Railway Commission. Dealing with the 'policy rate' of interest on loans charged to the Railway Department, it is pointed out that from 1920 onwards the increased cost of working the lines (notwithstanding 40 per cent increase in goods rates and 25 per cent in passenger fares), brought down net receipts below the 'policy rate' of 3¾ per cent, the total deficit in three years being £1,429,917. The Commission criticises adversely the manner in which funds are provided through Parliament, and states that the time occupied in finishing the railways has been unduly long." [193]

The Commissioners' report also included some comment as to the "Public discontent in regard to general travelling facilities on the railways of the Dominion", as reported by the Auckland Star:

"The evidence given on behalf of the public, a perusal of the time-tables, a record of the actual times kept by the trains, and statistics of train earnings show that, as a result of slow and infrequent services, general discontent exists, and the inhabitants of New Zealand do not make use of railways for the purposes of travel to the same extent that under ordinary circumstances they might be expected to do. The average number of journeys per head of population in the year, was — New Zealand, 21.08; Queensland, 35.82; South Australia, 47.46; and Western Australia, 51.27. We cannot but think that the reason for this disparity is to be found in the train service.

"On some parts of the system trains cannot be run at any great speed, by reason of grades and curves; but when it is found, as a sample, that on one line the only trains run in a day take two and a half hours to cover thirty-nine miles, it cannot be considered as a reasonable rate of progression, and it is not to be wondered at that the motor-car is used by everybody who possesses, or who can hire, such a vehicle, in competition with the rail." [194]

While acknowledging that much of the work planned for Auckland was needed, the Commissioners did not entirely agree that the extent of the improvements were justified:

"The reduction of grade alone is justification for the Auckland-Westfield deviation line, which is urgent also by reason of traffic increase. The double tracking of the existing line between Westfield and Penrose Junction is also a pressing necessity. While agreeing that a re-arrangement of approaching lines and of the stations and goods yards at Auckland and Wellington is needed, the Railway Commission considers that, 'The present traffic does not justify such expensive sidings and accommodation as the plan of the proposed new station and yards provides'.

"The Auckland passenger lay-out could be improved by the provision of a complete through-running station instead of a dead end main-line station, as shown on the plan. As the city grows there will be suburban passenger traffic from north to south, and vice-versa, and this could be provided for as well as the main-line services in one station. Whatever lay-out of yards and sidings may ultimately be decided upon, the work should only be carried out as traffic grows, care as a matter of course, being taken that any addition made from time to time conforms to the complete scheme." [195]

While the Commissioners seemed to counsel that a steady and planned approach was needed to achieve a cost-efficient railway service at Auckland, by September 1926, lobbyists such as the Northern Suburban Railway League saw the opportunity for a Northern railway outlet to be completed at about the same time as the new station, yards and Westfield deviation, again slipping away. This was despite so many, apparently logical, reasons for the proposed tunnel to Morningside to be started at once.

Some of those reasons were outlined by the Auckland Star at the time:

"During the last two or three months…a new phase of the question has cropped up, and one which gives undoubted proof that the work of piercing the tunnel, to enable the Morningside deviation to be carried out expeditiously, should be gone on with at once and without delay. On making inquiries and investigations a Star representative learned that if the proposed line is not commenced now trouble will be experienced in the near future.

"Discussing the work with engineers and others competent to express an opinion, it was pointed out that practically every truck of spoil from the tunnel leading to Morningside will have to be brought out through the new railway station yards which, it is anticipated, will be in complete working order by 1928. This state of affairs, it is contended, will seriously inconvenience the handling of railway traffic, particularly that of passengers, at the new station in Beach Road. Again it is an undoubted fact that in constructing and forming the new yards much spoil is required for filling-in purposes. The earth from the Auckland-Morningside tunnel would help considerably to solve that which will, it is anticipated, become an increasing difficulty as time goes on.

"There are several other valid reasons why the work of making the new northern outlet should be gone on with at once. There are over 2000 workers who use the present trains from Eden district daily, whilst it has been estimated by authorities that approximately 1,400,000 travellers use the trains during the year. There has been a phenomenal increase in the north line suburban season ticket-holders during the last few years, and figures prove that to-day Avondale has the largest booking of season tickets of any station in New Zealand, having now exceeded Petone's returns. Henderson is eighth or ninth on the list against all stations, and if the present rate of suburban building continues in those districts the figures will naturally show further large increases.

"People who were interviewed concerning the proposal to commence work now on the Morningside deviation pointed out to the Star representative that if the railways are to continue holding the present traffic against motor transport they must aim to give facilities to the travelling public. Under present conditions passengers from the suburbs mentioned have to travel by train two miles and a half further than is necessary, and by so doing add mileage, time, and fares—all of which favour the bus competitor.

"The tunnel scheme would, however, put the railway in a very advantageous position, as a station in Upper Queen Street would be practically in the centre of the business portion of the city, and it is estimated that three-fourths, or more, of the passengers would make this their terminal point. For instance, a train leaving, say, Upper Queen Street would be in Mount Albert while the tram or bus would only have reached the top of Symonds Street. Thus, with that great advantage, and also the saving in fares, the line would have a material gain over road traffic.

"Then, again, it was contended that the new Auckland station is not conveniently situated from the point of view of the average suburban dweller, as it is about a mile and a quarter out of the main business portion of the city. A glance at, the map of Auckland will show that the proposed station near the Town Hall will remove this difficulty, and it will serve as the best point of departure for suburbanites on the south as well as the north line. This will ensure that there will be no part of the line blank from a revenue point of view, as is largely the case with the Mount Eden-Auckland section.

"There is no central station at present, said Mr H. W. (sic –should be H A) Robertson, Hon. secretary of the Northern Suburban Railway League, when discussing the new line, and the first thing the Department will discover when this new Upper Queen Street station comes into use is the volume of business which has in the past been lost to it through lack of proper facilities, thus having congested the city areas and retarded suburban growth." [196]

The case for the Morningside tunnel was also substantiated by the report of the consulting engineers, Messrs Merz and McLellan, which was presented to the House, of Representatives with the 1926 Railway Statement:

"The experts (Mr E P Grove of Merz and McLellan) said, inter alia, that in dealing with suburban passenger traffic, the Auckland railway system was at a disadvantage, and the new station would not provide much improvement in that respect. To meet this difficulty it had been suggested that a new line, partly in tunnel, should be constructed from the new Auckland railway station to Morningside. It is proposed that this new line should link-up with the Westfield deviation by way of the new Auckland yard thus giving access to the city station from both north and south lines.

"Such a tunnel would clearly be of great value, the report continues, to passengers from the Henderson line and to passengers approaching the Westfield deviation. It was evident to Messrs Merz and McLellan that a frequent service of steam trains could not be worked through so long a tunnel as the northern outlet without grave inconvenience to passengers and to train crews. If, therefore, this new line is constructed, they said, electric working would be advisable, and would probably involve electrification of the whole suburban area.

"Continuing, the report says the general experience all over the world in dealing with suburban electrification has been that, within limits, an increase of traffic would follow an increase in facilities. It was the increased passenger receipts rather than a reduction in working expenses which in many cases had made suburban passenger electrification profitable." [197]

So by the close of 1926, it was obvious that the railways had to press on with the improvements found to be necessary by the Minister, the Commissioners and the consulting engineers if the downturn of passenger patronage was to be reversed enough to adequately compete with the trams, the buses and the motorcar. At this pivotal time, demand for an improved suburban railway service obviously existed, as did the support from Government, the railway leagues, business and, ultimately, thousands of disgruntled, but still potential, commuters.

There was also considerable pressure for a definitive plan from the community at large, or at least from those who could be affected by the projected route of the proposed Morningside deviation. The Newton Central School was a case in point, as reported by a very upbeat Auckland Star on 12 September 1927:

"Engineers in the employ of the New Zealand Railways have commenced work on the northern outlet from the new Auckland railway station. This has been the outcome of a report from the engineer-secretary of the Auckland and Suburban Drainage Board in which he stated that the Railway Department had been requested to arrange for the route of the projected railway in the vicinity of the Newton Central school ground to be definitely located. The reason given was to permit of an early decision being made with regard to a culvert proposed to be constructed in the watercourse along the south-eastern boundary of the school ground.

"The Newton Central School Committee have a considerable sum of money in hand for the purposes of improving the property, but they do not wish to proceed with the work till the survey of the line has definitely fixed its location, otherwise the whole of the work and expenditure of money on the school grounds might go for nothing. On July 22 (1927) an officer of the Railway Department visited the locality and discussed the matter generally with representatives of the Auckland City Council, Education Board and Drainage Board and now the work of fixing the line has commenced.

"One of the most interesting projects is the construction of the tunnel under the city to link up with the north line at Morningside. This tunnel, one mile and a half long, will give New Zealand its pioneer tube railway, and will mark a notable step in Auckland's development. An underground station will be built on this line in the vicinity of the Town Hall. The entrance to the main tunnel will be between Beach Road and Anzac Avenue.

"The tunnel will pass below the south-eastern corner of the Supreme Court building, under Government House grounds and the University College. At Princes Street the floor will be at a depth of 110 ft. It will pass below Albert Park and out the western side of the Drill Hall, crossing beneath Wakefield Street about midway between Rutland and Abercrombie Streets. At Wakefield Street the depth will be about 30ft, and this is the point at which it is proposed to erect the underground station. From Wakefield Street the tunnel will be on a straight line to its exit just beyond Newton Road, passing on part of the route beneath Karangahape

Road at a depth of 130 ft. From that point to its outlet the tunnel will be about midway between Karangahape Road and France Street." [198]

However, the survey process dragged on and, by June 1928, Newton Central School had not spent its money and was still waiting for an answer:

"The survey of the proposed new railway line between Auckland and Morningside is now in hand, but plans are not far enough advanced to enable the Railway Department to give a definite opinion to the Education Board as to the final location of the line through the Newton Central School ground. The Department is of opinion that it may be necessary to carry the line on the school side of the water course, and the board is advised to take no action in regard to expending money on ground improvements until the route of the line is definitely fixed." [199]

And then all bets were off following the general election of 14 November 1928 which resulted in the defeat of Gordon Coates' Reform Party by the Joseph Ward-led United Party. Accordingly, many of Coates' programmes were deferred, scaled back or cancelled altogether – especially once the Depression started to bite from late 1929.

Naturally, the new broom in the form of the replacement Railways Minister, William Burgoyne Taverner, found it necessary to undertake a survey of his portfolio, as he explained in his Railways Statement to the House of Representatives for the year ended 31 March 1929:

"Immediately on my assuming office I took the opportunity of making myself personally acquainted with so much of the railway system as circumstances permitted. In the course of my tour I received many representations regarding a variety of matters affecting the Department's operations — a large proportion of these had reference to improvements that were desired. So far as these requests involved the undertaking of new works, I found myself considerably restricted in meeting the requests by financial considerations. The very large commitments in which the Department was involved to carry out the extensive works that are now in hand and must be carried to completion absorbed practically the whole of the available finance." [200]

One of the representations received by the Railways Minister included what the Auckland Star referred to in its 21 May 1929 edition as:

"One of the largest in years…A deputation which he described as the most influential and representative with which he had been connected during his term of office, was this morning introduced by the Mayor of Auckland (Mr George Baildon) to the Minister of Railways (the Hon. W. B. Taverner) for the purpose of urging the importance of the Morningside railway deviation scheme.

"The deputation, which attended at the ministerial rooms in the Post Office buildings, represented the Northern Suburban Railway and Highways League, the Karangahape Road Business Men's Society, and twelve suburban and country local bodies and associations. In the words of the Mayor, the large deputation represented all shades of political opinion and all forms of business activity. The Postmaster-General (the Hon. J. B. Donald) occupied a seat at the ministerial table, and associated with the deputation were the Hon. J. G. Coates, Messrs. J. S. Fletcher, H. G. R. Mason, W. Parry, M. J. Savage, H. R. Jenkins, C. C. Munns, and A. Harris, M.P.'s.

"Mr H. A. Robertson, secretary of the Railway League, said that the league in 1912 submitted to the then Minister of Railways a request that northern people should be provided with a more direct route to and from the city than the circuitous way around Newmarket. A deviation between Auckland and Morningside was proposed. In 1924 the scheme was included in the schedule of works submitted to Parliament by the Hon. J. G. Coates, and upon its adoption was set down for commencement in 1928 with a view to being completed by 1932.

"After reviewing subsequent events the speaker urged the importance of proceeding with the work upon the following grounds: (1) Saving of time; (2) saving a great waste in haulage—about £15,000 per annum; (3) expansion of Auckland city; (4) the central station to be in the heart of the city; (5) relieving congestion that must occur whilst Auckland had only one main station; (6) avoiding a great inconvenience to northern and southern train users who would have to go to the new Auckland station; and (7) the gaining and retaining of railway passengers by virtue of quick service. This tunnel scheme, added Mr Robertson, is looked forward to by many thousands of people, and we respectfully request that you will authorise a start to be made at an early date.

"The Hon. Mr Coates, member for Kaipara, traced the steps by which the decision was reached to put in hand the Morningside tunnel scheme at a cost which was then estimated at approximately £600,000. Two important reasons why this scheme should be carried through were the extension of the North Trunk railway line from Whangarei to Okaihau (Bay of Islands) and the connecting of the Kirikopuni (Dargaville) branch line with the main line. The improved facilities which would be provided would affect not only Auckland city but also the whole of the Northern Peninsula. At present it was a frequent experience for trains from the North to reach Auckland behind time, and the speaker had travelled on trains recently when they had lost as much as three-quarters of an hour between Henderson and Auckland.

"In adopting the Morningside tunnel scheme, said Mr Coates, we felt that if we could provide fast services to and from. Auckland over distances of from 20 to 25 miles much more business would come to the railways. Although we did not stress the electrification of suburban lines for fear of frightening the public, we had in mind the possibility at some future time of fast suburban electric trains. The speaker said that partly because of the unemployment problem the late Government had anticipated that the work would be put in hand in 1929. There is no more important work, added Mr Coates, serving such a large and important area that I know of in the Dominion. The present losses in time are both irritating and unnecessary, and, while in the meantime the people of the North are prepared to put up with them, they are eagerly looking forward to the day when they will have a fast and expeditious train service.

"Mr E. H. Potter, Mayor of Mount Eden, pointed out that large quantities of electric power were about to become available from Arapuni. That power could be used for transport purposes, and if the Railway Department wished to make the railways pay they would need to electrify the suburban line, otherwise it would be found that motor transport would do the work. Nothing could compete against electrified railways from the city to Helensville and Pukekohe and other suburban points. The alternative was that the people would provide their own transport.

"Mr M. J. Bennett, president of the Karangahape Road Business Men's Association, on behalf of business men, urged that the undertaking should be regarded as urgent.

"The Minister thanked the Mayor and members of the deputation for meeting him in such a thoroughly representative way. I can assure you, he said, that we are quite alive to the urgency of making a decision in regard to this matter and that we shall not keep you waiting any longer than is absolutely necessary. You will realise, however, that before that decision can be made a good deal of work is necessary in the nature of very thorough investigations. The Minister said that during a recent visit to Auckland he went over the route of the proposed deviation. The scheme was one which could not lightly be undertaken and it was necessary that it should be considered on a reasonable commercial basis.

"The peak of competition between the railways and motor transport had not yet been reached and the Government did not want to do anything that would not be justified by results. He realised, however, the importance of transport in Auckland and he was glad to have been informed that the Transport Board desired to assist the Department in coming to a decision. Referring to the suggested electrification of lines the Minister said that in this the important question of outlay was involved.

"For instance, they would not expect motor bus services to be started unless there was reasonable prospect of adequate returns. If the proposed work were undertaken and there should be a loss the Railway Department would have to meet it. They must realise that a very heavy capital expenditure was involved in the interests of the metropolitan area.

"Mr Coates: Pardon me, sir, but the scheme was not intended primarily for the metropolitan area, but for the area in the North. The Minister: It is a metropolitan scheme in so far as it serves the city. Mr Coates: The major scheme was intended to serve both. The Minister: I will certainly regard it in its larger aspect. What is being done at the present time is to carry out investigations with a view to making a recommendation to Cabinet, and a decision will be given as soon as possible. In the meantime I ask that you will do me the honour of realising that I am interested in the matter, and I assure you that all you have said will have very full and earnest consideration." [201]

While members of the Auckland delegation were no doubt disappointed to hear that further investigations were necessary before construction of the Morningside tunnel could proceed, that disappointment was probably tempered somewhat after the Railways Department's financial statement, for the year ended 31 March 1929, was presented to Parliament. For a business that had grown so exponentially since the 1870s, the relatively small revenue and profit increases for the 1929 year were hardly prodigious, particularly on the eve of the Great Depression:

"Mr Speaker, — In presenting the Railways Statement for the year ended 31st March, 1929 I have the honour to report that the gross income from all sources was £8,747,975, an increase of £223,437 on that of the previous year, whilst the expenditure was £6,849,383, an increase of £164,260. The net earnings were £1,898,592, as compared with £1,839,415, an improvement of £59,177 on the results in the previous year.

"The revenue from passenger traffic totalled £2,124,746, as compared with £2,145,296 in the previous year, a decrease of £20,550, or 0.96 per cent. While these figures are more satisfactory than those for the previous year, when the decrease was £158,884, the fact must not be overlooked that the decrease in ordinary passenger traffic still continues. For the year under review the revenue from ordinary passenger traffic decreased by £148,476..." [202]

Fortunately for the sake of some progress, the Auckland railway station, goods yards and the eastern line to Westfield was nearing completion by January 1930 and would be completed that year. However, the Morningside railway deviation was abandoned, as reported by the Auckland Star on 18 January 1930:

"The decision of the Government that the Morningside tunnel shall not be built will be a disappointment to Auckland, but most citizens will be impressed by the reasons given. Since the scheme was propounded some years ago, when Mr Coates was Minister of Railways, it has been attractive. It offered a quicker route to the western suburbs and to the North. The detour by Newmarket has long been an irritation, and before Mr Coates adopted the tunnel scheme the alternative of duplicating the existing line was considered.

"The tunnel was estimated to cost £616,000, a little more than double the duplication, and the proposal was adopted in view of its decided advantages and the comparative costs of the two schemes. That, however, was in 1924. Mr Taverner took up the question when he succeeded Mr Coates a year ago, and caused a thorough investigation to be made of the proposal in all its bearings. He was criticised, for the delay, but his action was quite justified. Better by far that there should be delay than that the country should rush into unwarranted expenditure of such size.

"The lengthy statement by the Minister that we publish today shows that the main objections to the scheme are financial. The engineering difficulties he mentions are probably the least serious items on the list, but they, too, affect finance. If the tunnel could be constructed for £600,000, no doubt the Department's attitude would be wholly favourable, but the estimate is now £2,100,000. This, it is true, includes the cost of electrifying the whole of the Auckland suburban system — the Minister says the tunnel would have to be electrified, and it would be impossible to run one such unit in the midst of a steam system — and apparently the 1924 estimate did not embrace such a development.

"Two millions is a great deal of money, and even though the country obtained for it a new line shortening the route out of Auckland to the west and the north, and the electrification of the suburban area, this could be justified only by a reasonable certainty of an adequate return. Of this the Department does not feel assured. This shortening of the route, so Mr Taverner says, is not likely to have any influence on goods traffic, and increase, in passenger traffic would be 'highly speculative'.

"The public may find it difficult to accept these two estimates, but they are the considered opinion of the Department's professional advisers. Over all such projects as this hangs the uncertainty of transport development. Mr Taverner and his General Manager, Mr Sterling, probably feel that by the time this tunnel were completed motor transport might be even more popular than it is to-day, and that it might successfully compete against even this improved railway service.

"The Minister has also a harbour bridge in mind. If it were built it might alter the whole situation in respect to railway traffic to the North. The Department's case seems to us to be all too strong. The country cannot afford — at any rate at present — to spend two millions on such a work. The Minister is to be commended on the steps he has taken to reach his decision. We have repeatedly contended that thorough investigation of this kind should be applied to all railway projects. What has been done in this case should be done in all." [203]

As might be expected, not everyone agreed with the Minister's assessment of the economic viability and projected patronage of the Morningside deviation and, indeed, there were some who had their suspicions of how such an assessment was arrived at. For a start, the new Railways Minister, William Taverner, was a South Islander – a former Dunedin Mayor and long-serving Councillor – and so was bound to be viewed with some distrust insofar as his sympathies for Auckland progress was concerned.

Secondly, the Minister's readiness to concede railway's passenger transport business to the motorcar seemed a little too yielding for 1929 when road-based vehicles were still to assume any form of superiority and the future of both transport modes were open to regulation. In a somewhat circuitous fashion, the Auckland Star of 20 January 1930 both sympathised with the Minister's approach and posed the questions obviously being asked by its readers:

"Disappointment at the Government's decision on the Morningside tunnel is no adequate excuse for unfair criticism of the Minister's statement. It is suggested that the Government made up its mind first and found the reasons afterwards. If the Government's estimates are approximately correct — and it must be remembered that the Minister thinks that the figure for the actual building of the tunnel may be too low — the Government has a strong case against this particular scheme. It is more than three times the original estimate — or nearly twice as much if electrification is not counted — and in the meantime transport conditions, so far as the railways are concerned, have changed for the worse.

"It must be asked, however, what the Government proposes to do about the Northern line. Is there no alternative to this scheme? Let us hope there is one. If nothing is to be done, if access to the western suburbs is to remain exactly as it is — to say nothing of through traffic — with a single line, the roundabout route, and the backing at Newmarket, then the railway will lose still more traffic. If the Government admits that it can do nothing, this will be an invitation to other forms of transport to come in and take the business. Moreover, the reasons put forward for this Morningside decision throw into even sharper relief the objections to policy elsewhere. If the Government invites and acts upon the opinions of its professional advisers about the Morningside tunnel, why does it not do the same in respect to the completion of the South Island Main Trunk line?" [204]

Obviously, the Rt. Hon. J G Coates, now the Leader of the Opposition, was one of the strongest critics of the cancellation of the Morningside deviation and the non-electrification of the Auckland network, as recommended by all those studies undertaken during his tenure as Railway Minister.

"He (Coates) said that unless the railway lines near Auckland were electrified traffic would be diverted to the road. He considered that if the lines were electrified they would pay without further growth in traffic, that if the Reform Government had continued in power the matter would have been kept within a ten years' programme. Mr Coates mentioned that a report on electrification was presented to the Government in 1926 by Messrs Merz and McLellan and Co., consulting engineers, London. The report showed that if the suburban lines were electrified a great saving could be effected. Mr Coates said that other countries were moving fast in the direction of electrification of railways, as it was realised that quick services were a big inducement for people to travel by train." [205]

The Auckland Chamber of Commerce also made its disappointment known by way of a report generated by a committee appointed at a public meeting of protest. Details of the report were included in an article published by the Auckland Star on 15 March 1930:

"The report points out the difficulty of accounting for so wide a discrepancy between the Minister's estimate of £1,000,000 for the deviation and the 1924 estimate of £449,000, and goes on to refer in detail to a number of technical matters raised by the Minister. The construction of the deviation, continues the report, would result in a saving of at least fifteen minutes' running time between Auckland and stations on the Kaipara line, and Messrs Merz and McLellan have estimated, on the basis of experience in other parts of the world, that the shortening of the time between Auckland and Henderson to 40 minutes by electric train would make the suburbs served by this line so popular that there would be a 50 per cent increase in passenger travelling.

"There is also the saving to the community as a whole, in increased leisure that would result from the saving of time, the value of which cannot, of course, be assessed. This shortening of time would do much to bring back to the railways traffic which, with the discouragement of the present circuitous detour through Newmarket, has been driven to the roads. The new Auckland railway station is to be placed at a point very much further from the centre of gravity of the Auckland business and shopping area than the present station and, in view of this, it is only by the provision of a further station better serving this area, such as that contemplated near the Town Hall on the Morningside deviation, that substantially the whole of the present southern suburban traffic can be retained by the railways against bus and tram competition.

"The handling of the traffic to and from the new railway station is likely to create serious problems…and if the stream of traffic could be divided, a portion being diverted to a new station in the vicinity of the Town Hall instead of to the Beach Road station, the problems under this head would be greatly simplified. The Auckland public have shown themselves fairly definitely averse to feeder services involving the transfer between buses and trams, but with the change in the situation of the Auckland railway station the same state of affairs will arise out of the necessity of a change between tram and train.

"In this connection it may be of interest to note that the distance from the proposed tramway siding at the new railway station to the corner of Customs and Queen Streets is 54 chains, and the probable running time will be about four minutes, not allowing for any delays…to the corner of Queen and Wellesley Streets will be 90 chains, or under the most favourable conditions a running time of at least nine minutes. The trams will be called upon to handle practically the whole of the suburban railway traffic at the peak hour both for trams and trains. This will be found impossible, since even under the favourable conditions operating in Sydney not more than 100 passengers can be delivered by train per minute at the railway station. It would take many minutes even on this basis to dispose of the passengers arriving by a single suburban train arriving at Auckland." [206]

In order to facilitate a feeder service between Queen Street and the nearly-finished Beach Road station, the laying of a tram track loop was underway by June 1930, as reported by the Auckland Star:

"Work has been commenced on the construction of the tramway loop at the new Auckland railway station, and gangs of men are laying down the junctions, in the permanent tracks in Beach Road. The junctions are so placed that trams from the city will be able to turn straight into the station, load, proceed down the other ramp and turn back towards Queen Street instead of continuing in the direction of Parnell." [207]

But despite the tram link to the Beach Road station, concerns about the remote location of the station persisted even as far as the apparently-deaf ears of the House of Representatives during a debate on 29 August 1930:

"An appeal to the Government to take immediate steps to provide against a loss on suburban railway traffic that he predicted would otherwise result from the opening of the new Auckland railway station was made by Mr A. Harris (Waitemata) in the House of Representatives to-day. Mr Harris pointed out that the new station was three-quarters of a mile from Queen Street, and unless there were some connection with the city he contended the Department would surrender a lot of suburban traffic to the buses.

"A Member: Is the station in the wrong place? Mr Harris: Under present conditions it is, but had the Reform party remained in office the Morningside deviation would have been retained. The present Government, as a policy measure, decided against that deviation. He asked what the Department had in mind to retain the traffic that would otherwise be lost. There would be a serious loss of suburban traffic unless a loop-line were brought into the city." [208]

Waitemata MP Harris, persisted with his questions to the Government. In September 1930, not long before the completion of the Beach Road station, he continued to press for treatment that might just resuscitate the railway patient with some form of transport integration. However, even his suggested Band-Aid of a bridge to link the new station with the harbour ferry terminal was rejected:

"The construction of an overhead bridge from the new Auckland railway station over the line to the entrance of the Devonport vehicular ferry is not structurally practicable. This was the answer given by the Hon. W. A. Veitch, Minister of Railways, in the House to-day to Mr A Harris (Reform, Waitemata) who had suggested that a ramp of that nature should be erected.

"Mr Harris said the bridge would confer considerable benefits on the residents of North Shore and at the same time would not cost a great deal of money. It would provide an additional entrance to the railway station and bring it within easy access of the ferry service. The work also could be carried out before the opening of the new railway station within the next few weeks." [209]

However, by 25 September 1930, there seemed to be little money left in the railway kitty or, indeed, incentive to invest it, if additional Parliamentary questions asked that day can be considered to have had any legitimacy:

"Mr W. E. Parry (Labour, Auckland Central) asked in the House to-day if it was not a fact that thousands of pounds' worth of machinery imported from Australia for the Otahuhu railway workshops was lying rusting at the shops. He had been informed that at a cost of £50,000 at the outside sufficient machinery could have been acquired to deal with the country's railway work for the next 20 years, yet there had been huge capital expenditure, and suggestions were now current that a good deal of the equipment would rust instead of being used." [210]

"The attention of the Minister of Railways was called by Mr W. J. Jordan (Labour, Manukau) in the House to-day to the state of the railway permanent way in the Penrose district. It was pointed out that there had been a derailment in the locality recently and that other derailments had occurred previously. The staff was the same as it was 30 years ago notwithstanding that the traffic was much heavier. A special platelaying gang held for emergency work had been disbanded. The Minister was asked not to allow the track and rolling stock to be neglected as the safety of life and property was involved. Replying, the Hon. W. A. Veitch said that an examination of the permanent way would be authorised immediately, and Mr Jordan could rest assured that if any defects were found they would be remedied at once." [211]

In the meantime, the last trains arrived and departed from the old railway station on 16 November 1930, as reported by the Auckland Star the previous day:

"When the Auckland-Hamilton excursion train leaves to-morrow morning at 8.53 the old Auckland railway station will be closed for all time. The station was opened in 1885 and has done service for the City of Auckland for 45 years. To-morrow evening the first train to leave the new station will be the return Auckland-Hamilton excursion train at 6.35. It will be followed by the Limited express at 7 p.m.—ten minutes earlier than previously—and then the 7.40 p.m. Auckland-Wellington express will depart. The ordinary express from Wellington, which is due at Auckland at 6.38 a.m., will use the Westfield deviation as the first regular time-table passenger train, and it will be followed by the Hamilton-Auckland excursion train, which is due at 10.34 a.m.

"Both these trains will be piloted through the new station yards and will disembark passengers at the old station platforms for the last time. From Monday morning onwards all passengers and mixed trains will depart and arrive at the new station. Simultaneously with the opening of the new station the Westfield deviation will be brought into use for passenger trains. The North Auckland trains, and some of the suburban trains which serve the district between the city and Westfield, via Newmarket, will still use the Parnell tunnel route, but they, too, will be dispatched from the new station." [212]

Finally, on 24 November 1930, as reported by the Auckland Star:

"Auckland's new railway station was officially opened by the Hon. W A Veitch, Minister of Railways, this afternoon, in the presence of a large gathering of people representative of all shades of politics, as well as the business community and railway officials. The ceremony commenced at 2 p.m., and after a number of speeches the Minister of Railways opened the station building with a gold key, which was presented to him to commemorate the occasion. In the course of his speech, the Minister mentioned that criticism might be levelled against the location of the station and the relative positions of building and platforms; but these had been enforced by circumstances, which had had the fullest investigation.

"Incidentally, Mr Veitch mentioned that the cost of the Westfield deviation was £790,000. The cost of the complete rearrangement and reconstruction of the Auckland railway station with the yard and all appurtenances had been £1,250,000. Some of the leading items in that sum were: – Station building (including platforms, verandahs, passenger subways, retaining walls and forecourt), £365,000; new engine depot, £96,000; outward goods shed, £46,000; inwards goods shed, £22,000; signalling, interlocking and flood-lighting, £75,000; new yards, approximately £600,000. A very substantial offset to the cost of the project was the value of the old station site which had been abandoned." [213]

That the Minister chose to mention the criticism of the site of the new railway station as inconvenient during the opening ceremony certainly indicated just how vociferous that criticism had been, and would continue to be, well into the future. During the ceremony, the Leader of the Opposition tried vainly to deflect any criticism that his Government had been responsible for the decision to site the station at Beach Road by blaming the Railway Department's engineers and the 'Government of the day' without elaborating on the decisions that had actually been made some sixteen years previously.

"The Leader of the Opposition, The Rt. Hon. J. G. Coates, spoke of the fixing of the terminal point at the Auckland end. This point was fixed by the Department's engineers and approved by the Government of the day because it was convenient to the city, taking into consideration certain other improvements which would have to be made, such as better access to the North, and the delivery of the suburban passengers from the number of suburbs into the heart of the city.

"It would not be possible at the present time, or in 20 years' time, to handle the whole of the traffic of Auckland by road transport. The congestion would be too great. Electricity and quick services were necessary. Efficient, quick and up-to-date services were essential for users of the railway. They could not carry on their commerce without railways; the railways were not going out. It was essential to the business of the country to maintain rail services." [214]

Indeed, many railway critics saw the expected downturn of the Auckland railway business as a valid reason to introduce legislation that would regulate the whole of the region's transport facilities and needs.

Such was the view of Auckland MP, Michael Joseph Savage, as reported by the Auckland Star on the opening day of the new station:

"Speaking on behalf of Mr H. E. Holland, Leader of the Parliamentary Labour party, Mr M. J. Savage, M.P. for Auckland West, extended congratulations to the citizens of Auckland, and said he knew Mr Holland would agree that Auckland needed more than a railway station, which, he said, might remain as a monument to the memory of what might have been a useful railway service.

"Auckland, in common with other parts of the Dominion, needed a co-ordinated transport system that would get the best out of all forms of transport, both private and public. If the new Auckland railway station were to mark the passing of the railway system it seemed an expensive way of recording the people's preference for other forms of transport.

"There was no need to continue the struggle for supremacy between rail and motor services, said Mr Savage. Both were needed. It was only a matter of co-ordinating those services and preventing overlapping. There was no need to continue wasteful competition between services, rail and motor, running parallel. It had been said that the railways did not pay, but if motor services were forced to carry the capital charges of the roads over which they travelled, how many of them would pay at the present rates? If they were forced to become common carriers instead of being able to pick the eyes out of the traffic and leave the non-payable balance of it to the railways, there would be a different story to tell." [215]

By December 1930, road transport had been given a leg up and the 'eyes' certainly looked to it in droves. The relentless drive of road transport to congestion had started, and its ability to efficiently convey passengers throughout the region became very noticeable, very quickly – as reported by the Auckland Star:

"The fact that bus services are more in demand as the result of the removal of the Auckland railway station, and the increase in the scale of fares, is attested by the bus companies having found it necessary to place new vehicles on the road, particularly on routes skirting the railway lines serving the western and northern suburbs, and townships lying along the Great South Road. A noticeable feature of the increased bus business is that regular travellers form the majority of the new passengers. The

Auckland Bus Company has placed four more vehicles on the run between Henderson and Auckland and Glen Eden and Auckland during the rush hours, both mornings and evenings.

"The increased number of workers' tickets issued weekly shows that the increased business is made at the expense of the railways. No great increase has been shown in the number of casual passengers during the middle of the day. This was not anticipated, as the company carried a fairly large portion of the traffic prior to the increase in railway fares and the removal of the station to the new site. The company will be placing additional buses on the road within the next few months, and the first of the fleet will be put into commission on Wednesday.

"An improvement in the demand for tickets is also noticed by the Passenger Transport Company, which serves the southern outlying suburbs. The chairman of the company stated that the number of workers' tickets issued had been falling off during the past six months, but since the opening of the new station it had increased until more were being issued than at any time in the past. The company was anticipating even heavier traffic on the expiration of the season and monthly tickets held by regular travellers on the railways. The increase in the demand for the company's tickets was noticeable in all the districts served." [216]

Not surprisingly, revenue at the Auckland railway station was way down for the year ending 31 March 1931:

"Passenger tickets showed a decrease of 101,827..." [217]

In a paper entitled 'Auckland Suburban Railway System – Historical Background' (written in 1954 by an unidentified author but thought to be Sir Dove-Myer Robinson) illustrated:

"The extent to which the location of the station has affected suburban traffic...judged in general terms from the following statistics of season tickets accounted for by stations in the suburban area: (The term 'season tickets' includes all workers weekly and trip bearer tickets as well as monthly and other season tickets).

| Year Ended 31st March | Season Ticket Journeys | Journeys per 1000 Population | Population |
|---|---|---|---|
| 1920 | 3,096,800 | 20 | 155,000 |
| 1930 | 5,189,700 | 26 | 200,000 |
| 1940 | 2,970,000 | 12 | 240,000 |
| 1950 | 2,595,700 | 9 | 300,000 |
| 1953 | 1,964,400 | 6 | 325,000" |

"Even the present traffic is being maintained only because such low fares are being charged. The loss on the suburban service was officially stated in 1949 as being about £130,000 per annum. It is probably greater today, and it appears that suburban passengers are now being carried at somewhat less than half the actual cost. Other factors have influenced the trend following the shifting of the station site in 1930. The economic depression, the development of road transport, both public and private, and the transport difficulties during the war period, all have affected the situation. But any impressions that the total effect of all these factors has been as great as that caused by the shifting of the station site is soon dispelled by a comparison with similar figures to those above relating to the Wellington suburban area:-

| "Year Ended 31st March | Season Ticket Journeys | Journeys per 1000 Population | Population |
|---|---|---|---|
| 1920 | 2,963,000 | 28 | 106,000 |
| 1930 | 6,292,600 | 47 | 133,000 |
| 1940 | 8,701,900 | 54 | 162,000 |
| 1950 | 10,281,800 | 52 | 200,000 |
| 1953 | 9,497,700 | 45 | 210,000" |

"These figures speak for themselves. In particular, they show a decrease of over 75% in traffic on a population basis in the Auckland area since 1930, while the traffic in (the) Wellington area, despite all the other factors previously mentioned, practically kept pace with the growth in population up to 1953 and now in 1954 is ahead." [218]

But not only was the placement of the new Auckland railway station criticised, but also its allegedly ornate design and construction, as reported by the Evening Post:

"The expenditure on Auckland's ornate railway station came in for some vigorous criticism at the hands of the Chief Government Whip, Mr G. O. Munns (Roskill) in the House of Representatives yesterday during the Address-in-Reply debate.

"In countering Opposition attacks on the Government, Mr Munns had referred to some of the legacies the previous Administration had left the United Party on assuming office, to show the difficult time the Government had been through. One has only to look at the Auckland railway station, he said. A magnificent building for any country in the world! A Reform member: Are you not proud of it?

"Mr Munns: No, I am not proud of it. When I stand in the vestibule of the station I see no fewer than eleven electric clocks. Then there are bronze doors and inlaid floors. It seems to have been a shocking waste of money. When I see the station it makes me wonder what vision was in front of those responsible for the expenditure. Admittedly the old station was not suitable from the point of view of egress and access, but the terrific expenditure on that building seems to have been utterly unwarranted.

"Mr Munns declared that the location of the new station had meant an immense loss of revenue. On ordinary race days in Auckland between £200 and £300 used to be taken in fares but now the revenue on race days was between £17 and £19...the trouble was that the people were not going to the new station. They were using other means of transport." [219]

In fact, so desperate had the financial prospects for most of the national railway network become that the Government decided the whole operation should be managed by a Railways Board of five persons. The Board was empowered on 1 June 1931 by the Government Railways Amendment Act of April that year. The Act stipulated that the general functions of the Board:

"...shall be to carry on, control, manage, and maintain the Government railways to the end that the railways, while being maintained as a public service in the interests of the people of New Zealand and as an essential factor in the development of trade and industry, shall be so carried on, controlled, managed, and maintained on the most economical basis, having regard to the economic and financial conditions from time to time affecting the public revenues and trade and industry in New Zealand, with a view to obtaining a maximum of efficiency and maintaining a proper standard of safety and a reasonable standard of comfort and convenience for persons using the railways and any other services carried on in connection therewith." [220]

The Government Railways Amendment Act seemingly delegated the management of the railways to a non-governmental body as previous studies had seriously recommended. However, Parliament had not really forfeited control at all. Indeed, the Railways Board had simply become just another in a long line of report-generating vehicles as Clause 18(1) of the Act illustrates:

"Where after the commencement of this Act any special Act authorizing the construction of any Government railway is passed without a report by the Board on the proposed railway being first laid before Parliament no work in connection with such construction shall, save as such special Act expressly otherwise directs, be undertaken until a report by the Board respecting the railway so authorized is laid before both Houses of Parliament and a resolution approving such work is passed by both such Houses." [221]

Clauses 19 and 20 of the Act also offered up the Railways Board as a convenient buffer between the Railways Minister and those clamouring for improved services and infrastructure:

"19. No addition to or alteration, deviation, or improvement of any railway existing at the commencement of this Act or hereafter constructed shall be made, nor shall any work be done in connection therewith, except upon the recommendation of the Board.

"20. The Board on being satisfied that any railway or part of a railway can continue to be operated only under conditions that will result in the net revenue therefrom being insufficient to cover the working-expenses thereof, or on being satisfied that the continued operation of any railway or part of a railway is otherwise not in the public interest, may cease to operate the same, and with the approval of the Governor-General in Council dispose of the land and all other property of the Crown in respect of such railway or part of a railway." [222]

As might be expected for an organisation of such apparent power, there was no shortage of applicants for the five-man Board which was soon appointed and met for the first time on 17 June 1931. The Board's original members comprised Colonel James Jacob Esson CMG (Chairman – retired Civil Servant, Wellington), Sir James Henry Gunson CMG, OBE (Auckland businessman), Hon. Edward Newman (Marton farmer), Mr Daniel Reese (Christchurch businessman) and Mr George Walter Reid B.Com (Dunedin accountant). The General Manager of Railways, Mr H H Sterling, was appointed as the Board's Chief Executive Officer. [223]

Despite the additional barrier of the Railways Board placed between the aspirations of Northern Suburban Railway League and the Government, the League continued to lobby for the Morningside tunnel. This time, the League combined its efforts with those of the Highways League in suggesting to the Chamber of Commerce that such public works could utilise the Depression's unemployed. However, as reported by the Auckland Star on 30 October 1931, this approach did not find favour with Auckland's businessmen on this occasion:

"The belief that the time was now opportune once more to place the question of the Morningside tunnel before the present Government was expressed in a letter from the Northern Suburban Railway and Highways League which came before the Auckland Chamber of Commerce.

"The letter stated that the route had been proved to be a necessity as part of the Auckland- station scheme. It was understood that between 400 to 500 men could be employed for three years on the work, which would be of great value and would utilise unemployed men to great advantage. In that way the Railways Board would be saved a proportion of capital cost and when completed would save a large annual amount. The league desired to have the matter brought before the Unemployment Board and submitted a resolution for the approval of the chamber

"On the motion of Mr A. M. Seaman it was decided to reply that the time was inopportune, it being stated that such a move would be inconsistent with the chamber's demands for economy." [224]

The Railway League also sought the support of the Local Bodies and the New Lynn Borough Council was of course all in favour as per its response reported by the Auckland Star on 26 November 1931:

"A communication from the Northern Suburban Railway League expressed the opinion that the time was now opportune to place the Morningside tunnel scheme before the Government again. The scheme would provide work for 400 to 500 unemployed men for three years. If the unemployed were utilised the Railway Board would be saved a great deal of the capital cost.

"The following resolution to be forwarded to the Unemployment Board was submitted for the council's consideration:—'That we, the ratepayers and taxpayers of this borough, viewing with alarm the great army of unemployed who are doing work of (in many cases) unimportant and of little practicable value for the money Expended, do herewith submit to you and your board's earnest consideration a work of great importance to the progress of Auckland, its suburbs and the far north, the commencement of the Morningside Tunnel and duplication line to New Lynn.'—The council supported the resolution." [225]

But regardless of the merits of the case and the workforce available, entreaties for the Morningside deviation to be started continued to be sidetracked for a further three years. An example of how a Railways Minister could now avoid embarrassing questions, or delay making a decision, was reported by the Auckland Star on 26 September 1934:

"A request to the Government to proceed this year with improvements to the North Auckland railway outlet, including the Morningside tunnel, was made by Mr H. G. R. Mason (Labour, Auckland Suburbs) in the House of Representatives yesterday. The Minister of Railways, Mr Forbes, stated that he would confer with the Railways Board on the matter." [226]

A year later, the talkfest continued at a conference held on 30 September 1935:

"The desirability of the early prosecution of the Auckland-Morningside railway deviation was affirmed at a conference this afternoon of various local bodies interested in the project and representatives of the Auckland Chamber of Commerce. It was agreed to urge the Government to proceed with the work on the following grounds: (a) As far back as 1924 the scheme was stated by the then general manager of railways to be an economic proposition, in that it reduced distances and grades and provided more direct running. (b) It would directly and indirectly help in the solution of the unemployment problem. (c) It would provide direct access to and from Queen Street for all suburban passengers north and south, thus remedying the drift of traffic away from the railways owing to the present position of the Auckland railway station.

"The scheme, which involved the deviation of the North Auckland railway line by building a tunnel under the city from Beach Road to Morningside, was abandoned by the Government in January, 1930, because of engineering difficulties, the high cost of electrification, the fact that there would be no substantial saving in goods haulage, and the unpromising future of suburban railway transport at that time. Representatives of the Auckland City Council, the New Lynn Borough Council, the Chamber of Commerce, the Glen Eden, Henderson and Manurewa Town Boards and the Waitemata County Council were present.

"The deputy-Mayor, Mr Bernard Martin who presided, in outlining the object of the meeting and moving the motion which was carried, said that the Morningside tunnel had been dropped as one of the economy measures adopted by the Government as a result of the depression. Responsible Ministers recently had been stating that the Government intended to put in hand major public works, and he thought everyone would agree that the Morningside tunnel scheme was one that came under this heading and should meet with the approval of the Government. He was sure also that the scheme would meet with the hearty approval of the people of Auckland. It was obviously not satisfactory for people who lived north of Morningside to have to proceed south for some distance before being able to turn their heads in the direction of their own homes.

"In seconding the motion Mr George Lawson, Mayor of New Lynn, said that in his opinion the Morningside tunnel scheme should never have been taken off the railway programme. If it had been held up as an economy measure it should have been put back on the programme as soon as money was available. He agreed that the work could be undertaken as an unemployment relief scheme. The local bodies in the western suburbs had been battling for the tunnel for 20 years, and it was time the Government proceeded with it. It was absurd to think that passengers from these suburbs had to go round the city before being able to enter it by train. The prosecution of the tunnel scheme would be a distinct benefit to the city, and would also assist in the development of the suburbs.

"Mr A. G. Lunn (Chamber of Commerce) said that no one needed conversion to the scheme, as the advantages of it were so manifold. The time at present was particularly opportune to proceed with it, as money was available at a cheap rate, and in addition it would help to solve the unemployment problem.

"Mr W. A. Bishop (Waitemata County Council) said there was a great cry for work of national benefit, and he did not think there was any work round Auckland that would be more beneficial than the construction of the Morningside tunnel. The Railways Board would never get people in the western suburbs to travel by train to Auckland unless a more rapid service was provided. The Public Works Department was in the process of borrowing or had borrowed a sum of £500,000 to undertake more national work than the Unemployment Board had been undertaking, and in his opinion there was no better way of spending Auckland's share of that money than on the building of the Morningside tunnel and the electrification of the railways which ran in the direction of Swanson. If the tunnel was not built he predicted that in less than ten years it would be necessary to scrap the suburban railway service.

"Mr A. J. Routley (Glen Eden) also thought the time had arrived when the scheme should be gone on with as the work was of an economic nature. Anyone who had observed the suburban trains passing through Newmarket on their round-about way to the city must realise that there was no chance of the suburban railways paying their way. A more direct route to and from the city was required by people in the western suburbs, and they should press for it.

"Mr W. A. Corban (Henderson) said that the trains to Henderson used to consist of from 5 to 10 carriages, and now they had got down to about two carriages, and they were mostly practically empty. Any expenditure on the line would be wise, in his opinion.

"Mr H. A. Robertson (North Suburban Railway and Highways League) explained… The present was a most opportune time to bring the matter forward again, as the work was capable of absorbing from 300 to 500 men for three years, and money was available at a cheap rate. In addition the Railways Board could save £300,000 on the scheme, as electrification of the route would not be necessary, owing to the fact that soft coal could be used, or oil-driven engines similar to those secured for the Tawa Flat deviation could be employed. The scheme involved the erection of a station near Wakefield Street, practically in the heart of the city, and the deviation would save 20 minutes' travelling time for users of the trains from the western suburbs. It would mean a saving of £25,000 to the railways if the need to travel through Newmarket was eliminated, and this in itself would nearly provide the sinking fund for the tunnel scheme. It was absolutely necessary to press for the prosecution of the work at this juncture.

"The motion was carried and it was decided to write to the Prime Minister, Mr Forbes, the Minister of Railways, Mr Coates, and the

Railways Board urging the early commencement of the work, and to various local bodies in the metropolitan area enlisting their support in the move for the completion of the scheme." [227]

As might be expected, both the Chamber of Commerce and the Auckland City Council received less than a positive response to their entreaties:

"The Minister of Employment, Hon. H. T. Armstrong, has advised the Auckland Chamber of Commerce that the Government Railways Board, after reviewing the Morningside tunnel deviation scheme from all angles, had concluded that it was not an economic proposition. When the letter was introduced at the meeting of the Auckland Chamber this morning a member recalled that the board had previously seemed favourable to the scheme. Since then, however, it appeared that they had come to the opinion that it would not be an economical project. The letter was referred to the communications and transport committee to make a full inquiry into the matter.

"The Auckland City Council received a letter last evening from the General Manager of Railways in connection with a resolution passed by the council and adjacent local bodies urging the construction of the Morningside tunnel, stating that the matter had been considered, and the board concluded that the work would not be an economical undertaking. Under the circumstances the board would not recommend the Government to put the work in hand. The letter was received without discussion." [228]

No wonder there was no discussion. What was there to say after more than twenty years of putting one's case? Cruelly, there was a brief glimmer of false hope…from the first Labour Government which took office in late 1935 and was still feeling its way with politically-motivated, health and safety issues:

"The Morningside tunnel project, which was prominently before the Auckland public some years ago, is likely to be revived. The Minister of Public Works, the Hon. R Semple, stated to-day that the question of building the tunnel had not yet been seriously discussed by Cabinet, but would be considered in connection with the policy being carried out of improving communication by road and rail in the light of making the routes safer and shorter. The question will be considered seriously before long, said the Minister. Our policy is to give quicker and safer access to cities and towns by road and rail, and the Morningside tunnel comes into the scheme of things. My opinion also is that all tunnels adjacent to cities should be electrified, to get rid of the smoke and fume nuisance, which is unhealthy and objectionable in every way." [229]

Naturally, those represented by the dogged Northern Suburban Railway League also continued to pursue the Morningside deviation. In its edition of 9 July 1936, the Auckland Star published details of the League's persistence, some 22 years after the 1914 Hiley scheme – the scheme that had intended for the Beach Road station to be a far more suitable 'through' station than an arrested terminus and an economic and strategic disaster:

"A petition setting out facts for consideration in connection with the projected Morningside railway tunnel scheme has been forwarded to the Minister of Railways, the Hon. D. G. Sullivan, by the Northern Suburban Railway League. Owing to a misunderstanding a deputation representing the league was unable to meet the Minister during his visit to Auckland, and the secretary, Mr H. A. Robertson, has forwarded the reasons for his organisation's support of the scheme.

"Pointing out that the league had been advocating a more direct outlet than the existing line for 15 years Mr Robertson expressed the hope that they would soon see their ideal achieved by the Government's sanction and execution of this much-needed improvement for the advancement of the city. He adds that when the railway scheme for Auckland was designed and laid out, this outlet for the North was an integral part of the programme, and was passed and approved by Parliament in 1924. The cost of tunnelling work and the duplication of the line to New Lynn was then estimated at £616,000, and as wages to-day were on a par with those existing at that time, the Department should be able to save a considerable sum, as a grant or assistance could be obtained from the employment fund.

"We commend this work to you as a work of first importance, for the following reasons, states the petition: (1) The vital importance to the transport question of Auckland city; (2) shortening the distance of all north trains; (3) giving much needed facilities to the passengers of the southern, as well as the northern suburban residents; (4) saving of time; (5) saving of train mileage that costs the Department some £25,000 per annum; (6) The advent of the new rail car needs a two-way track; (7) Auckland, the largest city in New- Zealand, is the only city that is being served with a single line track for a very large proportion of its suburban traffic, and also the antiquated method of the tablet system is still operating, causing many vexations, delays and extra cost to the Department.

"Referring to the ever-increasing problem of transport in the city, the league considered that a station in Upper Queen Street and one on the other side of Karangahape Road would ease the congestion considerably. Again, the north of Auckland was rapidly increasing in productivity, the butter output alone representing 25 per cent of the Dominion's total supply. Many tons of fertilisers and various kinds of merchandise made the northern line to-day the best-paying proposition per train mile in New Zealand, it was stated. Any improvement to shorten or straighten the existing line would therefore soon be recouped by the Government.

"The establishment of the tunnel would allow workers to board their trains from the nearest station, going north or south, the time of travelling would be reduced by 20 minutes and the saving of train mileage was undoubtedly an all-important factor in the work of the Department, the league contended. With Auckland linked up by double rail tracks through the outer suburbs, and a glorified train service extended on a circuit, stated the petition in conclusion, the problem of overcrowding in the city would rapidly diminish. A duplication of the northern suburban line would therefore be a necessary adjunct." [230]

For as long as another Government and a new Railways Minister could possibly mean a fresh look at the matter, an unusually united Auckland continued to press for a start on the Morningside tunnel, as reported by the Auckland Star on 28 September 1936:

"A deputation, representing many interests in Auckland, this afternoon laid before the Minister of Railways, the Hon. D. G. Sullivan, representations for the construction of the Morningside tunnel and deviation. The deputation was composed of representatives of the Auckland Chamber of Commerce, the Northern Suburbs Railway League, the New Lynn Borough Council, the Glen Eden Town Board, the Waitemata County Council and the Henderson Town Board.

"The deputation was introduced by the Minister of Justice, the Hon. H. G. R. Mason, who referred briefly to the idea behind the project and its value to the people of Auckland.

"Mr A. G. Lunn, representing the Chamber of Commerce, pointed out that the scheme had been developed and proposed five or six years ago, when the depression was being felt seriously. He suggested that if it were now taken up it would employ a considerable amount of labour and would prove an economic practicability to the Railways Department. It would also provide more rapid access to the waterfront and so open up districts for the building of workers' dwellings. Thus it would prove of profit to the Railways Department.

"Dr E. P. Neale, secretary of the Chamber of Commerce, made the point that while there had been substantial improvements in suburban lines in the south there had not been so many in Auckland. When the Orakei deviation and new station were built it was part of the scheme to take the line north in a tunnel near the station, coming out in the Newton gully. That would have meant a saving in distance of one mile and a quarter, an easing in the grade from 1 in 40 to 1 in 80, and a saving in time of 15 minutes. He suggested the proposal formulated in 1924 had not had a fair hearing or received the consideration it deserved.

"A cross section of local body opinion was contained in the remarks of Mr George Lawson, Mayor of New Lynn, who said that no progress had been made on the north suburban lines for the past 20 years. The tunnel was authorised in 1924, but the scheme had not eventuated. There would be no material improvement in the running time on north suburban lines until the work had been completed. The building of the new station had made matters worse. The speaker contended that the northern suburbs had not been treated fairly in the matter; settlement had been retarded. Travelling time could be cut down by half if the line were duplicated and the tunnel made. There were hundreds of men on sustenance who could be put to useful work and return something to the State. In my opinion no better work could be undertaken by the Government, added the speaker." [231]

Despite the petitioners' sense of immediacy, the Government remained unresponsive, as reported by the Auckland Star on 20 February 1937:

"Towards the end of last year, the Minister of Railways, the Hon. D. G. Sullivan, assured a deputation representing local bodies and the Chamber of Commerce that he would have a fresh examination made into the Morningside tunnel scheme and the electrification proposals for the suburban railways, and that when the report was made available he would confer with Cabinet in the matter.

"In referring to the question this morning, the secretary of the Northern Suburban Railway League, Mr H. A. Robertson, said that since the deputation met the Minister on September 28 last, no further advice had been received with respect to the tunnel scheme. The Minister had also promised to consider the question of extending the time for the use of workers' weekly tickets on the railways till 9 a.m., but though the League had communicated with him in recent months no reply had come to hand. The league for years had urged that this concession should be made, as it felt confident that it would result in a large increase in passengers on the railways." [232]

Despite the silence from Wellington, similar entreaties continued at every opportunity, as reported by the Auckland Star:

"In view of the Public Works estimates now being prepared, the council resolved to write the Minister of Public Works in respect to the Morningside Tunnel deviation proposal. It will be pointed out that the Auckland- Henderson suburban line was the only main centre suburban line in New Zealand that was not either electrified or duplicated; that the line was seriously congested and Auckland the largest New Zealand city." [233]

And again, in August 1938..."The proposed railway tunnel between Morningside and Auckland is the subject of a further communication forwarded to the Minister of Railways, the Hon. D. G. Sullivan, by the Auckland Chamber of Commerce. This action was taken after the council of the chamber had received a reply from the Hon. H. G. R. Mason on behalf of the Minister, which stated that he was unable to give any definite information on the tunnel proposition at the moment. May we express the hope, states the chamber's reply, that your Departmental officers will treat the matter as one of reasonable urgency and that you will let us have a decision at an early date." [234]

Of course, by this time, the matter needed yet another report before any decisions could be made – as per the Minister's reply of September 1938 to the Auckland Chamber of Commerce:

"Every effort will be made to ensure the completion of a report on the scheme for providing a new route for northern railway traffic between Auckland and Morningside by means of tunnel under part of the city through the Arch Hill gully, according to advice contained in a letter from the Minister of Railways, the Hon. D. G. Sullivan, to the Auckland Chamber of Commerce. The Minister explained that a committee of the heads of the operating branches of the railways was appointed to report on the work, but the committee had not up to the present been able to complete its investigations. During the past year it had been called on to investigate many proposals, and the question had been which proposal could most conveniently be deferred." [235]

So there was yet another report to come, following yet another investigation by yet another committee. By 1940, with still no start having been made to improve Auckland's suburban railway network, the City's mayor suggested a half-measure which no doubt reflected the frustration felt by many when it was reported by the Auckland Star on 10 August that year:

"In order to assist in solving the passenger traffic problem in Auckland, a suggestion has been made by the Mayor of Auckland, Sir Ernest Davis, that there should be a re-arrangement in handling the suburban railway traffic, to enable suburban passenger trains to be brought approximately half a mile closer to the centre of the city.

"Sir Ernest suggests that the vacant railway land at the corner of Britomart Place and Beach Road should be used as the site of a suburban passenger station. There would not be need to erect elaborate buildings as covered platforms would meet the case for the present, and as the lines were already laid, the Department could no doubt adjust them to link with the main lines. The Mayor said that he realised that the problems facing the Auckland Transport Board were very real, and it was a highly technical subject calling for experience. He felt satisfied to abide by their judgment. But rail traffic was another matter and it seemed a simple question to deal with.

"He considered that the proposed change would revitalise suburban rail traffic, and it was easy to visualise electric trains running on the old main line to Newmarket and on the new line to Orakei. There was no question that the population was shifting eastward. He was certain that such a change would increase shopping in the city. Sir Ernest added that it was necessary to look ahead and plan accordingly. He looked forward to the time when all suburban traffic lines would be electrified, and the nuisance of the engine sheds on the Tamaki Drive done away with." [236]

The suggestion that a new station closer to the city centre naturally drew a reminder from Mr H A Robertson of the Northern Suburban Railway League, published in the Auckland Star several days later:

"I read with keen interest the comments made by Sir Ernest with reference to a railway station closer to the city. Some years ago the Northern Suburban Railway League—a league consisting of all the northern local bodies, the Auckland Chamber of Commerce and the Karangahape Business Men's and Ratepayers' Associations—impressed the then Government with the necessity of providing a new and quicker outlet for passengers and workers, pointing out that traffic congestion would inevitably be the outcome if the matter was left.

"In 1924, the Rt. Hon. J. G. Coates had the whole scheme passed as an Act of Parliament. Included in this scheme of works was the Auckland railway station and the Morningside tunnel, including a double line to New Lynn. The Auckland station was planned and built for this purpose, and had it proceeded according to plan there would not have arrived today any question of congestion. Sir Joseph Ward, who became Prime Minister, however, stopped this work. Later the world depression made finance difficult and thus the Forbes-Coates Government could not reinstate the scheme. The present Government had been waited upon on several occasions but unfortunately, to date, it has not seen the great benefit that this tunnel would be to the city.

"I quite agree with Sir Ernest that a station is required nearer the main centre of the city, and as one studies the map of Auckland, a station in Upper Queen Street would seem to be the centre, as it would serve both the city and Karangahape Road. I cannot agree, however, that a station at Britomart Place, as suggested, would be of great benefit. Further, as the

Auckland station was built for the purpose of providing a northern outlet on raised land, it would be well-nigh impossible for trains to leave Britomart Place and go north. The Railway Department is proceeding with the duplication of the line from Morningside to Swanson, and this work, which will be of great benefit for the quick working of trains, will be almost of no value owing to the bottle-neck at Newmarket. The scheme, therefore, becomes a matter of urgency to the Department as well as the public." [237]

Of course, as in a past era and during a previous war, by 1940, any public works urgency was soon subverted by wartime constraints and shortages of labour and materials. However, hopes remained for the construction of the Morningside tunnel as a post-war project, as reported by the Auckland Star on 28 September 1944:

"Reference to the future development of the Auckland city and suburban railway facilities is made by the Minister of Railways, Mr Semple, in a letter received by the Mayor, Mr Allum, this morning.

"I desire to inform you that the Morningside tunnel project is being included in a ten-year plan of railway development, which is being submitted by the Railways Department to the Government as part of the post-war rehabilitation programme, states Mr Semple. Regarding the question of electrification, Mr Semple states that any railway development schemes adopted will be carried out in the light of the most modern methods of railway operation known, with regard to the physical difficulties associated with the various works undertaken.

"The Morningside tunnel scheme was approved by Parliament in 1924, but was removed from the railway works schedule during the depression. It provided for a double-track underground line to avoid the route through Newmarket. Entrance to the main tunnel would be between Beach Road and Anzac Avenue. The tunnel would pass below the south-eastern corner of the Supreme Court building, under Government House grounds, and below Albert Park. At Wakefield Street, where the depth would be only 30 feet, an underground station would be provided. From Wakefield Street the tunnel would be on a straight line to its exit just beyond Newton Road. It would be 130 feet below Karangahape Road…The length of the tunnel would be a mile and a half." [238]

Summary

From the rejection of Felton Mathew's first vision of a railway line between Panmure and the Manukau Harbour in 1840, the development of Auckland's suburban railway network has been a woeful tale of political intrigue and jealousy, economic frailty, and general procrastination of such magnitude that expert and expensively-obtained advice was effortlessly circumvented and ignored as a matter of course.

As the country's transportation needs evolved, the parliamentary record has continued to be littered with decades of reports of enquiries, much of which have been debated, and decided, and not decided, and decisions reversed and reversed again. Consequently, despite the energy and money that had been expended on the country's railway system since the 1870s, the network remained vulnerable to the competition posed by all road-based transport systems, ranging from the first horse-drawn and electric trams to the final coffin nail of the motor car and buses of the twentieth century.

By 1940, an efficient Auckland suburban railway had been more or less discounted as a viable competitor, particularly after the misplacement of the city's main railway station. That was certainly the opinion of the Public News in 1932 when the paper commented:

"It is ironic that the railways, whose network girds the nation should fail Auckland on the last kilometre. Yet it is that short, downtown connection which could put Auckland public transport back on the rails. The railway's failure is marked by a splendid monument in Coromandel granite, Whangarei marble and New Lynn brick." [239]

By 1944, after decades of indecision, the Morningside tunnel proposal was once again on the political table. However, as detailed in Volume Two, Gas Pedal to Back-Pedal, there was still a great deal of procrastination to come…entangled in more nets of endless studies and reports.

*Chapter Seven*

# The Omnibuses - The Ancillaries Vie for Supremacy

"Some settlements, away from the iron tracks of the railway, would never have prospered without the rise of road transport. Service cars helped to spread a population which had previously been clustered around seaports or strung along the railways more widely." [1]

"...the bullock dray express was the first means of transit between Auckland and Onehunga and also from Riverhead to Helensville. A colonel who visited Auckland during the first term of Sir George Grey as Governor of the colony, in an interesting book written regarding his sojourn here, relates how they went on a trip in a bullock dray. Bedding was laid on the floor of the vehicle to make the journey more easy for the ladies who had to get to a Government House party, and did not want to walk through the mud.

"As Auckland progressed, a bus was run from the city to Parnell by the late Mr W. Crowther, and Hardingtons ran a service between Auckland and Onehunga. A bus service was also run to Ponsonby, Mr Joe Bainbridge being a very popular driver. Later Cobb and Co. ran buses between Auckland and Hamilton." [2]

"As the population increased, the omnibuses provided a passenger service from Auckland to Onehunga. Captain John Henry Hardington started the first regular public transport service in 1860 and by 1864 business had increased so much that the buses had to run hourly." [3]

Indeed, Captain Hardington was doing so well that, in June 1864, The New Zealand Herald was prompted to report:

"Hardington's New Omnibus — On Friday and Saturday a handsome new omnibus, drawn by a fine team of four horses, was seen about the town; the omnibus white, neatly picked out with quiet colours, of a good shape for comfort and room, and excellently ventilated along the roof, turned out to be Mr Hardington's new omnibus for Onehunga, in the place of one of the present less convenient vans. With such vehicles drawn by horses like those at present in use, Mr Hardington need fear no competition." [4]

Nevertheless, throughout the 1860s and beyond, there was a great need for competition, and the improvement and expansion of public transport throughout the growing city:

"Omnibus Conveyance — It is reported that a new claimant for the public patronage in this line is about to offer himself and that he is a practised driver in Australia, and will start omnibuses to Onehunga and Otahuhu. There is great room for improvement, and a little spirited competition will no doubt conduce to the public advantage and cause the class of carriages to resemble the omnibus which is, we hear, about to be placed upon the roads, which is undoubtedly a handsome public carriage.

"It is now too, that the suburbs of Auckland are increasing so rapidly, becoming necessary that omnibuses should ply between the town and Remuera, Parnell, Newmarket, and so on, so that people might build their houses further from town, and so lessen the scramble for land in its immediate vicinity." [5]

However, these horse-drawn conveyances were only as efficient and comfortable as the condition of the colony's roads would allow. By the early 1860s, the condition of Auckland's roads varied from awful to good, depending on the season and the terrain over which they were expected to support more frequent and increasingly heavier traffic. As The New Zealand Herald pointed out in an editorial published on 20 November 1863, as well as the transportation of passengers and mail, there were also troops and supplies to be despatched to the Waikato at that time:

"Speaking of the roads, when are they to be made good? Carts, waggons, and buses, are not stuck up, but stuck down now-a-days. The roads are fearful in some places, and endanger life and limb wherever you go. One of the buses got stuck at Papakura on Tuesday night, and passengers had to walk here, which they accomplished about nine o'clock instead of seven. 'Very pleasant, indeed, weather considered.' Then, again, one mail-coach met the same fate, just in sight of Drury, with similar results, and the mail would have been considerably behind time if it had not been for the kindness of a settler who brought it forward. Surely something should be done to put an end to these great evils if the war is to be carried on as it should be." [6]

Even for 'the respectable portion of the community', bus travel could be hazardous so it is hardly surprising that, during his final ride along the Great South Road in 1864, a somewhat less than respectable citizen, it was implied, twice succumbed to the triple whammy of over-indulgence and overcrowding over a rough patch:

"An inquest was held on Saturday, at the Settlers' Hotel, Otahuhu, on the remains of Jno. Birch, formerly of the Mauku Volunteers, who met his death from a fall from the Drury omnibus on the previous Thursday.

"Deceased, who was intoxicated was, it appears, riding on the top of the bus, and fell off into the road when nearly opposite Burton's. There were 12 passengers inside and thirteen on the outside, and there were no iron guards at the dies on the top of the bus. Near the Grange the deceased again fell off and one of the hind wheels passed over his groin. He died within 27 hours. It seems that other of the inside passengers were drunk, and that the driver, by his own admission on the inquest, receives passengers either drunk or sober, quite 'permiscuous like'. If buses are so crowded and if such a disreputable practise is pursued the sooner that a little healthy competition is started the better will it be for the respectable portion of the community who have to travel on the Great South Road. The Jury returned a verdict in accordance with the evidence." [7]

But as well as the possibility of not completing a journey alive, the limited space aboard these public conveyances could also greatly affect a passenger's comfort, as reported by The New Zealand Herald on 31 August 1864:

"Yesterday afternoon as a lady was coming into town by one of the Onehunga Buses, she was annoyed at receiving the full benefit of several blasts of tobacco smoke from a male passenger, although there are tickets in the inside of each Bus, prohibiting smoking. The gent observing the annoyance which he was occasioning remarked that he would go outside, 'Oh not at all,' replied the lady 'I shall go,' and quickly as said she was safely ensconced beside the driver, evidently greatly relieved at escaping from the rudeness of her fellow passenger." [8]

But while some prohibitions were often ignored, there were some safety aspects, considered absolutely essential today, that were purely voluntary in May 1868:

"To the Editor of the Herald. Dear Mr Editor, —I am very glad to see that some of the night buses now carry lamps, which is a very great convenience and comfort, and imparts an additional sense of security to those who have to travel by them after dark. Some of the vehicles, however, have not these lights, and I want you to tell me, Mr Editor, if there is a clause in any of the Acts to compel them to carry them, as well as all vehicles running after dark; if there is not, I think you will agree with me that there ought to be such a regulation in force. I must say, Mr Editor, that the bus drivers appear to be a very careful and obliging class of men, but you know if they travel in the dark a collision might occur, and that would be so very dreadful. —Yours, &c; Fanny." [9]

By the end of 1869, the public transport service provided by buses was still very patchy with overall coverage no doubt determined by the greater number of passengers able to afford a service to the more affluent suburbs. For instance, those living in the western suburbs, such as Dedwood (renamed Ponsonby in 1873), obviously had little choice but to walk:

"To the Editor of the Herald. Sir, — Amongst the other advances in civilization which Auckland has made within the last few years, how is it that no omnibuses have been laid on to the western suburbs? One paying line would, I should imagine, be found direct between the foot of Queen-street and Newton. Another would be found starting for the Union Bank, up Victoria-street, through Freeman's Bay and College-street to Ponsonby-road, thence by Franklyn and Wellington streets, into town again.

"With fares of 3d for all passengers within the city boundaries, and 6d for all passengers passing them, the speculation would be a success. The Dedwood district is rapidly filling up, and the very fact that public conveyances connected it with Queen-street, would render it still more attractive as a place of residence. There is quite as much room for a line of buses westward as there is to Parnell. The thing only wants trying with comfortable conveyances, not with express-vans as was done on a former occasion.—Yours, &c., Too Far to Walk. Newton, November 11." [10]

As well as any new routes, any sort of depot facilities or regular timetables for many of the bus services was still to be regulated by the City Board, the forerunner of the City Council. As competition increased, such regulations became even more important and, in this instance, a regular departure was required as a condition of standing at a point obviously convenient for prospective passengers:

"Applications were received from Mr Crowther and Mr John King, asking for permission to allow their buses to stand at the foot of Shortland-street. Some discussion arose and an opinion was expressed that so many buses standing at the bottom of Shortland-street was a great nuisance.

"Mr Sceats drew attention to the fact that Mr King did not run his buses regularly, but only just to suit his own convenience. Unless Mr King chose to run his vehicles regularly, he ought not to be allowed to stand at the bottom of Shortland-street. Mr George moved 'That a part of Shortland-street, near the Post-office, be set apart as a stand and that Mr Crowther's and Mr King's application be granted, on condition that they start a bus at least every half-hour'. Mr Staines moved, as an amendment, 'That the stand remain where it is'. The original motion was carried." [11]

As well as the City's early transport regulations, the original omnibus proprietors had also to contend with increased competition, as reported by The New Zealand Herald on 9 June 1870:

"A strong opposition has commenced running against Hardington's Onehunga line of omnibuses, by several parties with covered express vans. Mr Hardington has, for a long time, supplied the travelling public with commodious vehicles and civil drivers, at regular hours, but, judging by the amount of patronage bestowed on the opposition vehicles, the public are glad to travel at lower fares. A slight collision occurred in Onehunga on Tuesday between two of the rivals, which resulted in the loss of a wheel to one of them." [12]

Much as they have always done, those regulations also contained many financial pitfalls, tolls not being the least of them. However, as reported by The New Zealand Herald on 21 December 1871, those in the business of public conveyance were being given some financial incentive to expand their services:

"We are very glad to see that the request of the petitioners on the question of toll bar dues has been acceded to by the Superintendent, and that, in consequence, every public conveyance drawn by one or two horses will only be charged a shilling, with sixpence for every additional horse above two. It is some days since we drew public attention to the petition, which was most numerously and influentially signed, and we must say that we think the action of the Government most judicious in the matter.

"In consequence of this we may now expect to see omnibuses running regularly to Remuera, Mount Albert, and other suburban retreats, which will be of great benefit and convenience not only to residents in those localities, but also to many townspeople, who will thus he enabled to obtain the benefit of a trip to the regions of green fields at reasonable cost. We see that Mr Crowther will start a bus on the Remuera Road with the new year." [13]

But even as long ago as the 1870s, the growth of a business often outstripped a city's regulations (no matter how 'excellently governed') and its capacity to cope with rapid expansion and public need:

"Mr Hardington has been again summoned for an alleged breach of another city by-law, having come out successfully in the last case brought against him. This time he is charged with obstructing the traffic by having no less than three omnibuses opposite his premises on the morning of the departure of the Phoebe.

"It is well known that on the day in question there was an extraordinarily large number of passengers to be conveyed to the Phoebe at Onehunga, and the spectacle of so much bustle on that morning outside the Greyhound was cheering in the extreme, but Mr Hardington must answer to the city by-law for allowing such a commotion in the streets of this excellently governed city. The fact that Mr Hardington is mail contractor, and that in addition to the extra number of passengers he was conveying the mails for every port in New Zealand (except Napier) is entirely beside the question, and he must consult the by-laws at the risk of incurring the heavier penalties attached to delaying Her Majesty's mails.

"The case will come before the Court on Thursday, when it will no doubt be submitted that an obstruction was caused, although the contrary is the fact notwithstanding three whole omnibuses being outside the Greyhound at one time. This is the manner in which honest industry is fostered in this city." [14]

However, by the end of 1873, there came upon Auckland a revolutionary mode of travel that was to render irrelevant the omnibus competition existing to that time. But just who was in charge of this revolution, and had the revolution actually started?

"We scarcely feel competent of pronouncing whether the railway between Auckland and Onehunga was or was not officially opened on Saturday last. We know that the Messieurs Brogden and Sons issued a large number of invitations to the citizens of Auckland, their wives, relatives, and female friends. We know that the train left Fort Britomart at one o'clock, carrying a goodly company, and that upon arrival at the Onehunga terminus the company — ladies and gentlemen — were most hospitably entertained. We know that the whole affair passed off with great *éclat*: that his Honor Sir G. A. Arney, Chief Justice, his Honor the Superintendent, his Worship the Mayor, and many of our leading citizens, went out and came back; and that the occasion was in all respects most auspicious." [15]

Of course, even revolutions have to be paid for, and until the cost was competitive, it might not succeed, advised the Herald:

"But we are not in a position to say whether the line was opened upon the authority of the General or Provincial Governments, or simply upon the responsibility of the contractors; neither do we know who has had the fixing of the almost prohibitory tariff which is announced for the running of the line. We only know that it is very excessive; that complaints are loud and deep about it, and that very many people will prefer to use horse-conveyance to steam-power at the rate fixed for passenger traffic.

"It is probable the price for permanent transit will in time be considerably lowered. It is expedient it should. It must be borne in mind that the omnibuses run along a road on the line of which many hundreds of persons are dwellers. That the drivers pick up and drop passengers and parcels at any portion of it required. That they stop or drive on and accommodate their customers in all possible ways, short of delaying the journey to the inconvenience or annoyance of the majority of those using the conveyances.

"Unless the railway between this and Onehunga can compete against such odds, it will not subserve the purpose intended in the interests of the public. The journey to Onehunga and back on Saturday was rapidly performed. The carriages glided along the rails smoothly, and it was only in one or two places any oscillation was felt, and this only to a slight extent. But the sooner we know all about the time, in whose hands it is, who are responsible for its safe management, and what the permanent rate of tariff is to be settled at, the more satisfied and assured the public will feel. [Since the above was in type we are informed that the line will be worked by Messrs Brogden and Sons until April next, and that this firm will be held responsible for all matters connected with it until the time it is taken over by the Government.]" [16]

But regardless of just who the ultimate owners of the steam service to Onehunga and beyond were to be, the competition posed by the service was enough to persuade the veteran omnibus proprietor, John Henry Hardington, to sell up not long after that first run:

"Mr Hardington's horses, omnibuses, harness, lamps, &c. were auctioned to-day by Mr Alfred Buckland. There was a good attendance of bidders. The horses fetched fair prices, averaging from £10 to £30. The ordinary omnibuses fetched from £7 to £10, which appeared a sacrifice, considering that they cost £80 when new. The mammoth coach, which cost £280 was not sold. The sale realised about £1300, we believe." [17]

Nevertheless, the reins of the omnibus as a conveyance had not altogether been dropped and competition for public patronage continued and was never as fierce as among the omnibus drivers themselves. Not only did this result in injury but also the type of court proceedings reported by The New Zealand Herald on 6 January 1876:

"[Before R. C. Bantow, Esq., R.M.] Negligent Driving — W. White was charged with carelessly driving an omnibus on the Onehunga Road.

"J. T. Boylan deposed: I was a passenger in defendant's coach on the 20th November last. An accident occurred at Epsom. Gillham was driving another coach at the same place in the same direction. He was ahead of our vehicle. The coach I was in swerved off the metal on to the siding. I looked out of the window and saw the driver standing in the ditch. I opened the door to get out, as the horses appeared to be only walking, when just as I got on the step the horses gave a sudden start and I was pitched out, hurting my shoulder. I believe our driver was passing Gillham at the time. I don't think defendant was driving fast; he is a very careful driver.

"C. L. Long deposed: I was a passenger on the outside of defendant's coach on this occasion. I was thrown off and much hurt. Gillham's coach was just in front, and defendant was trying to pass. Gillham did not draw towards his side of the road, he kept the centre. There was not sufficient room left for defendant to pass. There would have been ample room if Gillham had kept on his proper side. There was no racing. It was necessary for White to pass at this place; he could not pull up in the act of passing.

"Defendant deposed: Gillham was before me. I overtook him on the road. We were not going fast. I called to Gillham that I wanted to pass. He would not give me room on the metal, and in pulling off on to the grass one of the wheelers slipped and fell, and I was put off the box. The coach then passed over some ruts. I should have passed safely if the horse had not slipped and I lost my seat. Case dismissed — R. Gillham was then charged with negligently driving. Mr Keetley appeared for defendant. The evidence was the same. The charge of negligent driving was not sustained. The Bench said if Gillham was obstructing the road there was another clause bearing on that." [18]

As well as the competition, the proprietors and drivers of public conveyances had also to contend with the rules and regulations meant to physically and financially protect their passengers, as illustrated by a letter to The New Zealand Herald in February 1876 and the Auckland Star later that year:

"To the Editor of the Herald: Sir, — Your correspondent, 'Sufferer', writes the trouble and bother of summonsing extortionate cabmen and carters, and therein he makes a mistake. He should let them summons him, after having tendered them their legal fare. So long as people will take no trouble, and put up with this system, so long will tricksters continue to take advantage (particularly of strangers). I have taken the trouble to look up the Corporation laws, and those who can afford the luxury of riding may learn that:

- No omnibus or city stage carriage may ply other than to the termini or route endorsed on its licence, under a penalty of 40s, and costs.
- Any owner or driver convicted of one offence may have the licence for the vehicle suspended; for two or more offences, revoked.
- Plying for hire without having the number of persons licensed to be carried, or carrying excessive number, or refusing to carry full number and luggage: penalty, 40s.

- Refusing or neglecting to drive any carriage within the prescribed space where directed (ten-miles radius from the General Post Office) at a speed not less than six miles per hour; penalty, 40s.
- Carrying passengers in any hackney carriage, during the hire thereof, without consent of the persons hiring: penalty, 40s.
- Agreement for excessive fares not binding, and any person who demands or exacts such charge is liable to a penalty of 40s, and to refund overcharge, if paid.
- No owner or driver, having agreed to take any fare for time, or to or from any place, shall refuse or neglect, under a penalty of 40s.
- Plying elsewhere than on standing, loitering, or causing any obstruction, or interfering with any other carriage or driver: penalty, 40s.
- Omnibuses must not stand or ply elsewhere than on standing, or who stop or delay on route, save in succession or turn penalty: 40s.
- Every driver who improperly delays or wilfully deceives any passenger as to route, or demands more than lawful fare, or who stops such carriage across any crossing, or blowing any horn or noisy instrument, or who shall smoke (after objection has been made by any passenger) penalty: 20s.
- Carrying any noisy or drunken person, furious driving, insulting language, damaging property penalty: £5, or three months' imprisonment.
- Fares must be painted upon every carriage under a penalty of £5.
- Carriage lights and lights inside stage carriages, under a penalty of 40s.
- All property left in carriages must be left at the office of the Town Clerk, under a penalty of £20.
- Every driver must produce card of fares, and have same displayed in carriage, under penalty of £5.

"The greater number of these regulations, it appears, also apply to carts and carters and, although it would appear the City Council have not enforced a great many of these necessary regulations, still the public will find they are amply protected against extortionate or dishonest drivers; so the real remedy lies with themselves. I am, &c., R. R." [19]

"With reference to a letter from the driver of an Onehunga omnibus, we learn that the carrying of any drunken person, or the serving of liquor to passengers, is an offence against the vehicle and passenger regulations of the city, for which the driver renders himself liable to a penalty of £5 and costs, and upon a second conviction, a risk of losing his licence. From the disinclination of persons to come forward and give information at the Police Court, a great deal of laxity exists among drivers in respect of the various regulations for the comfort and protection of travellers. A time will come, however, when these rules must be enforced." [20]

But while all omnibus and carriage proprietors and drivers were subject to the same regulations and penalties, each could at least compete by means of the services provided and the fares they charged. Quick by name and quick by nature, one omnibus proprietor soon saw the benefit of targeting numbers with a reduction of his fares for buses to and from the suburbs. (The following two articles also illustrate the growing preference for the term 'bus in place of omnibus. In time, of course, the apostrophe was dropped altogether.)

"Mr F. Quick has at last led the way in lowering the fare of the suburban 'busses. He has now added a fourth bus to the Ponsonby run. The 'busses start every quarter of an hour, two leaving for the Newton end and two for the Dedwood end. The fare is so low, that must close up all grumblers, who are worth a closing up. This will be a great boon to travellers. Tickets: are being issued daily. We are informed that 1000 have gone in a very short time. Mr Quick has written to San Francisco, for information regarding the most recent facilities in omnibus travelling. We wish Mr Quick every success in his new enterprise." [21]

Not to be outdone, services to the eastern suburbs were also improved at the same time:

"Mr Wm. Lundon started a handsome light omnibus to-day for the special purposes of carrying passengers and the mail between Auckland, Howick, and Panmure. The heavier 'bus, hitherto used for passengers, will come in two days in the week for the conveyance of luggage and goods. The new 'bus was built by Messrs Bruce and Bull, and is a credit to the builders. It is very tastefully painted and ornamented, carpeted and fringed, and one of the neatest vehicles of the kind that has yet been produced by our coachbuilders." [22]

Meanwhile, the main competition to the omnibus was raising its fares:

"The Onehunga people are loudly complaining that the new regulations connected with railway passengers and traffic instead of decreasing their burdens and increasing their convenience, go in an entirely opposite direction, as the fares to and from Onehunga for passengers have been suddenly increased. Of course, the omnibus proprietors running their conveyances between town and Onehunga are delighted, and, as a consequence, men may reasonably expect that the buses, and not the regular trains, will have the larger share of the passenger traffic if the railway fares are not reduced. On Saturday many of the passengers travelling on both the Mercer and Onehunga lines were informed that in future no copper tokens would be taken for the part payment of either goods or passengers." [23]

But the Auckland to Onehunga and Mercer Railway was finding it tough going, particularly after its management had been relocated to Wellington and to Government boffins who seemed to have little appreciation for local conditions and the competition affecting the profitability of its passenger and freight services.

By November and December 1875, not long after the main trunk line had reached Mercer, the railway returns did not show the profit expected of it:

"We have already drawn attention to the extraordinary result of the December working of the Auckland and Mercer railway. The returns for November showed a loss of £880 exclusive of interest on the cost. The returns for December show a further loss of £1,368, making a deficiency of £2,250 for only two months. In other words the expenses have exceeded the receipts by that amount.

"The working expenses bear for November the proportion of 153 per cent, to the receipts. For December they exceed 200 per cent. We are asked to believe, on behalf of the Government, that the wretched results for December are owing to floods which rendered repairs necessary and which stopped the traffic. We decline to accept the excuse. It is unreasonable on its face...The excuse is too palpably an afterthought to save Ministers from the blame which this railway business will justly bring upon them.

"When the railway policy was adopted, certain prospects were held out in connection with it. We have a right to ask that Ministers will either admit those prospects to have been based upon miscalculation, or that they will correct the mismanagement by which the prospects are being so grossly falsified. For our own part we believe that the present system must be put an end to without delay. The convenience of the customers of the railway and their interests must be the first consideration if the railway is not to be a disaster to the province. In the nature of a barren uniformity everything is to be centered in Wellington and no one is to have the least power in Auckland. The terminus is to be kept in an inconvenient place. The rates are to be so ill-calculated that the omnibus and the dray are preferred." [24]

By the end of December 1877, little had changed for Auckland's omnibus services as far as outside competition was concerned. As commented on by The New Zealand Herald of 28 December 1877, the inefficiency of the railway to provide an economical alternative continued to be a major concern:

"It will be admitted as a general rule, that a railway to be successful should be so managed, by means of an attractive tariff of charges and due consideration of public convenience, as to absorb the great bulk of the traffic, both of goods and passengers, and in effect to render successful competition by the ordinary road an impossibility. What has happened here in Auckland in regard to this very doctrine, indisputable as it is?

"Our railway management with its cast iron rule has simply tended to encourage competition. The ordinary road from Auckland to Onehunga, despite the railway, sees more omnibus traffic than it ever did. In a letter to Mr Tole, M.H.R., dated 21st September last, written by Mr Clayton, Chairman of the Newmarket Highway District, laid before the Railway Committee, the writer says that on that day the afternoon train from Onehunga arrived at Newmarket 'without a single passenger either first or second class.' 'Since the fares have been revised,' he adds, 'the traffic has lessened, whilst the 'buses that ply between Auckland and Onehunga are crowded with passengers inside and out.'

"Mr Clayton makes the common-sense practical suggestion, in keeping with the doctrine we have already ennuciated (sic), that the proper course is to make the fares such 'as to compete with the road traffic.' A general manager is wanted, with ability and judgment, farsightedness, and common sense practice, to make the line, defeat any competition, that any ordinary road can offer, and this is especially what is wanted in Auckland, where the road is seriously interfering with the growth of traffic by the rail; which is a condition of affairs that ought not to exist." [25]

Not that road-based transport had it all its own way at the time:

"If it is any use again to urge on the authorities the necessity for properly forming the new road on the reclaimed land between Customhouse-street and Parnell Railway Bridge, attention to its wretched condition is once more directed. Rugged, uneven, ill-formed, with no pretence to possessing a proper superficial curve, abounding in hollows, which become pools of mud after rain — the road is a disgrace. It cost, it is said, some £2000 to put it in the almost impassable state it now presents. About £100 more would make it fit for general traffic; would save a weary round to the omnibus horses and those of other vehicles, which have to be dragged up hills which this roadway, if decently formed, would enable them to avoid. The road has remained too long unfinished. Mention has frequently been made of the great necessity that exists for its completion, which would confer no small improvement on the traffic to and from Parnell. Surely the small additional expenditure required will now be granted." [26]

Nevertheless, the omnibus continued to prosper as Auckland's primary public transport system serving the suburban regions of the growing city. Until the introduction of the first horse-drawn trams in 1884:

"Horse drawn buses were the first form of regular public transport in the (Balmoral) area. Two services were running in the late 1870s with one serving Mt Eden Road while the other ran down Dominion Road. Around 1880 Mt Albert was also connected with the city by horse bus." [27]

*Chapter Eight*

# On Your Bike

Of course, throughout the late nineteenth century and later, there was still to be seen "...the occasional man or woman on horseback; and pedestrians and cyclists. By far the most widely used form of urban transport was 'shanks pony' – pedestrianism – but there had been a boom in cycling following the invention of the 'safety bicycle' in the 1880s." [1]

The advent of the bicycle certainly encouraged young women, in particular, to take to the streets but "Although the term 'bone-shaker' applied to the forerunners of the penny-farthing, it could equally well be applied to any bicycle. The state of the roads saw to that." [2]

But, despite the state of the roads, cycling became such a popular means of transportation and recreational pastime that, as such activities do, it soon attracted first the attention of the Auckland City Council, established in April 1871, and then the national tax gatherers at Parliament.

The Auckland City Council "...appointed its first traffic inspector in 1894, in an attempt to bring order to the increasing level of vehicular traffic in the central city area. From 1896, a licensing programme, initiated under the inspector, required bicycles to be registered with the Town Clerk and the registration number displayed on the bicycle." [3]

Not long after, what was to be described as a form of double taxation, justified as funding necessary for much-needed improvements to the cyclists' lot, was introduced to the House of Representatives as The Cycle Traffic Act 1898.

Ostensibly "...to provide for the Formation and Maintenance of Cycle Tracks, and the Regulation of the Cycle Traffic" [4] the Bill was introduced to Parliament in July of that year by Joseph Ward, MP for Awarua, Postmaster General, and later Prime Minister.

In general, the Cycle Bill called for every cycle owner living within seven miles of the main post office of certain town centres to register their conveyance with the local authority at a cost not exceeding five shillings per annum. This fee, less reasonable administration costs, was then to:

"...be devoted by the local authority to making and forming from time to time tracks for the use of cyclists in any portion of the cycle area to which the public have access, and so that as far as possible provision shall be made for keeping the cycle traffic on separate tracks, and apart from the ordinary vehicular traffic." [4]

During the first reading of the Bill, Mr Alexander Hogg, MP for Masterton, disagreed with the arbitrary nature of its provisions and said so:

"The object of the Bill, so far as he understood it, was to give local bodies the means of raising revenue for the purpose of constructing cycle-tracks. That object he thoroughly sympathised with. But what did the Bill really mean? It meant the imposition of a new tax, and he thought, considering the large number of taxes the people had to pay at the present time, there really existed no necessity for increasing those taxes for the object mentioned in this Bill." [5]

In what can now be viewed as a somewhat naïve statement, Mr Hogg went on to point out:

"From time to time efforts had been made to tax vehicles, but a tax of that kind was repugnant to the feelings of the people. What would be thought of a Bill to specifically tax perambulators? That could not be more objectionable than this measure." [6]

Mr George Fisher, MP for the City of Wellington, later responded:

"It was at present an offence under the Police Offences Act for women to drive perambulators along footpaths, but never yet had he seen a policeman 'game' enough to arrest a woman with a perambulator." [7]

Mr Frederick Flatman, MP for Geraldine:

"Bicycles were always useful, because people could get from one point to another in a very short time, and at far less expense than they could do by the use of horses. That was the object of a bicycle; and these machines ought to be able to go upon a road over which any other light vehicles could pass." [8]

Mr Roderick McKenzie, the MP for Motueka and later a Minister of Public Works and Mines:

"...was strongly of the opinion that that was the best thing to do with the cyclists, to let them go on the road, and let them take their chance amongst other wayfarers. He agreed with the leader of the Opposition, not only that cyclists were not yet sufficiently numerous to require legislation, but he was of the opinion that in the course of a few years these bicycles would be practically obsolete. In a few years' time they would probably have an improved motor-car, and if the cyclists were to have special roads, no doubt the honourable members for Ellesmere and Awarua, if they were members then, would want special tracks made for the motor-cars. He did not think it was at all likely the local authorities would be prepared to go on spending the ratepayers' money for that particular purpose." [9]

As we now know, 'special tracks' have been made for motor-cars, ad nauseam, and the bicycle did not become obsolete. Indeed, despite a continuing lack of dedicated cycle tracks and the poor quality of road surfaces, the bicycle encouraged young women, in particular, to take to the streets in greater numbers:

"For the first time, people had a means of personal transportation which they hadn't had since they gave up keeping horses." [10]

Before long, the importance of that 'means of personal transportation' would become the catch-cry for the promoters of a very different mode of conveyance and the independence it fostered. By the time of his death in 1934, Roderick McKenzie was indeed to see an 'improved motor-car', together with its 'special tracks' – along with a great number of other facilities, all well and truly paid for with 'ratepayers money'.

But before the motor car could "triumph…as the supreme form of land transport in this country", [11] the new conveyance had first to usurp the already well-established services provided by the trains, the buses and the trams.

## Chapter Nine

# The Dominance of the Centre Line - The Age of Trams

"The suburban development of Auckland depended on the availability of land, affordable transport and the desire of the middle class to move out of the crowded inner city." [1]

Not surprisingly, that dependence was soon recognised by the entrepreneurs of the time. Those businessmen sought to satisfy 'the desire of the city's middle class' by providing not only the land, but also a cheap means by which they could commute to and from it. However, they first had to obtain approval and certain concessions from the Auckland Improvement Commission (constituted by the Auckland Improvement (Albert Barrack Reserves) Act 1872), the Auckland City Council, and the various local bodies responsible for the areas into which they intended to project their public transport schemes.

One of the earliest of these supplications, by way of a letter of proposal to the Auckland Improvement Commission, was considered by the Commissioners and reported by the Auckland Star on 23 April 1873:

"A letter from Messrs O'Neill, Thomas and Co. was read, requesting the permission of the Commissioners to lay street tramways within the lands under their charge in terms similar to those proposed by the writers in an application to the City Council. The copy of the application to the City Council accompanied their letter.

"It stated that the advantages of street tramways having been sufficiently proved both in America and Europe, it had been suggested to them that similar advantages could be obtained for the city of Auckland by the proper introduction of a system of street tramways, and assuming that the street traffic of Auckland may be sufficient to guarantee a fair and reasonable return for capital, they would be prepared to undertake the construction of tramways in terms of the General Tramways Act 1872.

"The only privilege they require in consideration of the capital, time and labour expended will be the exclusive right to run on the rails a particular car with flanged wheels all other ordinary vehicles, carriages, cabs, carts, omnibuses, may use the rails at all times, with the simple condition that they shall move off when the rail car approaches so as to allow it to pass without obstruction or delay. The applicants are convinced that this style of locomotion will greatly facilitate traffic through the streets, will effect an important saving in city rates, and will in fact prove a boon of infinite value to the city of Auckland and the public generally. They further state that in the event of their carrying out the proposed works they will be prepared to give to the city ten per cent of the net profits which may arise from the undertaking after the company have realised 7½ per cent on their capital.

"They propose to commence operations within twelve months (the rails requiring to be imported) from the date of the City Council granting the authority to construct, and they will proceed with the operations without any delay and complete the tramway from Queen street, at the wharf, by Fort Britomart, Mechanics' Bay, Parnell to Newmarket, and afterwards to extend the tramway along other streets, and roads whereon they may appear necessary and capable of yielding a reasonable return. It was agreed on the motion of Mr Macready, and seconded by Mr Fenton, that the Board take the matter into consideration." [2]

But, some two years later, as reported by The New Zealand Herald of 23 November 1875, the construction of an Auckland tramway system had yet to start:

"A meeting of the Streets Committee of the City Council was held yesterday afternoon. It was decided to recommend to the Council that applications should be received in accordance with the Tramways Act of 1872 for the construction of a double line of tramway from Queen-street to Newmarket via Parnell, and a single line to Ponsonby. The result of the establishment of street tramways elsewhere has almost always been a happy one, and the substitution of cheap, light, and inexpensive vehicles for the omnibuses now in use will be hailed as a great boon by numbers of the inhabitants of this growing city." [3]

However, as would be the case for many years into the future, little progress was made on the public transport front during the 1870s. As the Auckland Star reported the following day, yet another tramway proposal was read and debated at the Auckland City Council meeting of 11 November 1880:

"Street Tramways – The following letter upon this subject was read:— Auckland November 10th, 1880. P. A. Phillips, Esq; Town Clerk, Auckland. Sir,—With reference to the above matter, I beg to lay before the Council the following, which may assist them in the discussion of this matter, and what I request from the Council:—I ask for a lease of the roads of the city of Auckland for a term of 21 years, for the purpose of constructing and working tramways or street railroads from and to the city and the suburbs thereof—and the same right will be asked from the several other Councils and local Boards for the purpose of extending into those several districts the system of communication aforesaid.

"That no travelling, steam, or other motor will be used along the streets of the city. With respect to the fares to be charged, these will be placed as low as possible, according to circumstances but I can here say that I shall be prepared to enter into an arrangement or undertaking that the cash fare shall at no time exceed the rate of threepence per mile. I shall be glad if the Board or Committee will proceed to the discussion of this matter during my absence.—I am, etc., H. H. W. Smith.

"Cr. Montague asked if Mr Smith had himself interviewed any of the highway boards upon the matter?—Cr. Waddell did not think he had. Cr. Montague said that he had seen Mr Smith on the previous evening, and that the gentleman then told him that he had interviewed Mr Evans (Chairman of the Ponsonby Board), who had informed him that there was not the slightest doubt that his Board would acquiesce in the agreement which he (Mr Smith) intended to make with the city.

"Mr Smith had also remarked that the Ponsonby line would be the first which he would lay down. Councillor Offer thought that it should be understood that they were not going to deal exclusively with Mr Smith. The construction of tramways should be open to competition. They had only affirmed the desirability of providing the city with a tramway system, and had not decided upon giving a monopoly to anyone. The matter should, in his opinion, be referred to the Works Committee without any reference to Mr Smith, for there were other parties as well as that gentleman willing, he believed, to go into such a scheme.

"Councillor Waddel remarked that no other one had the right of constructing tramways upon Smith's principle. Councillor Offer retorted that there were tramways constructed upon other principles. — Cr. Waddel said that that might be, but that according to Mr Smith's representations there was nothing equal to his system. It was noiseless, smokeless, etc.

"Councillor Goldie considered it advisable to secure all possible information on the subject from the South and elsewhere before arriving at any decision. He knew that some difficulties had been encountered in connection with it at Wellington, and as that was so it would be better for them not to commit themselves to anything which they might afterwards have cause to regret. He did not like the idea of making a test of the thing. It should be done permanently or not at all. They should have a guarantee that at any rate the tramway would be run for a certain number of years whether it paid or not; otherwise there was no use in driving off the stage carriages.

"Councillor Thompson said that he could quite understand the willingness of the Ponsonby Board to fall in with any arrangements which Mr Smith might make with the city, seeing that that district would have the benefit of the first line laid down. He was not aware, however, that any other Highway Board had been consulted.

"Councillor Montague observed that Mr Smith intended to leave by the outgoing mail for San Francisco, where his principals resided. The gentleman had told him that if a contract were arranged with him he would telegraph to England for the necessary material, and be prepared to proceed with the work in four months' time. The matter was then referred to the Works Committee, all possible information on the subject to be procured in the meantime." [4]

Ironically, the same Council meeting also accepted a petition for the standardisation of fares from Auckland's cab drivers – the established, legacy public transport providers soon to be forced to relinquish their relative monopoly of the city's steadily-narrowing streets:

"Councillor Offer presented a petition from the cab-drivers of Auckland, submitting a table of cab fares, which they thought easily understood and reasonable, viz: One-horse cab, 2s the first quarter of an hour, and 1s for every subsequent quarter of an hour; fare and a half from 8 p.m. until 8 a.m., time to count from stand back to stand whence engaged.

"Two-horse cabs 2s 6d the first quarter of an hour, and 1s 3d for every subsequent quarter of an hour; fare and a-half from 8 p.m. until 8 a.m., time to count from stand, back to stand whence engaged; cabs to be compelled to drive inside the ten mile radius by time – six miles per hour; the public to have the option of making special agreements.

"The petition went on to say that the new bylaws would not allow the cabmen to clear more than their bare expenses, and that, from their extent and complicated nature they were unworkable. The petitioners gave seriatim their opinion of the various bylaws. The petition was referred to the Works Committee." [5]

As an example of was to come, The New Zealand Herald described the intransigence felt by certain cabmen toward the city's bylaws on what must have been a particularly wet day in May 1883:

"Yesterday afternoon a number of the cabmen took shelter from the pitiless rain in a group under the Queen-street verandahs, leaving their cabs and horses unattended on the stand, when a constable doing duty ordered them to move on as obstructing the footpath. They passively resisted by ignoring the admonition…" [6]

In the meantime, with the formation in 1882 of the St. Heliers and Northcote Land Company Limited, even Queen-street verandahs would not be enough to protect Auckland's cabmen from the gathering storm of competition. Launched with a share capital of £125,000 at £1 per share, the first Directors of the St. Heliers and Northcote Land Company Limited included:

- William Aitken, a Glaswegian who settled in Auckland as a land and estate agent in 1855. (He was the appellant, referred to in Chapter Two, who's court action briefly invalidated the rate gathering activities of Auckland's Provincial Highway Boards in 1877).
- Graves Aickin, a chemist settled in Auckland in 1863 and opened a chemist shop in Karangahape Road in 1865. He was an Auckland City Councillor from 1879 to 1888 and President of the Auckland Chamber of Commerce in 1885.
- Joseph Bennett, agent
- Henry Brett, publisher
- Thomas Buddle, solicitor
- Joseph Lucas Clark, gentleman
- James M'Cosh Clark, merchant, who became the senior partner in Archibald Clark & Sons following the death of his father in 1875. In 1880, he was elected Mayor of Auckland for three years and also served as chairman of the Education Board and president of the Auckland Chamber of Commerce.
- D. B. Cruikshank
- Thomas MacFFarlane, magistrate
- Thomas Morrin
- Dr Purchas
- B. Tonks

In what must have been one of the earliest forerunners to an Auckland real estate blurb, the Prospectus of the St. Heliers and Northcote Land Company Limited proclaimed:

"The Company was originally projected for the purpose of acquiring blocks of good suburban land to be re-sold in lots suitable for residence sites, and recently, with the view of adding to the value of their lands by affording greater facilities of access, the Provisional Directors have entered into arrangements for providing a system of TRAMWAYS for the CITY and SUBURBS.

"An agreement has been made with the City Council by which the company has secured the 'Executive Right To Construct And Work Such Tramways For A Period Of Twenty-One Years' and the terms of the concession leave no room to doubt that the undertaking will be advantageous to the community, and profitable to the proprietors.

"The properties already purchased consist of several blocks of choice land, comprising the St Helier's Bay Estate of 620 acres, the Remuera Land Company's Estate of 117 acres, and the Northcote Estate of 1012 acres, amounting in all to 1749 acres; the whole being admirably adapted for villa sites, combining the advantages of extensive frontage to the Waitemata Harbour, picturesque scenery and soil of excellent quality, together with proximity to the city.

"The sales already effected have averaged £200 per acre in Remuera, and £120 at St Helier's, and land adjacent to the Northcote Estate has been recently sold at £100 per acre." [7]

The company's Prospectus offered further inducements to apply for the 60,000 shares still available by indicating that the provision of trams to these suburbs could increase the value of their land purchases by as much as "ten times the original cost". [8]

The Prospectus also advised that cars would be imported from Stevenson (probably John Stephenson & Co; tram builders of New York) and that Mr W. S. Totton, formerly of the Belfast Tramway Company, was to be in charge of the construction of the tramway which would provide a travel time of just 25 minutes between St Heliers and Queen Street. [9]

The launch of the St. Heliers and Northcote Land Company Limited came at an opportune time, not only in terms of the need for adequate public transport options, but also from an economic perspective, according to the stock and sharemarket report published by the Taranaki Herald on 5 August 1882:

"The sharemarket is dull, but prices remain at about previous quotations. A great number of new Companies have lately been projected in various parts of the Colony, and are now before the public. In Auckland, the Waiwera Hot Springs Company and the Union Oil, Soap, and Candle Company have been floated. The St. Heliers and Northcote Land Company, the Mutual Fire and Marine Insurance Company, and the Picton Coal Company, are candidates for public favor. In fact, there seems to be a Company fever in the Colony just now." [10]

In July 1884, the first horse-tram had an experimental run along Auckland's Queen Street and "…in August 1884 had opened the first section from the intersection of Customs Street, via Queen Street, Wellesley Street West, Hobson and Pitt Streets to Karangahape Road, thence to the Ponsonby Reservoir." [11]

But, as might be expected, not everybody welcomed this innovation of steel rails embedded along the centre line of city streets:

"A complaint by the (City Council) Inspector that cabmen refused to obey certain orders as to the position they were to take up during laying of tramways was referred to the Streets Committee for report." [12]

With no official provision for the continuing rights of the Council-licensed cabmen forthcoming, an increase in their resistance to this new technology was naturally to be expected. However, as a New Zealand Herald editorial of 26 July 1884 pointed out, the owners and drivers of cabs could not expect progress to wait for them:

"We have long had the privilege of paying a higher rate of cab fares than any people in any other place in the world. For this boon, it is thought, we are indebted to the fact that the cab interest is so ably represented in the councils of the city authorities. The spirit in which the cab regulations are drawn up leaves little room for doubt on the subject.

"It is not 'The fare is so-and-so,' but, in order that there may be no mistake as to who is master, 'There *shall* be paid'. Moreover, 'Every hiring *shall* be a continuous hiring' and Full Fare (this is very properly emphasised by capital letters) *shall* be paid until the cab return to the place from which it came', or something to that effect.

"If a man takes a cab to Newmarket and leaves it there he must pay for the return journey, even though the cabman get another 'fare' two minutes afterwards. We are not only allowed the privilege of doing this; it is thrust upon us, and we have no alternative but to do the generous thing. The paternal despotism of the City Council is a thing to marvel at and be thankful for. Like all other privileges, the cab privilege is doomed.

"Whether it is land or cabs, it is all the same thing; monopolies and rings most all sooner or later be broken up. When the trams run, if ever enough horse-power can be got to move them, a man will be able to drive half a mile, for something less than half-a-crown. And what will the cabmen do then?

"Many, no doubt, will return to the more lucrative, if less honourable, profession to which they were brought up. (It may safely be said in passing, that nobody was ever expressly educated and brought up for a cabman.) Only a portion of them, however, will have occasion to leave the ranks. Trams or no trams, cabs will always be wanted. All that a long-suffering people ask is that fares may be brought down to something like a reasonable scale. The effect of the new system will be to diminish the number of privately owned cabs. The cabmen will become drivers, and not owners of their cabs, and they can safely be left to arrange for themselves with their employers the sum that shall be paid for every hiring of a hackney carriage." [13]

The sense of 'doom' then felt by the cabmen, must have increased with the laying of every length of tram rail and finally when they lost their stands along Queen Street. As reported by The New Zealand Herald of 18 July 1884, it was a loss they did not take lightly:

"The Tramway Company were yesterday experimenting with the tramcars in testing the Queen-street section of the tramway, also the curves at the junctions, Wellesley and Lower Queen Streets. Mr Larkins, the contractor, and Mr Pudans, the company's traffic manager, were present during the experiments, and travelled up and down in the cars on the line. The work was found to be in good condition, and Mr Larkins having finished the above section, we may expect to see the cars running shortly.

"Yesterday Mr George Goldie, Sanitary Inspector, by order of the Town Clerk, gave the cabmen notice to 'move on' out of Queen-street, to make way for the Tramway Company. They were very indignant, and wanted to know where they were to go, and as that information was not forthcoming, they declined to budge from the proclaimed cab stand in Queen-street. What action the above high city officials will take remains to be seen." [14]

In the meantime, the names of the intransigent cabmen "...were taken and submitted to the City Council last night. The matter has been referred to the City Solicitor, the Mayor giving notice that he would move at the next meeting that the by law appointing the present cabstands be rescinded, and the appointment of new ones considered." [15]

As the cab drivers believed that their Council-issued licences entitled them to fairer treatment than had so far been accorded, 'difficulties' continued:

"A fresh difficulty occurred on Saturday between the cabmen and the Tramway Company's employees. When one of the tramcars went down Queen-street, the cabmen refused to move their vehicles out of the way. The names of the obstructionists were taken down, and one man named George Mitchell, who threw a stone at the tramcar, was arrested on a charge of insulting behaviour, whereby a breach of the peace might have been occasioned.

"The cabmen, it is understood, intend to test the question in a Court of law, as to whether they can be removed from the Queen-street cabstands hitherto set apart for them. A meeting of the cabmen takes place this evening at the Nevada Hotel, when business of importance, in connection with the above dispute will be brought before them." [16]

"The difficulty between the cabmen and the Tramway Company culminated in a fracas in Queen-street on Saturday afternoon. The cab drivers refused to move their vehicles from the stand, and the tram-carriages were brought to a sudden stop. One block occurred at the foot of Victoria-street and another at the junction of Queen and Wyndham streets. Fully one thousand people assembled in the thoroughfare, and during the scene that occurred, a man named Mitchell, who says he has only been in the colony several weeks, was arrested for throwing stones at one of the carriages. He was fined 10s and costs to-day. The cabmen hold a meeting to-night to consider their grievances." [17]

That meeting did indeed take place on the evening of 21 July 1884:

"A largely attended meeting of cab-owners and drivers was held last evening at the Nevada Hotel, for the purpose of considering the present difficulty regarding cabstands. Mr S Young occupied the chair, and in a few explanatory remarks stated the business for which the meeting had been called together, and in doing so he remarked that to have to move out of Queen-street would mean considerable loss to all concerned.

"He called upon Mr McLaughlan to read two petitions that had been prepared for presentation to the City Council, one of which had been drawn up by Mr T. Cooper, the solicitor. Mr McLaughlan read the petitions, and, after some discussion, the one prepared by Mr Cooper was adopted. That petition was to the effect that the cabmen had duly paid their license fees, and had obtained their licenses for the present year; that for a long time the laying of the tramway lines had seriously interfered with the business of the cabmen and although the cabmen had been advised that the Council had no power while the existing by-laws and regulations were in force to remove the cabs from Queen-street, yet they did move as asked whilst the lines were being constructed.

"But now that the tram lines were made, and Queen-street again available for traffic, the cabmen considered they had a right to occupy their old stand in Queen-street. On the 16$^{th}$ the following notice was received – 'You will have to clear out of Queen-street with your carriage tomorrow the 17$^{th}$ of July' – By order, Inspector Goldie.

"Believing that this notice was illegal, the cabmen declined to obey it. Understanding that new by-laws were contemplated to be made to remove the present stands to be removed from Queen-street the cabmen believed that stands could be obtained in Queen-street without interfering with the traffic of the tramways. Mr McLaughlan considered it very unfair to banish the cabs from the main thoroughfares to the by-streets which would be most inconvenient to the general public and especially so for travellers." [18]

However, it was not just the impending competition between the two transport systems to be reconciled. Some operational rules relating to this new technology with the capacity to carry scores of passengers at once, had also to be decided by the City Council:

"Letter from Secretary (of the City Council) to Tramway Company re by-law: That the stoppage for tramways in Queen-street be at the intersection of the following streets, viz., Custom, Fort, Shortland, Durham, Victoria, and Wellesley-streets, and by-law as submitted be approved.

"Some discussion took place in reference to the fourth clause concerning the tramway stopping places. (Councillors) La Roche, Holland, and Montague opposed the clause, and thought, in the interests of the public, that the convenience of the passengers should be considered to a greater extent. It would prejudice the success of the Company if passengers were only allowed to enter the car or dismount from it at the corners of streets, and it would be unfair if they were made to walk, unnecessarily, the length of the street. It would be a convenience to the public to hail a tram-car at any point they pleased.

"An amendment by Cr. Devore, providing for the addition of the words, 'and such other places in the western circuit as the Council may from time to time appoint,' was lost. Cr. Montague moved, as a further amendment, that the portion of the clause relating to stopping places be expunged, but this was also negatived. The report was adopted without amendment." [19]

Eventually, the new technology prevailed and the first tramcars started out on 11 August 1884:

"The Auckland Tramway Company commenced running their tram cars yesterday, on the section from the Waitemata Hotel, Lower Queen-street, to the Ponsonby Reservoir. Notwithstanding that the company can expect none of the 'through' traffic to Ponsonby till the line is completed, the cars were well patronised. Hitherto the people using the omnibuses between the two points abovenamed have paid 6d, and the alteration to 3d—or 2½d if a dozen tickets are purchased is a consideration in these dull times.

"No one will travel from Newton to town, or vice versa, when they can get carried for 2½d, so that the public will get habituated, as they do in San Francisco, to do all their travelling about in the city by means of the cars. As the same fare, 2½d, will take the visitor the round trip, the 'mashers' will find this circuit a cheap method of airing themselves. At present conductors are employed on the cars, but when the public are educated to the system of putting their fare in the box when they enter the tram-cars they will be dispensed with. In case any of the visitors try the 'sacred' concert dodge and slip in pennies instead of three-penny bits, there is a patent detective arrangement which arrests the penny and gibbets it on a glass dial till the full fare is paid. Yesterday there was a great run on tickets, which were purchased by the dozen, in order to get the discount. One gentleman purchased a pound's worth to start with." [20]

Indeed, there was plenty of interest in the new service and by the end of August it continued to expand as patronage increased and the resistance of the cabmen abated:

"The number of passengers carried by the Auckland Tramway Company, on the short section opened on Monday last was close on 500. It is contemplated to run extra and larger tramcars between three p.m. and dark so as to enable business people to get to their homes in the suburbs promptly on a ten minutes' service. The cabmen still 'hold the fort' on the eastern side of Queen-street but as the company are only working the single line at present, the obstruction occasions little inconvenience." [21]

"The Tramway Company intend to work the double line in Queen-street on and after Monday next, and introduce a fifteen minutes' service. The notice to the cabmen to move from the line terminates to-day. The company contemplate putting on the big car, which will hold forty passengers, in the evening, running it with three horses abreast. It is intended to fix further accommodation on the roofs of the cars in the same manner as is done in the omnibuses." [22]

But even as the cabmen seemed to give ground to the rail cars, by September 1884, they continued to demonstrate the ability of their more agile conveyances to circumvent the most rigid of city by-laws:

"Complaints have been made to His Worship the Mayor that the cabmen, especially of a night time, consult their own inclination rather than the city by-laws as to the places where they shall stand to await hiring. Certain places have been set apart for their sole use, but it would appear that these do not meet with their approbation, and they accordingly desert the unpopular spots, and congregate where the likelihood of a fare seemeth greatest. The Inspector has been instructed to see into the matter, and report to the next meeting of the Council." [23]

"Since the abolition of the old cab-stands in Queen-street and the appointment of the new ones, cabmen dissatisfied with their new positions to stand for hire have been in the habit of loitering about the thoroughfares in more favoured spots. Yesterday two of them were charged at the Police Court with breaches of the City By-law. "Mr George Goldie prosecuted on behalf of the City Council, and he pointed out the danger likely to arise if this sort of thing were allowed to continue when the tram cars ran more frequently. Nominal fines of 5s and costs were imposed, as the cases were merely brought to act as a warning." [24]

And, indeed, the tram cars did run more frequently. By April 1885, the Tramway Company's operations had become so successful that the planning and construction of second lines and loops was well under way:

"During the last few days Mr Cooke, Engineer to the Tramway Company, and some of his staff, have been engaged in marking out the second line of tramway in Wellesley-street, as that will be the first work gone on with, The plans in connection with this line—that contemplated at College road and Patteson-Street, and the extension of the loop lines under the concession recently granted by the City Council— will, we understand, be submitted to the Council at its sitting to-night for approval

"As College-road is not likely to be out of the hands of the contractor for six weeks, and Patteson-street is scarcely sufficiently consolidated to permit of the metals being put down yet, unless the Tramway Company is to be subjected to the annoyance experienced through the subsidence of the made ground opposite the Western Park gate, probably these two works will be left to the last. It is intended to commence laying down at once an extension of the tramway to Mechanics' Bay Bridge, and work it in connection with the Freeman's Bay line, which, in the first instance, will probably be run on to the foot of College Hill.

"The cars on that section will be one-horse cars, Mechanics' Bay and Freeman's Bay both being feeders to the Queen-street main line, and passengers from these points will get transfer tickets at Queen-street junction available for the day, so that the holders can transact their business in-Lower Queen-street, and then go on with any other car up town on their transfer. In order to work the beach and one-horse service and find accommodations for the 'leaders' required for the Wellesley-street grade, the company have again arranged for the occupancy of the Kamo Company's stables on the reclamations, thus rendering the company's depot stables Jervois-road, Ponsonby, wholly available for the additional horses required on the improved service of the western circuit, which it is anticipated will with a new timetable be inaugurated on Monday next.

"The leading feature of the new time-table is twenty-four additional trips per day – twelve each way – early extra trams in the morning to enable working men to get to Lower Queen-street before eight o'clock, and from about five to six in the evening, a nearly six minutes' service, ten trams being despatched in 65 minutes. There will be nothing but large cars and two-deckers ultimately used on the main line, the small cars being kept for the beach service, some 32 trips being run to Freeman's Bay daily. It is contemplated to commence the eastern circuit shortly by way of Wellesley-street East.

"The Wellesley-street second line, and the extension of the loop lines, which are immediately pressing, will not be done by contract, but by the company's own staff on day labour, under the supervision of their Engineer. The new line in Wellesley-street will be used as the down line, so as to have the advantage of the rougher metals on the down grade in the ensuing winter." [25]

Of course, as the capacity and coverage of the trams increased, so did the desperation of those cabmen who had, for so long, experienced only the competition that had existed between them. So, despite the earlier warning of the danger of cabs cruising the busier streets for fares, they continued to do so, as reported by The New Zealand Herald during it coverage of a City Council meeting in August 1885:

"Perambulating Hackney Carriages — Mr Aickin moved 'That the Legal Committee be requested to frame a by-law dealing with the prevailing objectionable manner in which hackney carriages perambulate streets soliciting hire, instead of remaining at the regular authorised stands'. He said since he first gave notice of this motion, a test case had been brought before the Court, but had not yet been decided, and the Inspector informed him that he did not think the present by-laws met the case.

"He pointed out the great inconvenience caused to traffic by this intolerable nuisance, and said they should try to prevent it. He would ask leave to add after the word 'by-law', 'if it be found necessary'. If it was found that the decision was against the Council, the Legal Committee could frame a by-law if it was necessary.

"Mr Devore seconded the motion. Mr Crowther suggested that the matter stand over till the decision of the Court was known, but Mr Aickin objected to Mr Crowther taking any part in this matter, as he was an interested person. He had seen his own cabs perambulating the street and he would leave it to his own good taste to let the matter go on its merits. He certainly had no more right to speak on this subject than he (Mr Aickin) had to speak on tramways. Mr Goldie said he would move the amendment, and also that it should include the regulation of the tramway traffic. Mr Crowther asked for a ruling whether he was out of order. The Mayor said he was not asked to rule, it was left to his own good taste. Mr Crowther insisted that he had a right to look after the interests of the business in which he was engaged." [26]

By November 1885, the Court delivered its 'Important Decision' as to the legality of 'perambulating cabs':

"Mr H. G. Seth Smith, R.M., gave judgment this morning in the case Goldie v. Ritchie, which was heard several weeks ago. The plaintiff, Mr Inspector Goldie, had received complaints of the nuisance of cabmen perambulating up and down Queen-street, to the hindrance of citizens crossing and re-crossing the streets. Mr Cotter appeared for the Council, and Mr Theo. Cooper, in defence, said that since the adjournment he had looked into the matter, and examined the by-laws, also the authorities referred to by Mr Cotter. He was convinced that a breach of the by-law had been committed by defendant.

"As the case affected the whole of the cabmen, and was a case of public interest, he had agreed with Mr Cotter to plead guilty, and for His Worship to impose a nominal penalty with Court costs. Mr Cotter said that was the arrangement; but if any cabman, after the announcement of this decision, should continue the objectionable practice of perambulating Queen-street, he would not escape so easily, as the Council would take immediate proceedings and press for the heaviest penalty. Defendant was ordered to pay the nominal fine of 1s and costs." [27]

Ironically, it would be the tramway's dominance of the centre line of these streets that would culminate in the demise of the trams when usurped by a predominance of motor vehicles some years later. In the meantime, obviously encouraged by the popularity of the City's new tram service, the citizens of Auckland's relatively remote north shore decided to emulate the enterprise, as reported by The New Zealand Herald on 14 August 1885:

"On Tuesday evening last a meeting of gentlemen interested in the construction of a tramway in the Devonport district was held at the Masonic Hotel, Devonport. It was convened by circular, and was numerously attended. Mr J. Lawson presided, and called upon Mr Knox, C.E., who had surveyed the route, to explain his plans and proposals, which he did by the aid of plans.

"The route he proposed was from the Victoria Wharf, along Beach-road to Cheltenham Beach, and thence to Narrow Neck, running via the Sheep Mount and Flagstaff Hill, by Victoria-road to Victoria Wharf. By this line the wants of the whole district would be met, and the Lake district also brought within easy distance. After allowing for every item of expenditure likely to occur, he reckoned the receipts would give a profit over expenses of 15 per cent, per annum. After a good deal of discussion, it was resolved to form a Devonport Tramway Company. Messrs Edson, Stark, Glenny, Cave, R. H. Duder, Mays, and E. W. Allison were appointed provisional directors, and they are to report to a meeting to be held on the 19th, at Mr Knox's office, Queen-street, Auckland, at three o'clock p.m. Mr Cave is Secretary *pro tem*. [28]

Accordingly, the Devonport tramway was officially opened on 25 September 1886:

"The Devonport tramway was formally opened on Saturday afternoon in the presence of a large number of shareholders and friends. The party assembled at the Devonport terminus, and from thence proceeded, in two cars, over the line as far as Cheltenham beach, general satisfaction being expressed with the easy travelling of the cars, which are of a somewhat novel character.

"On arrival at Cheltenham beach the party alighted, and after inspecting the Tramway Company's stables, partook of some refreshment. Mr Graves Aickin, Chairman of Directors, in declaring the tramway open to the public, said that, although the times were very dull, there was good reason to hope for the future success of their undertaking, for as North Shore was one of the most beautiful localities around the city, there was sure to be an increase of population there, if anywhere.

"They had on that occasion seen but a portion of the line which was to be extended considerably as funds would permit. The portion already constructed would certainly pay, and when extended it would pay better. He wished that all interested in the district would come forward and take a few shares, and thus assist the company, which had done its best to benefit the district without any special partiality.

"Mr M Niccol, Mayor of Devonport, referred to the rapid growth of the district which had now 3000 persons in an area of one square mile, and expressed his belief that the tramway would pay. No doubt Devonport would soon have a larger population and there was therefore good inducement to present owners of property to take up shares in the tramway company. Mr Aitkin returned thanks for the sentiments expressed by the Mayor and added that the company would always endeavour to carry out their undertaking to local bodies in the strictest manner.

"Mr McLeod proposed the health of Mr Knox, the engineer who was, he said, really the father of the tramway, having done a great deal of work in promoting the company, and bringing it to its present state. Mr Best, who has been the chairman of the North Metropolitan and a director of other English companies, said he had great experience in tramways, and felt every confidence in the success of the line just opened, and in the benefit it would be to the district.

"Mr Knox, in responding, said that though the tramway was economically constructed, it was carried out on sound and well-tried principles, and proofs of its working capacity could be found in several parts of the world. He was sure that with careful management there would be a handsome return for the capital invested, and he should not be afraid of meeting his directors in twelve months' time with a fair return for the expenditure. Votes of thanks were passed to Mr Cave, secretary *pro tem*, for his efforts in helping the movement forward, and to the Mayor and Council of Devonport. Messrs Bailey and Mays and others also spoke briefly expressing their wish that the company's venture would prove to be a successful one. After a vote of thanks to the chairman, the return journey was commenced and passed off pleasantly." [29]

In order to attract a comparatively small commuter population and, hopefully, a larger number of excursionists to the tram service, the Devonport Tramway Company almost immediately dropped its ticket prices, as reported by The New Zealand Herald on 26 November 1886:

"A new departure has been made by the Devonport Tramway Company, namely, the reduction of tickets for children to 1d each for the whole distance, and of tickets for adults, from wharf to wharf, to the same amount. Further information will be found in our advertising columns. This liberal action on the part of the company cannot fail to promote tramway traffic, and to induce pleasure-seekers to resort to the North Shore for a cheap day's outing." [30]

But, more incentive was obviously needed:

"In addition to the reduction in fares already made in the case of children, and the fares from wharf to wharf, the Devonport Tramway Company are now reducing the general tramcar fares from 6d to 4d return tickets. The recent reductions in fares have led to an increase in passenger traffic, and the directors have been led to make this further reduction in the confident hope that their endeavours to cheapen the rates of travel will ensure the company increased patronage." [31]

Sadly, the fare reductions were not enough to keep the Devonport Tramway Company on the rails and on 25 March 1887, Liquidators, Adam Porter and W. N. Buddle, were appointed. [32]

Later that month, the Liquidators "…accepted the tender of £650 of Messrs R & R Duder for purchase of the company's plant." [33]

Brothers Richard and Robert Duder operated a general store on Lake Road, a brickyard at Shoal Bay and a stable of race horses off Church Street, Devonport. While they may have picked up a bit of a bargain in the form of the Devonport Tramway, there was obviously some maintenance to be completed before the Devonport Council would permit them to continue the service:

"That the attention of Messrs R. and R. Duder should be called to the insecure and neglected state of the tram line, the Council intimating that before entertaining any request for consent to transfer the line must be put in good order, and that if necessary the Council, on application, will agree to the suspension of traffic for a time to permit of this being done." [34]

Once they were allowed to operate the tramway, the brothers wasted no time expanding the service and, by the following November, they were asking the Council to consider an extension of time to complete the line and for permission to construct a new loop at the foot of Devonport's Church Street. [35]

By 1900, there was apparently no shortage of passengers, particularly on race days, as illustrated by a letter of complaint published on 30 May of that year by The New Zealand Herald:

"To The Editor. Sir,—In common with other Devonport ratepayers I have been perfectly horrified, not only with the risk to human life, but also the cruelty to dumb animals, in connection with the last race meeting. This has occurred through the poor horses dragging overloaded 'buses up Persecution Hill, and afterward driven to the Lake up the hills on the Lake Road...B. Harrow." [36]

However, despite increasing passenger numbers, "Continual competition from horse-buses made for little tramways profits, but the downfall was said to have been land liabilities." [37]

As with rail and road construction, it was the profits that could be made from land sales that originally drove the tram network but "Tramway systems required a higher degree of capitalisation and organisation than earlier modes of public transport." [38]

"...it was an expensive undertaking: the laying of the tracks was arduous, the rails had to be imported from England, the first batch of cars was ordered from New York, the system was labour intensive and the motive power – horses – had to have grazing land and extensive stabling and feed storage. It was also fair game for criticism, with many complaints and difficulties attending the first few decades of its operation." [39]

The late 1880s was certainly not the best time to be investing, particularly in public transport. It was then that:

"The first systemic banking crisis in New Zealand's history occurred...The crisis was ostensibly the result of a long drawn out period of subdued growth beginning in the late 1870s – a period termed the 'Long Depression' by a number of economic historians. It is difficult to point to any single event that signalled an end to the euphoria and overtrading characteristic of the Vogel boom. Export prices peaked in 1875 for example, while land prices continued to increase until the early 1880s, as did the strong credit growth which underpinned the mortgage market. This decline in the economy's growth potential was eventually reflected in rural land prices, which declined over the course of the 1880s." [40]

As real estate sales collapsed across Auckland with the economic depression of the late 1880s, the St. Heliers and Northcote Land Company

Limited, now known as City of Auckland Tramways and Suburban Land Company Limited, faced increasing financial pressures.

"In 1893 the Bank of New Zealand Assets Company became the owner of the (Auckland City tramways) system by being the only bidder at an auction forced by the bank itself. The bank was to run the trams both under its own management and by leasing the management out to private transport operators." [41]

"For about twelve months the tramways were leased to Patterson Bros, a large horse-bus and carrying firm. Then in 1899 the British Electric Traction Company purchased the undertaking and the Auckland Electric Tramways Company was registered in London." [42]

But these ownership changes did little to improve the profitability of Auckland's tram services. There was still significant competition from horse buses better able to carry passengers to parts of suburbs not reached by the trams. "…residential development did not always proceed at a rapid pace and some lines were probably never successful financially…leaving the tramways to bear high fixed costs servicing low traffic areas for much longer than planned." [43]

However, despite the static nature of its financial fortunes, between 1896 and 1897, Auckland City's tram lines had expanded to a route length of some 11.39 kilometres and its trams carried 1,585,410 passengers. By 1900 the Tramway Company had extended its lines "…to Newmarket and Remuera with a branch line down lower Symonds Street and an extension to Epsom." [44]

By 1901, new technology, in the form of electric current, was set to replace the tramway's plodding horsepower and, by November 1902, that's just what it did – as reported by the Auckland Star on 17 November 1902:

"A little over fifteen months ago, on August 1, 1901, the first ground was broken in connection with the laying of the rails for the Auckland Electric Tramways Company—to-day saw the inauguration of the service. During the comparatively short interval the large sum of £120,000 has been spent locally in the laying of rails, the fixing of posts and wires, the erection of the power house and depots, etc.

"To this must be added the heavy sums spent in England and America for cars rails, posts, engines etc.; the total being sufficient to absorb the company's capital of £300,000. The lines laid measure about 20 miles, mostly double track; in single track there being about 34 miles of lines laid, all of this having been done in a little over a year, while the power-house and the depots have been put up in considerably less time.

"Several delays, altogether unavoidable by the company, have occurred, preventing the starting of the cars on the date fixed in the Order-in-Council giving authority for the service, June 1. A railway strike in America delayed the arrival of the rails, the machinery for the power station was delayed by lengthened trips of the New York steamers, and the wet weather hindered the work of laying the rails, so that nearly three months of unavoidable delay occurred.

"The proceedings in connection with the inauguration of the service opened at the power house in Albert-street at half-past twelve, when a large crowd of invited guests assembled within the building, examining the generator, the three large dynamos, and the switchboard from which the currents are worked…

"After the company had inspected the machinery contained within the power house Mr Paul M Hansen, attorney for the company, accompanied by Mr Alfred Kidd (Mayor), Sir John Logan Campbell, Mr H Wilson (town clerk), Mr James Stewart, C.E., Mr Carey, electrical engineer for the company, and Mr Turner, attorney for Messrs J. G. White and Company, ascended the platform from which the switches are worked, and after a selection had been played by Hunter's Garrison Band the generator was started going. A few minutes after Mr Hansen, on behalf of his company, requested Mr Kidd to turn on the electrical current for the line. Mr Kidd then depressed the lever by means of which the current was switched to the line amid loud applause.

"Addressing the company, Mr Kidd said that nothing during the term of his office had given him greater pleasure than to assist in opening that important work. On August 1st of last year he had the pleasure of turning the first stone in connection with the work, and they would remember that the day being gloomy and rainy. Mr Hansen remarked that he thought it was the angels weeping for gladness because the work had been started. When he (Mr Kidd) awoke this morning and found that it was raining again he could not help thinking that the angels were weeping for joy that the work was finished.

"The work was one of the largest undertakings carried out in New Zealand in connection with a private company or a municipality, and would do an immense deal of good to the city and its surroundings. (Applause) When they remembered the serious troubles which occurred during the execution of the work —bad weather, the winter having been the worst for continuous rain that he remembered, and all the work being outside, the disaster to the power house by the falling of a girder, the fire which destroyed a portion of the materials, and the strikes in America—

they would understand that the work had been delayed by no fault of the company.

"There was a little delay in the formation of the company, but both the company and the contractors had done all in their power to bring the matter to a successful issue in the time that was arranged. They would all agree that the delays which had occurred were unavoidable, because the company could not foresee them and provide against them. The work had not been skipped to save time...The work would cost nearly £450,000 and would do an enormous amount of good to the city and suburbs. About £130,000 had been spent locally, and already a large amount of good must have been done to the city by the expenditure of this large amount of money.

"The good that would issue from the cars would be inestimable. Workmen would be able to leave the crowded parts in the city and living as far away as Onehunga would be able to reach town in almost the same time as from the Three Lamps at present. They would all feel proud to think that Auckland was the first city in New Zealand to undertake that great work and bring it to a successful conclusion throughout the whole of the city and suburbs...The assembly then left the power house, and proceeded to the foot of Queen-street, opposite the Tramway Company's offices, where six cars were waiting to convey them to the Choral Hall, where luncheon was provided for the guests.

"Three of the cars were despatched from the Ponsonby depot early in the morning, and remained on the roadway until the party was ready to start. All the morning they were surrounded by crowds of people, and their attractive appearance, comfortable seating accommodation, and general elegance, were the subject of much favourable comment ... it is only necessary to add that on the street they look very attractive, the dark red panels contrasting well with the bright yellow sides and tops. The cars are not disfigured externally by advertisements, the number of the car and the monogram of the company being all which appears on the outside.

"A crowd numbering several thousand people gathered round the cars before the hour at which they were timed to start, 1.15 p.m. When all the cars were filled with guests, Mr Hansen stepped to the front of the first car, and addressing Sir John Logan Campbell, said that on behalf of his company he had the honour to ask Sir John to start the first electric tram car in this city. Knowing that to drive an electric car, or any other passenger vehicle in the city without a license was illegal, and further knowing that Sir John would not do anything against the law, he had taken the liberty to take out a motorman's license for Sir John, which he would ask the town clerk (Mr H. Wilson) to present. Mr Wilson then presented the license, which was handsomely bound in red leather, with silver corners and clasps.

"At the call of Mr Hansen three hearty cheers were given for Sir John Campbell, followed by three for Mr Hansen, called for by Sir John, and three for the Electric Tramways Company. Sir John, accompanied by Messrs Hansen, Kidd, Wilson and Carey then stepped aboard the platform of the car, and Sir John turned the lever which made the connection between wire and rail, thus starting the car.

"As he did so he said: 'Success to the Auckland Tramways Company. May its cars never cease to run in Auckland.' The car then moved off up Queen-street, amidst the cheers of the crowd, and followed by the other five ran up to the Choral Hall. The cars were insufficient to carry all the invited guests, and had to make a second trip. The passengers were all loud in their praises of the quiet, steady manner in which the cars ran, and of the comfort of the seating accommodation." [45]

According to the Auckland Star, in a commentary published the same day, the electric tramways placed Auckland among the most up-to-date cities of the world:

"The inauguration ceremony in connection with the completion of the electric tramways, held to-day, marks an important epoch in the history of Auckland. It brings us into line with the most up-to-date cities of the world in the matter of transit facilities and Auckland, with its wide area of land adapted for the erection of beautiful suburban residences, will profit more than most municipalities from the possession of fast and comfortable means of locomotion.

"The effect of electric tramways, wherever they have been put in operation, has been to decentralise the population. Lands four and five miles from the business centre become adapted even for the homes of workmen who have to make an early start in the morning, and they are thus enabled to live in cottages surrounded by pleasant gardens instead of being crowded into closely-built ugly and unhealthy streets.

"The overhead trolly (sic) system, which has been carried out in Auckland in a most effective and substantial manner by the Tramway Company, is now generally recognised as the most practicable and useful method of utilising electric traction for city traffic. After prolonged inquiries it was adopted by the great corporations of Glasgow and Liverpool, and is rapidly being applied to the other leading municipalities of the United Kingdom...We think the Auckland Tramways Company are entitled to unstinted praise for the excellence of the service, both with respect to permanent way, electrical installation, and cars, which they have supplied to Auckland. A mistake has, we think, been made in using centre poles instead of side poles in Khyber Pass, Manukau-road and the Customs-street entrance to Hobson-street. A change will certainly have to be made in the condition of the road at the latter point to prevent serious accident, and we had hoped that this would have been done before the tramways were opened.

"Taken as a whole, however, the service is one of which the city may well feel proud, and the hearty congratulations which were bestowed to-day on the manager, the contractors and others connected with carrying out this great undertaking were thoroughly well deserved. The terms of the contract with the Auckland Corporation secure cheap and rapid transit facilities for the public at no cost to the ratepayers, and although municipalisation is in the air, and much may be said in favour of public control of such services, there are reasonable grounds for believing that the citizens will have no cause to regret the bargain which has been made on their behalf." [46]

However, not all citizens going about their lawful business were completely happy with the new technology. As with the introduction of the original horse-drawn tram service, the new horseless trams caused a good deal of trouble – particularly for the horses which continued to transport people and haul goods throughout the city:

"This morning (24 November 1902) the electric cars commenced permanent running on the Newton-Ponsonby section, to the manifest delight of the travelling public. The down cars were rapidly filled, and although running every five minutes there were many left at the stopping places in Karangahape-road for want of room. This, however, did not matter much as another car was along in five minutes to pick up those who missed the preceding one.

"In some cases horses seemed to object to the machine that runs without apparent propelling power, and some circus play took place in Karangahape-road. A fine animal in one of the L.O'B. Timber Company's carts gave its driver some trouble as car after car ran past, but fortunately no accident occurred. About nine o'clock a horse in a trap at the foot of Wellesley-street also played up.

"As the 9.30 car was going up Wellesley-street a little mild excitement was caused when in front of the Opera House, owing to the rehostat (sic) getting warm and smoking, besides creating a peculiar smell. Someone ran out with a bucket of water in order to put out the fire, and shortly afterwards a hose arrived from the central Fire Brigade station.

"Fortunately Motor Inspector Neale arrived at this juncture and prevented the danger that exists from turning a stream of water on to electrical apparatus. Mr Carey, electrical engineer to the Tramway

Company, in conversation with a 'Star' representative subsequently explained that to have turned the hose on would be dangerous to the man with the nozzle as water, being a strong conductor of electricity, the current would travel through the stream and give a shock, added to which the water would ruin the electrical equipment by short circuiting, as water only increases an arc instead of diminishing it.

"The cause of the rehostat (sic) getting warm was not due to any defect in the car equipment, but to one of the new motor men running on resistance up hill. The thing was easily remedied, and there was absolutely no danger to passengers, as the cars are insulated. Evidently the Fire Brigade must not turn the hose on to electrical equipment without being advised by one of the officers of the company. In the event of a fire on the line of the tramways one of the company's inspectors will be always present while the current is on. The company will also have an emergency crew with a waggon to work the fire appliances.

"Several times during the day horses got frightened at the unusual sight of a car running along without horses attached to it. Early in the morning a commercial traveller's trap was upset in Ponsonby-road owing to the horse becoming excited as a car passed by, but no one was hurt. In Karangahape-road, near the top of Pitt-street, a horse ridden by a young man was startled by an electric car, and jumped aside upon the footpath, with the result that he slipped on the hard pavement, fell upon his rider, and broke his leg.

"A loaded cart of the Northern Boiler Milling Company, drawn by two horses, at tandem, in Karangahape-road this morning, was approaching Pitt-street when the horses were startled by an approaching electric car The leader ran round upon the footpath, and was on the point of entering the bar passage of the Naval Hotel, when a man caught him by the bridle and stopped him. A large crowd of women and children, who were standing at Pitt-street corner watching the cars, were considerably frightened. Fortunately, no damage was done." [47]

Progressively, "...tram lines were laid connecting Mt Eden, Balmoral, Kingsland and Mt Albert with the city. By 1908 tram lines had been laid part way down Mt Eden Road..." [48]

In the 1904 Official Yearbook, New Zealand's Registrar General claimed that Auckland was one of the most progressive cities in the Colonies by virtue of its tramway system. However, that progress came at quite a cost including the provision of rolling stock, equipment and track maintenance; wages; and electric power. Indeed, during the first years of the twentieth century, the city's tramway system was the biggest consumer of electric power, then supplied by steam power stations.

"Tramway systems required a higher degree of capitalisation and organisation than earlier modes of public transport… Suburban local authorities, especially in Auckland, often added to capital costs by insisting on road improvements when the tracks were laid." [49]

In 1910, the average capital outlay in New Zealand per mile of line was about £12,000 with the largest part of this cost resulting from the provision of the tracks, overhead wires, and supporting standards. Much of that infrastructure had also to be provided along with the facilitation of another new technology – the telephone and the telegraph:

"Residents on the Great North Road, Eden Terrace to Kingsland, and Epsom sections of the electric tramways service, are anxiously looking forward to the completion of these circuits, and wondering at the delay in providing them with the same travelling facilities enjoyed by those living in the city and adjacent suburbs.

"There is an inclination to blame the Auckland Electric Tramways Company for the delay in completion, but it may be mentioned that they are in no way blameworthy, the position being that they are compelled to stay the work until the Telegraph Department have raised the telegraph and telephone wires, a by no means small undertaking. When this has been done the fixing of the remaining overhead wires for the tramway will be pushed forward as rapidly as possible, and the services opened." [50]

And as the web of tram lines fanned out to the suburbs, the cost of those lines, ancillary equipment, and maintenance increased:

"The Auckland Electric Tramways Company will shortly be proceeding with one or two of the extensions of the existing lines. Mr Hansen, attorney to the company, informs us that the Herne Bay Road extension, at Bayfield, in the Ponsonby district, will be the first of these works to be taken in hand, and it is expected that this section will be open for traffic in about two months' time.

"The length is about half-a-mile, and the work of construction will occupy only about three weeks, but it is expected to be about five weeks before the contractors start work. The next extension will be the Remuera section, and this will probably be followed by the Mount Eden and Mount Roskill extension, but this has not yet been finally decided upon. The steepness of some portions of the lines, and the sharp curves at the head or foot of several of these gradients has had a marked effect on the wheels of the cars which have been running since the system was inaugurated in November last.

"The considerable wear of the wheels is stated to be largely accountable for the great noise which is made by the cars whilst in motion. It is intended to fit the cars with new wheels, 100 of which have already arrived. A second hundred will arrive shortly, and a further hundred will come to hand about September.

"It is expected that the noise attendant upon the traffic will be greatly reduced by the removal of the old wheels, but Mr Hansen states that so far as Queen-street is concerned, the rumbling is largely due to the hard asphalt surface of the street, whilst the numerous verandahs also act as so many sounding boards, and thus assist to increase the noise, which has of late been much remarked upon. Subsidences have occurred in a few weak spots along the tram lines, and these are now being repaired. The base is being excavated and made much stronger than formerly in order to prevent a recurrence of the subsidences." [51]

The expansion of the tramway system was not just one of a geographical nature. A wide-ranging debate as to whether or not the trams should be allowed to run on Sundays was finally settled, but only just, by a poll of Auckland's citizens that took place on the last day of September 1903:

"The poll on the proposal of the Auckland Electric Tramways Company to run their cars within the city boundaries on Sundays took place yesterday, and resulted in the citizens giving their sanction to the Sunday trams by the narrow majority of 22 votes.

"The great interest evinced in the question during the last fortnight, and which had become particularly keen during the last few days, had given an indication that the poll would be a heavy one, and the results of the voting fully justified the general expectation in this respect. Out of a total of 12,301 names on the municipal electors' roll, which was the basis of the referendum, 8024 voters exercised their privilege. There were 136 informal votes, thus leaving 7888 valid votes, of which 3955 were cast in favour of the Sunday trams and 3933 against.

"Polling commenced at the various booths at nine a.m., and from this hour a steady stream of voters passed in and out throughout the day. The heavy rain which had been falling during the preceding night had cleared off, and, with the exception of a slight shower or two during the forenoon, the weather remained fine during the day. Both parties had a large and well organised staff of workers engaged, and in each case no efforts were spared in the endeavour to secure a victory. The staff working for the proposal included about 20 tramway officials, who were off their ordinary duty, and who volunteered their services for the occasion.

"Representatives of religious bodies and some of the labour organisations were also active, and a spirited contest was carried on. The usual election boxes were placed in front of each booth, and the main plan of operations was conducted from these centres, at which voters were supplied with their numbers, as well as advice, both documentary and verbal, as to how to record their votes on the momentous question of the day.

"A goodly number of vehicles, each bearing the ribbon badge, were at work on both sides, and these were busily engaged from an early hour, in conveying voters to and from the booths. The tramcars, which were placarded with the words, 'Vote for the Sunday trams, the People's Carriage', also conveyed a large number of electors to the booths, where inspectors handed out tickets enabling them to complete the (trip?) without paying a second fare. Two constables were stationed by Inspector Cullen at each booth, but there was very little occasion for their presence, the contest, keen as it was, being conducted with good humour throughout.

"The pros and cons of the question were eagerly debated in front of the booths, and the large number of women who vigorously advocated the advantage of the 'people's carriage' was generally commented upon, especially at the Federal Hall, where the voting was heaviest, and where the larger of the two majorities in favour of the proposal was obtained. During the afternoon a very large number of women recorded their votes, but a great influx of male voters commenced to set in shortly after five o'clock when the men left off work. The officials were then kept busy up till the hour of the closing of the poll, but everything passed off without a hitch, the ample arrangements made by the returning officer, Mr T. Ussher, being excellently carried out by his deputies and their assistants.

"As the returns at the various booths were announced they were posted in front of the Herald Office, where they were awaited by a very large and excited crowd of people, which extended right across Queen-street on to the opposite footpath, as well as for about 50 yards along the street. When the final result was compiled and placed on the notice board, great jubilation was manifested, loud cheers being sent up from amongst the crowd. The excitement continued to prevail for a few minutes, but the crowd gradually dispersed, and within a quarter of an hour Queen-street was itself again. Mr Hansen, managing director of the company, was loudly cheered when the result of the poll was announced, and as he subsequently walked down Queen-street he was accorded a further ovation.

"Mr Hansen states that the time-table for the Sunday tram service, which will extend over the whole of the lines, will be submitted to the City Council at its meeting to-night, and advertised before the end of the week. The cars will be running throughout the city and suburbs on Sunday next, the service being about a half-hour one. The cars will start to run at twenty minutes past twelve p.m., thus affording church-goers, Mr Hansen says, the opportunity of riding home." [52]

Unfortunately, tragedy was to strike the tramways on Christmas Eve 1903:

"The full enjoyment of the Christmas season was marred for Auckland by the most serious accident that has occurred in the history of electric traction in this city. Two cars, carrying together about 150 people, collided violently on the New North Road, near the George-street stopping-place, and, as a result three persons lost their lives; at least, three others are, at the time of writing, in a critical condition, and the list of casualties altogether numbers over 50, exclusive of those who merely received skin wounds or a slight shock, from which they speedily recovered.

"Of the three persons who received fatal injuries one was killed instantly, another died within an hour of the accident, and the third fatal result occurred yesterday forenoon. The immediate cause of the accident was that a double-decked car got beyond the control of the driver, rushed downhill, and crashed into a car coming up behind it, completely wrecking the latter car and carrying away the under part of the former.

"The accident occurred at about a-quarter past eight on Christmas Eve, when the double-decked car No. 39, in charge of Fred Humphrey, motorman, was going from Kingsland to Auckland. Everything seems to have gone well till coming up Eden Terrace. Just before the loop-line was reached the car was stopped, and the brake apparently refusing to work the huge car, to the consternation of the passengers, started backward, being carried downhill by its own weight. As she gained speed the long arm, which establishes connection between the overhead wires and the motors on the car, became detached from the current wire, and the car began to slip still more rapidly downhill.

"Immediately the contact with the overhead wire was broken the lights inside went out, and the car gaining impetus at every yard and rushing on in darkness threw the passengers, on board into a state of high frenzy. Those passengers who kept their wits about them state that the motorman and conductors did their utmost to minimise what was practically beyond the power of man to prevent. In complete darkness the car rushed downhill at a terrific speed, swaying from side to side, its loose parts rattling and jarring, and above all were the frantic shouts of the men, the screams of the women, and the crying of terrified children.

"On the car dashed, down past the brightly-lighted stores by the roadside, which seemed themselves to appear and disappear out of the darkness, on past the Mount Roskill Road, and then the dark car plunged down into the darkness of the unlighted road towards the Rocky Nook bowling green, and shot round the bend. Then it was seen, and not till then, that there was a car in the way, an up-car from Kingsland, and full of passengers. The glare of the lamp shone out immediately car 39 shot round the corner, but it was then too late for the up-car motorman (Ernest Thompson) to do more than reverse, which he seems to have done with remarkable celerity and presence of mind.

"But the collision was inevitable, the cars met, there was an awful crash, followed by piercing shrieks and agonised groans, and instantly all was in utter darkness. For the space of half-a-second, perhaps, there was complete, silence, and then the cries and groans broke out afresh, and with renewed intensity. For some time all was in darkness, as there was no connection between the cars and the wires overhead. Lights were fetched from neighbouring houses, and then it was seen what a terrible wreck had been made of the cars.

"Stout iron-frame work was twisted up like wax, woodwork was smashed to splinters from the size of matches to great pieces 4ft and 5ft long, which pierced the passengers, jammed up in car No. 32, which was the car run into. The sight was one that will never be effaced from the experiences of those who witnessed it – the oncoming car roaring as it sped along the metals in the darkness, the crash, and the tearing away of the ends of the cars when they met.

"The lights flashing about caught the smashed glass lying in the roadway, and lighted up the wreckage of the cars. People were being dragged out of the broken windows of the cars, and in the dark some of those who fell got trampled upon. Just after the accident a car, which was at the Kingsland terminus, came up, and shed a brilliant light on the scene, which enabled the work of rescue to proceed with greater facility.

"Inside the combination car No. 32 there was still to be seen a heap of struggling people, who were almost inextricably mixed up with the seats, every one of which was torn from the floor by the shock, and in some cases pinning the passengers down. The forepart of the roof of this car was torn off, but where the front seats were there was jammed the iron work of the double-decked car, while the motor of car No. 32 was smashed inwards and upwards, and thrust up into the car a mass of confused metal rods, bolts, and plates.

"The winding staircase of the double-decked car was torn off from beneath, and the whole of it hung, dangling from the top. Not a pane of glass remained whole in either car, and not a seat but what was not wrenched from its fastenings. A crowd very quickly gathered round, but there seemed to be some hesitancy displayed by bystanders before proceeding to the assistance of passengers. Someone made a start, and then the work went on quickly enough. People were carried off bleeding to the stores along the roadside, extending from the scene of the accident to Eden Terrace, where Mr Haslett's chemist's shop is situated.

"The scene reminded one of a battle, for so quickly were the injured attended to on the spot that the place seemed filled with bandages and people almost within a few minutes of the catastrophe. The roadway and the cars were strewn with hats and jackets, baskets and parcels, sticks and umbrellas. These were all taken charge of by the police, who were promptly on the scene." [53]

An inquiry into the accident was quickly undertaken and its conclusions reported by The New Zealand Herald on 7 January 1904:

"The inquiry into the circumstances connected with the fatal tram accident of Christmas Eve was concluded yesterday at the Magistrate's Court. When the Court met the parties intimated that they had no further evidence to lead and the coroner proceeded to sum up to the jury the evidence taken during the past week. He said all the legal gentlemen present at the inquest, including those representing the Auckland Electric Tramways Company, had given the jury every opportunity to inquire into the state of the company's rolling stock, the methods used by them, and generally into the working of the company's lines.

"The public was indebted to the jury for the patience, care and earnestness which they had brought to bear on the whole inquiry. They would have no difficulty in arriving at a verdict as to the cause of death...but they were also asked, to decide whether any blame is attachable to any of the employees of the Tramways Company, and whether the accident was due in any way to the state of the company's rolling stock, and whether they were blamable (sic) in the matter.

"As to Motorman Humphrey, who was in charge of the car that ran away, the duty of the jury would be to inquire very carefully into his conduct and give their verdict in accordance with the evidence. Humphrey had borne a good character. He had been thought by his employers to be a capable driver of an electric car and he appeared to have received the usual instruction as a motorman.

"It would be for the jury, besides considering the conduct of Humphrey, to consider whether, in their opinion, the instruction given to Humphrey — and in fact, to other motormen — was sufficient to qualify him or them for their duties and for such an emergency as the running back of this car.

"He (the coroner) wished to point out to the jury that Humphrey had not attempted to get out of his responsibility by misrepresentation or perjury – in fact, his own statement was to all intents and purposes a confession of his incapacity to deal with such an emergency, and of his responsibility for the accident.

"There was nothing in the evidence to show how the ratchet brake became unworkable, nor anything to lead one to suppose that the track brake would not have acted if called upon. The jury would have to decide on the conduct of this motorman and say if he was incompetent, and, further, if he was negligent and disobeyed orders by leaving his car as he did.

"That he was incompetent and lost his nerve was evident. The incompetence may not have been so much his fault as that of his employers, but his leaving his post and proceeding to the other end of the car to try the brake there, when he was bound to remain at the handles was his own act and if the jury found that an act of negligence on the part of the motorman it would, the coroner thought, amount to manslaughter, and the jury might find a verdict accordingly.

"If, however the jury believed that the motorman left the car and ran to the other end because he thought the conductor incompetent, it might be only an error of judgment. According to the law, as it now stands, however, the fact of the coroner's jury not finding a verdict of manslaughter did not prevent a prosecution taking place afterwards.

"There was no evidence of any dereliction of duty on the part of the conductor in charge of the combination car No. 32. The motorman in charge of that car, according to the evidence, shut off the power, applied the emergency brake, and jumped off, and the jury might note the fact that he did not reverse the car. His case might be considered somewhat similar to that of the captain of a ship – bound to remain on the car, at any rate, as long as he could do anything for the safety of the passengers. Of course, that was only remotely connected with the cause of the death of the three victims, but he pointed the matter out to the jury for their consideration.

"Then there was the question whether any blame was attachable to the Auckland Electric Tramways Company, through the conduct of other officers not immediately connected with the cars...the evidence did not disclose any imperfections in the company's rolling stock, the whole evidence before the jury being, as far as it went, that the stock is in good order and up-to-date, including the brakes. There was also evidence that the cars and brakes were inspected every night, and if the jury was of opinion that the brakes, etc., were of up-to-date construction and in thorough repair, he believed it would tend to allay public anxiety on this question.

"Another question was whether sufficient care had been taken in the selection and examination of motormen and conductors. There was some evidence that the employees of the company, both, motormen and conductors, were not sufficiently conversant with the use of the brakes, and that seemed to him to have contributed to some extent to the cause of this collision and the consequent death and suffering. It was clear that Motorman Humphrey's knowledge of the use of the electric brakes was defective. He did not know, he said, whether what had been called the ordinary emergency brake would or would not stop a car when running backward, while, as a matter of fact, the jury had been told that it would not, and that another operation would have to be performed.

"The probability was that Humphrey's want of knowledge contributed to cause the confusion which Humphrey said existed when the car ran away. One of the conductors (Carson) told the jury that he did not understand the brakes, even the mechanical brake.

"Then Motorman Moyes, who was a motorman employed to instruct other men, stated that he never taught the candidates the use of the backward electric brake. He was taught it in Sydney, and understood its use but also understood that it was not in force here, and he mentioned what appeared to be a fact, that it was not in the book of rules.

"That may not have directly affected Humphrey, but it appeared that some motormen had not been instructed in the use of this brake. Mr Carey, electrical engineer to the Tramways Company, made an explanation that it was thought by him and other electrical experts that it was better not to insert the explanation of the use of that brake in the book of rules. No doubt that was their opinion, but it was clear that sufficient care had not been taken otherwise, apart from the book of rules, to draw the attention of the company's servants to this brake.

"Any opinion the jury was prepared to give on this question would be sent on to the proper authorities. With regard to the City Council, it appeared that the motormen had the Council's license to drive a motor-car. The Council granted the license as a matter of form on a certificate from the Tramways Company's officers that the man was competent, and he thought the jury would agree with him that the Council could hardly be expected to undertake an examination with a view to testing the competency of the men.

"Mr Campbell (counsel for motorman Humphrey) said he wished to make an observation with regard to the coroner's direction to the jury on the question of manslaughter. There was nothing in the evidence to show that Humphrey's getting off the car was the cause of the collision at all, and he (Mr Campbell) interpreted the law to mean that a man must be found to have been grossly negligent or guilty of recklessly negligent conduct to justify a verdict of manslaughter.

"Mr Tole (Crown Prosecutor appearing on behalf of the police) said no man could be convicted of manslaughter for a mistake if he acted to the best of his judgment and ability, however unfortunate his judgment might be, but at the same time a person had to exercise ordinary care, skill, and diligence, and it was the absence of ordinary precaution or care that made, negligence culpable. Mr Brabant S.M. (acting as coroner) directed the jury that if they found gross negligence it was manslaughter. If not, it was an error of judgment, or, in common language, losing his head.

"The jury retired at ten minutes past one, and gave their verdict at half-past three, as follows:

"That Miss Anne Young Hogarth met her death on the night of December 24, 1903 on double-deck car No. 39 travelling from Kingsland to Auckland, by the trolley arm breaking away from the conductor, the said trolley arm, becoming unmanageable, striking Miss Hogarth on the head and causing her death. That the death of Benjamin Lindsay and the death of William Caley were caused through the colliding of car No. 39 and car No. 32 on the night of December 24, 1903.

"The jury find that the cause of the collision was the ratchet brake failing to act, causing Motorman Humphrey to lose his head, and through his want of knowledge be did not use the other brakes at his command.

"The jury added the following rider: That in consequence of the steep grades in and around Auckland the use of the double-deck cars should be discontinued. They also recommend that the Tramways Company's mode of teaching motormen and conductors is inadequate, and more stringent measures should be adopted. Lifeguards should be attached to the cars with as little delay as possible. The jury believe that the brake power on the cars is quite satisfactory when in proper order and in the hands of those who understand their use. They also believe that the motormen and conductors should be subject to a medical examination as to their fitness. They are also of opinion that the speed of cars on downgrades should be reduced." [54]

So the jury did not find motorman Humphrey guilty of manslaughter. However, its recommendations certainly called for better training of tramways staff charged with the safe and comfortable transportation of an increasing number of passengers through streets filled with the comings and goings of pedestrians and horse-drawn vehicles of all kinds.

During the early 1900s, there were a number of collisions between tramcars and horse-drawn conveyances when the latter unexpectedly strayed onto the tram lines and giving the cars little time to stop, despite their relatively slow speed. In many cases, the reinsman would have heard the noisy trams approaching and would have known the lines were close, yet lacked that fine control of the horse just as the conveyances converged.

In time, that clank of the tramcar would be greatly reduced, much to the relief of the general citizen's hearing but not to that of the accident-prone pedestrian and lazy horseman. By mid-1904, new technology was set to reduce the noise pollution of the tramway system, as reported by the Auckland Star:

"Speaking to the managing director of the Auckland Electric Tramways Company this morning on the subject of the noise of the cars, one of our staff was told by him that wooden sleepers had little effect in deadening the noise, which was caused by chipped wheels.

"Mr Hansen said that the system followed by his company — rails placed on concrete foundations — was that followed in most parts of America, and it proved perfectly satisfactory. In the case of Auckland, considerable trouble has been caused by the subsidences of the soil, particularly in Queen-street, and it has been found advisable to place wooden sleepers under the concrete at certain points in order to prevent further subsidence. In parts where the foundation is firm no trouble is experienced.

"The Auckland Electric Tramways Company is expecting here shortly a large number of steel-tyred wheels, which are to replace the iron wheels which are at present being used. The fault of the latter is that they chip easily — a piece of hard metal on the rail will raise the wheel and let it fall with a jar on the track, and the wheel chips. One chip means that others will follow quickly, and soon the wheel has a hundred points in it. Hence the jar and grind of the cars along the road. No amount of filing will remedy the defect, and the only alternative is to get the steel-tyred wheels. With these there should be a minimised noise, for even if an injudicious motorman causes the tyre to skid and flatten the emery wheel soon trues it up.

"Mr Hansen says that the experience of his company is that of others in America and other parts of the world. He says the noise of the cars is wholly attributable to the chipping of the wheels through loose metal on the roads. The vibration causes as much harm to the cars as annoyance to the public, and the company intends to replace the old wheels as early as possible. Some of the Onehunga cars are already so fitted." [55]

However, the problem of chipped wheels and the noise they caused was not the only one to be faced by the Auckland Electric Tramways Company during 1904. Disputes about wages and conditions were also very much to the fore:

"The dispute between the Auckland Electric Tramways Company and their employees in respect to the rate of wages and conditions of labour again occupied the attention of the Arbitration Court—His Honor Mr Justice Chapman and Messrs Brown and Slater —sitting at the Supreme Court Buildings yesterday.

"The evidence of the men was continued, the first witness called by Mr Way being A. W. Comer, a motorman, who stated that he had been in the employ of the Auckland Tramways Company since the inauguration of the service. He said he was engaged to come to New Zealand from Sydney, the rate of pay being 8s, with a promise of an additional 6d at the end of three months. The increase never took effect.

"Witness bore out the statements of other employees in respect to the high cost of living in Auckland as compared with Sydney. He considered Sydney men were very much better off. Since his arrival in Auckland he had been presented by passengers with a gold medal for his prompt action in applying the emergency brake when the life of a little girl was in jeopardy, thus preventing a fatality.

"It was the custom in Sydney to pay the motormen for all hours that they were on duty, but in Auckland the men were signed off when waiting during the progress of sports or entertainments (other than at the theatres, where the stay was only brief), and received no pay for such time. The men received no holidays, and it was a fair and just demand that a week's vacation should be given on full pay once a year. On general holidays the men had to work very hard to cope with the increased traffic. The men had to get their meals in the best way they could. In Sydney this kind of thing was managed better, spare hands taking the place of motormen and conductors during mealtime. The time devoted to meals was not deducted from the hour shift in Sydney.

"Edwin Thackeray, a spare motorman, said he had been employed by the company in his present capacity for six months, his earnings ranging from 15s to £1 per week. He was a married man with one child. Sunday was his best day. He had to attend at the barn at a quarter-past six a.m., half-past eleven a.m., and a quarter-past two p.m. On each occasion when the last car had gone out if he were not wanted he could go…Continuing, witness said he had to remain at the barn for about four hours per day. He did not consider it right that a man should have to hang about so much without payment.

"To His Honor: He learned his profession as motorman at Portland, Oregon, and had since driven cars in San Francisco and Oakland, California, during a period extending over several years. Moreover, he had acted as instructor to motormen, and had had experience in Coventry, England.

"In Oregon his wages equalled 10s 5d per day, and living was far cheaper. Indeed in no part of the world had he found living to be so expensive as in Auckland. The work in America was considerably lighter, and the men had intervals of rest at the end of each trip. The work was also carried out under more comfortable conditions. There was not the petty officialism so rampant in Auckland. A motorman in America had confidence in himself and worked so as to give satisfaction both to himself and to his employers. Here he was subjected to continual annoyances on the part of petty officials, who did not thoroughly understand the business.

"Patrick MacManemin, motorman, stated that formerly he was employed as a horse-car driver on the Newmarket line, making eight trips per day, as against thirteen- at present, and enjoying fifteen minutes' rest after each round trip, whereas at present there were practically no stops at all. Under the old system there was considerably less anxiety, and the cars were much more easily handled. Accidents were very rare with the horse-cars. The conditions of labour, both for driver and conductor, were better under the old system.

"At present he and his mate relieved one another at meal hours, which meant, that he was tied to the service for the whole day. He worked ten hours per day on the horse cars, and received £2 2s per week. To Mr Scott: The increased pay he now obtained did not counterbalance the advantages of the old car service, as the mental strain was now greater. There was more anxiety, and the work in the winter-time was colder, owing to the increased speed. He had decreased in weight a stone.

"Amos Hollingsworth, motorman, stated that he had had five years' experience in Boston, U.S.A., in driving electric cars. The Auckland service was a very hard one. Never had he worked such long stretches. Taking this into account, and also the exorbitant cost of living in Auckland, he considered he was decidedly better off when in America. Living expenses were, in fact, out of all proportion to the wages earned, and he had to draw upon his private resources." [56]

There was also the matter of whether or not the Auckland Electric Tramways Company could continue to run the trams for another two years – an extension to be decided by Auckland's citizens as per the provisions of the Tramways Act 1894. The Second Schedule of that Act required the local authority to ascertain the decision of its ratepayers before granting any further concessions to the tramway company.

The ratepayers poll was conducted on 26 April 1904, and the results published by The New Zealand Herald the following day:

"A poll of Auckland city electors was taken yesterday on the proposal to grant the Auckland Electric Tramways Company an extension of their concession for two years, representing the period occupied in laying the lines and preparing to run the cars after the original concession was granted.

"The poll was taken in the form provided by the Tramways Act, namely, that only those who desired to forbid the granting of the concession were required to vote. It required a third of the voters on the roll to effectually forbid, and as there were 10,745 voters on the roll the number required by those opposed to the additional two years was 3582. There was very little interest taken in the poll, and the total number of votes only reached 1483, so that in due course the City Council will formally grant- the extension for two years." [57]

Not only could the Auckland Electric Tramways Company continue for another two years but not long after this extension was granted, the Arbitration Court also settled, for a year at least, the pay rates and conditions under which its employees were to work:

"The Arbitration Court to-day delivered its award in the dispute between the Auckland Electric Tramways Company and the Union of employees. Following are the terms of the award:

"1. Hours of Work: The hours of work shall be eight hours per day for all employees, but the employer shall have the right to call upon any employee to work for one hour more on any day, paying for the time so worked at ordinary rates. All time worked beyond nine hours, shall be paid for at time and. a half rates. All time worked on Sundays shall be paid for at time and a half rates. Any men called upon to work on Christmas Day or Good Friday shall be paid at double time rates.

"2. The employer shall have the option of relieving any man for meal time for a maximum of one hour, the time of such relief to be deducted in the computation of the man's time. In cases where the option is not exercised relieving mates are to be allowed to agree to relieve each other for meal time; failing such agreement the men shall work throughout the shift.

"3. Rates of Wages: The following shall be the minimum rates of wages payable to the several classes of employees: Motormen, 1/ per hour; conductors, 10½d; switchmen, 10½d; assistant switchmen (boys), 5d per hour; trackmen, 11¼d; car examiners, 10¾d; firemen at power-station, 1/; all general labourers, including car cleaners, 10½d." [58]

But despite labour costs, a fatal accident, and high maintenance and infrastructure outlay, the Electric Tramways Company was nevertheless able to make a profit in its first year of operation – at least enough to pay the Council its due. However, as a 'Resident of Twenty Years' pointed out in a letter to the editor of The New Zealand Herald, published 13 July 1904, the Council was unwise to penalise the reason for the Tramways Company's success – the extreme popularity of the service it provided:

"TO THE EDITOR. Sir, — It was recently officially announced that the sum of £2013, the amount of the City Council's share of the profits earned by the electric trams, had been forwarded to the Council by the company, and I for one am pleased to see that the trams have been such a success, but I cannot understand why the Council are so rigorous in the persecution of the company re the matter of overcrowding. Probably the Council see that a big mistake was made in granting concessions to a company instead of owning the trams themselves, and intend adopting a dog-in-the-manger policy harassing the company all they possibly can.

"Instead of doing so, the Council should assist the company all in its power. The Council is already, and will be, thousands of pounds better off each succeeding year the Tramways Company is running here, as is proved by the following: In our old mode of travelling, viz., by horse trams and buses, the City Council did not receive more than £500 per annum, if that much, for the right to run over the roads, licenses for trams, buses, drivers, and conductors, and at the same time had to keep the whole road in repair.

"Now the Electric Tramways Company pays the Council £400 per annum for the right to run on the road, about £2500 in rates, taxes, and licenses for cars, drivers, and conductors, £2013 as a share of profits for the first year's work, besides keeping 16ft or 17ft of the road in repair (the roads were never so good as since the trams have been running), total cash paid, £4913, being an advance of £4500 on the old income. The Council is apparently not satisfied with this, but is persecuting the company for overcrowding, with the object of bringing more money into the treasury in the way of fines.

"Now, re the overcrowding past and present. When we had the old horse cars and (omni)buses running it was an every-day occurrence to see those vehicles packed, to their utmost carrying capacity, people hanging on to steps, or wherever they could get a foothold or handgrip, the poor brutes of horses having to struggle up Wellesley-street, which was painful for one to witness. Yet no prosecutions ever followed. Now, if an electric car has six over the number there is a cry out and a prosecution. Let the Council give the Tramways Company a rest, and set their minds on the urgent requirements of the city for the general health, viz., drainage and a destructor. — I am etc., A Resident of 20 Years." [59]

Apart from what it paid the Auckland City Council, the Auckland Electric Tramways Company had also to account to its owner, the London-based, British Electric Traction Company. However, according to The New Zealand Herald's British correspondent's report, published on 16 August 1904, the British Electric Traction Company was well pleased with the success of its investment thus far and plans were well advanced for the enhancement of its Auckland service:

"London, July 16. Several references to the Auckland Electric Tramways Company were made at last Monday's meeting of the British Electric Traction Company which was held at Winchester House. Sir Charles Rivers Wilson, who presided, in moving the adoption of the report and balance-sheet, said that their large investment in the Auckland Electric Tramways, amounting to £287,360, had during the year become productive, a dividend having been paid of 4½ per cent. They considered that this would improve, and that it would prove a very valuable investment.

"Mr P. M. Hansen, speaking of the Auckland Electric Tramways, in which the British Electric Traction Company is largely interested, stated that when the undertaking was purchased by the British Electric Traction Company five years ago it was yielding no interest whatever on the small capital of £40,000, and now it was paying interest on almost £600,000. (Applause) The people of Auckland fully appreciated what had been done for them. They had not come forward when the capital was wanted, but they had quite changed their minds, and if the time came when the British Electric Traction Company felt disposed to part with their interests they could rest assured there would not be much difficulty in finding willing buyers in New Zealand.

"Mr Godsell, of Taranaki, endorsed all that Mr Hansen had said. Auckland had been revolutionised by these tramways, and his only complaint was that the British Electric Traction Company would not sell their shares. The trams in Auckland had been a success from the first day they had started. A city like Auckland was the very place to develop the tram system, for there was a British population that would not walk a yard if they could help it, and the people would just as soon pay 3d as they would 1d. (Laughter)

"You wish to know my views as to the prospects of petrol as a rival to electricity for tramway working? said Mr P. M. Hansen, managing director of the Auckland Tramways, in the course of a long conversation yesterday. I certainly think that petrol would be no good on tramways in a city like Auckland. The roads are too hilly, and there is too much intermediate traffic. That would mean constantly calling upon the petrol motor for reserves of power which it does not possess. You see, the starting involves the hardest pull, and these frequent starts would prove a heavy tax on a motor that did not possess a large margin of power. A new regenerating motor, which stores up for use the electric power generated by its own motion, is being tried on behalf of our company. If that should prove a success, it should make greatly for enhanced economy of working.

"Then four out of the twelve new cars which were ordered are now all ready for shipment, and will go out by the next direct steamer, while the others will follow shortly. Further, the new 100-h.p. engine, which is being built for us, is well in hand, and will, it is hoped, be delivered in New Zealand before the end of the year. It has been somewhat delayed in construction owing to the fact that all the manufacturers that construct electric plant are so crowded with orders that they have to work at high pressure, and even then find it difficult to keep up the requisite supply." [60]

But, of course, whenever profits are generated by successful enterprise, there are always parties looking on from the wings, eager to partake of a slice of the pie. Those suburban councils which were so eager to have their boroughs pierced by tram rails and to prosper from the additional business they would generate were no exception.

Their parochial view, as reported by the Auckland Star on 13 September 1904, was one that was to compromise many growth proposals that could otherwise have benefitted the greater Auckland region:

"A discussion took place at the meeting of the Grey Lynn Borough Council last night upon the question of the right of local bodies to a proportion of the City Council receipts from the Tramway Company. In response to a request from the Grey Lynn Council for a share of the license fees of tramway drivers, the town clerk, Auckland, wrote stating that the fees collected from the Tramway Company were expressly provided for by the deed of delegation between the Auckland City Council and the Auckland Electric Tramways Company Limited.

"The Mayor, Mr J. Farrell, considered the Grey Lynn Council should take a step forward in this matter, and invite other local bodies to take combined action with the Grey Lynn Council to recover a proportion of the fees received by the Auckland City Council. The answer from the City Council seemed to him very like bluff. They were willing to pay the city a percentage for collecting license fees, but wanted their proportion of such fees. He also thought they should see if the outside bodies were not also entitled to a share of that £2000 profit paid by the Tramway Company to the city. It was impossible to calculate only the city traffic, as the income from the tramways must greatly come from people residing in outside districts.

"Mr C. McMaster said the City Council had no power to override an Act by a deed of dedication. The Act provided that the Council should receive a proportion of the license fees. He did not think even Parnell would refuse to join in this matter. The Mayor: No, if there is anything to be made out of it, Parnell will, I feel sure, agree to join with us. It was agreed to write to the other local bodies upon this matter, with the object of taking combined action." [61]

In the meantime, just over two years since its first tram trundled up Queen Street, the Auckland Electric Tramways Company continued to prosper thanks to the popularity of the service it provided to a growing population of commuters and suburban residents. Just how popular the tram service had become was divulged by the company's Managing Director, P. M. Hansen, during an interview published by The New Zealand Herald on 6 January 1905:

"The exceptionally heavy traffic over the Auckland Electric Tramways Company's lines during the recent holidays, and the steady increase in the travelling public at ordinary times formed the subject of an interview which a representative of the Herald had with Mr P. M. Hansen, the managing director of the company, in the course of which Mr Hansen threw a great deal of light upon the workings of the system.

"Reference was made by the interviewer to the company's operations during the past year, and Mr Hansen was asked how many passengers were carried during 1904. We carried last year,' replied Mr Hansen, 'about 18 million passengers, which was an excess of five million passengers over 1903...these figures are not like those given for some other places...the passengers carried on the Auckland sections paid, not 18 million pennies only, but fares ranging from 1d to 6d each...The cars ran altogether close upon 17 million miles, which will show the enormous strain placed on our rolling stock. This is- especially heavy considering the very hilly nature of the country with which we have to deal in Auckland.'

"Considering the enormous numbers of people we have carried, and the heavy mileage run we have every reason to be very satisfied with last year as regards mishaps, for no person was killed for which the company or its servants were to blame, and, beyond those who were in the collision between a Kingsland car and a steam roller in Symonds-street, very few persons, indeed, have received injuries. I regard the low percentage of accidents, when compared with the business done, as very satisfactory indeed.

"We had to deal with three very heavy days last year. The first was the great, football match between England and Auckland at Alexandra Park, when we carried 81,171 passengers in one day. The next was the second day of the Agricultural Show, Saturday, when we carried 89,712 passengers, and last Christmas Eve we beat all previous records by carrying 98,023 passengers. But in considering these figures you must not forget that on such heavy days it is impossible to collect all the fares, consequently the number of passengers carried must have been higher than the figures I have given you.

"We have to make special preparations for such emergencies. You must understand that the heaviest part of the burden rests upon the shoulders of Mr M. F. Carey, the chief engineer, and his assistants. Unless the engines in the power-station are properly looked after, the machinery in the cars in perfect order, and the overhead construction kept up to the mark, unless, in short, every one of the innumerable details of the system, whether in the power-house, the overhead wires, the track, and the car itself, is in absolutely perfect order, and every care and precaution taken, the whole system will be at once thrown out of gear, to the loss of the company and the annoyance and inconvenience of the travelling public.

"You will see, then, how much depends upon the general management, which has to make all sorts of preparations to arrange satisfactory time-tables, to prepare and instruct the additional men required, to furnish spare men, to give special instructions, and issue special warnings to all the men on duty, so as to ensure the personal safety of the travelling public, and to meet their convenience as far as possible.

"On what may be called 'big' days, (we would employ) all (the cars) we have. For instance, on Christmas Eve we ran the whole 47 cars, and there was practically no breakdown of any car during the whole day. Of course we have, up to the present, been at great disadvantage to deal with the heavy traffic of the last fortnight as we would like, but in the course of this month we shall have running the new car built by Messrs Cousins and Atkin, and seven more cars coming from Home will be added to the rolling stock, and when we get them we shall be far better able to deal with any extraordinary rush of traffic.

"We are quite aware that some of the cars now running are not so smart as to outward appearance as they might be, but for several months past we have been unable to lay them up for painting, etc., in consequence of the demands of the traffic, but as soon as the 12 new cars are running—four are now here on the lines — then we shall be able to lay up other cars, and so get all the cars into spick and span condition, and in every respect equal to the best systems anywhere in the world. We employ 47 cars, six of which are double-deckers. These last require each six men daily, working in two shifts, in all 36 men; then the 41 cars requiring four men each daily, employ 164 — there are 200 men; the engineer's staff, trackmen, car cleaners, inspectors, and clerical staff, etc., bring up our employees to some 360 men. The conversation then veered round to a variety of subjects germane to the running of a big tramway service, and the child passenger was referred to.

"I have been struck," said Mr Hansen, "by the extraordinary number of children in Auckland who are particularly fine for their age. Really, it is amazing to see. The sturdy youngsters who, as their mothers solemnly assure the conductors, are under three (and therefore travel free), and the strapping boys and bouncing girls who are under 12 (and therefore travel half-fare), have particularly impressed me with their stature. Yes, the size of the children of Auckland is remarkable when compared with the ages given on a car," Mr Hansen reflectively observed." [62]

While Mr Hansen would certainly have been pleased to see the introduction then of the variety of identity cards required to be shown in the 21st century to obtain any kind of travel fare concession, he was not to know that his company's encouragement of the omnibus as a feeder service to the trams would ultimately be responsible for the replacement of the trams altogether.

This encouragement was expressed by Mr Hansen in a letter to the Parnell Borough Council:

"The Tram Service: In answer to the Council's letter asking the Auckland Electric Tramways Company to carry out the extension of the tram service to Gladstone Road and St. Stephen's Avenue, Mr Hansen wrote intimating that the company was not prepared at present to proceed with the extension. He added that he understood arrangements were being made for a (omni)bus service to act as feeders to the trams, and that the company would be prepared to subsidise the service. The company's right to carry out the extension would expire in May, and he suggested that the Council should apply to the Government for a two-years' extension of time." [63]

Had he known that the horse power of those omnibuses would eventually be supplanted by the internal combustion engine, powering far more efficient transporters than his single-minded trams, he may not have suggested that the Auckland Electric Tramways Company could subsidise such an ancillary service. But such are the vagaries of life that, in 1905, it would have been thought absurd that such a thriving business as that then provided by the Tramways Company could ever be replaced.

However, to keep pace with the demand, there was a need for more tramcars, as illustrated by a plea from the Auckland City Council's Finance Committee:

"The report of the Finance Committee, containing the following clauses, was adopted: — Auckland Electric Tramways Company Limited, submitting supplementary time-table for approval: Time-table approved; the Tramways Company to be again pressed to make early provision for the increasing traffic by at once placing orders locally for more tramcars." [64]

As another indication of just how busy the tramways had become, those additional trams were ordered almost immediately, as reported by The New Zealand Herald on 12 October 1905:

"Twelve out of the thirteen new cars which were ordered by the Auckland Electric Tramways Company Ltd., some months ago, have now been placed upon the lines and it is expected that the thirteenth car, which will bring the total number of cars in the company's service up to 56, will start running by the end of the present week.

"The company, however, although they have increased the service so substantially, are still making further provision for Auckland's requirements. By the last San Francisco mail, Mr Paul Hansen, managing director for the company, received instructions from the London directors to order four more cars, and to place the order locally. Mr Hansen, accordingly, is taking steps to place the order forthwith. When these additional cars are in use, Auckland will have a daily service of 60 cars, or 50 per cent more cars than are running in Wellington." [65]

However, while this transport revolution continued to embed itself in the highways and byways of New Zealand's main cities, other parts of the world were a very important, one step ahead:

"Passenger traffic in London has been revolutionised within the past few months. In Piccadilly, Oxford-street, Trafalgar Square, the Strand, and on practically every main route of traffic in the metropolis, huge new motor-'buses may be seen adroitly threading their way among, and swiftly forging far ahead of, the old-fashioned and out-of-date horse 'buses.

"Famous as is the London 'bus driver's skill in driving, the motor-'buses seem to gain as much by the marvellous way in which they are able to pick their way among the horse traffic as from their vastly superior speed. There are already considerably more than a hundred motor-'buses running on the main I routes in the heart of London, more than a thousand more are actually on order and being rushed to completion as quickly as possible; while the old horse 'bus companies have been forced by the remarkable success of the new vehicle to arrange for transforming their three thousand 'buses from horse to mechanical traction.

"On the ranks motor-cabs are fast displacing the familiar hansom and the slow four-wheeler, and the Cabmen's Union has opened a motor school where the London Jehu may learn the business of chauffeur. Motor carriages are all the rage in society, and traders are going in largely for motor traction. And the awakening is not confined to London. In every part of the country its influence is being felt in one form or another, the throb of the motor-'bus being heard even in the remote villages.

"In order to meet the increased competition the railway companies are discarding steam for electricity, and they are opening up new sources of traffic by providing motor services as feeders. It is, however, in the development of the road carriage that the chief feature of the transit transformation in England lies. In the urban and rural districts the self-propelled 'bus is generally admitted to be the public conveyance of the future. It has already proved its utility in the linking up of villages and small towns which are either not served at all or indifferently served by the railways." [66]

However, Auckland transport was not entirely behind the times. While the central city continued on with both horse-drawn omnibuses and electric trams, the North Shore had replaced its original tramway with steam motor buses as early as 1904:

"The inauguration of the steam motor bus service between Devonport and Lake Takapuna took place yesterday afternoon. The event was naturally regarded as one of considerable interest to the residents of the Takapuna district. The service, which has been established by the North Shore-Takapuna Motor 'Bus Company, begins running this morning, and in order to suitably commemorate the event, yesterday's inaugural ceremony was arranged.

"The syndicate, composed of some enterprising local residents, have issued a time-table which comprises a convenient service between the Victoria Wharf, at Devonport, and the Lake, the times of starting from and arriving at the wharf being arranged to work in with the running of the ferry boats.

"Three 'buses are at present in commission, the two large ones being, Chelmsford cars, built to the 'Ideal' design by the Cousins and Atkin Carriage Factory Limited. These cars are most substantially built and neatly finished, with spring seats and specially-strong solid rubber tires. The cars are fitted with 30 h.p. steam motors, with an ordinary working pressure of 350lb, the heating power being supplied automatically by kerosene. Each of these cars, which are named respectively the Pupuke No. 1 and No. 2, are licensed to carry 16 passengers, and they will be constantly engaged in the Devonport-Lake service.

"The third car, a Serpolette, is a very handy runabout which will carry nine passengers, and will be used for auxiliary services, or as an adjunct to the main service, as occasion may require. Two other Serpolette cars, each carrying twelve passengers, have been ordered by the syndicate, and are due to arrive in about a fortnight by the Kaikoura. There will thus be then five cars available for the service. The time occupied in the journey between Devonport and the Lake will be about twenty minutes. The Serpolette car covered the distance yesterday in fourteen minutes but, including stoppages for taking up and setting down passengers, it is expected that the first-mentioned period will be about the average working time." [67]

Meanwhile, in central Auckland, the Auckland Electric Tramways Company continued to enjoy a virtual passenger monopoly with its electric trams despite some difficulty maintaining a fleet sufficient to meet the increasing demand. By mid-1906, the company also found its operations increasingly threatened by the subsidence of city streets. After some debate with the City Council, an agreement had been reached whereby the tramways company would re-enforce its lines with supporting piles driven into those road sections affected.

Naturally, there was a cost involved and liability for that cost depended on the cause of the subsidence, a point argued between the tramways company and the City Council ad nauseam:

"The City Council at its meeting last evening received a letter from Mr P. M. Hansen, managing director of the Auckland Electric Tramways Company, on the Queen-street sewer and subsidences. Mr Hansen, after replying to the Council's letter on the subject and the report on the sewer made by the city engineer (Mr W. E. Bush), goes on to say:—

"The city engineer in his report addressed to you, dated July 25 last, practically admits all the defects of the sewer as set forth in my letter to you of July 4. But it is difficult to understand his subsequent point of view when he says in effect, that the sewer generally is in a very fair condition, and much better than I had expected to find it from the tone of Mr Hansen's letter. The rather optimistic tone of reassurance adopted by the city engineer in his report no doubt resulted in the statements that the condition of the Queen-street sewer was 'not so desperate' as my company's 'somewhat alarmist report' led people to believe, and that: 'apparently the sewer only requires some small repairs to put it in order.'

"I can, however, assure your Council that the reports contained in my letters of July 4- and 18th are certainly not exaggerated, but, on the contrary, as we know now, they fall far short of disclosing to your Council the very bad state of affairs that really exists. Since the receipt of the city engineer's report above referred to, and in consequence of your letter to me under reply, we arranged for a complete survey and thorough inspection of the sewer with its branches by some of our consulting engineers, and in the following I give you a brief summary of the results of our investigations:

"(1) The condition of the sewer and drain pipes between Shortland-street and Victoria-street is not only as stated in my letters, but the negligence disclosed in one particular part of the sewer below Victoria-street is even worse than we considered it to be at our first inspection.

"(2) The portion of the sewer between Shortland-street and Custom-street, shows not only the-defects as already stated, but further examinations have proved to us conclusively that it is generally in a ruinous condition; in fact, we consider it our duty to inform your Council that our engineers are unanimous in their opinion that that portion of the sewer is in a very dangerous condition and unsafe to carry the street traffic.

"(3) In respect to the portion of the sewer between Custom-street and Shortland-street, if piles were now driven, as approved by the Council, the condition of the sewer is such that its collapse would undoubtedly be precipitated.

"(4) As far as the portion of our tracks between Shortland-street and Wellesley-street is concerned the subsidence is partly due to the defects of the sewer and to leaky and blocked-up drains, as well as to the entire absence of any adequate drainage to the road bed.

"(5) The subsidence of our tracks between Custom-street and Shortland-street is undoubtedly due to the long and continued neglect and default in leaving the sewer—which was originally badly constructed —in its present ruinous and unsafe condition. This by itself is sufficient to account for the settlement of the tramlines. Besides leaky and blocked-up drains and the defective construction of the road bed have naturally accentuated the trouble.

"(6) It is by no means the tramlines alone that suffer from the neglect or default as pointed out above: the street surface adjacent is distorted and irregular in many places, and the asphalt, during rain, shows more numerous and deeper hollows as time goes on.

"In this unfortunate position of affairs I feel compelled very respectfully and reluctantly to inform you that my company holds the city liable for all past, present, and future damage done to our undertaking in consequence of the neglect or default of the body corporate to provide for and under Queen-street and maintain a complete and efficient system of drainage.

"The Mayor (responding to Mr Hansen's letter): Councillors may trust that this matter has received very careful consideration from the engineer, and he has consulted the city solicitor, and I may say the Council need not be alarmed at its responsibilities in the matter. I therefore formally move that a reply be sent to the Tramways Company disclaiming all liability, such reply to be drafted by the city solicitor. The motion was carried unanimously without further comment." [68]

As well as the dispute between the tramways company and the City Council as to which entity was responsible for the failure of the sewage and roading system to support the increasingly heavier traffic, the tramways company continued with its struggle to supply the requisite number of cars – to its cost, according to an Auckland Star report of 12 October 1906:

"The matter of the number of cars provided by the Auckland Electric Tramways Company has been before the Auckland City Council for some time, and notice was given some months ago to the company to provide additional cars, of which, so far, two have been provided.

"This number being considered inadequate to the requirements of the city, the matter was referred to the Finance Committee, who reported to last night's meeting as follows:—Your committee recommend that, in view of the traffic inspector's report that the Tramways Company had only supplied two extra cars in response to the Council's notice, and as in the opinion of the Council such additional number does not adequately meet the requirements of the traffic, notice be given to the Auckland Electric Tramways Company Limited, that the Council intends to proceed to recover the fine of £8 per day it imposed by the deed of delegation for the default of the company in not running on the tramways cars for the conveyance of passengers according to the Order-in-Council and the said deed." [69]

By the end of November 1906, the City Council received advice from the Auckland Electric Tramways Company Limited that the company had "...received advice from London to order additional cars; that they will have three additional cars ready by the beginning of December, 1906, and 8 radial cars by the 5$^{th}$ of January, 1907." [70]

However, by 1 December, only one new car was ready with five others still under construction. Accordingly, at a meeting held on 6 December 1906, "...The Finance Committee of the Council...recommended, that in accordance with the city solicitor's opinion the time of 60 days mentioned in the Council's notice to the Tramways Company be extended by one calendar month, and that the city solicitor be instructed to take action to enforce the penalty of £8 per day for every day thereafter during which the default in providing sufficient rolling stock continued.

"The Mayor (Mr A. M. Myers) said the amount that would have to be paid by the company up-to-date would be about £328. He believed the decision would meet with the approval of the Council, and he urged them to adopt it. The Finance Committee had gone very carefully into the matter, and would not inflict the fine were they not satisfied that there was neglect on the part of the Tramways Company and further, that unless the Tramways Company expedited matters the company would be asked to contribute a good deal more. He thought the Council would be able to establish the claim in a court of law. This decision would conclusively show that the Council were in earnest in urging the Tramways Company to fulfil their duties in providing sufficient cars for the accommodation of the public. (Hear, hear.)

"The company had certainly neglected to do so and had not taken seriously, if he might say so, the recommendations of the Council in that connection. The committee had only inflicted the penalty because of the neglect on the part of the Tramways Company in not using the expedition that the Council might expect, on the part of the company.

"Mr H. M. Smeeton said the decision would be thoroughly approved by all in the city. He did not think the citizens knew of the earnest endeavours made by the Council to get the Tramways Company to fulfil their duties. The fine would convince the Tramways Company that they would have to bestir themselves and supply the number of cars the Council demanded. Mr M. Casey: It is certainly an easy way of getting money. (Laughter) He was delighted to think that they could ease the ratepayers by getting money from the Tramways Company."[71]

While Councillor Casey might have thought it easy money, the truth was that the Auckland City Council received a share of the Tramways Company's profits as per the deed of delegation that existed between them. The Council also benefitted greatly from the political profit generated by a tramway that provided an efficient transport service to its citizens. That had to be far more important than the paltry £328 penalty that could be collected from the Tramways Company struggling with its own success and that of the City.

That success was acknowledged by Mr C. G. Tegetmeier, chairman of directors of the Auckland Electric Tramways Company Limited, during a visit to Auckland during early 1907:

"Matters relating to the Auckland tramway service formed the subject of an interview which a Herald representative had on Saturday with Mr C. G. Tegetmeier, chairman of directors of the Auckland Electric Tramways

Company, who is about to return to London after spending several weeks in Auckland, in connection with the affairs of the company.

"As might be expected, he is greatly impressed on his present visit with the great progress made by Auckland during the past seven years. The prosperity of Auckland, said Mr Tegetmeier in a preliminary observation, seems to be established on a very solid basis. This remarkable prosperity is indicated perhaps in no clearer manner than by the numbers of people who travel on the tramways — a number which has proved to be altogether beyond the expectations, based on the experience of tramway systems in England and other countries.

"This may be to a large extent explained by such local circumstances as the hilly nature and the climate of Auckland, but it must also be largely due to the fact that the people have the money in their pockets. The Auckland people, then, patronise the tramcars to a greater extent than the Home people in proportion to population? Oh certainly. The experience in England never led us to anticipate such an enormous traffic here." [72]

That 'enormous traffic' continued to generate handsome profits for the Auckland Electric Tramways Company Limited and of course the Auckland City Council, particularly after a proposed change to the way their dividend was to be calculated. By 1907, further expansion by way of additional cars and electricity generation was also planned:

"London, May 3. The meeting of the Auckland Electric Tramways Company will be held on the 7th inst., and the directors have just issued their report for 1906. It is stated that the total revenue for the year amounted to £132,364, as compared with £122,995 for the previous year. The traffic receipts, which amounted to £130,336, show an increase of £8457.

"After deducting all expenses chargeable to revenue, including £14,255 for interest on the debenture stock, and providing for the rental and percentage of profits payable to the Auckland City Council amounting to £3246, and after setting aside £10,000 to meet depreciation, there remains a surplus of £33,583, making with the £3018 brought forward from the previous account, an available balance of £36,601.

"The report goes on to say that, differences having arisen between the Auckland City Council and the company with regard to the system formerly adopted to arrive at the profits earned within the city, upon which the City Council is entitled to a percentage, a new method has been suggested by the company which it is believed will meet the City Council's views.

"To meet increasing traffic five additional cars have been added during the year; these will during the present year be increased by a further 12 cars, making the total rolling stock 72. The Board have decided to take in hand the construction of the extension of about three miles in the Mount Eden Road district, referred to in the last report, immediately the necessary powers are obtained. To cope with the demand to be created by the above extensions and to meet the increased traffic, further plant, capable of an output of 600 kilowatts, will be installed during the year." [73]

In the meantime, the commuter crush continued – a situation not helped by a work-to-rule implemented by tramway employees intent on improving their pay and conditions:

"The decision of the tramway employees to rigidly adhere to the municipal by-laws, and allow no passengers on cars in excess of the authorised number, again caused much inconvenience and annoyance yesterday. Generally speaking, the public have accepted the situation with equanimity, but the situation at five o'clock last evening was very acute when the usual rush for cars took place. On the Parnell and Herne Bay sections there was a scene of much confusion, and the general stampede for seats resembled more of a football scrimmage than peaceful citizens following their daily avocation.

"Even chivalry was forgotten. 'Might is right' seemed to be the accepted motto, and fragile women were remorselessly carried willy-nilly into the cars or ruthlessly pushed aside. Their discomfort was also intensified by the drenching rain and the muddy state of the roads. Many passengers of both sexes boarded the cars when in motion near the terminus, only to get off again when the cars came to a standstill, the licensed number having secured their seats earlier." [74]

But tramway employees were not the only participants partly responsible for the 'usual rush for cars'. Those politically responsible to its citizens for improvement also had an agenda of their own:

"The proposal of the Auckland City Council to allow a certain number of strap hangers on the tramcars has excited a good deal of comment. It was stated at the meeting of the Council that the by-law would benefit suburban residents by allowing them to get home earlier than at present, while when the end of the first section was reached, the majority would be enabled to secure a seat.

"With a view to ascertaining the attitude likely to be taken up by the suburban bodies through whose districts the trams pass, a Herald reporter yesterday had a number of interviews with the representatives of such bodies. The chairman of the Remuera Road Board (Mr J. R. Dickson) referred to the resolution passed by his Board, and which decision has already been published. The Board had, he said, instructed its solicitors to draw up a by-law empowering the Board to prohibit strap hanging, and to allow only those in the cars who can find seats. As soon as that by-law comes into force the Board would prosecute the Tramways Company for any breach inside the Board's area, which extended from Newmarket to Green Lane. The Board was acting in conjunction with others, and the members were distinctly of opinion that it would not be advisable to allow strap hangers, because if they did so they would be allowing the Tramways Company to evade that portion of the deed of delegation which provided that sufficient cars should be furnished for the needs of the residents.

"Referring to strap hangers within One-tree Hill district, Mr Burton believed his Board would agree to all the recommendations because the outcry of the residents of the district was so great regarding the shortage of cars. The great difficulty was between the hours of 7.45 and 8.30 in the morning, when the cars bound for Auckland were insufficient to convey the incoming passengers from the One-tree Hill district.

"The same thing happened from Auckland between 4.45 and 6.15 in the afternoon, while on Saturday evenings, between 6.30 and 7.30 the same shortage was noticed. Great difficulty was also experienced by residents attending the theatre in the evening. On all occasions, when there were public gatherings Alexandra Park, the local residents were so inconvenienced that many of them were often delayed from one to two hours in getting home.

"It was believed by Mr W. R. Bloomfield, chairman of the Epsom Road Board, that it was in the interests of the travelling public, as a whole, that every person should have a seat in a tramcar, and no strap hangers should be allowed. This was a means of having more cars provided." [75]

However, by September 1907, the congestion issue had become so chronic that the Auckland City Council, at least, acceded to the Electric Tramways Company's change of by-laws, allowing cars to carry more passengers than those who could be seated:

"A special meeting of the Auckland City Council was held this morning in respect to the by-laws regarding tramway traffic recently passed by the Council.

"On the motion of Mr Bagnall, seconded by Mr Hutchison, the following resolutions were carried: (a) That the Auckland City Council doth hereby by special resolution intend to operate as a special order resolve that the by-law lodged the 23rd August, 1907, of the Auckland Electric Tramways Company Limited, repealing by-laws 2, 14, and 15 of the said company be confirmed...The by-laws in question are those prohibiting the carriage of more passengers than seats are provided for." [76]

Despite its ultimate acceptance in 1907 of what is, today, an accepted practice of standing passengers, some members of the Auckland City Council must, at that time, have suffered from a good deal of Antipodean angst concerning the overall running of the City's tramways. Following the transmission of the Council's concerns to the principal shareholders of the Auckland Electric Tramways Company, what was described by The New Zealand Herald as an 'important letter from London' was duly received by way of a reply.

This letter, seemingly the first indication that the Auckland City Council was considering public ownership of the tramways, was duly laid before the Council at its meeting held on 21 November 1907:

"One of the most important letters received for a considerable time in relation to tramway matters was laid before the City Council at the meeting last evening by the Mayor (Mr A. M. Myers), who had received it from Mr Tegetmeier, chairman of directors of the Auckland Electric Tramways Company. The letter was dated London, September 27, and was a reply to communications forwarded by the City Council on July 24 last.

"After acknowledging receipt of the Council's letter, Mr Tegetmeier went on to say: Your letter refers in general terms to the present unsatisfactory position of the Auckland Electric Tramways but except for the reference to the alleged insufficiency of the rolling stock and electric plant to deal with the passenger traffic there are no indications in the letter as to the ground for speaking of the present position of the tramways as unsatisfactory. It is true there has been some friction with the men but this, it would appear, has arisen entirely from the men's dissatisfaction with the recent award of the Arbitration Court, and I would suggest that the dissatisfaction of the public to which you refer is largely attributable to the course which the men have adopted.

"I need not assure you that the directors of the company have always endeavoured, and will continue to use their best endeavours, to reduce as much as possible any causes tending to give dissatisfaction to the local authorities or to the public. With regard to the specific complaints as to the insufficiency of the rolling stock and electric plant, I would beg to refer you to the letter of the company to the Auckland City Council of the 6th inst. in which the Council were informed of the measures that had been taken to largely increase the number and efficiency of the cars and the capacity of the plant at the power station...

"I fully appreciate the point you refer to that owing to questions of policy in regard to the tramways having to be settled in London, some little time must necessarily elapse between the initiation of such questions and their settlement, but such time spent on the consideration of large questions of policy is not a disadvantage, and I submit that with a capable general manager on the spot, who is empowered to deal with all details concerning the working of the system, and who has had considerable tramway experience in this country, and having the advantage of the co-operation of a resident director who has been associated with the Auckland tramways since their initiation, and is acquainted with the conditions, such questions should be of infrequent occurrence.

"I also recognise the fact to which you refer that inasmuch as many public services in New Zealand are owned either by the Government or the local authorities, there may be a certain amount of antagonism to private ownership of undertakings of the character of tramways. The directors have therefore taken into serious consideration the suggestion which you have submitted that negotiations should be entered into between the company and the local authorities for the transfer of the rights and properties of the company to a local tramways board and we have consulted with the British Electric Traction Company who are the principal shareholders in the Auckland Electric Tramways Company.

"The directors of the British Electric Traction Company have reminded us that the local authorities originally had the opportunity of taking up the tramways undertaking, but they decided to leave the risk of investing the very considerable capital involved in establishing the undertaking to those who were prepared to take that risk, and that subsequently, when the Auckland Tramways Company had to be capitalised, an opportunity was given to the investing public to subscribe for the shares at par, but out of the £300,000 of ordinary shares issued only an insignificant proportion was subscribed for by others…

"Having thus taken very considerable risks and succeeded in establishing a successful undertaking, the principal shareholders do not at all favour the proposal that they should now sell out before they have had sufficient time to reap the fair reward of their enterprise, and they would very much prefer that the company should continue to work the tramways under the terms and for the period of the concessions which, as you are aware, is until June 30, 1932, in respect of the tramways within the city of Auckland, and until June 30, 1934 in respect of the tramways in the suburbs, at which dates the local authorities have the right to purchase such portion of the undertaking as is within their respective district at its then value as a going concern.

"If, however, it is the desire of the citizens of Auckland that the tramways should now be owned and worked by or on behalf of the various local bodies interested, the principal shareholders will in deference to such wish offer no objection to the directors of the Auckland Tramways Company negotiating with the local authorities for the sale of the rights and property of the company on an equitable basis, having regard to the terms and tenure of the concession, and to the profit-earning capacity of the undertaking.

"The paid up share and debenture capital of the company is now £635,100, and the divisible profits last year, after payment of rental and percentage of profits to the Auckland City Council, amounting to £3246 and after providing £16,915 for repairs and maintenance, and £10,000 for depreciation, were £47,838.

"Of the above-mentioned capital £50,000 was raised during the current year, and is being expended, and further liabilities are being incurred on the extensions now in course of construction, and upon the increased rolling stock and plant. It may be expected that this additional capital expenditure and the growth of population in the districts served will result in increasing profits.

"In reply to your question, I have, therefore, to state that the directors of the Auckland Tramways Company will be prepared to negotiate for the transference of the whole of the rights and property of the company subject to the purchasers discharging its liabilities for such a sum as if invested at 4¼ per cent, per annum will yield an annual return from December 31 last equal to last year's profits of the company for the remaining term of the concessions, and return the share and debenture capital in full at the end of that period.

"In reference to your suggestion that we should send a representative to Auckland at the earliest possible moment, with full authority to deal with the whole question, I venture to express the opinion that it would be better that an agreement in principle should, in the first instance, be arrived at either by letter or cable, as I consider that this course would be both more expeditious and less likely to lead to misunderstanding.

"The Mayor's suggestion to refer the letter to the Finance Committee was approved." [77]

By the time of the ordinary general meeting of the Auckland Electric Tramways Company Limited was held in May 1908, the proposal for a municipal buy-out was still on the table awaiting a response from the Auckland City Council:

"London, May 22. Last Wednesday Mr C. G. Tegetmeier presided at the tenth ordinary general meeting of the Auckland Electric Tramways Company, held at Donington House. Lieutenant-Colonel Burton, late of Auckland, was present. In moving the adoption of the directors' report the chairman said the issued share capital stood at £350,000, the amount having been increased early in the year by the issue of £50,000 in six per cent, preference shares.

"Nearly the whole of these shares were taken up in Auckland, and it was satisfactory to note the increasing extent to which the capital of the company was being acquired by local investors. At the present time about £154,000 of the capital was held in New Zealand by about 400 shareholders...In regarding their increase in capital expenditure, it had to be remembered that when the company was formed it was not, and could not have been, anticipated that the traffic would develop to such a remarkable extent as it had. To carry, as they did last year, passengers equal in number to 300 times the whole of the population of the district, and on several occasions, with a population of 75,000, to carry over 110,000 in one day, was, he thought, quite exceptional in the record of tramway undertakings...

"For the current year the results up to the present showed considerable improvement on last year. For the period up to April 24, on an increased car mileage of 40,700, they had carried nearly a million more passengers and taken £5749 more in traffic receipts.

"There was one matter he should refer to, and that was the suggestion that had been submitted to them by the Mayor of Auckland that they should enter into negotiations for the sale of the company's undertaking to a local tramways board, who would obtain legislative authority to acquire and work the concern on behalf of and for the benefit of the various local bodies interested.

"The Mayor referred to the fact that in the three other principal cities of New Zealand the tramways were owned by the municipalities, and he suggested that the antagonism which existed in New Zealand to the private ownership of anything of the character of a tramway concession was intensified in the case of the Auckland tramways by the fact of the ownership being in the hands of a company having its headquarters and a large portion of its capital held outside the country...

"After very full consideration, and with the concurrence of the principal shareholders, they had informed the Mayor that if it was the desire of the citizens of Auckland that the tramways should be owned and worked by or on behalf of the various local bodies interested, the directors would be prepared to negotiate for the disposal of the rights and property of the company on an equitable basis." [78]

However, by September 1908, the City Council was more intent on prosecution than procurement as it sought damages from the Auckland Electric Tramways Company at the Auckland Supreme Court on 3 September 1908:

"The action brought by the Auckland City Council against the Auckland Electric Tramways Company Limited for £784 damages for alleged breach of the deed of delegation and Order-in-Council, in failing to provide sufficient cars, was commenced at the Auckland Supreme Court yesterday, before Mr Justice Edwards.

"The plaintiff Council, in its statement of claim, alleges that since November 7, 1907, and for some time prior thereto, the Tramway Company has failed to comply with the deed of delegation and Order-in Council in so far that it has not provided to the satisfaction of the Council a sufficient number of cars to meet the requirements of the traffic; that on July 19, 1907, the Council gave written notice to the company calling its attention to the inadequate supply, and requiring it to provide two additional cars by August 31, and three more by October 31; that by November 7 the company had only provided two of the five cars mentioned, and that Council then gave the company notice that a breach had been committed, and gave it 60 days in which to rectify matters...

"In the next clause the Council asserts that the company had not, on January 7, 1908 (the date of the expiration of the 60 days' notice), and up till May 2 (the date of instituting proceedings), provided the additional number of cars required, and the Council claimed the amount specified as damages, at the rate of £8 per day, as provided for under the deed of delegation or Order-in-Council.

"The company, in its statement of defence, denies that on November 7, 1907, or at any time before or since, it made default, in complying with the conditions of the deed of delegation or Order-in-Council. It denies that it has not provided a sufficient number of cars to the satisfaction of the Council, that it has not secured to the public the full benefit of the undertaking, and further, that, it is a condition of the deed or Order-in-Council that the company shall use or maintain to the satisfaction of the plaintiff a sufficient number or quantity of passenger cars to subserve the purposes of the undertaking.

"For a further defence, the defendant company says that it is provided in the deed of delegation that whenever anything is to be done or supplied by the company, subject to the approval or satisfaction of the Council, such approval shall not be unreasonably arbitrary, and it shall be sufficient if the thing done or supplied is substantially in accordance with what is ordinarily observed under similar circumstances.

"It alleges that the Council has unreasonably and arbitrarily withheld its approval of the number of cars used by the company, inasmuch as it has required it to provide a greater number of cars than were reasonably necessary and, further, that it has substantially complied with the notice of

July 19, inasmuch as orders for the cars specified were at once placed, and the same were completed as soon as possible, and supplied before June 30, 1908. A further ground for defence is that the time-tables submitted from time to time and approved by the Council have been duly carried out by the company." [79]

Not surprisingly…"When the case of the Auckland City Council v the Auckland Electric Tramways Company Limited was called on at the Supreme Court yesterday morning, Mr Thos. Cotter, counsel for the plaintiff body, said he had very great pleasure in announcing that since the adjournment the previous day, the parties had met and had arrived at the following terms of settlement —

"1. The plaintiffs witnesses having stated that the present car service is sufficient, the defendants admit that it is fairly open to question whether their service of cars until April, 1908, was sufficient within the terms of the deed of delegation of June 25, 1900.

"2. The plaintiffs do not dispute that the question of sufficiency is to be determined as provided by the deed of delegation, namely, 'If the thing done or supplied shall be substantially in accordance with what is usually or customarily done, or supplied, in similar cases or under similar circumstances.'

"3. The defendants pay into Court the sum of £100, and £75 costs, which the plaintiffs accept in full settlement of all matters in question in this action. The notice of March 27, 1908, to be deemed cancelled.

"His Honor: I think it is a very proper settlement. Indeed, it was on my mind to suggest such a settlement to the parties, inasmuch as it is admitted that there is a sufficient service now by the persons best qualified to judge, namely, the Mayor and other witnesses, and I suppose the object of the action in the beginning was to ensure the same.

"Mr Bell (for the Tramways Company): Our real difficulty was that as the action was framed, it was to assert that the City Council was the sole test, and there was no limit to the determination by the Council what was necessary, but when we found that the Council did not question the statement in paragraph 2 of the settlement, we were only too glad to admit that it was open to question, until our recent acquisition of cars, whether we had complied with the deed of delegation.

"His Honor: I am very glad the parties have seen their way to settle it. An order, in terms of the settlement, was entered accordingly." [80]

Despite such bureaucratic interruptions, the business of the Auckland Electric Tramways Company Limited continued to expand:

"In a table attached to its annual report, the Auckland Electric Tramways Company furnishes a return of the number of passengers, etc., for the year which closed on December 31, 1908. The number of cars working was increased from 71 in 1907 to 87 last year, and the number of passengers carried increased from 22,474,537 in 1907 to 26,144,320 in 1908.

"The average receipts per passenger worked out at 1.47d in 1907 and 1.50d in 1908, while the average expenditure per passenger in 1907 was 0.88d and in 1908 0.92d, the proportion of expenses to receipts increasing from 60 per cent, in 1907 to 61 per cent, in 1908. The number of route miles increased from 19.2 in 1907 to 22.3 in 1908, the single lines from 6.99 to 8.15, and the double lines from 12.21 to 14.15. The traffic receipts showed the satisfactory increase of £26,129 12s 9d." [81]

By 1910, trams were still viewed as the best alternative to the lumps and bumps of both the horse-drawn and new motor-omnibus services. That's one of the reasons why a new tram service, this time powered by steam, was established as a means of conveying ferry passengers between the wharf at Bayswater and Takapuna. The inauguration of the new service was described by the Auckland Star on 22 December 1910:

"The running of the new service between Auckland and Takapuna, by steam-tram and ferry, was commenced this morning without any formal opening. The first trip was made at 7.15 a.m., and thereafter hourly, the number of passengers being such as to indicate that the service will be well patronised when the public become used to it.

"The newly-built steamer Pupuke, which now connects Auckland with Bayswater and the steam tram, is a commodious vessel, licensed to carry 738 persons, and stated to be somewhat faster than any other ferry-boat now plying in the harbour. The tramway, which is eleven miles in length, is divided into eleven penny sections, and the journey round the lake, which is made every other trip, takes slightly less than an hour. The line is equipped with six cars and two engines, the number of cars used being varied according to requirements. The ferry is met at the Bayswater wharf hourly from 7.30 a.m., the 8.30 trip being the first round the lake." [82]

So, by the close of 1910, ferries, motor-omnibuses and both steam and electric trams were successfully transporting an increasing number of passengers to and from a geographically- expanding area. But with so many vehicles competing for road space and passengers, frequent accidents were bound to occur. Tram passengers scrambling between the sidewalk and their central roadway conveyances were particularly at risk:

"On 17 March (1911), a young woman crossing Queen Street to catch a tram was knocked down and run over by a passing motorist. She was not seriously injured, but the motorist was charged with, 'Having driven a motor car on Queen Street at a speed likely to be dangerous to the public'. In a show of excessive zeal the prosecution called 16 witnesses who variously assessed the vehicle's speed between 8 and 12 MPH." [83]

But despite the growing motor-car competition, the chairman of the Auckland Electric Tramways Company, C. G. Tegetmeier, was very optimistic as to the future of both his company and Auckland:

"London, November 5 (1910). During the course of his speech in his capacity as chairman at the half-year's meeting of the Auckland Electric Tramways Company, Mr C. G. Tegetmeier remarked that the progress of Auckland in the last three or four years in everything that constituted material prosperity had been very marked, and there were grounds for the confident anticipation that there was a period of still greater expansion and prosperity ahead. The results of the operations of the company for the six months to June 30 last afforded very gratifying evidence of the continued expansion and progress of the company's business: more than a million more passengers had been carried and the traffic receipts were £6463 higher than in the first six months of 1909.

"Taking the population of Auckland and the districts served at 100,000, it would be seen that they were carrying the whole population more than 300 times in the course of the year. It was no unusual thing for the number of passengers carried in one day to total more than the whole of the population. Working expenses were necessarily higher, although, proportionately to the increase of the mileage run, they showed a satisfactory decrease, the ratio of expenses to receipts having gone down from 62 per cent to 59 per cent." [84]

Of course, to keep pace with the demand for its services, not only was a continuous supply of cars needed but, particularly as the routes were extended, the plant that powered the system had also to be expanded. At a time when electric power was just coming into its own, the maintenance of the power stations included the installation of new devices, such as switching equipment, generators and pumps, almost as soon as they were invented.

"The Auckland Electric Tramways Company has now 99 trams in service, the 99th having been tested and passed yesterday. Another one, making 100 in all, is almost completed. Having registered a century, the company is still scoring freely. The 101st car is being built by the company itself, an order is being placed for 10 more locally, and for five at Home. When these are completed the company will have 116 trams. When these are all in service their total carrying capacity will be very much greater than that of the cars of any other system in New Zealand. All the new cars are being built to carry 52 passengers seated, and are after the pattern of the large cross-seated trams which have lately been built, which have proved the most suitable for local conditions.

"A large addition has recently been made to the power-house of the Tramways Company, and the installation of additional plant has just been completed. The new plant consists of a 600-kilowatt alternator and a 500-kilowatt motor generator. Space is left, in the extension of the building for a 1000-kilowatt alternator, and the order for this is now being placed.

"In the boiler-house there have also been extensions of the plant, among them a Davis-Perett oil-eliminating plant, for extracting all the oil which water may have gathered from the machinery before it is sent back to the boilers. The same water can thus be converted into steam over and over again without disadvantage. The oil is separated by electrical methods and the water is passed over sand and shingle.

"In showing a reporter round the premises yesterday, Mr F. E. de Guerrier, engineer to the Tramways Company, pointed out an ingenious apparatus which has just been installed and which conveys the coal from the point at which it is tipped to the furnaces by mechanical means and without handling. The same apparatus can be used to bring the ashes back.

"The old pumping station has been abandoned, and in the new pumping station, next (to) the morgue, are three circulating pumps, with room for a fourth. Each pump is capable of delivering 1500 gallons of water per minute. Two high-tension cables have been laid to Epsom, and the sub-station there is now in use. In it are two motor-generators. Power is generated at the power-house at 5500 volts. The motor-generators receive this and generate current at 550 volts, the ordinary tramway voltage. The chief economy in having a sub-station is in the cost of copper mains." [85]

Nevertheless, by July 1911, such apparent progress was still not enough to satisfy the Auckland City Council's expectations. So, politically motivated or otherwise, and for the second time in as many years, the Council once again sought some legal restitution:

"The City Council decided a fortnight ago to prosecute the Auckland Electric Tramways Company for certain alleged breaches of the deed of delegation. At last night's meeting a copy of the notice to be served upon the company was forwarded by the city solicitor (Mr Thomas Cotter) for signature. The notice set out that if the Council's requirements are not supplied within 60 days the Council will exercise the powers conferred upon it under the deed of delegation and will take legal action against the company on the ground that it had not provided a sufficient number of cars to the satisfaction of the Council, and had failed to keep such cars as had been in use in good order and condition.

"Mr J. J. Walklate, general manager of the Auckland Electric Tramways Company, wrote notifying that cars Nos. 102, 103, and 104 had been delivered from the builders, and had been placed in commission. He had received further advice from London regarding the shipment of remaining trucks and underframes for the other cars ordered, and expected to be able to improve slightly upon the dates of delivery mentioned in his letter of May 30. In any event every effort would be made to hasten the completion of the cars. The Mayor remarked that the company was evidently 'putting its best leg forward'." [86]

Indeed, the Tramways Company did appear to be trying, despite the bureaucratic interference and the frustratingly slow decision-making process of government agencies, as reported by The New Zealand Herald on 10 December 1910:

(During the previously-reported review of the tramway company's operations for the six months to June 30 1910, the chairman, C. G. Tegetmeier, referred) "...to the item 'legal and other expenses in connection with brakes inquiry, £826 16s 8d'...the chairman recalled the fact that more than three years' ago the New Zealand Government appointed a Royal Commission to inquire into the question of the brakes on the company's cars. Consequent upon the report of the Commission, the sanction of the New Zealand Public Works Department was obtained to equip two of the cars with the latest improved air brake, which, the company was advised, would be most suitable for the conditions which prevail in Auckland.

"Actual experience in the working of the brake extending over a period of some months proved satisfactory, alike to the company's officers and to the men in charge of the cars, who were directly concerned in the efficiency and reliability of the brake, and the directors were desirous of equipping the whole of the cars with a similar type of brake at a cost of approximately £12,000. The Public Works Department, however, were not prepared to give the necessary permission, and as a result of some controversy the New Zealand Government appointed a second Royal Commission to investigate the matter.

"The members of the Commission had their first sitting in April, and they took very exhaustive evidence in the principal cities of New Zealand where electric tramways were operated, and in their report they concurred in the adoption by the company of the type of brake which the company for some time previously had been willing and anxious to install. They had not yet had the approval of the Public Works Department to the measures proposed for giving full effect to the recommendation of the Royal Commission, but so soon as that had been received the work of installing the air brake upon all the cars would be taken in hand and completed with all possible despatch." [87]

However, bureaucratic interference in the private business of the Auckland Electric Tramways Company wasn't confined to just the City Council. The Government also sought control of the country's tramways services by means of the Tramways Act 1908. This Act essentially set the ground rules for the establishment, construction, and running of suburban tramway systems throughout the country.

For instance, the Act forbade a local authority in charge of a tramway from entering into any dealings, such as the raising of loans for the system's expansion, without first obtaining the permission of its ratepayers. While not seen to have any immediate relevance to the privately-owned, Auckland tramway service, that requirement would prove to be of crucial importance after the city had acquired ownership a decade or so later.

In the meantime, amendments to the 1908 Tramways Act legislated in 1910 and 1911 were of more immediate concern to the Auckland City Council. The 1910 amendment was of particular concern as some of its provisions directly impinged on the revenue-earning capacity of the Council:

"The Tramway Amendment Bill was reported to the House of Representatives today by the Labour Bills Committee, which recommended that the Bill be allowed to proceed with amendment…Very voluminous evidence was taken by the committee when the Bill was under consideration. The printed report of the evidence occupies 250 foolscap pages, and included in it are statements of witnesses representing the Auckland City Council and the Auckland Tramways Company.

"Mr P. M. Mackay stated that the Auckland City Council took strong exception to two important principles incorporated in the Bill — first, the encroachment upon the power of local bodies by the centralising of matters of local importance in the Minister; and second, the insecurity given to municipal contracts when the provisions of deeds can so simply be overridden by regulations made by the Governor.

"Clause 3 empowered the Minister to authorise any proper person to inspect any tramway, its rolling stock, plant, appliances, and machinery, and on the report of such person that any alterations, repairs, or additions are required to insure the safety of the public or employees, or to meet the reasonable requirements of the traffic, the Minister may order those alterations, repairs, or additions to be made accordingly. All this power, said Mr Mackay, was already held by the Council under its deed of delegation, and had been constantly exercised by it ever since the initiation of the electric tramways. The clause was, therefore, a distinct encroachment on the power of the local body, and practically cancelled the provisions of the deed of delegation between the Council and the company.

"In exercising its power in the past the Council had found itself hampered in securing an increase in rolling stock as quickly as was desired by the delay which had taken place in Wellington in approving of the plans of the proposed cars, and naturally dreaded greater delays if mere local matters are to be centralised in Wellington.

"In clause 12 the power of the Council to license tramcars is entirely taken away and transferred to the Minister. Apart from any other consideration, this would mean a loss in revenue of £200 per annum, and the agreement between the company and the Council in the deed of delegation referring to this matter was set aside, which was a matter of great moment to a local body which had had an honest pride in the security of its contracts and deeds.

"Mr Mackay concluded: In making this statement for the consideration of the committee, I desire on behalf of the Auckland City Council to enter a most respectful, but emphatic, protest against the underlying principle of the Bill which deprives the local bodies of their control of what is essentially local traffic, and hence a matter of local government, and also sets aside the provisions of deeds merely by regulations made by the Governor." [88]

But what a government might take with one hand, it sometimes lets slip with the other, as it did with the Municipal Corporations Amendment Act 1913 which became law on 1 February 1914.

In essence, the Act allowed city and borough councils to "...establish, maintain, and regulate" a number of services for its citizens and that included, as per Clause 27(1) "...a service for the conveyance of passengers and goods to and from any place within the borough, or, with the consent of any neighbouring local authority, between any place within the borough and any place within the district of that local authority..."

While Clause 27(3) of the Municipal Corporations Amendment Act stated, "Nothing herein shall authorize a Council to construct any tramway or railway," the previous Clause 27(2) was of great significance to Auckland's existing tramway system in that it permitted a council to establish, maintain, and regulate "services for the purpose of extending or supplementing the service of the said tramway, or of serving areas not served or not adequately served by the said tramway."

And, of even greater significance to the future of all established modes of transport, Clause 27(2) allowed for:

"The establishment and maintenance of a ***motor service*** for the purpose only of serving areas not served or not adequately served by the tramway shall not be in contravention of this subsection, notwithstanding that part of the course of such service is through streets in which the said tramway is laid, and which are served by the said tramway." [89]

Naturally, the Auckland Electric Tramways Company vehemently opposed Clause 27 of the Municipal Corporations Amendment Act prior to its enactment and the company had its share of supporters fearful that any City Council competition could jeopardise the future success of the tramway system. This letter to The New Zealand Herald, published on 24 October 1913, sums up an uneasiness apparently felt by a number of concerned citizens:

"Sir, — Would you allow me a little space in your paper for a few words on above. I wonder if many of the people of this town have noticed of late the position which the Council has taken up towards the Auckland Electric Tramways Company. If they have been reading the newspapers they must see that the Council is pinpricking the Tramways Company at every turn. This, to my mind, is not a very proper policy to be taken by the Council under the circumstances.

"As we all know at the time the Auckland Electric Tramways Company started operations in this town they did so at a big risk. They sunk large capital in a venture which was the first of its kind started in New Zealand, and they gave the people a tramway service second to none in this part of the world. Now, after a success has been made of the venture the City Council is regretting the deal made by the then Council, who sold their rights, because at the time they were frightened to take a risk themselves.

"Even had they taken the risk and run the trams themselves I'm quite safe in saying that the system would not be the success it is to-day. This is proved by the non-success of the trams run by the councils in other towns of New Zealand. Now the Tramways Company want, in a small way, to protect their interests for the remaining term of their lease, and also to protect the City Council when the trams become their property, but the Council is up in arms.

"I would like to point out to the Council that they should remember before making things unpleasant for the Tramways Company that the said company has about 700 men employed in this town, whose wages, amounting to a big sum, are spent among the business people of Auckland.

"If the City Council believe they have made a bad deal they ought now to bury the hatchet, and not retard the Auckland Electric Tramways Company in giving the people of this city an ever-improving system, so that when the Council's time for management comes along they will have a first-class service handed over to them. E. J. Banon. 30 Upper Queen Street, Auckland." [90]

In its report of continuing profits later that year, the Auckland Electric Tramways Company reassured its shareholders and customers that the company was not only providing the best of all possible services but that it would continue to meet the demand with a systematic expansion of its infrastructure. That demand was expected to increase even more with the scheduled opening of the Auckland Exhibition in December 1914.

"The sixteenth ordinary general meeting of the Auckland Electric Tramways Company Ltd was held at the registered offices of the company Electrical Federation Offices, Kingsway, London, W.C., on Thursday, October 9, 1913, Mr C. G. Tegetmeier, chairman of the company, presiding.

"The chairman said Gentlemen, — moving the adoption of the directors' report and the statement of accounts, I should like to preface my remarks by expressing the satisfaction felt by my colleagues and myself in being able to present to you a statement of accounts which shows in such a high degree a continuance of the progress that has characterised the business of the company since the commencement of the undertaking.

"Our traffic receipts last year amounted to £257,591, which was £28,449, or 12 per cent more than in the preceding year. We have become accustomed to seeing our traffic receipts increase year by year, but although the route mileage worked last year was only slightly in excess of the previous year, the result of the year shows a greater proportionate increase than we have ever had in any one year over the immediately preceding year...

"As I have told you on the last few occasions that I have had the pleasure of addressing you, the time was approaching when we should have to meet considerable expenditure for reconstruction of our permanent way. Last year extensive renewals were carried out, and the expenditure amounted to £34,844...For the next few years the expenditure will continue heavy, though not perhaps to the same extent as last year.

"We are fortunate in having provided out of past profits for expenditure of this nature, but the necessity for continuing the provision still, of course, exists, and out of last year's revenue we have allocated £25,000 or £5000 more than in the preceding year, to the renewals account...On the other side of the balance sheet the capital expenditure is the principal item that calls for remark, and this shows an increase during the year of £115,304. A large portion of this expenditure was the cost of new cars, on which we spent during the year a total of nearly £50,000.

"At the beginning of the year we had 126 cars in stock. This number was increased during the year to 156, and we had five more approaching completion at the end of the year. One reason why we have made this very liberal addition to our cars is that during the current twelve months an Exhibition on a considerable scale is to be held in Auckland commencing in December next. It will remain open for some months, and there is no doubt that while it is open there will be a large increase in traffic requirements. I am glad to say that we have at last received the approval of the Public Works Department to running coupled cars. This will enable us to make much more effective use of the smaller cars which were acquired in the early days of the undertaking." [91]

By 1913, it had been common for horse-drawn omnibuses and cabs to supplement the tramway system by carrying passengers to and from the line to their homes and workplaces, as necessary. However, by the second decade of the twentieth century, horsepower was increasingly being replaced by motor power – a development that, unbeknownst to the directors of the Auckland Electric Tramways Company at the time, would eventually replace their business altogether.

But while Mr Tegetmeier was not in a position to recognise the impending danger posed by Auckland's motor-omnibuses during his October 1913 address, he nevertheless hedged his bets by indicating that their use could be a future business proposition for the Tramways Company:

"The site of the Exhibition is not directly on our tramway route, and at the request of the Exhibition authorities we have agreed to run a service of motor-omnibuses connecting the tramway lines at two different points with the Exhibition entrance. We have acquired six motor vehicles of the most up-to-date design for this purpose, and they will cost approximately £5000.

"We hope that they will to a large extent pay for themselves during the time the Exhibition is open, but we do not expect much from them after it is over, and it is entirely with the object of furthering the success of the Exhibition by facilitating access to it that we have obtained them. With the conditions prevailing in Auckland, and with an efficient tramway service providing continuous communication from the centre of the city through all the main thoroughfares, we do not think there is scope for the profitable operation of motor-omnibuses. However, if there should be opportunity in the future of running motor vehicles in Auckland to advantage, the company is not likely to leave it to others to take advantage of." [92]

In the meantime, there was enough to do to maintain the tramway service to a standard that would meet the needs of Auckland's commuters, as the optimistic Mr Tegetmeier stated in his summation of the company's affairs:

"It is not to be expected that the company can keep pace with the ever-growing traffic requirements of Auckland without expending capital. Increased requirements on the part of the public and increased capital expenditure on the part of the company to meet them have been distinctive features of the company's progress since the commencement, and we can look back with satisfaction to the fact that as further capital has been expended, the outlay has always proved remunerative..." [93]

However, the optimism of 1913 was to be somewhat tempered by the events of the following year, as described by the chairman of the Auckland Electric Tramways Company, Mr Tegetmeier, on 22 October 1914:

"The outstanding feature in connection with the company's business during the twelve months covered by the accounts was the strike in New Zealand which, commencing in October of last year as quite a small affair among the Waterside Workers, was quickly turned into the most serious industrial upheaval that the country had ever experienced. The effect of the strike upon our business was very considerable, not only in a diminution of receipts, but also in a large increase of expenses. The tram service was stopped entirely for eighteen days, from November 8 to 25.

"It is fortunate, perhaps, that the question of our men joining the strike did not arise, for working had to be discontinued owing to the exhaustion of our coal and the impossibility of obtaining further supplies. Work was resumed immediately coal could be obtained, and by that time the failure of the general strike was apparent, although the so-called leaders of labour did not declare the strike off till a month later. The loss of traffic receipts occasioned by the stoppage may be estimated at approximately £15,000. Our receipts were also adversely affected earlier in the year, by the prevalence of an epidemic among the Maori population which was officially termed small-pox, and although there were no fatal, or even serious, cases among the European population, the protective measures adopted by the health authorities, and the scare among the residents, affected the volume of traffic to a very marked extent.

"The traffic created by the Exhibition, which was held in Auckland during the summer months, helped our receipts on the tramways, but not to the extent we had anticipated. Our total traffic receipts amounted to £271,701, which is £14,110 more than in the preceding year, and the number of passengers carried increased from 40,300,000 to 42,100,000, which, as I have before remarked, represents an average of more than the whole population every day.

"Dealing with the revenue account, our expenses show a large increase, and for the first time in our experience the increase is greater than the increase in our traffic receipts. The principal item to account for this is power and running expenses, which are £118,130 or £18,320 more than in the preceding year. This is due to several causes. In the first place we ran a greater number of car miles during the year, notwithstanding the stoppage during the strike. The cost of running was also largely increased for some time after the strike by the much higher price we had to pay for coal. In order to maintain the services large quantities of coal had to be purchased at a cost of over £2 a ton, as compared with, the normal average price of about 14s. It may be interesting to state that our consumption of coal averages over 500 tons a week." [94]

Of course, as one would expect from a private company that had provided a service to the public for so many years that, once their profits were affected by public matters beyond their control, they would seek some relief or, at least, appreciation. This hope was expressed by Mr Tegetmeier in connection with the additional extensions soon to be provided by his company:

"At the present time we are discussing two or three extensions, one of which, an extension of about half-a-mile in Upper Queen Street, the centre of the city, we have agreed to carry out at the request of the Auckland City Council. This extension will be an expensive one to construct, as it will involve a good deal of special work in junctions and crossings, and we would rather be without it, as it will be difficult to work, and we do not expect that it will bring any material increase to our revenue. We quite realise that public convenience will be served by the extension, but we think that the company's willingness to meet the wishes of the council in the public interest should receive proper recognition, and, where possible, reciprocation." [95]

With his closing remarks, Mr Tegetmeier again expressed his optimism for the continuing success of the Auckland tramways business despite the uncertainties of the Great War:

"With regard to the immediate future, it is of course impossible to say what effect the war will have upon our business, but I should not expect that it will affect the position in Auckland or in New Zealand generally to any serious extent..." [96]

However, closer to home, a war of a different sort – one of bureaucracy, waged between local and national Government – did disrupt the Auckland Electric Tramways Company business, as reported by The New Zealand Herald on 21 August 1915:

"Provision for meeting the difficulty which has arisen in connection with the opening of the extension of the Auckland tramway system to Mount Albert, is made in the Tramways Amendment Bill which was introduced in the House of Representatives this afternoon by the Minister for Public Works, the Hon. W. Fraser, and which was passed through all its stages in that Chamber.

"The Minister, in asking for urgency for the Bill, said that the measure dealt with a purely technical matter. The Order-in-Council containing the authorising order in regard to the tramway extension in Auckland had been issued after the extension had been approved by the Public Works Department, but the Auckland Electric Tramways Company had inadvertently omitted to notify that there was a double line of rails. Consequently, the authorising order was invalid, and, although the new line had been finished, it could not be used.

"A large number of people, about 4000 he was told, wished to use the line, but the company could not run the cars without an authorising order. The Bill, which would overcome the difficulty, provided that the authorising order might be modified by allowing he construction of double tramway lines in lieu of single ones." [97]

And despite the optimism expressed by the Tramway Company's Chairman during his 1914 address, the events of the following year did, in fact, affect the company's profits:

"An interesting review was given by Mr C. G. Tegetmeier, chairman of the Auckland Electric Tramways Company, in moving the adoption of the (1915) annual report at the yearly meeting of shareholders in London. Since the company started running cars in 1902, said Mr Tegetmeier, this was the first time the company had not been able to point to an increase, and generally to a large increase, in the company's revenue, over that of the preceding year.

"The war had affected their business in Auckland, as in one way or another it had affected commerce and industry in all parts of the Empire. A comparison with the preceding year might be somewhat deceptive, because in that year there had been extra traffic, due to the Auckland Exhibition, to increase their receipts, and, on the other hand, the discontinuance of running for 18 days during the strike, to reduce them. It was probable, however, that the effect of these two causes upon the gross receipts was to counterbalance each other.

"The accounts covered a period of 11 months of war-time, and closely following upon the outbreak of war there was noticeable decline in the volume of traffic. The tendency in that direction became more pronounced as the year went on; and was still continuing." [98]

Compared to the previous year's outlook, there was also a noticeable change of mind regarding the Tramway Company's use of motor-buses, as explained by Mr Tegetmeier during his end of 1915 address to the board and shareholders:

"The total traffic receipts amounted to £267,793 — a decrease of £3908 compared with the previous year. The whole of that decrease, however, was in respect of their motor-buses, the receipts from the tramways being a few hundred pounds more than in the preceding year, although there was a slight decrease in the number of passengers carried. The motor-omnibuses were acquired specifically for the purpose of facilitating the Exhibition traffic, and on the close of the Exhibition their running was almost discontinued.

"During the year the company had endeavoured to find scope for their profitable use but their experience had proved that under the conditions which prevailed in Auckland it was not possible to operate them remuneratively for passenger traffic, and it was proposed to dispose of them as soon as a suitable opportunity could be found. It was not to be expected that they would realise what they cost." [99]

There were also the first indications that, regardless of the war, the cost of doing business in the remote antipodes was becoming increasingly more difficult:

"It was unfortunately the case that the company had to pay English income tax upon the whole, of its profits, notwithstanding the fact that its profits were earned exclusively in New Zealand and were heavily taxed there, and were likely to be much more heavily taxed in the future. That was one of the many anomalies that pressed very hardly upon companies such as theirs. This was not the time — and he feared it might not be the time for a long while to come — to think of raising capital for new developments, however promising they might be, and even if capital were available the great rise in the cost of all materials and the adverse influences affecting the normal growth of their traffic receipts emphasised the desirableness of restricting expenditure to the needs of the present." [100]

One of the more obvious consequences of the Electric Tramways Company's spending restrictions was the extension of its lines in the City and to the farthest reaches of its various boroughs, as reported by The New Zealand Herald on 10 October 1916:

"The improbability of any further tramways extensions in the city or suburbs being undertaken by the Auckland Electric Tramways Company whilst the war lasts was made clear yesterday by Mr J. J. Walklate, general manager of the company, in a statement he made in reply to some inquiries on the subject. The reasons governing this limitation of expansion on the part of the company were also given.

"What chiefly concerned the company just now, Mr Walklate said, was how to procure the materials and plant necessary to keep the tramway system running. At the present time exports of engineering supplies and plant from Home were being subjected to very stringent criticism before manufacturers were allowed to supply them, and, further, before shippers were allowed to ship them.

"The point apparently was to distinguish between what was necessary to keep industries going, and what was for new work which could and must necessarily be deferred until conditions were easier. So far as New Zealand requirements were concerned the Ministry for Munitions was assisting in the matter by communicating with the High Commissioner in London in cases where any doubt as to absolute necessity for exports from Britain might otherwise exist in the minds of the British authorities.

"For the reasons given, Mr Walklate said, further extensions and duplications of the Auckland tramway services were suspended, and to a certain extent also renewals of lines. So far the Tramways Company had managed very well, having been so fortunate as to be able to procure everything absolutely essential to the maintenance of its services. He was hopeful of being able to continue to do this in the future." [101]

But while the growth of the tramways system may have slowed, the speed of its cars had not – a fact that had not escaped the notice of the police on what must have been a particularly quiet day for murders, burglaries and prostitution:

"An interesting case brought under a city by-law dealing with the speed of tram cars in Queen Street was heard at the Police Court yesterday morning before Mr F. V. Frazer, S.M. Walter Beck, a motorman employed by the Auckland Electric Tramways Company Ltd. was charged that he drove a tramcar in Queen Street on January 6 last at a greater speed than nine miles an hour. Mr J. R. Reed, K.C., represented the defendant and the Tramways Company, and intimated that defendant admitted that he drove the car at more than nine miles an hour.

"Sergeant Alex Matthews, in his evidence, said that on Saturday, January 6, 1917, he saw a double tram, marked 'special' being driven up Queen Street at terrific speed. He estimated the speed at about 30 miles an hour. Witness saw the defendant later and asked him why he travelled so fast. He replied that he was unaware that there was any speed limit for trams in Queen Street. Evidence was also given by Constable Kearney.

"Mr Reed said the by-law under which the case had been brought was passed in 1907, and there had never been the slightest attempt, until the present, to enforce it. The Auckland tramcars, counsel stated, were so constructed that they had only two speeds. The half-speed produced a rate of 12 miles an hour. At full-speed the rate would be increased on the flat to 19 miles an hour, and beyond that it could not be made to go, except on a down-hill grade. The only way the motorman could comply with the by-law was by starting cars at half-speed, and then letting the lever back. By this means a jerky progress, averaging nine miles an hour, might be attained.

"Looked at from a public point of view, added Mr Reed, it would be a very backward step if we were compelled to run our cars within nine miles an hour. It would mean an additional four minutes going up Queen Street, and at least a dozen extra cars would be necessary to cope with the traffic at the busy periods of the day in consequence of the delay.

"Senior-Sergeant Rutledge explained that the case had not been brought to harass the company, or to make it comply with the by-law, but because the car in question was run by the defendant at a speed not consistent with public safety.

"Mr J. J. Walklate, manager of the Tramways Company, stated that he had made a test in Queen Street with the two cars, and it was found impossible to go at a higher speed than 19 miles. If the by-law were strictly observed it would be impossible to run a service in Queen Street. The main thoroughfare was particularly free from accident, only two fatal accidents having occurred during the last 15 years.

"He did not consider it was dangerous to run a tramcar in Queen Street at 19 miles an hour. The highest speed of trams up Queen Street was about 18 miles an hour. Mr Reed said the company had submitted a time-table to the council, which had adopted it. This provided for a 45 minutes' service between Auckland and Onehunga, and if the nine-mile speed limit had to be observed in Queen Street the company simply could not maintain the service.

"Mr Frazer said a speed of nine miles seemed to him to be an unreasonable rate to which to limit an electric tram, although it might have been right enough for the old horse trams. He would not like to say definitely that the by-law was invalid until he had inquired into the legal position, and he would reserve his decision." [102]

In the meantime, while 1917 was to be another year of increased patronage, and therefore record revenue, it was also to be a particularly expensive year for the Auckland Electric Tramways Company, as outlined by the company's chairman, Mr C. G. Tegetmeier, during his address to the 20th ordinary general meeting held in London on 20 November 1917:

"The main features of the year's operations, as disclosed in the accounts are the substantial increase in receipts and the almost equal increase in working expenses. Our traffic receipts amounted to £282,697, which is £7914 more than in the preceding year, and is the highest amount we have yet taken. It represents nearly £2 10s per head of the population per annum. There was a corresponding increase in the number of passengers carried, which reached a total of 43,351,000, or nearly a million more than in the preceding year.

"At our meeting last year, when dealing with the figures we then had before us, I referred to the growth of our traffic receipts in spite of the adverse conditions arising out of the war, which might have been expected to cause a diminution in the number of passengers and consequently in the traffic receipts, instead of the increase of £7000 which we were then able to show.

"These adverse conditions have not varied much during the past year, and it is a cause for congratulation that, while we are a long way from showing the expansion we had been accustomed to in pre-war years, yet the increase of £15,000 in our traffic receipts during the past two years has been sufficient to make up for the unavoidable increase in expenses which we have had to meet.

"The figures I have quoted indicate the extent to which the riding habit has developed in Auckland, where it is much in excess of what we are accustomed to in this country. There are, I think, very few towns in this country where the tramways can show over two hundred rides per head of the population per annum, and in the majority of cases the number is very considerably less.

"In Auckland the number for last year is nearly 400. The development of the tramways is, no doubt, one explanation of the development of tramway riding, and in some measure we may regard it as a case of supply creating demand, for we see that our tramway system in Auckland, nearly all of which is double track, provides one route mile of tramway for about each 4000 of the population. Another explanation is to be found in the greater spending capacity of the community consequent upon the higher level of wages which prevails there.

"The time will come and we hope soon — when we shall once more enjoy, the blessings of peace. The many men who have left Auckland to share in the defence of the Empire and of liberty will return to industrial activity, and we may, I think, anticipate with confidence that the development of traffic which we have experienced during the war period will make still greater progress when we have returned to peace conditions. In the meantime…Our business during the past year has been carried on under considerable difficulties, particularly with regard to the supply of materials and the shortage of suitable labour. These difficulties...have been intensified by the abnormally wet weather which was experienced in Auckland for most of the year.

"During the year 34 of our employees left for military service, making a total of 121 since the beginning of the war. Their places were necessarily filled by inexperienced and untrained men, with the result that the volume of work performed fell off and its cost increased. The strike of coalminers in New Zealand, which took place in April Inst. affected our supplies of fuel to such an extent that it was found necessary to curtail our services, but in spite of this the total car mileage run throughout the year shows a slight increase over the preceding year.

"The revenue account shows that the main increase in our expenses for the year was in the item 'power and running expenses' which amounted to £117,083, or £5835 more than in the preceding year. The increased cost is nearly all due to the higher scale of pay to our men, which I referred to at our last meeting, and which was still further increased in April last. Administration and general expenses are £496 more than in the preceding year, and amounted to £27,811. The increase is more than accounted for by the increase in the item 'New Zealand income and land taxes' which amounted to £15,233, or £1249 more than we paid in the preceding year, and £10,290 more than we paid in the year 1915.

"Under New Zealand laws, income tax is levied on the taxable income of companies and not on the individual shareholders in the companies. As a consequence, the whole of the profits of the company are subject to income tax on the highest scale, although it is no doubt the case that a very large number of the 855 ordinary shareholders we have in New Zealand would have to pay a much lower rate on their individual incomes, of which the profits distributed by the company form part.

"It is no doubt an easy thing for those who are affected by taxation to criticise its incidence, but as a company serving a public need, and with a statutory limit upon the price we can demand from the public for our services, we may, I think, consider with some reason that the New Zealand system presses upon our shareholders somewhat unfairly. It is certainly an anomaly that a similar enterprise in New Zealand, if carried on by a municipality, is entirely exempt from taxation." [103]

That was the second year in a row that the Auckland Electric Tramways Company had referred to the cost of doing business in far off Auckland – particularly the unfairness of the high taxation to which the company was subject despite its provision of a necessary public service. There was also mention of the higher employment, supply of maintenance materials and the wet weather. Throughout 1918, the company also remained under a great deal of pressure to extend and improve its services, as reported by The New Zealand Herald on 20 June 1918:

"The complaints concerning the suburban tramway services which were discussed at special meeting of representatives of the Mount Roskill and One-tree Hill Road boards some weeks ago were referred to at the meeting of the One-tree Hill Road Board last night, when a letter from Mr J. J. Walklate, manager of the Auckland Electric Tramways Company, in reply to representations was read.

"The letter stated that the tramway services had recently been carefully examined and improved, particularly at the rush hour at five o'clock, and the writer trusted that the additional cars which had been put in would have the effect of removing the cause of the complaints referred to. The board decided that, in view of the fact that the services to the outlying suburbs have not been at all adequately improved, the matter should not be allowed to rest, and the chairman was authorised to endeavour to arrange a meeting of the Mayors of Newmarket, Mount Eden and Onehunga and the chairman of the Mount Roskill Road Board, for the purpose of approaching the City Council with a request that a united effort be made to bring the tramway service up to the required standard." [104]

In the meantime, by July 1918, the five o'clock rush continued to test the tramways service:

"An additional car to meet the demands of the five o'clock rush has been provided by the Auckland Electric Tramways Company. This car will run a trip to Symonds Street section, and return in time to run another trip to the Royal Oak at 5.25 p.m. The Mayor, Mr J. H. Hanson, stated yesterday that in a further communication received by him from the general manager of the company...the latter had...since arranged for another car to run at about five o'clock, making a total of 111.

"The Mayor said that the council had the matter under consideration, and had the assurance of the general manager of the company that everything that could reasonably be required would be undertaken by the company. The council would, as far as lay in its power, and in a reasonable way, see that public facilities in the matter of tramway traffic would be adequately met." [105]

While more cars could be provided to ease the congestion, it was obvious by the end of 1918 that the city was rapidly outgrowing its main transport system. Nevertheless, there were to be no extensions of the tramway lines in the foreseeable future, as reported by The New Zealand Herald on 9 January 1919:

"No extensions of the tramway service are at present contemplated by the Auckland Electric Tramways Company. When questioned upon the subject yesterday, the general manager, of the company, Mr J. J. Walklate, said that no applications for extensions had been received from local bodies, while, in any case, should extensions be desired, it was exceedingly doubtful as to whether the necessary material would be available for many months to come." [106]

A lack of material following the war meant that, despite undertakings, the duplication of a line to the more immediate suburbs had also to be deferred, as discussed at a City Council meeting on 20 February 1919:

"In reply to a question as to when the duplication of the Grey Lynn tramway line would be undertaken, the company stated there was no immediate prospect of the work being done. The reason given was the inability to procure sufficient rails for maintenance of existing tracks, in consequence of which the company could not consider the duplication of single lines. The Public Services Committee recommended that the council remind the company of its promise to undertake the duplication of this line as its first work, after the war and ask that the work be put in hand as soon as possible." [107]

However, by mid-February 1919, the public had more to delay their travel than just an apparent shortage of cars on single-track lines when the employees of the Auckland Electric Tramways Company went on a go-slow in support of their case for improved wages and conditions. This action obviously resulted in chaos:

"The dispute between the tramwaymen and the Auckland Electric Tramways Company was brought home to the travelling public yesterday in an unpleasant manner. A decision on the part of the men to 'ease-up' resulted in a much slower service than the customary one being run. During the rush hours from 5 p.m. onwards, the inconvenience to the public was accentuated by some of the men failing to bring out the extra cars usually employed at that time. The result was that there was only a partial service to cope with the large numbers of persons who wished to return to their homes.

"The trouble commenced with the first cars out, and continued until the last cars had reached the barns at night. Not only did the early trams from the suburbs crawl along the route to the city, but in many cases they passed street corners where would-be passengers were waiting, leaving them lamenting...Many women and girls suffered seriously from the impossibility of obtaining seats in the out-going cars.

"Several elderly ladies were reduced to real distress at the prospect of having to walk home after their vain struggle to catch a car. One who had been refused admission to an Onehunga car ran after it from Customs Street to the chief post office, even then failing to achieve her object.

"A girl of about 14, carrying a baby, tearfully approached a tramways official begging him to tell her how she could get home to Ponsonby. 'They won't let me on the cars,' she cried. The man appealed to could do no more than point to a tram just coming down Customs Street, and the child ran towards it with her burden." [108]

Of course, such a situation could not continue for long and a settlement between the city, the tramways company and its employees was reached after only three days. However, it was not a settlement set to please everyone, as anticipated by The New Zealand Herald:

"The intimation of a settlement of the tramways dispute will be received with great satisfaction. The agreement reached with the Mayor yesterday involves immediate consideration by the City Council of some increase in tramway fares, but this is a matter which would probably have had to be faced under any method of granting higher pay to the tramway men.

"All that need be said on that point now is that it would have been better for all concerned had the city's relations to the Tramways Company been considered calmly and apart from any temporary dislocation of the public service. Any open consideration of the men's claims for higher wages at the present time would have opened up the question of fares, and it is regrettable that the dispute was not so conducted as to give the City Council, and the suburban bodies if necessary, the opportunity of deliberately reviewing their respective positions under the deeds of delegation.

"The go slow policy adopted on Friday made that impossible, and in the circumstances as they then presented themselves Mr Gunson is deserving of the thanks of the whole city for his prompt, vigorous, and successful action. Until full information is available it should be assumed that the Mayor has safeguarded the city's interests and that such fares as he has undertaken to recommend the council to approve will not be a gift to the Tramways Company but a concession to enable it to pay a sufficient wage to its employees without loss to its shareholders. The company's case for the right to increase fares and the extent to which the wages concession to the men justifies an alteration will no doubt be fully discussed in the City Council and will then be open to public criticism. Meantime it is good news that the go slow tactics are being abandoned from to-day." [109]

As anticipated, the proposed fare rise to pay for the increased wages bill certainly attracted criticism from the public. Should commuters pay some of the Tramways Company's costs in order that the company might retain its profit margin? A group formed to protect society thought not:

"The fact that an increase in tramway fares is involved in the tentative agreement between the company and the union was discussed by the Council of the People's Protection Society last evening. Opinions were expressed that the public should not be taxed to pay extra wages to the men and that the company, whatever was the extra cost of wages, should stand by its original agreement. It was felt that great care should be taken to safeguard the interests of the public, and that any concession made to the company should not exceed the amount required to cover any increase in wages." [110]

By April 1919, the Auckland Electric Tramways Company still had 12 years before its option to run the tramways by way of its deed of delegation with the City Council expired. However, by the end of the war, it had become obvious to the Tramways Company that doing business in faraway New Zealand was not going to get any easier and its misgivings presented the Council with the opportunity to take over the transport system.

Indeed, the Council was given the option to buy the tramways business with that option expiring on 30 June 1919. But the Council was not its own man where such public services were concerned. It needed the co-operation and ultimate consent of the City's local bodies before a final decision could be made and that was never to be a foregone conclusion. Not when each of those bodies, including various roads boards, had their own agendas and remunerative interests to protect:

"A special meeting of the Mount Eden Borough Council was held last evening to consider a letter from the General Manager of the Auckland Electric Tramways Company (Mr Walklate) asking for the formal consent of the Council to the sale of the tramways to the City Council.

"The Mayor (Mr C. Hudson) presided over a good attendance of members. Mr Hudson said he had attended the meeting called by the Mayor of Auckland (Mr J. H. Gunson) in connection with the proposal, and the position was fully explained. He had submitted it to the Borough Solicitor, and a reply was received, stating that the Mount Eden Borough Council's consent would in no way affect its rights under the deeds of delegation. The Council would be able to exercise the same rating powers on the City Council as at present on the company. The conditions of purchase, however he said, should be that the two bodies enter into a covenant by which the City Council promises to adhere to the conditions of the deed of delegation.

"He proposed a resolution as follows, which was carried unanimously:

"That this Council consents to the transfer of the rights, privileges, and responsibilities held by the Auckland Electric Tramway Company, under the deeds of delegation from this Council, provided always that the City Council will enter into a covenant or agreement that they will observe, fulfil and perform all the covenants, agreements and obligations on the part of the company, contained in the deeds of delegation granted by this Council in respect to the tramways of this district, and also subject to the conditions that the rating liability of the Tramway Company be taken over by the Auckland City Council so that this Council shall be able to exercise the same rating powers on the Auckland City as they now do on the company." [111]

The One Tree Hill Road Board also viewed the purchase of the tramway as the way forward:

"Brief reference to the proposal of the City Council to purchase the tramway service was made at last evening's meeting of the One-Tree Hill Road Board. In discussion, the opinion was expressed that there was no doubt that the City Council would get better value in regard to plant now than in 12 years' time…it was stated that the project would be in the interests of the Greater Auckland scheme. Discussing the matter later, the chairman of the board, Mr H. Dobbie, said the feeling of the ratepayers of the district was favourable to the proposed purchase, seeing that it contained possibilities for the extension of the tramways." [112]

In the meantime there was also agreement as to the sale from London:

"The debenture holders of the Auckland Electric Tramways Company have passed a resolution assenting to the sale to the Auckland City Council." [113]

However, the option to buy was not undertaken without some inquiry and debate, as reported by the Auckland Star on 24 May 1919:

"The City Council yesterday took the definite step, which under the circumstances had become inevitable, of deciding to purchase the Auckland Tramway Company's property, subject to the approval of the ratepayers.

"Before coming to this decision, the Council asked Mr William Ferguson, of Wellington, an engineer whose name and work are known throughout the Dominion, to report whether the Council would be justified in purchasing at the price and on the terms set out in the option. It was necessary, before the Council should finally decide to purchase, that it should have an expert opinion on the condition of the tramway system as a working concern." [114]

Among many important positions held by William Ferguson (1852-1935), he had been a member of the Institute of Local Government Engineers of New Zealand, a founding member of the New Zealand

Society of Civil Engineers and Chairman of the National Efficiency Board.

"Although he received no public honours, he had been responsible for the design of many important public engineering works in Wellington, and his ability had been recognised in requests for advice from throughout the country." [115]

In his 'Option of Purchase and Valuation' report provided to the Council in May 1919, William Ferguson warned:

"The weakest part of the undertaking is the power stations are of old design," but his report then went on to assure the Council, "hydro-electric power would be available within a very few years."

Ferguson's report then continued in a positive tone as he described the existing track of some 27.13 miles as being in excellent condition, the overhead system in good order, rolling stock as satisfactory, buildings as suitable, and the repair shops as quite modern. [116]

After commenting on William Ferguson's report, the Auckland Star article went on to raise some questions as to the management of the tramways once the City Council had assumed control:

"Mr Ferguson begins by saying that the earnings of the undertaking in the past have been ample to provide for the interest on the debentures which will be issued if the Council takes it over, and goes on to consider the value of the assets. It is his opinion, after a careful inspection, that the system has been well maintained and that its condition quite warrants the Council in paying £1,180,000 for it, which will be approximately the total amount of the purchase money.

"It now remains for the ratepayers of the city to sanction the issue of debentures for the purchase of the system. They are not likely to refuse. The advantages of public ownership of such a public utility are plain to everybody, and Mr Ferguson's report is an assurance that good value will be given for the debentures issued. The question, however, is complicated by the fact that the city is taking over a system of transportation that benefits outside districts as well as the city, and will extend to other districts as time goes on. We have no information yet as to the exact manner in which the tramways are to be controlled, except that the present manager is to be retained for five years, a decision which will be approved of by the citizens.

"We presume that the City Council, being responsible for the purchase money, means to control the system, but we are not sure whether this would be the best permanent method to adopt, seeing that there are extensive and widening interests in the trams outside the city. The alternative to City Council control would be the establishment of a

Tramway Board on the lines of the elective body which manages the Christchurch system. Attention should be given to this question as soon as possible." [117]

Indeed, the ratepayers, or at least a comparatively few of them, did sanction the City Council's purchase of the tramways by way of a poll undertaken on 11 June 1919, as reported by The New Zealand Herald the following day:

"The proposal that the Auckland City Council should purchase the tramways was carried at yesterday's poll of the ratepayers by a majority of 1672 votes. A striking lack of interest was shown in the polls, only about 20 per cent of the 14,000 ratepayers entitled to vote exercising the franchise.

"The result of the poll is to give sanction to the City Council's proposal to raise a debenture loan of £1,250,000. All that is now required to enable the transaction to be completed between the council and the Auckland Electric Tramways Company is the consent of the suburban local bodies." [118]

In the same edition, The New Zealand Herald commented on both the poor turnout and the co-operation of the various local bodies necessary to make a success of the tramways:

"A reliable indication of public opinion on the question of municipalisation of the tramways is no doubt conveyed by the result of yesterday's poll, though it is a matter for regret that so small a proportion of the ratepayers cast their votes. In view of the magnitude of the issue, and of the judgment and care with which the negotiations have been conducted, the City Council was entitled to the personal assistance of every ratepayer who approved its policy.

"As it was, nearly 80 per cent of the electors were content with the presumption that those with a keener appreciation of their civic responsibilities would be sufficiently numerous to carry the proposal against whatever opposition might appear. In spite of this indifference, the result of the poll was an endorsement of the council's policy by a majority of nearly four votes to one, and doubtless a fuller poll would have given an even more positive decision.

"No very serious obstacle now remains to prevent the transfer of the tramway services to municipal control. The consent of one or two of the suburban authorities has still to be obtained, but the Mayor of Auckland was apparently successful at Tuesday's conference in persuading them that the interests of their districts would be as fully safeguarded by the City Council as by the Tramway Company, and that any claims for further concessions would prejudice the interests of the whole community." [119]

However, while it all looked good for a successful municipal acquisition of the Auckland tramways service, the problem of chronic congestion remained. This was graphically described by a commuter, 'Decent Service', in his Letter to the Herald, also published on 12 June 1919:

"Sir, — For several Saturdays I have gone out to Kingsland and returned to Page's corner at about five o'clock. Now that the football season is well on its way I notice that there are crowds of footballers waiting at the above stop by five o'clock, and it is an impossibility to get a train there.

"Mothers with children could not jostle them in with this crowd of men. Two weeks ago an elderly lady was helped by a very kind stranger, who made three attempts to get her on a car. He asked the young men to give the old lady a. chance, but this was of no avail, as their one object seemed to be to board the tram. One would have thought they were trying to save their lives the way they rushed at the car. Last Saturday was a special match, and there must have been three carloads at five o'clock, but of course no cars at the right time and place. I made up my mind to get on a down car and go to Mount Albert terminus. This I did. There were 25 others in our car. Is this state of things to be tolerated for ever?

"When coming back we were full up and people were standing long before we got to Page's corner. The Tramway Company must have lost a lot of fares, as hundreds walked. Why not have extra cars running to Kingsland and back on Saturdays. I do trust that those who are inconvenienced – and there must be hundreds — will worry till this is rectified. Decent Service." [120]

But, apart from a time-table review and the laying on of more cars at peak times, there was little more that could be expected from the new tramways owners, at least in the short term. That was clearly explained by Auckland's Mayor, J H Gunson, as he and his Council dealt with the administrative hurdles of assuming control of such a complex transport service:

"Mr W. J. Holdsworth (Councillor) said he had interviewed the general manager of the (Tramways) company, Mr J. J. Walklate, that day. He was glad to announce that the time-table was now under review and that a number of extra cars were to be provided which would do much to alleviate the congestion in the rush hours.

"Mr Gunson said some of the local bodies seemed to have thought that as soon as the council owned the tramways they were going to be revolutionised – that the council would double the number of cars, and remove all causes for complaints. Of course, it stood to reason that no radical changes in the services could be made immediately, except for the one Mr Holdsworth had mentioned. The council could simply take over the tramways as a going concern, maintain the services, and effect reforms gradually. Certainly seven or ten extra cars were to be put on at once, and he was quite sure the Public Services Committee would bend its best energies to improving the services." [121]

But there wasn't just the need for more cars. There were also lines to be extended and double-tracked – work and associated costs that had now become the responsibility of the City Council and which would, for many years, cause much disharmony between it and the boroughs through which the tramway ran. In his report to the City Council of 26 June 1919, the Mayor, Mr Gunson, described some of the work that would be continued following the Council's acquisition of the tramways:

"(a) Anzac Avenue extension from Beach Road to Lower Symonds Street. This is in accordance with the Council's policy, and represents requests recently submitted. (b) Grey Lynn duplication. The Council has long pressed for this work, (c) Relaying rails, Manukau Road, Epsom. This is required in connection with paving works already authorised, and the company had this under negotiation, (d) Duplication Dominion Road. This is a work postponed by the company, which they have recently had under consideration and is much needed, being similar to Grey Lynn." [122]

On 1 July 1919, the Auckland City Council finally took over the city's tramway system, as reported by The New Zealand Herald on 30 June 1919:

"The working of the Auckland tramways by the Electric Tramways Company will cease after to-day. The service will be taken over by the City Council tomorrow, July 1, in accordance with the terms recently agreed upon. The present general manager, Mr J. J. Walklate, will continue to act in a similar capacity on behalf of the council. At the meeting of the council on Thursday last it was intimated that a number of extra cars would be run during rush hours, after the change in control, and it is possible that some of these will be in commission to-morrow.

"The electric tramways service was commenced by the company on November 24 1902. The purchase price agreed upon between the council and the company is £1,143,750, subject to certain small adjustments. The ratepayers have authorised the raising of a debenture loan of £1,250,000, to meet the cost of acquiring the service." [123]

However, while all control of Auckland's tramways was assumed by the City Council on 1 July 1919, payment for its acquisition had still to be financed through the issuance of debenture stock. By January 1920, that payment had still to be finalised:

"A statement covering the municipal purchase of the tramways from the Auckland Electric Tramways Company was placed before the City Council last evening by the Mayor, Mr J. H. Gunson. This showed that the amount of 'purchase money' had been ascertained to be £1,229,462 19s 7d. This sum represented the amount due from the council to the company in accordance with the agreement for sale and purchase.

"It was recommended that the council authorise the issue of the debentures under the tramway loan for the sum of £1,250,000 of which sum debentures be paid to the company to the value of £1,229,462 19s 7d subject to all legal matters involved in the transaction being referred to the city solicitor.

"The chairman of the Public Services Committee, Mr W. J. Holdsworth, moved that the issue of debentures, and the payment to the company of the amount due, be authorised. He said this was the natural sequence to the taking over of the tramways business by the council. He thought the Mayor should feel gratified at the fact that the figures worked out as they did, seeing that his estimate had been so accurate. He believed the citizens would not regret the step the council took in acquiring the concern, and they had a very fine asset in the tramways, which the council would be able to control in their interests.

"Mr P. M. MacKay, in seconding the motion, said he thought the citizens and the council ought to be proud of the fact that they had a man in the civic chair who had put through the largest transaction ever completed in the Dominion. There was no doubt the city had a very good asset in the tramways and that would be proved as time went on. He paid a tribute to the business acumen of the Mayor." [124]

Finally, by March 1920, the financial transaction was nearly complete with the physically demanding issuance of the debenture bonds:

"The purchase of the Auckland electric tramways system by the City Council has, in the concluding stages of the transaction, entailed an amount of physical strain and monotonous work on the part of the Mayor, Mr J. H. Gunson, and the city treasurer, Mr J. S. Brigham, that few people will have either contemplated or imagined. The payment for the undertaking and plant, etc., is being made in debenture bonds to which the written signatures of both the gentlemen named had to be attached.

"To liquidate the purchase and provide an extra sum for tramway extensions, costs, etc., debentures to the total value of £1,250,000 have been prepared, in bonds of £100 each. The Auckland Electric Tramways Company's share of the sum referred to is £1,227,201. Thus, in order to make the bonds negotiable, Messrs Gunson and Brigham were faced with the irksome and somewhat stupendous task of signing their names 12,500 times, that being the number of securities for £100 each which had to be got ready for issue to the company and to the public.

"Six mornings were devoted to the work by the two official signatories, and on each occasion two or three hours were spent in the process. The Mayor proved to be the speedier writer of the two, accomplishing the uninteresting undertaking at an average of about 800 signatures an hour, though at times he exceeded that rate.

"He and the treasurer each had an assistant occupied in blotting their names as they wrote them, while two other assistants were employed in numbering the bonds and preparing them for record purposes. A total of 9cwt of paper was used in the printing of the debentures. The whole of them were completed this week, and a final settlement with the company will be made in the course of a day or two. In this historic purchase the City Council secured 160 tramcars, 27,130 route miles of track, powerhouse and plant, car barns, etc., all of which were taken over as a going concern." [125]

By December 1923, The New Zealand Herald was of the opinion that the municipal takeover of the city's tramways had been a very good move for all concerned:

"The increased stir of holiday traffic in and about Auckland this season reveals the qualities and defects of the attractive city's different systems of transport. Many of the qualities are now most prominent in the improved tramways service, but the improvement, rather than making for complacency, emphasises the necessity for further development and an accelerated extension of service. It is to be noted at the outset that business enterprise has promoted the improvement and development of the city's electric tramways system. Local government has realised that an improved service encourages traffic, and increases revenue and profit. Last year, for example, a record revenue of over £530,000 was obtained. It is a pity that general government, in the matter of railway facilities, should be content to wait always on more propitious times.

"Auckland administrators are spending about half a million sterling on additional extension, and duplication of the tramway system. And even this progressive expenditure must be regarded as an instalment only of the total capital required for future expansion. The growth of Greater Auckland is still ahead of the service, which in recent years has not been laggard in development.

"Improvement and extension of the service has practically been continuous since the date of purchase. Tracks have been duplicated on several routes; some extensions have been completed in record time; renewal of tracks and plant has been very extensive; many new cars have been put into commission; and the whole service has been reorganised and brought up to a high standard of efficiency. Almost a quarter of a million sterling has been spent or is being expended on development, while the latest loan authorities amounting approximately to £280,000, will increase the total capital expenditure to £1,725,000.

"Financially, results have justified municipal enterprise. Public appreciation of the notable improvements is still rather less than perfect; it is depreciated, as a rule, during the rush, hours, the citizens overlooking the fact that the jostling and crowding on such occasions should be accepted as the growing pains of a city in the making. Under progressive and efficient control, Auckland's tramway system is now easily the largest municipal business concern in the Dominion. It far exceeds in traffic and revenue any one of the services in the other centres. It employs nearly 1200 workers; has 180 cars in commission; and transports over 30 miles of double track, 52,000,000 passengers a year.

"Apart from the extensive tramways developmental works recently completed and those in hand, representing an expenditure of over £250,000, the city ratepayers on November 28 last sanctioned the raising of an additional £280,000 (part of loan authorities aggregating £710,000) for further extensions and improvement of the tramway system. This new programme of work will cover a period of four years by which time, judging from the present rate of Greater Auckland's expansion, there will be clamant need for more and still more extension of the electric tramway service.

"To realise the prospect of future needs it is only necessary to make a tour of Greater Auckland and note the extent of residential settlement in areas which must eventually be brought within the scope of electric tram service. Hundreds of houses are being built in anticipation of such transport, while thousands of sections are on the market with the same prospect mentioned as a factor of future profit.

"Beyond each of the present terminal points of the tramways system land is being subdivided for a keen demand for residential plots. The talk everywhere is 'the cars are coming or are sure to come in the near future'. Meanwhile, plans have been projected and financial provision authorised for a very substantial programme of important extensions and general development. In addition to extensions provision has been made for the purchase of 20 new cars, at a cost of £70,000, and extensive additions to the Roskill workshops for maintenance and overhaul, and for the building of new cars, aggregating £32,000." [126]

Before the 1920s, competition between horse-drawn conveyances and the trams had been quickly settled by the public's overwhelming preference for the latter. However, as the number of motor vehicles traversing Auckland's improving road surfaces increased, motor buses soon became the alternative service, augmenting and extending the trams.

"Indeed, in the early years, most motor services, like the horse-drawn services which had preceded them, tended to be ancillary to the rail network. Service cars (the first motorised buses and taxis) carried passengers to and from railway stations, and to and from areas where rail had never penetrated. The first motor bus services were ancillary to the tramways." [127]

As the registration of Auckland motor vehicles increased from less than 1000 in 1913 to some 12,000 by 1923, their increased presence began to influence more than just the railed conveyances. The habits of wayward pedestrians crossing busier roads had also to be regulated:

"The enforcement of the new regulations for the control of pedestrian traffic was the cause of considerable activity in the city yesterday, particularly at the intersection of Queen and Customs Streets. Four traffic inspectors were stationed there, one at each corner, and they were kept very busy directing people into the passages marked by broad white lines for crossing the street.

"At times there was quite a crowd of onlookers watching the efforts of unsuspecting pedestrians to cross at other than the stipulated places, only to be checked by a vigilant inspector and guided into the right path. The arrangement worked well, but some interference was caused through vehicles, which were waiting for instructions from the policeman on points duty, pulling up between the white lines, instead of halting before reaching them." [128]

There were also the hazards posed by the operating systems of these motor vehicles, the effects of which, it was suggested, could be offset with the implementation of more modern building materials:

"The risk of fire occurring on the ferry wharf at Devonport as the result of oil dripping from motor cars awaiting the vehicular ferry steamer was impressed upon the Auckland Harbour Board yesterday in a report from the traffic manager. It was stated that the timbers of the wharf were very dry and were being rendered highly inflammable by a gradual soaking in oil.

"The suggestion was made that the Devonport Borough Council should be asked to set aside a portion of the street outside the wharf gates for the accommodation of a queue of motors. The Hon. E. W. Alison and Mr J. Henderson seized the opportunity to advocate the early erection of a new concrete wharf at Devonport. The board referred the traffic manager's suggestion to the Works Committee." [129]

The greater presence of motor buses and other modes of transport along city streets also generated some serious concerns for the Auckland City Council which was committing so much to the upgrade of its tramways:

"The Auckland City Council has taken a very practical course in the matter of meeting competition from motor transport. It has decided to go into the business on its own account. Tenders have been invited for the supply of 10 motor-omnibuses, which next year (1924) are to serve as feeders of the tramway service.

"This new feature of municipal enterprise will be studied with very close interest, in view of the fact that several of the outer suburban municipalities have been informally discussing the question of introducing the trackless trolley system of transport. It may be assumed that if the City Council's experiment with motor-omnibuses, which are now a prominent feature in the Old World, be a commercial success, the trackless trolley system will not be favoured in Greater Auckland, though opinion for its introduction has considerable support in the North Shore boroughs.

"The relative merits of different systems of auxiliary tramway services were discussed recently at a meeting of city rate-payers on the eve of the latest poll on loan proposals. On that occasion the Mayor of Auckland, Mr J. H. Gunson, explained that, after giving careful consideration to a detailed report by the tramways manager, Mr A. E. Ford, it had been held that the motor-bus, due to its mobility compared with the trackless trolley, offered the most useful field for feeding the more popular electric tramway system and developing routes which, as yet, scarcely warranted the cost of tramway construction. The opinion of the council has now been given practical expression, and a start on the projected auxiliary transport service will be made next year with a fleet of ten single-deck motor-buses." [130]

The Auckland City Corporation Tramways Manager, Albert Edward Ford, later undertook a substantial tour of investigation to the United States, Canada, Great Britain, Europe, and Australia. Between June 1926 and January 1927, Albert Ford's paramount objective was to collect information about the interaction between trams and motor-omnibuses operating in those countries and the different systems of traffic control and regulation in place.

Long before Google and Wikipedia, such an overseas jaunt was the only practical way to discover, first-hand, what the rest of the world was doing and how successful their methods were. Some of the findings contained in Ford's 1927 report concluded that motor buses depreciated far faster than electric trams and that the operation of the former depended too much on the volatile cost and supply of petrol.

His findings were almost identical to those of the first member of the Auckland City Council's staff to be sent on an overseas tour of investigation, Walter Ernest Bush, the Council's Engineer from 1906 to 1929. Following his trip through the United States of America, Canada, and Great Britain, Bush provided the Council with a report dated 3 March 1920 in which he observed:

"Generally, it may be stated that to cope with the passenger traffic of large cities the tramway system is still needed, and for countries where petrol or other motor-spirit has to be imported, where electricity can be generated from coal or water-power, it would be foolish to depend altogether upon the motor-bus for transportation, apart from railways; but if it can be shown that motor-buses can give a regular and adequate service for less cost than a tramway system, the motor-bus will ultimately oust the tramway.

"That point for most cities has not yet been reached, but there are few cities where motor-buses cannot be used with great advantage to supplement and help develop electric tramways, and therefore the trams and buses should be under one control, and the City Council will be well advised to protect itself from competition which can only prove harmful in the long run to the best interests of the travelling public." [131]

Seven years later, Ford was more concerned about the duplication of tram and bus services on Auckland's main streets and suggested that a way of decreasing congestion and increasing tram speeds could be accomplished as in Sydney, where the parking of cars in main thoroughfares was prohibited.

However, he admitted, "Buses are here to stay but not as a replacer of trams but as an augmenter by developing or providing services in streets not served by trams and in districts so sparsely populated as not to warrant the high capital outlay for tramways...the corollary is that trams must remain." [132]

Ford backed this view with a quote from a W H Sawyer, then President of the American Railway Association, "...there is increasing evidence that the tramcar is economically the backbone of a properly co-ordinated transportation system, and that it should continue to handle the bulk transportation needs of the cities...my observations lead me to fully subscribe to such a conclusion," commented Ford. [133]

– Hardly a comment likely to impress another Ford – one by the name of Henry, who was then mass producing public transport's nemesis.

While such overseas jaunts as those made by Albert Ford were then considered to be a cost-effective way of obtaining a comprehensive picture on which could be based the best, long term decisions, the later alternative, much favoured by both local bodies and the Government, was to pay overseas consultants to visit New Zealand, assess its problems and provide a comprehensive report recommending how to proceed.

Unfortunately, just as, to some extent, it proved to be in the case of the advice provided by Bush and Ford, the millions of dollars spent on consultants were to be wasted on advice rarely accepted. Instead of decisions based on sound observation, the future of public transport was to be decided by politicians and others keen to perpetuate what an Auckland Star article of 26 December 1924 described as '...an illusion of progress':

"The telephone, the motor car, and wireless do more than annihilate distance; they destroy rest and reflection. They create, like the merry-go-round, an illusion of progress." [134]

But, to the detriment of the future of public transport, increasing numbers of motor cars and motor buses stimulated that illusion of progress to such an extent that a great deal of what, today, is referred to as 'spin' was necessary to promote the merits of the tram service.

For instance, an Auckland Star article, published 15 July 1924, continued to maintain that the tramways would remain the major public transportation mode of the future – but only if the road-user cost of providing the tram service was equal to the costs incurred by other conveyances:

"In many big cities of the world the motor bus is throwing out a determined challenge to the electric tramcar as the most popular and successful form of transport. In some instances the trams appear to be yielding temporarily to the fierce rivalry of their mobile competitors, in other cases they are holding their own, and again, in several cities, the tramcar has, after a strenuous tryout, resumed its old status as the most dependable and cheapest form of urban transport.

"Notwithstanding the grouch about rush-hour inadequacy which is heard all over the world from the tram traveller, when it becomes a matter of quick and steady transport at cheap rates of large masses of passengers at congested periods of the day, the electric carriage on rails is an ever constant standard of reliability. But the public loves novelty, even in travelling, and for a while is willing to pay for it.

"Here in Auckland the tramcar appears in no immediate danger of being supplanted, but the construction of long stretches of concrete roading has presented opportunities which the motor bus is now eagerly seizing. It is a case of getting in while the going is good, for it is obvious that the civic authorities, after spending hundreds of thousands on a tramway system, and more hundreds of thousands on concrete highway are hardly likely to sit quietly and allow motor buses to run the community owned tramcars out of profit on roads built and maintained by public money.

"At last Thursday night's meeting of the City Council the Mayor presented a memorandum on the subject of the control of and fees for the license of motor buses, with a proposal for seeking legislation granting local authorities wider powers in this matter than they now possess.

"Following this the memorandum is being sent to all the district local authorities, including the county councils, with a covering letter asking if they will be represented at a conference if the City Council calls one in Auckland as soon as the Motor Vehicles Bill is available.

"When spoken to on the subject to-day, the Mayor (Sir James Gunson) declared that the Council faced the future with equanimity, and that it was warranted in so doing on two grounds. Firstly, he said, the tramway service is efficient and over the section of the city in which it operates offers a means of public transport second to none. It is regular, fast, and efficient, and cannot be usefully displaced by any competition that may arise from the motor buses.

"There is no doubt whatever, added Sir James, that in distant portions and in areas not served by the trams the motor bus has come to stay, and will fulfil a useful function in meeting public needs. The Council recognises this, and it is now just a question how far it will engage in the motor bus form of transport. It has ten motor buses on order, and may possibly order a very large number more. The one question that is concerning the Council, and which must shortly be considered, is that of the control and license fees for buses.

"Those who know nothing at all about the question are still aware that under the principle created by the concession in 1899 and up to 1901 by the City Council to the British Electric Tramways (sic - Traction) Company the trams pay what is equivalent under normal conditions, for the upkeep and maintenance of the centre of the road, an annual charge of £250 per annum per tramcar.

"During recent years, and, in fact, continuously since 1919, the Council has spent a sum approaching £500 per tramcar per annum on this work. But that has been abnormal. The normal figure for maintenance of the road is about £250 per car. This is the sum which is also represented by the terms under which the city deals with the other boroughs, such as Mount Eden and Mount Albert.

"It is therefore one of general principle and policy, and not one alone affecting the city. It follows that either this obligation must be waived, or else motor transport in respect to other portions of the road, namely the concrete surface laid by the city, must pay its share for the use of that concrete in the shape of fees relative to what are paid by the tramcars. It is desired on behalf of the Council to make this position emphatically clear, and the future policy for the carrying out of which legislation may be sought, in order that those interested in private buses, and who think of operating more, may understand that they are not going to be allowed the use of the road promiscuously without adequate control and substantial fees.

"If all forms of transport were on the same footing, as in common justice they should be, then the trams as at present operating in Auckland will hold their own against all competitors and developments. In stating this policy it should be made clear, said the Mayor, that no reference is made to, and there is not involved the question of, the capital cost and maintenance of the tram rails and overhead gear. This is all part of the tramway system.

"What is referred to is the road surface obligations for the full width of the double track and for fifteen inches on either side of it, which falls upon the tramway concern, and which portion is also used by all other traffic without restriction. In fact until recently, when concrete roads were constructed, vehicles used the tram track more than any other portion of the road. This created an inequitable obligation on the tramway undertaking, the finances of which are separate and distinct from all the other accounts of the corporation. The system has got to pay on its own merits, and it must not therefore be involved unduly in charges and obligations of an excessive character, from which other forms of transport are relatively exempt

"This is obviously so unjust and inequitable, especially with the enormous development of motor traffic that, and in this one may speak for all the tramways in the Dominion, the existing anomalies must, in common equity, shortly be corrected. Another phase of the question of motor passenger transport was quite soundly raised at the council meeting last Thursday, and that was that it is an impracticable proposition for 200 motor buses to operate in the city areas.

"Streets such as Queen Street will not carry the traffic, as there is no room for them, unrestricted and uncontrolled as they are. This must be obvious to anybody. On the other hand, the council will shortly have 200 tramcars, all under effective control and rapidly moving, while, at the same time creating no congestion." [135]

The 'Motor Vehicles Bill' referred to in the Star article was the Motor-Vehicles Act 1924 which came into force on 1 January 1925 "...to provide for the Registration, Licensing, and Regulation of the use of Motor-vehicles" including "...every motor-coach or motor-omnibus." [136]

But as well as registration and licensing costs, the owners and drivers of private and goods-delivery motor vehicles, coaches and omnibuses were being charged top dollar to traverse the land, albeit to ostensibly fund the roads on which that traverse was taking place.

Motor-bus operators also faced hurdles of another sort – particularly as, from about 1922, the buses increasingly attracted commuters away from the less convenient, less comfortable, and slower trams. This preference for bus transport is best illustrated by the Police Court proceedings of 23 September 1925. This newspaper report also highlights an official partiality toward the established trams as the prime people-mover of the day:

"Several bus drivers were charged in the Police Court yesterday with allowing their buses to be overcrowded. The first case taken was against Henry Johnstone, a driver for the Royal Motor-bus Company. A traffic inspector gave evidence that he boarded defendant's bus in Symonds Street. There were nine passengers standing inside. This was four more than were allowed by the City Council by-laws.

"Cross-examined by Mr Meredith, who appeared for the defence, witness said the bus in question was the only one of the buses owned by the Royal Company that was overcrowded on this occasion. The company was apparently trying to observe the by-law.

"Mr Meredith: Do not the public themselves give a little difficulty Do they like being told not to get on? —No, they do not like being told not to get on. Mr Meredith: Have you not seen trams loaded back and front, and filled up chock-a-block?

"Witness: For all I know they may be employees of the department. Have you heard of any prosecutions lately for overcrowding of trams ?—I have heard suggestions of prosecution.

"Mr Meredith said it was recognised that overcrowding had to be stopped as far as possible. This company had more buses than any other and the worst that could be said against it was that on this evening there were four passengers too many in one bus. The driver was in a pretty hopeless position and the case should be dismissed as trivial. The fact that other persons who were not being prosecuted were committing the same offence in aggravated form could be regarded as an extenuating circumstance. The trams were at present notoriously guilty of packing the people on and stuffing them in, in every possible way. That was an infinitely more flagrant breach than the defendant was guilty of.

"The company was attempting to obey the by-law, but the fact that overcrowding was allowed on the trams made people attempt to crowd on the buses. After being warned off by the driver they sometimes climbed on as the bus moved off. Only a technical breach had been committed and in view of the fact that gross breaches were being committed by others it would be a hardship if defendant were convicted.

"Mr Cutten (the Magistrate) said no doubt the by-law was a very difficult one for the drivers to comply with, but there was a very good reason for it, and it should be obeyed. As these cases would act as a warning defendants would be convicted and ordered to pay costs." [137]

By 1925, it was obvious that tramway operators, such as the Auckland City Council, needed more than just by-laws to reduce the competitive edge of the motor buses. In order to promote their concerns and discuss solutions, the tramway operators organised a conference at Wellington – a forum by which they hoped to convince Parliament that some form of national legislation to regulate motor-omnibus traffic was required to deal with what The New Zealand Herald of 5 August 1925 described as an invasion:

"The motor-omnibus by invading city streets and competing for the patronage of the travelling public has created a problem in which most of New Zealand is interested. There has been a disposition in Auckland to contend that the City Council has shown special animus against competitors with its own tramway service every time it has done anything to control the activities of the motor-omnibus.

"The absurdity of this attitude is proved by the nature of a conference just held in Wellington, attended by representatives of all tramway authorities in New Zealand as well as by delegates from some towns which have no tramway services, but are interested nevertheless in the development of motor-omnibus transport. Much more was involved there than the anxieties of the Auckland City Council. The fact is that the motor-omnibus is not only a factor of increasing weight in the transport of passengers; it is a new and often disturbing element in city traffic wherever it has gone beyond the elementary stage of development.

"It has now been established beyond question that municipal authorities throughout New Zealand feel the need for some measure of control over the motor-omnibus. They have decided this in conference and placed their decision before the Prime Minister. The deputation which met Mr Coates brought to him concrete proposals for the licensing and control of motor-omnibus services.

"Mr Coates remarked at one stage that the core of the problem was to assure the most economical and efficient system of passenger transport. That sums up the whole situation exactly. In places where tramway systems have been long in operation, are owned by the community, and by unprofitable working would cast new burdens upon the citizens, their existence as fixed assets ought to be recognised.

"Some limitation of omnibus competition is not unreasonable in such circumstances. It is all very well to contend, as people have done, that motor transport is the method of the future, that tramways are obsolescent, and that, to put it bluntly, they should be scrapped if they cannot hold their own against unrestricted competition. That contention cannot be allowed quite so lightly as it is advanced, having regard to the amount of public money involved and to the fact that most of it is loan money.

"What should be determined in such cases is where the greatest good of the public lies then, provided that the right method of determination has been adopted, all parties should be made to accept the decision, even if the result was curtailment of the ambitions and plans of those who operate omnibus services. Taking Auckland as an example, the field of operation is a wide one. With some measure of control it might be divided among the competing services with advantage to both and to the public.

"Two things are quite apparent. There must be some sort of control, for experience both in New Zealand and elsewhere proves the necessity. Secondly the power should not be solely in the hands of the local authority, since in many instances it owns the tramway system and thus stands in an invidious position. Local body officials and officers of the Public Works Department are to confer, gathering and collating all the information available. Armed with the results, the Government will endeavour to meet the situation, thus helping local authorities to grapple with a problem which has become Dominion-wide in its incidence, giving rise to a Dominion-wide demand for its solution." [138]

By late 1925, the Public Works Department had drafted the proposed legislation to regulate motor-omnibus traffic but the Department's proposals had a long way to go before they could become law. They first had to face a good deal of opposition from the private bus proprietors, their employees, stakeholders (such as coach builders and the suppliers of petrol, spare parts, and tyres) and, of course, those passengers who had quickly become accustomed to the more convenient, comfortable, and speedier rides provided by motor power.

"A strong protest against the proposals for the regulation of motor-buses recently drafted by the Public Works Department, was made yesterday by a deputation representing the Auckland Omnibus Association, which waited upon the Chamber of Commerce. Mr (George) Grey Campbell (representing the private bus owners association) said the action of the Auckland Tramways Committee through its chairman, in making representations to the Prime Minister concerning the effect of buses on trams, was well known. This had been the direct reason for the proposals, and Mr Coates had promised to bring down regulations to cope with the situation.

"The association felt it had a right to put its view of the question regarding municipal and Governmental enterprise in transport competition before the Chamber of Commerce. Capital invested in buses in Auckland amounted to £250,000, over 200 buses being registered. It was a fair average to say that each bus cost £1000, although some were valued at £2000. There were 300 drivers employed, and if the regulations were enforced their effect would be widely felt. The fact that the regulations were being brought down by Order-in-Council was a matter for protest. The matter of transportation should receive the attention of Parliament as a whole.

"The inception of the bus services, Mr Campbell said, had seen a more efficient running of the trams, and fares were cheaper. If the City Council were suffering any loss, the public had gained. Because tramway buses had failed, and private buses had been successful, that was no reason why private enterprise should be blamed. Bus services had been directly responsible for opening up outer districts. Auckland buses carried about 40,000 people a day, or 14,000,000 a year. The council had not decided to use buses until private vehicles had worked roads which were out of the way of tram services.

"Referring to the effect the regulations would have if passed, Mr Campbell said the results would be more serious than at first supposed. Very wide powers were proposed to be vested in the licensing authority. It would be most unfair if the City Council was allowed to control routes and fares. It. was contended licensing authority should consist of representatives of all local bodies interested in transportation, and should be presided over by a magistrate. The clause would restrict trade, and would force the buses off the road.

"The handing to the City Council of almost all the power on the Appeal Board made that body entirely wrong in its constitution. All appeals should go to the Supreme Court. Another complaint was that the council buses were not covered by the regulations. Mr L. J. Keys referred to the large number of people who had built houses in the outer suburbs now that they were brought into touch with the city by the buses." [139]

Any restriction of trade, particularly that which favoured one form of transport over another and which operated to the detriment of its customers, was obviously of great concern to those who promoted the concepts of free and competitive enterprise.

"Opposition to the bus regulations, which were denounced as being tyrannous, unjust and un-British, was expressed at a public meeting addressed by Messrs A. Hall Skelton and E. Stevenson, secretary of the Anti-Bus Regulation League, in the Civic Square last evening. The attendance was not very large and the speakers were subjected to a good deal of interruption.

"The following resolution was declared carried: — This mass meeting of Auckland citizens denounces the motor-bus regulations as a piece of communistic tyranny unparalleled in British history. We further pledge our solid support to the motor-bus owners in their worthy efforts to combat the un-British and unjust attack which has been made upon them. This meeting also congratulates the Mount Eden, Mount Albert and Onehunga Borough Councils on their opposition to these unfair regulations." [140]

"The debate on the Address-in-Reply was resumed in the House of Representatives this afternoon by Mr G. W. Forbes, Leader of the National Party...Mr Forbes proceeded to criticise the motor bus regulations. He acknowledged the necessity for some regulation but if the regulations were designed merely to destroy competition with the tramways then he thought them unwise. Competition was the soul of trade and anything that aimed at the destruction of that principle was to be deprecated. He hoped the House would carefully analyse the regulations when they came up for discussion." [141]

The first step to that discussion occurred on 10 July 1926 when Parliament elected a Select Committee to consider the proposed motor-omnibus regulations and the petitions of some 85,828 persons and the evidence of thirty witnesses in connection with those petitions. As reported by the Auckland Star, the appointment of committee members was not without some controversy:

"There was something of a squabble when the Prime Minister moved the election of a committee of the House to consider the question of the bus regulations, Mr A. Harris (Waitemata) rising to say that the personnel of the committee was not one that might be expected to deal with the matter in the most strictly impartial way. These regulations were of vital importance to a very big section of the community, and the utmost impartiality should he shown by the Parliamentary Committee dealing with them.

"The committee consists of Messrs J. S. Dickson, P. Fraser, G. W. Forbes, H. E. Holland, E. J. Howard, E. P. Lee, C. E. Macmillan, M. J Savage, T. K. Sidey, H L. Tapley, Hon. K. S. Williams, and the Premier (Gordon Coates)". [142]

The Select Committee's first public hearing was held on 21 July 1926 and there was so much public and press interest that the meeting had to adjourn to a larger room after fifteen minutes:

"All parts of New Zealand were represented, including all the main Municipal authorities. Mr E. P. Lee, the chairman of the Committee, presided, and the following members were present: The Hon. K. S. Williams, Messrs E. H. Potter, M. J. Savage, P. Fraser, C. E. Macmillan, G. W. Forbes, J. Dickson, T. K. Sidey, E. J. Howard, H. L. Tapley, and H. Holland. The chairman apologised for the absence of the Prime Minister on account of indisposition.

"Mr P. Fraser said that there seemed to be a general recognition that the regulations were necessary, and he suggested that the evidence should be confined to the main points at issue. The chairman said that he did not intend to prevent free discussion of the whole matter, which was of great public interest.

"Mr William George McDonald presented the case on behalf of the Wellington motor-bus proprietors. The bus proprietors throughout New Zealand had a general objection to the Regulations...The Regulations came upon us as a bombshell, declared Mr McDonald.

"He thought that the time was ripe for Regulations controlling the whole system of transport in New Zealand. It was felt that the Regulations had been conceived with the sinister design of putting the bus people out of business. If the local authorities wanted to exercise a monopoly over the transport service of the cities or elsewhere, they should do so, but they had not stated that that was their desire.

"He, personally, was opposed to monopoly, as he thought it was not in the best interests of the community. There were three clauses in the Regulations, as originally published, that would constitute a municipal monopoly of transport. One was that relating to the licensing authority. Under the Regulations, the licensing authority would be quite within its rights in refusing a license unless the Council came to the conclusion that their own trams were not giving the desired service...the effect would be to put them out of business.

"Witness then dealt with the provision for the extra fare of 2d. If that had been put into effect it would have put him off the roads but as a matter of fact that provision never had been carried out. Since then the clause dealing with the 2d fare had been amended and now it was left to the licensing authority to say whether the extra fare should be imposed or not.

"They had to apply for a license each year, and they were faced with the prospect of having a different body of men to deal with every two years. To-day they had a licensing authority which did not impose the 2d extra fare, but tomorrow they might have to deal with a body which favoured the imposition of the extra fare.

"Mr McDonald complained of the unreasonableness of the Regulations regarding insurance. Although motor-bus proprietors did not object to provision being made for insurance, if it were reasonable, the Regulations meant that his company (the Wellington and Suburban Bus Company) would have to carry a cover of £250,000. At the conference a floating policy had been suggested by the proprietors, limiting the cover on any one bus to from £15,000 to £20,000.

"He thought that if the insurance question had been left to the proprietors they could have fixed it up satisfactorily. But don't think that the insurance clause is going to put us out of business, said Mr McDonald. You are going to load us with very heavy premiums, but we are going to carry on. Mr McDonald said that his petition was supported by fourteen or fifteen thousand people, and he would like the opportunity to call evidence expressing the views of the public." [143]

When the Select Committee hearings resumed the following day, it was time for the Auckland transport situation to be examined:

"The committee decided to deal with the petition lodged by the Auckland bus proprietors. Mr Grey Campbell, representing the Auckland bus proprietors, gave evidence in support of the Auckland petition.

"In Auckland there were 180 privately-owned buses engaged in the city and suburbs. They employed over 500 men, and the capital value of the buses and accessories was over £500,000. The bus position in Auckland had changed considerably in recent years. The two main companies in Auckland were the Royal Motor Company and the Mount Eden Company, each with a fleet of 30 buses. They objected to the licensing authority being interested in any way in the transport business, as it was against the principles of British law and justice.

"A virtually interested competitive party should not control bus competition. Moreover, it was a recognised principle that a minority should not rule. The licensing authority in Auckland could not possibly be an impartial body. As an alternative to the present licensing authority he suggested there should be an independent authority representative of all interests concerned, such as borough councils, town, boards and county councils. Another alternative was the election of the licensing authority by popular vote in the same manner as a power board was elected.

"They objected to the penal fare, said Mr Campbell, as it would have the effect of putting the bus companies out of business. It would mean raising the prices on buses in outside districts and that would prevent public patronage. The natural result would be that buses would have to go off the roads. The penal fare was not called for by the circumstances in Auckland at present.

"It had been claimed that the buses were causing a loss to the tramways, but the evidence was against that. Last year, it was stated, Auckland had .lost £3000 on the tramways, but he challenged the figures, and called for a full investigation of the position. The bus proprietors were certain that any losses that had been occasioned had been due to the operations of the municipally-owned bus service.

"The privately-owned buses had not been responsible for any loss on the tramways. Furthermore, the City Council in 1925 had reduced their fares with the avowed object of smashing the bus competition. How could the private bus owners be charged with being the cause of the loss when the loss on the tramways was due to the action of the City Council itself? The loss on the tramways had also been due to increased running costs.

"The bus proprietors had never objected to the insurance clause, said the witness, and they believed insurance should be made compulsory. Where there was a large fleet of buses there should be provision for a blanket policy. Municipal buses should come under the regulations in the same way as those privately owned. They were not objecting to competition, but they asked that all their competitors should be put on the same basis as themselves.

"The buses in Auckland, he urged, served the public, and if they were forced to go off the road the public would suffer. It had been said they were pirates; that they had gone into districts where the trams had been pioneers and had taken the cream of the trade, but, rather, the boot was on the other foot. He quoted an instance where the City Council had followed private enterprise into one district and had reduced the fares in an endeavour to put the private company's buses off the road. It was patent, he declared, that the Auckland City Council could not fully cope with the traffic that was operating.

"In answer to Mr H. Holland, witness said the population of Auckland had increased very considerably in recent years, and the competition of the buses had not made the tramways an unprofitable concern. He said private buses were paying, and he thought they would continue to pay if there was no interference. Replying to Mr E. J. Howard, witness expressed the view that the majority of the people of Auckland were behind the bus proprietors.

"Mr C. E. Macmillan: Don't you think the regulations were framed in the interests of the general public? Witness: No, they were framed to protect the tramways.

"Replying to further questions by Mr Potter, witness said it was a fallacy to suggest that the Auckland people owned the tramways, for they had been laid down by borrowed capital, and the interest was therefore going outside New Zealand, whereas private buses were owned in New Zealand.

"Mr G. W. Forbes: If the question of the regulations was put to the popular vote, what do you think would be the result in the Auckland district? Witness said he believed the vote would be overwhelmingly in favour of the buses." [144]

Additional evidence favouring private bus transport was delivered to the Committee that day: "…further evidence on behalf of the Auckland bus proprietors was heard. Mr F. C. Martin, manager of the Royal Company…stressed the hardship that would result from the operation of the penal clause.

"To Mr E. H. Potter, witness said that the bus service had been started because of the unsatisfactory tram service to Onehunga. Mr Potter: Did the council put on buses in opposition to yours? Witness: Yes, on June 10 last. Witness added that his buses were well patronised, while the municipal buses went practically empty.

"Mr Potter: Has your service had the effect of opening up a number of residential areas?

"Witness: Yes. Witness added that if the buses went off the road, there would be a repetition of the old football match at five o'clock every night and people would have to wait half an hour before getting their tram home.

"Mr Potter: Before the bus competition started there was a by-law preventing people from standing on the rear of tram cars?

"Witness: Yes.

"Mr Potter: That was in the interests of public safety?

"Witness: Yes.

"Mr Potter: Since the competition started, that by-law has been revoked?

"Witness: Yes.

"To Mr G. W. Forbes, witness said that people preferred to ride in the buses. Mr Forbes: Wouldn't the public prefer to pay the extra fare and continue to ride in the buses?

"Witness: Well, you know the public. They are peculiar, and every twopence counts at the end of the month.

"Replying to Mr E. P. Lee (chairman), witness said it had not been a competition of fares, but of service. Private enterprise could not live if the regulations were enforced with regard to fares.

"Mr S. Gray, Town Clerk of Mount Eden Borough, said his council opposed the regulations on the ground that they gave a monopoly to the City Council. The districts outside Auckland would be controlled by the City Council, a position which amounted to taxation without representation. The private bus services had been of great value to Mount Eden, as they had had the effect of opening up a big area which lay beyond the tram terminus. It used to be a perfect nightmare to get out of Auckland at five o'clock. Before the buses came on the scene there had been continual demands by the outside districts of Auckland for improved tram services. It was only since the arrival of the buses that the tram service had been improved. About one-third of Mount Eden lay outside the tram service.

"Mr Meredith, a shareholder of the Royal Company...objected to the regulations on two main grounds. The licensing authority should not be an interested party, and the penal fare clause would put buses out of business. The regulations were plainly against public interest. He said Auckland's transport system was hopelessly inadequate at present. There was no congestion, and people were taken right to their homes. That the public appreciated the bus service was shown by the response made to a request for signatures to a petition. Witness detailed various attacks made on buses by the council framing a special by-law, subsequently amended by the Supreme Court, also by a reduction of fares and the waiving of certain by-laws dealing with the control of traffic. It had to be remembered that buses had induced a lot of traffic which did not exist before, also it had to be borne in mind that the roads were the property of the general public and not merely of municipal undertakings." [145]

"Witness (Mr Meredith) suggested that there should be an elective transport board. Transport to and from work was a matter of public interest and it was essential that the public interest should not be jeopardised. It had been suggested that the buses had robbed the trams of a lot of traffic, but it had to be remembered that the buses had induced a lot of traffic which did not exist before. Mr Meredith added that he did not regard trams as an absolute necessity. Motor transport could cope with the position, provided there were sufficient buses." [146]

That was certainly not the opinion of the Auckland City Council, as expressed to the Select Committee by its representative, Mr Thomas Bloodworth:

"For buses to run alongside the trams and try and pick up passengers en route would result in an economic waste. The buses should be made to work in districts where they could serve a useful purpose. The increase in traffic in Auckland City had been remarkable within the last six years, and it was for members of the council, as administrators, to see if some of that traffic could not be eliminated. The council submitted that it was the motor-omnibuses that should be eliminated. It is not a question of municipal transport and private transport working together in the tramway area, said Mr Bloodworth. It is a question of which of the two shall survive, for both cannot." [147]

Coincidentally, the same opposition to a collaborative scheme utilising both municipal rail and private motor-bus services was also being debated across the Tasman, as reported by The New Zealand Herald on 27 July 1926:

"[from our own correspondent Sydney] The Government appears to be looking for trouble in all directions...if the Government carries out the proposals of one of its Ministers to prevent the buses from picking up passengers along the tram routes, except during the peak periods of traffic, there will inevitably be an outcry on the part of the public.

"The Government is not, as was feared in some quarters, going to create a monopoly for itself in the bus traffic, but the trams are a losing proposition, and as the incursion of the buses is held to be largely responsible for it, the Government is going to cut out the buses in the slack periods along tram routes and compel the public to squeeze into trams already overcrowded.

"If the public desire buses – and they do desire them, judging from the way they patronise them – then they will insist upon the use of them at all hours, and not merely during the peak periods. People are already packed like sardines on Sydney's trams at almost any hour of the day on almost any of the busy services. To crowd more people into them by cutting out buses, simply in order that the Government can pull up its deficit on the trams, will be for the Government to invite trouble. This is something that will touch the public immediately, like the income tax." [148]

But the proposals to regulate private buses in favour of the tramway system would not just tax the travelling public. There were a number of suppliers who had set up businesses and invested heavily in the future of motor transport while some municipalities, such as Auckland's North Shore, remained unsure as to what type of public transport future they should be investing in. The continuing Select Committee hearings provided a forum for these uncertainties, some of which were reported by The New Zealand Herald on 28 July 1926:

"Mr G. B. Beaver, company manager, representing the Auckland motor body builders, said the advent of the motor had increased the business of body builders very considerably, and they had improved their plant and machinery. In recent years they had also been able to reduce the prices of motor body work by from 40 to 50 per cent, but it appeared that the regulations would mean that all their work would go for naught. Already the regulations had resulted in (a) big check to the industry, and staffs had to be reduced.

"Mr J. D. Morison, Mayor of Takapuna, said the configuration of his borough did not allow of a bus service. They felt they could not have an electric tram service as well as a bus service. At present the district had a private steam tram service, and the Borough Council held an option of purchase over that service, as well as the harbour ferry service. The council had been advised not to purchase the system unless it could secure control of the bus service. Witness admitted that a bus service was required up to a certain point, such as for feeding trams, but it was not required on the main roads. He urged that the regulations should be put into effect.

"In replying to Mr E. H. Potter, Mr Morison said that the price which the Tramway Company was asking for its service was £65,000.

"Mr Potter: And you will have to spend a considerable amount of money in alterations if you are going to electrify the trams?—Yes.

"Mr Archibald Slinger, engineer for the Takapuna Borough Council, said that the difficulty they were up against at present was caused by intensified traffic. "He agreed that an electrified tram service was the only satisfactory service so far as Takapuna was concerned, and it could be made to pay if there was protection against buses. To Mr Potter witness said it would probably cost £150,000 to purchase the present trams and electrify them.

"Mr Thomas Bloodworth, a member of the Auckland City Council and Auckland Power Board, said the-council urged that the motor regulations in their original form or with slight modification were essential to the continued existence of the tramway system. Under the present system of free competition by motor-buses they were carrying on at a loss and were threatened with an increasing loss as time went on. If the loss on the tramways were such that a rate had to be levied to meet it, such a rate would cripple the finance of the city, and would thus tend to hinder progress.

"The City Council contended that the competition with private buses which was the cause of the loss was unnecessary, as the city's transport service could deal with the traffic offering within the tramway area. The council had to see that all interests received due consideration. It could not allow any one section in pursuit of its business to so monopolise any facility or to interfere with the rights of others. The council had to spend huge sums of money in making and maintaining roads and had spent huge sums in widening streets.

"It had under contemplation several other schemes of like nature, all designed to give facilities to all forms of necessary transport. No council could allow those facilities to be used by private omnibus interests in a manner which would impair and speedily ruin the tramway service.

"After referring to the purchase of the tramway system by the council and the capital involved Mr Bloodworth said he wanted to make it clear that if bus competition was allowed the tramway system would have to be scrapped. After careful examination of all evidence available the City Council was satisfied that no other transport facilities were yet available which could supersede the tramways on their essential merits, notwithstanding what the motor bus proprietors might say to the contrary."
[149]

Threatened by what was to become a swarm of motor-powered transport, the Auckland City Council had little choice, in the meantime, but to publicly protect its investment when speaking to the Select Committee. This was despite the Council's private reservations as to the ultimate future of the city's tramway system. The Council's stance may not have been entirely in the best interests of the travelling public, particularly the commuter. However, from an economic standpoint, it had little option but to protect its investment in the city's tramway system and what it ultimately saw as the investment of its citizens. That this investment in public transport had been essential in the first place came in for some scrutiny by certain members of the Select Committee:

"Mr Thomas Bloodworth, representing the Auckland City Council, who gave lengthy evidence yesterday, was examined by members of the committee.

"Mr Fraser: Was it essential that the tramway service should be taken over by the Auckland City Council?—I think so. The service under the private company was not satisfactory.

"Mr Fraser: Do you think the price paid for the tramways was too high? – The Auckland City Council acted on the advice of experts.

"Mr Potter: In reference to the purchase of the trams, is it not a fact that the shareholders in the company at that time received 24s in the £?—I was not a shareholder and I am unable to say.

"Mr Potter: Do you think the trams were purchased at a price that any private syndicate or company would have paid?—I think that under the circumstances then existing no syndicate or private company would have purchased the trams at any price whatever.

"Mr Potter: Did the City Council lightly view bus competition?—I regret to say it did." [150]

However, in contrast to the City Council's allegations that private bus operators were solely to blame for an expected deterioration in the fortunes of the tramways, some interpreted the competition generated as having had a more positive result:

"The evidence of Arthur Mason Gould, a solicitor, of Auckland, was continued before the Motor-bus Regulations Committee yesterday afternoon. In his evidence, Mr Gould gave the results of an analytical examination of balance-sheets and reports submitted to the Auckland City Council in regard to the working of the trams and buses, his object being to show that the loss sustained by the council was due rather to a reduction in fares than the opposition of private buses.

"Mr Gould submitted that there was no danger of the trams having to be scrapped as a result of private competition. Actually, the number of passengers carried on the trams had increased since the buses began running. It had been estimated that the running of the municipal buses had resulted in a loss of £34,000. The witness urged that there was no need for further regulations, as there already existed an amazing tangle of legislation which was in need of simplification." [151]

Nevertheless, for another two weeks, the Select Committee continued to hear various witnesses for and against the enactment of legislation to regulate motor-omnibus operations. On its final sitting day, the 18th of August 1926, the Committee dealt mainly with correspondence before closing the inquiry to "...commence its deliberations." [152]

Those deliberations were duly completed and the Select Committee's recommendations were tabled by its Chairman, Mr E. P. Lee, in the House of Representatives on 1 September 1926. Some of Mr Lee's comments during the presentation of his Committee's recommendations included:

"...he referred to the reports which had been submitted to the committee dealing with the conditions as they existed in other countries. Both in England and Australia there was legislation restricting the bus competition with the tramways. The tramways must not be jeopardised, as over £6,000,000 was invested for which the people of the Dominion were responsible.

"The-private bus owners had been well within their rights in starting services in competition with the tramways. It had been shown that these services were needed, especially in Auckland, where there had been great congestion at rush hours. Unfortunately the Auckland City Council, for some reason, did not remedy the trouble by supplying the transportation that was needed. Its excuse was that it was unable to have tramcars built in time. It might have had valid reasons, but the fact remained that transport was needed and the private buses came in to supply it. The proposal now was to remove them. If that were done and the tramway authorities were given an exclusive right to conduct the service, it would be only fair that those who had maintained services in the interests of the public should be adequately compensated." [153]

In its editorial comment on the Select Committee's recommendations, The New Zealand Herald agreed with the Committee that the control of private motor-omnibus services was necessary and that legislative action was the best means of doing that. But, according to the Herald, time was of the essence and legislation had to be proceeded with straight away:

"Therefore no dilatoriness can be excused, no plea of a session near its end and a rush of business to be done can be accepted...Without some decisive action by the Legislature, the present chaotic situation with every form of transport a law unto itself will continue. There is neither reason nor excuse for delay. All the parties have been fully heard. Their evidence has been sifted, the judgment has been given. It remains for Parliament to act. There can be no conceivable justification for closing the session without doing as the committee recommends, giving statute form to the rules for transport control.

"One of the speakers in the discussion of the report said that tramways systems had been established by the inquiry as still unrivalled for rapid mass transport. The whole substance of the committee's finding endorses this. Accepting it means admitting that for Greater Auckland a tramway system is indispensable. It is even more important for the outer suburbs than for the city. Therefore these suburbs should shoulder some responsibility for an essential service which, temporarily at least, is in difficulties. Whether they like the idea or not, the challenge has been flung to them.

"If this plan is adopted, if all those who depend on the service share responsibility for it, a satisfactory solution may be found, reconciling the claims of tramway and motor-omnibus, so that with both functioning there will be adequate and well-regulated transport services for the people. That is, or should be, the main consideration beneath everything affected by the motor-omnibus regulations." [154]

Unfortunately, the best interests of 'the people', certainly those of Auckland, were not necessarily the 'main consideration' when the final clauses of the Motor-omnibus Traffic Act 1926 were determined and passed into law on 1 November of that year. While the Act protected the people's investment in its tramway system, that protection would eventually prove to be transitory as the City's population grew and areas of settlement expanded.

In line with the Motor-omnibus Traffic Act's national coverage, the country was divided into 13 motor-omnibus districts, each responsible for the annual licensing of motor-omnibus operators by means of a licensing authority. The regulatory sting, as far as the protection of the trams was concerned, was sheathed in Clauses such as 6(2), 6(3) and 7:

"In determining whether or not any such application should be granted, the licensing authority shall take into consideration any existing or proposed facilities for the transport of passengers within the area proposed to be served, the condition of the roads or streets proposed to be traversed and the normal traffic thereon, and all other relevant considerations.

"No license shall be granted in respect of any motor-omnibus unless the licensing authority is satisfied on the report of an Inspecting Engineer that the vehicle conforms to the requirements of any regulations for the time being in force as to the design and construction of motor-omnibuses, and is in a fit condition, all proper regard being had to the safety and comfort of passengers, to be licensed as a motor-omnibus.

"Before disposing of any application under the last preceding section the licensing authority shall give public notice thereof in one or more newspapers, and shall give to every other local authority in the motor-omnibus district and to every public authority or person engaged in carrying on a tramway or motor-omnibus service in that district an opportunity to be heard; and every such local or public authority or person shall have a right of appeal under section sixteen hereof from the determination of the licensing authority."[155]

Clause 10 of the Act also sought to ensure that motor-omnibuses could not charge lower fares than trams along the same route:

"With respect to every motor-omnibus service authorized to be carried on pursuant to this Act the licensing authority shall prescribe the routes to be traversed, the time-tables to be observed, the fares to be charged, and such other conditions and matters as may be prescribed by regulations under this Act, or as the licensing authority thinks proper.

"For the purpose of fixing the fares as aforesaid in respect of any route the licensing authority may divide the route into two or more sections, and in any case where a motor-omnibus service is provided for an area that may conveniently be served in whole or in part by an existing tramway or motor-omnibus service, carried on by any local or public authority, it shall be the duty of the licensing authority so to fix the fares that the fares charged in respect of the carriage of an adult passenger by the motor-omnibus over any route or section thereof (however such fares may be computed) shall be at least twopence more than the corresponding fare charged in respect of the existing service."[156]

In fact, if any motor-omnibus operator was found to be "...in substantial competition with any tramway service or motor-omnibus service carried on by any local or public authority..." it was obliged by Clause 15(1) of the Act to sell to that local or public authority "...all motor-omnibuses and other property used by him exclusively for the purposes of the service, at a price to be agreed on between the parties, or, in the event of their being unable to agree, at a price to be fixed by a Compensation Court under the Public Works Act, 1908..."[157]

In the case of Auckland's Royal Motor-Bus Company, the Compensation Court granted "...the company £21,275 17s 2d as payment for the taking over of the concern by the City Council. This amount practically divides the difference between the claims of the opposing parties. The bus company valued its property, including 28 buses, garage at Onehunga to accommodate 18 buses, and garage in St. Mark's Road for ten buses, at £29,675. The City Council on the other hand offered £14,620..."[158]

Cuts to various bus services soon followed, and little time was given for any protest:

"Strong criticism of the action of the Auckland City Council in discontinuing the bus service to Mangere was expressed at a meeting held under the auspices of the Mangere Progressive Association...Speakers stated that when the City Council took over the Royal Motor-Bus Company's plant the service was cut down to a feeder bus from the Onehunga tram terminus, but even this was later withdrawn on the ground that it was being run at a loss. It was complained that the council had treated the district very badly, and that the feeder bus had been withdrawn at ridiculously short notice."[159]

But the non-competitive provisions of the Motor-Omnibus Traffic Act came too late for the North Shore tramway. By April 1927, the tramway from Bayswater, which by then had been extended to include Milford, was experiencing financial difficulties and had been placed in receivership. The service ceased to operate on 26 April 1927, following its acquisition by the Devonport Ferry Company. In its report at the time, the Auckland Star recorded the poignant change from steam tram to motor bus:

"Under the new arrangement the steam tram will cease to operate, their passing being signalised this morning by a little ceremony at Takapuna, when one of the engines was decorated with a wreath of carrots, onions and rhubarb. The attached card was inscribed: 'Well done, thou good and faithful servant.' The ceremony was decorously carried out, and a moving picture machine was at hand to record a permanent impression of the event. From Bayswater a fleet of four 'Red' buses and Mr A. H. Smith's eleven 'Yellow' buses will operate to convey passengers to and from Takapuna while there will also be ten limousine cars on the service between Devonport and Takapuna." [160]

Nor was the Bayswater tramway able to benefit from later legislation which, by way of the Motor-spirits Taxation Act 1927, also provided for "...the imposition of Customs Duties on Motor-spirits and for the Allocation of the Revenues derived therefrom" at the initial rate of 4d per gallon. Ninety-two percent of the revenue collected (after expenses) was to be paid into the Revenue Fund of the Main Highways Account and the balance "...apportioned among those Borough Councils in whose districts there is a population of six thousand or upwards..."

Initially, the first petrol tax was only levied on motor-spirits used to fuel motor vehicles and other users could apply for a refund. [161]

But, despite the Motor-Omnibus Traffic Act, the fuel tax, registration and licensing fees:

"Motor buses drew traffic away from tramway services and given their cheaper costs of operation were able to serve low-density residential areas away from the fixed tram routes. Most bus operators were not affected by the legal obligation of tramway operators regarding fares and frequency of service but were able to charge what the traffic would bear." [162]

In what was supposed to have been a further boost to the future of Auckland's tramways, the City Council asked its ratepayers for permission to raise a special loan with which to fund an ambitious expansion of the service. However, the poll, taken on 17 August 1927 was not expected to be as successful for the tramways as those taken in previous years. The Auckland Star anticipated this in its comment a month before the poll:

"The transport issues that the City Council will place before the city ratepayers next month will have to meet several adversaries and by its handling of the question the Council is hardly giving its cause the best of chances. The problem of transport is more confused than ever before.

"The Council is asking for an extension of tramway tracks at a time when the future of this form of transport is doubtful. It is placing several extension proposals of varying size, and in the eyes of citizens varying merit, before the ratepayers in one lump, so that it will be impossible for a ratepayer to approve of one and vote against another. Denied this choice, will ratepayers not be disposed to reject the lot?

"Further, it is asking the city ratepayer to assume liability for costly capital extensions that will benefit other districts as well as his own, but these districts will not incur any liability. Hitherto the city ratepayer's liability for transport losses has been a theoretical affair, but the balance-sheet for the last twelve months has made an addition to the rates a practical possibility.

"The city ratepayer will ask himself why he should vote for works that will benefit areas that at present cannot be rated for loss on operation.

"Lastly, the figures put before the Council in respect of these undertakings show heavy estimated losses during the first three years— £53,000 for all proposals, and £31,000 for the three extensions beyond the city area. If the City Council wishes its proposals to have a fair chance of success it will have to give ratepayers more information —such, for example, as reasons why feeder buses will not suffice for extensions — more latitude in voting, and some guarantee that the burden of liability for transport losses is not going to rest solely on the city area for an indefinite period." [163]

So, by 1927, not only was the future of the tramways as a public transport facility threatened by the motor buses purposely put in place to supplement the trams, but the ability of the City Council to finance an expansion that would allow the trams to compete with those motor buses was also restricted by the City's local body structure.

The City had grown all these appendages – boroughs whose existence and growth had been greatly facilitated by the skeletons of transport systems, such as the tramways and, to a lesser extent, the railway. However, over the years, these boroughs became increasingly independent of the central city. It would not be until the formation of the Auckland Regional Authority in 1963 that a more realistic, regional perspective of transport planning was attempted.

As detailed in Part 2 of this history, attempts to unify all local bodies for the greater good of the Auckland isthmus continued to 1989 when the Auckland Regional Authority became the Auckland Regional Council and the Auckland Regional Transport Authority was formed. But even with the formation of these administrative bodies, the parochialism of Auckland's local bodies continued to affect the efficiency and growth of the region throughout the 1990s and beyond.

This was summed up by Bruce Jesson in his book, 'Only Their Purpose is Mad':

"Public transport is one of the most disagreeable features of life in Auckland. Few major cities can have a transport system as bad. There are various reasons for this. Local government is so fragmented in Auckland that it is virtually impossible to bring a region-wide view to regional problems. And, for many decades, there has been a systematic bias toward spending money on motorways and roads." [164]

It was not until 2010 that Auckland City and its various local bodies would be consolidated into a 'super city' – a joining of all regional prejudices that must finally and surely result in a public transport system to serve and satisfy all...?

In the meantime, the crucial poll of Auckland City's ratepayers was set to take place on 17 August 1927. That was the date on which the future of the tramways system as a viable public service was to be decided by a public which represented a comparatively small proportion of those now inhabiting the much larger Auckland region far from the beachhead of the 1840s.

By definition, those ratepayers were eligible to vote because they owned property close to the central city and few would need to commute daily to the likes of Mount Roskill or the depths of Mount Eden Road. When a trip to the suburbs was necessary, city ratepayers were more likely to drive their own motor vehicle as Dr G. T. Bloomfield described in his 1975 history of Urban Tramways in New Zealand:

"Increasing private car ownership affected tramway usage for recreational and social purposes in the evenings and at weekends." [165]

Particularly when compared to the ageing and overcrowded trams, that 'increasing private car ownership', that 'illusion of progress', was also a concept of the future that Auckland City's ratepayers would have found difficult to disregard when it came time to cast their ballots.

In an attempt to remind ratepayers of the public legacy they could lose if they rejected the City Council's loan proposals for the tramways expansion, the Council published a comprehensive history and profile of the city's tramways just before the August poll.

The August 1927 edition of the Municipal Record (Official Organ of the Auckland City Corporation, New Zealand) included a good deal of historical information and photographs in its eighteen pages:

"People who are transported long distances at cheap rates in splendid modern vehicles, safely, comfortably and rapidly, have to thank James Outram, the English engineer, who was really the father of 'tramways'.

"In 1775 he advised the Duke of Norfolk to pull up the wooden rails in common use in the Duke's Sheffield collieries, and to lay down L-shaped cast iron rails, spiked to cross sleepers. The first Outram rails were laid down in 1776, and were known as "Outram Ways." ...In course of time, the first two letters of the name "Outram" were discarded, and we thus get our universally known word 'tramways'. The first tramway for passengers in the world was through the streets from Harlem to New York in 1832...Liverpool was the first large town to adopt street passenger tramways in 1868." [166]

But as well as the promotion of the trams as Auckland's future transport solution, the Municipal Record also contained a lot of propaganda critical of the competing motor-omnibuses:

"No one doubts that the 'bus has come to stay, but it will not stay as a substitute or rival of trams...Petrol 'buses can never permanently compete against trams. It is universally held by American authorities that the tram car is the backbone of properly co-ordinated transport systems, and that it will continue to carry the bulk of passengers. It is well to remember as showing that even the high grade 'buses (such as the Auckland Municipality use as tram feeders) wear out quickly and become obsolescent. It is generally held that the best 'buses should be written down over a five years' life, and inferior 'buses over an even shorter term. The depreciation cost of the 'bus in comparison with the tram is very high." [167]

The mechanical deficiency of a motor-omnibus, compared to that of a tram car, is also graphically illustrated in the centre pages of this edition of the Municipal Record which displays photographs contrasting the 'Multitudinous Parts of Motor Omnibus Engine' with those of 'A Sturdy Servant – Showing Rigid Construction of Tram Car Equipment'...

"Here is seen an Auckland-made (tram) Car, staunch, strong, safe and reliable. A glance at the photographs, showing the working parts of the tram car and the working parts of a motor 'bus, will convince the citizen of the superiority of his citizen-owned vehicle." [168]

Whether or not many readers of the Municipal Record accepted its premise of superior tram transport is not known. However, on the day of the ratepayers' poll, 17 August, 1927, an otherwise innocuous accident could have been taken as an ominous sign of things to come:

"While running to board a city-bound tram car about 12.45 this afternoon Mr Peter Whelan (35), of 14, Ligar Place, Grafton, was knocked down by a motor vehicle. He was taken to the Hospital by the St. John Ambulance and admitted with injuries to the head and concussion. His condition is not considered to be very serious." [169]

The poll result was reported by the Auckland Star the following day:

"Auckland ratepayers rejected the City Council's tramways loan proposal of £500,000 by a majority of 881 at the poll which was taken yesterday. The result of the voting was as follows:

"For: 3427 Against: 4308 Majority against: 881. At the city booths the opposition to the proposal was decisive, and at the greater number of the suburban booths also majorities were recorded against the loan... The poll was a heavy one, and the city and suburban vote showed that much interest had been aroused in the proposal. The Mayor (Mr George Baildon) said that the matter had been fully placed before the ratepayers, and they must accept full responsibility for any necessary modifications of policy which must follow from the decision of yesterday. He was not prepared at the moment to say whether a modified scheme would be put to the ratepayers in the near future." [170]

The same edition of the Auckland Star also stated its opinion as to why the poll had failed:

"Four considerations defeated the loan proposals yesterday: doubt about the future of trams; uncertainty about city transport finance; objection to the City taking on fresh liability for the benefit of outside districts; and the throwing of all the proposals into one issue. There were ratepayers who, if they could, would have voted for the improvements within the city, but who felt obliged to reject the programme because they objected to the other items. The Council did its best with its case, and though its activities did not convince a majority, these probably had much to do with the increase in the number who took the trouble to vote. Yet what a reflection on the state of citizenship it is that on an issue like this only 35 per cent of voters went to the poll!

"The Council will now have to proceed with its task of making accounts balance. The system is in a state of readjustment, and it may be some time before stability is reached. The wider question, what should be the ultimate policy of ownership and control, is brought nearer by yesterday's result; and if the City Council is wise it will before long take the outside bodies into its full confidence, ask for their views, and endeavour to frame a permanent policy which will meet future needs. Yesterday's rejection is only a check; no one supposes that city transport will stand still indefinitely." [171]

Nevertheless, "This was the start of Auckland's car dependence. It was not the first nor the last time that Auckland ratepayers have revolted against contributing to the region's land transport infrastructure." [172]

While the results of the 1927 poll did not bring city transport to a standstill, the future of the tramways as a public service had certainly been compromised, both by the poll result and the poor voter turnout. Official statistics, published later that year, also seemed to reflect a growing acceptance of the transport revolution by a public quite naturally mesmerised by the incomparable motor car and the potential for independent and speedier travel that it promised. Those statistics, measuring the past use of the trams, were published by the Auckland Star on 14 November 1927:

"The following points in connection with electric tramways stand out sharply: (a) The relative tendency for the use made of tramways to decline;

(b) the tendency for the annual capital charges to increase and for the gross surplus to decrease.

"This conclusion is reached by the Government Statistician, after a review of the problems of urban transport. He says that the increasing use of the motor car and omnibus as a means of transport in the Dominion has complicated the problem. Indeed, the inevitable problem which accompanies all revolutions in the means of transport viz., the duplication of costly services — has already been dealt with by legislation inhibiting the operations of privately-owned omnibuses in certain areas The general consideration of the question of urban transport has focused considerable attention on the electric tramways in the Dominion. The growth of tramway traffic is shown in tabular form, rising from 82,865,000 in 1911 to 167,600,000 in 1927. Passengers carried have more than doubled, but the population has grown by but 60 per cent since 1911.

"It is significant that the number of passengers carried shows a very slight movement between 1921-22 and 1922-23, and that they actually remained constant between 1923-24 and 1924-25, and again between 1925-26 and 1926-27. These figures are all the more significant when it is considered that the index number for the population served moved up 5 points between 1923-24 and 1924-25, and by 3 points between 1925-26 and 1926-27. It would be idle to suggest that the demand for passenger transport decreased during the periods under discussion.

"The conclusion that the demand for tramway transport actually waned for the years mentioned is irresistible, more particularly when the index numbers relating to the average number of trips per annum per head of population are considered. These figures actually declined from 121 in 1920-21 to 120 in 1921-22 and 119 in the following year. After a recovery to 122 in 1923-24 the index number for 1924-25 sank as low as 118, to rise again in 1925-26 and 1926-27 to 129 and 127 respectively.

"There has been a decided decline since 1923-24 in the percentage of the gross surplus to the capital outlay on the trams. In 1923-24 this figure stood at 11.07 per cent, but every subsequent year has seen a decrease recorded, until in 1926-27 it had fallen to 5.21 per cent. This decline is particularly noticeable, and indicates substantial changes in general tramway finance.

"Only a cursory glance at the figures for revenue and operating expenses is necessary to show that the principal cause of the phenomenon under discussion is the fact that the revenue has not kept pace with the operating expenditure. To ascribe this lagging behind in the revenue to any particular cause would require a great deal more data than is available in these statistics, but the tendency for the number of passengers carried to remain stationary over certain periods during the last five years appears to be the prime cause.

"Proceeding with the examination of the gross surplus in relation to other debits in the way of capital charges, a rapid drift in tramway finance during the last few years is disclosed. This may be due to changes in the methods of arranging the finances or to increasing competition from motor transport. There appears to be every reason to suppose that the latter is the more potent force." [173]

While the Government Statistician's figures relate to tram services throughout the country, there is no doubt that the conclusions reached certainly applied to the Auckland situation in 1927. But while these figures show tram patronage to have at least become static, of greater significance to the City's provision of any future public transport service, had to be the reduction of profit shown.

For the first time since the start of Auckland's electric tramways, the need to upgrade the service and maintain its car fleet and infrastructure was soon to cost more than expected receipts. By February 1928, the formation of a Transport Commission to look at how tramway extensions and the Auckland region's other transport needs could be financed was proposed.

In the meantime, the Auckland Star outlined the contributions then made by the various local bodies and reported that not all were in favour of extending the tramway lines:

"Definite advice regarding the sitting of the proposed Transport Commission is not yet available, but reports indicate that the inquiry will commence early next month. One of the matters that will come before the commissioners for consideration is the question of tramway extensions in Auckland, said Mr J. A. C. Allum, chairman of the Tramways Committee of the City Council, to-day. He added that the council had already decided that extensions were necessary and estimates had been prepared in connection with the proposed tramway developments.

"On the tramway routes at present in use the tramways department had paid to the City Council and suburban local bodies for the past year rates which were as follows: City, £3881; Mount Albert, £571; Onehunga, £10; One Tree Hill, £518; Newmarket, £106; Mount Roskill, £565; Mount Eden, £292. In addition to paying rates to the extent of £5045 last year for the use of the portion of the roadway occupied by the tram tracks, the department was also required to keep its part of the surface in proper order, explained Mr Allum.

"From the point of view of the outside local bodies, it was stated this morning that the roading improvements put in hand some years ago, and the concrete roads which had been completed, had the effect of protecting the tram tracks as well as giving an excellent surface for heavy traffic. The result was to assist the tramways department.

"Mr E. H. Potter, Mayor of Mount Eden, said that the travelling public paid in fares the whole of the cost of maintaining the track and the interest and sinking fund on the capital sunk in the undertaking. When the company was bought out by the city corporation some of the districts were much smaller than they were to-day and they had since shown marked growth. Large sums had been spent on the roads, and, as far as Mount Eden was concerned, the spread of population meant that only two-thirds of the district was now being served by the trams.

"At the request of the City Council, continued Mr Potter, the Mount Eden Borough Council extended the concrete road beyond the tram terminus to the borough boundary, a promise being made that tramway extensions would follow later. Special work was done in order to help with the tramway foundations and the re-grading was greater than would have been otherwise provided for. Recently the people had shown their preference for a bus service beyond the tramway limits, and the desire was that their needs should be met." [174]

Indeed, many of Auckland's local bodies resented the setting up of a Transport Commission by the Government because they felt such a Commission would favour the then current transport arrangements managed by the Auckland City Council. And the Government wasn't that keen to become involved in what it saw as local government affairs either.

"Several suggestions have been made in Parliament recently that the Government should interest itself in Auckland transport questions. Mr Jordan, for instance, has quoted again the recommendation of the Motor Omnibus Regulations Committee that a metropolitan transport board should be set up in Auckland, with the obvious inference that the Government should move in the matter.

"Mr Potter, also, has directed official attention to Auckland transport conditions. All that can be said in answer to these contentions has already been said. The Government, answering earlier questions about a transport board, said that the question was purely an Auckland one, and that any legislation to give effect to the committee's recommendation must be set on foot in Auckland. What else could the Government do?

"The recommendation said that the board should have power to take over the tramway and omnibus undertakings of the City of Auckland. Is the Government to legislate in such a direction irrespective of what the City of Auckland, owner of these enterprises, thinks about the proposition? If such a thing were suggested touching any other branch of municipal enterprise, there would be a tremendous outcry led, it may be suspected, by those who are inferentially urging Government interference with Auckland civic affairs.

"Transport conditions in the metropolitan area cannot be regarded as satisfactorily settled now, but they never will be by any solution arbitrarily imposed by the central Government. To attempt this would be a violation of the whole spirit of local government by local authority as New Zealand knows it." [175]

Nevertheless, the lobbying pressure of a number of Aucklanders and their political representatives eventually resulted in a Government proposal to set up a commission to inquire into and report upon Auckland's transport service, its present and future requirements, and the means by which those requirements may be best provided for. The Commission was appointed on 4 April 1928 and reported to both Houses of the General Assembly on 11 June of that year. [176]

But well before that appointment, local bodies had already decided they did not want to debate "…the relative advantages and costs of trams, railless trams, buses, and other means of transport" but the "…constitution of an elected Transport Board…" on the grounds that "To set up a commission to consider the relative advantages of different methods of traction would cloud the issue and obscure the real solution." [177]

As the Auckland Star reported on 24 February 1928:

"The resentment of the outside local bodies to the present transport arrangements controlled by the Auckland City Council found expression last evening when twenty-three suburban local body representatives assembled at the Mount Eden Borough Council offices to discuss the question of what attitude they would take towards the commission on transport proposed to be set up by the Government." [178]

That attitude was summed up at a meeting of the New Lynn Town Board held on 13 March 1928:

"The transport question was once more a subject of discussion at the meeting of the New Lynn Town Board last evening. The chairman (Mr W. S. Titchener) referred to the proposed transport commission and the attitude likely to be adopted by the outside local bodies. He contended that the proposed commission would serve no good purpose and had not been asked for by the outside local bodies, who possessed a population equal to that of the city area.

"The City Council sought and approached the Government for a monopoly in transport and, no doubt, at the same time promised to give a good service. The Government gave the city the monopoly without consulting the outside local bodies. The service was bad, and the

Government had failed to keep the council up to what was their undoubted promise. It might be found that the commission would be merely a 'whitewashing' business. He contended that the setting up of a Transport Board to control the metropolitan services as one big job, instead of a series of little ones, was the only solution to the transport problem...

"Mr Akehurst said the (tramways) Department had shown their incompetence because they had never attempted to increase their turnover, but increased their charges and consequently reduced their customers. They changed their time-tables and put on special buses without notifying the public." [179]

As previously noted, the Commission of Inquiry to inquire into and report upon the passenger transport problems of the Auckland metropolitan district was nevertheless appointed on 4 April 1928. The Commissioners appointed included:

"Mr J. S. Barton, S.M., of Wanganui (chairman); Mr W. G. T. Goodman, traffic manager, of Adelaide and Mr Alfred Edward, retired superintendent of traffic, Sydney.

"The order of reference provides for inquiry into the present transport services of the district, its present and future requirements, and the means by which these may be best provided for. In particular the commissioners are asked to investigate:

"(a) The adequacy, efficiency and suitability of the existing transport system maintained by the Auckland City Council and other existing transport services, as regards administration, equipment, working and financial provisions.

"(b) The working and effect in the district of the provisions of the Motor-Omnibus Traffic Act, 1926, and its regulations.

"(c) The working and effect in the district of other statutes and regulations affecting vehicular transport.

"(d) The suitability for the district of motor-omnibus transport, either in conjunction with or as an adjunct to tramway transport.

"(e) The most suitable form of transport for localities within and localities beyond the tram termini; whether services for such localities should be feeder services or through services or a combination of both; whether and to what extent such services should be conducted by local bodies or any other public management or by private enterprise; and whether and to what extent such services should be under the control of local bodies or any other public control.

"(f) The desirability of establishing a transport board for the district or any part of it, and if so, with what constitution, powers of control, powers of undertaking transport services and means of obtaining funds for its purposes, and whether such a board, if established, should take over all or any existing transport services, and if so upon what terms.

"The areas affected are the City of Auckland, the Borough of Newmarket, the Borough of Mount Eden, the Borough of Mount Albert, the Borough of Onehunga, the Borough of Otahuhu, the New Lynn Town District, the Glen Eden Town District, the Henderson Town District, the Ellerslie Town District, the Mount Roskill Road District, the One Tree Hill Road District, the Mount Wellington Road District, the Panmure Township Road District, and such areas in the vicinity of Auckland not included in the foregoing district, but exclusive of localities on the north shore of Waitemata Harbour, as in the opinion of the commission should be included in any general consideration of the transport of passengers in the districts mentioned or any substantial portion of them." [180]

Given the importance and expanse of the inquiry, it is surprising that "The commission's report is returnable to the Government by May 26." [181]

But perhaps it was a time for fast action, if not panic, on the part of the Auckland City Council – a situation elaborated on by the tramways manager, Mr A. E. Ford, during his appearance at the subsequent Commission of Inquiry's hearings:

"On the City Council's transport operations for the year ended March 31 (1928), the deficiency was approximately £41,500, a profit of £18,500 on the tramways being more than offset by a loss of about £60,000 on the bus undertaking.

"In giving these figures to the Transport Commission yesterday while under cross-examination, Mr A. E. Ford, tramways manager, said it should be remembered that they were only approximate and subject to audit. A comparison with the previous year showed that tramways receipts had increased by £11,000, and there had been a similar increase in the losses on the bus undertaking. The tramways had a credit balance for 1926-27 of £7385, and the bus portion of the transport system, a debit balance of £48,125. There had been a credit of £2467 at the opening of that year and a debit balance of £38,273 at its close. The debit balance for the two years thus mounted to almost £80,000.

"Regarding future policy, Mr Ford said that bus services which were incurring exceptional losses must be withdrawn, but all districts in the metropolitan area must be provided with reasonable services. By that, he meant services which were an adjunct to the main system. If residents were willing to subsidise services that were a hopeless loss the Tramways Department would be willing to co-operate." [182]

As part of the evidence later provided by Mr Ford to the Commission, he advised:

"In October, 1923, he reported to the Mayor (then Mr J. H. Gunson) upon the need of preparing to meet bus competition in Auckland. The first tram route affected by the competition was from Surrey Crescent to Pitt Street. Nothing was done to meet the competition, although witness repeatedly urged the need of taking steps to restrain it. When the transport problem began in earnest in the following April the city was faced with losses on its tramways undertaking. For a very considerable time to come, he said, the trams must continue to be the backbone of the transport system.

"Mr Johnstone (Counsel for the Auckland City Council): Did you take steps to break the competition? — Yes. You recommended a reduction in fares? — Yes. Did that help the position? — Yes. You ran an increased mileage? — Yes. Restrictions were put on bus traffic by excluding it from Queen Street? — Yes. That assisted the trams, although the restrictions were made in the interests of traffic regulation? — Yes. Witness added, however, that the position was not substantially improved and conferences were arranged at which an effort was made to obtain legislation to regulate motor bus traffic." [183]

Indeed, it was obvious throughout much of the Transport Commission's hearings that the Auckland City Council believed it was the rightful body to license and regulate all public transport services throughout its region. This was made patently obvious by Mr John Andrew Charles Allum, then Chairman of the Council's Tramways Committee, when he stated at the inquiry:

"The Auckland City Council considers there is no justification for the setting up of a Transport Board, or any other authority to assume control of its tram services. The only argument that could be suggested in favour of the proposed board, pointed out Mr Allum, was that all persons using the transport system would have representation upon the board controlling the whole of the transport district. He maintained, however, that the representation was unnecessary, and may well be ineffective." [184]

Later to be a distinguished, long-serving Mayor of Auckland, John Allum, demonstrated his knowledge of public affairs and his foresight when he stated further to the Commission:

"The policy which the council has pursued is the only one that anybody controlling transport could adopt, and the city can only view with alarm any proposal which is calculated to deprive its present area, comprising the bulk of the population and the material wealth of the transport district, of the preponderance of power to which its importance entitles it...Should it be thought desirable that such representation should be given, the (Council) suggests that it can be obtained by the creation of a greater Auckland." [185]

Unfortunately for the maturity of Auckland as a world-class city, John Allum's concept of a 'greater Auckland' as a means to settling the City's growth issues was not to be achieved for more than 80 years. During that time, the self-interests of its satellites and of those in power at Wellington would continuously fragment the City's need for a 'preponderance of power' to its detriment and that of the country as a whole.

At a later hearing of the Transport Commission, John Allum singled out the Mount Eden Borough as an example of the lack of co-operation he referred to:

"Difficulties arising out of the lack of co-operation on the part of outside bodies was the subject of cross-examination by Mr Rogerson, when Mr J. A. C. Allum, chairman of the Tramways Committee of the City Council, continued his evidence before the Transport Commission yesterday afternoon. Witness stated that Mount Eden's attitude was, in effect, that the borough did not realise its responsibility in transport matters and did not give the city the co-operation and assistance it was entitled to. There was 'polite' hostility... He did not thing (think) that if the outside local bodies were taken into partnership, the lack of confidence would be removed.

"Mr Allum said that both he and the Tramways Committee had considered the question of a transport board, and he had already stated that the City Council objected to handing over the tramway undertaking to any authority other than one controlling a greater Auckland. Progressive amalgamations of outside bodies, he added, should continue, and finally the difficulties would disappear." [186]

In 1928, there were also others working against what was then described as the City Council's 'municipal autocracy'. The feeling was summarised by an Auckland Star comment published on 10 May 1928:

"We have no intention of discussing the work of the Transport Commission till its labours are completed, but a statement made by one of the witnesses yesterday seems to us to require a little passing comment.

"Councillor J. A. C. Allum, chairman of the Tramways Committee, was explaining the City Council's policy, and referred to the defeat of the tramways extension loan proposals. The Council, he said, still holds that the proposed extensions are essential and are urgently required, and it therefore considers that legislation should be passed empowering it to raise money for extensions approved by the Public Works Department and the Local Government Loans Board 'without the necessity of taking a poll'.

"We do not know how far the other members of the City Council share these views, but we protest against them emphatically. Mr Allum had apparently forgotten that councillors are elected by the ratepayers to carry out a policy which the ratepayers have endorsed. They have no authority and no official existence apart from the approval of the ratepayers, and yet, according to Mr Allum, they now claim the right to over-ride the decision of the ratepayers by statutory means and to impose fresh financial burdens upon them against their considered judgment and their declared will.

"Such an assumption of autocratic power would be ridiculous if it were not at the same time dangerous. We hope that Mr Allum will come to recognise the folly and futility of such absurd pretensions, which are wholly inconsistent with our established methods of municipal administration, and utterly incompatible with the democratic principles on which our systems of local and national self-government are based." [187]

The possibility of subsidising the tramways service as a necessary public function was a political concept yet to be fully debated. In the meantime, it seemed so much easier and cheaper for some to welcome the motor bus and the roads it needed. However, with an investment in the tramways service to protect, the City Council was not so eager to embrace the bus, apart from where it was needed as a feeder service to the trams.

The anti-competitive penalties imposed on the private bus services by the 1926 Motor-omnibus Traffic Act, particularly those relating to penal fares which ensured that motor-omnibuses could not charge lower fares than trams along the same route, were widely criticised by the suburban local bodies and bus passengers.

That criticism was described to the Transport Commission by the local bodies' representative, Mr Northcroft:

"Continuing his address before the Transport Commission on behalf of Suburban Local Bodies yesterday, Mr Northcroft said the imposition of the penal fare may or may not have been justified on the policy of expedience. However, there could be no doubt it was a process of strangulation of the privately run buses. In effect the Government said: 'If you choose to continue you may do so, but with the handicap of the penal fare in the race for traffic.' The fact that it is done elsewhere does not make the legislation any more virtuous. The City Council did not take steps to create a monopoly within its own borders, but on the other hand secured a monopoly over the whole of the metropolitan area.

"There would have been less criticism had the City Council obtained control by some proper licensing authority within the metropolitan area. The City Council was a competitor for transport trade, and it would have been more proper and less unjust. The grievance and sense of injustice was not confined to bus operators, but to those people who resided in districts where the buses ran. Those people find themselves in an unenviable position regarding transport facilities to-day, and the council should be compelled to show justification for having the buses off the roads. Feeder buses were not a success. They have been irritating to the residents. In some cases the buses had gone completely off, and in others very unsatisfactory feeder services obtain (sic).

"Criticising the figures of running costs of the buses as set out by Mr Ford and Mr Allum, Mr Northcroft said the various types of buses were not treated separately. On the other side of the bus balance sheet there was the same unsatisfactory position. There was a time when the earnings of the buses was given with some particularity. It might not be too much to say that the Tram Department was a tram department, and had little sympathy with the buses. Without in any way making an accusation of deliberate falsification of records, it could be said that whenever trams and buses figure, the trams have been favoured. Every assistance was given the trams, but the buses were discouraged and neglected.

"Special concession tickets for the buses are obtainable only with the utmost difficulty. The buses are not wanted, and it would appear that the Tramways Department is only concerned with proving its case, which is that buses should be put off the roads. 'It seems to me,' continued Mr Northcroft, 'that the tram profits have been consistently overstated. Sufficient provision has not been made for depreciation." [188]

Additional evidence as to the dissatisfaction with the way public transport was being run by the City Council to the detriment of outlying suburbs was given by Mount Eden's Mayor, Ernest Potter:

"In the evidence submitted to the Transport Commission yesterday afternoon by the second witness for the suburban local bodies, Mr Ernest Herbert Potter, Mayor of Mount Eden, the proposal for a transport board was dealt with at length.

"Mr Potter, in a written statement, dealt with the history of transport, making special reference to the period of private motor-bus enterprise. He said that the legislation to restrain private operations had been a severe setback to the outside districts, and bitter feeling developed because of the fact that the transport undertaking was vested in the body representative of the city only.

"The view taken was that the city had transport for its own requirements and was not greatly concerned about adjacent districts. There was also dissatisfaction as it was thought that the interests of the smaller local areas were being subordinated to the tramways. Regarding the negotiations between Mount Eden Borough Council and the City Council for extension of the Dominion Road and Mount Eden tramlines, Mr Potter said that the City Council had undoubtedly broken its agreement, and it appeared possible that the city ratepayers would reject future loans for extensions, as had been done last year.

"Mr Potter denied that there was any hostility between his borough and the city. He attributed the present troubles to the system of ownership and control…He regarded the tram services at present maintained on Mount Eden and Dominion Road routes as satisfactory, but said that the feeder buses beyond the termini were most unsatisfactory.

"Would you have buses running right into town? asked Mr Johnstone (for the City Council). Witness: Yes. And would you let them pick up passengers on the way? — Yes, subject to the penal fare.

"Mr Johnstone: Have you not said that transport is not a thing for municipalities at all, and did not your council actively support the bus proprietors? — Yes, but only for the outer areas, beyond the tramway routes…there was sufficient area and population outside the tram limits to support the buses…A settlement of the transport question would do much for trade, for health and for progress…and would remove the sense of injustice which so many people have at the present time." [189]

In its defence, the City Council continued to state its difficulties in terms of its lack of resources to serve the whole of the metropolitan area, as explained to the Commission by one of its Councillors, Mr Eady:

"L. A. Eady, a member of the Auckland City Council, in evidence, supported the idea of passenger transport, in common with other related public utilities serving the metropolitan area, being controlled and managed by a metropolitan aspect. He said that the transport services was a major regional utility and said that the present dissatisfaction with passenger transport facilities in the outer areas was not the result of mismanagement by the Auckland City Council, the Tramways Committee, or the tramways manager. It was rather the effect of the anomaly of a local body with but local powers and limited boundaries, endeavouring to serve an extensive metropolitan area without penalising its own ratepayers." [190]

This need for all of the Auckland region's transport system to be controlled by a single entity continued to be touched upon throughout the Transport Commission's hearings. As pointed out by Alfred George Lunn, former president of the Auckland Chamber of Commerce, in his submission to the Commission, such a controlling body was not a new concept in New Zealand:

"The problem does not arise in Wellington or Dunedin…because suburban local governing bodies have amalgamated with the city, but in the case of Auckland it is the general feeling of the commercial community that a public trading utility like transport, operating both in the city and in suburban local governing areas, should be in the hands of a permanent commission or elective board representative of the whole metropolitan area and not merely the area comprised within the city boundaries.

"That the question of extension of transport facilities to the outer area, was dependent upon the favourable vote of city ratepayers on a loan proposal was the position referred to by Mr Lunn in expressing the view that the majority of the city ratepayers were already adequately provided with transport facilities, and would not vote in favour of tramway extensions. He added that there was, at the present time, greater possibilities than in the past of extensions proving unremunerative and therefore, burdensome to the city but not to the outer suburban areas mainly concerned.

"This, he submitted, had accentuated the grievance of the outer areas against city control, and an additional grievance arose from the fact that the City Council had been largely responsible for the legislation inimical to motor-omnibus traffic. Many outer areas owe their recent expansion to the development of bus transport, Mr Lunn said and the taking over of such facilities by the city, followed by a drastic curtailment of transport facilities is regarded as an injustice by the people who have been induced by the previously existing services to settle in the outer area." [191]

As the Transport Commission hearings continued, so did the debate about the advantages and otherwise of an amalgamation of all the Auckland region's local bodies or a single transport authority to manage the transport needs of the entire Auckland region – the 'metropolitan scheme'.

"Two witnesses were before the Auckland Transport Commission this morning. Mr R G Clarke, ex-chairman of the One Tree Hill Road Board, who gave evidence for the outside local bodies, and Mr Tom Bloodworth, a former member of the Auckland City Council, who came forward as an independent witness to advocate the metropolitan scheme.

"It is impossible to secure satisfactory results under the present system of control by the City Council, said Mr Bloodworth...He considered that Greater Auckland in accordance with the council's idea would never be achieved by voluntary amalgamation, except when local authorities became embarrassed financially or otherwise, and in that case the City Council did not always want them. He did not think the Government would ever give consent to amalgamation by compulsion. If complete amalgamation came about voluntarily or by legislation, however, the council would be so overwhelmed by a mass of detail administration that it would be more impossible to give attention to larger matters than it had been in the recent past.

"Greater Auckland as proposed by the City Council is a dream impossible of realisation, said Mr Bloodworth, and even if it were possible it would not give the desired results in transport and other (illegible) matters. He added that a separate transport board would be in the same position as the council when it took over the tramway service in 1919, and would have a big undertaking on its hands, with no financial reserves and the need of immediate heavy expenditure.

"Mr Bloodworth said that the trams were now absolutely dependent on the Power Board for motive power; the Power Board drew a big revenue from the trams; the two services were interwoven, were in a sense the same service or the same kind of service; and the area served by the Power Board was approximately the area that should be served by a transport board. Both services would belong to the same people; the same ratepayers would be security for each, controlled by the one board; economy in administration would be possible, which would be very difficult if each were controlled by a separate body." [192]

While an amalgamation of power supply and tramway services were to be one of the alternatives suggested by the Transport Commission in its final report, the overall administrative role of such a body over the whole transport system posed too many difficulties and was therefore discounted.

In its report, the Commissioners provided an overview of how electric power had been supplied to the tramways from the beginning:

"Power for the tramways was supplied from a power-station in Hobson Street, and there was a substation at Green Lane Road, Epsom. In February, 1920, however, the Council gave effect to a proposal to combine the tramway power station with the electricity-supply system, and to generate the whole of the city and suburbs' requirements from the King's Wharf Power-station.

"In 1921 a proposal was made for the amalgamation of the city and surrounding bodies into one Power Board, and this culminated in the passing of the Auckland Electric-power Board Act, 1921-22, which provided for the sale of the electrical undertaking of the Auckland City Council to the Auckland Electric-power Board, the date of the transfer being 30th June, 1921; but it was not until the 31st March, 1924, that the tramway system commenced to purchase all its power from the Auckland Electric-power Board." [193]

Continuing his evidence to the Transport Commission:

"Mr Bloodworth said that the city had failed to meet the bus competition, because it adopted the wrong methods, and it secured the legislation to control private enterprise only after a strenuous two years of work. Witness referred to the report of Mr W. E. Bush, city engineer, prepared after an investigation abroad in 1919, and said that the portion regarding roads had been adopted, with the result that concrete thoroughfares had been rapidly laid down, but the warning regarding bus competition was ignored, showing how blind the council was in providing roads that gave the opening for competition without seeking protection by legislation." [194]

That competition provided by unregulated, private bus companies, running more than 100 buses on chosen, profitable routes, reached its peak in late 1926 when the Motor-omnibus Traffic Act of that year came into force. By then, even the City Council's own fleet of some thirty motor buses imported new from England to provide feeder services to the tram routes had become a burden, with their running costs reducing the annual profit that the tram services had always made on their own. At the same time, commuters travelling to and from the growing, outer suburbs soon grew tired of changing between trams and feeder buses at the tram termini.

Understandably, they preferred to be able to commute by means of a single mode of conveyance and not have to jostle for another seat half way to work or home.

As more concrete roads extended to suburbia, beyond the reach of the tram, private motor buses soon became that mode of convenient conveyance. This competition and the loss incurred by the Council's own bus fleet resulted in an overall tramways loss of £15,474 for the year ending 31 March 1925 – the first loss ever recorded by the Auckland Electric Tramway system. [195]

With the passing of the 1926 Motor-omnibus Traffic Act, "It was the option of the (private) bus-owners to either sell their vehicles to the Corporation (Auckland City Council), or retain them and operate them subject to the provisions of the Act." [196]

Most bus companies opted for the latter so that "The eventual position was that the Council was loaded with 106 buses, comprising eleven various types in varying conditions. The amount paid for the buses, land, garages, and plant taken over was £61,507." [197]

However, while the Council was able to overcome most of its competition by buying it, "Owing to their general unsuitability and disrepair is found it necessary to maintain fifty-two of the 106 buses taken over so that sufficient can be relied upon to actively operate. This leaves fifty-four buses which, due to their state of repair and unsuitability, are not being used. The evidence showed that it has cost the Council £12,500 to rehabilitate the buses taken over. The accounts for the year ended 31st

March, 1928, show that the tram section, after providing for interest, sinking fund, and all payments, resulted in a credit of £18,943, and the bus section on the same basis a loss of £64,029." [198]

Consequently, during the hearings before the Auckland Transport Commission, the City Council was anxious to convince the Commission that a single body (preferably the Council) should be responsible for the management and regulation of all forms of transport operating throughout the whole Auckland region. This concept was of course tantamount to adopting the utopian ideal of the 'metropolitan scheme' referred to earlier as a 'dream too far'.

This became increasingly obvious as the various representatives of Auckland's suburban local bodies spoke to the Commission of their mistrust of the City Council's motives. Much of this mistrust stemmed from the introduction of the 1926 Motor-omnibus Traffic Act which the local bodies believed "...was and is the special instrument of the Auckland City Council, and was enacted solely on considerations relating to the Auckland City Council. This belief has made its contribution to the atmosphere of mistrust which prevails in Auckland." [199]

"The case for the suburban local bodies was continued before the Transport Commission yesterday afternoon, when further argument was advanced in opposition to feeder bus services...Putting forward the views of the New Lynn Town Board, Walter Leigh Titchener (chairman) claimed private enterprise ran buses at a lower running cost than the City Council. The (Town) board believed that had the latter not interfered with transport facilities in its district, it would still be enjoying a satisfactory service, which would have a tendency to become stronger with increased population.

"The board was of the opinion that all buses on the main highway should run right through to the city from the outer districts. Feeder services were detrimental to the adequacy and efficiency of services, and seriously impaired their earning power. In addition, there was no adequate saving in running costs, and passengers were greatly inconvenienced." [200]

There were men of broader vision heard by the Commission...men who saw beyond the inconvenience of feeder services and the savings of shillings and pence that were promised by town boards and local bodies:

"I think that the boundaries of the City of Auckland should be extended so as to include all local districts between the Waitemata and Manukau harbours and between the Tamaki and the Whau, said Mr Alfred S. Bankart, merchant, of Auckland, in giving evidence at the Transport Commission to-day.

"Mr Bankart said that he had been closely associated with two former mayors — Sir John Logan Campbell and Sir Arthur Myers. He strongly favoured the Greater Auckland scheme originally brought down by Sir Arthur Myers, and considered that there should be one strong central body administering municipal affairs in the area included within the extended boundaries.

"Witness said that considerable economy should thus be achieved, by reduction of overhead expenses and greater efficiency in management. To bring under one control all municipal activities, including the trading utilities, witness said, would tend to lessen and possibly, to destroy the jealousy and ill-will which existed when local bodies dealt with the city and even amongst themselves.

"In the amalgamations that had taken place there had been a gain to the districts concerned and also to the city, and none of the amalgamated areas wished to secede. Witness did not favour the setting up of separate boards to deal with public utilities, because of the multiplicity of control that would follow, and also because valuable sources of revenue would be removed from the municipal council.

"To the chairman (Mr J. S. Barton, S.M.) witness said that, as the development of Auckland approached the ideal of contiguous local bodies, there would gradually be a willingness on the part of the suburban boroughs to hand over their responsibilities to a major body." [201]

While the greater argument brought before the Transport Commission related to the competition that had arisen between the City's trams and motor buses, there was the occasional mention of a greater threat to both public transport services – the private motor car:

"The varying fortunes of a bus venture in the Birkenhead district were outlined (to the Auckland Transport Commission) by Mr Thomas Smith, manager of the Marine Suburbs Bus Company.

"According to Mr Smith a horse-drawn bus service was started in 1914 and was subsequently converted into a motor bus service. The service operated at the outset under subsidy from the borough council, but later a limited liability company was formed. The company paid no dividend for the first two years, six per cent for the next two years, ten per cent for five years, on a paid-up capital of £2200. In 1924 the company was reconstructed and the nominal capital of the present company is £20,000. The service was always acknowledged to be in the first rank. Efficiency was its first consideration.

"In 1925 opposition appeared for the first time and before the matter was adjusted by the Licensing Authority and Transport Appeal Board the company had suffered a loss of £2000. Higher fares, operating in 1927, gave the company better prospects, but on account of the opposition of 'pirate' motor cars the company decided to withdraw the whole of the service on February 29 of this year (1928), and since then the district has been without adequate transport service." [202]

But it was not just the conveyance of passengers that needed some form of organisation and regulation. As the Auckland Transport Commission hearings drew to a close, there was also the matter of the regulation of heavy goods traffic to consider. As motor lorries became larger and their loads heavier, their transportation of goods along less robust roads needed to be consistently regulated throughout the Auckland region.

After six weeks of hearings, the Commission had heard enough of the need for the formation of a 'greater Auckland' to solve the region's transport problems but here was an instance where a fragmented regulatory regime would certainly prove to be impractical:

"With the object of proving that the regulation of heavy traffic in the Auckland metropolitan district by a number of small local authorities acting independently was not in the best interests of the public or the carriers, and was in many respects impracticable, a lengthy statement was produced by William Edward Anderson, secretary of the Auckland Master Carriers' Association.

"The main point was that the regulations relating to classification of roads should not apply in the Auckland metropolitan area. A scheme was outlined for the protection of the more lightly constructed roads and streets and the administration of the motor-lorry regulations in that area. It was suggested in that connection that a central authority should be appointed as an Auckland Metropolitan Traffic Control Board, either under the wing of the Auckland City Council or the Public Works Department, or as a newly-constituted body, but preferably under the City Council.

"Such authority should be empowered to declare any road in the area to be not available for any through traffic exceeding a certain weight, and running beyond a given speed. The authority should also fix suitable signs to any roads to which such declarations applied, and should administer generally the motor regulations in the area, including the employment of inspectors. It was suggested that under the scheme outlined all roads would be available for the use of all motor vehicles, subject to certain restrictions, so long as they were engaged in carting goods into or out of an area, but heavy through traffic would be compelled to use the roads best able to carry it." [203]

The final sitting of the Auckland Transport Commission occurred on 14 June 1928, as described by The New Zealand Herald:

"The three commissioners solemnly took their seats again yesterday, when Mr Barton, addressing an audience of two, announced that no notice of further evidence had been given, and there was no reason why the hearing should not be formally closed. Good progress is being made with the compilation of the commission's report, which is returnable to the Governor-General by June 25. The commissioners are working long hours at their office at the Town Hall." [204]

But while the Commissioners worked so diligently, representatives of the city's suburban local bodies wasted no time recommending to their local bodies the Commission's expected finding that a Transport Board should be formed. They lobbied for City Council support but, as a first sign of its resistance to the relinquishing of its transport responsibilities, the Council would have none of it until the Commission had reported:

"Deeming the whole question *sub judice*, the Auckland City Council has declined to state its opinion on the proposals for a transport board laid before its representatives by those of the suburban bodies…the council is not prepared to express its opinion on the proposals…until the commission has given its report and recommendations.

"In the course of his final address, Mr Meredith (for the suburban bodies) said the transport board scheme submitted to the City Council this week, was an answer to the council's charge of unfriendliness on the suburban bodies' part. Their attitude, he claimed was entirely fair and reasonable. In the proposals they recognised the city was entitled, at any rate, at the outset, to a larger share of representation than the suburban districts. They also acknowledged the city had taken over the transport system at a time of crisis, and had done so in the interests of the whole metropolitan area. They did not seek to bargain about finance, but suggested the new board should simply occupy the City Council's position as a transport authority." [205]

So the stage was set with the players waiting in the wings – the suburban councils ready to rehearse as part of the transport board they expected would be recommended but the City Council, fearing the worse, only too willing to wait for direction. That direction came when the report of the Transport Commission was finally presented to Parliament on 27 July 1928.

The report provided a detailed overview of the task faced by the Commissioners and the various solutions they considered before indeed recommending the incorporation, by a special Act of Parliament, of an Auckland Transport Board to control the district's traffic:

"We believe that there should be one authority, with a virtual monopoly, owning and controlling transport facilities and transport within the said district, but with power, where it seems to that authority desirable, to permit and regulate private services which connect with the places outside its area." [206]

The Board was to consist of ten members, eventually to be elected by the ratepayers in the respective areas of:

(1) The City of Auckland as at present constituted (six members)
(2) The Boroughs of Mount Eden, Newmarket, and Mount Albert (two members)
(3) The Borough of Onehunga and the Road Districts of One Tree Hill, Mount Roskill, Panmure Township, and Mount Wellington, and the Town District of Ellerslie (two members) [207]

However, of all the possible solutions put to the Commission during its hearings, the creation of an Auckland Transport Board was not its first choice:

"To our minds the solution of this difficulty is a simple one. It lies in the voluntary abandonment of the parochial and arbitrary boundary-lines and the amalgamation of all the contiguous local authorities with the city. We can find no other opinion expressed by any outside and impartial observer." [208]

"...evidence was adduced from a body of responsible well-informed citizens who are working towards the ideal of civic unity and are satisfied that their efforts will tend to the fulfilment of the hopes that we have herein expressed. In the case of two of the witnesses, for instance, we led them to the logical conclusion of their scheme with some attention to detail, and each admitted that it involved the eventual disappearance of the present local bodies and the institution of a bicameral form of self-government for Greater Auckland. We are satisfied that that ideal must be attained, and when it is, it does not much matter what name is given to the civic authority that embodies and administers the ideal.

"The district covered by the Transport Board whose constitution we have advocated contains ten municipal authorities, 103 Councillors, five Mayors, five Chairman of local bodies, ten administrative officers, and ten staffs of municipal officers, with the relative engineers, road foremen, works foremen, legal and other professional advisors. All of those persons have immediate relations and friends.

"In those districts where the separationist policy holds sway, these persons and their friends, with their personal ambitions and personal interests, constitute a formidable group of citizens, unified by these ambitions and interests, keenly awake to their protection. So far, they are likely to be assisted in preserving the existing state of things by the natural conservation and the usual apathy of the remaining citizens of their areas.

"This is the problem that lies before those who wish to educate the community to the adoption of better methods." [209]

While the amalgamation of all the local bodies to form one municipal city was their prime recommendation, that solution was one of five considered by the Commissioners and which included:

"(1) That the ownership and control of the transport facilities should be left with the Auckland City Council…

"(2) As in (1), but advantage taken and use made of the provisions of sections 49 to 54 of the Municipal Corporations Act, 1920. The suggestion is that, pursuant to these provisions, members of the adjoining local authorities should become co-opted members of the Tramway Committee of the Auckland City Council.

"(3) The city's boundaries might be enlarged by the absorption of the independent contiguous local bodies, until its political area is nearly, if not quite, coincident with the area of the transport district as already defined.

"(4) A new Board or other controlling body could be created to take over the control of transport facilities within the traffic district as already defined.

"(5) As a variation of method (4), the powers and rights of an existing Board—viz., the Auckland Electric-power Board—might be enlarged so as to enable it to take over transport as one of its functions, and thereby avoid the disadvantages attaching to the creation of another body with borrowing and rating powers." [210]

By a process of elimination, the Commission finally opted for the Transport Board but, "…we have to say that we are of opinion that that method which we believe to be best in principle must be eliminated as politically impossible. We refer to method (3), which involves the creation of Greater Auckland.

"It has been made abundantly clear to us by the evidence that there is no chance at all of the citizens of Auckland district agreeing at the present time or in the near future to amalgamate all the local bodies into one city. We agree with the opinion expressed by many witnesses that there should be no attempt to effect that purpose by legislative compulsion.

"We think that any attempt in that direction would be viewed as a violation of the principle of self-government in a matter in which the principle should rule, and that this would raise such a spirit of discontent and resentment as would make the working and administration of the new body impossible.

"We have elsewhere expressed our opinion of what we believe to be the narrow, short-sighted policy, the lack of true civic pride and public spirit, which magnifies the importance of any local benefits that may attach to the present system and is blind to the advantages of amalgamation. This is a matter which is entirely in the hands of the citizens of Auckland and district, and until a spirit of co-operation and unity has been cultivated sufficiently to dissipate the present unhappy and arbitrary divisions the discord and difficulties which are inherent in those divisions will continue...

"That leaves us with one method, and it becomes our affirmative proposal. We accept it and put it forward with regret, because we have been led to it not by the constructive application of positive principles, but by a progressive elimination that leaves nothing else. The problem that we have to meet arises out of modern traffic developments, and it is an urgent problem. As we have already pointed out, it will not wait until the civic constitution of the people affected will allow it to be related to modern methods of municipal administration: we have therefore no alternative but to relate it to older methods." [211]

Referring in their report to the constitution of the city's Water and Electricity Boards as previous examples of the city's disunity, the Commissioners viewed their proposed Transport Board as a compromise.

"If the terms 'transport facilities' and 'Transport Board' are substituted for 'water' and 'Water Board', that extract describes accurately the position as it reveals itself to us. The eyes are still shut, and the arguments for an ad hoc unity are still based on difficulties that are born of an alliance of disunity and suspicion." [212]

Unfortunately, the leaders of Auckland's various municipalities were to lack a collective vision for many decades and, as a result, the city's growing population would never experience the transport alternatives available to the citizens of the more advanced cities of the world.

In the meantime, the Commissioners recommended "...that the Board shall take over as a going concern, as from the 1st April, 1928, the tramway and motor-omnibus services of the Auckland City Council, with all the assets, rights, and equipment, on the basis of the City's Tramway Department balance-sheet as on the 31st March, 1928." [213]

It was the opinion of the Commissioners that "...for localities within the tram termini the tram itself affords the most suitable form of transport.

"For mass transport in city and closely settled suburban areas there is a clear preponderance of evidence in favour of the view that the tram-car is the best form of conveyance. It is, as compared with other forms of transport on similar work, reliable, safe, and cheap. Its carrying unit is a car with a large seating capacity. Its ability to carry great loads at peak time was expressed before us somewhat epigrammatically in the statement that 'it may be overcrowded, but it cannot be overloaded'.

"There was some evidence to the contrary; there was some evidence in favour of the petrol-driven motor-omnibus; but there is easily a great preponderance of the view we have expressed, and we find accordingly.

"For services beyond the tram termini, the pneumatic-tired petrol-driven motor-omnibus is by an equally general consensus of opinion the best form of transport as a public conveyance for passengers." [214]

If only the boundary between the patronage of trams and the motor buses could be so finely defined but, of course, it couldn't – simply because commuters to and from the suburbs not served by the trams were understandably reluctant to change from one to the other service part way through their journey. The fare disparity between the tram and bus services on different routes also made anything other than a through service completely impractical yet a bus route that paralleled a tramway for any distance would continue to perpetuate the wasteful competition the Commissioners sought to eliminate.

If the various local bodies of Auckland could not agree to provide the wherewithal to provide for the efficient management of district-wide transport regime, then the Commissioners hoped that its suggested Transport Board would, with its "...exclusive right to construct, manage, maintain, and operate tramways, and shall have the exclusive right to maintain, manage, and operate motor-and-horse-omnibus services, and any like passenger service, by any vehicle plying or standing for hire for the conveyance of passengers at separate fares within the said district..." [215]

In its summation of the Transport Commissioner's report, The New Zealand Herald was certainly of the opinion that the Commission had done the best it could:

"Too lengthy to be considered in any more detail, the report can be summed up as a judicial and practical finding in the transport position of Auckland. The central recommendation, that of a transport board, is not the ideal solution, as the commission frankly confesses. By the manner in which it delivers its finding it shows how acutely and clearly it has summed up strength and weakness in the situation it surveyed, and engenders confidence in the proposals it makes for handling the transport problem of Auckland in the future." [216]

But even if the city in question was other than Auckland, there were bound to be those who felt anything but confidence in the Commission's proposals. Understandably, those representing the motor bus interests were somewhat apprehensive:

"The finding of the commission has caused the Passenger Transport Company to ask what its position will be in running its services under two licensing authorities. Mr N. B. Spencer, chairman of directors of the company, said the formation of a board was a satisfactory move, but he considered difficulties would arise with regard to the company's services which would not be wholly in the board's district.

"Part of the run would come within the Otahuhu Borough Council district and, from the company's viewpoint, it would have been a great advantage to include Otahuhu in the board's district. At present the company's services all came within the No. 1 Licensing Authority's area and he questioned whether compensation would be available for the company should it be unable to comply with the conditions of licences issued by the board. The company would be running under licence from a board which would own the trains and would be competitors." [217]

However, before a Transport Board of any sort could be established, the City Council and the adjacent local bodies had to agree on how that could best be done. According to The New Zealand Herald of 29 August 1928, that would not happen until 'certain fundamental facts' were acknowledged:

"Though the first meeting between the City Council and the suburban representatives, to consider the Transport Commission's report, was unable to make even the first step toward a conclusion, the discussion was not wholly unprofitable. It revealed very clearly the impossibility of proceeding with a conference including the whole personnel of the City Council, and it emphasised the necessity of recognition by the council that, if any progress is to be made, it must acknowledge certain fundamental facts.

"The first is that the subject of the commission's report and the subject for consideration by the conference is not the ownership and operation of the municipal transport system, but the problem of passenger transport in Greater Auckland. The second is that the responsibility for that transport must be spread over Greater Auckland... it does require the council to formulate a precise conception of its views." [218]

Unfortunately, the issue of 'ownership and operation of the municipal transport system' remained a priority for some councillors who, as part of their attempt to retain control, sought justification for their views from the ratepayers by means of a tramway loan which, if granted, would perpetuate the status quo. In the meantime, vacillation and confusion reigned:

"Another deadlock has been the unfortunate result of last night's meeting of the City Council and representatives of the suburban local bodies. From the council side there came the suggestion that the city ratepayers should be asked to sanction a tramway loan. If they did so, the council would continue to carry on its transport enterprise: if the loan were rejected, then the transport board would be accepted.

"If the council, or those members who favour the suggestion, mean this as a test of the whole issue, they propose to offer it in an impracticable way, for a loan referred to the ratepayers in those circumstances would not have the faintest possible chance of acceptance; not because the ratepayers are necessarily strongly in favour of a transport board, but because they would undoubtedly refuse to endorse loan proposals offered in such an atmosphere of unreality.

"In any event the suburban bodies would have none of the new idea. They demanded a transport board or nothing, an attitude that normally would favour their having the second choice — nothing — granted.

"Viewed from the angle of the general public, the position seems to be that the City Council cannot make up its mind to any policy. It is divided in its counsels. A majority is obviously hostile to the plan which has become a fixed idea with the other local bodies. Between them the parties have produced a simple deadlock, as was shown at last night's meeting.

"Meantime the transport system, which admittedly needs reorganisation and more equipment, gets neither. Through the antagonism between the parties the public of the Greater Auckland area stands to suffer more than it did in the period of worst confusion." [219]

Many of the City's leaders appeared to treat the proposals of the Auckland Transport Commissioners as a starting point from which to float their own ideas of how the City's transportation problems could best be alleviated. This was despite the exhaustive and expensive inquiries undertaken by the Transport Commission – a recurring response to such studies that was to hamper the progress of too many municipal and national causes.

Some observed the futility of it all, as reported by The New Zealand Herald on 14 September 1928:

"All the proposals are panic proposals — grasping at straws, said Mr T. Bloodworth, who, in addressing a meeting last evening under the auspices of the Remuera Ratepayers' Association, censured the City Council's suggested alternatives to plain adoption of the Transport Commission's report. He made an appeal to the parties affected by the finding of the commission to meet in conference on a basis of equal representation for the purposes of discussion.

"No one can say just what the report of the Transport Commission cost, said Mr Bloodworth…The cost, must, however, be in the region of £4000 to £5000. Whether it is worth it, the future will decide. The main recommendation of the commission upon which all the report rests is for a special transport board, and that the City Council is not prepared to accept, said Mr Bloodworth.

"Instead, it puts forward proposals, some of which are expressly ruled out by the commission and others which have been rejected by the ratepayers and local bodies. For, instance, the City Council, after arguing all along that the ratepayers of outer local bodies shared no responsibility in transport service, now suggested city ratepayers should again be asked to sanction a loan of £500,000 which had previously been rejected." [220]

Finally, some two months after the publication of the Transport Commission's findings, "The Auckland City Council, at a special meeting...unanimously approved of a decision previously made in committee, to approve of the findings of the Transport Commission in regard to a transport board..." [221]

As a result, agreement was soon reached between the Council and the suburban local bodies with the Auckland Star reporting:

"...the Auckland transport problem is much nearer solution, as the formation of a transport board has been agreed upon, and steps are to be taken to secure the necessary local legislation to bring it into force." [222]

A week later, opposition to the setting up of a transport board had been overcome and the Auckland Transport Board Bill had been drafted:

"The Auckland Transport Board Bill, containing 89 clauses, which has been prepared by the City Council and outside local bodies, follows very closely the recommendations of the Transport Commission.

"The district under which the board will have jurisdiction comprises the Auckland city, the boroughs of Mount Eden, Mount Albert, Newmarket and Onehunga, the Road districts of One Tree Hill, Mount Roskill, Mount Wellington and the town districts of Ellerslie and Panmure. Provision is made for the inclusion of other districts on agreement of the board and the local body concerned. There will be ten members of the board, six representing the city, two representing Mount Eden, Mount Albert and Newmarket, and the other two the remaining districts.

"All the City Council's tramway and bus business is to he handed over to the board, including loan undertakings and sinking fund. The board is to have a transport monopoly in its district, but has power to license private buses." [223]

By early October, only a few amendments were needed to ready the Auckland Transport Board Bill for its Parliamentary introduction:

"Agreement was reached this morning at the final conference of representatives of the Auckland City Council, the suburban local bodies and the Auckland members of Parliament concerning the Auckland Transport Bill. It has been agreed that the first board shall be nominated, and that it will hold office until the municipal elections in 1931. The constituent local authorities are to have the right to appoint new members to the board if they so desire after the elections to be held next May

"The proposal to set up a transport board to control passenger transport in the metropolitan area is to be subject to the approval of the ratepayers in the suburban districts, who are to take a poll on the question when the city ratepayers are being asked to give their sanction to the scheme. A clause is to be introduced into the bill to safeguard existing bus services, such as those conducted by the Passenger Transport Company and by Mr Keys." [224]

The Auckland Transport Board Bill was passed as the Auckland Transport Board Act 1928 in the early hours of 6 October 1928. Some of the Act's defining clauses included:

"*3. Constitution of district---*

*(1) The City of Auckland, together with the Boroughs of Mount Eden, Mount Albert, Newmarket, and Onehunga, the Road Districts of One Tree Hill, Mount Roskill, Mount Wellington, and Panmure Township, and the Town District of Ellerslie shall for the purposes of this Act form one district, to be known as the Auckland Transport District.*

"*57. Board to purchase transport undertaking of Auckland City Council---(1) The Board shall on a date to be arranged between the Board and the City Council, but within one calendar month from the date of the first meeting of the Board, take over as a going concern the tramway and motor-omnibus undertaking of the City Council, with all lands, buildings, plant, and other assets used and enjoyed in connection therewith, including all sinking funds held on behalf of the City Council in respect of loans relating to the undertaking, and with the benefit and subject to the burden of all contracts and obligations of the City Council in connection therewith, including the loan indebtedness of the City Council in relation to the said undertaking.*

"*(2) The said undertaking shall be taken over by the Board as from the first day of April, nineteen hundred and twenty-eight, and the City Council shall be deemed as from that date to have been carrying on the same for and on behalf of the Board, and all payments made, moneys received, and obligations entered into by the City Council in relation thereto, including subsidies and other commitments and undertakings in favour of the employees or any association of the*

*employees in the said undertaking, shall be deemed to have been so made, received, and entered into on behalf of the Board, and the City Council shall account and be entitled to indemnity accordingly.*
Powers of Board
*"58. Board to have sole and exclusive right to construct and operate transport undertaking---Subject to the provisions of this Act, the Board, upon taking over the tramway and motor-omnibus undertaking of the City Council, shall, notwithstanding any provision to the contrary contained in any Act, have the sole and exclusive right to own, acquire, construct, maintain, manage, and operate tramways, and shall also have the sole and exclusive right to maintain, manage, and operate motor-and horse-omnibus services and any like public-passenger-conveyance services by any vehicle plying or standing for hire for the conveyance of passengers at separate fares within the district:*
*"Provided that the Board may from time to time and for such period, not exceeding five years, and subject to such conditions as the Board may impose, grant to any person the right to maintain, manage, and operate motor-or horse-omnibus services or any like public-passenger-conveyance services within the district and require the payment of fees in respect of such right, whether by way of annual fees or otherwise."* [225]

However, the Auckland Transport Board Act 1928 was not to take effect until certain approvals were obtained, including:
*"76. City Council may approve Act---(1) Nothing in this Act contained shall have any force or effect, and the polls mentioned in this section shall not be taken unless and until the City Council by resolution approves this Act, and the City Council shall within fourteen days from the passing of this Act hold a special meeting to consider and determine such question.*

*(2) The City Council shall within forty-two days from the passing of this Act take a poll of the ratepayers of the City of Auckland upon the question as to whether or not this Act shall come into operation.*

*(3) The local authorities of the constituent districts other than the City Council shall within forty-two days from the passing of this Act take a poll of their respective ratepayers upon the question as to whether or not this Act shall come into operation.*

*(4) Such polls shall be taken under the provisions of the Local Elections and Polls Act, 1925, and all the provisions of that Act shall apply accordingly."* [226]

Fortunately, for the future of Auckland transport, the majority of the City Council and those City and suburban ratepayers, who bothered to vote, approved of the Transport Act, as reported by the Auckland Star:

"Approval of the Auckland Transport Board Act was expressed at a special meeting of the Auckland City Council yesterday afternoon, after a discussion had taken place. When a vote was taken there were three dissentients, Messrs. W. H. Murray, A. J. Stallworthy and G. Knight. It was decided to take a poll of the city ratepayers on October 31, provided that that date was suitable for the suburban local bodies for the taking of a poll in their; areas." [227]

"The ratepayers in the city and suburbs decided yesterday by a big majority that the proposed Auckland Transport Board should be set up to control transport. The aggregate voting showed that there were nearly six to one in favour of the proposal. A feature of the polls was the unanimity of ratepayers that a transport board should be established, although only about 17 per cent of the ratepayers on the collective rolls recorded their votes." [228]

The inaugural meeting of the Auckland Transport Board took place on the morning of 22 December 1928. At that meeting, John Allum was elected as the Board's founding chairman, a position he was to hold until 1943, and Mr G. Baildon was appointed his deputy. The remainder of that first Board comprised Messrs E. J. Phelan, M. J. Coyle, A. J. Entrican, G. Ashley, F. S. Morton, J. Wood, E. H. Potter and L. E. Rhodes.

"After thanking the members for electing him as the first chairman, Mr Allum reviewed the recent history of transport in Auckland, and said they were about to conclude the largest and probably the most important transaction which has taken place in the history of Auckland. In the first place, said Mr Allum, I desire to say that the members elected by the City Council accept their positions not as delegates of the City Council, but as members of a partnership created to deal with transport problems in the Auckland metropolitan district.

"The Motor-omnibus Traffic Act, 1926, no longer has effect in this district, and under its own special Act this board has wide powers in dealing with traffic matters. In this connection, the board, in issuing licenses to private operators, can make terms and conditions which, while being just and fair to the private operators, will not prejudice the board as owner of the public utility." [229]

Unfortunately for the new Transport Board, the management and regulation of Auckland's public transport was not to be as straightforward as all that. During the time taken to decide on and then form a Board, commuters had become increasingly used to the motor bus services which not only extended almost to their door but were also so much quicker than taking a tram. And, as explained by 'Anti-Waste' in a letter to The New Zealand Herald, published 11 January 1929, time is money:

"Sir, —In reading the account in the Herald of business transacted at the new Transport Board meeting I was particularly struck by the statement that 50 more trams were needed and another £500,000 to complete proposed extensions, etc. As a large city ratepayer I suggest that before we make too many permanent extensions and irrevocably sink money in them we want to have a jolly good think.

"I have asked numbers of people affected as to their opinions of the extensions and in most cases the reply is, 'Oh, good idea, it will increase values in our street. Will it pay? Oh, I don't think so because most of us use the bus, as it saves a lot of time.'

"Now this is the wrong idea. If the trams are not going to pay we are better without them; high land values are, on the whole, bad. My eyes have been opened during the last four years to the enormous waste of passengers' time in trams. In my own case I could not afford to come into town by tram, even if the extension was made right through to my door and the Kohimarama bus service was compelled to charge an exorbitant penal fare.

"A business man's time around about nine in the morning and six at night is worth a lot more than 2d or even 6d for 15 to 30 minutes wasted. The Kohimarama bus service delivers me home in 15 to 17 minutes, whereas I could not get home by the trams, as at present run, even with the extension from the Remuera terminus, in under 35 minutes, if all goes well — 40 minutes would be nearer the time. In four years' travelling on the buses I have never once been delayed a minute and am so pleased with the service that, except on special occasions, I never consider coming into town in my own car. (The saving on a similar lone run like Onehunga is also about 20 minutes.)

"If the present type of tram extensions are made and the Kohimarama and such-like services refused a licence for these areas the result will be that people like myself will go into town in our own motor-cars and the present bad traffic congestion will be made worse, to the detriment of all, including the trams." [230]

As well as the motor buses, the tramway system was also under threat from the 'trackless tram' – the trolley bus powered by the same electrical grid that served the railed trams. Trolley buses were first introduced at Wellington by the City Council in 1924 but replaced by the more manoeuvrable motor buses about eight years later. Nevertheless, to the 1929 commuter aboard an Auckland tram, the trackless tram still promised so much more convenience, the saving of time and, perhaps ahead of its time, an economy of resources – as observed by 'Anti-Waste':

"We certainly want to use New Zealand power if possible. With all our roads concreted wherever the trams go is it not practical to have some form of trackless trams, which could be used in the same way as the Kohimarama buses, on long distance through trips, first stop, say, Victoria Avenue.

"This is not possible at present, as they follow behind each other, and the slowest every-stop-tram sets the speed of the fastest. Apart from mere passengers the holding up and the wearing out of brakes of commercial trucks, etc., due to trams wrongly stopping in the middle of the road is a big loss to commerce. With trackless trams they could pull up at the side of the road and more trips would be made with the same tram, and would naturally need less men and trams to give better service. The enormous total of passengers' time saved would go a long way toward scrapping a lot of the old and inefficient tramway methods of transportation. Anti-Waste." [231]

While most Auckland commuters seemed obsessed with the time that could be saved by driving their own automobile or catching the bus, instead of the tram, an Auckland Star article of 15 January 1929 sought to bring them back to earth with a description of what once had been:

"Auckland's trams and municipal buses will be formally taken over by the newly-formed Transport Board to-morrow. The board is now actually in possession, but to-morrow is the formal and legal date upon which the change-over starts.

"Methods of transport are just now matters of the keenest difference of opinion, and nobody can prophesy the outcome, but all can agree that the board has come into existence at an extremely interesting time. There has been such a tremendous change in the methods of transport since the city of Auckland had tramways that people who were not born before the days of the motor car and the motor bus can have no idea of the leisurely way Auckland used to get about in the 'eighties, and even in the 'nineties.

"When one is whisked from one side of the town to the other in a fleet taxi one wonders how old Aucklanders could afford the time to make a leisurely voyage out to Onehunga, say, in one of those four-wheelers—the last of which departed from Shortland Street a year or so ago.

"And then the horse buses. The journey from Queen Street to Parnell or the Three Lamps occupied more time than most city workers now devote to their lunch. Those quaint old vehicles used to go down Queen Street at a sober walk, picking up passengers and breaking into a decorous trot when the Customs Street corner was reached. One does not remember that any of the drivers ever had to face a charge of furious driving.

"It was in 1884 that Aucklanders first had the privilege of riding in a tram car, a horse-drawn one, but still, a tram car, with a real conductor and tickets, and all. Looking at a photograph of one of these strange little contraptions one realises that they must have been very small. There were only five windows aside and each window meant a passenger. Five people on the platform meant a crowd. As the wheels were very near the middle and there was a good overhang fore and aft, this weight on the platform caused the vehicle, travelling at anything over two knots, to pitch exactly like a boat in a swell. These strange ark-like affairs were drawn by two horses, with an extra one hitched on at the foot of Wellesley Street for the pull uphill.

"A tram horse, when it was retired from the track, was generally considered to be the last word in 'doneness'. However, Aucklanders got a lot of pleasure out of this stone-age method of transport, and old hands still recall with something like awe the enormous crowds that used to be carried when there was a specially exciting football match at Potter's Paddock, which is the Alexandra Park of to-day. But Auckland must have trams, and the new Transport Board takes over at a time when it requires very sound management indeed, and also vision to keep the system abreast of the great changes that are taking place all over the world." [232]

By 1929, the government-owned railway service to those suburbs north and west of the city was also set to expand. Construction of the new train station at Beach Road was due to be completed by the end of 1930 and, although it would soon be cancelled, the old proposal to construct a tunnel under the city to link up with the northern line at Morningside, with another station at the Town Hall, was then very much a possibility.

But for many commuters such as 'Anti-Waste' the expectation of an efficient and cost-effective transport solution was not to be met by the new Transport Board's preferred choice of railed over motor transport. Despite its protestations to the contrary, the Board seemed to be mesmerised by the glare of tram headlights and the legacy system's need for more rolling stock and extended lines.

The Auckland Star summed up the situation in its publications of the 17th and 18th of January 1929:

"Although many buses have been provided for under the old tramway policy, which, by the way, has also been placed before the Transport Board, it is quite clear that the main recommendations are for a large loan expenditure in regard to trams. Considering the present state of the public mind, it is doubtful whether a loan of this character would be sanctioned by the ratepayers. The public will want to know, and rightly so, what the board proposes to do in respect to the huge losses on bus services before they agree to further loan expenditure." [233]

"The Board had before it last night three major proposals—a programme of extensions and additions to cost £638,000, a change to universal threepenny fare, and the introduction of electric trolley buses. It wisely decided that its duty was to provide additions to rolling-stock and urgent extensions of lines, before considering any readjustment of fares. The Board can hardly go beyond the advice of its expert advisers, and these are against the introduction of another form of vehicle.

"The great problem before the Board is tramway extension, and the first task of the Board is to define the lengths to which this should go. It cannot be expected to do this at one meeting, or even in two, yet the matter is urgent; for necessary works should be put in hand at once, and provision made for the extra plant. From the tramway point of view the situation is improved by the creation of the Board, for the city ratepayer is no longer expected to back extensions put in for the benefit of outside districts, but the question how far trams should be used for long distance transport is as difficult as ever to decide."

"Take the Dominion Road and Mount Eden Road extensions. They would serve a growing district and be a great convenience to people who now have to take a feeder bus. But how far beyond should trams eventually go? Mr Ford says that these extensions will relieve feeder buses. But as settlement thickens beyond these termini, will not the demand for feeder buses from these points grow? And what is the policy to be about through buses from the city? The sound general policy is a judicious mixture of trams and buses, but just where the line should be drawn it is extremely difficult to say. Moreover, the policy of extension both of trams and buses in the western suburbs should be partly governed by the new railway line." [234]

Of course, while the debate raged, the proverbial horse, in the form of an increasingly mobile population attempting to make some progress along the City's congested streets, had already bolted and time was quickly running out. Some, like 'Safety First' who had his or her Letter to the Editor published by The New Zealand Herald on 23 January 1929, seemed to see more practical solutions somewhat quicker than the Transport Board seemed likely to:

"Sir, — Now that the Transport Board is likely to extend some of the tramlines would it not be a good idea, in the interest of pedestrians and traffic alike, to lay the new lines close to the footpaths on each side of the road, then passengers could step from the tramcar on to the footpaths. All vehicular traffic would then be in the centre of the road, and so do away with traffic having to stop for tramcars, and eliminate any further need for safety zones. In this way the maximum of safety would be afforded tram passengers, and traffic would be speeded up on the roads and so avoid congestion. Safety First." [235]

But while the Transport Board had some logical reasons for simply extending the tramway before venturing into new transport frontiers, it did so by ignoring overseas trends that promised future flexibility similar to that suggested by 'Safety First'..."The adoption of trackless electric trams was opposed by the Auckland Transport Board last evening, when, in so far as Auckland is concerned, it had adverse reports before it from the (tramways) general manager, Mr A. E. Ford, and the (tramways) engineer, Mr F. E. de Guerrier.

"Mr Ford said the railless electric trolley buses were developed in England a few years before the war, but during the war no progress was made. During recent years further development had taken place in England, and to a lesser degree in America, and to-day high-powered vehicles, both single and double deck, fitted with air brakes, and a body similar in design to a petrol-bus body, were manufactured. A low loading-line chassis had also been evolved for these vehicles much on the same lines as a modern omnibus chassis.

"The railless car was installed as a substitute (for obsolete trams), making use of the overhead equipment, electric supply service, and also the permanent pavement put down by the local authority. It was generally agreed that many of the small towns would not have had trams in the first instance had motor-omnibuses been available to give the necessary transport facilities. Having installed electric tramways it was more economical to make use of overhead trolley equipment with railless omnibuses than to dismantle the trolley wires and feeders, and to provide petrol omnibuses.

"The principal advantages of electric omnibuses were simplicity and reliability of equipment, which was similar to that of a tramcar; elimination of gear changing; low maintenance costs compared with motor-buses; and operation by electric power produced in the country instead of by imported fuel.

"Their principal disadvantages were that they must be operated on certain fixed routes and they had not the flexibility of a petrol omnibus, while where trolley wire equipment with the necessary feeders did not exist, this had to be provided, and represented additional capital costs... it appeared that the transport position in the board's area did not warrant the installation of another type of vehicle, but could be best and most economically dealt with by modern tramcars and modern petrol buses.

"The chairman, Mr J. A. C. Allum, said it was only two years since Mr Ford had returned from a tour on which he had made a close study of all forms of transport, and besides the knowledge he had gained with regard to the trackless trams he had the benefit of the technical press and of other expert experience. He did not condemn the trackless tram right out, but he did say it was not applicable to Auckland. Such trams would have to be used only as feeders or along alternative routes. They could not run on the same routes as the other trams." [236]

Nevertheless, some such as Mr W. L. Titchener, chairman of the New Lynn Town Board, a district that had only the train service and the motor bus to provide public transport at that time, had other ideas as to what type of transport would best serve the commuters of the western suburbs:

"The trains run at infrequent intervals and there are numerous delays, exasperating to the travelling public. The trains have their own stopping places and passengers have to walk to those stations no matter what the distance, even though the rails might be at the very back door of a traveller's residence.

"How different with the buses! They stop right along the concrete roads and pick up and set down people at their very doors. If a new settlement springs up the buses can serve the district at no extra cost, while with the trains it means huge expense in laying down permanent way. I am strongly of opinion that the Transport Board should appoint a bus manager, who should be quite distinct from the tramways manager. If it is to be competition between buses and trams, let it be a question of the survival of the fittest. The public themselves will be the judges.

"The Ilford (England) Borough Council recently purchased seven small tramway concerns with a view to pulling up the rails to make way for motor transport on the roads. The public is being gradually educated up to the point where they value the quick bus services, and it may be difficult to obtain public sanction for tramway extensions." [237]

While the Transport Board Chairman called for patience and time for his Board to consider the various options and decide on those that would best serve the region's transport interests, it would seem that many shared Mr W. L. Titchener's views that motor buses were the answer, particularly for the City's more distant suburbs. These views were also shared by many commuters, as expressed in various 'Letters to the Editor' at the time:

"While the City Council owned the trams there were two essential injustices in the position. Firstly, the owners of the trams were made the arbiters of the conditions under which their rivals, the buses, should run.

Secondly, the local body elected by one area was given control over the transport, and therefore the destiny, of a number of surrounding areas. Those who think that now a Transport Board has been set up it merely remains to support its proposals whole-heartedly should remember that of the two injustices the first remains exactly as it stood, and the second has been only partly removed.

"While New Lynn, Glen Eden, Henderson, Otahuhu, Papatoetoe and Manurewa are not represented the board must bear in mind that most of the fastest growing suburbs are excluded. Another reflection should be that the larger the capital sunk in the trams the smaller the inducement to the board to hold the balance between trams and buses. The setting up of the board is a step in the right direction, but other steps equally urgent remain to be taken. Transport." [238]

"Sir,—On reading the report of the Transport Board I was surprised to learn that a deputation had gone to the meeting to advance Avondale's claim for trams. Mr W. J. Tait, acting as spokesman, stated that 1106 ratepayers signed a petition in favour of tramway transport, but I am pretty confident that if a proper vote was taken after this question had been thoroughly discussed the balance would come out greatly in favour of buses, provided the fares remained reasonable, and the service adequate.

"Trams may be all right to serve the inhabitants of Mount Albert Road, but what about the Waterview people and all the thickly populated area from Oakley Estate to the proposed tram route. Those who have travelled by tram from the city to Mount Albert terminus know what a slow method transport this is, and yet it is proposed to extend this service for miles further. Buses can cover the whole of the populated area, while tramways are confined to a specified route unless an enormous amount of money is expended for branch lines, and I contend that at the present time, while a few minor improvements could be made to our bus service, we are being well served. Didn't Sign." [239]

However, despite the public's apparent preference for motor bus transport, the running of buses as a public service was not paying its way. The loss was so bad that, pending its raising of a loan to extend its tramlines to Avondale via Mount Albert, bus services to the western suburbs could no longer be provided by the Transport Board, as reported by The New Zealand Herald of 31 January 1929:

"Faced with a loss of £38,131 on its omnibus undertakings during the nine months ended on December 31, the Auckland Transport Board, meeting in committee last evening, decided to cease all its western suburban services beyond Avondale as from March 31. Private enterprise is to be invited to take over the services to New Lynn, Glen Eden and Henderson after that date.

"The board had before it a comprehensive report by the (now Transport Board) manager, Mr A. E. Ford, recommending a revision of fares, sections, terminal points and time-tables on various routes, but, after defining its policy with regard to the western services, the board decided to defer consideration of the balance of the report for three months. 'We will then know the position in regard to tram extensions and development generally,' said the chairman, Mr J. A. C. Allum. 'We must first see how we stand on our loan proposals'. In moving that the Henderson, Glen Eden, Smith Street and Hutchinson Avenue services should cease from March 31, Mr Allum said it had always been his opinion that those routes would be better left to private enterprise." [240]

As might be expected, not all Board members agreed with their Chairman:

"Criticism of the action of the Transport Board in transferring certain bus services to private ownership drew a spirited reply at a meeting of the Transport Board yesterday. Mr M. J. Coyle drew attention to an opinion expressed by Mr F. S. Morton to the effect that the board was too ready in many cases to cede its rights when private firms were applying for permission to run bus services.

"The Transport Board is prepared to give private enterprise a chance in various directions and private enterprise signifies it is ready to take it, but now it is said we are doing the wrong thing,' said Mr Coyle. 'We are condemned…for giving these services away. I cannot understand it. I am strongly in favour of private enterprise running the buses in the outer area beyond the trams, and I say it will give the people a better service than this board can give.'

"Attacks upon the board were replied to by the chairman, Mr J. A. C. Allum. 'If there has been any humbug talked in this city in the last two years it has been about transport,' he said. I am sick and tired of this eternal nonsense about private enterprise – that we must not enjoy any privileges not enjoyed by private enterprise.

"I have done all I can to see that private operators get a fair deal, but this is a public undertaking in which £2,000,000 is invested, and every member of the board has a lot more responsibility in connection with it than any private feeling he may hold. The only duty I see before me is the protection of the ratepayers, added Mr Allum. It is wrong to use the powers we possess to let this undertaking be in any way impaired. Yet I am getting nothing but abuse for having acted in such a manner." [241]

Despite their chairman's insistence that the Transport Board's obligation to the interests of ratepayers should come first, some Board members nevertheless feared that concessions given too readily to private enterprise would be viewed unfavourably by the public:

"It is a remarkable admission of incompetency that, with the advantages and resources within the realm of this board, we are to throw out the news to the public that private enterprise is to be invited to do something we cannot do, said Mr F. S. Morton. It is an admission that we cannot do our job, and we will be made a laughing stock.

"Mr E. J. Phelan urged that the board should run the bus services, even at a considerable loss, until it had made its tramway extensions. Let private enterprise serve that area, including Avondale, until Avondale gets electrified railways or tramway extensions,' advised Mr Potter. I know private enterprise can live on us, said the chairman, who added that the G.O.C. Company had testified in Court that it made its services pay by the revenue gained on tram routes." [242]

And nothing had changed in that regard. As it always had, the tram service was still paying its way and providing its new owners, the Auckland Transport Board, with a profit of sorts. That profit had greatly offset the continuing losses incurred by the buses:

"The statement of accounts prepared by the Auckland Transport Board for the nine months, ended December 31 last (1928) reveal a profit of £986 on the combined working of trams and buses. In yesterday's issue, this amount was attributed to the trams, but the profit in that department is considerably greater. For the nine months ended December, 1927, the entire undertaking showed a deficit of £40,178, and, in view of the fact that the buses have since been run at a heavy loss, amounting in nine months to £38,000, the surplus now returned on the undertaking as a whole can be viewed with satisfaction." [243]

Based on those figures, it is easy to see that, from a purely business point of view, further investment in the City's profit-making tram service was a simple choice for the Transport Board to make:

"The Auckland Transport Board decided at a special meeting yesterday (12 February 1929) to apply to the Local Government Loans Board for authority to raise £300,000 by way of loan for the purpose of carrying out the first section of the four years' programme of tramway improvements, drawn up at its last meeting. The work to be done during the first two years comprises the construction of the Point Chevalier, Dominion Road and Remuera tramway extensions, the Onehunga duplication, the railway station and Stanley Street loop, together with the purchase of 25 new trams and 10 new buses and provision for new plant and workshops additions." [244]

But the decision to raise a loan for tramway extensions wasn't one based on commercial considerations alone. There was plenty of local support for a continuation of tramway services and its steady expansion:

"In order to refute a rumour that Remuera residents are opposed to the Auckland Transport Board's loan proposals, involving extensions to the tram tracks beyond the Remuera, Point Chevalier and Dominion Road termini, a large deputation of residents of the eastern portion of Remuera waited upon the board yesterday and expressed unanimous approval of the scheme.

"Regret at the decision of the Auckland Transport Board to limit its proposed loan to £300,000, instead of asking for the full amount required to serve the whole area, was expressed by Mr E. F. Jones, chairman of the Mount Roskill Road Board, last evening.

"Mr Jones said he had no objection to the proposed extensions to Point Chevalier and elsewhere, but he knew what human nature was, and he could not help thinking that when these services were established the residents therein would take little or no interest in extensions to other suburbs. He moved that the Mount Eden Borough Council should be asked to convene a meeting to recommend the Transport Board to bring out a complete scheme in one loan proposal.

"Mr S I. Goodall also said he thought it advisable to go for one loan to cover the whole scheme, for it would not be necessary to have the whole of the works done simultaneously. The wider the area the more support the loan would receive. The motion was carried." [245]

At this point, there was little doubt that public opinion was mostly in favour of the Transport Board's plans to extend the tramway service, providing the motor bus, privately owned or otherwise, could be used to supplement the trams where necessary. Yet to be debated and decided was just how much ratepayers were willing to borrow, and eventually repay, to implement those plans. For some, the choice was simple – don't borrow anything to fund what they believed was fast becoming an obsolete transport system. Many of these opinions were expressed by way of letters to the editor:

"Sir,—Is it not time the Auckland ratepayers awoke to the position re transport and thought well before they committed themselves to further huge loans, especially on a system that is rapidly taking second place in the chief cities of the world. The Auckland rates are now very high compared with other towns in New Zealand and they certainly have no advantages. The Transport Board is the City Council, as is well realised, the members of which will exercise their powers and force their rule to the bitter end at whatever cost. The ratepayers of the western suburbs pay rates on a good concrete road to travel on. They had a splendid bus service run, not at a loss, until a year ago.

"The City Council, or Transport Board, has now decided to hand the service over to private enterprise, but on such restricted and impossible conditions that no private company would dare to take it over. The City Council well knows that nothing but a through service will satisfy the busy suburbanites, who cannot waste too much time in travelling.

"The finding of the commission and all details are very fresh in our memories and it was with grave apprehension and sore misgivings that we saw those determined opponents of motor-buses tightly clutching the reins of the Transport Board. Would another petition, this time to Sir Joseph Ward, restore to us our British, or perhaps I should say our natural right, of travelling to and from the city how we wish? Never Say Die." [246]

"Sir, —In reply to 'Felix' (a previous letter writer) and other critics, I still contend the Transport Board should be content with its present lines and equipment, and allow motor transport to serve all the other districts, and run to and from the city. Felix gives copious figures of electric-car extensions in a few towns in America, but for every one of the extensions he mentions in America I can give at least ten of existing bus services in America being extended and new routes opened. Can he give one example of any city or township laying down tramway lines as a new enterprise?

"I have just returned from a trip round the world and have had my eyes opened in regard to transport. I was all over Great Britain, America, Canada and the Continent, and was in London for months and did not see a tramline or tramcar anywhere. I travelled all over London in large double-decker motor-buses. If London had tramlines in the streets traffic could not carry on. The buses run alongside the footpaths, pick up their passengers and off like a shot. That is proper transport. There are five thousand motor-buses running in the London streets by one company alone, to say nothing of other bus services. It is very wearying to be in one of the long lines of tramcars toiling up Symonds Street at a walking pace every evening from five o'clock, and to see the few motor-buses which are allowed to run to outside suburbs leaving us miles behind. Business.

"Sir, —A deputation which waited on the Transport Board, asking for the extension of the Remuera tramway to the city boundary, claimed that all the people living on that route would be in favour of the extension, except those who had shops at the terminus. I live between the two points named and shall do my utmost to hinder the tram extension and vote against any loan for that purpose. It seems to me the people living between the terminus and the city boundary and on to St. Heliers have already a better service than the tram service can ever be. Ratepayer." [247]

Details of the loan alternatives were explained by the New Zealand Herald on 27 February 1929:

"Two issues are to be submitted to the ratepayers by the Auckland Transport Board when authority to borrow for tramway and plant extensions is being sought. The ratepayers will be asked to vote on a loan of £300,000 for the first works on the board's programme, and also, alternatively, on a loan of £625,000, the sum estimated as being necessary to carry out the full programme. The board had previously decided to submit only the loan of £300,000 to the ratepayers in the first instance, and to leave the second part of the programme for their endorsement at a later date.

"This decision came before the board again yesterday for confirmation. The chairman, Mr J. A. C. Allum, advised that the intention of the board to seek the approval of the Local Government Loans Board in regard to the loan of £300,000 had been advertised, and no objections had been received. He moved that the board's previous decision should be confirmed. Speaking with regard to the prospects of the loan being carried, Mr Allum said success would depend very largely on votes of the ratepayers in the districts already served by the trams. He said the proposals had been unanimously endorsed by the press." [248]

In the meantime, solutions to the traffic congestion already plaguing the inner city were being sought. One such proposal, considered to be 'the boldest stroke yet', was described by the New Zealand Herald of 4 March 1929:

"The boldest stroke yet contemplated in Auckland for solving the traffic outlet problem is pictured in the perspective reproduced on this page, illustrating the vital proposal to link Upper Queen Street with Belgium Street by a subway under Karangahape Road.

"The proposal, yet to be finally considered by the Auckland City Council, will, it is claimed, greatly simplify traffic conditions at one of the city's busiest and most awkward intersections, and, as far as tramway routing is concerned, will make possible speedier connection between the city and the south-western suburbs of Dominion Road, Edendale, and Mount Albert." [249]

"PROPOSED SUBWAY FROM QUEEN STREET TO BELGIUM STREET TO RELIEVE TRAFFIC CONGESTION
"A sketch plan of the new proposal showing how traffic could pass under Karangahape Road and link up with the New North Road through Belgium Street without adding to the congestion at Grafton Bridge and in Upper Symonds Street." [249]

The striking aspect of this 1929 illustration is not just the proposed underpass but the design's provision for motor vehicles to supplement the tramway beneath Karangahape Road. The sketch is also notable for its absence of motor buses which, by then had more or less been restricted to routes that rarely included the city centre.

But while tram and motor bus transportation operators had seemingly reached an agreement of sorts as to the territorial disposition of its services, there remained the spectre of the private motor car and, in its more competitive form – the taxi.

By 1929, the new form of the horseless carriage for hire was not only increasingly competing with trams and buses for passengers but, as motor vehicles became more affordable, their private use began to influence public transport use. The consequences of this were not entirely appreciated by some serving on the Transport Board:

"A suggestion that the Auckland Transport Board should intervene in the present taxi war was made by the Motor-omnibus Proprietors' Association yesterday. In a letter to the board, the secretary, Mr G. Grey Campbell, said the latest movement of the taxis to charge at the rate of five miles for 2s we consider brings them into the scope of the Transport Board Act.

"They are running over the routes of many of the licensed bus services at these rates. This will be an infringement of the licence granted by the board. We understand that one taxi company is preparing to go into the Ellerslie district, pick up fares there and convey them any distance up to five miles for 2s, continued the letter. As their operations within the tramway area will, no doubt, have a serious effect on tramway revenue if allowed to continue, we would ask the board to take the necessary-steps to prevent buses infringing the rights granted under the Transport Board Act to existing concerns.

"The chairman, Mr J. A. C. Allum, said the Transport Board had no control over taxis, which could do as they pleased as long as they plied for hire and charged for the use of the car and not per passenger. Mr A. J. Entrican said it was purely a taxi war, which could not last for long.

"Mr L. E. Rhodes: It is only a temporary measure and will adjust itself. I admit we may be losing a certain amount of revenue, but if the people can get a cheap ride in a motor-car we should let them enjoy themselves while it lasts. (Laughter)" [250]

But the advent of motor transport was no laughing matter. It was serious business, if the figures were to be believed:

"Some illuminating figures concerning the growth of the motor industry in New Zealand were quoted by the Prime Minister, Sir Joseph Ward, in his capacity as president of the Wellington Automobile Club, at a social function held by the club last evening.

"Probably no branch of our commercial, industrial and social life, said Sir Joseph, has made such strides as the use of motor-cars and vehicles. They have come to form an important part of the attributes of modern life and business. That this was so was evident from the totals of registrations as at March 31 last (1928), as follows:

|  | North Island | South Island |
|---|---|---|
| Cars | 82,360 | 48,196 |
| Commercial Vehicles | 19,809 | 8,970 |
| Cycles | 21,846 | 15,398 |
| Total | 124,015 | 72,564 |

"The number of new registrations during the year ended March 31 was 27,674, being 18,739 motor-cars, 4167 commercial vehicles and 4768 motor-cycles. The record for registrations during any one month was reached in December, 1928, when 3685 new registrations were effected. The development of motor transport had been accompanied by a considerable expansion in the motor and cycle industry, as the following figures showed:

|  | 1918-19 | 1927-28 |
|---|---|---|
| Persons employed | 1,366 | 4,483 |
|  | £ | £ |
| Salaries and wages | 193,149 | 860,065 |
| Value of output, repair Work, etc. | 571,074 | 1,919,359 |
| Value of land, buildings, Plant and machinery | 714,271 | 2,234,950 |

"The motor import trade also showed great expansion, said the Prime Minister. The motor spirit imported in 1918 totalled 10,725,149 gallons, and in 1928 54,540,440 gallons. The respective values were £829,869 and £1,655,457.

"The number of motor vehicles imported in 1918 was 3094 and in 1928 it was 18,787. The value of these was £451,444 and £2,766,919 respectively. Motor-cycles imported in 1918 totalled 1122, valued at £53,444 and the number imported in 1928 was 3558, valued at £173,397.

"The extent to which motor transport services in the Dominion had been developed was shown by the following figures for November, 1928, in respect to vehicles employed in the omnibus services, passenger car services and freight services:—Number of vehicles, 2215; value, £1,027,927; persons employed, 2950; passengers carried 1,982,220; freight carried 84,866 tons.

"If these figures were multiplied by 12 it would be seen what a huge figure was represented by the operations for one year. The motor industry was here to stay. There was plenty of room for motor vehicles and railways, and both these great branches of transport could move along side by side without friction." [251]

Obviously believing that to be true, those devoted to the status quo of Auckland's tramway network, were reassured by the Local Government

Loans Board's acceptance, in April 1929, of their main proposals to borrow most of the funds needed to expand and improve that network. But there were some limits imposed:

"Approval of the bulk of its loan proposals involving the borrowing of £526,600 has been received by the Auckland Transport Board from the Local Government Loans Board. The latter has deferred a decision on the proposed loan of £58,400 for the Avondale tramway extension and has declined to approve the borrowing of £40,000 for the purchase of 20 new buses. It is expected that loan proposals will be submitted to a ratepayers' poll on May 8." [252]

"The Local Government Loans Board has deferred consideration of the proposal to borrow £58,400 for the extension of the tram tracks to Avondale, apparently on the ground that the district is being amply served by buses and trains and that the proposed construction of the Morningside tunnel (still to be started nearly 90 years later) will provide an improved service with electric trains. It has laid down the principle that any new buses required must be purchased out of revenue and not by borrowed capital." [253]

Long before the great number of motor vehicles yet to cram Auckland's roads could be imagined, the debate as to whether public money should be spent on motor vehicles or the trams still seemed fairly straightforward to most – as a letter to the Auckland Star, published 5 April 1929, indicated:

"I noticed it was reported in Tuesday's Star that the chairman of the Transport Board said ratepayers liked to have a say in the expenditure of money. I should think they do. The attempt of the board to bolster up and add to the present electric car system as against the quicker and more mobile motor transport does not meet with the approval of the people of Auckland, as exemplified by the sixty thousand residents* who signed a petition in favour of motor transport.

"What the residents of Auckland require is motor transport to all the outlying suburbs, and the sooner the board realises this, the better. Now that they are saddled with the present tram lines and cars let them make the best use of what they have, but if motor buses are good enough for London (one company alone having five thousand on the road), why cannot we have them? I am not writing this in the interests of any motor bus proprietors. I do not know one of them. The Transport Board can run the buses if they like. I am merely one of the sixty thousand (practically the adult population of Auckland) who asked for motor bus transport as against the present slow electric tram car system. Common Sense." [254]

*[The letter writer is referring to the more than 85,000 persons nationwide who opposed the proposed Motor-Omnibus Regulations of

1926 and who signed petitions presented to the Motor-Omnibus Regulations Committee for consideration.]

If that bias toward motor-omnibus transport was to sway the majority of ratepayers to vote against the Transport Board's proposal to borrow the £526,600 needed to expand the tramway service, as happened with the loan proposal put to the ratepayers in 1927, then it must surely prove to be the death knell for Auckland's trams.

Accordingly, the Transport Board was keen to reassure the public that the trams remained a viable and essential service that was costing them nothing to support:

"The Transport Board welcomes the very fullest investigations into its affairs by this body and similar bodies, stated Mr J. A. C. Allum, chairman of the board, explaining the loan proposals to members of the council of the Auckland Chamber of Commerce yesterday.

"Mr Allum said the undertaking of the board had now reached its critical stage; it would either go ahead or go back. They could face the public and say they had an undertaking which was now paying its way. I wish to emphasise that the Auckland transport system has not cost ratepayers a penny, Mr Allum added. Neither directly nor indirectly has any money been received from rates. The system has been kept going from fares. The whole of the undertaking was worth to-day what was paid for it, plus the amount expended on improvements. Many of the extensions that were proposed would be immediately profitable." [255]

Such promotion was extremely important as a much larger majority was needed in this poll compared to that taken in 1927, as an article in the Auckland Star of 3 May 1929 explained:

"The Transport Board loan proposals, which are to be voted on next week, are causing much interest from end to end of the wide transport district. There are many varying opinions as to the result and members of the board are doing everything possible to secure the carrying of the loan. It is not generally known that the loan must have a three-fifths majority to ensure its success, and in certain quarters this is considered a difficult hurdle. If it were a loan proposal made by the City Council, as formerly, a bare majority only would be required. A three-fifths majority for local bodies other than boroughs is needed for the carrying of loan proposals." [256]

The New Zealand Herald was in no doubt as to the importance of the tramway and its need to have the necessary funds to continue and expand its services. Long before the present-day, mass media methods of promotion, it was commentary such as this that so often influenced public opinion:

"To the reasonable man the only choice is whether the £526,600 programme shall be authorised in whole or in part. To deny the board capital urgently needed for wholly essential purposes would be as disastrous as it would be absurd. The alternative would be stagnation in transport just when progress is insistently demanded by all circumstances.

"It is no use suggesting that if refused authority for tramway extensions the board could establish more omnibus services. It cannot borrow to buy buses because the Loans Board refuses to permit this. It has not the capital resources to buy the vehicles without borrowing. Even if it could, what would the position be? It runs certain omnibus services now. They regularly return a loss. Tramway profits are at present covering that loss. If it increased the ratio of omnibus to tramway services, it would be multiplying the losses without increasing the profits to meet them.

"Whatever the respective merits of tramways and Motor-omnibuses, the fact remains the tramway services in Auckland do pay their way, returning a profit which should make it possible, once conditions are stabilised, to give further concessions to the public. The Transport Board is acting in harmony with the policy of transport authorities the world over in preferring railed traffic as the only satisfactory form of transport to move people in the mass." [257]

In what could be described as natural for Auckland affairs, that harmony did not quite extend to many of the City's citizenry, as demonstrated during a Town Hall meeting held two days before the Transport Board poll was to take place:

"Remarkable scenes were witnessed in the Town Hall concert chamber last evening when over 1000 people were addressed on civic affairs by Mr J. R. Lundon and Mr W. H. Murray, members of the Auckland City Council. For nearly three and a half hours the large audience hooted and jeered almost incessantly.

"The police were called in three times and one man was removed from the hall. Opinion was sharply divided among the audience and at times the meeting was completely out of control, speakers being shouted down by men and women, who stood up waving their arms and hurling abuse at those on the platform.

"The climax came when Mr J. A. C. Allum, who recently resigned his position as chairman of the Transport Board* and whose policy was being severely criticised, entered the hall and walked to the platform. He was faced by an audience which had lost nearly all semblance of control, and although a few cheered the rest were exceedingly hostile. Mr Allum was allowed to speak between outbreaks of jeering…Several moments elapsed before the uproar subsided sufficiently for Mr Allum to speak. Shouting above the uproar he said:—I have only one message for you. On Wednesday you are asked to vote on a matter of vital importance to Auckland. I am before you with no particular interest; you have beaten me, but I tell you it, is in your interests to support the undertaking which is yours. If you want to preserve the £2,000,000 you have in this undertaking, you will record your vote.

"Someone mentioned buses, and this was the sign for greater noise than ever. Quite unheard except by those near him Mr Allum shouted: I am not going to be frightened by the big stick waved by a small section of the community. I refuse to be intimidated by interested parties. I smell benzine, and I do not like it, he added, amid howls and screams from both men and women…the meeting was brought to a sudden close at 11.15 by the extinguishing of the lights in the hall. There was a rush for the doors, but the lights went on again while the crowd departed." [258]

*After failing to regain his seat on the Auckland City Council a few days before this meeting, John Allum had tendered his resignation as founding Chairman of the Auckland Transport Board. However, his resignation was not considered until after the May 8 poll, the results of which reinforced his position, as outlined by a letter to the Editor of The New Zealand Herald, published 14 May 1929:

"Sir: — Even the bitterest opponents of Mr Allum concede his undoubted capability as a business man, and the overwhelming majority in favour of the loan proposals is surely an endorsement of his policy as chairman of the Transport Board, and a good reason for the council to do some hard thinking before they accept his resignation. There is no doubt that the fearless attitude of Mr Allum at Mr Lundon's meeting, in answering questions, and in some cases giving the lie direct to his opponents, was the deciding factor in the poll on the loan proposals. The spontaneous ovation which greeted Mr Allum as he walked up the hall and mounted the platform was a great tribute to his courage from a meeting crammed with opponents.

"It was a striking instance of the inherent fairness of a British crowd, in demanding a hearing for a man who has been attacked in his absence, and who has undoubtedly been misrepresented by the highly-coloured effusions of his opponents. In the interests of the ratepayers, Mr Allum should undoubtedly remain on the Transport Board to help carry out the policy he has inaugurated, and which has been endorsed so emphatically at the recent poll. Transit." [259]

Indeed, the poll proved to be an emphatic endorsement of the Transport Board's plans and loan proposals:

"Auckland ratepayers yesterday voted overwhelmingly in favour of the Transport Board's loan proposals. The proposal to borrow £526,000 to carry out tramway extensions and improvements was approved by 3 votes to 1, and the alternative proposal to raise £280,000 to carry out half the programme received 4 votes to 1.

"Immediate steps will be taken to raise the capital required, the first call being made on the New Zealand money market. Few loan proposals of recent years have excited so much interest. Polling was extremely heavy under the circumstances, nearly 18,000 ratepayers, or 47 per cent recording their votes out of an aggregate roll of 38,000. The estimate includes about 1600 informal votes. The result of the voting was as follows:

Proposal No. l: For 12,190 Against 3,925 Majority 8,265
Proposal No. 2: For 11,989 Against 2,988 Majority 9,001

"A three-fifths majority was required to carry the proposals and the margin was comfortably exceeded at every polling place. The approval was more emphatic in the districts expecting to be served by the proposed tramway extensions, but voting was solidly in favour even in those other districts which are to receive no direct benefit. Ellerslie and Panmure, for instance, voted 3 to 1 for the proposals and Newmarket nearly 4 to 1. City ratepayers voted fairly consistently for the loans." [260]

The New Zealand Herald also saw the results of the poll as an expression of confidence for the future of railed passenger transport, relegating motor buses to a subordinate position in the opinion of the travelling public:

"For the second time, the ratepayers of the metropolitan area have given their sanction by an overwhelming majority to the policy and principles upon which the Auckland Transport Board was established. Six months ago they endorsed the proposal that a special organisation should be created to control passenger transport throughout an area comprising ten local government districts. On that occasion 85 per cent of the votes recorded, about 9260, were in favour of the issue.

"The board's programme for the prosecution of developments that have been delayed by vain controversy and confusion of counsels has now been endorsed at a much heavier poll. The provisional returns do not disclose the exact dimensions of the poll, but there were over 16,000 votes recorded on the major issue and nearly 15,000 votes on the alternative proposal. Of the former, 75 per cent were in favour and, of the latter, 80 per cent. There could scarcely have been a more emphatic vindication of the board's policy, a more decisive repudiation of the attacks that have been made upon the board or a more pronounced condemnation of the efforts to handicap its progress by fomenting unreasoning prejudices against its members.

"This result is not due to an exceptional preponderance of voting in part of the district overshadowing substantial opposition elsewhere. In every constituent district, both proposals received more than the three-fifths majority required by the defect in the legislation, and the vote was equally decisive in districts which, had a short-sighted view been taken, were less interested than those in which the loan is actually to be expended. Another satisfactory feature is the rejection of the fiction of domination by the City Council. In one case, the suburban polls gave a relatively higher majority than the city; in the other, the voting was in almost exactly the same proportions.

"The result has another important implication. The board asked for authority to spend £526,600 wholly upon the development of electric tramways—extensions, rolling-stock and equipment. It has not entirely discarded Motor-omnibuses, but these are to be relegated to a subordinate position. In this respect, also, a clear mandate has been given by the ratepayers. Had they been seriously disturbed by prospects of railed transport being superseded, their apprehension would have been reflected in the casting of their votes. Instead, an overwhelming majority has recorded its confidence in the reliability and stability of electric tramways as the most economical means of serving the needs of Greater Auckland. The Transport Board and the citizens of Auckland have good reason for gratification over the result." [261]

While much of the voter approval for the Transport Board's policies could be attributed to the positive stand taken by its Chairman, John Allum, the recent loss of his City Council seat had put his Chairmanship of the Board in doubt. Nevertheless, his subsequent resignation was not accepted and he continued as Chairman of the Transport Board until 1943.

As a result of the loan proposal poll, John Allum's optimism continued:

"Gratification at the overwhelming endorsement of the policy of the Transport Board was expressed last evening; by the chairman of the board, Mr J. A. C. Allum. It remains for the ratepayers of Auckland to get right behind the great transport undertaking which they own, and continue to improve the position of its affairs, he said. The result of the poll should open a brighter era for Auckland's transport and mark the commencement of greater prosperity for this publicly-owned system. One effect of the sanctioning of the loan proposals would be the elimination of most of the costly feeder bus services, although a certain number of buses would continue to be run to meet adequately the transport requirements of all quarters of the city." [262]

However, despite the apparent consensus represented by the loan proposals poll, meeting 'the transport requirements of all quarters of the city' in the face of entrenched 'village pump' parochialism was unlikely to be a smooth ride. The paving of a united way forward was not always facilitated by the Transport Board itself, as illustrated by a letter to the Auckland Star published 17 May 1929:

"In deciding yesterday that preference of employment be given to men with at least three months' residence in the Transport district the Transport Board has been guilty—unwittingly perhaps—of extreme parochialism.

"Not that it is the only local body to sin in this respect. The example was set them on a smaller scale by at least one 'little tin-pot local body', as the Mayor described them, when imposing restrictions and the curse is coming home to roost. No one can blame the Transport Board for placing some restriction to prevent local unemployed being shouldered out, but that protection should, in my opinion, at least embrace the whole Auckland metropolitan area.

"The transport district is too narrow. Take, for instance, the New Lynn, Glen Eden and Henderson districts, and others; large numbers of the unemployed, including ex-City Council employees temporarily unemployed, live in these districts. They have been consistently encouraged to do so for the public benefit in order to avoid congestion and slum areas in the city proper, and so on.

"Now the Transport Board, one of the largest employers of labour in the city, definitely penalises them for making their homes in the suburbs. It is no fault of theirs; rather their regret that the arbitrary fixing of the transport area boundaries has left them outside the pale. Many workers have already abandoned their homes in these suburban districts through unemployment and other causes, and decisions such as that made by the Transport Board are going to make it still harder for those who remain.

"Already in Glen Eden alone there is a large number of empty and abandoned houses, and if other large city employers, the Harbour Board, for instance (many of whose employees live in the suburbs), follow the example of the Transport Board, we shall all have to pack up and take rooms in the city. I trust that the Transport Board will reconsider its decision in the best interests of the whole community.

"The Transport Board is the first board formed in the Auckland district since the advocates of the metropolitan boards' scheme (Messrs Holdsworth, Bloodworth and others) took the field, and I am sure that they never contemplated any metropolitan board signalising its birth by such an unjust decision as the one in question. I, for one, stand for the Greater Auckland scheme after this in preference to the metropolitan one if every board formed in the Auckland district is going to restrict employment to residents within its own actual boundaries. J. H. Hayes." [263]

Others predicted that the conflict between public passenger transport (the trams) and that offered by private enterprise (the motor buses) would continue despite an expressed intention to co-operate for the greater good of the region.

The Mayor of Mount Eden and Transport Board member, Ernest Potter, indicated as much when commenting on the poll result:

"The approval of the loan proposals…by the ratepayers in the board's area is, to my mind, a vote of confidence in the board system of government, and definite evidence of genuine public desire to advance an essential service in the larger area. Transport is a utility service, inter-borough in operation, and, properly developed, will promote progress through the advantages of efficient facilities as between town and country.

"The co-operation by the board with private ownership is essential in the greater field of transport. The growth of Auckland, added Mr Potter, has been especially rapid and motor transport has spread the population. This has created problems which can only be met by a board which has, as its chief aim, an adequate service with reasonably cheap fares." [264]

But not all Transport Board members were as happy with the decisions being made, including the purpose for which the proposed finance was to be raised. During his resignation speech to the Onehunga Borough Council, One Tree Hill, Mount Roskill and Mount Wellington Road Boards, and Ellerslie and Panmure Town Boards, which he represented as a Transport Board member, Mr P. S. Morton "…complained of the scant support given him during his term of office, although he had done his best to advance suggestions that he considered would tend towards an efficient and payable transport system.

"His reason for opposing the recent loan proposals was that he believed the methods of the management of the board were absolutely obsolete. If the system was not paying to-day, how could it be expected to do so when interest, sinking fund and working charges on the loan would absorb £80,000 a year? Either fares had to be increased to meet this extra charge or else a rate would have to be levied over the whole transport area. Had his advocacy for trolley cars been listened to the extensions provided for in the loan could have been accomplished for a little over one-third of the amount estimated.

"Discussing his position on the board Mr Morton said: 'I have been hopelessly in the minority. I feel I have gone there and done my best to bring about conditions that would improve transport for the outside areas. I have done my best and cannot do any more." [265]

Speaking of trolley cars…the resigning P. S. Morton was not the only Aucklander who could foresee the impending termination of parallel lines. This opinion was illustrated by a letter written to the Auckland Star by an E. Stevenson published on 5 June 1929:

"The message just received from Mr Ernest Yates (of Arthur Yates Seeds), who is now in London, that trams on rails are in disfavour all over the world and that both London and Paris are seriously considering pulling up all their rails and replacing them with trackless trams only confirms the convictions of those of us who believe that the carrying of the recent loans will put Auckland back at least twenty years in transport matters.

"All these extensions could have been put in with trackless trams at less than half the cost and the trackless tram could continue along the route of the present trams into the city. As the rails become worn out all our trams could be gradually made trackless. Unfortunately the present Transport Board will not listen to anything but rail trams. The ratepayers have never had a chance to vote on anything but rail trams and inside six or seven years exactly the same problem will present itself. There is a large population beyond the trams calling out for better transport. Further tram extension, except linking up all the heads along the Mount Albert-Epsom Roads, will be out of the question, as trams are too slow for long distances. The transport muddle in Auckland is getting worse. E. Stevenson." [266]

At the same time, the future of trams as a mass transportation system was also being debated in Sydney, as reported by the Auckland Star on 12 June 1929:

"The (Australian) Government has no intention of scrapping its trams, declared the Minister for Local Government, Mr Bruxner. On the contrary, it intends to ensure the complete co-ordination between trams and buses through the new Transport Board. Mr Bruxner pointed out that he had received information from Britain showing that the trams there were not being scrapped. The tendency was rather to extend them. It was a wild statement to say that London was scrapping its tramways system, while in America, as in Britain, it was found that neither trams nor buses could adequately cope with the growing traffic. Precisely the same conditions applied to Sydney." [267]

In the meantime, whether trams were the future or not, it was time to spend the money as if they were:

"The Local Bodies Loans Board has approved the Auckland Transport Board development loan of £526,600, which has a term of 20 years, with a 3 per cent sinking fund, and a maximum interest rate of 5 per cent." [268]

"An Order-in-Council consenting to the raising of the Transport Board's loan of £526,600 for tramway extensions and development purposes has been published in the Gazette. The board is taking immediate steps to raise the money. The first two works to be put in hand are the extensions of the tram tracks at Point Chevalier and Dominion Road. The length of sections and scale of fares to be charged on these routes were fixed by the board at its meeting yesterday." [269]

Well before the citizens' May poll was known, and the subsequent loans approval granted, the Auckland Transport Board had approved plans for the construction of larger tramcars. This was plainly stated in a letter of 8 February 1929, written by the Auckland Transport Board Manager, A. E. Ford, to the Engineer-In-Chief and Transport Under-Secretary (F. W. Furkert):

"With further reference to my conversation with you when you were in Auckland some weeks ago. I have now to inform you that the Board has approved of the construction of 25 tramcars, subject to the approval of the Local Government Loans Board and the ratepayers…Our cars are 7'6" overall width, which gives the statutory clearance of 1'3" between the side of the car and the centre poles. We find that cars 7'6" wide are too narrow to give the requisite modern day comfort both in seating accommodation and passage room…It is expected that after the above 25 cars are completed, a further 25 will be put in hand, and I will be glad to know if you will support an application for an increased width of 6 inches for the new cars." [270]

While improving passenger comfort was no doubt a prime consideration for Mr Ford, larger tram cars and lines extended further into the suburbs could only mean a greater capacity to carry more paying passengers at the expense of competitors.

The Government's cancellation of the proposed Morningside rail tunnel project in early 1929 provided the Auckland Transport Board with the opportunity to extend its tram services west to Avondale, an extension it had previously deferred pending the Morningside decision. However, another loan, and permission to raise that loan, would have to be first obtained from the ratepayers enrolled in the districts controlled by the Transport Board, as explained by an Auckland Star article of 5 August 1930:

"Ratepayers in the Auckland Transport Board's district will be asked tomorrow to approve a scheme for the extension of the tram tracks to Avondale. It is proposed to raise £58,000 with which to carry out the work. The trams to Avondale would follow the New North Road from the Mount Albert tram terminus. Should the poll be successful, Avondale residents will be able to make the run to the city without breaking their journey as they have to do at present with the feeder bus service…The poll is not a local one, as some people imagine, but only those people who are on the ratepayers' roll of the various districts in the board's area are entitled to exercise their franchise. Approximately 50,265 people are entitled to vote.

"The purpose in submitting the loan proposal is to replace the existing buses by trams, said Mr J. A. C. Allum, chairman of the Transport Board. There is no question of establishing a new transport service. Mr Allum added the time was overdue for the extension, for it would serve not only Avondale but also the large area between Mount Albert and Avondale, which in recent years had become an important residential district.

"Regarding the suggestion that the trams to Avondale would compete with the railways, Mr Allum said that the railways did not cater for the bulk of the people living in the one and a half miles between the Mount Albert and Avondale stations. The purposes for which railway and road services were created were dissimilar. The railways catered for people desiring to travel from one district to another, and the stops were relatively far apart. On the other hand, trams and buses carried passengers from point to point on the route and stops were frequent.

"The inconvenience of the new railway station for suburban traffic was too well known to need emphasis. Work on the present programme had been expedited in order that the board might do its share in meeting the unemployment situation. If the ratepayers gave the authority now sought it could continue to employ a large number of men. It was fair to point out that at the poll taken in May 1929 the people of Mount Albert and Avondale loyally supported the loan proposals for extensions in other districts." [271]

And, of course, they did the same again:

"The ratepayers in the Auckland Transport Board's district approved the Avondale tramway extension proposals yesterday by 3825 votes to 1544. Seventy-two per cent of the votes cast were in favour of the proposal, giving a margin of 606 votes in excess of the three-fifths majority required. As a result of the ratepayers' sanction a start will be made early next year to extend the tramlines from Mount Albert to Avondale at an estimated cost of £58,400. The chairman of the Transport Board, Mr J. A. C. Allum, stated last evening that plans and specifications would be prepared immediately and materials would be ordered in time to put the work in hand early in the New Year.

"Although the voting was not as solidly in favour of the proposal as was the case when the board's main programme of tramway extensions was submitted to the ratepayers last year, there were majorities in its favour in every district except Ellerslie. Overwhelming support was forthcoming from Avondale, which will benefit most by the extension, 674 votes being recorded for the proposal and 124 against. Substantial majorities in favour of the extension were also recorded at Point Chevalier, 163 to 82, and at the Chamber of Commerce in the city, 309 to 172. There were 50,265 persons entitled to vote, of whom 5400, or 10 per cent, exercised their privilege.

"Mr Allum, who expressed his pleasure at the result of the poll, said it was hoped to complete the Mount Eden tramway extension as far as Landscape Road and also the Richmond Road extension early in the New Year. In the meantime the Edendale extension and also the extension of the Mount Eden line along the Three Kings Road to Mount Albert Road, now made possible by the sanctioning of the Mount Roskill Road Board's proposal for the permanent reconstruction of the Three Kings Road, would probably be commenced in October, leaving the Garnet Road extension, planned by the board a few days ago, and the Mount Albert-Avondale extension for the early part of next year. That would complete the board's programme of extensions." [272]

Of course, the Transport Board's programme of extensions had to be paid for and that required both local and overseas investors:

"Advertisements are being published by the Bank of New Zealand, giving particulars of a 5½ per cent loan of the Auckland Transport Board. It is stated that the particulars are issued to comply with the regulations of the Stock Exchange, and are not intended as an invitation to subscribe to the loan.

"The issue consists of £100,000 in bearer debentures of £100 each, with principal and interest payable in London. Redemption is at par in July 1950, at the Bank of New Zealand, London. Under authorisation by the Auckland Transport Board the bank is negotiating the sale of the debentures at £99 per debenture. This issue forms part of an authorised borrowing of £526,600 for the purposes of Point Chevalier, Dominion Road and Remuera and other tramway extensions, railway station and Stanley Street loops, Onehunga duplication, 25 new trams, 10 new buses, additions to workshop and plant, and for loan expenses." [273]

While investment in any endeavour is not without risk, there were many investors who obviously still believed in the predominance of railed public transport. This was despite some evidence that other cities, including Christchurch, were favouring the more adaptable trolley bus to meet their future transport needs. As reported by The New Zealand Herald on 28 December 1931, the comments of the General Manager of the Christchurch Tramway Board, Mr F. Thompson, did not auger well for the future of the country's tramways:

"Wherever I have gone I have found tramway organisations in financial difficulties, said Mr F. Thompson, general manager of the Christchurch Tramways Board, who returned to New Zealand by the Aorangi yesterday after a tour of Great Britain, Canada and the United States.

"All kinds of factors are operating against tramways, but the most serious, in my opinion, is the private motor-car...This is so equally in England and America. Car-owners not only prefer to use their own vehicles, but in a spirit of hospitality they take further patronage from the trams by filling their cars with friends. All I have seen confirms me in the belief that the Christchurch Tramways Board has done wisely in running trolley buses, as trackless trams are called, said Mr Thompson.

"Mr Thompson said that trackless trolleys found favour especially in cases where the tram tracks had reached the stage when expensive renewals were called for. Although they did not possess quite the mobility of petrol buses, they were a very attractive proposition in a country like New Zealand, where petrol cost practically twice as much as in England. Moreover, there were no petrol fumes which, in some of the narrow streets of London, made the air obnoxious on warm days. Depreciation cost less because the parts of the trolley bus were fewer and the life of the vehicles was longer because wear and tear were less.

"A very important consideration lies in the fact that the trolley car meets the preferences of a public which has become used to rubber movement on rubber wheels, added Mr Thompson. A very considerable section of the public would sooner ride on rubber than on steel, even when the steel tracks are well laid. Mr Thompson said that for the reasons mentioned he could foresee trolley buses solving many of the problems of transport in New Zealand." [274]

The Auckland Star of 28 December 1931 also referred to Mr Thompson's findings and compared them with the Auckland situation:

"The impressions received on his tour of Britain, Canada and the United States by the general manager of the Christchurch Tramways Board should be noted by our own Transport Board and by the public. Mr Thompson has found tramway organisations everywhere in financial difficulties, and he is very favourably disposed towards the trolley bus— that is, the bus that is run by electricity, but does not use rails. He considers that his own Board has done wisely in introducing trolley buses and that this form of vehicle will solve many of our transport problems.

"It may be pointed out that the British Royal Commission on Transport, set up in 1928, regards tramways as obsolescent if not obsolete, and recommends that no more be laid down. In Auckland tramways are still being built, and though it is reasonably certain that the Avondale extension will be the last, one cannot help feeling apprehensive about the financial result of this and recent works. Mr Thompson's full report to his Board should be of equal importance to Auckland." [275]

Nevertheless, work commenced on the Mount Albert-Avondale tramway extension on 31 April 1931 and the line was officially opened on 30 January 1932:

"Another important district was linked with Auckland's tramway system this afternoon when the Mount Albert-Avondale extension of one mile and a half was officially declared open for traffic. Those present at the opening ceremony included Mr J. A. C. Allum, chairman of the Transport Board…In the course of his remarks Mr Allum said that in addition to joining an important district to the tramway system, the through service to the city would undoubtedly prove a great convenience to a large number of residents.

"The length of the extension was 1.55 miles, and it was proposed to maintain a minimum 16-minute service during the slack hours of the day and a 10-minute service at rush hours. Extra cars would be put into service when traffic warranted. As was invariably the case when tramways were constructed, considerable improvements had been made in the thoroughfares traversed.

"Not only is the opening of the Mount Albert-Avondale extension important in itself, but it marks the completion of the important programme of tramway extensions carried out by the board after endorsement by the ratepayers. Some 11½ miles of double tram tracks have been laid by the board, and the total mileage of double track in the Auckland system is now 44½ miles, a distance equal to that from Auckland to two miles past Mercer. The board has also put 40 new tramcars in service and more are in course of construction. These new vehicles are a credit both to those who designed and built them.

"We have reached a new stage of normality, and our affairs must be adjusted to meet it, said the chairman. The revenue of the undertaking, like that of other trading concerns, has fallen, but I am glad to say that the board has been able to make arrangements to meet the reduced income. In extending the tramway to Avondale it is not considered that this is the permanent method of transport for those who wish to make the through trip to the city. The primary object of the tramway is to serve short distance passengers, and the ultimate means of transport from here to town will be by means of electrified railway running through the Morningside tunnel.

"However, it is obvious that this work must await a substantial increase in population, and in the meantime the Avondale trams will serve both the short and long distance riders. In conclusion, may I say that the best way to show your appreciation of the tramway extension to Avondale is to use it." [276]

While by the early 1930s, initiatives such as the Morningside rail tunnel were still contemplated as viable solutions to Auckland's long-term, public transport needs, the City's civic leaders had resigned themselves to the fact that such plans were then financially out of reach. They were also seen as a step too far in terms of meeting the needs of static, if not diminishing, passenger numbers.

At the same time, local authorities, such as the Auckland Transport Board, had to service its debt commitments – pay for at least some of what it had already accomplished before more work could be contemplated. The situation was summed up by an Auckland Star comment published on 31 May 1933:

"Through four and a half years, since transport in the Auckland metropolitan area was brought under the control of a special Board, there has been a continual struggle to make the system pay. The problem lies in operating a tramway service economically in the thinly-populated areas. Auckland's tramways are an example of the cost of developing ahead of population, and it is probably true that the system to-day, with its 45 miles of double-track, is sufficient for the needs of nearly a million people.

"Certainly experience has shown that there can be no more extensions, and that it is essential to consolidate and improve within the existing limits. When the tram routes were extended by the Board a few years ago it was expected that an increase in traffic would follow, but conditions have prevented such a result.

"In the past year the only course open was to meet the fall in revenue by curtailing the services, and, as the annual accounts presented yesterday show, the anticipated deficit for the year has been thus cut in half. The loss of slightly under £11,000 is an improvement on the previous year, when the Board was behind to the extent of £18,300, and, to give ground for hope, it was indicated that revenue had been steadier in recent months. It seems reasonable to predict that an increase in traffic, bringing about a better revenue position, will come as soon as there is an improvement in general conditions.

"Meanwhile a tight hand must be kept upon expenditure, and the possibility of reducing the loan overhead is to be fully explored. Like some of the other large authorities, the Transport Board loses more through the rise in the exchange rate than it is able to save by conversion of its internal debt, and its difficulty is a reminder of the urgent need of securing some concession from the overseas lender.

"With over two-thirds of its loans domiciled abroad, the Board is more interested in that aspect of the problem than in a New Zealand conversion, important though that may be, and until some solution is reached the anomalous position exists that some of our leading public bodies have to pay higher interest rates than do many smaller authorities. In the aggregate local bodies owe to Britain over £17,000,000, and in regard to the whole of this sum they are at the same disadvantage as the State in dealing with its external debt. Individual action cannot be taken, and the only course is to deal with the question, when the time is opportune, on a national scale." [277]

A local body debt of £17 million could be viewed as insignificant in terms of the country's total indebtedness, incurred in pursuit of some fifty years of growth, were it not for the fact that 'over two-thirds' of that money had been sourced from overseas' investors.

In that respect, little had changed since the 1880s when one of New Zealand's original settlers, Thomas Russell, returned to London and established the New Zealand Land Mortgage Company Limited, described as: "...a tangible expression of Russell's belief that money raised in Britain on debentures at low interest rates must inevitably produce profits when farmed out at the high mortgage rates ruling in New Zealand – and in the process enrich promoters and directors." [278]

At the time, "The editor of the London *Standard* referred to the new company (the New Zealand Land Mortgage Company Limited) as the latest of a very long series of such instruments for procuring capital to sustain the industry and credit establishments of the most debt-ridden spot on earth, without exception." [279]

At any time, the repayment of overseas debt can be influenced by either favourable or adverse currency exchange rates. Even the apron-stringed relationship between Mother England and New Zealand was not enough to ensure the continued financial parity of the English and New Zealand pound.

By 1933, the New Zealand pound was worth only about four-fifths of an English pound – a considerable difference to those in England who had invested in the expected growth and prosperity of New Zealand. One of those British investors included the Alliance Assurance Company Limited which sought what it believed was due through the courts:

"The hearing of the case, the Alliance Assurance Company Ltd., against the Auckland City Corporation and the Auckland Transport Board, was continued before the Court of Appeal today. The question under argument is whether all interest payments in London and sums payable on redemption of debentures issued by the City Corporation when the tramway system in Auckland was taken over by the corporation in July, 1919, should be made in English or New Zealand currency.

"In addressing argument to the Court Mr Barrowclough, for the plaintiff company, submitted that there was no difference between the English pound and the New Zealand pound. He adopted the views of the majority of the House of Lords in the case of the Adelaide Electric Supply Company, Ltd., against the Prudential Assurance Company, Ltd., that there had been differences between New Zealand and English currency as a means whereby a debt could be discharged, but that the symbol "£" had been and always was the same, whether applied to English or to New Zealand currency.

"He further contended that there had never been any Statute or Act in law having the effect of a Statute which altered the New Zealand pound from the New Zealand pound. New Zealand currency had always been linked with that of England, and we had not yet broken away from the financial and currency system that was brought to New Zealand from England by our forefathers.

"In opening the case for the defendants this morning, Mr A. H. Johnstone, K.C., submitted three propositions for the consideration of the Court: —(a) That at all material times there was a New Zealand pound separate and distinct from the English pound; (b) if the contention 'A' were sound then, as a matter of construction, the pound referred to in the contract now under consideration was the New Zealand pound; (c) that, speaking of the pound as money of account, whether the New Zealand pound was the same as the English pound or not, as a matter of construction, having regard to the provisions of the Local Bodies Loans Act, 1913, under which the debentures were issued, the amounts payable under the debentures were payable in New Zealand currency." [280]

Unfortunately, neither the Appeal Court nor the Privy Council, before each the case was later heard, saw it that way:

"The dismissal by the Judicial Committee of the Privy Council of the appeal of the Auckland City Council and the Auckland Transport Board against the judgment of the New Zealand Court of Appeal in the tramway loan case was announced in a Press Association cablegram from London yesterday.

"No details of the terms of the decision have been received. Judgment in favour of the debenture holders in a case brought by the Alliance Assurance Company Limited against the Auckland City Council and the Auckland Transport Board was given by the New Zealand Court of Appeal last June. The point at issue was whether principal and interest on debentures domiciled in London should be paid in English currency or in

New Zealand currency. The Court held that payments must be made in English currency.

"Debentures for £1,227,200 were issued by the City Council when it purchased the Auckland tramways, and liability for them was later assumed by the Transport Board. Holders had the option of requiring payment of the principal and interest in Auckland or in London. In respect of debentures worth nearly £1,000,000, the option was exercised in favour of London. The Local Bodies Loans Act, 1913, gave authority for raising money out of New Zealand, and from that time until the date of the contract in 1920 there was no separate New Zealand pound. Pending the reserved judgment of the Privy Council the interest payments have been made in sterling." [281]

As well as the additional cost incurred by the overseas exchange difference, in 1936, the Auckland Transport Board had also to absorb another expense very much attributable to a maturing society – the advent of the 40-hour week:

"Good progress has been made with the training of the extra staff, which will be necessary when the 40-hour working week comes into operation on the Auckland tramways on September 6. A total of 126 extra conductors have been receiving tuition, and 60 conductors will have the opportunity to move up to motormen. At present the Auckland Transport Board's employees have a working week of a minimum of 48 hours, and it is estimated that the change over to the 40-hour week will involve the board in an extra expense of £44,546 for a full year." [282]

Some 21 years after the Auckland City Council had acquired its tramway service from the Auckland Electric Tramways Company, it was time to make good on the debentures issued. Payment was made on 1 July 1940 – in sterling, of course – but some of that payment was achieved by means of another loan, and there were still other loans outstanding.

"The repayment of that portion of the Auckland city tramway loan of £1,250,000 which was due in London on July 1 was the subject of reports to the Auckland Transport Board yesterday. Summarising the position, the chairman, Mr W. H. Nagle, said the board had exchanged an oversea indebtedness of £916,250 for an internal indebtedness of £425,000 which it had contracted to pay in the next 10 years. The board still had owing in England about £601,000.

"Mr C. R. Gribble, secretary, reported that the money for repaying the loan was handed to the Bank of New Zealand for transference to London on July 1. The balance then due for redemption amounted to a total face value of £733,000…The cost of redemption with exchange at 25 per cent was £916,250.

"This amount was found as follows: — By sinking funds in the hands of the Auckland city sinking fund commissioners, £747,330; by the board, £168,920. The board's portion of the payment was made up of a loan from the Bank of New Zealand, and the utilisation of moneys received from the sale of properties, the balance being met from the sinking fund deficiency reserve.

"The only amount still outstanding under this particular loan of £1,250,000 was £3600 issued at 6 per cent and due on January 1, 1943. Mr Nagle said the board and the city had every reason to be satisfied with the transaction and with the work of the sinking fund commissioners, to whom a vote of thanks was later passed. In the bonds of the board the British investor had had an excellent investment. He had been paid his full interest in sterling and now the principal had also been paid in sterling." [283]

Despite every reason to be satisfied with the transaction, the bottom line was that the Transport Board and the tramways was still very much in debt and, as a result, would probably have struggled to add to and improve its services.

As it happened, the war was set to impose austerity and shortages on every enterprise operating in the cities of the colonies and, ultimately, their citizens. The Auckland Transport Board wasted no time distributing the burden, as reported by the Auckland Star on 12 July 1940:

"The decision of the Auckland Transport Board to apply for an Order-in-Council authorising higher maximum fares was referred to briefly in the House of Representatives last night by the Minister of Transport, Mr Semple. The Minister was referring to the need for conserving petrol.

"Mr Doidge (Opposition, Tauranga): Are you going to let the Auckland tramways put their fares up 1d?

"The Minister: I have no jurisdiction.

"Mr Doidge: They are going to ask you for authority.

"Mr Richards (Government, Roskill): You can leave that to the Auckland public." [284]

Taxi fares were also set to rise but that was much to the consternation of many operating in the taxi industry who wished to remain a competitive alternative to the public transport services provided by the cities. As published by the Auckland Star on 12 July 1940, it was the opinion of one such taxi operator, that the Minister of Transport's professed policy of transport co-ordination and co-operation was contradicted by his approval for a fare increase:

"The public should be made aware upon whom the responsibility for increased taxi fares lies, stated Mr F. Drumm, manager of the Atta Taxi Company, commenting to-day on the decision of the Minister of

Transport, the Hon. R. Semple, to uphold a decision given by the Metropolitan Licensing Authority on May 27. The new scale approved by the Authority and, in terms of the Minister's judgment, held by the Minister to be justified, leaves the fare at 1/6 for the first mile, as at present, with a charge of 6d extra for each additional half-mile, instead of each additional mile.

"The scale was to have come into force on June 15 but no effect was given to the decision because an appeal was lodged by a taxicab licensee against the Authority's decision. This was referred to the Minister in the nature of a test appeal. The Minister has shown amazing inconsistency in dismissing the appeal, said Mr Drumm. Throughout his tenure of office as Minister of Transport Mr Semple has persistently demanded co-ordination of the transport services and impressed on operators the necessity of co-operating to reduce costs and eliminate waste. Recently he said that while this was desirable in normal times it had become a national duty in the present emergency because by it petrol would be conserved.

"The case for a unified system which he has now dismissed provided a practical method of putting into effect all the advantages of the Minister's declared policy. It was shown that the necessary facilities were available for the immediate co-ordination of the taxi service. Estimates of the savings to be effected were submitted and showed that the proposed increased fare would not be necessary if the unified system were in operation.

"While rejecting the appeal the Minister again repeated his desire for the utmost co-operation in the industry, but considered this would be best achieved by the voluntary action of the operators. Surely it was obvious to Mr Semple that the appeal to him was made necessary solely because a section of operators refused to co-operate. The evidence showed, however, that the overwhelming majority of the operators favoured the proposed system, and the appeal was in effect an invitation to him to assist them in implementing the Minister's own professed policy. Instead, he has decided in favour of the minority who opposed it.

"The decision of the Metropolitan Licensing Authority against which the appeal was lodged was an extraordinary contradiction of the interim report made by that body during the proceedings. The authority then declared it was convinced by the evidence submitted that a unified system was desirable and necessary and that failing it being voluntarily adopted within a limited time by the operators, steps would be taken to enforce it. For an unexplained reason the final decision completely reversed this finding.

"Mr Drumm added that the Atta Company has strenuously opposed increased fares throughout the proceedings and indicated methods of avoiding this course. The authority, while admitting the desirability of the proposed system, refused to act on it, he said, thereby approving the increased fare." [285]

But, in stark contrast to the austerity-driven fare increases to come, 1937 Auckland was about to provide a free transport service thanks to the marketing acumen of the Farmers' Trading Company:

"A 21-years agreement was sealed on Monday between the Auckland Transport Board and the Farmers' Trading Company Limited for a three-minute trolley bus service from the company's store in Hobson Street, down Victoria Street West, along Queen Street, and up Wyndham Street to the store (states the New Zealand Herald). The company is to pay the total cost of four trackless vehicles and equipment not exceeding £14,000, and an annual sum not to exceed £2500.

"All vehicles and equipment are to be the property of the board, and the drivers will be in the board's employ. If the wages or the hours of the men are increased or reduced there is provision in the agreement for proportional adjustments. Three of the buses will give a continuous service, and four on Fridays, the board to maintain the vehicles in good running order and to indemnify the company against all claims by passengers." [286]

Not long before the world order was to regress to warfare, Auckland transport accelerated forward and provided the city's shoppers with their Christmas present of free trolley buses – as reported by The New Zealand Herald on 19 December 1938:

"The new electric trolley bus service from the city to the Farmers' Trading Company Limited in Hobson Street, will be started to-day. Four buses have been provided for the free service, but it is not anticipated that more than three will be required for the first few days of this week. The buses will run continuously each week-day from 9 a.m. to 5 p.m. The ordinary Friday time-table will be from 9 a.m. to 9 p.m., and that on Saturday from 9 a.m. to noon. The round trip from the foot of Wyndham Street to Hobson Street, and back via Victoria Street and Queen Street, takes four minutes. Each of the new buses, which are attractively finished in yellow and green paint, has a seating capacity for 36 passengers. Twelve drivers have been trained for the service and were recently granted licences." [287]

While the Farmers' trolley buses certainly proved to be a success for the retailer, shoppers, and the Auckland Transport Board, it wasn't until September 1949 that trolley buses replaced any of the city's trams. Those trams running to Herne Bay were the first to be replaced and Auckland closed its last tram route on 29 December 1956.

Summary

The history of Auckland's trams, as illustrated by the preceding narrative, is not meant to be an exhaustive account and certainly lacks the nostalgia with which many historians have portrayed the era. And an era it certainly was – featuring a unique mode of transport as different from its petrol-fuelled replacement as the horse-drawn version it had replaced.

The importance of the trams to the development of Auckland was emphasised by Dr G. T. Bloomfield in his article, 'Urban Tramways in New Zealand 1862-1964' published by the New Zealand Geographer in 1975:

"The role of the tramway in shaping the pre-1940 areas of New Zealand metropolitan cities was a significant one. Extensive residential areas with a common style of house, long commercial strips along arterial roads, and many of the features of the central business district bear continued witness to an important mode of public transport." [288]

In his article, Dr Bloomfield also explained why the trams had to go:

"The economics of tramway operations, already difficult in the late 1920s, were almost impossible by 1950. Operating costs were high, all the systems were largely obsolete in the equipment and the routes did not reach far enough to the new residential suburbs and employment centres which emerged during and after the war. Capital investment required for a modernised and viable system was too great in comparison with the more flexible bus operations. Even if some cities had decided to continue, the supply of new equipment would have posed major difficulties for the tram and equipment manufacturers of Britain and the United States were diversifying or going out of business." [289]

*Chapter Ten*

# The Motor Car Cometh

"The transition from horse-drawn to motorised transport was completed by the end of World War 1, when 160,000 horses were sent overseas, never to return. And it has been said with some accuracy that New Zealanders went overseas on horseback and returned in cars." [1]

The introduction of the first motor-powered vehicle was quickly recognised as a source of revenue for the Government – to be regulated, and therefore, by definition, taxed. Indeed, the first motor cars imported into New Zealand by businessman and politician, William McLean, in March 1898, barely had time to overheat before the first motor-car-related, licensing Act was passed in October of that year.

Known as The McLean Motor-Car Act, the legislation was described as "An Act to authorise William McLean to use Motor-cars, and enable other Persons to obtain Permits and Licenses for a like Purpose, and also to authorise the Storage of Inflammable Substances used in driving such Motor-cars.

"Whereas William McLean, of Wellington, Commission Agent, acting for himself and others, lately arranged for the introduction into the colony of motor-cars: And whereas it is doubtful whether in the existing state of the law motor-cars can be lawfully used on the public roads and streets, and it is expedient that power should be given to use motor-cars on such roads and streets: …" [2]

As well as the regulatory and licensing rules it contained, The McLean Motor-Car Act included a number of fundamental clauses requiring motor-cars to carry an audible signalling device, exhibit a light during the hours of darkness, and restricting their speed along a public highway to no more than twelve miles an hour. As the importation of racier vehicles continued, the McLean Motor-Car Act was repealed and replaced by The Motor Cars Regulation Act 1902. This Act replaced the 12 mph speed restriction with:

"The person in charge of a motor-car shall not permit such car to travel along a road, street, or public highway at a greater rate of speed than is reasonable." [3]

But…"For all the stir they created, and regardless of how miraculous they must have seemed to the crowd who gathered to watch them, the first cars landed in Wellington in March 1898 were feeble affairs. They had primitive engines, unreliable leather clutch linings and chronically fallible belt drives. They were capable of hauling a couple of adults along on level ground at around 12 miles per hour; but add more passengers, or ask them to tackle a hill, and they were sure to let you down. Both Wellington cars, along with the first to reach Auckland, shortly found themselves packed off to Christchurch where the flat landscape promised to be more congenial to their technical limitations." [4]

As we now know, the 'technical limitations' of those first, motorised monsters didn't last and it wasn't long before their effect on southern roads was observed by a contributor to the Otago Daily Times of 25 July 1914:

"The rapid deterioration of main and arterial roads in our dominion has been the cause of many an anxious hour to county councils, road boards, and also to motorists. To say that our roads are in a bad state as present is to make a very mild statement, as a short journey either north or south of our city will quickly demonstrate.

"Motor traffic is held to account largely for this, and rightly so. Watch a piece of road on a wet day; small pools of water denote where hollows exist. Along comes a motor car, the tyres search out these hollows, and splash water and mud out on either side. Along comes another car. The same process is repeated, each car cutting deeper than its predecessor and before long that portion of road is full of pot holes. This is what is continually going on our roads.

"The Motors Bill which the Government has brought down has as its aim the righting of this injustice. The imposition of a tax that is considered equitable will find motorists quite ready to pay their full share of the cost of putting matters on a fair basis, but there is a considerable amount of controversy as to the right way to levy this tax.

"The Government in its Bill pins its faith to a schedule with horse-power as a basis. In this it follows the English Act. In accepting horse-power as a governing unit, however, it ignores the weight of a car, and weight of load is a factor to be considered in the determination of the amount of damage which any vehicle will cause a road.

"Another suggested method of levying a motor tax is by an import duty on tyres, this being termed a tyre tax. This form of taxation has many advantages, including a very important one — namely, ease of collection, the machinery being already complete for this purpose. It, too, can deal automatically with the speed problem. It is well known that speed as well as weight destroys a road, and it is equally well known, to motorists at all events, that speed work soon ends the life of a tyre, so that a driver who is careful with his tyres is also handling the road carefully, while the reckless driver, who has no regard for the well-being of the road, is penalising himself by wearing out his tyres." [5]

But despite the increasingly urgent need to hold motorists to account for the construction and maintenance of the country's roads, the proposed Motors Bill of 1914 did not eventuate. The First World War and resulting shortages significantly curtailed the growth of motor transport and, anyway, there were far more important issues to deal with – the roads.

From one's 21st-century, tarmac perspective of mudless surfaces, it is at first difficult to understand why tram lines were chosen to support the city's first bulk-passenger conveyances. However, for a relatively less bumpy, albeit relatively slow ride across town, the perpetual smoothness of rails was a far better alternative to the horse-drawn omnibuses and hackney cabs "…which had to run over the uneven loose metal roads before concrete and tar-seal roads became a reality." [6]

"Throughout the nineteenth century the best city streets consisted of crushed scoria spread on the beaten clay or earth." [7]

"Auckland, in particular, was poorly served by its roads at the turn of the century and even at the end of the First World War New Zealand still had a large percentage of dirt roads…" [8]

"Soft soils and plentiful rainfall are the worst enemies of good roads. No amount of gravel can prevent carts and wagons from sinking up to their axles during the wettest months of the year…The only practical solution was to give the roads a durable waterproof surface by spraying bitumen on top of the gravel." [9]

Trouble was, the only bitumen available at the end of the 1890s and early 1900s was acquired as a waste product from coking coal used for the making of gas for street lighting. As a result, there was only enough to tar-seal short stretches of a town's main shopping and commercial streets each year at reasonable cost. The availability of bitumen was further compromised as electricity came to replace gas as the main lighting source.

"…supply and demand forces continued to make bitumen expensive and it was only after the first world war that growth in the demand for motor-spirits would exceed the growth in demand for bitumen sufficiently to reduce the price of bitumen by a significant amount." [10]

"By 1901 the patience of the ratepayers had worn thin over the Council's inaction concerning upgrading the city roads. Since the 1880s, people had complained of the clouds of choking dust created by the two inch blue metal used in road repair. Only the lower part of Queen Street and some surrounding streets had been laid with asphalt coated blocks, but the arrival of horse trams forced the Council to upgrade inner city roads.

Two pressure groups, The Auckland Cycle Roads League and the Auckland Good Roads League, continuously petitioned for smoother road surfaces.

"Finally, the Council contracted the Neuchatel Asphalt Company to lay Auckland's first asphalt road surface in Queen Street at a cost of £27,492. When the task was completed a year later, the company claimed the new surface was 'non-absorbent, near-noiseless and easily-cleanable'." [11]

"In 1902 Auckland possessed only one paved street; there are now (in 1922) thirty-three streets laid in either asphalt, wood blocks, or concrete, as well as a large number of macadamised roads. The failure of a supply of good road metal retarded Auckland's progress in road making, but the substitution of concrete has had successful results, and the Council has given authority for a large number of streets to be laid in this material, and the work is now being proceeded with." [12]

To help pay for the country's roads, another 'Motors Bill' was put forward in 1921, as the Auckland Star of 1 February of that year reported:

"The advent and rapid increase in the use of motors has made it necessary for somebody to look after the national highways. This is the main reason behind the Government scheme of road construction and maintenance which is described in outline by Hon. J. G. Coates, who states that a Bill is now being drafted to embody the policy mapped out by the Government.

"By this Bill he said, the Government sought, not to interfere with local control of the main roads, but to get a greater uniformity in maintenance work than was existing at present. The way of doing this was to define exactly the area to go under the jurisdiction of each local body, and to get each body to elect a board or commission to control the main roads in its area. The scheme further proposes to set up a fund to augment the sums already granted for the maintenance of the Dominion's main roads, and this fund will be derived from a motor or a tyre tax." [13]

With the passage of the Customs Amendment Act in December 1921, the general tariff for rubber tires, rubber tiring, and inner tubes of rubber for pneumatic tires was as high as 25 per cent of proportionate value of the goods – a considerable additional cost for the motorist who, by 1925, was also paying a ten per cent import duty on British-made cars and some 25 per cent on those from America. [14]

But while the erosion of tyres and a road's surface was then considered to occur in some equal proportion, the replacement cost of a tyre hardly equated to the replacement of a length of highway. Another form of compensation to be paid by the motorist was therefore needed, and duly took the form of a comprehensive national scheme '...to make Provision for the Construction, Reconstruction, Maintenance and Control of Main Highways'.

This ideal was finally facilitated by means of the Main Highways Act 1922 which appointed a Main Highways Board overseen by the Minister of Public Works. The Act divided New Zealand into highway districts administered by District Highway Councils comprised of local officials from the Public Works Department and the county councils. The councils submitted road construction and maintenance proposals to the Main Highways Board for consideration and funding.

The funds dispensed by the Main Highways Board originated from the Main Highways Account, which consisted of the Main Highways Revenue Fund and the Main Highways Construction Fund. The Main Highways Revenue Fund derived its funds from:

"(a.) All moneys appropriated by Parliament out of the Consolidated Fund for the purposes of main highways, being not less than the sum of thirty-five thousand pounds...(b.) All moneys received as Custom duties imposed in respect of rubber tires, rubber tiring, and inner tubes of rubber for pneumatic tires...(c.) All moneys received by the Crown under any Act in respect of the licensing of motor-vehicles...(d.) All moneys paid to the Board by any local authority in respect of the maintenance and repair of any main highway..." [15]

The Construction Fund consisted of:

"(a.) All moneys borrowed by the Minister of Finance...(The Act allowed the Minister of Finance to borrow such moneys as may be required for the purposes of the construction of main highways...not exceeding in aggregate the sum of three million pounds)... (b.) All moneys appropriated by Parliament out of the Public Works Fund for the purposes of main highways, being not less than the sum of two hundred thousand pounds...(c.) All moneys lawfully transferred from the Revenue Fund...(d.) All moneys paid to the Board by any local authority in respect of the construction or reconstruction of any main highway..." [16]

"The impact of the new regime on the quality of main roads in New Zealand was immediate. The proportion of metalled to unmetalled roads rose from 1925, and from 1926 tarsealed surfaces began to appear...Between 1924 and 1929 the number of passengers carried by rail had been slashed by nearly a half...Goods could now be carried over longer distances..". [17]

Nevertheless, jurisdictional confusion continued to affect the repair of those roads unable to cope with the increasing loads they were expected to carry. As reported by The New Zealand Herald on 26 May 1923, neither the Government nor the City Council cared to take responsibility for what was one of the country's main trade thoroughfares at the time:

"An appeal for assistance in maintaining the section of the main South Road within their boundaries was made to the Prime Minister yesterday by a deputation representing the Manurewa, Papakura, and Papatoetoe Town Boards.

"The chief complaint, as submitted by the Rev. W. C. Woods, was that this road was being used by heavy commercial vehicles plying between Auckland and the towns to the south, and that this traffic was so seriously damaging the roads that it was becoming impossible for the districts concerned to face the heavy maintenance charges. Mr Woods said the condition of the road had become shocking, and almost unsafe. They wished to know whether the Government could come to their aid with any large sum of money. Mr Massey said he could not do this. He asked whether the county councils were doing anything. Mr Woods replied that the Franklin County Council had put its section in admirable condition, but the Manukau county and the other districts concerned had a most atrocious road.

"Licenses paid by the vehicles complained of were collected by the City Council, and it was thought this money should be divided equitably over the district. The Town Boards had considered the erection of toll-gates as a solution, and contemplated the framing of by-laws which would interfere with this heavy class of traffic.

"Mr Massey said the main roads problem was a serious one, as it had to be tackled right through the Dominion, and would involve the expenditure of millions. He did not think it possible to raise all the money required at present. New Zealand's credit in London was good, but if he tried to raise a huge sum, and it was found that good value for the money was not being obtained, the Dominion's credit would suffer. He wanted to avoid that. He thought the county councils could do a great deal more than they were doing. They were not justifying themselves if they expected the Government to do all the work.

"Mr Massey indicated that there would be some changes in the future which would help such bodies as those represented on the deputation. He agreed that it was absurd to carry ten-ton loads over such roads as the main South Road, and thought no road in New Zealand would carry them. It would not be hard to get Parliament to restrict such loads if that were necessary. He also agreed that there should be some adjustment in the matter of the collection of fees by one body." [18]

The same edition of The New Zealand Herald commented:

"Local authorities and their constituents will be gratified by the Prime Minister's sympathy with the suggestion that restrictions should be placed on heavy motor traffic. The damage to the Main South Road, to which Mr Massey's attention was directed, is unfortunately typical of a condition that constitutes one of the most serious aspects of the general roading problem. The difficulty is that while the roading of the Dominion is largely in a primitive condition, demanding a very heavy expenditure to meet essential needs, there is an increasing volume of heavy motor transport which only substantial concrete pavement can sustain.

"As a result, new construction is being so seriously damaged that it will have to be replaced long before the original cost can be discharged. Mr Massey is doubtful of the Government's ability to finance the comprehensive roading programme that all recognise to be essential. There can be no doubt whatever that the country cannot afford to make roads capable of carrying vehicles of unlimited weight, and it is equally certain that it cannot afford to have the roads that are within its means shattered by transport of this class.

"The problem has been already too long neglected. It should be examined by the competent authorities such as a conference of national and local engineers and limits of loading fixed within the capacity of a standard form of road construction. Upon that basis, it should be possible to determine the necessary restrictions. Whether the latter is effected by legislation, such as Mr Massey suggests, or by increasing the powers of local authorities, there should be a wide margin of safety in favour of the road. Until our main roads are able to carry the farmer's waggon and the light pleasure car without delay or misadventure, the loading of motor transport must either be distributed among small vehicles or returned to the railways." [19]

Another jurisdictional matter included the provision of 'good road metal' which, in some cases, was influenced by parochial interests – forever a stumbling block to the City's growth:

"The Waitemata County Council is contemplating the raising of loans for the purpose of carrying out important road proposals, and is faced with the problem of obtaining sufficient supplies of first-class metal for this work. There are two quarries in the county but they are the property of groups of ridings and at various times it has been suggested that these deposits—the Oakley quarry and the Waitakere quarry—should be taken over as county undertakings.

"When these quarries were acquired it was found that only certain ridings could benefit from opening them up. Special orders were therefore passed limiting the cost of maintenance and capital in respect of the

Oakley quarry to the Wainui, Takapuna, Kumeu, Waitakere, Waikumete and Waipareira ridings and the Waitakere quarry to the Titirangi, Kaukapakapa, Kumeu, Mairetahi, Waikumete, Waipareira and Waitakere ridings.

"At the meeting of the council yesterday the chairman, Mr F. W. Grigg moved two motions providing that the Government be asked to insert in the Washing-up Bill (end of the Parliamentary year Bill designed to include clauses that would tidy up miscellaneous matters omitted during the year, unfinished business, or passed legislation needing minor corrections) a clause authorising the rescission of these special orders.

"He said that the council was about to raise loans involving some thousands of pounds for road metalling and metal had to be provided for the main highways. It was evident that the council would have the money to spend but not the material for carrying out the work.

"In the past, ridings that had been excluded from the benefits of the special order had wanted metal that could have been supplied at the time, but owing to their having no interest in the quarries they had been shut out from supply. The time had now arrived when a comprehensive scheme should be embarked upon to ensure an adequate supply of metal for all ridings and this could not obtain so long as parochialism such as created by the present method existed." [20]

Such a strategic resource as road metal could not long be controlled by ridings and local bodies which, by October 1925, could be requisitioned as per the Public Works Amendment Act of that year. Clause 4 of the Act stipulated:

"Where any public work has been authorized to be carried out by or on behalf of His Majesty and gravel or stone is required in the construction of such work, any land may be taken under the principal Act for the purposes of a gravel-pit or quarry to be used in connection with such work, or the Minister may, by his servants or agents, after twenty-four hours' notice to the occupier, enter on any such land, other than land occupied as a garden or ornamental shrubbery, and dig and take any stone, gravel, or other material therefrom.

"Reasonable compensation shall be paid for any injury done to or material taken from the land entered upon, and in the event of any dispute the amount thereof shall be determined in manner set out in Part III of the principal Act." [21]

The first Annual Report of the Main Highways Board, for the year ending 31 March 1925, described the roading situation faced by the Board at that time:

"The advent of the motor-car entirely changed the complexion of the roading problem in New Zealand, as elsewhere, and the cry for better roads arose very shortly after motor transport became an appreciable factor. Later on, with the rapid increase in the use of motor-vehicles, particularly heavy ones, the position became acute, and it was soon quite evident that the type of road that was suitable for slow-moving horse-drawn traffic was inadequate." [22]

But despite the inadequateness of many of the country's roads, the lorry's ability to deliver door-to-door, at least over the shorter distances, ensured that it would soon succeed the railways as the prime freight mover. Cheaper freight charges also proved to be a 'factor to be reckoned with' and of serious concern to the railways, as reported by The New Zealand Herald on 18 September 1923:

"The fact that motor transport was a factor to be reckoned with in competition with the railways was brought before the Minister for Railways, the Hon. J. G. Coates, to-day in an instance quoted by the chairman of directors of the Kaipara Dairy Company, Mr Hanson.

"In asking that the rail freight on butter be reduced, Mr Hanson said the present departmental charge was over 20s per ton from Helensville to Auckland. On the other hand, his company had been offered a contract for cartage by motor lorry at 14s a ton. Before accepting the offer, the directors would like to know what the railway department would do in the matter.

"Mr Coates replied that the railway tariff was being revised and the Dairy Company would he notified of any decision at an early date." [23]

Revising the railway tariff to meet the competition was an obvious option. However, the Government also had other means by which it could reduce the competitiveness of road transport operators. For instance, there was the licensing regime imposed by the Motor-Vehicles Act 1924 which came into force on 1 January 1925 "...to provide for the Registration, Licensing, and Regulation of the use of Motor-vehicles." [24]

The Act required every motor-vehicle used on any road or street to be registered and licensed and the drivers of those motor-vehicles were also required to be licensed. All licences were to be renewed annually, all at a cost, of course. For every motor-cycle: 10s; for every private and public motor-car: £2; for every motor-coach or motor-omnibus: £5; for every one-ton truck with pneumatic tires on all wheels: £2; for every motor-lorry fitted with solid tyres: £5; and for every motor-lorry fitted with pneumatic tires on all wheels: £3.

As part of "Generally regulating motor traffic on roads and streets and public places..." and "...prescribing the rules under which they may be used…" the 1924 Act allowed for the Governor-General, by Order in Council, to provide for "…the granting of different classes of motor-drivers' licenses, and the conditions under which such licenses may be granted." [25]

While under the 1924 Act, motor-vehicle registration fees and fines were to be paid into the Government's Main Highways Account to the credit of the Main Highways Revenue Fund, drivers' licence fees and any fines imposed by local authorities were collected by and paid to the local authority in whose district the licence was issued and fines incurred.

The 1924 Motor-vehicles Act was unashamedly an early example of the user-pays principle – forever a tax on road users with which to build and maintain their thoroughfares. However, the administration costs of registration and licensing largely offset the revenue obtained, so the Act was never meant to be "…the best application of the principle" as explained by the then Minister for Public Works, the Hon. J. G. Coates during the months leading up to its eventual passage:

"The principle of taxation involved in the Bill was that the user should pay for the maintenance of the roads. The Bill would probably provide for a flat tax per motor vehicle, but that was not the best application of the principle. If possible, he hoped the user would be made to pay through a petrol tax, which was the fairest way in his opinion.

"He thought ways could be found for exempting petrol used for launches and machinery, especially farm machinery. Mr Coates made an especial appeal to the farmers not to raise a howl at the very mention of a petrol tax, as he thought exemptions could be provided for the petrol used for milking, etc. It must be recognised that the whole system of motor taxation had to be remodelled. If the roads for petrol vehicles could be provided, no one he thought, would be quicker to realise the direct gain from good roads than the motorist, and he would probably also be found ready to pay for them, recognising that it paid him to do so by the saving in car and tyre wear, petrol and time." [26]

Minister Coates' anticipated opposition to his petrol tax proposal was not slow in coming. Even the motorist, through his organisations such as the Canterbury Automobile Association, "…moved that a letter be sent to the Minister protesting against the proposal, and also that the South Island Motor Union be asked to enter its protest." [27]

However, Council members of the Canterbury Automobile Association seemingly had motives for their opposition that did not include the main purpose of the proposal:

"Mr F. W. Johnston said he was very much against the idea of the tax. In reality it was a breach of faith on the part of the Minister who, at a conference with motoring bodies in Wellington, had agreed to keep to a single tax on tyres. If he considered it necessary to impose a tax on petrol, he should first have approached the bodies with whom he had made his first agreement, and not broken away completely without consulting them.

"Mr R. W. Lockhead said he protested against the principle involved in a petrol tax for it would lead to trafficking in petrol. Mr H. G. Livingstone said he was against a petrol tax. The proposed tax was open to all kinds of dodges and the Government was being beaten in numerous ways already by people planning evasions of the present forms of taxation. It was unnecessary to add petrol to the list. In his opinion the tyre tax was the best in every way." [28]

By 1926, the future need for roads capable of supporting vastly larger traffic volumes and weights than the 'farmer's waggon and the light pleasure car' remained grossly unanticipated.

In 1922, New Zealand imported some 3,436 British and American motor vehicles. The number of imports steadily increased with 12,302 imported in 1923; 15,654 in 1924; and 16,537 during the first eleven months of 1925. [29]

In order to compete with the preferential import tariffs enjoyed by British car makers, the American firm of General Motors registered its own company, General Motors New Zealand Limited, in January 1926 and soon after commenced the construction of two vehicle-assembly buildings on a site at Petone. With a floor area of some 80,000 square feet, one of those buildings was then described as having the largest single floor in the Dominion.

By that time, the Ford Motor Company was already importing vehicle chassis, engines, and bodies for assembly at Wellington and Timaru. [30]

In the meantime, there was still only the revenue derived from the tyre tariffs and the 1922 Main Highways Act, and the registration and licensing fees obtained from the provisions of the 1924 Motor-vehicles Act with which to build and maintain the country's roads and it was not enough.

As a result, road planning and construction continued to be governed largely by cost, with little vision for the future transport needs of the country, as reported by The New Zealand Herald on 4 August 1926:

"The Main Highways Board does not specially advocate bitumen or any particular road-making material, according to a statement made in the House to-day by the Prime Minister Mr Coates. He said the board recommended a material only after it had ascertained the volume of traffic and the class of road that was required. The whole question was controlled by costs, especially the rate of interest and the term of the loan.

"Naturally the board did not encourage a local body to go in for a very expensive class of road if another class would do. It had obtained information from all parts of the world and it went carefully into every case. It did not advocate bitumen when the volume of traffic justified a more expensive material, nor did it favour bitumen as bitumen. It considered only the traffic and the cost per mile." [31]

The effects of traffic and the cost of roading were vehemently debated during the House of Representatives' Ways and Means Committee resolution to amend the Customs Tariff to provide for a duty of 4d per gallon on motor-spirits. The debate, which took place on 31 October 1927, included:

"The Hon. Mr Williams (Minister of Public Works) said,-Sir, the necessity of collecting additional revenue by means of a petrol-tax arises from the fact that the enormous increase in petrol-driven vehicles has brought about the position that the revenues already provided are entirely inadequate to maintain an efficient road system. In the Public Works Statement I showed that the County Councils, even with the assistance received from the Main Highways Board, are not in a position to maintain the roads up to the standard the traffic demands; and experience shows that the roads will go back unless further funds are provided.

"Apart from that, the great bulk of the money received through the road-tax has been going to the Main Highways Board, to the detriment of secondary settlers' roads in the various counties Not only is that so, but some of the larger localities have demanded better roading facilities adjacent to their cities; and it is wiser to try to meet these different requests in the general scheme of working, rather than allow too many local schemes to come into being and then have between the different localities a disconnected link, which would be very difficult indeed to deal with.

This tax is therefore being imposed to meet those two points – the difficulties that the local bodies find themselves in and the desire of the larger localities to have better facilities adjacent to towns.

"As regards the point of the increase in the cost of roading, I think I dealt with it fairly well in the Statement. It shows that in 1924 the cost was $51 a mile; in 1925 $75; and in 1926, $111. The progressive increase is due to the additional number of cars in use and the extra travelling done by the cars. It has also been pointed out that the county rates have risen rapidly, and that even now, with the heavy rates, we have reached the position that if no further taxation is imposed the main roads will go back, and the subsidiary roads also will go back to a still greater extent. We have had representations too from the smaller boroughs showing how they are placed owing to the traffic through the boroughs, and that they are not in a position to maintain their roads up to anything like a reasonable standard. Motorists have so far been catered for in the general scheme only as regards long-distance traffic." [32]

The Motor-spirits Taxation Act 1927, "An Act to provide for the Imposition of Customs Duties on Motor-spirits and for the Allocation of the Revenues derived therefrom", was eventually passed on 15 November of that year.

The Customs duty imposed a tariff of 4d. on every gallon of imported motor-spirit and it was included in the retail price to consumers after the first day of February 1928. [33]

The Act provided for certain exemptions from the tax, including motor-spirit purchased to operate milking machines and for general farm work, launches, and motor vehicles used by local bodies for the maintenance of roads. A later amendment of October 1928 exempted an 'agricultural tractor' allowed to use a road or street "…when proceeding to or from a farm". [34]

All revenue from the tax on motor-spirit was paid into the Consolidated Fund from which administrative costs and successful applicants for exemption were paid. Ninety-two per cent of the remainder was then paid into the Revenue Fund of the Main Highways Account (established under the Main Highways Act 1922). The balance (eight per cent) was then to be "…apportioned among those Borough Councils in whose districts there is a population of six thousand or upwards, in amounts bearing to each other approximately the same proportions as exist for the time being between the populations of the several boroughs." [35]

By 1930, the tariff on motor-spirits had been increased to 7d a gallon, a rate that began to impact the operating costs of those using the new and maintained roads, as reported by the Auckland Star of 23 July 1930:

"It seems inevitable, said Mr J. A. C. Allum, chairman of the Auckland Transport Board, that the substantial increase in the petrol tax will be reflected in higher omnibus fares. I am already advised by the private omnibus interests that, although they absorbed the tax of 4d a gallon, it will be impracticable for them to bear the additional amount imposed by the new tariff, 7d a gallon.

"The Auckland Transport Board also bore the 4d a gallon tax without passing any of it on, but I am afraid that the new tax will make it necessary for the board seriously to consider the bus fares. Fortunately the number of buses used by the board is being steadily reduced, and will be still further reduced in proportion as the tramway extensions come into operation." [36]

Naturally, the age-old method of tax avoidance – indeed, the avoidance of any payment at all – prevailed:

"Benzine thieves are getting bolder. The syphon method is now being abandoned in favour of one much more expeditious. The thief undoes the drain plug at the bottom of the car's rear tank, lets the benzine pour into a large container and is off in a few minutes. Two cars were robbed in this manner in a street in Wellington the other night, and the tank of another in the neighbourhood also was drained. Altogether 25 gallons of spirit was taken. A lack of street lights makes the operations of thieves comparatively easy." [37]

The Minister of Finance did not have to rely on darkness to facilitate his draining of "…such amount or amounts, not exceeding in all the sum of five hundred thousand pounds…out of the net revenues derived during that year from Customs duty on motor-spirits and otherwise payable pursuant…to the Motor-spirits Taxation Act, 1927, into the Revenue Fund of the Main Highways Account established under the Main Highways Act, 1922." [38]

Although Section 37 of the Finance Act 1932 became the Minister's plug through which he could drain funds considered necessary for other purposes, "…no direction shall be given by the Minister that would reduce the amount which in his opinion is necessary to meet the proper requirements of that (Revenue) Fund." [39]

The Eighth Annual Report of the Main Highways Board for the year ended 31 March 1932 revealed just how quickly the Board's Revenue Fund had grown and, therefore, how vulnerable it had become to selective plundering, as needed:

"Revenue from the proceeds of tax on tires and tubes, registration and licence fees of motor-vehicles and the motor-spirits tax:

| 1924-1925 | 1925-1926 | 1926-1927 | 1927-1928 |
|---|---|---|---|
| £465,164 | £336,737 | £507,413 | £688,980 |
| 1928-1929 | 1929-1930 | 1930-1931 | 1931-1932 |
| £1,303,178 | £1,442,226 | £1,745,536 | £1,688,075 |

"Expenditure by the Board for the year ended 31 March 1932 totalled £1,701,884 including £529,393 and £320,341 spent on North and South Island roads, respectively. [40]

Of course, the higher petrol costs and other fees and taxes paid by the motorist not only meant more funds were available for the roads but also reflected an increase in operating costs for the private passenger and freight services – all to the benefit of the trams and the trains.

Nevertheless, the competition for passengers and freight continued to intensify, as described by an Auckland Star article of 2 January 1931:

"The steady decline in railway receipts recently announced is due principally to a factor which low prices for primary products will not explain away. Figures available from the Department of Transport show how substantial is the business conducted by road vehicles in competition against the rail.

"The private car, giving tremendously improved travel facilities, has developed the 'travel habit', but the gain has not gone to the railways, because there is a car to every ten persons in New Zealand to-day, compared with one to every 17 in the year 1925.

"Motor trucks in 1925 were estimated to be giving a freight service equal to 48,000,000 ton miles per annum. The same enumeration to-day places the ton-mile factor at over 200,000,000 miles. Service cars on the long distance routes are not serious competitors of the rail on a price basis, but their elasticity in providing convenient transport has given them the advantage." [41]

As the ability of road vehicles to carry freight and passengers over longer distances increased, speed of delivery also became a competing factor for rail to contend with. And there was no shortage of drivers to show just how competitive they could be, as reported by the Evening Post on 3 January 1931:

"A very fine high-speed performance by a small car was completed this morning, the run from Wellington to Auckland being completed in under 14 hours. The car, a standard Rover saloon, of 10 horse-power, driven by Mr Barrow and Mr Power (no others were on board) left Thorndon just as the Limited pulled out at 7.15 p.m. yesterday. The weather was anything but good, but in spite of the road route being considerably longer than the rail (470 miles, as against 426), the car beat the train to Auckland by 27 minutes." [42]

But competition was a necessary component of commercial enterprise to some, and not a problem requiring some form of legislative redress:

"The growth of expenditure on railway transport and the increasing competition between rail and road transport were two of the problems dealt with by Mr W. A. Gray in an address on 'Transport Problems in New Zealand,' which he gave at a meeting of the Economic Society of New Zealand and Australia last evening.

"The advantages which the railways possessed over the canals— convenience, speed and flexibility—were the basis on which motors were challenging the railways said Mr Gray. Motor transport had already proved its claim to be the most effective all-round form of transport yet invented, and most of the expenditure on it could easily be justified. As between roads and railways, the recognition that the former now offer in the main a more efficient system does not solve the problem, concluded

Mr Gray. For a long time to come co-ordination must be sought between the rival methods, but not to the extent of eliminating competition." [43]

But there were many who sought to protect the railways from the rivalry that not only affected their jobs, but also the long-term investment of the country's taxpayers, as reported by The New Zealand Herald on 27 July 1931:

"At a meeting of the Auckland branch of the Amalgamated Society of Railway Servants on Saturday, the following resolution was carried: That this meeting views with grave concern the serious opposition of private bus and motor companies against the State-owned railways, and agrees with the finding of the Communications and Transport Committee of the Auckland Chamber of Commerce in so far as it condemns unrestricted competition with railways, and favours a central authority to safeguard the interests of the railways against the long-distance competition.

"We are further convinced that the taxpaying community in general should display a more eager tendency toward protecting the greatest developmental agency in this Dominion, as there is approximately £60,000,000 expended in railways construction, and the interest must be borne by the taxpayers, irrespective of the ultimate triumph of its serious challengers and damaging competitions." [44]

The Government agreed that the country's railway investment required protection from the competition posed by road transport and responded with the Transport Licensing Act, 1931 "...to make Better Provision for the Licensing and Control of Commercial Road Transport Services other than Tramways."

Just as the Motor-omnibus Traffic Act of 1926 protected the publicly-owned tramways from rival buses, the Transport Licensing Act did the same for the publicly-owned railways facing increasingly stiffer competition from coaches and trucks conveying their passengers and loads more efficiently along better roads.

The Act created the four transport and licensing districts of Auckland, Wellington, Christchurch and Dunedin – overseen by a Central Licensing Authority appointed by the Minister of Transport.

Those parts of the Act which pertained to the carriage of passengers included:

"26. (1) In considering any application for a passenger-service license the Licensing Authority shall generally have regard to –

*(a)* The extent to which the proposed service is necessary or desirable in the public interest; and

*(b)* The needs of the district or districts as a whole in relation to passenger-transport, – and if it is then of opinion that the proposed

service is unnecessary or undesirable it shall refuse to grant a license.

"30. (2) Where desirable in the public interest the Licensing Authority may so fix the fares and time-tables as to prevent wasteful competition with alternative forms of transport of any kind (if any), and may impose such conditions as it thinks fit to ensure that passengers shall not be taken up or shall not be set down, except at specified points, or shall not be taken up or shall not be set down between specified points.

"30. (3) Notwithstanding anything contained in the foregoing provisions of this section, the Licensing Authority shall, where necessary, so fix the fares that the fares charged (however computed) for the carriage of adult passengers over any route or section thereof within an area that may be conveniently served in whole or in part by an existing tramway service carried on by any local authority or other public body shall be at least twopence more than the corresponding fare charged in respect of the tramway service." [45]

Many parts of the Act referring to the carriage of passengers also pertained to the carriage of goods. Certain goods services routes and districts could also be declared 'controlled areas' in which the competitiveness between road and rail could be better regulated.

"45. (1) The Governor-General may from time to time, by Order in Council published in the *Gazette,* declare any transport district or districts or any part or parts of any such district or districts, or any route or routes through any district or districts or any part or parts thereof, specified or defined in such Order, to be a 'controlled area' for the purposes of this Part...

"48. The Licensing Authority of a controlled area, before granting any goods-service license or renewal of a goods-service license, –

*(a)* May call upon the applicant therefor (whether or not at the time of making such application he was actually carrying on the service to which it relates) to furnish to the satisfaction of the Licensing Authority proof that his liability in respect of loss of or damage to any goods that may be conveyed by such service is covered by insurance or otherwise to such extent as the Licensing Authority deems reasonable, having regard to the nature and extent of such service; and

(b) Shall require the applicant to produce proof of his having paid all license and other fees then due and payable under any Act or any regulation or by-law in respect of the motor-vehicles to be used in connection with the goods-service." [46]

The provisions of the Transport Licensing Act 1931 were not only overtly protective of the public transport systems of tram and rail, as were their purpose, but the Act was also notable for the number of its requirements readily changeable By Order in Council, without further reference to Parliament.

But, despite the Act's somewhat harsh regulatory interference in private enterprise, John McCrystal, in his book, 'On the Buses in New Zealand', observes that the Act was welcomed by many in the passenger transport industry: "Holding a licence was tantamount to a guaranteed niche in the marketplace, enabling operators to venture capital on their businesses with a greater degree of confidence than they had hitherto felt in the dog-eat-dog, cut-throat environment of the 1920s." [47]

Unfortunately, the depression decade of the 1930s was hardly the time for either private or public enterprise to venture capital. As previously noted, the railways was doing so badly that, in June 1931, the Government appointed a Railways Board of five persons to manage the whole operation.

Empowered by the Government Railways Amendment Act of 1931, The Board was appointed, "…with a view to obtaining a maximum of efficiency and maintaining a proper standard of safety and a reasonable standard of comfort and convenience for persons using the railways and any other services carried on in connection therewith." [48]

A year later, improvements to the Railways' bottom line were evident, but only after some retrenchment. In the meantime, road vehicles continued to seriously compete for the railways' passengers and freight, as reported by The New Zealand Herald on 17 May 1932:

"The following statement is submitted by the Railways Department in reply to a letter by Mr F. A. Carlisle, published in the Herald of May 7:—

"Mr Carlisle seems to have an impression that because the present economic condition of New Zealand has necessitated a halt in the construction of several lines and readjustments in certain branch services, the Railways Board is pursuing a policy detrimental to the public welfare. Such an opinion is contrary to the judgment of many representative men who have commended the board's success in improving the financial position of the railways.

"Save our railways was a phrase used by Mr Carlisle. That is the task which the board and the executive officers are accomplishing. The Prime Minister has indicated that in these difficult times it is not only a case of saving the railways; it is also a matter of saving the State (in the financial sense). Economies effected in the working of the railways during the past financial year amounted to more than £1,000,000 which otherwise would have been an addition to the taxpayers' burden. By this careful policy the net revenue of the railways was also improved by £150,000 for the year.

"With the new low scale of fares and extra provision for the comfort of passengers, the railways management is doing everything possible to draw more traffic. The satisfactory result of this policy is seen now in a noticeable 'back to the rail' movement among the public. Unfortunately, the railways are still handicapped by road competition on a basis which is far from equitable, and they also suffer from the short-sighted attitude of persons who expect to have the benefit of the low freight rates of the railways for heavy goods and to give preference to motors for other articles.

"Necessarily the capacity of the railways to serve the public must be related to the measure of support available. As common carriers the railways are obliged to accept any kind of freight offered. The list of commodities reaches a total of nearly 3000, including many low-rated articles which the motors shun. The road vehicles have the privilege of selecting the business which suits them." [49]

Perhaps additional regulations were required to further protect the railways' business? By August 1933, the Commissioner of Transport seemed to think so: "Economic aspects of State regulation of transport were touched upon by the Commissioner of Transport, Mr J. S. Hunter, in an address delivered to the Victoria University College Commerce Society this evening. He dealt particularly with the competition to the railways posed by road transport:

"The case for the regulation of transport rested fundamentally on the fact that transport belonged to that group of industries known as public service monopolies, Mr Hunter said. Motor transport did not perhaps conform to the conditions determining a public service monopoly to quite the same extent as the railways and tramways did, but obviously when competition developed between public motor services and other services the question arose whether the control exercised over them was to be relaxed, similar control extended over road services, or whether some midcourse should be adopted.

"In New Zealand, where the railways are State-owned and where the investment of public money represents some £60,000,000, it would undoubtedly produce chaos in our industry and trade if unregulated competition held sway, said Mr Hunter. Could we afford to see the deficit on our railways increase from £1,500,000 and our road bill to greater than the £8,000,000 it is-today? We could not afford it. We have no alternative but in the national interest to extend regulation to motor transport.

"The chief disadvantage of State regulation of transport is that any form of regulation must retard progress. There is always a tendency to maintain the status quo against new advances. The motor interests claim that regulation means bolstering up the railways. This argument is quite sound, but it misses the point. The question is not whether road or rail services, for instance, shall prevail, but what arrangements yield the maximum benefits to the public.

"I would direct your thoughts, Mr Hunter continued, to the following points: (1) Whether as a step further in the regulation of transport an investigation on lines of the Salter committee in Britain and its prototype in America would not serve a useful purpose in New Zealand in determining what proportion of our growing road bill should be met by taxation levied on the motor vehicle. (2) Whether there is not room for greater unification in the control of the various transport services in the Dominion through a single tribunal. (3) Whether there is not need for some co-ordinating authority to direct investment in transport facilities in the channels of greatest productivity." [50]

An attempt to satisfy at least two of those proposals was announced by the Minister of Transport, the Hon. J. G. Coates, on 29 March 1934:

"The appointment of the Transport Co-ordination Board was announced today by the Minister of Transport, the Hon. J. G. Coates. The personnel of the board is Sir Stephen Allen, chairman, Mr Lisle Alderton (Auckland) and Mr H. B. S. Johnstone (Otago, South Canterbury). Members of the board are appointed under the authority of the Transport Law Amendment Act of last session for a term of three years.

"In addition to hearing and determining appeals, which was formerly the function of a separate tribunal, the Transport Appeal Board, the board will, of its own initiative, or at the request of the Minister, make investigation into transport questions as it or the Minister deems necessary. The board is required to report to the Governor-General through the Minister the result of its investigations, and to make such recommendations as it thinks fit for the purpose of securing the improvement, co-ordination, development and better regulation and control of all transport facilities ...

"The importance to New Zealand of careful handling of all major transport questions, continued Mr Coates, was to be found in the fact that 35 per cent of the Dominion's public debt was represented by commitments of public money invested in railways, roads, harbours and tramways." [51]

One of the first investigations undertaken by the Transport Co-ordination Board concerned the matter of motor vehicle taxation, as reported by The New Zealand Herald on 5 October 1934:

"An investigation of motor taxation was commenced to-day by the Transport Co-ordination Board. Five days have been set aside for the purpose, and evidence will be tendered by various interested organisations, among them the Municipal Association, the Railways and Main Highways Boards, the Master Carriers and Customshouse Agents' Federation, the Omnibus Proprietors' Association, the Road Transport Alliance, the Motor Trade Federation, the Counties' Association, and the Farmers' Union.

"Evidence was tendered this morning by Mr W. G. Walkley on behalf of the North and South Island Motor Unions. He submitted that the level of motor taxation was now unreasonably high, that the manner in which it was applied was unsound in principle, and that double taxation was now being borne by the motorist.

"This, he said, was unjust. The annual taxes per vehicle had been increased by 1000 per cent since 1923. The original petrol tax of 4d a gallon, he recalled, was introduced in 1927. It was now 10d, plus surtax, and all the additional taxation was imposed for the benefit of the national exchequer, and the original plan that all revenue from petrol tax must be used on the roads had been ignored by later legislation." [52]

In case they didn't know, Mr Walkley was also keen to inform the Transport Co-ordination Board that the motor car was no longer an expensive novelty to be taxed as such:

"There seems to exist in the minds of many people an extraordinary misconception that if a person possesses a motor vehicle he is necessarily possessed of means above the average, said Mr W. G. Walkley, representative of the North and South Island Motor Unions, in giving evidence before the Transport Co-ordination Board which is inquiring into motor taxation at the instance of the Government.

"Mr Walkley said he preferred the term 'possession' rather than 'ownership' because a great many people who drove motor-cars had bought them on the hire-purchase plan...Twenty-five years ago such an assumption of means would have been right, but to-day the motor-car is so commonly used that ownership, if it indicates anything, does not necessarily indicate affluence...It is pointed out that ownership of a motor vehicle does not indicate ability to pay the punishing taxation now inflicted on the motorist..." [53]

Further submissions reinforcing the view that a motor car could no longer be considered a luxury item, but one of necessity, were made to the

Transport Co-ordination Board by the New Zealand Motor Trade Federation:

"After quoting the latest figures in respect of the occupations of owners of motor vehicles given in the 1934 report of the Commissioner of Transport, the New Zealand Motor Trade Federation asserted that the number of vehicles owned and used for pleasure purposes alone was very small. Because a small percentage were used for pleasure purposes, the assumption that motor cars were articles of luxury was unsound and even absurd." [54]

Subsequent submissions to the Transport Co-ordination Board's inquiry into motor taxation included those for and against any changes to the status quo:

"Joint submissions were presented to the Transport Co-ordination Board today on behalf of the New Zealand Road Transport Alliance and White Star services, representing commercial operators of both passenger and goods vehicles.

"The main relief sought was the abolition of heavy traffic fees. It was maintained that the petrol tax was the only form of taxation of motor transport which fairly measured highway usage. It was submitted that existing methods of taxation had outlived their usefulness and should be replaced by a simplified system which was calculated to ensure the future welfare of the whole Dominion." [55]

"When the Transport Co-ordination Board's inquiry into motor taxation was resumed to-day the Main Highways Board submitted a statement expressing the opinion that there should be no revolutionary alterations in motor taxation. Although some adjustments might be desirable, no proposal which was likely to deplete the Highways Board's funds should be entertained." [56]

The Main Highways Board certainly had good reason to fear any further erosion of its funds, as explained by a New Zealand Herald report of 6 February 1935:

"The North Island Motor Union has made another protest against the Main Highways Board being charged interest on advances received in its accounts. In another aspect this is not a new grievance, but the union's protest is intensified by the fact that the special taxation, imposed in the first instance for roading purposes, is now being levied upon to the extent of £500,000 a year for the benefit of the Consolidated Fund.

"As this has been done for three successive financial years, there is substance for the remark that it has become an annual practice. The Motor Union suggests that there is danger of the Highways Board funds becoming chaotic because of such things. Whether that risk is imminent or not, it is certain that the special financing of highway construction and maintenance has already departed seriously from the simplicity and singleness of purpose first designed for it.

"At the outset the revenue fund was supposed to receive the proceeds of the tyre tax and of motor registration and licence fees. It was also to be granted £35,000 a year from the Consolidated Fund. When the petrol tax was first imposed the entire net proceeds were to be divided between the board and various cities and boroughs in the proportion of 92 per cent and 8 per cent. Further the Construction Fund was to receive at least £200,000 a year from the Public Works Fund. All this money was to be available for direct expenditure on highways.

"Many changes have been made in the past four or five years. The annual £500,000 raid has already been mentioned. In 1930 the £35,000 grant to the Revenue Fund and the annual transfer of £200,000 from the Public Works Fund to the Construction Fund were discontinued. Since that date the board has been charged interest on £1,226,000 already received from the Public Works Fund by annual transfers.

"An increase in the petrol tax was made for the benefit of the Consolidated Fund. This did not directly affect the board's finances, but it changed what had previously been a single-purpose levy into one which is partly for roading purposes and, partly in effect a luxury tax – though it bears on much more than pleasure motoring. Again certain rating subsidies were placed on the board's funds instead of the Consolidated Fund. Thus, what started as a simple system of special taxation wholly intended for roading has developed such complications that the word chaotic is not inappropriate, though it applies more to the income of the Highways Board than to its accounts." [57]

Indeed, at a time when the increasing use of motor vehicles was becoming more of a necessity, that proportion of the tax take referred to as a 'luxury tax' side-lined into Government coffers, was described as 'intolerable' and a 'burden' by those representing motorists:

"The motorists' taxation burden reached the colossal sum of £5,336,537 last year (1934), states the president of the North Island Motor Union, Mr W. O'Callaghan, in a memorandum on motor taxation, and this load was carried by a class comprising only 15 per cent of the Dominion's population.

"In 1923 the Government collected from the motor vehicle owner the modest sum of £795,062. Last year's huge figure comprised petrol tax £2,712,884; 25 per cent exchange on motor imports, £939,129; customs duty on motor vehicle parts, tyres and lubricating oils, £795,618;

registrations and licence fees, £365,614; sales tax on motor imports, £283,292; heavy traffic fees, £180,000 and drivers' licences, £60,000...

"To-day the automobile associations ask the Government for immediate relief to the extent of at least 2d a gallon of the petrol tax, adds Mr O'Callaghan. In the light of the foregoing figures it is submitted that any fair-minded person will agree that the motor vehicle owner has every reason to feel dissatisfied with the present punishing and discriminatory taxation he is carrying." [58]

The Transport Co-ordination Board's inquiry into the taxation of motor transport was completed and its report delivered to the Government on 18 December 1934. Unfortunately for motorists, the Board's comprehensive findings did not completely agree with their view that motor transport taxes were 'punishing and discriminatory':

"We have now dealt with all the points brought before us which were relevant to the inquiry, and we wish finally to summarize our conclusions and recommendations. They are as follows:—

(1) Taxation upon the motor industry is heavy in common with taxation generally in the present times.
(2) Import duty on motor-vehicles and parts has not been criticized seriously, and calls for no special comment.
(3) Fees payable for registration, transfer of ownership, annual licenses, and drivers' licenses are not unreasonable.
(4) The existing scale of heavy-traffic license fees requires adjustment.
(5) Taxation on motor fuel, having regard to all the surrounding circumstances, is not excessive, and any increase beyond the present levy would probably bring into operation the principle of diminishing returns.
(6) Taxation of motor fuel does not provide a complete measure of road usage. A combination of motor-fuel tax and heavy-traffic fees represents the most equitable form of motor-vehicle taxation.
(7) The percentage of the motor-fuel tax which is now allocated to cities and larger boroughs, combined with a share of heavy-traffic license fees and drivers' license fees, provides a fair allocation for the construction and maintenance of main-highway continuations within their areas.
(8) If motor-fuel taxation is to be considered in relation to any standard of road construction and maintenance, it is essential that the national system of highways in the Dominion be completely classified. It does not appear possible to co-relate motor-taxation with road construction and maintenance over our national system of highways

until such highways have been so classified, and a general roading standard has been fixed." [59]

Consequently, one the Board's recommendations included:

"That no reduction in motor-taxation be granted except in conformity with a reduction of taxation in other directions as improvement in conditions in the Dominion may warrant." [60]

Following the Transport Co-ordination Board's report and recommendations, the Motor Vehicles Amendment Bill 1934-1935 was introduced to Parliament on 5 April 1935. In accordance with some of the Board's findings, the Bill contained some important changes to the way motor vehicles were to be taxed, as reported by the Auckland Star on 5 April 1935:

"An important reclassification of motor vehicles for taxation purposes is provided in the Motor Vehicles Amendment Bill, which was introduced in the House of Representatives by Governor's Message last night. The Minister of Finance, Mr Coates, intimated that there was no intention of rushing the bill through this session.

"The principal effects of the amendment are as follow:—(1) All motor vehicles consuming motor spirits and using the roads for the greater part of their time will pay taxation through the petrol tax, annual license fees and, in the case of heavy vehicles, heavy traffic fees; (2) all motor vehicles not consuming motor spirits will pay taxation through a mileage tax based on their actual road mileage; (3) those motor vehicles which consume motor spirits, but are used on roads for only a small portion of their total use, will now be able to be exempted from license fees, motor spirits tax and heavy traffic fees, but they can be required to pay a mileage tax based on the use they make of the roads." [61]

Following the passage of the Motor Vehicles Amendment Act 1934-1935, the taxation changes took effect on 1 June 1935. However, as well as taxation, the Transport Co-ordination Board had a much larger transport issue to deal with – one that highlighted the very essence of transport management and an issue that has never been reconciled since, to the detriment of the whole country in terms of transport efficiency and cost-effectiveness.

The Board's concern was plainly stated in their first annual report of August 1935:

"Before leaving the question of co-ordination, we desire to bring to your notice an important aspect of the problem which we consider requires attention. We refer to the necessity of co-ordinating the activities of the various bodies which control the finance and construction of capital works in the transport field. We are of the opinion that any future major constructional work in the transport field should be examined from the standpoint of the economic effect of existing transport services. It is true that this step will not assist in the co-ordination of the existing facilities, but it will at least have the effect of preventing the perpetuation of past errors in the duplication of transport facilities, thereby inviting unnecessary competition with services which in many cases have proved to be entirely satisfactory.

"The most striking aspects of the existing financial control are the great diversification of authority controlling the expenditure of money in transport development and the lack of economic co-ordination between the various conflicting fields of transport construction. We refer in general terms to the construction of railways supplanting coastal shipping services, to the development of main highways promoting direct competition with the railway service, the development of small harbours at the expense of elaborately equipped major ports, and the projected expenditure on airports which may affect all other forms of transport.

"We quote the following observation of Mr J. B. Eastman, the Federal Co-ordinator of Transport for the United States of America, after an exhaustive examination of the transport position in that country: 'If no thought is given to the development of a well-co-ordinated national system of transportation, and Government money is poured into the construction of new means of transportation without regard to the effect upon those which already exist in the greatest profusion, and if, on top of all this, competition between rival forms of transportation is allowed to run riot, there can be no ultimate end but complete demoralization with injury to all and benefit to none." [62]

Needless to say, the Transport Co-ordination Board's comments were well-founded, given the parochialism and cronyism that had shaped the country's transport history to that point. One of the more recent instances of competitive 'riot' occurred during late 1934, resulting in a number of appeals to the Transport Co-ordination Board:

"A large number of appeals has been received by the Transport Department against the recent decision of the No. 2 Licensing Authority, which declined to renew the great majority of licenses for motor transport firms running between Auckland and the Waikato and Thames. It granted three licenses, declined 13, and restricted another 13 to local areas, preventing a through run to Auckland. It is understood that approximately 40 motor vehicles are adversely affected by the decision, against which there is the right of appeal. The operators are entitled to continue the services until their appeals are heard. The Transport Co-ordination Board, which is now the Appeal Board...is expected to make arrangements to hear the appeals in Auckland subsequently." [63]

In line with their common-sense reasoning of what constituted competition in terms of the principles of the Transport Act, the Transport Co-ordination Board subsequently reversed most of the No. 2 Licensing Authority decisions in favour of the motor transport firms.

"In reversing most of the decisions recently made by the No. 2 District Transport Licensing Authority, the Transport Co-ordination Board has set out in some detail its conception of the principles of the Act in so far as they relate to the licensing and control of commercial goods services. It is a timely pronouncement in view of the somewhat confused state of mind of the community upon this important matter.

"The board's reasoned judgment dismisses the idea that any licensing authority may prohibit a service simply to eliminate competition. Public interest is bound up in the fortunes of the railways because millions of borrowed money have been invested in them. It would, however, be contrary to the principles through which commerce has progressed if competition that secures an adequate measure of support could be suppressed at the stroke of a pen.

"Local authority must not exceed that of the legislature, and, in the opinion of the board, this has been attempted by the No. 2 district. The Co-ordination Board discusses the import of the words 'desirable' and 'necessary' and points out in favour of certain road transport services, that the factors of speed, time of operation, suitability for carriage of particular goods, general convenience, or a combination of any of these factors, might be of inestimable benefit to the residents of the district served.

"One test of desirability, says the board, is surely the extent of public patronage. It reaffirms the opinion that the railways are entitled to such consideration and protection as is comparable with the service they are rendering to the public, but fails to find in the Act the intention that road services running parallel with the railways should be eliminated as a form of special protection.

"It argues that, notwithstanding the contention of the Railways Board that there is 'overwhelming desirability' in regard to rail transport, no form of transport can have a vested right which would stand in the way of progress toward a more economic and convenient form..." [64]

While the Transport Co-ordination Board's reversal of the No. 2 Licensing Authority's decisions related more to the conflict then existing between the country's public railway service and privately-operated goods vehicles, the Board's preference for fair competition also applied to the realm of public transport. In particular, the Board's laissez-faire views extended to the growing competition between the Government-owned railways, the municipal trams and privately-owned bus services.

But, unfortunately for the Board's intended 'progress toward a more economic and convenient form', the newly-elected (December 1935) Labour Government and its Transport Minister, Robert Semple, had other ideas:

"The whole transport system is most unsatisfactory, said the Minister of Transport, Hon. R. Semple, in announcing the immediate suspension of the functions of the Transport Co-ordination Board pending the enactment of new legislation reconstructing the scheme of transport control.

"The Transport Board is to issue no more licences or hear any more cases of any kind — in other words they do not exist as far as their functions are concerned, the Minister said. Mr Semple explained that he early appreciated the need to co-ordinate rationally road, rail, sea and air services in the best interests of the country generally. He had therefore conferred with the Cabinet, which set up a committee comprising the Minister of Railways, Hon. D. G. Sullivan, the Minister in charge of the Tourist and Publicity Departments, Hon. F. Langstone, and himself, with the general manager of railways, Mr G. H. Mackley, the commissioner of transport, Mr G. C. Godfrey, and the engineer-in-chief of the Public Works Department, Mr C. J. McKenzie.

"This committee was making a complete investigation and had cabled to Queensland and South Africa, as well as other parts of the Empire, seeking information regarding transport experiences and laws, to assist drafting fresh New Zealand legislation, which it was hoped would be ready for the next session. The Minister condemned cut-throat competition, with accompanying sweated labour, and also expressed dissatisfaction at the present legislation, which made a Minister 'just a rubber stamp'. [65]

So, once more during Auckland's transport history and, indeed, that of the country, the politicians had overruled and succeeded a Government-appointed advisory board – the decisions of which apparently had not found favour with its new political masters. The reason for the Minister's decision in this case seemed obvious to at least one commentator:

"The opinion that the Transport Co-ordination Board as at present constituted had tended to favour the private operator rather than the railways in road transport appeals that had come before it, was expressed last night by an Auckland solicitor who has been closely associated with transport licensing work. He recalled that the board had allowed the restoration of several services which had failed in appeals to the former Transport Appeal Board, and last April reversed the decisions of the No. 2

District Licensing Authority, which had refused renewals of licences for 26 goods services between Auckland and southern districts. In his opinion the need was not so much the abolition of the board, as its reconstitution with supreme control over all forms of transport. Although at present it could deal with road and air services, travel by sea and rail was outside its control." [66]

However, as reported by The New Zealand Herald on 13 February 1936, the Minister was in no mood to consider any reconstitution of the Transport Co-ordination Board. Indeed, in keeping with his reputation as a hands-on, get-things-done individual, Robert Semple intended to do things his way:

"I will not allow the Transport Co-ordination Board to sit again, said the Minister of Transport, the Hon. R. Semple, to-day in replying to a deputation from the New Brighton Borough Council. The Christchurch Tramway Board recently decided to discontinue a bus service to part of New Brighton and residents of the area decided to appeal to the Transport Co-ordination Board. As this board is suspended, the council approached the Minister.

"Mr Semple said the matter would not be long delayed but he would not allow the Co-ordination Board to sit again. He advised the deputation to send an appeal and petition to him at Wellington. As soon as possible Parliament would review the whole matter and in the meantime the board would not be allowed to make decisions." [67]

True to his word, central control by the Minister was soon to be established with the introduction of the Motor-vehicles Amendment and the Transport Licensing Amendment Acts of 1936:

"The complete reorganisation of the transport system of New Zealand will be brought about by two bills which the Minister of Transport, the Hon. R. Semple, will introduce during the coming session of Parliament. The main points of the bills, as indicated by Mr Semple to-day, are:—

"The number of transport licensing authorities is to be reduced to four, one in each of the main centres. The Transport Co-ordination Board is to disappear, and all appeals made direct to the Minister. Better wages and conditions and shorter hours of work will be ensured for employees in the transport services. A saving of between £7000 and £8000 a year will be made in the administration of the Transport Act. Closer co-operation and co-ordination between transport services will be provided for, and cut-throat competition will be prevented. The Minister alone shall have power to grant licenses for air transport services.

"One organisation will be set up to control traffic in the whole of New Zealand apart from the metropolitan areas, and the existing system of county councils and borough councils having power to draw up by-laws for the control of traffic will be abolished. A set of by-laws covering the whole of New Zealand, except the metropolitan areas, will be drawn up and a proper system of control instituted." [68]

Section ten of the Transport Licensing Amendment Act retrospectively abolished the Transport Co-ordination Board as of 1 April 1936 and it was heard of no more. But the empowerment of one Government minister authorised to decide complex transport matters did not proceed without opposition, some of which was reported by the Auckland Star and The New Zealand Herald on 20 May 1936:

"The opinion that it would be better to have the control of transport entrusted to a board rather than to leave wide and ultimate powers in the hands of a Minister was expressed by Mr R. A. Wright (Independent, Wellington Suburbs) in the second reading debate on the Transport Licensing Amendment Bill in the House to-night.

"What I don't like is the fact that the transport services of New Zealand are to be controlled by the Government of the day—by the Minister, he said. Mr Wright said that in making his protest he was speaking impersonally, and was making no personal reflection on any member of the Government. His point was that it was unwise for the Minister to be the sole judge in regard to the transport system of New Zealand, especially when the Government was an interested party by owning and controlling the railway system.

"Under the proposed system, appeals would be made to the Minister. He stressed the difficulties there would be when particular friends were concerned. Mr Semple replied that he would not be prompted by individuals' influence. Mr Wright said that human nature was the same all over the world, and he pointed out the difficulties of the Minister having to make a decision between personal friends, neither of whom was wrong." [69]

"A general criticism of what he referred to as the restrictive proposals in the Transport Licensing Amendment Bill was voiced by the Rt. Hon. J. G. Coates (Opposition—Kaipara) during the second reading debate on the measure in the House of Representatives to-night. It has been laid down that the object of any transport system must be to ensure that the public is provided with the cheapest and most efficient form of transportation, Mr Coates said. History reveals successive replacements of one form of transportation by another, and the Minister himself, in his historical review of transport in New Zealand, has admitted that argument.

"We are far removed from the days of the stage coach and the bullock team. Does not the Minister realise that by protecting the railways he may be protecting something already growing obsolete in certain directions?

Road transport can only he developed by having a right to expand. Under the Government's legislation it will be denied that right.

"There was power in the bill, Mr Coates continued, for the setting up of one-man authorities, instead of the existing tribunals, and by Order-in-Council the number of authorities and number of transport districts could be reduced. One man, presumably a civil servant responsible to the Minister and the Government of the day, could be charged with the licensing of transport. It might be said that only a simplification of method was proposed, but the inherent danger was that of political control.

"A study of the bill forced the conclusion that the proposed alterations in the constitution of licensing authorities were only a piece of legislative bluff. The Minister was given power to over-ride the decisions of the authorities and would become a dictator of transport, with power to suspend or revoke existing licences by star chamber methods...

"The Government is denying freedom and attempting to abolish any suggestion of competition, which is the key to improved conditions and services. It appears to take the view that transport problems resolve themselves into a question of rail versus road. This view is almost criminal in its narrowness. There should be no question of warring interests. It should not be rail versus road, but rail and road." [70]

In his reply to opposition criticism of the Transport Licensing Amendment Bill, the Minister of Railways, Hon. D. G. Sullivan, did not claim the ability to anticipate future transport preferences. That was just as well, because he was wrong (or at the very least, his vision fell very much short of that which was promised):

"No infringement of the rights of road operators is contemplated by the Government, according to a statement by the Minister of Railways, Hon. D. G. Sullivan, during the second reading debate on the Transport Licensing Amendment Bill, which was continued in the House of Representatives to-day...

"Apparently Mr Coates believed that the railways were obsolete and could not recover lost ground...The Minister said he was not going to pose as a prophet, but he thought Mr Coates was overlooking the possibilities of the rail-car, which would probably prove a very valuable means of winning back to the railways a substantial percentage of the traffic now carried by private motor-cars.

"Personally, I would sooner ride in a rail-car than a motor-car, Mr Sullivan added, and I think that when we get the cheaper and more comfortable service which the rail-car can provide, thousands will adopt that means of transport. There is no doubt in my mind that the rail-car is more attractive than buses or ordinary trains." [71]

Following the defeat of a last-minute amendment advocating that appeals from the licensing authority should be heard by a magistrate and not by the Minister of Transport, the Transport Licensing Amendment Bill was passed by the Legislative Council and became law on 1 June 1936. The appointees responsible to the Minister of Transport for the four district licensing authorities were named three weeks later:

"Four district licensing authorities have been appointed by the Government under the new Transport Licensing Amendment Act, and they will take the places of the former central licensing authorities and will have power to grant passenger service licences and to exercise jurisdiction in respect of transport affairs under Ministerial control...

"All the men appointed were of wide general experience, had a sound knowledge of the districts which they would administer, were 100 per cent loyal to the policy of the Government, and were sympathetic toward the transport situation." [72]

During May and June 1936, Parliament also had the Motor Vehicles Amendment Bill to consider. While this Bill was somewhat less contentious than the Transport Licensing Amendment Bill, the legislation still provided for a more rigid control of motor vehicles, their owners, and drivers, as reported by The New Zealand Herald on 26 May 1936:

"The nationalisation of traffic regulations and traffic inspection are two of the major provisions of the Motor Vehicles Amendment Bill, which the Minister of Transport, Hon. R. Semple, hopes to be able to bring down before Parliament adjourns for the short winter recess.

"Unless we can get proper control over road traffic we have no chance of reducing the number of accidents on the roads, Mr Semple said. I regard this as one of our most urgent needs. The bill will give us power to take this control and to ensure that all vehicles on the roads shall reach an adequate standard of mechanical fitness.

"We cannot go on killing people at the present rate and I am satisfied that scores of fatal accidents on the roads are due entirely to the lack of proper control and inspection. Mr Semple said the bill would provide for a nationalised system of traffic inspection and a nationalised schedule of traffic laws which would apply all over the Dominion..." [73]

But while the nationalisation of motor traffic regulation was criticised by many, few could argue with legislation that sought to protect those potential victims of the motor car mayhem to come:

"The hit and run motorist came under the scathing lash of the tongue of the Minister of Transport, Mr Semple, when explaining in the House of Representatives on Saturday the provisions contained in the Motor Vehicles Amendment Bill. A clause is included, he said, that increases the maximum penalty to which a motorist is liable when he is involved in an accident and fails to stop. This is a most serious problem in New Zealand and throughout the world.

"Under existing law the maximum penalty was three months' imprisonment and a fine of £20, he said. That was insufficient for a 'hit and run' motorist, and the bill provided for a maximum penalty of five years, or a fine not exceeding £500. Mr Semple said a severe penalty was needed. A man who was intoxicated while in charge of a motor car and knocked somebody down and left him to die on the road was a potential murderer, and should be punished.

"Such a mishap might, on the other hand, be due to accident, but it was the duty of every citizen to stop his car and take the injured person to the nearest hospital. Men and women had been left on the road to die but their lives might have been saved had they been taken at once to a hospital. Men who were guilty of such a cowardly crime presented a problem here and elsewhere, and the bill was designed to make the penalty fit the offence. Accidents were liable to increase in proportion to the increased number of cars on the road." [74]

But, what did the Bill do for the rights and obligations of pedestrians?

"An appeal for consideration of the pedestrian was made by Mr J. A. Lee (Government —Grey Lynn) during the second reading debate on the Motor Vehicles Amendment Bill in the House of Representatives to-day. Mr Lee explained that he would not have intervened in the debate but being one of the last remaining 'tribe of pedestrians' he was anxious to sing his swan-song before the speed of the motor-car was increased.

"For some uncanny reason those who in this age of whizz want to chase their tails by the internal combustion method seem to be wholly contemptuous of the pedestrian, Mr Lee said. The pedestrian is expected to be a machine. He must always have his wits about him, but at the same time he is expected to be so much of a dullard that when he steps out on to the road he must have only one idea in his head —he must be asking is there a motor-car coming.

"But surely we are going to be allowed a little bit of time in which to walk and dream. We should not assume that it is the right of the pedestrian all the time to have to see that he dodges the car and that it is the right of the motorist to take it for granted that there might not be someone else on the road. As it is, the poor dreamer who walks out on to the road is a pedestrian. As such he is a tartar. The only crime he has committed is that of being a human being and not a machine.

"Mr Lee referred to fast traffic in the vicinity of Parliament Buildings and said it was a wonder that there were not more by-elections. Members of Parliament must be agile to dodge speeding motor-cars that tore down the roads near the building.

"I do not want to be let loose on the roads on the understanding that I have no right there, Mr Lee added. Yet it has been said during this debate that the pedestrian has no right on some of our roads. Surely it is time that those who are not motorists in New Zealand should assert that the human being has a right to be a human being and that the duty of motorists is to have such control over their cars that if the pedestrian does take a step to the right or left because he wants to dream a little he should be safe. Surely we are not going to say 'well done' because a motorist catches him in the back.

"Mr Lee prophesied that if pedestrians did not assert their right the day would come when the motorist would decorate his cars with some indication of the number of scalps he had taken. He was a little doubtful about the proposal in the bill to increase speed. The motorist usually claimed that the faster he could go the safer it was. It was difficult to see that the claim was just." [75]

Many of the requirements contained in the amendments to the Motor Vehicles Amendment Act 1936 persist today, in the form of 'warrant of fitness' inspections and the perils of buying used vehicles, as reported by The New Zealand Herald on 23 July 1936:

"Various amendments to the Motor Vehicles Amendment Bill were introduced in the House of Representatives by Governor-General's Message to-day and circulated in the form of a supplementary order paper. The alterations in the bill follow generally the lines of a statement made yesterday by the Minister of Transport, the Hon. R. Semple, who said that in the main the bill had been well received by local bodies and other organisations by which it had been discussed.

"A clause in the original bill providing for the registration of bicycles has been deleted. In explaining the amendment the Minister said it had been deemed wise to leave the registration of bicycles to local bodies. Under another amendment the Minister has power to revoke any local body by-law which in his opinion may be unreasonable or undesirable in its relation to motor traffic.

"There is also power for regulations to be made providing for the periodical examination of motor-vehicles at a fee not exceeding 5s for each examination...A provision designed to protect purchasers of second-hand cars was included among the amendments. The Minister said it enabled a prospective purchaser of a used car to investigate its history by looking up the register on payment of a fee of 1s. A great deal of fraudulent dealing was going on in respect of second-hand cars, and the amendment had been inserted to protect the public." [76]

The Motor Vehicles Amendment Act was subsequently passed by the House of Representatives on 23 July 1936. Various sections of Bill came into force later that year, including the maximum speed limit of thirty miles an hour in populated areas, effective from 1 September 1936.

Of course, the regulation of a vehicle's speed is pointless when the road ahead is choked with knotted lines of motor cars, trucks and buses, as described by correspondence to the Evening Post published on 10 November 1936:

"We are letting ourselves be tied in traffic knots everywhere by the failure to take time by the forelock. With more cars to the mile of road than any other country, we are only just beginning to see that a great extension of motorways is the only alternative to a blood-stained congestion. And all the time, we are spending millions just to keep the unemployed alive and let them stand at street corners.

"The above is taken from a recent issue of the Observer (English), a paper not famed for any help for the motorist. This Dominion (writes H.D.B. to The Post) is in the same predicament, and we, too, should sit up and take notice. Latest records show that there are 216,000 registered cars in New Zealand, not far from one to six of the population, and rapidly heading for second place in world car density. A fine-day holiday such as Labour Day a week or two ago finds the road load factor at its maximum, and we find ourselves ready to endorse the statement quoted above with perhaps more besides.

"Readers of English and Continental periodicals and magazines will know that the coming of the motor-car has almost overwhelmed traffic controlling authorities in all civilised countries. At home here our traffic congestion problems may be divided into two classes, the first the jam in city streets; second, the unyielding procession on the highways. It is, of course, admitted that the difficulty which our road engineers have had to meet is in the attempt to reconcile modern traffic requirements to the coach roads of colonial days already laid down.

"New Zealand is a comparatively easy country to road. Our traffic troubles have been progressive in their incidence. Could we have foreseen the development ten or fifteen years ago, and given the necessary courage, our highways today would have been both able to accommodate the traffic and some millions of money saved. Road engineers and we have a fair share of the best of them, are after all public servants, and must do, generally, what they are told. It is public opinion therefore that we must mould into modern road sense." [77]

While the terms, 'modern road sense' and 'modern traffic requirements', conveyed little more in 1936 than they do now, the truly modern difference in the twenty-first century is, of course, one of scale. As the first century of Auckland's journey drew to a close and the traffic problems of the 1930s were allowed to 'progress in their incidence', that incidence was nothing compared to the later decades of motor vehicle indulgence, when the demand for private and commercial mobility quickly surpassed the availability of public transport and the quality roads needed to magic-carpet the faster and heavier vehicles.

This eventual predominance of one mode of transport over another was almost entirely due to the lack of any comprehensive plan by which the city's transport systems could be integrated and governed as one unit. Instead, the various transport systems continued to compete for infrastructure and patronage, regardless of their respective places in the wider landscape.

Too often, it was the political patronage, and of course the funding that support attracted, that determined the success or otherwise of transport-related enterprises. That seemed to be the case with the construction of Auckland's new 'Municipal Transport Station' which was officially opened at what is now 'Britomart' on 13 September 1937, as reported by the Auckland Star:

"The severing of a blue and white ribbon with a pair of silver scissors by the Mayoress of Auckland, Lady Davis, marked the official opening this afternoon of Auckland's new transport terminal on the old railway site. The ceremony, which introduced a new era as far as the control of both bus and service car transport is concerned, was largely attended by members of the public, representatives of the Auckland City Council, transport interests, and suburban local bodies.

"Throughout yesterday the station was used by buses and service cars which cater for a big portion of Auckland's travelling public, and from to-day the full services on the various routes radiating from the city were in operation. Everything worked smoothly, and there was not a semblance of confusion at the long covered platforms which are a feature of the new station…

"…Mr F. W. Schramm, M.P. for Auckland East,…said the traffic problem in New Zealand was still in its infancy, and predicted that in Auckland it would become very acute in years to come. The station would tend to lessen the congestion which was bound to occur in the future, particularly in Lower Queen Street…

"Mr N B. Spencer, chairman of the Auckland Omnibus Proprietors' Association, said the terminal marked a very important milestone in the history of passenger transport in Auckland. The transport operators had long felt the want of a central transport terminal, but nothing could be done while they had annual licenses only, and the transport business was in a state of uncertainty. However, the transport business had now settled down, and was taking its rightful place in the life of the people, thus making possible the building and financing of the station.

"The Mayor, Sir Ernest Davis, said it was worthy of comment that in a swiftly-moving age, in which one advancement was rapidly succeeded by another, the city of Auckland had not failed to keep closely abreast, on the question of road passenger transport facilities, with modern practice oversea, and the result was the provision of a fine transport station. It had outstanding features to give it the right to rank alongside the latest termini in other countries, and which, in accordance with the policy of the corporation, recognised future as well as current requirements..." [78]

Then again, appearances can be deceptive, as per the 'unexpected' comments of the Auckland Omnibus Proprietors' Association chairman:

"An unexpected note was struck at the official opening ceremony of Auckland's new transport station to-day by Mr N. B. Spencer, chairman of the Auckland Omnibus Proprietors' Association. We consider that if the City Council had taken more notice of the views of those operating the transport services the result would have been a much more efficient terminal, which would have cost the operators a great deal less, said Mr Spencer.

"The terminal is costing the operators about £70 a week, including an annual payment of £550 towards the capital cost of the buildings. The terminal has not cost the council a penny piece. Everything is paid by the operators. Mr Spencer said it was felt that they should have had platforms like the up-to-date stations in England where the buses run right through. However, they would carry on and do their best. The operators had to pay for everything.

"There were a couple of interjections at this stage, and in reply to one Mr Spencer said that operators had agreed at the moment not to increase the fares and to carry on. He hoped that the station would be a success, and would be used more and more by the public as time went on. The Mayor, Sir Ernest Davis, said in reply that he thought the remarks had been a little inopportune. The City Council had given all the points great consideration." [79]

However, as time went on, there came another war during which there was an artificial lull in motor vehicle usage. The lull was mainly due to a shortage of resources such as petrol, as reported by the Auckland Star on 5 October 1939:

"Petrol restriction has introduced some people, who hitherto have used nothing but their cars for travel, to new modes of transport. A Wellington woman, mother of a near-adult family, rode in a bus last week for the second time in her life, though she has lived many years in a suburb served by bus as well as by railway." [80]

Then, when the war came to an end, the 1930's concept of a magic carpet to transport New Zealanders about and between the country's larger cities took on the weave pattern of exclusivity in the form of a motorway system.

Principally based on those built in America, motorways were then thought to be the solution needed to deal with the growing motor vehicle congestion of the world's cities. On 17 March 1945, the Auckland Star published an overview, written by its London correspondent, about the motor vehicle traffic decisions faced by the 'Mother' country and therefore, by implication, soon to be faced by New Zealand:

"In a few years, or sooner, motoring, for the million will again be in full swing in Great Britain. More motoring for many more millions, in fact. Some motor car manufacturers are ready with their immediate post-war programmes. Output, it is reported, can begin in a small way three months after the war ends. That trickle will quickly become a flood. New models made by new methods will come pouring from the factories in ever-increasing numbers. The Government have estimated that 20 years after the end of the war there will be four times as many cars on the roads as there were in 1939…

"Four times as many cars; four times as much congestion; four times as many accidents! Is that a logical sequence? The answer must be 'Yes' — so long as modern traffic is constricted by the inadequate road system that wasted so much time and money, and levied toll of so many lives before the war. What is the primary cause of road accidents in normal times? Most people will say at once: Speed. But this is only partly, true. The real answer is: Speed in the wrong place.

"A fast aeroplane is no more dangerous than a slow one in its proper medium. An express train is just as safe as a goods train, because it has the track cleared before it. But high-speed travel on the roads of this country is definitely dangerous, because the average road, with its twists, bends, crossings and blind corners, its pedestrians and it mixed traffic, is the wrong place for speed.

"What is the remedy? Not to limit the speed of motor cars or to design low-powered engines. That would be a retrograde step in an age of fast travel. It would also be as great a burden on British cars in the export market as is the existing system of taxation.

"The only way is to build, and to begin building as soon as possible, a completely new system of motorways linking the most important centres and reserved for the exclusive use of motor traffic. Upon these great wide highways speed would be unrestricted." [81]

*Afterword*

Nowadays, few Auckland drivers, travelling upon their 'great wide highways', could describe their speed as 'unrestricted'. On the contrary, while the forecasted flood of motor cars certainly eventuated, the infrastructure needed to efficiently divert the torrent through and about the city did not. This is despite the millions of dollars spent on countless transport studies, committees, and reports commissioned over many decades.

Indeed, parliamentary and local council archives remain littered with the advice and recommendations reported by Royal Commissions, tribunals, and experts. Unfortunately, that advice was rarely accepted or deemed to be unsuited to agendas already decided. Too soon, studies became paper skeletons to be entombed and over-buried by fresh debates, commissions of inquiry, and more reports.

It is this utter disregard for expensive, professional advice commissioned so many times during the city's first century that astounds more than the apparent lack of capital, the effects of two world wars and depressions, and even the parochialism and commercial self-interest allowed to stymie many worthwhile projects.

Unfortunately for the transport aspirations of New Zealand, and Auckland in particular, consensus was too often sabotaged by both national and local parochialism. The national prejudice that existed between the North and South Islands was exhibited early during the railway building process, at a time when the fortunes and aspirations of southern cities such as Christchurch and Dunedin rivalled those of Auckland and Wellington.

Indeed, the rivalry was such that a Northern Association was formed in Auckland in December 1864, with the objective "…to take steps to secure the separation of the Province of Auckland from the Southern portion of the Colony of New Zealand." [82]

That didn't happen, but an active fight for a fair share of the treasury purse continues today, too often to the detriment of national prosperity.

Obviously, when infrastructure finance is tight, as it always has been, some local partiality and commercial interest can be forgiven or, at least, understood. When the spanning of the Waitemata was again proposed during the 1920s, the owners of the Devonport Ferry Company had legitimate reasons to object. So did members of the Auckland Harbour

Board who claimed a bridge would interfere with plans to expand their activities westward to the upper reaches of the harbour. Eventually, some semblance of national and regional consensus resulted in the building of the bridge but long, long after it was so desperately needed.

That's not to say a self-centred pursuit of commercial profit has not benefited Aucklanders in general, and resulted in a better city far removed from the first tents erected on the beach by Hobson. There's no doubt that by way of the railways, the trams, Grafton Bridge, the Harbour Bridge, the Newmarket Viaduct, and the Sky Tower, the city has indeed come a long way.

Nevertheless, Aucklanders cannot travel between those city icons much faster than when they relied on the horse-drawn trams of 1900. By the time the last tram clanked to oblivion on 29 December 1956, the motor car and the motor bus had prevailed and the age of a much slower form of congested chaos had dawned. This was despite the advice of a string of well-paid experts who continued to advocate the building of those 'great wide highways' – but not without an equal investment in public transport.

While patronage of Auckland's public transport services (trams, trains, ferries and buses) had substantially decreased since the war years and the advent of the motor car, there were still some 60 million, public-transport passenger trips recorded during 1960. Buses with their greater route flexibility and carrying capacity were the logical replacement for the trams.

However, without the dedicated road space that the trams had enjoyed, buses have only added to the congestion and the frustration of motorists vying for their share of the highway and byway.

Those motorists might now travel in greater comfort, depending on the standard of motor vehicle they can afford – but faster? Not at all.

## References

**Waka Paddle to Gas Pedal**
**The First Century of Auckland Transport – 1840 to 1940**

1. McCrystal, John. (2007). On the Buses in New Zealand - From Charabancs to the Coaches of Today. Wellington, Grantham House Publishing & Bus and Coach Association.

### Introduction
1. (1914). Railway Improvements. The New Zealand Herald and Daily Southern Cross. Auckland. Volume LI. Edition 15705. 4 September 1914. P.6.

### Chapter One
### The Inland Waterways – Paper Canals
1. Petrie, H. (2006). Maori Enterprise: Ships and Flour Mills. City of Enterprise. I. Hunter and D. Morrow. Auckland, Auckland University Press. P.38.
2. Hooker, B. (1987). "An Early Auckland Transport Plan Rediscovered." Auckland-Waikato Historical Journal No. 50: PP. 32-34.
3. (1884) Auckland-Onehunga Canal. Te Aroha News. Te Aroha, Waikato. Volume 1, Edition 51. 24 May 1884. P.6.
4. (1908) Auckland and Manukau Canal Act. General Assembly of New Zealand. 10 October 1908.
5. (1903). Untitled. Auckland Star. Auckland. Volume XXXIV, Edition 193. 14 August 1903. P.4.
6. (1909). Auckland Harbour Board - Waitemata-Manukau Canal. The New Zealand Herald. Auckland. Volume XLVI, Edition 14187. 9 October 1909. P.6.
7. (1909). Improvements In Transport. Auckland Star. Auckland. Volume XL. Edition 37. 12 February 1909. P.4.
8. (1914). Inland Waterways - Commission Of Inquiry. The New Zealand Herald. Auckland. Volume LI. Edition 15579. 9 April 1914. P.8.
9. (1914). Bridge Over Harbour - Between City And Suburbs. The New Zealand Herald. Auckland. Volume LI. Edition 15588. 21 April 1914. P.8.
10. (1919). The Projected Canal. The New Zealand Herald. Auckland. Volume LVI. Edition 17154. 7 May 1919. P.8.
11. (1920). Inland Waterways - The Suspended Commission. Auckland Star. Auckland. Volume LI. Edition 54. 3 March 1920. P.8.

12. (1920). Ferro Bridge Over Tamaki. <u>Auckland Star</u>. Auckland. Volume LI. 20 July 1920. P.6.
13. (1920). Inland Waterways - Waikato River Navigation. <u>The New Zealand Herald</u>. Auckland. Volume LVII. Edition 17580. 20 September 1920. P.6.

**Chapter Two**
**Across the Waitemata – The Ferries**
1. (1926). Bridging The Waitemata - The Story Of The Ferries. <u>Auckland Star</u>. Auckland. Volume LVII. Edition 220. 16 September 1926. P.11.
2. Mackay, J. A. (1973). "Early Takapuna and Transport on the North Shore." <u>Historical Journal Auckland – Waikato</u>. Volume 22. April 1973. P.2.
3. (1860). Shipping Intelligence. <u>Daily Southern Cross</u>. Auckland. Volume XVII. Edition 12. 27 March 1860. P.3.
4. (1860). Pleasure Trips By Steam. <u>Daily Southern Cross</u>. Auckland. Volume XVII. Edition 1275. 9 March 1860. P.3.
5. (1860). The Steamer Emu. <u>The Colonist</u>. Nelson. Volume IV. Edition 320. 13 November 1860. P.2.
6. (1860). Shipping Intelligence - Port Of Auckland. <u>Daily Southern Cross</u>. Auckland. Volume XVII. Edition 1350. 16 November 1860. P.2.
7. (1865). Launch Of The Enterprise. <u>The New Zealand Herald</u>. Auckland. Volume II. Edition 611. 27 October 1865. P.4.
8. (1867). The Stokes' Point Ferry <u>The New Zealand Herald</u>. Auckland. Volume IV. Edition 989. 15 January 1867. P.4.
9. (1870). Launch Of The New Ferry Steamer Devonport. <u>The New Zealand Herald</u>. Auckland. Volume VII. Edition 2116. 5 November 1870. P.6.
10. (1870). Untitled. <u>Auckland Star</u>. Auckland. Volume I. Edition 290. 14 December 1870. P.2.
11. (1872). Auckland Harbour Board. <u>Auckland Star</u>. Auckland. Volume III. Edition 826. 10 September 1872. P.2.
12. (1872). North Shore Ferry. <u>Daily Southern Cross</u>. Auckland. Volume XXVIII. Edition 4691. 5 September 1872. P.3.
13. (1872). The New Ferry Company. <u>Auckland Star</u>. Auckland. Volume III. Edition 824. 7 September 1872. P.2.
14. (1872). The Takapuna. <u>Auckland Star</u>. Auckland. Volume III. Edition 856. 2 December 1872. P.3.

15. (1873). Auckland And North Shore Steam Ferry Company. The New Zealand Herald. Auckland. Volume X. Edition 2796. 14 January 1873. P.3.
16. (1873). The Takapuna. Auckland Star. Auckland. Volume IV. Edition 900. 25 January 1873. P.2.
17. (1873). The Ferry Company. Auckland Star. Auckland. Volume IV. Edition 1074. 1 July 1873. P.2.
18. (1874). Auckland And North Shore Steam Ferry Company. The New Zealand Herald. Auckland. Volume XI. Edition 3815. 3 February 1874. P.3.
19. (1881). The New Steam Ferry Company. The New Zealand Herald. Auckland. Volume XVIII. Edition 6183. 16 September 1881. P.5.
20. (1881). Untitled. Auckland Star. Auckland. Volume XII. Edition 3480. 1 October 1881. P.2.
21. (1881). Untitled Editorial. Auckland Star. Auckland. Volume XII. Edition 3487. 10 October 1881. P.2.
22. Laxon, W. A. (1993). Ewen William Alison Dictionary of New Zealand Biography Te Ara - The Encylopedia of New Zealand. Volume 2.
23. (1888). The Rival Ferry Steamers. Auckland Star. Auckland. Volume XIX. Edition 8. 11 January 1888. P.5.
24. (1889). Devonport Steam Ferry Company (Limited) - Annual Meeting. Auckland Star. Auckland. Volume XX. Edition 43. 20 February 1889. P.5.
25. Laxon, W. A. (1993). Ewen William Alison. Dictionary of New Zealand Biography Te Ara - The Encylopedia of New Zealand. Volume 2.
26. (1925). Forty-Four Years Faithful Service. The New Zealand Herald. Auckland. Volume LXII. Edition 19207. 22 December 1925. P.15.
27. (1929). Devonport Ferry Service - Letter To The Editor. Auckland Star. Auckland. Volume LX. Edition 167. 17 July 1929. P.18.
28. (1940). Devonport Ferry Dividend. Evening Post. Wellington. Volume CXXIX. Edition 136. 10 June 1940. P.12.
29. (1881). Untitled Editorial. Auckland Star. Auckland. Volume XII. Edition 3391. 13 June 1881. P.2.
30. (1920). Waterways Development. Auckland Star. Auckland. Volume LI. Edition 230. 25 September 1920. P.7.

## Chapter Three
**Auckland Canals and the Inland Waterways Commission**
1. (1920). Inland Waterways - Commission Appointed. <u>The New Zealand Herald</u>. Auckland. Volume LVII. Edition 17656. 17 December 1920. P.7.
2. (1921). Inland Waterways - Commission Starts Work. <u>The New Zealand Herald</u>. Auckland. Volume LVIII. Edition 17752. 11 April 1921. P.6.
3. (1921). Proposed Canal. <u>Auckland Star</u>. Auckland. Volume LII. Edition 100. 28 April 1921. P.1.
4. (1921). Report of the Auckland Canals and Inland Waterways Commission. Wellington. 25 August 1921. P.2.
5. ibid. P.3.
6. ibid. P.5.
7. ibid. PP.5 & 6.
8. ibid. P.6.
9. ibid. P.8.
10. ibid. P.9.
11. ibid. P.18.
12. ibid. P.19.
13. ibid. P.20.
14. ibid. P.24.

## Chapter Four
**The Harbour Bridge**
1. (1926). Bridging The Waitemata - The Story Of The Ferries. <u>Auckland Star</u>. Auckland. Volume LVII. Edition 220. 16 September 1926. P.11.
2. (1931). Nothing New - Harbour Bridge Scheme. <u>Auckland Star</u>. Auckland. Volume LXII. Edition 152. 30 June 1931. P.12.
3. (1921). Inland Waterways - Discussion On Report. <u>The New Zealand Herald</u>. Auckland. Volume LVIII. Edition 17963. 13 December 1921. P.8.
4. (1921). Untitled. <u>Auckland Star</u>. Auckland. Volume LII. Edition 300. 17 December 1921. P.6.
5. (1921). Waitemata Bridge - Harbour Board's View. <u>The New Zealand Herald</u>. Auckland. Volume LVIII. Edition 17773. 5 May 1921. P.6.

6. (1929). The Morningside Tunnel - Letter To The Editor. The New Zealand Herald. Auckland. Volume LXVI. Edition 20164. 26 January 1929. P.16.
7. (1924). Span Across Harbour. The New Zealand Herald. Auckland. Volume LXI. Edition 18841. 16 October 1924. P.10.
8. (1926). Bridge Over Harbour. The New Zealand Herald. Auckland. Volume LXIII. Edition 19273. 11 March 1926. P.10.
9. (1926). Opinion At Newmarket. The New Zealand Herald. Auckland. Volume LXIII. Edition 19273. 11 March 1926. P.10.
10. (1926). Proposed Harbour Bridge. The New Zealand Herald. Auckland. Volume LXIII. Edition 19277. 16 March 1926. P.7.
11. (1926). Bridging The Waitemata. Auckland Star. Auckland. Volume LVII. Edition 58. 10 March 1926. P.8.
12. (1926). Harbour Bridge Scheme. The New Zealand Herald. Auckland. Volume LXIII. Edition 19291. 1 April 1926. P.10.
13. (1926). Bridging The Waitemata. Auckland Star. Auckland. Volume LVII. Edition 58. 10 March 1926. P.8.
14. (1926). Bridge Over Harbour - City Council's Attitude. The New Zealand Herald. Auckland. Volume LXIII. Edition 19268. 5 March 1926. P.13.
15. (1926). Bridging The Waitemata - Irresponsible Bodies. Auckland Star. Auckland. Volume LVII. Edition 65. 19 March 1926. P.9.
16. (1926). Bridge Over Waitemata - Support At Birkenhead. Auckland Star. Auckland. Volume LVII. Edition 59. 11 March 1926. P.10.
17. (1926). Harbour Bridge Scheme. The New Zealand Herald. Auckland. Volume LXIII. Edition 19291. 1 April 1926. P.10.
18. (1926). Million By Lottery. The Press. Christchurch. Volume LXII. Edition 18746. 17 July 1926. P.14.
19. (1926). Bridge Over Harbour - Lottery Scheme Rejected. The New Zealand Herald. Auckland. Volume LXIII. Edition 19416. 26 August 1926. P.10.
20. (1926). Harbour Bridge. The New Zealand Herald. Auckland. Volume LXIII. Edition 19323. 10 May 1926. P.7.
21. (1926). Bridge Across Harbour - British Capital Interested. The New Zealand Herald. Auckland. Volume LXIII. Edition 19423. 3 September 1926. P.10.
22. (1926). A project to span the harbour with a bridge... Auckland Star. Auckland. Volume LVII. Edition 228. 25 September 1926. P.21.
23. (1926). Bridging The Harbour - Trade Expansion Scheme. Auckland Star. Auckland. Volume LVII. Edition 244. 14 October 1926. P.10.

24. (1926). Harbour Bridge Scheme - The Experience Of Sydney. <u>The New Zealand Herald</u>. Auckland. Volume LXIII. Edition 19492. 23 November 1926. P.12.
25. (1927). The Harbour Bridge - Petition To Parliament. <u>The New Zealand Herald</u>. Auckland. Volume LXIV. Edition 19548. 29 January 1927. P.12.
26. (1927). Mount Eden Council. <u>The New Zealand Herald</u>. Auckland. Volume LXIV. Edition 19722. 23 August 1927. P.11.
27. (1927). Onehunga Affairs. <u>The New Zealand Herald</u>. Auckland. Volume LXIV. Edition 19716. 16 August 1927. P.12.
28. (1927). News Of The Day - Mount Albert Donations. <u>Auckland Star</u>. Auckland. Volume LVIII. Edition 199. 24 August 1927. P.6.
29. (1927). Letters To The Editor - The Harbour Bridge. <u>The New Zealand Herald</u>. Auckland. Volume LXIV. Edition 19625. 2 May 1927. P.12.
30. (1927). The Road To The North. <u>The New Zealand Herald</u>. Auckland. Volume LXIV. Edition 19658. 9 June 1927. P.14.
31. (1928). A Harbour Bridge - Attitude Of Mr Coates. <u>The New Zealand Herald</u>. Auckland. Volume LXV. Edition 19849. 20 January 1928. P.13.
32. (1928). The Harbour Bridge - Letters To The Editor <u>The New Zealand Herald</u>. Auckland. Volume LXV. Edition 19850. 21 January 1928. P.14.
33. (1928). Harbour Bridge Scheme. <u>The New Zealand Herald</u>. Auckland. Volume LXV. Edition 19861. 3 February 1928. P.10.
34. (1928). The Harbour Bridge - Letter To The Editor. <u>The New Zealand Herald</u>. Auckland. Volume LXV. Edition 19873. 17 February 1928. P.14.
35. (1928). Big Bridge Project. <u>Auckland Star</u>. Auckland. Volume LIX. Edition 42. 20 February 1928. P.16.
36. (1928). Of National Importance. <u>Auckland Star</u>. Auckland. Volume LIX. Edition 165. 14 July 1928. P.17.
37. (1928). Road Conditions - The Harbour Bridge. <u>The New Zealand Herald</u>. Auckland. Volume LXV. Edition 19998. 14 July 1928. P.10.
38. (1928). Delays At Devonport. <u>The New Zealand Herald</u>. Auckland. Volume LXV. Edition 20112. 24 November 1928. P.10.
39. (1929). The Harbour Bridge - Highways Board's View. <u>The New Zealand Herald</u>. Auckland. Volume LXVI. Edition 20178. 12 February 1929. P.12.
40. (1928). Trans-Harbour Bridge. <u>Auckland Star</u>. Auckland. Volume LIX. Edition 204. 29 August 1928. P.11.

41. (1928). Spanning The Harbour. <u>Auckland Star</u>. Auckland. Volume LIX. Edition 236. 5 October 1928. P.5.
42. (1929). The Harbour Bridge - City Support Sought. <u>The New Zealand Herald</u>. Auckland. Volume LXVI. Edition 20152. 12 January 1929. P.12.
43. (1928). Harbour Bridge - Letter To The Editor. <u>The New Zealand Herald</u>. Auckland. Volume LXV. Edition 20072. 9 October 1928. P.14.
44. (1928). Harbour Bridge Scheme. <u>The New Zealand Herald</u>. Auckland. Volume LXV. Edition 20080. 18 October 1928. P.14.
45. (1929). Favoured By Premier. <u>Auckland Star</u>. Auckland. Volume LX. Edition 131. 5 June 1929. P.3.
46. (1929). Profoundly Disappointed. <u>Auckland Star</u>. Auckland. Volume LX. Edition 131. 5 June 1929. P.3.
47. (1929). Premature - Harbour Bridge Scheme. <u>Auckland Star</u>. Auckland. Volume LX. Edition 138. 13 June 1929. P.7.
48. (1929). Waitemata Bridge. <u>Auckland Star</u>. Auckland. Volume LX. Edition 142. 18 June 1929. P.6.
49. (1929). Bridge Construction. <u>The New Zealand Herald</u>. Auckland. Volume LXVI. Edition 20297. 3 July 1929. P.11.
50. ibid.
51. (1929). A Stone Wall - Nothing Being Done. <u>Auckland Star</u>. Auckland. Volume LX. Edition 176. 27 July 1929. P.20.
52. (1929). Harbour Bridge Scheme - The Preliminary Work. <u>The New Zealand Herald</u>. Auckland. Volume LXVI. Edition 20338. 20 August 1929. P.8.
53. (1929). The Harbour Bridge - Investigating The Project. <u>The New Zealand Herald</u>. Auckland. Volume LXVI. Edition 20343. 26 August 1929. P.12.
54. (1929). The Harbour Bridge. <u>Auckland Star</u>. Auckland. Volume LX. Edition 203. 28 August 1929. P.6.
55. (1929). Harbour Bridge - Personnel Of Commission. <u>Auckland Star</u>. Auckland. Volume LX. Edition 209. 4 September 1929. P.10.
56. (1929). The Harbour Bridge - Investigating Project. <u>The New Zealand Herald</u>. Auckland. Volume LXVI. Edition 20352. 5 September 1929. P.14.
57. (1929). The Harbour Bridge - Selection Of The Site. <u>The New Zealand Herald</u>. Auckland. Volume LXVI. Edition 20363. 18 September 1929. P.13.
58. (1929). Who Will Pay? <u>Auckland Star</u>. Auckland. Volume LX. Edition 230. 28 September 1929. P.9.

59. (1929). Must Be Reasonable. <u>Auckland Star</u>. Auckland. Volume LX. Edition 230. 28 September 1929. P.21.
60. (1929). Harbour Bridge - Three Investigators Appointed By Cabinet. <u>Auckland Star</u>. Auckland. Volume LX. Edition 240. 10 October 1929. P.10.
61. (1929). The Harbour Bridge - Commission Criticised. <u>The New Zealand Herald</u>. Auckland. Volume LXVI. Edition 20387. 16 October 1929. P.13.
62. (1929). Bridge Commission. <u>Auckland Star</u>. Auckland. Volume LX. Edition 247. 18 October 1929. P.5.
63. (1929). Scope Of Inquiry. <u>Auckland Star</u>. Auckland. Volume LX. Edition 248. 19 October 1929. P.9.
64. (1930). Waitemata Harbour Transit Facilities (Report of Royal Commission Appointed To Inquire Into). New Zealand Government. Wellington. 22 April 1930.
65. (1931). Jubilee Of Ferries. <u>The New Zealand Herald</u>. Auckland. Volume LXVIII. Edition 20901. 17 June 1931. P.12.
66. (1935). Harbour Bridge - City Council Attitude. <u>The New Zealand Herald</u>. Auckland. Volume LXXII. Edition 22035. 15 February 1935. P.10.
67. (1931). Auckland Harbour Bridge Empowering Act. General Assembly of New Zealand. 9 November 1931.
68. ibid.
69. (1935). Harbour Bridge - City Council Attitude. <u>The New Zealand Herald</u>. Auckland. Volume LXXII. Edition 22035. 15 February 1935. P.10.
70. (1931). Harbour Bridge - Conference To-Day. <u>Auckland Star</u>. Auckland Volume LXII. Edition 295. 14 December 1931. P.9.
71. (1932). Harbour Bridge Plans. <u>The New Zealand Herald</u>. Auckland. Volume LXIX. Edition 21104. 11 February 1932. P.10.
72. (1932). Harbour Bridge - Finance Difficult. <u>Auckland Star</u>. Auckland. Volume LXIII. Edition 79. 4 April 1932. P.8.
73. (1932). Harbour Bridge - Negotiations Fail. <u>Auckland Star</u> Auckland. Volume LXIII. Edition 211. 6 September 1932. P.5.
74. (1932). No Capital Available. <u>Evening Post</u>. Wellington. Volume CXIV. Edition 59. 7 September 1932. P.6.
75. (1932). Harbour Bridge - Efforts To Raise Money. <u>Auckland Star</u>. Auckland. Volume LXIII. Edition 217. 13 September 1932. P.8.
76. (1932). The Harbour Bridge - Letter To The Editor. <u>Auckland Star</u>. Auckland. Volume LXIII. Edition 219. 15 September 1932. P.6.

77. (1932). The Harbour Bridge - Dissension At Meeting. <u>The New Zealand Herald</u>. Auckland. Volume LXIX. Edition 21290. 17 September 1932. P.13.
78. (1932). Harbour Bridge - Local Body Control? <u>Auckland Star</u>. Auckland. Volume LXIII. Edition 231. 29 September 1932. P.8.
79. (1932). The Harbour Bridge - Letter To The Editor. <u>The New Zealand Herald</u>. Auckland. Volume LXIX. Edition 21303. 3 October 1932. P.13.
80. (1932). Harbour Bridge Scheme. <u>The New Zealand Herald</u>. Auckland. Volume LXIX. Edition 21305. 5 October 1932. P.12.
81. (1932). Harbour Bridge - Local Body Conference. <u>Auckland Star</u>. Auckland. Volume LXIII. Edition 237. 6 October 1932. P.11.
82. (1932). Gloves Must Come Off. <u>Auckland Star</u>. Auckland. Volume LXIII. Edition 244. 14 October 1932. P.8.
83. (1932). Useful Schemes Urged. <u>The New Zealand Herald</u>. Auckland. Volume LXIX. Edition 21362. 10 December 1932. P.14.
84. (1932). Bridge Proposal - Director's Resignation. <u>The New Zealand Herald</u>. Auckland. Volume LXIX. Edition 21347. 23 November 1932. P.12.
85. (1932). The Harbour Crossing. <u>Auckland Star</u>. Auckland. Volume LXIII. Edition 305. 24 December 1932. P.14.
86. (1933). Only Wasting Time. <u>Auckland Star</u>. Auckland. Volume LXIV. Edition 21. 26 January 1933. P.10.
87. (1933). Harbour Bridge Company. <u>Auckland Star</u>. Auckland. Volume LXIV. Edition 45. 23 February 1933. P.5.
88. (1933). Harbour Bridge - Circular To Shareholders. <u>The New Zealand Herald</u>. Auckland. Volume LXX. Edition 21433. 6 March 1933. P.6.
89. (1933). Harbour Span <u>Auckland Star</u>. Auckland. Volume LXIV. Edition 142. 19 June 1933. P.8.
90. (1933). Harbour Bridge - Company's Announcement. <u>Auckland Star</u>. Auckland. Volume LXIV. Edition 193. 17 August 1933. P.10.
91. (1933). Harbour Bridge Plan. <u>The New Zealand Herald</u>. Auckland. Volume LXX. Edition 21617. 9 October 1933. P.10.
92. (1933). Letters To The Editor - Harbour Bridge. <u>The New Zealand Herald</u>. Auckland. Volume LXX. Edition 21640. 4 November 1933. P.15.
93. (1933). The Harbour Bridge. <u>Auckland Star</u>. Auckland. Volume LXIV. Edition 266. 10 November 1933. P.6.
94. (1933). Never Brighter - Bridge Prospects. <u>Auckland Star</u>. Auckland. Volume LXIV. Edition 290. 8 December 1933. P.8.

95. (1934). Harbour Bridge Scheme. <u>The New Zealand Herald</u>. Auckland. Volume LXXI. Edition 21716. 3 February 1934. P.14.
96. (1934). Harbour Bridge Scheme. <u>The New Zealand Herald</u>. Auckland. Volume LXXI. Edition 21741. 5 March 1934. P.4.
97. (1934). Devonport Out. <u>Auckland Star</u>. Auckland. Volume LXV. Edition 57. 8 March 1934. P.10.
98. (1934). Harbour Bridge Plan. <u>The New Zealand Herald</u>. Auckland. Volume LXXI. Edition 21764. 2 April 1934. P.12.
99. (1934). Scheme Fizzling Out. <u>Auckland Star</u>. Auckland. Volume LXV. Edition 109. 10 May 1934. P.16.
100. (1934). Harbour Bridge - Question Of Finance. <u>The New Zealand Herald</u>. Auckland. Volume LXXI. Edition 21802. 17 May 1934. P.13.
101. (1934). The Harbour Bridge - Letter To The Editor. <u>Auckland Star</u>. Auckland. Volume LXV. Edition 119. 22 May 1934. P.6.
102. (1934). Harbour Bridge - Interest On Loan. <u>Auckland Star</u>. Auckland. Volume LXV. Edition 134. 8 June 1934. P.5.
103. (1934). Harbour Bridge - Local Bodies' Conference. <u>Auckland Star</u>. Auckland. Volume LXV. Edition 182. 3 August 1934. P.9.
104. (1934). Harbour Bridge - Question Of Finance. <u>The New Zealand Herald</u>. Auckland. Volume LXXI. Edition 21903. 12 September 1934. P.13.
105. (1934). Harbour Bridge Scheme - Local Body Interest. <u>The New Zealand Herald</u>. Auckland. Volume LXXI. Edition 21941. 26 October 1934. P.11.
106. (1934). Harbour Bridge Plan. <u>The New Zealand Herald</u>. Auckland. Volume LXXI. Edition 21951. 7 November 1934. P.9.
107. (1934). Harbour Traffic. <u>The New Zealand Herald</u>. Auckland. Volume LXXI. Edition 21963. 21 November 1934. P.13.
108. (1934). Ferry Traffic - Changes In Five Years. <u>Auckland Star</u>. Auckland. Volume LXV. Edition 280. 26 November 1934. P.9.
109. (1934). Harbour Bridge Scheme - Financial Negotiations. <u>The New Zealand Herald</u>. Auckland. Volume LXXI. Edition 21973. 3 December 1934. P.11.
110. (1935). The Harbour Bridge - Negotiations Proceeding. <u>The New Zealand Herald</u>. Auckland. Volume LXXII. Edition 22022. 31 January 1935. P.12.
111. (1935). Harbour Bridge - City Council Attitude. <u>The New Zealand Herald</u>. Auckland. Volume LXXII. Edition 22035. 15 February 1935. P.10.

112. (1935). Surprised And Hurt. <u>Auckland Star</u>. Auckland. Volume LXVI. Edition 39. 15 February 1935. P.3.
113. (1935). Harbour Bridge - London Negotiations. <u>The New Zealand Herald</u>. Auckland. Volume LXXII. Edition 22041. 22 February 1935. P.10.
114. (1935). Harbour Bridge - Offer From Germany. <u>The New Zealand Herald</u>. Auckland. Volume LXXII. Edition 22041. 22 February 1935. P.10.
115. (1935). Harbour Bridge - £400,000 Wanted. <u>Auckland Star</u>. Auckland. Volume LXVI. Edition 55. 6 March 1935. P.9.
116. ibid.
117. (1935). Harbour Bridge - Company Criticised. <u>The New Zealand Herald</u>. Auckland. Volume LXXII. Edition 22201. 30 August 1935. P.14.
118. (1935). Harbour Bridge - Finance From Australia. <u>Auckland Star</u>. Auckland. Volume LXVI. Edition 240. 10 October 1935. P.9.
119. (1935). Harbour Bridge Plan - Raising The Capital. <u>The New Zealand Herald</u>. Auckland. Volume LXXII. Edition 22256. 2 November 1935. P.15.
120. (1935). Harbour Bridge - May Start Next Easter. <u>Auckland Star</u>. Auckland. Volume LXVI. Edition 262. 5 November 1935. P.8.
121. (1935). Harbour Bridge - Commencement Unlikely. <u>The New Zealand Herald</u>. Auckland. Volume LXXII. Edition 22266. 14 November 1935. P.12.
122. (1935). Gloomy Prophet - Vote For First Time. <u>The New Zealand Herald</u>. Auckland. Volume LXXII. Edition 22268. 16 November 1935. P.16.
123. (1935). Letters To The Editor - Harbour Bridge. <u>The New Zealand Herald</u>. Auckland. Volume LXXII. Edition 22285. 6 December 1935. P.16.
124. (1935). Harbour Bridge - Company's Annual Meeting. <u>The New Zealand Herald</u>. Auckland. Volume LXXII. Edition 22290. 12 December 1935. P.15.
125. (1936). Harbour Bridge Delay. <u>The New Zealand Herald</u>. Auckland. Volume LXXIII. Edition 22366. 12 March 1936. P.13.
126. (1936). No Support. <u>Auckland Star</u>. Auckland. Volume LXVII. Edition 80. 3 April 1936. P.3.
127. (1936). Letters To The Editor - The Harbour Bridge. <u>The New Zealand Herald</u>. Auckland. Volume LXXIII. Edition 22386. 4 April 1936. P.17.

128. (1936). Harbour Bridge - New Campaign Launched. <u>The New Zealand Herald</u>. Auckland. Volume LXXIII. Edition 22431. 29 May 1936. P.14.
129. (1936). Harbour Bridge - Company Criticised. <u>The New Zealand Herald</u>. Auckland. Volume LXXIII. Edition 22439. 8 June 1936 P.12.
130. (1936). Harbour Bridge - Prime Minister's View. <u>The New Zealand Herald</u>. Auckland. Volume LXXIII. Edition 22451. 22 June 1936. P.12.
131. (1936). Harbour Bridge - National Undertaking. <u>Auckland Star</u>. Auckland. Volume LXVII. Edition 162. 10 July 1936. P.8.
132. (1936). Support Refused. <u>Auckland Star</u>. Auckland. Volume LXVII. Edition 191. 13 August 1936. P.16.
133. (1936). Harbour Bridge - County Support Sought. <u>The New Zealand Herald</u>. Auckland. Volume LXXIII. Edition 22498. 15 August 1936. P.12.
134. (1936). Harbour Bridge - Board's Neutral Attitude. <u>The New Zealand Herald</u>. Auckland. Volume LXXIII. Edition 22501. 19 August 1936. P.12.
135. (1936). New Plan. <u>Auckland Star</u>. Auckland. Volume LXVII. Edition 266. 9 November 1936. P.9.
136. (1936). Bridge Justified. <u>Auckland Star</u>. Auckland. Volume LXVII. Edition 266. 9 November 1936. P.9.
137. (1936). Harbour Bridge Plan - Attitude Of Minister. <u>The New Zealand Herald</u>. Auckland. Volume LXXIII. Edition 22573. 11 November 1936. P.14.
138. (1936). Letters To The Editor - The Harbour Bridge. <u>The New Zealand Herald</u>. Auckland. Volume LXXIII. Edition 22575. 13 November 1936. P.15.
139. (1937). Letters To The Editor - Vehicular Ferry. <u>The New Zealand Herald</u>. Auckland. Volume LXXIV. Edition 22634. 23 January 1937. P.17.
140. (1937). Plain Talk <u>Auckland Star</u>. Auckland. Volume LXVIII. Edition 58. 10 March 1937. P.8.
141. (1937). Some Day - A Harbour Bridge. <u>Auckland Star</u>. Auckland. Volume LXVIII. Edition 149. 25 June 1937. P.9.
142. (1937). Ferry Terminals. <u>The New Zealand Herald</u>. Auckland. Volume LXXIV. Edition 22798. 4 August 1937. P.10.
143. (1937). The People's Forum - The Harbour Bridge. <u>Auckland Star</u>. Auckland. Volume LXVIII. Edition 138. 12 June 1937. P.16.

144. (1937). Letters To The Editor - The Harbour Bridge. <u>The New Zealand Herald</u>. Auckland. Volume LXXIV. Edition 22851. 5 October 1937. P.13.
145. (1937). Letters To The Editor - Overtaxed Ferries. <u>The New Zealand Herald</u>. Auckland. Volume LXXIV. Edition 22874. 1 November 1937. P.14.
146. (1937). Letters To The Editor - The Harbour Bridge. <u>The New Zealand Herald</u>. Auckland. Volume LXXIV. Edition 22878. 5 November 1937. P.15.
147. (1938). Harbour Transport. <u>The New Zealand Herald</u>. Auckland. Volume LXXV. Edition 22927. 4 January 1938. P.10.
148. (1938). Letters To The Editor - The Harbour Bridge. <u>The New Zealand Herald</u>. Auckland. Volume LXXV. Edition 22938. 17 January 1938. P.12.
149. (1938). Letters To The Editor - Harbour Traffic. <u>The New Zealand Herald</u>. Auckland. Volume LXXV. Edition 23065. 16 June 1938. P.17.
150. (1938). Harbour Transport - Prime Minister's View. <u>The New Zealand Herald</u>. Auckland. Volume LXXV. Edition 23221. 15 December 1938. P.16.
151. (1939). Crowded Ferries. <u>Auckland Star</u>. Auckland. Volume LXX. Edition 22. 27 January 1939. P.14.
152. (1939). Harbour Bridge - Delayed Conference. <u>The New Zealand Herald</u>. Auckland. Volume LXXVI. Edition 23391. 6 July 1939. P.14.
153. (1939). Ferry Cessation. <u>The New Zealand Herald</u>. Auckland. Volume LXXVI. Edition 23409. 27 July 1939. P.17.
154. (1939). Ferry Cessation - Emphatic Protest. <u>The New Zealand Herald</u>. Auckland. Volume LXXVI. Edition 23419. 8 August 1939. P.11.
155. (1939). Harbour Bridge - Urgent Necessity. <u>The New Zealand Herald</u>. Auckland. Volume LXXXVI. Edition 23434. 25 August 1939. P.12.
156. (1939). Northcote Women. <u>The New Zealand Herald</u>. Auckland. Volume LXXVI. Edition 23455. 19 September 1939. P.12.

## Chapter Five
### Trails Through the Fern
1. Barr, John. (1922). The City of Auckland New Zealand 1840-1920. Auckland. Whitcombe & Tombs Limited.
2. (1850). Highways And By-Ways Daily Southern Cross. Auckland. Volume V. Edition 278. 26 February 1850. P.2.
3. Woolston, A. (1996). Equal to the Task - The City of Auckland Traffic Department 1894-1994. Auckland. Auckland City Council & New Zealand Police. P.16.
4. (1871). The Highway Boards Empowering Act. New Zealand. Statute VIII. 16 November 1871. P.39.
5. (1875). The Highway Boards Empowering Act (No. 2). Bill No. XXV. Clause 3.
6. (1877). The Auckland Highway Districts Validation Act. Bill No.1. General Assembly of New Zealand. 9 October 1877.
7. (1877). Political Intelligence. Otago Daily Times. Edition 4819. 28 July 1877. P.2.
8. (1877). Special Telegrams. Waikato Times. Volume X. Edition 797. 26 July 1877. P.2.
9. ibid.
10. (1877). The Auckland Highway Districts Validation Act 1877. Bill No. 1. General Assembly of New Zealand. 9 October 1877.
11. (1877). Parliament. Southland Times. Edition 2844. 28 July 1877. P.2.
12. (1877). Main Roads. The Bay of Plenty Times. Volume VI. Edition 528. 6 October 1877. P.2.
13. (1858). The Public Works. Daily Southern Cross. Auckland. Volume XV. Edition 1176. 5 October 1858. P.3.

## Chapter Six
### Trails of Steel – The Railway
1. Ball, Anne Stewart. (2009) "Beginning days of a railway: James Stewart and the Auckland to Drury railway." Manukau Topics: transport. Manukau City Council – Manukau Libraries. Accessed 12 July 2013 from http://www.manukau-libraries.govt.nz/EN/ManukauOurHistory/ManukauTopics/Pages/Beginningdays.aspx.
2. (1863). Provincial Council. Daily Southern Cross. Auckland. Volume XIX. Edition 2005. 19 December 1863. P.4.

3. (1863). The Auckland and Drury Railway Act 1863. Bill No.2. Clause IV. General Assembly of New Zealand. 14 December 1863.
4. ibid. Clause XI.
5. (1864). Auckland And Drury Railway - Letter to the Editor. The New Zealand Herald. Auckland. Edition 1. 1 April 1864. P.4.
6. (1864). The Auckland And Drury Railway - Tenders. Daily Southern Cross. Auckland. Volume XX. Edition 2097. 9 April 1864. P.5.
7. (1864). The Auckland And Drury Railway - Spectemur Agendo. The New Zealand Herald. Auckland. Volume 1. Edition 210. 15 July 1864. P.3.
8. ibid.
9. (1864). Auckland And Drury Railway - Acceptance of Tenders. The New Zealand Herald. Auckland. Volume 1. Edition 285. 11 October 1864. P.5.
10. (1864). Untitled. The New Zealand Herald. Auckland. Volume 1. Edition 290. 17 October 1864. P.4.
11. (1864). Auckland And Drury Railway - Local Tenders. Daily Southern Cross. Auckland. Volume XX. Edition 2316. 22 December 1864. P.4.
12. (1864). Editorial - 1864 Overview. The New Zealand Herald. Auckland. Volume II. Edition 355. 31 December 1864. P.3.
13. (1865). Turning The First Sod Of The Auckland And Drury Railway. Daily Southern Cross. Auckland. Volume XXI. Edition 2365. 17 February 1865. P.5.
14. ibid.
15. (1865). The Auckland And Drury Railway. Daily Southern Cross. Auckland. Volume XXI. Edition 2464. 13 June 1865. P.5.
16. Hodgson, T. (1992). The Heart of Colonial Auckland 1865-1910. Auckland, Random Century New Zealand Limited. PP.56 & 57.
17. Stone, Russell C. J. (2005). Auckland Business, 1841 - 2004: Myth and Reality City of Enterprise. Ian Hunter & Diana Morrow. Auckland, Auckland University Press. P.234.
18. Simpson, Tony (1992). Shame and Disgrace - A History of Lost Scandals in New Zealand. Auckland, Penguin Books. P.74.
19. Stone, Russell C. J. (2006). Auckland Business, 1841 - 2004: Myth and Reality City of Enterprise. Ian Hunter & Diana Morrow. Auckland, Auckland University Press. P.234.

20. Stone, R. C. J. (2013). Dilworth, James. <u>Encyclopedia of New Zealand - Dictionary of New Zealand Biography</u>. Accessed 7 June 2013 at http://www.TeAra.govt.nz/en/biographies/2d11/dilworth-james.
21. (1866). Railway Compensation Case. <u>Daily Southern Cross</u>. Auckland. Volume XXII. Edition 2645. 9 January 1866. P.4.
22. (1866). Railway Compensation Court - Dilworth v Auckland and Drury Railway Commissioners. <u>Daily Southern Cross</u>. Auckland. Volume XXII. Edition 2704. 17 March 1866. P.6.
23. (1866). Events of the Month. <u>The New Zealand Herald</u>. Auckland. Volume III. Edition 740. 29 March 1866. P.5.
24. (1866). The Auckland And Drury Railway Company v Dilworth. <u>Daily Southern Cross</u>. Auckland. Volume XXII. Edition 2732. 26 April 1866. P.4.
25. (1866). Dilworth v Auckland And Drury Railway. <u>Daily Southern Cross</u>. Auckland. Volume XXII. Edition 2738. 3 May 1866. P.4.
26. (1866). Auckland Provincial Council - Railway Accommodation Works. <u>The New Zealand Herald</u>. Auckland. Volume IV. Edition 953. 3 December 1866. P.5.
27. (1866). Auckland And Drury Railway - Report to the Provincial Council. <u>Daily Southern Cross</u>. Auckland. Volume XXII. Edition 2652. 17 January 1866. P.5.
28. ibid.
29. ibid.
30. (1866). Railway Commissioners Report - Editorial. <u>The New Zealand Herald</u>. Auckland. Volume III. Edition 682. 20 January 1866. P.4.
31. ibid.
32. (1866). Report Of The Present State And Progress Of The Railway Works. <u>Daily Southern Cross</u>. Auckland. Volume XXII. Edition 2903. 14 November 1866. P.6.
33. (1872). Auckland And Drury Railway. <u>Daily Southern Cross</u>. Auckland. Volume XXVIII. Edition 4689. 3 September 1872. P.3.
34. Dieffenbach, Ernest. (1843). <u>Travels In New Zealand</u>. London, John Murray. P.281.
35. Jesson, Bruce. (1987). <u>Behind the Mirror Glass</u>. Auckland, Penguin Books (N.Z.) Limited. P.13.
36. ibid. P.18.
37. (1870). The Immigration and Public Works Loan Act 1870. Bill No. LXXX. General Assembly of New Zealand. 13 September 1870.

38. Simpson, Tony (1992). <u>Shame and Disgrace - A History of Lost Scandals in New Zealand</u>. Auckland, Penguin Books. P.50.
39. (1871). Arrival Of The Colonial Treasurer. <u>Daily Southern Cross</u>. Auckland. Volume XXVII. Edition 4370. 17 August 1871. P.2.
40. (1871). Vogel Papers - Editorial. <u>The New Zealand Herald</u>. Auckland. Volume VIII. Edition 2379. 9 September 1871. P.2.
41. (1871). Railway Construction. <u>Otago Daily Times</u>. Dunedin. Edition 3025. 17 October 1871. P.3.
42. ibid.
43. (1871). Opposition to Brogden Contracts - Editorial. <u>The New Zealand Herald</u>. Auckland. Volume VIII. Edition 2424. 1 November 1871. P.4.
44. (1871). The Railway Scheme. <u>Otago Daily Times</u>. Dunedin. Edition 3080. 20 December 1871. P.2.
45. Higgins, Leonard S. (1978). "The Brogden Pioneers of the Early Industrial Development in Mid-Glamorgan." <u>National Library of Wales Journal</u> Volume XX Issue 3. 3 September 1978. PP.240-252.
46. (1872). Visit of James Brogden. <u>Auckland Star</u>. Auckland. Edition 1208. 5 January 1872. P.3.
47. (1872). Auckland And Waikato Railway - Strike Of The Workmen. <u>Auckland Star</u>. Auckland. Volume III. Edition 633. 22 January 1872. P.2.
48. (1872). Railway Strike - Editorial. <u>Auckland Star</u>. Auckland. Volume III. Edition 633. 22 January 1872. P.2.
49. (1871). The Truck System - Editorial. <u>The New Zealand Herald</u>. Auckland. Volume VIII. Edition 2455. 7 December 1871. P.2.
50. Barr, John. (1922). <u>The City of Auckland New Zealand 1840-1920</u>. Auckland. Whitcombe & Tombs Limited. P.103.
51. Baker, William. (1930). "Fifty-Seven Years Ago Auckland's First train." <u>The New Zealand Railways Magazine</u> Volume 5. Issue 7. 1 December 1930. Accessed 2 October 2010 at http://www.nzetc.org/tm/scholarly/tei-Gov05_07Rail-tl-body-d16.html.
52. Lee, Mike. (2010). People turn out to show car not the only way to travel. <u>New Zealand Herald</u>. Auckland. 19 September 2010.
53. (1874). Editorial - Sunday Trains to Onehunga. <u>The New Zealand Herald</u>. Auckland. Volume XI. Edition 3802. 19 January 1874. P.2.
54. ibid.
55. Ringer, Bruce. (2009) "The railway renewed: 150 years of railways in Manukau." <u>Manukau Libraries</u>. Auckland. Accessed 12 July 2013 at http://www.aucklandlibraries.govt.nz/EN/heritage/localhistory/count.

56. (1871). The Kaipara Railway Act 1871 (Disallowed). Bill No. 7. Auckland Provincial Government. Session XXVI. 31 January 1871. Clause 4.
57. (1871). The Kaipara Railway. <u>Daily Southern Cross</u>. Auckland. Volume XXVII. Edition 4222. 24 February 1871. P.2.
58. (1871). Delay to the Kaipara Railway - Editorial. <u>The New Zealand Herald</u>. Auckland. Volume VIII. Edition 2264. 28 April 1871. P.2.
59. (1871). The Kaipara Railway Terminus - Letter to the Editor. <u>The New Zealand Herald</u>. Auckland. Volume VIII. Edition 2267. 2 May 1871. P.3.
60. (1871). Kaipara Railway - To Be Or Not To Be. <u>The New Zealand Herald</u>. Auckland. Volume VIII. Edition 2268. 3 May 1871. P.3.
61. (2013). John Lamb. <u>New Zealand Maritime Index</u>. Auckland, New Zealand Maritime Museum. Accessed 29 July 2013 at http://www.nzmaritimeindex.org.nz/izref.php?refid=999990008.
62. (1871). Kaipara Railway - To Be Or Not To Be. <u>The New Zealand Herald</u>. Auckland. Volume VIII. Edition 2268. 3 May 1871. P.3.
63. (1871). The Kaipara Railway Bill - Editorial. <u>The New Zealand Herald</u>. Auckland. Volume VIII. Edition 2268. 3 May 1871. P.2.
64. (1871). Kaipara Railway Act Disallowed - Editorial. <u>The New Zealand Herald</u>. Auckland. Volume VIII. Edition 2269. 4 May 1871. P.2.
65. (1871). Kaipara Railway Termini - Report By The Provincial Engineer. <u>The New Zealand Herald</u>. Auckland. Volume VIII. Edition 2281. 18 May 1871. P.2.
66. (1871). Kaipara Railway - Report By Henry Wrigg. <u>Daily Southern Cross</u>. Auckland. Volume XXVII. Edition 4293. 18 May 1871. P.3.
67. (1871). The Kaipara Railway - Letter to the Editor from Practical. <u>The New Zealand Herald</u>. Auckland. Volume VIII. Edition 2285. 23 May 1871. P.3.
68. (1871). Difficulties Of The Northern Settlers. <u>The New Zealand Herald</u>. Auckland. Volume VIII. Edition 2350. 7 August 1871. P.3.
69. (1871). The Kaipara Railway - Construction to Proceed. <u>The New Zealand Herald</u>. Auckland. Volume VIII. Edition 2352. 9 August 1871. P.5.
70. (1871). The Kaipara Railway - Turning of the Sod Ceremony. <u>Auckland Star</u>. Auckland. Volume II. Edition 508. 26 August 1871. P.3.
71. (1871). The Kaipara Railway - Turning of the First Sod Ceremony. <u>The New Zealand Herald</u>. Auckland. Volume VIII. Edition 2372. 1 September 1871. P.3.

72. (1871). The Kaipara Railway - Turning The First Sod. <u>Daily Southern Cross</u>. Auckland. Volume XXVII. Edition 4383. 1 September 1871. P.3.
73. (1928). Transport Problem - Bullock Dray Express. <u>Auckland Star</u>. Auckland. Volume LIX. Edition 303. 22 December 1928. P.11.
74. (1875). Opening of the Kaipara Railway. <u>Auckland Star</u>. Auckland. Volume VI. Edition 1779. 27 October 1875. P.2.
75. (1876). Excursion To Kaipara And Back. <u>Auckland Star</u>. Auckland. Volume VII. Edition 1856. 28 January 1876. P.2.
76. (1881). Death Of Captain Casey. <u>Auckland Star</u>. Auckland. Volume XII. Edition 3410. 7 July 1881. P.2.
77. ibid.
78. (1882). The Kaipara Steamship Company Limited. <u>The New Zealand Herald</u>. Auckland. Volume XIX. Edition 6514. 3 October 1882. P.6.
79. (1911). Kaipara-Waitemata Canal. <u>The New Zealand Herald</u>. Auckland. Volume XLVIII. Edition 147689. 7 September 1911. P.5.
80. Stone, R. C. J. (1973). <u>Makers of Fortune</u>. Auckland, Auckland University Press. Oxford University Press. P.14.
81. ibid.
82. Woods, N. S. (1935). "The Birth of Our Railways - The Great Public Works Policy of 1870 Part III. <u>The New Zealand Railways Magazine</u> Volume 10. Issue 3. 1 June 1935.
83. Noonan, Rosslyn J. (1975). <u>By Design: A brief history of the Public Works Department, Ministry of Works 1870-1970</u>. Wellington. Government Printer. P.47.
84. (1876). The Public Works Act. Bill No. L. New Zealand House of Representatives. 31 October 1876. Clause 34.
85. ibid. Clause 100.
86. Simpson, Tony (1992). <u>Shame and Disgrace - A History of Lost Scandals in New Zealand</u>. Auckland, Penguin Books. P.52.
87. Noonan, Rosslyn J. (1975). <u>By Design: A brief history of the Public Works Department, Ministry of Works 1870-1970</u>. Wellington. Government Printer. P.36.
88. ibid. P.47.
89. ibid. P.48.
90. Simpson, Tony (1992). <u>Shame and Disgrace - A History of Lost Scandals in New Zealand</u>. Auckland, Penguin Books. P.52.
91. (1879). Public Works Policy. <u>West Coast Times & Lyttelton Times</u>. Hokitika. Edition 3349. 23 December 1879. P.2.

92. Heatley, Dave. (2009). The History and Future of Rail in New Zealand. Wellington, New Zealand Institute for the Study of Competition and Regulation Incorporated. June 2009.
93. (1880). The Report Of The Railway Commissioners. The New Zealand Herald. Auckland. Volume XVII. Edition 5830. 27 July 1880. P.5.
94. Ontrack. "Chronological History". Accessed 2 October 2010 from www.ontrack.govt.nz/ABOUTUS/HISTORY/pages/Chronologi...
95. Stone, R. C. J. (1973). Makers of Fortune. Auckland, Auckland University Press.
Oxford University Press. PP.119 & 120.
96. (1880). Opening Of The Kaipara Railway. The New Zealand Herald. Auckland. Volume XVII. Edition 5730. 30 March 1880. P.5.
97. (1880). The Kaipara Railway. The New Zealand Herald. Auckland. Volume XVII. Edition 5698. 21 February 1880. P.5.
98. (1881). Opening Of The Kaipara Railway. Auckland Star. Auckland. Volume XII. Edition 3418. 18 July 1881. P.2.
99. (1880). The Neglect Of The North. Auckland Star. Auckland. Volume X. Edition 3057. 6 February 1880. P.3.
100. (1880). Editorial - Neglect of the North Auckland District. The Evening Star. Auckland. Volume X. Edition 3052. 31 January 1880. P.2.
101. (1901). Amalgamation Of Railway Leagues. The New Zealand Herald. Auckland. Volume XXXVIII. Edition 11704. 13 July 1901. P.3.
102. ibid.
103. (1911). Suburban Railways - An Unsatisfactory Reply. The New Zealand Herald. Auckland. Volume XLVIII. Edition 14835. 11 November 1911. P.8.
104. (1911). Trains To Avondale - Better Service Wanted. The New Zealand Herald. Auckland. Volume XLVIII. Edition 14870. 22 December 1911. P.7.
105. (1912). Suburban Train Services - An Indignation Meeting. The New Zealand Herald. Auckland. Volume XLIX. Edition 14930. 1 March 1912. P.4.
106. (1882). Otahuhu Train. The New Zealand Herald. Auckland. Volume XIX. Edition 6291. 16 January 1882. P.4.
107. (1878). Untitled - Editorial. The New Zealand Herald. Auckland. Volume XV. Edition 5036. 7 January 1878. P.4.
108. (1885). Untitled - New Railway Station. The New Zealand Herald. Auckland. Volume XXII. Edition 7406. 14 August 1885. P.4.

109. Auckland Transport. "Britomart - Chapter 1 - The Historic Land 1600-1959." <u>Britomart Transport Centre - Where Rail Meets The Road</u>. Auckland. Accessed 1 January 2010 at www.britomart.co.nz/history1.html. P.5.
110. (1908). Motor Car and Train. <u>The New Zealand Herald</u>. Auckland. Volume XLV. Edition 13897. 3 November 1908. P.4.
111. (1913). Railway Crossings - Prosecutions For Trespass. <u>The New Zealand Herald</u>. Auckland. Volume L. Edition 15381. 16 August 1913. P.8.
112. O'Hara, W. K. (1927). "The Development Of Auckland's Railway Station." <u>The New Zealand Railways Magazine</u> Volume 2. Issue 2. 1 June 1927. P.8. (Reprint Edition: Victoria University of Wellington New Zealand Electronic Text Collection.)
113. (1909). The Railway Station - New Yard Arrangements. <u>The New Zealand Herald</u>. Auckland. Volume XLVI. Edition 14108. 9 July 1909. P.6.
114. (1911). Suburban Trains and the Station. <u>The New Zealand Herald and Daily Southern Cross</u>. Auckland. Volume XLVIII. 3 August 1911. P.6.
115. (1912). Auckland Railway Station - No Funds For New Building. <u>The New Zealand Herald</u>. Auckland. Volume VLIX. Edition 15066. 8 August 1912. P.7.
116. O'Hara, W. K. (1927). "The Development Of Auckland's Railway Station." <u>The New Zealand Railways Magazine</u> Volume 2. Issue 2. 1 June 1927. (Reprint Edition: Victoria University of Wellington New Zealand Electronic Text Collection.)
117. (1920). Engineer's Retirement - Long Record Of Service. <u>The New Zealand Herald</u>. Auckland. Volume LVII. Edition 17534. 28 July 1920. P.8.
118. (1926). Mr D. T. McIntosh - Obituary. <u>Auckland Star</u>. Auckland. Volume LVII. Edition 273. 17 November 1926. P.18.
119. (1914). Auckland Railways - New Station Question. <u>The New Zealand Herald</u>. Auckland. Volume LI. Edition 15656. 9 July 1914. P.8.
120. (1914). Mr Bradney Supports Scheme. <u>The New Zealand Herald</u>. Auckland. Volume LI. Edition 15748. 24 October 1914. P.9.
121. Hiley, E. H. (1914). Report On New Zealand Government Railways. Wellington. 1 August 1914.
122. ibid.
123. ibid.
124. ibid.

125. ibid.
126. ibid.
127. (1915). The Parnell Tunnel - An Engineering Feat. <u>Evening Post</u>. Wellington. Volume LXXXIX. Edition 59. 11 March 1915. P.3.
128. Hiley, E. H. (1914). Report On New Zealand Government Railways. Wellington. 1 August 1914.
129. ibid.
130. (1914). Railway Improvements. <u>The New Zealand Herald and Daily Southern Cross</u>. Auckland. Volume LI. Edition 15705. 4 September 1914. P.6.
131. ibid.
132. (1914). Mr Hiley Praised. <u>The New Zealand Herald</u>. Auckland. Volume LI. Edition 15748. 24 October 1914. P.9.
133. (1914). Mr Hiley's Report - Good Points and Expensive Suggestions. <u>Free Lance</u>. Wellington. Geddis & Blomfield. Volume XV. Edition 741. 12 September 1914. P.8.
134. (1914). Members' Keen Interest. <u>The Press</u>. Christchurch. Volume L. Edition 15064. 4 September 1914. P.10.
135. (1915). The Waterfront Railway. <u>Auckland Star</u>. Auckland. Volume XLVI. Edition 61. 12 March 1915. P.4.
136. ibid.
137. ibid.
138. (1915). Hand Of The Spoiler Already At Work. <u>Auckland Star</u>. Auckland. Volume XLVI. Edition 62. 13 March 1915. P.9.
139. (1915). The Foreshore Railway. <u>Auckland Star</u>. Auckland. Volume XLVI. Edition 63. 15 March 1915. P.4.
140. (1915). Hand Of The Spoiler Already At Work. <u>Auckland Star</u>. Auckland. Volume XLVI. Edition 62. 13 March 1915. P.9.
141. ibid.
142. (1915). The Other Way Out. <u>Auckland Star</u>. Auckland. Volume XLVI. Edition 63. 15 March 1915. P.2.
143. (1915). Railway Outlet - Foreshore Scheme. <u>The New Zealand Herald</u>. Auckland. Volume LII. Edition 15874. 22 March 1915. P.7.
144. (1915). The Waterfront Scheme. <u>The New Zealand Herald</u>. Auckland. Volume LII. Edition 15874. 22 March 1915. P.4.
145. (1916). The Railway Station. <u>The New Zealand Herald</u>. Auckland. Volume LIII. Edition 16389. 17 November 1916. P.6.
146. ibid.
147. (1916). Railway Station Site. <u>The New Zealand Herald</u>. Auckland. Volume LIII. Edition 16401. 1 December 1916. P.9.

148. (1918). Suburban Railway League - New Lynn Branch Formed. <u>Auckland Star</u>. Auckland. Volume XLIX. Edition 158. 4 July 1918. P.7.
149. Hiley, E. H. (1914). Report On New Zealand Government Railways. Wellington. 1 August 1914.
150. (1860). The Nelson Examiner. <u>The Nelson Examiner and New Zealand Chronicle</u>. Nelson. Volume XIX. Edition 40. 19 May 1860. P.2.
151. (1926). New Railway Outlet To North Auckland. <u>Auckland Star</u>. Auckland. Volume LVII. Edition 210. 4 September 1926. P.10.
152. (1919). North Auckland Railway - The Suggested Deviation. <u>The New Zealand Herald</u>. Auckland. Volume LVI. Edition 17180. 6 June 1919. P.5.
153. (1919). Suburban Railway League (To the Editor). <u>Auckland Star</u>. Auckland. Volume L. Edition 146. 20 June 1919. P.3.
154. (1921). North Auckland Route - Shortening The Line. <u>The New Zealand Herald</u>. Auckland. Volume LVIII. Edition 17797. 2 June 1921. P.9.
155. Gustafson, Barry. (2012). Massey, William Ferguson. <u>Dictionary of New Zealand Biography - The Encyclopedia of New Zealand</u>. Accessed 30 October 2012 at http://www.teara.govt.nz/en/biographies/2m39/massey-william-ferguson.
156. (1921). Auckland Of The Future - Moving The People Around. <u>Auckland Star</u>. Auckland. Volume LII. Edition 169. 18 July 1921. P.6.
157. (1922). Northern Railway - Suggested Deviation. <u>The New Zealand Herald</u>. Auckland. Volume LIX. Edition 18164. 9 August 1922. P.11.
158. ibid.
159. (1922). Suburban Train Service - Extended Area Desired. <u>The New Zealand Herald</u>. Auckland. Volume LIX. Edition 18164. 9 August 1922. P.11.
160. Hiley, E. H. (1914). Report On New Zealand Government Railways. Wellington. 1 August 1914.
161. (1922). The Railway Muddle. <u>The New Zealand Herald</u>. Auckland. Volume LIX. Edition 18280. 22 December 1922. P.6.
162. (1922). Railway Congestion - Suburban Sufferings. <u>The New Zealand Herald</u>. Auckland. Volume LIX. Edition 18282. 26 December 1922. P.6.

163. (2011). Compensation talk after Cup transport debacle. <u>The New Zealand Herald</u>. Auckland. 10 September 2011.
164. (1923). Heavy Train Traffic - Probable Easter Record. <u>The New Zealand Herald</u>. Auckland. Volume LX. Edition 18364. 3 April 1923. P.6.
165. (1923). Suburban Railways - Improvements Wanted. <u>The New Zealand Herald</u>. Auckland. Volume LX. Edition 18409. 26 May 1923. P.10.
166. (1923). Behind The Times. <u>The New Zealand Herald</u>. Auckland. Volume LX. Edition 18409. 26 May 1923. P.8.
167. ibid.
168. (1923). Auckland Railway Outlet - Editorial. <u>The New Zealand Herald</u>. Auckland. Volume LX. Edition 18507. 18 September 1923. P.6.
169. Bassett, Michael. (2013). Coates, Joseph Gordon. <u>Dictionary of New Zealand Biography - The Encyclopedia of New Zealand</u>. Accessed 6 June 2013 at http://www.TeAra.govt.nz/en/biographies/3c24/coates-joseph-gordon.
170. (1923). Auckland Railway Outlet - Editorial. <u>The New Zealand Herald</u>. Auckland. Volume LX. Edition 18507. 18 September 1923. P.6.
171. (1923). New Northern Outlet - Suggested Railway Line. <u>The New Zealand Herald</u>. Auckland. Volume LX. Edition 18514. 26 September 1923. P.10.
172. (1923). Northern Railway Outlet - Editorial. <u>The New Zealand Herald</u>. Auckland. Volume LX. Edition 18515. 27 September 1923. P.6.
173. (1923). Railway Outlets. <u>Auckland Star</u>. Auckland. Volume LIV. Edition 231. 27 September 1923. P.4.
174. (1924). Railway Congestion - Platform Inadequate. <u>The New Zealand Herald</u>. Auckland. Volume LXI. Edition 18600. 7 January 1924. P.8.
175. (1924). Railway Travel - Figures For Holidays. <u>The New Zealand Herald</u>. Auckland. Volume LXI. Edition 18604. 11 January 1924. P.8.
176. ibid.
177. ibid.
178. (1924). Railways And Roads - Co-Ordination Policy. <u>The New Zealand Herald</u>. Auckland. Volume LXI. Edition 18600. 7 January 1924. P.8.

179. (1924). Road Or Railway - Anxiety In Waipu. <u>Auckland Star</u>. Auckland. Volume LV. Edition 31. 6 February 1924. P.8.
180. (1924). Railway Improvements - Minister's Tour Of Lines. <u>The New Zealand Herald</u>. Auckland. Volume LXI. Edition 18626. 6 February 1924. P.8.
181. (1924). Auckland Railway Station. <u>The New Zealand Herald</u>. Auckland. Volume LXI. Edition 18626. 6 February 1924. P.8.
182. (1924). Railway Commission. <u>Evening Post</u>. Wellington. Volume CVII. Edition 128. 31 May 1924. P.7.
183. (1924). A Railway Commission. <u>Evening Post</u>. Wellington. Volume CVII. Edition 120. 2 June 1924. P.6.
184. (1924). £6000 Commission. <u>Auckland Star</u>. Auckland. Volume 55. Edition 161. 9 July 1924. P.10.
185. (1924). New Railway Station - Deviation To Westfield. <u>The New Zealand Herald</u>. Auckland. Volume LXI. Edition 18764. 18 July 1924. P.12.
186. (1924). The Railways - Improvement Plans. <u>Auckland Star</u>. Auckland. Volume LV. Edition 235. 3 October 1924. P.9.
187. (1924). Railway Improvements. <u>Auckland Star</u>. Auckland. Volume LV. Edition 235. 3 October 1924. P.4.
188. (1924). New Route To North - Tunnel Under City. <u>Auckland Star</u>. Auckland. Volume LV. Edition 235. 3 October 1924 P.9.
189. (1924). Suburban Railways - Work Of Electrification. <u>The New Zealand Herald</u>. Auckland. Volume LXI. Edition 18868. 17 November 1924. P.8.
190. (1924). Commission's Report - In Administrator's Hands. <u>The New Zealand Herald</u>. Auckland. Volume LXI. Edition 18891. 13 December 1924. P.10.
191. (1924). What Will Fay And Raven Say? <u>NZ Truth</u>. Edition 989. 8 November 1924. P.5.
192. (1924). Our Railways. <u>Auckland Star</u>. Auckland. Volume LV. Edition 306. 26 December 1924. P.8.
193. (1924). Auckland's New Station - Railway Revenue. <u>Auckland Star</u>. Auckland. Volume LV. Edition 306. 26 December 1924. P.8.
194. (1924). Trains Need Speeding Up - Why The Public Grumble. <u>Auckland Star</u>. Auckland. Volume LV. Edition 306. 26 December 1924. P.8.
195. (1924). Auckland's New Station - Big Scheme Not Justified. <u>Auckland Star</u>. Auckland. Volume LV. Edition 306. 26 December 1924. P.8.

196. (1926). New Railway Outlet To North Auckland – Handling Suburban Traffic. <u>Auckland Star</u>. Auckland. Volume LVII. Edition 210. 4 September 1926. P.10.
197. ibid.
198. (1927). Northern Outlet - Railway Beneath City. <u>Auckland Star</u>. Auckland. Volume LVIII. Edition 215. 12 September 1927. P.10.
199. (1928). New Railway Line - Auckland To Morningside. <u>Auckland Star</u>. Auckland. Volume LIX. Edition 144. 20 June 1928. P.8.
200. Taverner, William B. (1929). Railways Statement. Department of Railways. Wellington, New Zealand Government. Accessed at http://atojs.natlib.govt.nz.
201. (1929). Morningside Tunnel - Deputation To Minister. <u>Auckland Star</u>. Auckland. Volume LX. Edition 118. 21 May 1929. P.9.
202. Taverner, William B. (1929). Railways Statement. Department of Railways. Wellington, New Zealand Government. Accessed at http://atojs.natlib.govt.nz.
203. (1930). No Morningside Tunnel. <u>Auckland Star</u>. Auckland. Volume LXI. Edition 15. 18 January 1930. P.8.
204. (1930). The Railway Decision. <u>Auckland Star</u>. Auckland. Volume LXI. Edition 16. 20 January 1930. P.6.
205. (1930). Electrification Of Railways. <u>Auckland Star</u>. Auckland. Volume LXI. Edition 16. 20 January 1930. P.7.
206. (1930). Abandoned Tunnel - Morningside Deviation. <u>Auckland Star</u>. Auckland. Volume LXI. Edition 63. 15 March 1930. P.12.
207. (1930). Work Commenced - Railway Station Loop - Provision For Trams. <u>Auckland Star</u>. Auckland. Volume LXI. Edition 142. 18 June 1930. P.10.
208. (1930). New Railway Station - Loss Of Traffic Feared. <u>Auckland Star</u>. Auckland. Volume LXI. Edition 204. 29 August 1930. P.5.
209. (1930). New Railway Station - Overhead Bridge Proposal. <u>Auckland Star</u>. Auckland. Volume LXI. Edition 227. 25 September 1930. P.8.
210. (1930). New Machinery Lying Idle? <u>Auckland Star</u>. Auckland. Volume LXI. Edition 227. 25 September 1930. P.8.
211. (1930). Penrose Railway Line - Immediate Examination. <u>Auckland Star</u>. Auckland. Volume LXI. Edition 227. 25 September 1930. P.8.
212. (1930). Last Day's Use - Old Railway Station. <u>Auckland Star</u>. Auckland. Volume LXI. Edition 271. 15 November 1930. P.9.
213. (1930). Officially Opened - Auckland Railway Station. <u>Auckland Star</u>. Auckland. Volume LXI. Edition 278. 24 November 1930. P.8.
214. (1930). Fixing The Site - Department's Reasons. <u>Auckland Star</u>. Auckland. Volume LXI. Edition 278. 24 November 1930. P.8.

215. (1930). Transport Legislation Needed. <u>Auckland Star</u>. Auckland. Volume LXI. Edition 278. 24 November 1930. P.8.
216. (1930). More Bus Traffic - At Railways' Expense. <u>Auckland Star</u>. Auckland. Volume LXI. Edition 290. 8 December 1930. P.9.
217. (1931). Railway Revenue - Auckland Returns Down. <u>Auckland Star</u>. Auckland. Volume LXII. Edition 85. 11 April 1931. P.6.
218. Unidentified (1954). Auckland Suburban Railway System. Auckland. (Copied from the archives of Sir Dove-Myer Robinson, Auckland City Library.)
219. (1931). An Expensive Legacy - Auckland's Railway Station. <u>Evening Post</u>. Wellington. Volume CXII. Edition 14. 16 July 1931. P.13.
220. (1931). Government Railways Amendment Act 1931. Bill No. 4. New Zealand House of Representatives. 28 April 1931.
221. ibid. Clause 18(1).
222. ibid. Clauses 19 & 20.
223. (1931). Railways Board. <u>Auckland Star</u>. Auckland. Volume LXII. Edition 139. 15 June 1931. P.8.
224. (1931). Morningside Tunnel - Attitude Of Business Men. <u>Auckland Star</u>. Auckland. Volume LXII. Edition 25. 30 October 1931. P.12.
225. (1931). Local Bodies - New Lynn Borough Council. <u>Auckland Star</u>. Auckland. Volume LXII. Edition
226. (1934). Railway Works - North Auckland Outlet. <u>Auckland Star</u>. Auckland. Volume LXV. Edition 228. 26 September 1934. P.9.
227. (1935). Tunnel Scheme - Morningside Plan. <u>Auckland Star</u>. Auckland. Volume LXVI. Edition 231. 30 September 1935. P.9.
228. (1935). Morningside Tunnel - Railways Not Favourable. <u>Auckland Star</u>. Auckland. Volume LXVI. Edition 301. 20 December 1935. P.17.
229. (1936). Railway Outlet - Morningside Proposal. <u>Auckland Star</u>. Auckland. Volume LXVII. Edition 148. 24 June 1936. P.8.
230. (1936). Tunnel Scheme - Morningside Hopes. <u>Auckland Star</u>. Auckland. Volume LXVII. Edition 161. 9 July 1936. P.8.
231. (1936). Tunnel Scheme - Morningside Plan. <u>Auckland Star</u>. Auckland. Volume LXVII. Edition 230. 28 September 1936. P.3.
232. (1937). Morningside Tunnel - Report Still Awaited. <u>Auckland Star</u>. Auckland. Volume LXVIII. Edition 43. 20 February 1937. P.12.
233. (1937). Morningside Deviation. <u>Auckland Star</u>. Auckland. Volume LXVII. Edition 176. 27 July 1937. P.3.
234. (1938). Morningside Tunnel - Chamber Urges Action. <u>Auckland Star</u>. Auckland. Volume LXIX. Edition 183. 5 August 1938. P.8.

235. (1938). Morningside Tunnel - Report To Be Completed. <u>Auckland Star</u>. Auckland. Volume LXIX. Edition 211. 7 September 1938. P.12.
236. (1940). Suburban Traffic - Suggestion By Mayor. <u>Auckland Star</u>. Auckland. Volume LXXI. Edition 189. 10 August 1940. P.11.
237. (1940). Railway Problem - Site Of The Station. <u>Auckland Star</u>. Auckland. Volume LXXI. Edition 192. 14 August 1940. P.10.
238. (1944). Tunnel Scheme - Post-War Proposal. <u>Auckland Star</u>. Auckland. Volume LXXV. Edition 230. 28 September 1944. P.6.
239. Auckland Transport. "Britomart - Chapter 1 - The Historic Land 1600-1959." <u>Britomart Transport Centre - Where Rail Meets The Road</u>. Auckland. Accessed 1 January 2010 at www.britomart.co.nz/history1.html. P.9.

## Chapter Seven
### The Omnibuses - The Ancillaries Vie for Supremacy

1. McCrystal, John. (2007). <u>On the Buses in New Zealand - From Charabancs to the Coaches of Today</u>. Wellington, Grantham House Publishing & Bus and Coach Association. P.7.
2. (1928). Transport Problem - Bullock Dray Express. <u>Auckland Star</u>. Auckland. Volume LIX. Edition 303. 22 December 1928. P.11.
3. Mogford, Janice C. (1977). <u>The Onehunga Heritage</u>. Auckland, Auckland City Council. Revised Edition. 1990.
4. (1864). Untitled - Hardington's New Omnibus. <u>The New Zealand Herald</u>. Auckland. Volume I. Edition 188. 20 June 1864. P.3.
5. (1864). Untitled - Omnibus Conveyance. <u>The New Zealand Herald</u>. Auckland. Volume Unstated. Edition 160. 18 May 1864. P.3.
6. (1863). Untitled. <u>The New Zealand Herald</u>. Auckland. Volume I. Edition 4. 20 November 1863. P.4.
7. (1864). Inquest At Otahuhu. <u>The New Zealand Herald</u>. Auckland. Volume I. Edition 110. 21 March 1864. P.4.
8. (1864). Spirited Conduct. <u>The New Zealand Herald</u>. Auckland. Volume I. Edition 250. 31 August 1864. P.4.
9. (1868). The Parnell And Remuera Buses. <u>The New Zealand Herald</u>. Auckland. Volume V. Edition 1406. 20 May 1868. P.4.
10. (1869). Omnibuses For Dedwood. <u>The New Zealand Herald</u>. Auckland. Volume VI. Edition 1820. 13 November 1869. P.5.
11. (1870). City Board - Buses. <u>The New Zealand Herald</u>. Auckland. Volume VII. Edition 2058. 30 August 1870. P.3.

12. (1870). Untitled. <u>The New Zealand Herald</u>. Auckland. Volume **VII**. Edition 1994. 9 June 1870. P.3.
13. (1871). Toll Bar Regulations. <u>The New Zealand Herald</u>. Auckland. Volume VIII. Edition 2467. 21 December 1871. P.2.
14. (1873). Untitled. <u>Auckland Star</u>. Auckland. Volume IV. Edition 925. 25 February 1873. P.2.
15. (1873). Untitled. <u>The New Zealand Herald</u>. Auckland. Volume X. Edition 3779. 22 December 1873. P.2.
16. ibid.
17. (1874). Untitled. <u>The New Zealand Herald</u>. Auckland. Volume XI. Edition 3826. 16 February 1874. P.2.
18. (1876). Onehunga R M Court – Wednesday <u>The New Zealand Herald</u>. Auckland. Volume XIII. Edition 4414. 6 January 1876. P.4.
19. (1876). Cab And Cart Fares. <u>The New Zealand Herald</u>. Auckland. Volume XIII. Edition 4453. 21 February 1876. P.3.
20. (1876). Untitled. <u>Auckland Star</u>. Auckland. Volume VII. Edition 1911. 3 April 1876. P.2.
21. (1876). Untitled. <u>Auckland Star</u>. Auckland. Volume VII. Edition 1913. 5 April 1876. P.3.
22. (1876). Untitled. <u>Auckland Star</u>. Auckland. Volume VII. Edition 1928. 24 April 1876. P.2.
23. (1877). Untitled - Editorial. <u>The New Zealand Herald</u>. Auckland. Volume XIV. Edition 4881. 9 July 1877. P.2.
24. (1876). Untitled - Editorial. <u>The New Zealand Herald</u>. Auckland. Volume XIII. Edition 4444. 10 February 1876. P.2.
25. (1877). Untitled. <u>The New Zealand Herald</u>. Auckland. Volume XIV. Edition 5028. 28 December 1877. P.2.
26. (1878). Untitled - Editorial. <u>The New Zealand Herald</u>. Auckland. Volume XV. Edition 5036. 7 January 1878. P.4.
27. (2008). Matthews & Matthews Architects, R. A. Skidmore Urban Design & Lisa Trutman. Balmoral Shopping Centre Character Heritage Study. Auckland. Auckland City Council. November 2008. P.22.

**Chapter Eight – On Your Bike**
1. McCrystal, John. (2007). <u>On the Buses in New Zealand - From Charabancs to the Coaches of Today</u>. Wellington, Grantham House Publishing & Bus and Coach Association. P.15.
2. Johnson, David. (1991). <u>Auckland City Life - A Celebration of Yesteryear</u>. Auckland, David Bateman Limited. P.22

3. Bush, Graham W. A. (1980). Moving Against the Tide. Palmerston North, The Dunmore Press Limited. P.159.
4. (1898). The Cycle Traffic Act 1898. Bill No. 24-1. General Assembly of New Zealand. 1 January 1899. Clause 7.
5. Hansard (1898). Cycle Traffic Bill. House of Representatives. Wellington. 7 July 1898. P.295.
6. ibid. P.295.
7. ibid. P.297.
8. ibid. P.295.
9. ibid. P.294.
10. Ellyard, David. (2007). Who Invented What When. Sydney, New Holland Publishing Australia Pty Limited.
11. Holcroft, M. H. (1979). Carapace - The Motor Car in New Zealand: A Roadside View. Dunedin, John McIndoe Limited. P.82.

**Chapter Nine**
**The Dominance of the Centre Line - The Age of Trams**
1. (2008). Matthews & Matthews Architects, R. A. Skidmore Urban Design & Lisa Trutman. Balmoral Shopping Centre Character Heritage Study. Auckland. Auckland City Council. November 2008. P.12.
2. (1873). Auckland Improvement Commission - Street Tramways. Auckland Star. Auckland. Volume IV. Edition 1017. 23 April 1873. P.3.
3. (1875). Untitled. The New Zealand Herald. Auckland. Volume XII. Edition 4377. 23 November 1875. P.2.
4. (1880). City Council. Auckland Star. Auckland. Volume XI. Edition 3218. 12 November 1880. P.3.
5. ibid.
6. (1883). Untitled. The New Zealand Herald. Auckland. Volume XX. Edition 6713. 24 May 1883. P.4.
7. St Heliers & Northcote Land Company Limited. Auckland Tramways: Prospectus of the St Heliers & Northcote Land Company Limited. Auckland City Library: Sir George Grey Collection. Auckland. 1882.
8. ibid.
9. ibid.
10. (1882). Stock and Share Market. Taranaki Herald. New Plymouth. Volume XXX. Edition 4103. 5 August 1882. P.2.

11. Stewart, Graham. (1973). The End of the Penny Section - A History of Urban Transport in New Zealand. Wellington, A H & A W Reed Limited. P.27.
12. (1884). City Council. The New Zealand Herald. Auckland. Volume XXI. Edition 7031. 30 May 1884. P.6.
13. (1884). Calamo Currente. The New Zealand Herald. Auckland. Volume XXI. Edition 7080. 26 July 1884. P.1 (Supplement).
14. (1884). Untitled. The New Zealand Herald. Auckland. Volume XXI. Edition 7073. 18 July 1884. P.4.
15. (1884). Untitled. Auckland Star. Auckland. Volume XXVI. Edition 4426. 18 July 1884. P.2.
16. (1884). Untitled. The New Zealand Herald. Auckland. Volume XXI. Edition 7075. 21 July 1884. P.4.
17. (1884). Untitled. Auckland Star. Auckland. Volume XXVI. Edition 4427. 21 July 1884. P.2.
18. (1884). Meeting Of Cabowners And Drivers. The New Zealand Herald. Auckland. Volume XXI. Edition 7076. 22 July 1884. P.6.
19. (1884). City Council. Auckland Star. Auckland. Volume XXVI. Edition 4426. 18 July 1884. P.2.
20. (1884). Starting Of The Tramways. The New Zealand Herald. Auckland. Volume XXI. Edition 7094. 12 August 1884. P.5.
21. (1884). Untitled. The New Zealand Herald. Auckland. Volume XXI. Edition 7095. 13 August 1884. P.4.
22. (1884). Untitled. The New Zealand Herald. Auckland. Volume XXI. Edition 7108. 28 August 1884. P.4.
23. (1884). Untitled. The New Zealand Herald. Auckland. Volume XXI. Edition 7121. 12 September 1884. P.4.
24. (1884). Untitled - Editorial. The New Zealand Herald. Auckland. Volume XXI. Edition 7133. 26 September 1884. P.4.
25. (1885). Untitled - Editorial. The New Zealand Herald. Auckland. Volume XXII. Edition 7316. 30 April 1885. P.4.
26. (1885). City Council. The New Zealand Herald. Auckland. Volume XXII. Edition 7406. 14 August 1885. P.6.
27. (1885). Perambulating Cabs - Important Decision. Auckland Star. Auckland. Volume XXVI. Edition 266. 16 November 1885. P.2.
28. (1885). Untitled. The New Zealand Herald. Auckland. Volume XXII. Edition 7406. 14 August 1885. P.4.
29. (1886). Devonport Tramway Company. Auckland Star. Auckland. Volume XVII. Edition 227. 27 September 1886. P.3.

30. (1886). Untitled. <u>The New Zealand Herald</u>. Auckland. Volume XXIII. Edition 7805. 26 November 1886. P.5.
31. (1886). Untitled. <u>The New Zealand Herald</u>. Auckland. Volume XXIII. Edition 7816. 9 December 1886. P.4.
32. (1887). The Supreme Court - A Heavy Sitting in Chambers. <u>Auckland Star</u>. Auckland. Volume XVIII. Edition 72. 26 March 1887. P.8.
33. (1887). Untitled. <u>The New Zealand Herald</u>. Auckland. Volume XXIV. Edition 7909. 30 March 1887. P.6.
34. (1887). Devonport Borough Council. <u>Auckland Star</u>. Auckland. Volume XVIII. Edition 139. 14 June 1887. P.5.
35. (1887). Devonport Borough Council. <u>Auckland Star</u>. Auckland. Volume XVIII. Edition 257. 1 November 1887. P.2.
36. (1900). Tram Lines On The North Shore. <u>The New Zealand Herald</u>. Auckland. Volume XXXVII. Edition 11385. 30 May 1900. P.7.
37. Stewart, Graham. (1973). <u>The End of the Penny Section - A History of Urban Transport in New Zealand</u>. Wellington, A H & A W Reed Limited. P.32.
38. Bloomfield, Dr. G. T. (1975). Urban Tramways in New Zealand 1862-1964. <u>New Zealand Geographer</u> Edition 31. P.100.
39. Hodgson, T. (1992). <u>The Heart of Colonial Auckland 1865-1910</u>. Auckland, Random Century New Zealand Limited. P.54.
40. Hunt, Chris. (2009). "Banking crises in New Zealand - an historical perspective." <u>Reserve Bank of New Zealand Bulletin</u> Volume 72. Issue 4. 4 December 2009. PP.30 & 32.
41. Hodgson, T. (1992). <u>The Heart of Colonial Auckland 1865-1910</u>. Auckland, Random Century New Zealand Limited. P.56.
42. Stewart, Graham. (1973). <u>The End of the Penny Section - A History of Urban Transport in New Zealand</u>. Wellington, A H & A W Reed Limited. P.32.
43. Bloomfield, Dr. G. T. (1975). Urban Tramways in New Zealand 1862-1964. <u>New Zealand Geographer</u> Edition 31. P.112.
44. Lowe, David. <u>Auckland 1900 - A Pictorial Entertainment</u>. Auckland. The Lodestone Press. P.32.
45. (1902). The Electric Trams - Inaugral Function - A Successful Run. <u>Auckland Star</u>. Auckland. Volume XXXIII. Edition 273. 17 November 1902. P.7.
46. (1902). The Electric Trams. <u>Auckland Star</u>. Auckland. Volume XXXIII. Edition 273. 17 November 1902. P.6.
47. (1902). Electric Tram Cars - Public Service Started. <u>Auckland Star</u>. Auckland. Volume XXXIII. Edition 279. 24 November 1902. P.5.

48. (2008). Matthews & Matthews Architects, R. A. Skidmore Urban Design & Lisa Trutman. Balmoral Shopping Centre Character Heritage Study. Auckland. Auckland City Council. November 2008. P.22.
49. Bloomfield, Dr G. T. (1975). Urban Tramways in New Zealand 1862-1964. New Zealand Geographer Edition 31. PP.100 & 107.
50. (1903). The Electric Tramway Service. The New Zealand Herald. Auckland. Volume XL. Edition 12163. 8 January 1903. P.5.
51. (1903). The Electric Tramways - New Extensions. The New Zealand Herald. Auckland. Volume XL. Edition 12314. 4 July 1903. P.5.
52. (1903). The Sunday Trams - Close and Exciting Contest. The New Zealand Herald. Auckland. Volume XL. Edition 12390. 1 October 1903. P.5.
53. (1903). A Christmas Eve Disaster - Tram Cars Crash Together at Rocky Nook. The New Zealand Herald. Auckland. Volume XL. Edition 12454. 26 December 1903. P.5.
54. (1904). The Tramway Accident - Completion of the Inquiry. The New Zealand Herald. Auckland. Volume XLI. Edition 12464. 7 January 1904. P.6.
55. (1904). The Electric Tramways. Auckland Star. Auckland. Volume XXXV. Edition 87. 12 April 1904. P.5.
56. (1904). Auckland Tramways Dispute The New Zealand Herald. Auckland. Volume XLI. Edition 12555. 22 April 1904. P.3.
57. (1904). The Tramway Poll. The New Zealand Herald. Auckland. Volume XLI. Edition 12558. 27 April 1904. P.5.
58. (1904). Tramway Dispute. Auckland Star. Auckland. Volume XXXV. Edition 117. 17 May 1904. P.5.
59. (1904). The City Council and the Tramways Company. The New Zealand Herald. Auckland. Volume XLI. Edition 12606. 13 July 1904. P.3.
60. (1904). Auckland Electric Trams - Talk with Mr Hansen. The New Zealand Herald. Auckland. Volume XLI. Edition 12635. 16 August 1904. P.6.
61. (1904). Tramway Fees And Profits - Suburban Bodies' Claim. Auckland Star. Auckland. Volume XXXV. Edition 219. 13 September 1904. P.3.
62. (1905). Auckland Electric Trams - How The System Is Worked. The New Zealand Herald. Auckland. Volume XLII. Edition 12757. 6 January 1905. P.3.
63. (1905). Borough Councils - Parnell. The New Zealand Herald. Auckland. Volume XLII. Edition 12779. 1 February 1905. P.6.

64. (1905). Auckland City Council. The New Zealand Herald. Auckland. Volume XLII. Edition 12960. 1 September 1905. P.7.
65. (1905). Auckland's Tram Service - To Be Increased to Sixty Cars. The New Zealand Herald. Auckland. Volume XLII. Edition 12995. 12 October 1905. P.5.
66. Smith, W. Lints. (1905). London's Traffic Revolution. The New Zealand Herald. Auckland. Volume XLII. Edition 13033. 25 November 1905. P.1.
67. (1904). Takapuna Motor 'Bus Service - Inaugral Run to the Lake. The New Zealand Herald. Auckland. Volume XLI. Edition 12738. 15 December 1904. P.6.
68. (1906). Queen-street Sewer - Letter By Mr Hansen to City Council. The New Zealand Herald. Auckland. Volume XLIII. Edition 13270. 31 August 1906. P.6.
69. (1906). Tramway Matters - Shortage of Cars. Auckland Star. Auckland. Volume XXXVII. Edition 238. 12 October 1906. P.3.
70. (1906). Tramway Matters. Auckland Star. Auckland. Volume XXXVII. Edition 274. 23 November 1906. P.3.
71. (1906). City Council And Tramway Company. The New Zealand Herald Auckland. Volume XLIII. Edition 13354. 7 December 1906. P.6.
72. (1907). Auckland Tramways - Interview With Mr C G Tegetmeier. The New Zealand Herald. Auckland. Volume XLIV. Edition 13403. 4 February 1907. P.6.
73. (1907). Auckland Electric Tramways - Surplus of £33,583 FOR 1906. The New Zealand Herald. Auckland. Volume XLIV. Edition 13460. 10 June 1907. P.5.
74. (1907). The Tramway Difficulty - Vigorous Protests. Auckland Star. Auckland. Volume XXXVIII. Edition 166. 13 July 1907. P.6.
75. (1907). Overcrowded Tramcars - Attitude of Local Bodies. The New Zealand Herald. Auckland. Volume XLIV. Edition 13503. 30 July 1907. P.6.
76. (1907). The Tramway By-Laws - Confirmed By City Council. Auckland Star. Auckland. Volume XXXVIII. Edition 224. 19 September 1907. P.5.
77. (1907). Auckland Tramways, Question of Ownership. The New Zealand Herald. Auckland. Volume XLIV. Edition 13602. 22 November 1907. P.6.
78. (1908). Auckland Tramways - Meeting of Shareholders. The New Zealand Herald. Auckland. Volume XLV. Edition 13788. 29 June 1908. P.6.

79. (1908). The Tramway Case - City Council's Action. <u>The New Zealand Herald</u>. Auckland. Volume XLV Edition 13846. 4 September 1908. P.6.
80. (1908). The Tramway Case - Action Settled. <u>The New Zealand Herald</u>. Auckland. Volume XLV. Edition 13847. 5 September 1908. P.6.
81. (1909). Auckland Tramways - The Year's Return. <u>The New Zealand Herald</u>. Auckland. Volume XLVI. Edition 14082. 9 June 1909. P.8.
82. (1910). Auckland-Takapuna Service - Started To-Day. <u>Auckland Star</u>. Auckland. Volume XLI. Edition 303. 22 December 1910. P.5.
83. Woolston, A. (1996). <u>Equal to the Task - The City of Auckland Traffic Department 1894-1994</u>. Auckland. Auckland City Council & New Zealand Police. P.31.
84. (1910). Auckland Tramways - Great Growth of Traffic. <u>The New Zealand Herald</u>. Auckland. Volume XLVII. Edition 14549. 10 December 1910. P.5.
85. (1910). The Tramway Service - A Hundred Cars. <u>The New Zealand Herald</u>. Auckland. Volume XLVII. Edition 14561. 24 December 1910. P.8.
86. (1911). The Tramway Service - Shortage of Cars. <u>The New Zealand Herald</u>. Auckland. Volume XLVIII. Edition 14744. 28 July 1911. P.8.
87. (1910). Auckland Tramways - Great Growth of Traffic. <u>The New Zealand Herald</u>. Auckland. Volume XLVII. Edition 14549. 10 December 1910. P.5.
88. (1910). The Tramways Bill - The City Council's Powers. <u>The New Zealand Herald</u>. Auckland. Volume XLVII. Edition 14523. 10 November 2010. P.6.
89. (1913). Municipal Corporations Amendment Act 1913. General Assembly of New Zealand. Statute No. 62. 15 December 1913.
90. (1913). The City Council And The Tramways. <u>The New Zealand Herald</u>. Auckland. Volume L. Edition 15439. 24 October 1913. P.4.
91. (1913). Auckland Tramways - Satisfactory Year. <u>The New Zealand Herald</u>. Auckland. Volume L. Edition 15468. 27 November 1913. P.4.
92. ibid.
93. ibid.
94. (1914). Auckland Tramways - The Maori Epidemic - Work of the Past Year. <u>The New Zealand Herald</u>. Auckland. Volume LI. Edition 15784. 5 December 1914. P.4.
95. ibid.

96. ibid.
97. (1915). Mount Albert Trams. The New Zealand Herald. Auckland. Volume LII. Edition 16002. 21 August 1915. P.9.
98. (1916). Auckland Tramways - No Increase This Year. Auckland Star. Auckland. Volume XLVII. Edition 2. 3 January 1916. P.7.
99. ibid.
100. ibid.
101. (1916). Auckland Tramways - Extensions Suspended. The New Zealand Herald. Auckland. Volume LIII. Edition 16356. 10 October 1916. P.9.
102. (1917). Speed of Trams The New Zealand Herald. Auckland. Volume LIV. Edition 16461. 10 February 1917. P.9.
103. (1918). Auckland Tramways - The 20th Annual Meeting. The New Zealand Herald. Auckland. Volume LV. Edition 16750. 17 January 1918. P.6.
104. (1918). Suburban Tram Service - Demand For Improvement. The New Zealand Herald. Auckland. Volume LV. Edition 16881. 20 June 1918. P.7.
105. (1918). The Five O'Clock Rush. The New Zealand Herald. Auckland. Volume LV. Edition 16893. 4 July 1918. P.4.
106. (1919). The Tramway Service - No Extensions In View. The New Zealand Herald. Auckland. Volume LV. Edition 17054. 9 January 1919. P.4.
107. (1919). The City Council - Tramway Services - Grey Lynn Duplication. The New Zealand Herald. Auckland. Volume LVI. Edition 17091. 21 February 1919. P.6.
108. (1919). Time No Object - City Trams Slow Down. The New Zealand Herald. Auckland. Volume LVI. Edition 17086. 15 February 1919. P.8.
109. (1919). Tramways Settlement. The New Zealand Herald. Auckland. Volume LVI. Edition 17087. 17 February 1919. P.6.
110. (1919). The Tramway Services - Point of View of Public. The New Zealand Herald. Auckland. Volume LVI. Edition 17088. 18 February 1919. P.4.
111. (1919). Sale of City Tramways - Mount Eden Consents. Auckland Star. Auckland. Volume L. Edition 97. 24 April 1919. P.9.
112. (1919). Purchase of Trams - Support At One Tree Hill. The New Zealand Herald. Auckland. Volume LVI. Edition 17126. 3 April 1919. P.8.
113. (1919). Commercial - Auckland Tramways. The New Zealand Herald. Auckland. Volume LVI. Edition 17172. 28 May 1919. P.5.

114. (1919). The Tramways. <u>Auckland Star</u>. Auckland. Edition 123. 24 May 1919. P.6.
115. Stace, F. Nigel. (1996) "William Ferguson - Biography." <u>Dictionary of New Zealand Biography</u> The Encyclopedia of New Zealand. Volume 3. Accessed 9 December 2013 at http://www.teara.govt.nz/en/biographies/3f4/ferguson-william.
116. Ferguson, William. (1919). Option of Purchase and Valuation/City of Auckland and the Auckland Electric Tramways. Auckland. Auckland City Council.
117. (1919). The Tramways. <u>Auckland Star</u>. Auckland. Edition 123. 24 May 1919. P.6.
118. (1919). Purchase of Tramways - Sanction By Ratepayers. <u>The New Zealand Herald</u> Auckland. Volume LVI. Edition 17185. 12 June 1919. P.6.
119. (1919). The Tramways Poll. <u>The New Zealand Herald</u>. Auckland. Volume LVI. Edition 17185. 12 June 1919. P.6.
120. (1919). Tramway Service - Letter to the Editor. <u>The New Zealand Herald</u>. Auckland. Volume LVI. Edition 17185. 12 June 1919. P.9.
121. (1919). Tramways Purchase - Extension of Services. <u>The New Zealand Herald</u>. Auckland. Volume LVI. Edition 17198. 27 June 1919. P.8.
122. (1919). Taking Over Trams - Transition Arrangements. <u>Auckland Star</u>. Auckland. Volume L. Edition 152. 27 June 1919. P.8.
123. (1919). Auckland Tramways - Change of Ownership. <u>The New Zealand Herald</u>. Auckland. Volume LVI. Edition 17200. 30 June 1919. P.6.
124. (1920). Tramways Purchase - The Financial Position. <u>The New Zealand Herald</u>. Auckland. Volume LVII. Edition 17375. 23 January 1920. P.4.
125. (1920). Tramways Purchase - Signing Of The Bonds. <u>The New Zealand Herald</u>. Auckland. Volume LVII. Edition 17430. 27 March 1920. P.6.
126. (1923). Auckland Tramways - History And Progress. <u>The New Zealand Herald</u>. Auckland. Volume LX. Edition 18593. 28 December 1923. P.9.
127. McCrystal, John. (2007). <u>On the Buses in New Zealand - From Charabancs to the Coaches of Today</u>. Wellington, Grantham House Publishing & Bus and Coach Association. P.8.
128. (1923). Local And General News. <u>The New Zealand Herald</u>. Auckland. Volume LX. Edition 18371. 11 April 1923. P.10.
129. ibid.

130. (1923). Auckland Tramways - History And Progress. The New Zealand Herald. Auckland. Volume LX. Edition 18593. 28 December 1923. P.9.
131. Bush, W. E. (1920). Report to Auckland City Council on his tour of investigation through the United States of America, Canada and Great Britain. Auckland. 3 March 1920. PP.29 & 30.
132. Ford, Albert Edward. (1927). Tramways & Omnibus Services - Auckland City Corporation Tramways. Auckland. 3 March 1927.
133. ibid.
134. (1924). Distractions of Wireless. Auckland Star. Auckland. Volume LV. Edition 306. 26 December 1924. P.4.
135. (1924). Tram And Bus Rivalry. Auckland Star. Auckland. Volume LV. Edition 166. 15 July 1924. P.7.
136. Motor-vehicles Act 1924. General Assembly of New Zealand. Bill No. 39. 6 November 1924.
137. (1925). Overcrowded Buses. The New Zealand Herald. Auckland. Volume LXII. Edition 19131. 24 September 1925. P.13.
138. (1925). City Transport Control. The New Zealand Herald. Auckland. Volume LXII. Edition 19088. 5 August 1925. P.8.
139. (1925). Motor-Bus Control - The Regulations Opposed. The New Zealand Herald. Auckland. Volume LXII. Edition 19209. 24 December 1925. P.13.
140. (1926). Buses On Tram Routes - The Regulations Opposed. The New Zealand Herald. Auckland. Volume LXIII. Edition 19346. 5 June 1926. P.10.
141. (1926). Debate In The House. The New Zealand Herald. Auckland. Volume LXIII. Edition 19367. 30 June 1926. P.14.
142. (1926). An Innocent Abroad. Auckland Star. Auckland. Volume LVII. Edition 162. 10 July 1926. P.10.
143. (1926). Bus Control - Petitions To Parliament. The Press. Christchurch. Volume LXII. Edition 18750. 22 July 1926. P.11.
144. (1926). Buses In Auckland - Regulations Objected To. The New Zealand Herald. Auckland. Volume LXIII. Edition 19387. 23 July 1926. P.12.
145. (1926). Buses And Trams - Select Committee Inquiry. Auckland Star. Auckland. Volume LVII. Edition 173. 23 July 1926. P.5.
146. (1926). Buses In Auckland - Competition With Trams. The New Zealand Herald. Auckland. Volume LXIII. Edition 19388. 24 July 1926. P.12.
147. (1926). Bus v Tram - Effects of Competition. Evening Post. Wellington. Volume CXII. Edition 24. 28 July 1926. P.12.

148. (1926). Buses And Trams - Position In Sydney. <u>The New Zealand Herald</u>. Auckland. Volume LXIII. Edition 19390. 27 July 1926. P.12.
149. (1926). The Bus Regulations - Views Of Auckland Bodies. <u>The New Zealand Herald</u>. Auckland. Volume LXIII. Edition 19391. 28 July 1926. P.13.
150. (1926). Auckland Tramways - Effects Of Bus Traffic. <u>The New Zealand Herald</u>. Auckland. Volume LXIII. Edition 19392. 29 July 1926. P.13.
151. (1926). Bus Regulations - Further Evidence Before Committee. <u>Evening Post</u>. Wellington. Volume CXII. Edition 26. 30 July 1926. P.10.
152. (1926). Bus Regulations - Written Evidence And Suggestions. <u>Evening Post</u>. Wellington. Volume CXII. Edition 42. 18 August 1926. P.11.
153. (1926). The Bus Regulations. <u>Auckland Star</u>. Auckland. Volume LVII. Edition 207. 1 September 1926. P.10.
154. (1926). Motor-Omnibus Control - Editorial. <u>The New Zealand Herald</u>. Auckland. Volume LXIII. Edition 19421. 1 September 1926. P.10.
155. (1926). Motor-omnibus Traffic Act 1926. General Assembly of New Zealand. Bill No. 67. 11 September 1926. Clauses 6(2), 6(3) & 7.
156. ibid. Clause 10.
157. ibid. Clause 15(1).
158. (1927). Royal Motor-Buses. <u>The New Zealand Herald</u>. Auckland. Volume LXIV. Edition 19642. 21 May 1927. P.12.
159. (1927). Mangere Bus Service. <u>The New Zealand Herald</u>. Auckland. Volume LXIV. Edition 19750. 24 September 1927. P.12.
160. (1927). Takapuna Transport - New Ferry Service Operates From Tomorrow. <u>Auckland Star</u>. Auckland. Volume LVIII. Edition 96. 26 April 1927. P.10.
161. (1927). Motor-spirits Taxation Act 1927. General Assembly of New Zealand. Bill No. 47. 15 November 1927.
162. Bloomfield, Dr. G. T. (1975). Urban Tramways in New Zealand 1862-1964. <u>New Zealand Geographer</u> Edition 31. P.112.
163. (1927). The Tramways Poll. <u>Auckland Star</u>. Auckland. Volume LVIII. Edition 171. 22 July 1927. P.6.
164. Jesson, Bruce. (1999). <u>Only Their Purpose Is Mad</u>. Palmerston North, Dunmore Press Limited. P.177.
165. Bloomfield, Dr. G. T. (1975). Urban Tramways in New Zealand 1862-1964. <u>New Zealand Geographer</u> Edition 31. P.112.

166. Auckland City Corporation. (1927). "Special Tramways Number." <u>Municipal Record</u>. Volume Three. Issue Two. August 1927. P.10.
167. ibid. P.6.
168. ibid. PP.8 & 9.
169. (1927). Running For A Tram - Man Knocked Down. <u>Auckland Star</u>. Auckland. Volume LVIII. Edition 193. 17 August 1927. P.5.
170. (1927). Loan Rejected - Heavy Tramways Poll. <u>Auckland Star</u>. Auckland. Volume LVIII. Edition 194. 18 August 1927. P.8.
171. (1927). The Rejected Loan. <u>Auckland Star</u>. Auckland. Volume LVIII. Edition 194. 18 August 1927. P.6.
172. (2008). "Auckland". Retrieved 7 December 2008 from http://www.petroltax.org.nz/akmotorways.html.
173. (1927). Demand Less Now. <u>Auckland Star</u>. Auckland. Volume LVIII. Edition 269. 14 November 1927. P.9.
174. (1928). Trams And Transport - Commission Next Month. <u>Auckland Star</u>. Auckland. Volume LIX. Edition 39. 16 February 1928. P.8.
175. (1927). Auckland Transport. <u>The New Zealand Herald</u>. Auckland. Volume LXIV. Edition 19771. 19 October 1927. P.10.
176. Auckland Transport Commission. (1928). Report of the Auckland Transport Commission. Wellington. H.-33. 11 June 1928.
177. (1928). Transport Problem. <u>Auckland Star</u>. Auckland. Volume LIX. Edition 46. 24 February 1928. P.8.
178. ibid.
179. (1928). Suburban Transport - Metropolitan Board. <u>Auckland Star</u>. Auckland. Volume LIX. Edition 62. 14 March 1928. P.10.
180. (1928). Auckland Transport: Commission Of Inquiry. <u>Auckland Star</u>. Auckland. Volume LIX. Edition 82. 7 April 1928. P.9.
181. ibid.
182. (1928). Heavy Bus Losses. <u>Auckland Star</u>. Auckland. Volume LIX. Edition 105. 5 May 1928. P.12.
183. (1928). Dead Mileage. <u>Auckland Star</u>. Auckland. Volume LIX. Edition 107. 8 May 1928. P.8.
184. (1928). Transport Control - Board Not Justified. <u>Auckland Star</u>. Auckland. Volume LIX. Edition 108. 9 May 1928. P.8.
185. ibid.
186. (1928). Ratepayers' Decision. <u>Auckland Star</u>. Auckland. Volume LIX. Edition 110. 11 May 1928. P.5.
187. (1928). Municipal Autocracy. <u>Auckland Star</u>. Auckland. Volume LIX. Edition 109. 10 May 1928. P.6.
188. (1928). Sauce For The Goose. <u>Auckland Star</u>. Auckland. Volume LIX. Edition 114. 16 May 1928. P.9.

189. (1928). Buses And Trams - Outer Area Interests. <u>Auckland Star</u>. Auckland. Volume LIX. Edition 115. 17 May 1928. P.8.
190. (1928). Greater Auckland - An Anomalous Position. <u>Auckland Star</u>. Auckland. Volume LIX. Edition 118. 21 May 1928. P.9.
191. (1928). Entirely Illogical. <u>Auckland Star</u>. Auckland. Volume LIX. Edition 119. 22 May 1928. P.9.
192. (1928). Impossible Dream. <u>Auckland Star</u>. Auckland. Volume LIX. Edition 120. 23 May 1928. P.9.
193. Auckland Transport Commission. (1928). Report of the Auckland Transport Commission. Wellington. H.-33. 11 June 1928. P.5.
194. (1928). Clogged With Detail. <u>Auckland Star</u>. Auckland. Volume LIX. Edition 121. 24 May 1928. P.8.
195. Auckland Transport Commission. (1928). Report of the Auckland Transport Commission. Wellington. H.-33. 11 June 1928. P.8.
196. ibid.
197. ibid.
198. ibid. P.9.
199. ibid. P.37.
200. (1928). Feeder Bus Services. <u>Auckland Star</u>. Auckland. Volume LIX. Edition 125. 29 May 1928. P.8.
201. (1928). Transport Maze. <u>Auckland Star</u>. Auckland. Volume LIX. Edition 132. 6 June 1928. P.8.
202. ibid.
203. (1928). Inquiry Ends Today - Transport Commission. <u>The New Zealand Herald</u>. Auckland. Volume LXV. Edition 19967. 8 June 1928. P.13.
204. (1928). Formally Closed. <u>The New Zealand Herald</u>. Auckland. Volume LXV. Edition 19973. 15 June 1928. P.13.
205. (1928). Transport Board Plan. <u>The New Zealand Herald</u>. Auckland. Volume LXV. Edition 19968. 9 June 1928. P.10.
206. Auckland Transport Commission. (1928). Report of the Auckland Transport Commission. Wellington. H.-33. 11 June 1928. P.20.
207. ibid. P.22.
208. ibid. P.9.
209. ibid. PP.27 & 28.
210. ibid. P.20.
211. ibid. PP.20-22.
212. ibid. P.10.
213. ibid. P.26.
214. ibid. PP.18 & 19.
215. ibid. PP.24 & 25.

216. (1928). The Transport Report. <u>The New Zealand Herald</u>. Auckland. Volume LXV. Edition 20010. 28 July 1928. P.10.
217. (1928). Greater Auckland Aspect. <u>The New Zealand Herald</u>. Auckland. Volume LXV. Edition 20011. 30 July 1928. P.11.
218. (1928). Auckland's Transport. <u>The New Zealand Herald</u>. Auckland. Volume LXV. Edition 20037. 29 August 1928. P.10.
219. (1928). Transport Confusion. <u>The New Zealand Herald</u>. Auckland. Volume LXV. Edition 20049. 12 September 1928. P.12.
220. (1928). Auckland Transport - Need To Reach Agreement. <u>The New Zealand Herald</u>. Auckland. Volume LXV. Edition 20051. 14 September 1928. P.16.
221. (1928). Transport Problem - Formation of Board. <u>Auckland Star</u>. Auckland. Volume LIX. Edition 223. 20 September 1928. P.9.
222. (1928). Nearer Solution - The Transport Problem. <u>Auckland Star</u>. Auckland. Volume LIX. Edition 224. 21 September 1928. P.10.
223. (1928). Transport Bill - Proposed Legislation. <u>Auckland Star</u>. Auckland. Volume LIX. Edition 230. 28 September 1928. P.5.
224. (1928). Transport Agreement - Auckland Bill Amended. <u>The New Zealand Herald</u>. Auckland. Volume LXV. Edition 20069. 5 October 1928. P.12.
225. (1928). Auckland Transport Board Act 1928. General Assembly of New Zealand. Bill No. 44. 9 October 1928. Clauses 3, 57 & 58.
226. ibid. Clause 76.
227. (1928). Transport Act - Approved By City Council. <u>Auckland Star</u>. Auckland. Volume LIX. Edition 242. 12 October 1928. P.11.
228. (1928). Transport Board - Approved By Ratepayers. <u>Auckland Star</u>. Auckland. Volume LIX. Edition 259. 1 November 1928. P.9.
229. (1928). Transport Board - First Meeting Held. <u>Auckland Star</u>. Auckland. Volume LIX. Edition 303. 22 December 1928. P.7.
230. (1929). Tramway Extensions. <u>The New Zealand Herald</u>. Auckland. Volume LXVI. Edition 20151. 11 January 1929. P.12.
231. ibid.
232. (1929). Transport Board - Formal Change To-Morrow. <u>Auckland Star</u>. Auckland. Volume LX. Edition 12. 15 January 1929. P.8.
233. (1929). Bus Services - Transport For Suburbs. <u>Auckland Star</u>. Auckland. Volume LX. Edition 14. 17 January 1929. P.9.
234. (1929). Transport Problems. <u>Auckland Star</u>. Auckland. Volume LX. Edition 15. 18 January 1929. P.6.
235. (1929). Tramway Extensions. <u>The New Zealand Herald</u>. Auckland. Volume LXVI. Edition 20161. 23 January 1929. P.14.

236. (1929). Trackless Trams. <u>The New Zealand Herald</u>. Auckland. Volume LXVI. Edition 20157. 18 January 1929. P.13.
237. (1929). A Bombshell. <u>Auckland Star</u>. Auckland. Volume LX. Edition 19. 23 January 1929. P.8.
238. (1929). Transport Board - Position Of The Outer Suburbs (To the Editor). <u>Auckland Star</u>. Auckland. Volume LX. Edition 21. 25 January 1929. P.6.
239. (1929). Trams To Avondale. <u>The New Zealand Herald</u>. Auckland. Volume LXVI. Edition 20164. 26 January 1929 P.16.
240. (1929). Big Loss On Buses. <u>The New Zealand Herald</u>. Auckland. Volume LXVI. Edition 20168. 31 January 1929. P.13.
241. (1929). City Transport Policy. <u>The New Zealand Herald</u>. Auckland. Volume LXVI. Edition 20185. 20 February 1929. P.12.
242. (1929). Big Loss On Buses. <u>The New Zealand Herald</u>. Auckland. Volume LXVI. Edition 20168. 31 January 1929. P.13.
243. (1929). Trams And Buses. <u>The New Zealand Herald</u>. Auckland. Volume LXVI. Edition 20175. 8 February 1929. P.10.
244. (1929). Tramway Extensions - Confirming Loan Scheme. <u>The New Zealand Herald</u>. Auckland. Volume LXVI. Edition 20179. 13 February 1929. P.12.
245. (1929). Tramway Extensions - Opinion In Remuera. <u>The New Zealand Herald</u>. Auckland. Volume LXVI. Edition 20185. 20 February 1929. P.13.
246. (1929). Transport Services - Letter To The Editor. <u>The New Zealand Herald</u>. Auckland. Volume LXVI. Edition 20173. 6 February 1929. P.14.
247. (1929). The Transport Board - Letters to The Editor. <u>The New Zealand Herald</u>. Auckland. Volume LXVI. Edition 20188. 23 February 1929. P.14.
248. (1929). Transport Loans - Alternative Proposals. <u>The New Zealand Herald</u>. Auckland. Volume LXVI. Edition 20191. 27 February 1929. P.12.
249. (1929). Bold Traffic Scheme. <u>The New Zealand Herald</u>. Auckland. Volume LXVI. Edition 20195. 4 March 1929. P.13.
250. (1929). The Taxicab War - Omnibus Owners Protest. <u>The New Zealand Herald</u>. Auckland. Volume LXVI. Edition 20209. 20 March 1929. P.15.
251. (1929). The Motor Industry - Great Growth Outlined. <u>The New Zealand Herald</u>. Auckland. Volume LXVI. Edition 20232. 17 April 1929. P.14.

252. (1929). Tramway Extensions. The New Zealand Herald. Auckland. Volume LXVI. Edition 20222. 5 April 1929. P.12.
253. (1929). Loan For Transport - Approval of Proposals. The New Zealand Herald. Auckland. Volume LXVI. Edition 20224. 8 April 1929. P.10.
254. (1929). The Transport Loan. Auckland Star. Auckland. Volume LX. Edition 80. 5 April 1929. P.6.
255. (1929). City Transport System - The Loan Proposals. The New Zealand Herald. Auckland. Volume LXVI. Edition 20234. 19 April 1929. P.12.
256. (1929). Transport Loan - Poll Next Week. Auckland Star. Auckland. Volume LX. Edition 103. 3 May 1929. P.8.
257. (1929). Transport Board Loans The New Zealand Herald. Auckland. Volume LXVI. Edition 20247. 6 May 1929. P.10.
258. (1929). Transport Board Poll - Uproar At Town Hall. The New Zealand Herald. Auckland. Volume LXVI. Edition 20248. 7 May 1929. P.13.
259. (1929). The Transport Board - Letter To The Editor. The New Zealand Herald. Auckland. Volume LXVI. Edition 20254. 14 May 1929. P.12.
260. (1929). The Transport Loan - Both Issues Approved. The New Zealand Herald. Auckland. Volume LXVI. Edition 20250. 9 May 1929. P.10.
261. (1929). The Transport Loans. The New Zealand Herald. Auckland. Volume LXVI. Edition 20250. 9 May 1929. P.10.
262. (1929). Early Start On Work. The New Zealand Herald. Auckland. Volume LXVI. Edition 20250. 9 May 1929. P.10.
263. (1929). Transport Board And Employment. Auckland Star. Auckland. Volume LX. Edition 115. 17 May 1929. P.6.
264. (1929). Vote Of Confidence. Auckland Star. Auckland. Volume LX. Edition 108. 9 May 1929. P.11.
265. (1929). Transport Board - Mr Morton's Resignation. Auckland Star. Auckland. Volume LX. Edition 124. 28 May 1929. P.12.
266. (1929). Auckland Transport. Auckland Star. Auckland. Volume LX. Edition 131. 5 June 1929. P.6.
267. (1929). Tram Services - Sydney Seeking Co-Ordination With Buses. Auckland Star. Auckland. Volume LX. Edition 137. 12 June 1929. P.7.
268. (1929). Loans Approved - Auckland Transport. Auckland Star. Auckland. Volume LX. Edition 133. 7 June 1929. P.3.

269. (1929). New Tram Extensions. <u>The New Zealand Herald</u>. Auckland. Volume LXVI. Edition 20279. 12 June 1929. P.12.
270. Ford, A. E. (1929). New Cars & Statutory Clearance Whilst In Service. Letter to F. W. Furkert, Engineer In Chief & Transport Under-Secretary. National Archives. Auckland. 8 February 1929.
271. (1930). Trams To Avondale? <u>Auckland Star</u>. Auckland. Volume LXI. Edition 183. 5 August 1930. P.5.
272. (1930). Tram Poll Carried - Avondale Extension. <u>The New Zealand Herald</u>. Auckland. Volume LXVII. Edition 20636. 7 August 1930. P.10.
273. ibid.
274. (1931). Transport In Cities. <u>The New Zealand Herald</u>. Auckland. Volume LXVIII. Edition 21066. 28 December 1931. P.3.
275. (1931). Transport Changes. <u>Auckland Star</u>. Auckland. Volume LXII. Edition 306. 28 December 1931. P.6.
276. (1932). Two Sections - New Tram Extension. <u>Auckland Star</u>. Auckland. Volume LXIII. Edition 25. 30 January 1932. P.11.
277. (1933). Transport Accounts. <u>Auckland Star</u>. Auckland. Volume LXIV. Edition 126. 31 May 1933. P.6.
278. Stone, R. C. J. (1973). <u>Makers of Fortune</u>. Auckland. Auckland University Press. Oxford University Press. P.184.
279. Ibid.
280. (1936). The Pound Symbol - Currency Dispute. <u>Auckland Star</u>. Auckland. Volume LXVII. Edition 67. 19 March 1936. P.8.
281. (1937). Tramway Loan - Appeal Dismissed. <u>The New Zealand Herald</u>. Auckland. Volume LXXIV. Edition 22638. 28 January 1937. P.10.
282. (1936). Getting Ready - Forty-Hour Week. <u>Auckland Star</u>. Auckland. Volume LXVII. Edition 197. 20 August 1936. P.8.
283. (1940). Tramway Loan - London Repayment. <u>The New Zealand Herald</u>. Auckland. Volume LXXVII. Edition 23703. 9 July 1940. P.9.
284. (1940). Auckland Tram Fares. <u>Auckland Star</u>. Auckland. Volume LXXI. Edition 164. 12 July 1940. P.9.
285. (1940). Auckland Taxis - Increase In Fares. <u>Auckland Star</u>. Auckland. Volume LXXI. Edition 164. 12 July 1940. P.8.
286. (1937). Auckland Trolley Bus Service. <u>Evening Post</u>. Wellington. Volume CXXIV. Edition 12. 14 July 1937. P.12.
287. (1938). New Trolley Buses - Service Starts To-Day. <u>The New Zealand Herald</u>. Auckland. Volume LXXV. Edition 23224. 19 December 1938. P.12.

288. Bloomfield, Dr. G. T. (1975). Urban Tramways in New Zealand 1862-1964. <u>New Zealand Geographer</u> Edition 31. P.120.
289. ibid. P.114.

**Chapter Ten**
**The Motor Car Cometh**
1. McCrystal, John. (2007). <u>On the Buses in New Zealand - From Charabancs to the Coaches of Today</u>. Wellington, Grantham House Publishing & Bus and Coach Association. P.29.
2. (1898). The McLean Motor-Car Act 1898. General Assembly of New Zealand. Bill No.62. 28 October 1898.
3. (1902). The Motor Cars Regulation Act 1902. General Assembly of New Zealand. Bill No.14. 1 October 1902.
4. McCrystal, John. (2007). <u>On the Buses in New Zealand - From Charabancs to the Coaches of Today</u>. Wellington, Grantham House Publishing & Bus and Coach Association. P.16.
5. (1914). Motor Taxation And Good Roads. <u>Otago Daily Times</u>. Dunedin. Edition 16135. 25 July 1914. P.10.
6. Stewart, Graham. (1996). <u>Always A Tram In Sight - The Electric Trams of New Zealand 1900 to 1964</u>. Wellington, Grantham House Publishing. P.5.
7. Keenan, Michael. (2006). Financial Management Strategies In The Auckland Gas Company 1862-1915. <u>City of Enterprise - Perspectives On Auckland Business History</u>. Ian Hunter and Diana Morrow. Auckland, Auckland University Press. P.73.
8. MacLean, Pam & Joyce, Brian. (1971). <u>The Veteran Years of New Zealand Motoring</u>. Wellington. A. H. & A. W. Reed Limited. P.21.
9. "The Taranaki Toll Roads 1906-1925." Retrieved 21 November 2008 from www.petroltax.org.nz/tollroads-2.html.
10. ibid.
11. Woolston, A. (1996). <u>Equal to the Task - The City of Auckland Traffic Department 1894-1994</u>. Auckland. Auckland City Council & New Zealand Police. P.27.
12. Barr, John. (1922). <u>The City of Auckland New Zealand 1840-1920</u>. Auckland. Whitcombe & Tombs Limited. PP.199 & 200.
13. (1921). For Good Roads. <u>Auckland Star</u>. Auckland. Volume LII. Edition 27. 1 February 1921. P.5.
14. (1925). Items Of Interest. <u>Evening Post</u>. Wellington. Volume CX. Edition 149. 21 December 1925. P.11.

15. (1922). Main Highways Act 1922. General Assembly of New Zealand. Bill No. 47. 31 October 1922.
16. ibid.
17. McCrystal, John. (2007). On the Buses in New Zealand - From Charabancs to the Coaches of Today. Wellington, Grantham House Publishing & Bus and Coach Association. P.32.
18. (1923). Main South Road - Burden Of Counties. The New Zealand Herald. Auckland. Volume LX. Edition 18409. 26 May 1923. P.10.
19. (1923). Heavy Motor Traffic. The New Zealand Herald. Auckland. Volume LX. Edition 18409. 26 May 1923. P.8.
20. (1924). Metal For Highways. The New Zealand Herald. Auckland. Volume LXI. Edition 18764. 18 July 1924. P.10.
21. (1925). Public Works Amendment Act 1925. New Zealand House of Representatives. Bill No. 47. 1 October 1925.
22. Main Highways Board. (1925). First Annual Report Of The Main Highways Board. Wellington.
23. (1923). Rail Versus Motor - Lorry Transport Cheaper. The New Zealand Herald. Auckland. Volume LX. Edition 18507. 18 September 1923. P.8.
24. (1924). Motor-vehicles Act 1924. General Assembly of New Zealand. Bill No. 39. 6 November 1924.
25. ibid.
26. (1924). Motor Vehicles Bill. The New Zealand Herald. Auckland. Volume LXI. Edition 18600. 7 January 1924. P.8.
27. (1924). Petrol Tax Opposed. The New Zealand Herald. Auckland. Volume LXI. Edition 18604. 11 January 1924. P.8.
28. ibid.
29. (1926). New Motor Industry. The New Zealand Herald. Auckland. Volume LXIII. Edition 19231. 21 January 1926. P.11.
30. ibid.
31. (1926). Materials For Roading. The New Zealand Herald. Auckland. Volume LXIII. Edition 19397. 4 August 1926. P.14.
32. (1927). Customs Tariff Amendment - Duty On Motor-Spirits. Committee of Ways and Means. Wellington. New Zealand House of Representatives. 31 October 1927. PP.435 & 436.
33. (1927). Motor-spirits Taxation Act 1927. New Zealand House of Representatives. Bill No.47. 15 November 1927.
34. (1928). Motor-spirits Taxation Amendment Act 1928. New Zealand House of Representatives. Bill No.24. 6 October 1928.

35. (1927). Motor-spirits Taxation Act 1927. New Zealand House of Representatives. Bill No.47. 15 November 1927.
36. (1930). Higher Bus Fares. <u>Auckland Star</u>. Auckland. Volume LXI. Edition 172. 23 July 1930. P.8.
37. (1930). Benzine Thieves Active. <u>The New Zealand Herald</u>. Auckland. Volume LXVII. Edition 20622. 22 July 1930. P.10.
38. (1932). Finance Act 1932. New Zealand House of Representatives. Bill No.11. 10 May 1932.
39. ibid.
40. Main Highways Board. (1932). Eighth Annual Report of the Main Highways Board. Wellington. Main Highways Board.
41. (1931). Rival To Railways. <u>Auckland Star</u>. Auckland. 2 January 1931. P.2.
42. (1931). Beating The Limited. <u>Evening Post</u>. Wellington. Volume CXI. Edition 2. 3 January 1931. P.12.
43. (1931). Transport Competition. <u>The New Zealand Herald</u>. Auckland. Volume LXVIII. Edition 20908. 25 June 1931. P.10.
44. (1931). Services By Road. <u>The New Zealand Herald</u>. Auckland. Volume LXVIII. Edition 20935. 27 July 1931. P.11.
45. (1931). Transport Licensing Act 1931. General Assembly of New Zealand. Bill No.38. 11 November 1931.
46. ibid.
47. McCrystal, John. (2007). <u>On the Buses in New Zealand - From Charabancs to the Coaches of Today</u>. Wellington, Grantham House Publishing & Bus and Coach Association. P.46.
48. (1931). Government Railways Amendment Act 1931. Bill No. 4. New Zealand House of Representatives. 28 April 1931.
49. (1932). Saving The Railways. <u>The New Zealand Herald</u>. Auckland. Volume LXIX. Edition 21184. 17 May 1932. P.10.
50. (1933). Transport Competition - Case For Regulation. <u>The New Zealand Herald</u>. Auckland. Volume LXX. Edition 21561. 4 August 1933. P.11.
51. (1934). Supreme Board - Transport Control. <u>Auckland Star</u>. Auckland. Volume LXV. Edition 75. 29 March 1934. P.15.
52. (1934). Motor Taxation. <u>The New Zealand Herald</u>. Auckland. Volume LXXI. Edition 21923. 5 October 1934. P.13.
53. (1934). Cars And Affluence. <u>The New Zealand Herald</u>. Auckland. Volume LXXI. Edition 21923. 5 October 1934. P.13.
54. (1934). Cars And Income. <u>Auckland Star</u>. Auckland. Volume LXV. Edition 242. 12 October 1934. P.16.

55. (1934). Taxing Of Petrol - Best For Motor Transport. Auckland Star. Auckland. Volume LXV. Edition 239. 9 October 1934. P.8.
56. (1934). Motor Taxation - No Change Desired. The New Zealand Herald. Auckland. Volume LXXI. Edition 21925. 8 October 1934. P.10.
57. (1935). Roading Finance. The New Zealand Herald. Auckland. Volume LXXII. Edition 22027. 6 February 1935. P.10.
58. (1935). Motorists' Burden. The New Zealand Herald. Auckland. Volume LXXII. Edition 22062. 19 March 1935. P.11.
59. Transport Co-Ordination Board. (1935). Transport Co-Ordination Board - First Annual Report. Wellington. 1 August 1935. P.25.
60. ibid.
61. (1935). Motor Taxation - Important Change. Auckland Star. Auckland. Volume LXVI. Edition 81. 5 April 1935. P.7.
62. Transport Co-Ordination Board. (1935). Transport Co-Ordination Board - First Annual Report. Wellington. 1 August 1935. P.8.
63. (1935). Many Appeals. Auckland Star. Auckland. Volume LXVI. Edition 22. 26 January 1935. P.12.
64. (1935). Transport Control. The New Zealand Herald. Auckland. Volume LXXII. Edition 22079. 8 April 1935. P.8.
65. (1936). Transport Board - Work Suspended. The New Zealand Herald. Auckland. Volume LXXIII. Edition 22339. 10 February 1936. P.8.
66. (1936). Transport Board - Favouring Private Enterprise. The New Zealand Herald. Auckland. Volume LXXIII. Edition 22339. 10 February 1936. P.8.
67. (1936). Bus Service Stopped. The New Zealand Herald. Auckland. Volume LXXIII. Edition 22342. 13 February 1936. P.10.
68. (1936). Overhaul. Auckland Star. Auckland. Volume LXVII. Edition 69. 21 March 1936. P.10.
69. (1936). Too Much Power? Auckland Star. Auckland. Volume LXVII. Edition 118. 20 May 1936. P.10.
70. (1936). Trouble Certain. The New Zealand Herald. Auckland. Volume LXXIII. Edition 22423. 20 May 1936. P.15.
71. (1936). Transport Bill - Road Services. The New Zealand Herald. Auckland. Volume LXXIII. Edition 22425. 22 May 1936. P.11.
72. (1936). Transport Act - Four Appointments. The New Zealand Herald. Auckland. Volume LXXIII. Edition 22449. 19 June 1936. P.10.

73. (1936). Road Traffic - Reducing Accidents. <u>The New Zealand Herald</u>. Auckland. Volume LXXIII. Edition 22428. 26 May 1936. P.10.
74. (1936). Hit And Run. <u>Auckland Star</u>. Auckland. Volume LXVII. Edition 134. 8 June 1936. P.9.
75. (1936). The Age Of Speed. <u>The New Zealand Herald</u>. Auckland. Volume LXXIII. Edition 22440. 9 June 1936. P.13.
76. (1936). Motor Traffic. <u>The New Zealand Herald</u>. Auckland. Volume LXXIII. Edition 22478. 23 July 1936. P.13.
77. (1936). Tied In Knots. <u>Evening Post</u>. Wellington. Volume CXXII. Edition 114. 10 November 1936. P.13.
78. (1937). New Bus Terminal - In Full Use. <u>Auckland Star</u>. Auckland. Volume LXVIII. Edition 217. 13 September 1937. P.8.
79. (1937). New Bus Terminal - Criticised. <u>Auckland Star</u>. Auckland. Volume LXVIII. Edition 217. 13 September 1937. P.8.
80. (1939). Novelty Of Bus Travel. <u>Auckland Star</u>. Auckland. Volume LXX. Edition 235. 5 October 1939. P.6.
81. (1945). 100-M.P.H. Motoring. <u>Auckland Star</u>. Auckland. Volume LXXVI. Edition 65. 17 March 1945. P.16.
82. (1864). Auckland – Separation Movement In Auckland. <u>The Colonist</u>. Nelson. Volume VIII. Edition 749. 30 December 1864. P.3.

# Index

Adelaide Electric Supply Company, Limited, 435
Ahern, Mr., 167
Aickin, Graves, 266, 274, 276
Aitken v Bremner, 104
Aitken, William, 104, 266
Akehurst, Mr., 380
Albatross, steam ferry, 18
Alderton, Lisle, 460
Aldridge, E., 44, 51
Alexandra Park, 406
Alison, Alex senior, 10
Alison, Ewen and Alexander, 16
Alison, Hon. E. W., 47, 57, 275, 348
Allen, Sir Stephen, 460
Alliance Assurance Company Ltd v Auckland City Corporation & Auckland Transport Board, 434
Allingham, R. J., 38
Allum, John Andrew Charles, 244, 377, 382, 385, 403, 409, 411, 415, 417, 420, 421, 422, 424, 429, 432, 453
Amalgamated Society of Railway Servants, 456
American Railway Association, 350
Anderson, William Edward, 392
Anti-Bus Regulation League, 358
Arbitration Court, 295, 297, 313
Archibald Clark & Sons, 266
Armstrong, Hon. H. T., 238
Arney, Sir G. A., 251
Arthur Yates Seeds, 427
Arthur, T. B., 30

Ashdowne, Captain C. G., 80
Ashley, G., 403
Atkinson, H., 4
Atta Taxi Company, 437
Auckland and Drury Railway, 107, 112, 113, 116, 117, 119, 121, 128, 130, 138, 143, 151, 155, 495, 496
   first sod turned, 117
   land purchase, 119
   land speculation, 129
   strike, 138
   tenders, 114
   truck system, 140
Auckland and Drury Railway Act 1863, 107, 111, 117, 130
Auckland and Manukau Canal Act, 4
Auckland and Mercer Railway
   extension to southern stations, 142
Auckland and North Shore Steam Ferry Company Limited, 14, 15, 16, 18
Auckland and Suburban Drainage Board, 218
Auckland Automobile Association, 35, 55, 57, 83, 89, 95, 97
Auckland Bus Company, 231
Auckland Cab Drivers
   petition to Council 1880, 265
Auckland Canals and Inland Waterways Commission, 21, 28, 29, 48, 485

Auckland Chamber of Commerce, 186, 225, 234, 235, 238, 242, 243, 266, 356, 386, 420
   Communications and Transport Committee, 456

Auckland City Council, 29, 33, 43, 45, 55, 59, 65, 68, 72, 75, 76, 77, 78, 83, 87, 91, 93, 94, 105, 183, 184, 186, 218, 236, 238, 259, 262, 263, 299, 300, 303, 306, 308, 309, 310, 312, 313, 315, 318, 321, 323, 324, 329, 340, 342, 344, 349, 350, 355, 361, 363, 365, 366, 367, 370, 378, 379, 381, 382, 385, 387, 388, 392, 395, 396, 400, 403, 414, 415, 421, 422, 435, 476, 477, 495, 509, 510, 511, 513, 514, 515, 517, 518, 527
   autocratic power, 384
   created April 1871, 105
   municipal autocracy, 383
   omnibus corporation laws, 253
   Public Services Committee, 344, 345
   public transport profit & loss 1928, 389
   Streets Committee, 263, 268
   Tramways Committee, 377, 382, 383, 386

Auckland Cycle Roads League, 444

Auckland Electric Power Board, 365, 388, 395
   King's Wharf Power-station, 388

Auckland Electric Tramways Company, 279–346, 279–346

Auckland Electric-power Board Act, 1921-22, 388

Auckland Exhibition, 326, 327, 328

Auckland Good Roads League, 444

Auckland Harbour Board, 4, 6, 7, 14, 23, 29, 44, 50, 51, 52, 53, 55, 59, 67, 68, 72, 85, 87, 92, 93, 96, 166, 179, 183, 188, 348, 481
   Harbour Bridge opposition, 44

Auckland Harbour Bridge, 5, 24, 66, 224
   Australian Finance, 80, 81, 88
   English Finance, 35, 69, 79, 82
   German Finance, 79
   lottery, 34, 35, 40
   petition, 37, 42
   tolls, 32, 36, 45, 79

Auckland Harbour Bridge alternative, 67

Auckland Harbour Bridge Association, 40, 41, 43, 44, 46, 50, 53, 55, 58, 59, 61

Auckland Harbour Bridge Commission, 53, 54, 55, 86

Auckland Harbour Bridge Commissioners, 52

Auckland Harbour Bridge Committee, 32

Auckland Harbour Bridge Company Limited, 58, 60, 61, 62, 64, 67, 68, 69, 71, 72, 75, 76, 77, 79, 80, 82, 86

Auckland Harbour Bridge Design 1926, 35

Auckland Harbour Bridge Empowering Act 1931, 58, 77

Auckland Harbour Bridge Royal Commission, 51, 76

Auckland Highway Districts Validation Act 1877, 104

Auckland Hospital Board, 94

Auckland Improvement (Albert Barrack Reserves) Act 1872, 262
Auckland Improvement Commission, 262
Auckland Main Trunk Railway League, 162
Auckland Master Carriers' Association, 392
Auckland Metropolitan Traffic Control Board, 392
Auckland Motor Body Builders, 364
Auckland Omnibus Proprietors' Association, 356, 476
Auckland Post Office, 168
Auckland Province
   separatism proposed 1864, 480
Auckland Provincial Council, 143
Auckland Provincial Highways Act 1862, 104
Auckland Railway
   eastern outlet, 181
   expectations 1924, 205
   past realities, 179
   political control, 180
   traffic, 184
Auckland Railway Station, 115, 166, 168, 170, 171, 186, 206, 215, 216, 222, 226, 429
   Beach Road, 172, 177
   Beach Road - opened 1930, 229
   Britomart 1885, 167
   congestion, 203
   construction starts 1924, 209
   contract, 188
   costs 1930, 229
   Easter 1923 congestion, 197
   funds unavailable, 171
   inefficiency, 194
   location effect on patronage, 231
   monument to public transport failure, 230
   northern outlet 1927, 218
   Queen Street - last trains 1930, 228
   relocation proposal 1878, 166
   relocation to Britomart Place, 242
   Upper Queen Street, 177
Auckland Regional Authority, 372
Auckland Regional Council, 372
Auckland Regional Transport Authority, 372
Auckland Supreme Court, 121
Auckland to Helensville Railway opens, 153
Auckland Town-planning Association, 51, 53, 55
Auckland Tramway Company, 271
   expansion by 1900, 279
Auckland Tramways Committee, 356
Auckland Transport
   history, 405
Auckland Transport Board, 55, 221, 243, 379, 382, 393, 395, 398, 403, 406, 408, 410, 412, 414, 415, 417, 419, 420, 422, 423, 427, 429, 430, 433, 435, 437, 439, 453, 523
   a compromise, 396
   accepted by Auckland City Council, 400
   debentures issued, 430
   inaugral meeting 1928, 403
   parochial employment conditions, 425

plans endorsed by poll 1929, 422
tram & bus takeover 1929, 405
transport monopoly, 400
Auckland Transport Board Act 1928, 401, 402, 403
Auckland Transport Commission, 391
Auckland Transport Commissioners, 399
Auckland-Manukau Canal, 67
Austin, Mr., 124
Avondale Road Board, 190

Baber, Mr., 124
Baddeley, Mr., 124
Bagnall, H. N., 187, 312
Baildon, George, 46, 187, 219, 374, 403
Bailey, Mr., 277
Bailey, W., 4
Bainbridge, Joe, 246
Baker, William, 141
Baldwin, British Prime Minister, 36
Ball, Mr., 126
Bank of New Zealand, 430, 436
Bank of New Zealand Assets Company, 279
Bankart, Alfred S., 390
Banking Crisis 1880s, 278
Banon, E. J., 326
Bantow, R. C., 252
Barrow, Mr., 455
Barrowclough, Mr., 435
Bartlett, A., 6
Barton, J. S., 380, 391, 393
Beaver, G. B., 364
Beck, Walter, 332
Beckham, Thomas, 121, 124
Beddoes, Mr., 13

Begg, J., 21
Behind the Mirror Glass, 131
Belfast Tramway Company, 267
Bell, Fred A., 26
Bell, Mr., 318
Bennett, Joseph, 266
Bennett, M. J., 201, 221
Best, Mr., 276
Birch, Jno., 248
Birkenhead Borough Council, 6, 30, 31, 33, 68, 77, 87
Bishop, W. A., 65, 237
Blake, E. V., 53
Blampied, Mr., 41
Blandford, G., 114
Bloodworth, Thomas, 33, 53, 61, 65, 363, 365, 387, 388, 399
Bloomfield, Dr G. T., 373, 440
Bloomfield, W. R., 312
Bond, J. S., 7
Boylan, J. T., 252
Brabant, Mr., 293
Breakwater Road, 167, 169, 177, 188
    railway crossing accident, 167
Bremner, Alexander, 104
Brett, Henry, 266
Brigham, J. S., 345
Brinsden, F. W., 187
British Electric Traction Company, 279, 299, 314, 352
British Royal Commission on Transport, 431
British Trade Facilities Act, 36
British Treasury, 73
Britomart, 167
Brogden, James, 136
Brogden, Messrs John & Sons, 133, 135, 140, 251, 252
    history, 137
    railway contracts, 133, 136

Brogden's Navvies, 138
Brookfield, Mr., 121
Brown and Slater, Messrs, 295
Bruce and Bull, Messrs, 255
Bruxner, Mr., 427
Buckland, Alfred, 252
Buckland, Mr., 110
Buddle, Thomas, 266
Burgess, Captain Isaac, 9
Burns, Robert, 36
Burton, Lieutenant-Colonel, 315
Burton, W., 187, 312
Bus Services
   Municipal Transport Station, 476
   Public v Private, 411
Bush, Walter Ernest, 306, 350, 389
   transport overview 1921, 191

Cabmen
   flout by-laws, 272
   perambulate their hackney carriages, 274
Cadman, Mr., 110
Caldwell, D. R., 4
Caley, William, 293
Callan, Philip, 12
Cameron, R., 4
Campbell, George Grey, 356, 360, 417
Campbell, Mr., 164, 165, 292
Campbell, Sir John Logan, 120, 280, 281, 391
Canterbury Automobile Association, 450
Carey, M. F., 280, 283, 292, 302
Cargen Hotel, 171
Carlisle, F. A., 458
Carr, E. J., 187
Carruthers, Mr., 138

Carson, tram conductor, 292
Casey, Captain, 152
   death, 153
Casey, M., 187, 309
Castleton, L. C., 32
Cave, Mr., 275, 276
Chapman, Mr. Justice, 295
Cheeseman, Thomas, 112, 118, 125, 126, 129
Chelmsford cars, 305
Christchurch Tramway Board, 430, 469
City Board, 249
City Board of Commissioners, 119
City of Auckland Tramways and Suburban Land Company Limited, 279
Clark, James M'Cosh, 266
Clark, Joseph Lucas, 266
Clark, M. A., 4
Clarke, R. G., 387
Clay, T. B., 164
Clayton, Mr., 257
Coates, Rt. Hon. Joseph Gordon, 34, 36, 39, 47, 74, 81, 199, 201, 204, 205, 208, 210, 220, 225, 229, 243, 355, 358, 444, 449, 450, 451, 460, 465, 470
Cobb and Co., 246
Cochrane, A., 164
Cochrane, Joseph, 124
Comer, A. W., 295
Commissioner of Transport, 459, 462
Compensation Court, 370
Consolidated Fund, 462
Cooke, Mr., 273
Cooper, Captain, 126
Cooper, Theodore, 270, 275
Corban, W. A., 237

Cotter, Thomas, 275, 318, 321
Counties' Association, 461
Cousins and Atkin Carriage Factory Limited, 305
Cousins and Atkin, Messrs, 302
Coyle, M. J., 162, 164, 403, 411
Craig, J. J., 4
Crookes, S. A., 33
Crowther, W., 246, 249, 250, 274
Cruikshank, D. B., 266
Cullen, Inspector, 287
Customs Amendment Act 1921, 444
Cutten, Mr., 355
Cycle Tracks, 259, 260
Cycle Traffic Act 1898, 259

Darlow, W. B., 85, 98
Davidson, N. S., 76
Davis, Lady, 476
Davis, Sir Ernest, 87, 92, 186, 187, 188, 242, 477
Davis-Perett oil-eliminating plant, 321
Dawson, P. H., 94
de Guerrier, F. E., 321, 408
De Latour, Mr., 105
Debt
  Local Body, 434
  National, 434
  public debt 1934, 460
Dempsey, J., 187
Dennen, P., 69
Devonport Borough Council, 91, 348
Devonport Steam Ferry Company Limited, 10, 16, 18, 19, 45, 47, 48, 55, 57, 76, 90, 92, 96, 98, 370, 480
Devonport Tramway Company, 275, 277

Devonport, steam ferry, 13, 15
Devore, Councillor, 271, 274
Dickson, J. R., 311
Dickson, J. S., 358
Dieffenbach, Ernest, 131
Dieffenbach's 'Travels in New Zealand, 151
Dignan, Mr., 126
Dilworth, James, 117, 120, 122, 129
District Highway Councils, 445
Dobbie, H., 340
Doidge, Mr., 437
Donald, Hon. J. B., 220
Dorman, Long and Company, 58, 59, 61, 62
Drumm, F., 437
Drury, Captain, 28
Duder, R. H., 275
Duder, Richard & Robert, 277
Duke of Norfolk, 373

Eady, L. A., 386
Eagle, steam ferry, 17
Eastman, J. B., 466
Economic Society of New Zealand and Australia, 455
Edgar, Matthew, 150
Edgar, Samuel, 149
Edson, Mr., 275
Education Board, 218
Edward, Alfred, 380
Edwards, Justice, 317
Emu, paddle steamer, 10
Ennis, L., 59
Enterprise, steam ferry, 11, 15
Entrican, A. J., 33, 187, 403, 417
Epsom Road Board, 312
Esson, Colonel James Jacob CMG, 234
Evans, Mr., 264

Farmers' Trading Company
   trolley bus service 1938, 439
Farmers' Union, 461
Farrell, J., 300
Fay, Sir Samuel, 206, 209, 212, 213
Federal Co-ordinator of Transport, USA, 466
Felton and Orr, 78
Felton, T. A., 78
Fenton, Judge, 104
Fenton, Mr., 263
Ferguson, William, 7, 21, 340
Finance Act 1932, 454
Finlayson, Thos., 4
First World War, 6
Firth, Josiah Clifton, 120
Fisher, George, 260
Fitzroy, Robert, 101
Flatman, Frederick, 260
Fletcher, J. S., 54, 220
Foley, Mr., 109
Forbes, George William, 235, 237, 358, 362
Ford Motor Company, 451
Ford, Albert Edward, 349, 350, 381, 385, 407, 408, 411, 428
   1927 Report, 349
Ford, Henry, 350
Foreshore Destruction, 181
   Campbell's Point, 181
Fort Britomart, 107, 112, 141, 166, 251
Fowlds, Mr., 201
Franklin County Council, 446
Fraser, George, 6
Fraser, P., 358, 366
Frazer, F. V., 332, 333
Free Lance, 180
Freeman, E., 164

Freeman, Ralph, 60
Furkert, F. W., 53, 54, 428
Furness, Arthur J., 4

Gallaugher, Mr., 110
Gardner, C. F., 189, 190
Gemini, steamer, 152
General Motors New Zealand Limited, 451
   vehicle-assembly 1926, 451
General Tramways Act 1872, 262, 263
Gentlemen of Fortune Limited Circle, 120, 193
George, Mr., 109, 249
Gilbert, W. S., 93
Gillham, Mr., 252
Gillies, Mr., 121
Gillies, Supreme Court Judge, 104, 105
Glen Eden Town Board, 240
Glenny, Mr., 275
Godfrey, G. C., 468
Godsell, Mr., 299
Golden, W. R., 45
Goldie v. Ritchie, 274
Goldie, George, 264, 269, 270, 272
Goodall, S I., 413
Goodman, W. G. T., 380
Gould, Arthur Mason, 367
Goulding, Mr , 129
Government Railways Amendment Act 1931, 458
Grafton Bridge, 31
Graham, George, 111
Graham, Robert, 117
Grandison, Mr., 164
Gray, S., 363
Gray, W. A., 455
Grayson, A., 83

Great South Road, 110
Greater Auckland scheme, 84, 383, 387, 390, 391, 395, 398, 425
Green, S., 91
Greville, R. H., 50, 51, 97, 99
Grey Lynn Borough Council, 300
Grey, Sir George, 9, 104, 166, 246
Gribble, C. R., 436
Grierson, C. K., 53
Grigg, F. W., 448
Grove, E. P., 212, 217
Guiniven, John, 48, 63, 64, 71, 73, 74, 77, 81, 86, 91, 95, 96, 98, 99
Gummer, W. H., 48
Gunson, James Henry, 187, 188, 234, 338, 339, 343, 345, 349, 352, 382

Hadfield, A., 31, 84
Hall-Skelton, A., 187
Hamilton Chamber of Commerce, 21
Hammond, Mr., 10
Hams, Charles, 76, 82
Hansen, Paul M., 280, 281, 285, 287, 294, 299, 301, 303, 304, 306
Hanson, J. H., 336
Hanson, Mr.
   Kaipara Dairy Company, 449
Harbour Bridge Association, 94
Harbour Bridge Empowering Act, 65
Harding, Samuel, 107, 127, 138
Hardington, John Henry, 141, 250, 252
Hardingtons, 246, 250
Harkin's Point, 144

Harris, Alexander MP, 28, 34, 42, 46, 47, 49, 52, 65, 69, 71, 73, 74, 81, 82, 94, 220, 227, 358
Harris, C., 69
Harrison, Surveyor, 4
Harrop, Mr., 108
Harrow, B., 278
Hayes, J. H., 426
Heather, H. D., 7, 187
Henderson Town Board, 240
Henderson, J., 348
Henderson, Mr., 138
Henderson's Mill, 158
Herries, Hon. Sir William Herbert, 7, 20, 171, 172, 190
Heslop, G. W., 15
Higgins & Bloomfield, Messrs., 116
Highway and Roads Boards
   formed in Auckland Province, 103
   powers, 103
Highway Boards Empowering Acts 1871 & 1872, 103
Highways Act 1867, 103
Highways Act 1874, 104
Highways League, 234
Hiley Report, 174, 180, 186, 192, 201
   public comment, 178
Hiley, Ernest Haviland, 1, 172, 174, 175, 176, 183, 188, 209
   interview, 184
   retires, 191
Hobson, William, 3, 101, 151
Hogarth, Miss Anne Young, 293
Hogben, Julius, 79
Hogg, Alexander, 260
Holderness, D., 7
Holdsworth, W. J., 343, 345

Holland, H. E., 230, 271, 358, 361
Hollingsworth, Amos, 296
Holmes Brothers, 11, 12, 14
Hope, Mr., 138
Hornibrook, M. R., 88, 95
Hornibrook, M. R. Proprietary Limited, 88
Houghton, C. V., 4
Howard, E. J., 358, 361
Hudson, C., 339
Humphrey, Fred, 288, 290
Hunter, A., 21
Hunter, J. S., 459
Hunter's Garrison Band, 280
Hutchison, G. W., 63, 74, 77, 78, 312

Ilford (England) Borough Council, 409
Immigration and Public Works Act 1870, 132
Immigration and Public Works Loan Act 1870, 132
Inland Waterways
   Canals, 3
Inland Waterways Commission, 6, 7, 8, 20, 86
Institute of Local Government Engineers of New Zealand, 340
Irwin, M., 82

Jackson, G. A., 37
Jacob's Ladder, 141
Jagger, F., 4
Jenkins, H. R., 220
Jesson, Bruce, 131, 372
John Stephenson & Co, 267
Johnston, F. W., 450
Johnstone, A. H., 435
Johnstone, H. B. S., 460

Johnstone, Henry, 354
Johnstone, Mr., 382, 386
Jones and Adams, engineers, 36, 41
Jones, E. F., 413
Jones, F. J., 204
Jones, S., 35
Jordan, W. J., 228, 378
Jull, A. E., 43

Kaipara Dairy Company, 449
Kaipara Railway, 143, 178
   excursions, 152
   miscarried public work, 147
   opened, 152
   political favour, 145
   Riverhead terminus, 144
   second survey, 144
   sod-turning ceremony, 150
   the battle of the termini, 145
   to proceed, 150
Kaipara Railway Act 1871, 143
   disallowed, 146
Kaipara Steamship Company Limited, 153
Kamo Company stables, 273
Karangahape Business Men's and Ratepayers' Associations, 243
Karangahape Road Business Men's Society, 220
Karangahape Road subway, 415
Kearney, Constable, 332
Keetley, Mr., 253
Kelleway, N., 31
Kenah, J W, 167
Kenah, W, 167
Keys, L. J., 357, 401
Kidd, Alfred, 280
King, F. M., 6
King, John, 249

King, Mr., 109
Kitson, Hon. Roland D., 60
Knight, G., 187, 403
Knox, Mr. (surveyor), 275, 276
Knox, R., 164, 165
Kohimarama bus service, 404
Kreeft, Captain F. C., 10, 11
Krupps, 79

La Roche, Councillor, 271
Labour Day Committee, 38
Labour Party, 81, 96
Lady Bowen, steamer, 150
Laissez-faire, 131, 213
Lamb, John, 146, 148
Lamb's Landing, 144
Lambden, J., 194
Land Clauses Consolidation Act, 123, 130
Land Speculation, 131, 151, 160
   primary industry, 119
Lands Clauses Consolidation Act, 121, 124
Langstone, Hon. F., 468
Larkins, Mr., 269
Lawson, George, 236, 241
Lawson, J., 275
Leagues
   formation of, 161
Leck, Mr., 15
Lee, E. P., 358, 362, 367
Lee, J. A., 473
Lee, Mike, 142
Leyland, J., 4
Licensing Authority and Transport Appeal Board, 391
Lindsay, Benjamin, 293
Littlejohn, J., 84, 85
Livingstone, H. G., 451
Local Bodies Loans Act 1913, 435

Local Bodies' Harbour Bridge Committee, 68, 71, 74
Local Government Loans Board, 383, 412, 415, 419, 427
Local Improvement Act 1858, 103
Lockhead, R. W., 451
London *Standard*, 434
Long Depression, 278
Long, C. L., 253
Loring, Commodore, 11
Lundon, J. R., 421
Lundon, William, 255
Lunn, Alfred George, 236, 240, 386
Lynch, Mr., 108
Lyon, William John (Jack), 82

MacAndrew, James, 156
Macdonald, J., 68
Macfarlane, Mr., 166
MacFFarlane, Thomas, 266
Macindoe, C. G., 87
MacKay, P. M., 187, 323, 345
Mackenzie, H. K., 7
Mackley, G. H., 468
MacManemin, Patrick, 296
Macmillan, C. E., 358, 361
Macready, Mr., 263
Main Highways Account, 445, 450
Main Highways Act 1922, 103, 445, 451, 453, 454
Main Highways Board, 39, 42, 43, 79, 445, 448, 451, 461, 462
   Annual Report 1932, 454
Main Highways Construction Fund, 445, 463
Main Highways Revenue Fund, 445, 450
Main South Road, 446

Mangawara–Piako Canal, 23
Mangere Progressive Association, 370
Marchbanks, James, 53
Marine Department, 7, 60
Marine Suburbs Bus Company, 391
Marks, Arthur W., 32, 36, 40
Martin, Bernard, 80, 236
Martin, F. C., 362
Martin, R., 75, 76, 77, 98
Masefield, T. T., 15, 26
Mason, Hon. H. G. R., 54, 220, 235, 240, 242
Masonic Hotel, Devonport, 275
Massey, William, 1, 6, 171, 179, 190, 198, 446, 447
Master Carriers and Customshouse Agents' Federation, 461
Mathew, Felton, 3, 101, 106, 244
Matthews, Sergeant Alex, 332
Mauku Volunteers, 248
May, Mr., 125
Mays, Mr., 275, 277
McCrystal, John, 458
McDonald, Captain Coll, 53
McDonald, William George, 359
McElwain, P., 187
McIntosh, Daniel Thomas, 168, 169, 171, 176
McKenzie, C. J., 204, 468
McKenzie, Roderick, 260
McLaughlan, Mr., 270
McLean Motor-Car Act, 441
McLean, William, 441
McLeod, Mr., 276
McMaster, C., 301
McVilly, R. W., 191, 195, 204
Mechanics Bay Viaduct, 119

Melbourne Government Steam Inspectors, 10
Mellor, Peter, 74
Melville, Miss E., 33, 187
Mennie, J. M., 4
Meredith, Mr., 354, 363, 393
Merz and McLellan, Messrs, 212, 225
   Report to Parliament 1926, 217
Metcalfe, H. H., 182, 184, 185
Metropolitan Licensing Authority, 438
Michaels, R. T., 187
Midland Railway, 169
Midland, East Coast, and North Auckland Railways, 200
Millar, John Andrew, 170
Mills, G., 74, 75, 77, 79, 87
Mitchell, George, 269
Mitchelson, Hon. E, 161
Mollyhawk, steam ferry, 19
Montague, Councillor, 264, 265, 271
Moore, R. F., 40, 41
Moore-Jones, S., 187
Morison, J. D., 365
Morningside deviation, 29, 189, 201, 202, 211, 215, 218, 219, 220, 224, 226, 234, 235, 241, 244, 406, 419, 428, 432
   abandoned 1930, 223
   lack of funds, 191
   petition 1936, 239
   proposed route, 194
   revived 1935, 238
   uneconomic 1935, 238
Morrin, Thomas, 120, 266
Morton, F. S., 403, 411, 412
Morton, P. S., 426

Motor & Cycle Industry Employment 1928, 418
Motor Bus
  as auxiliary, 193
  control called for 1925, 355
  licensing, 352
Motor Bus Proprietors' Insurance, 360
Motor Cars Regulation Act 1902, 441
Motor Import Trade 1918-1928, 418
Motor Omnibus Regulations Committee, 378
Motor Trade Federation, 461
Motor Vehicles
  congestion England, 475
  congestion New Zealand, 475
  fraudulent second-hand dealing, 475
  heavy goods regulation, 392
  hit and run, 472
  Imports 1922-1925, 451
  licensing 1925, 449
  maximum speed limit imposed 1936, 475
  motorists' tax burden 1934, 463
  no longer an expensive novelty 1934, 461
  pedestrians' rights & obligations, 473
  petrol tax, 43, 450, 452, 463
  petrol thefts 1930, 454
  pirates, 392
  registration and licence fees, 463
  registrations 1928, 417
  registrations increase 1923, 348
  revenue 1924-1932, 454
  Serpolette, 305
  tax, 444
  taxation, 461
  tyre tax, 442, 444, 451, 463
Motor Vehicles Amendment Act 1934-1935, 465
Motor Vehicles Amendment Act 1936, 472, 475
  national bicycle registration rejected, 474
Motor Vehicles Bill, 352
Motor-omnibus Proprietors' Association, 417, 461
Motor-omnibus Regulations Committee, 358, 367, 420
  recommendations 1926, 367
Motor-omnibus Traffic Act 1926, 368, 370, 380, 384, 389, 403, 456
Motor-omnibuses
  Auckland City Council purchase, 349
Motor-spirits Taxation Act 1927, 371, 453, 454
Motor-vehicles Act 1924, 353, 449, 451
Motor-vehicles Amendment Act 1936, 469
Mount Albert Borough Council, 32, 38
Mount Albert Land Sales, 158
Mount Albert-Avondale tramway extension, 432
Mount Eden Borough, 383
Mount Eden Borough Council, 38, 64, 339, 378, 385, 413
Mount Eden Company, 360
Mount Roskill Road Board, 336, 413, 430
Moyes, Motorman, 292
Municipal Association, 461

Municipal Corporations Act 1920, 395
Municipal Corporations Amendment Act 1913, 324
Municipal Record
   Official Organ of the Auckland City Corporation, 373
Munns, C. C., 220
Munns, G. O., 232
Murray, G. W., 187
Murray, W. H., 403, 421
Mutual Fire and Marine Insurance Company, 267
Myers, Arthur M., 171, 179, 185, 309, 313, 391

Nagle, W. H., 436
Nathan, L. D., 4
National Efficiency Board, 341
National Railway Network, 133
National strike 1913, 328
Neale, Dr E. P., 240
Neale, Motor Inspector, 283
Nerheny, P. J., 187
Neuchatel Asphalt Company, 444
Nevada Hotel, 269
New Brighton Borough Council, 469
New Lynn Borough Council, 235, 236, 240
New Lynn Town Board, 379, 390, 409
New Munster, 102
New Ulster, 102
New Zealand Company, 131
New Zealand Court of Appeal, 435
New Zealand Land Mortgage Company Limited, 434

New Zealand Motor Trade Federation, 462
New Zealand Road Transport Alliance, 462
New Zealand Society of Civil Engineers, 341
Newman, Hon. Edward, 234
Newmarket Highway District, 257
Newton Central School, 218
Niccol & Son's Shipyard, 14
Niccol, George, 18
Niccol, H., 14, 15
Niccol, M., 276
Nicholson, W., 10
No. 2 District Transport Licensing Authority, 466, 467, 469
North and South Island Motor Unions, 461
North Auckland Railway League, 161
North Island Main Trunk Railway League, 161
North Island Motor Union, 462, 463
North Shore
   Proposed Borough amalgamation, 72
   Steam motor buses 1904, 305
North Shore Bridge Company, 6, 26, 27
North Shore-Takapuna Motor 'Bus Company, 305
Northcote Borough Council, 59, 65, 67, 68, 72, 74, 98
Northcote Estate, 267
Northcote Women's Progressive League, 100
Northcroft, Mr., 384
Northern Association, 480

Northern Boiler Milling
Company, 284
Northern Railway, 159, 178
   opened to Kumeu &
     Helensville, 159
   patronage 1912-1921, 193
   traffic increased, 190
   tunnel outlet, 171
Northern settlers
   disheartened, 149
Northern Suburban Railway and
Highways League, 220
Northern Suburban Railway
League, 162, 163, 189, 190, 191,
193, 198, 201, 215, 217, 234,
239, 243
   New Lynn branch, 189

O'Callaghan, W., 463
O'Connor, D., 10
O'Halloran, Arthur, 19
O'Hara, W K, 168
O'Meara, F. G., 31
O'Neill, Charles Gordon, 144,
145, 146, 148, 149
O'Neill, Thomas and Co.,
Messrs, 262
Offer, Councillor, 264, 265
Oliver, Richard, 156
One Tree Hill Road Board, 340,
387
Onehunga Borough Council, 38,
426
Onehunga Line, 109, 127
   first train 1873, 141
   popularity & etiquette, 142
O'Neill, J., 108
One-tree Hill Road Board, 336
Osprey, steam ferry, 17
Otago Central and the Midland
Line, 156

Otahuhu Borough Council, 398
Otahuhu railway workshops, 227
Outram Ways, 373
Outram, James, 373

Pakeha colonisation, 3
Parker, Mr., 164
Parkinson, W., 73
Parnell Borough Council, 303
Parnell Railway Bridge, 257
Parnell Tunnel, 119, 141, 169,
171, 176, 228
Parochialism, 30, 31, 49, 84, 425,
447
Parochialism and Cronyism, 466
Parr, Hon. Christopher James,
70, 183, 191
Parry, Mr., 7
Parry, W. E., 220, 227
Passenger Transport Company,
231, 398, 401
Patterson Brothers, 279
Paul, Robert, 197
Pedestrian Traffic, 348
People's Protection Society
Council, 339
Perambulator Tax, 260
Phelan, E. J., 403, 412
Phillips, P. A., 263
Phoebe, steamer, 250
Picton Coal Company, 267
Pollen, Dr., 110
Porter, Adam & Buddle, W. N.
Liquidators, 277
Potter, Ernest Herbert, 221, 359,
362, 365, 366, 378, 385, 403,
412, 426
Potter's Paddock, 406
Powell, E., 42
Power, Mr., 455
Prickett, Mrs J., 69

Private Bus Owners Association, 356
Progress, an illusion of, 351
Provinces of New Zealand, 102
Provincial Council, 27, 103, 107, 114, 129
Provincial Councils Powers Act 1856, 103
Prudential Assurance Company, Limited., 435
Public News, 245
Public Petitions Committee, 47
Public Services Committee, 337
Public Transport
  bus losses 1928, 410
  London 1905, 304
  profit & loss 1928, 381
  statement of accounts 1927/1928, 412
Public Works Act 1876, 155
Public Works Act, 1908, 370
Public Works Amendment Act 1925, 448
Public Works Department, 51, 53, 54, 86, 89, 105, 204, 237, 322, 327, 330, 356, 383, 392, 445, 468, 500
Public Works Fund, 57, 445, 463
Pudans, Mr., 269
Pukaki Creek, 7
Pupuke, steam ferry, 319
Purchas, Dr., 266

Queen Street sewer
  report 1906, 306
Queen-street, 102
Quick, F., 255
Quick, George, 17

Rail v Omnibus, 252, 257

Rail v Road, 128, 160, 168, 214, 216, 221, 223, 454, 455, 458, 459, 471
Rail v Trams & Road, 204
Railway Appropriation Bill, 108
Railway Board of Commissioners, 119, 121
Railway Department, 22, 25, 165, 183, 186, 187, 189, 199, 458
  Fay & Raven Report 1924, 214
  financial restrictions, 219
  improvement statement 1924, 210
  infrastructure 1879, 155
  operations 1880, 158
  parochial & political interests, 156
  passenger patronage 1924, 214
  public service monopoly, 459
  Royal Commission 1879, 157
  Royal Commission 1924, 206, 214
  Royal Commission 1924 costs, 208
  Statement 1929, 219, 222
  Treasury's control, 213
Railways Amendment Act 1931, 233
Railways Board, 233, 237, 458, 461, 467
Ransom, Hon. Ethelbert Alfred, 50, 54
Ranson, C., 4
Rattray, Captain, 109
Raven, Sir Vincent, 206, 209, 212, 213
Reed, J. R., 332
Rees, Mr., 105
Reese, Daniel, 234
Reform Party, 191, 219

Reid, George Walter, 234
Reid, John, 9
Remuera Land Company Estate, 267
Remuera Ratepayers' Association, 399
Remuera Road Board, 311
Rennie, J. C., 65, 77
Representative Constitution to the Colony of New Zealand, 102
Rhodes, L. E., 32, 403, 417
Richards, Mr., 437
Ridings, R., 124
Road Freight v Rail Freight, 449
Road Transport Alliance, 461
Roads
  bitumen, 443
  congestion 1929, 404
  congestion forecast 1930, 229
  costs 1924-1926, 452
  early, 443
  first asphalt surface, 444
  Government or Local Body responsibility, 445
  macadamised, wood blocks, & concrete, 444
  metal shortages, 447
  motorways needed 1936, 475
  motorways the future, 478
  planning & construction 1926, 451
  toll-gates considered 1923, 446
  unsafe for speed, 478
Robertson, H. A., 191, 193, 198, 201, 220, 237, 239, 241, 243
Robinson, Sir Dove-Myer, 231
Rogerson, Mr., 383
Rollo, T. M., 72
Ronayne, T., 162, 163, 172

Rooney, Mr., 129
Rosetta, merchantman, 11
Ross, Mr., 109
Rough, Captain David, 101
Routley, A. J., 237
Rowe, Mr., 110
Royal Motor Bus Company, 354, 360, 362, 370
Rugby World Cup, 197
Rural Land Settlement, 113
Russell, Thomas, 120, 434
Rutledge, Senior-Sergeant, 333

Salter Committee, 460
Savage, Rt. Hon. Michael Joseph, 81, 85, 90, 91, 95, 97, 220, 230, 358
Sawyer, W. H., 350
Sceats, Mr., 249
Schramm, F. W., 476
Scotchman, steam ship, 146
Scott, Mr., 296
Seaman, A. M., 235
Semple, Rt. Hon. Robert, 83, 89, 238, 437, 468, 469, 470, 472, 474
Sergeant, Captain H. H., 7, 29
Sheehan, John, 143, 152
Shepherd, Mr., 124
Shortland street, 102
Sidey, T. K., 358
Sinclair, Dr. Andrew, 120
Skeates, E. G., 30, 33, 34, 37, 42
Skelton, A. Hall, 358
Slinger, Archibald, 365
Smeeton, H. M., 309
Smerdon, G., 31
Smith, A. H., 371
Smith, H. G. Seth, 274
Smith, H. H. W., 264
Smith, Thomas, 391
Smith, W. H., 4

Somerfield, F. J., 13
South Island Main Trunk line, 225
South Island Motor Union, 450
Southern League, 134
Spencer, N. B., 398, 476, 477
St Helier's Bay Estate, 267
St. Heliers and Northcote Land Company Limited, 266, 267, 279
Staines, Mr., 249
Stallworthy, A. J., 403
Stallworthy, J., 154
Stark, Mr., 275
Sterling, H. H., 223, 234
Stevenson, E., 358, 427
Stewart, James, 107, 123, 124, 127, 138, 280
Stout, Robert MP, 156
Strack, F. W., 78
Stringer, Sir Walter, 61, 62
Suburban Railway
  Auckland to Onehunga and Mercer, 256
  congestion, 185
  congestion, 196
  electrification, 202
  improvements needed, 165
  Northern Line, 211
  Northern Line, 189
  Northern Line, 224
  Northern Line, 240
  Northern Line patronage 1926, 216
  Onehunga line opened 1873, 251
  passenger traffic, 199
  patronage down 1923/1924, 204
  Royal Engineers, 189
  station relocation, 186
  Town Hall deviation, 190

Westfield Line, 171, 210, 215, 228, 229
Sullivan, Hon. D. G., 239, 241, 242, 468, 471
Sydney Harbour Bridge, 37, 58, 59, 62, 93

Tait, W. J., 410
Takapuna Borough Council, 30, 35, 66, 72, 81, 83, 98, 365
Takapuna, steam ferry, 14
Tamaki River Bridge, 7, 109
Tamaki Road Board (West), 103
Tapley, H. L., 358
Taverner, William Burgoyne, 219, 223, 224
Taxis
  bus war, 417
  fares 1940, 437
Te Aroha News, 3, 4
Teasdale, J. B., 7
Teed, D, 182
Tegetmeier, C. G., 309, 313, 315, 320, 322, 326, 328, 329, 330, 333
Telegraph Department, 285
Thackeray, Edwin, 295
Thompson, Councillor, 265
Thompson, Ernest, 289
Thompson, F., 430
Thompson, M. E., 30
Thornton, D. B. JP, 124
Titchener, W. S., 379
Titchener, Walter Leigh, 390, 409
Toka Toka, 145
Tole, Mr., 257, 293
Tomlinson, M. C., 26
Tonar, J. B., 40
Tonks, B., 266
Toroa, steam ferry, 18
Totton, W. S., 267

Town Hall deviation, 189
Trams v Motor Buses, 299, 347
   propaganda, 374
   road sharing, 352
Tramway Amendment Bill 1910, 323
Tramways
   100-car milestone, 320
   40-hour week introduced 1936, 436
   accident inquiry 1904, 290
   Auckland City Council suit, 317
   Auckland City Council's share, 298
   Auckland optimism, 320
   Auckland revolutionised, 299
   cabmen resist, 268
   cabmen's petitions 1884, 270
   car construction 1929, 428
   Christmas Eve tragedy, 288
   chronic congestion, 343
   City Council's option to buy, 339
   congestion 1907, 312
   debentures repaid 1940, 436
   failing as a main transport system 1918, 336
   fall in revenue 1933, 433
   fare rises 1940, 437
   first fire, 283
   first horse tram 1884, 267
   first passenger tram 1832, 373
   first tram run 1884, 271
   future compromised by 1927 poll, 375
   go-slow 1919, 337
   horse fright, 283
   horses, 406
   land sales, 278
   last tram 1956, 440
   loan 1929, 412, 415, 419
   loan judgement, 435
   loan proposal 1928, 399
   North Shore, 275
   North Shore 1910, 319
   North Shore opens 1886, 275
   North Shore steam tram ends, 370
   omnibus feeder service, 303
   Option of Purchase and Valuation 1919, 341
   passengers carried 1908, 319
   poll 1904, 296
   poll 1919, 342
   poll 1927, 373
   poll 1929, 420
   poll 1930, 428
   poll result 1927, 374
   prospering 1905, 301
   Purchased by Auckland City Council 1919, 344
   Queen Street speeds, 332
   Royal Commission - brakes, 322
   special loan poll, 371
   statistical growth, 376
   stimulating residential settlement 1923, 347
   strap hangers, 311
   Sunday service referendum, 286
   Sydney 1926, 364
   ticket prices, 271
   Tramway Board, 342
   Union Award 1904, 297
   unrivalled for rapid mass transport, 368
   wheel noise, 285
   work-to-rule, 311
Tramways Act 1894, 296
Tramways Act 1908, 323

Tramways Amendment Bill 1915, 330
Tramways v Buses, 406, 409, 421, 427
   a win 1929, 424
   public hearing 1926, 359
   Sydney 1929, 427
   Transport Commission's view 1928, 396
Tramways v Private Motor-car, 417, 431
Tramways v Railways 1930, 429
Transport Appeal Board, 460
Transport Commission, 377, 378, 383, 384, 388, 390, 400
   appointed 1928, 379
   Commissioners, 380
   order of reference, 380
   report of 1928, 398
   report of 1928, 393
Transport Committee 1936, 468
Transport Co-ordination Board, 461, 465, 467, 469
   abolished 1936, 470
   appeals, 466
   appointed 1934, 460
   first annual report 1935, 465
   laissez-faire views, 467
   motor taxation inquiry, 462
   report 1934, 464
   suspended 1936, 468
Transport Law Amendment Act 1933, 460
Transport Licensing Act 1931, 456, 458
Transport Licensing Amendment Act 1936, 469, 472
Transport Licensing Authorities reduced 1936, 469
Transport Services

cut-throat competition condemned 1936, 468
Trolley Buses, 404, 407, 408, 426, 430, 431
Turner, Mr., 280

Unemployment Board, 61, 62, 71, 74, 79, 80, 81, 234
Union Oil, Soap, and Candle Company, 267
United Party, 219
Ussher, T., 287

Vaile and Sons, Messrs., 4
Vehicular Ferry Traffic 1934, 76
Veitch, Hon. W. A., 227, 228
Victoria University College Commerce Society, 459
Victoria, paddle steamer, 17
Vogel, Sir Julius, 132, 136, 154
   British loan, 133
   visit to Britain, 133
   Vogel boom, 278
   Vogel scheme, 154

Waddell, Councillor, 264
Waikato Railway, 110, 166
Waikato River, 5
Waikato River Board, 8, 22
Waikato River Navigation and Vigilance Committee, 21
Waikato War, 107
Waitemata and Manukau Canal Promotion Co. Ltd., 4
Waitemata Bridge Committee, 31, 32, 33, 35, 36, 37
Waitemata County Council, 37, 41, 65, 77, 79, 83, 84, 85, 164, 236, 237, 240, 447
Waitemata Electric Power Board, 55, 85

Waitemata Flour Mill and Biscuit Factory, 146
Waitemata Harbour Bridge Association Incorporated, 96, 97, 99
Waitemata–Kaipara (Helensville) Canal, 22, 153
Waitemata–Manukau Canal, 4, 7, 22
Waitoa Highway District Board, 104
Waiuku–Waikato Canal, 23
Waiwera Hot Springs Company, 267
Walker, Mr., 129
Walklate, J. J., 322, 331, 333, 336, 337, 343, 344
Walkley, W. G., 461
Wallace, W., 6
Walton, Edward C., 20, 67
Ward, Sir Joseph, 46, 48, 49, 50, 51, 52, 172, 243, 259, 414, 417
Warnock, J. A., 187
Washing-up Bill, 448
Waste Lands Commissioner, 125
Watson, J. E., 7
Way, Mr., 295
Weaver, Mr., 124
Wellington and Suburban Bus Company, 360
Wellington Automobile Club, 417
Wellington Motor Bus Proprietors, 359
Whangarei County Council, 87
Whelan, Peter, 374

Whitaker, Frederick, 120
White and Company, Messrs J. G., 280
White Star services, 462
White, W., 252
Whitmore, Hon. Colonel G. S., 166
Whitney, Captain A., 6
Wilford, Hon. T. M., 49
Williams, Hon. K. S., 358, 452
Wills, C. H. M., 60, 85
Wilson, H., 280, 281
Wilson, Sir Charles Rivers, 299
Wilson, W. R., 4
Wily, H. E. R. L., 8
Winstone, Geo., 4
Witheford, J. H., 19
Wood, J., 403
Wood, Reader, 124
Woods, Rev. W. C., 446
Woodside Township, 12
Wrigg, Henry, 145, 147, 148
Wright, R. A., 470
Wynn, Mr., 108, 121, 126
Wynyard, Colonel, 9
Wynyard, M. H., 50, 51, 61

Yarnall, J. W., 75
Yates, Ernest, 427
Young, S., 270
Young, Sir Alexander, 79

www.ingramcontent.com/pod-product-compliance
Lightning Source LLC
Chambersburg PA
CBHW060526010526
44107CB00059B/2608